An Introduction to Operations Management

An Introduction to Operations Management: The Joy of Operations covers core topics of operations management, including product and service design, processes, capacity planning, forecasting, inventory, quality, supply chain management, and project management. Das provides a clear, connected, and current view of operations management and how it relates to a firm's strategic goals.

Students will benefit from the real-world scenarios that foster an understanding of operations management tasks. Without relying heavily on statistics and mathematical derivations, the book offers applied models and a simple, predictable chapter format to make it easy to navigate.

Students of introductory operations management courses will love this practical textbook. A companion website features an instructor's manual with test questions, as well as additional exercises and examples for in-class use.

Ajay Das is a Professor in the Operations Management group at Zicklin School of Business, Baruch College, New York, USA. He has hands-on industry experience in operations and supply chain management and has published extensively in top-tier scholarly and professional journals, including the *Journal of Operations Management* and the *International Journal of Operations and Production Management*.

An Introduction to Operations Management

The Joy of Operations

Ajay Das

Routledge
Taylor & Francis Group

NEW YORK AND LONDON

Please visit the companion website for this title at www.routledge.com/cw/das

First published 2016
by Routledge
711 Third Avenue, New York, NY 10017

and by Routledge
2 Park Square, Milton Park, Abingdon, Oxon OX14 4RN

Routledge is an imprint of the Taylor & Francis Group, an informa business

Library of Congress Cataloging in Publication Data
A catalog record for this book has been requested

ISBN: 978-1-138-88457-1 (hbk)
ISBN: 978-0-7656-4582-1 (pbk)
ISBN: 978-1-315-71520-9 (ebk)

Typeset in Times New Roman
by Apex CoVantage, LLC

Printed and bound in the United States of America by
Edwards Brothers Malloy on sustainably sourced paper

To students everywhere—soar high, and every teacher's heart will soar with you!

To all teachers—for lighting the fire, and showing the way,

To Surita and Karan—for their love, patience, and the time they allowed me,

and most of all,

To my departed parents, Aloka Das and Dr. Shailendra Mohan Das.
The older I get, the more reasons I find to thank you.

Contents

Figures

Tables

Statistical Tables

Take-Away Boxes

Preface

Preface for Students

What should *Taylor Swift* do? She can do one of three possible concerts next season. As her business manager (lucky you), which one would you suggest she do? Turn to Chapter 13, "Managing Projects," page 575, to find out how to impress celebrities and make friends using your project selection capabilities.

Goldman Sachs has hired hotshot you as a commodity analyst. How do you see rare earth minerals prices over the next six months, your mentor there asks? Turn to Chapter 5, "Business Forecasting," page 169, for some solid pointers.

"How're things going?" asks your boss in your new gig at *Tesla Motors* manufacturing. Well, what does she mean exactly, you nervously muse? Probably not how well your last date went. Learn core process performance metrics—Productivity, Yield, Flow Time, Flow Rate, Capacity Utilization and Inventory Turns. And how to measure, analyze, and report how "things are going"? Turn to Chapter 4, "Managing Processes," page 123, to get some quick but rigorous answers.

Apple's watch deliveries are getting delayed because of supplier issues. As *Tim Cook*'s handpicked new hire, you need to come up with some brilliant moves, fast. Turn to Chapters 10, "Supply Chain Design," and 11, "Managing Supply Chains," to get some great, do-able ideas.

Your boss at *Hi-Cost Hospital* has been keeping large inventories of expensive drug applicators. She says, "It will be catastrophic if we run out!" But the hospital is under tremendous cost pressure. Is there a way to stock less without adversely affecting patient service? Turn to Chapter 8, "Managing Inventory," page 312, to find out.

FB receives a lot of feedback from users—they want speed, security, privacy, storage, portability, ease of use, and other goodies. Now put on your hat as FB's new operations person (*hey, you're a great prospect—everyone wants you!*). How would you prioritize and convert the many voices of the customer into actual product features? Use the House of Quality tool and Kano's customer satisfaction model to get a great start (Chapter 9, "Managing Quality," page 374, and Chapter 3, "Process and Service Design," page 82, respectively).

Such challenges will come at you, fast and furious, in your work life. No matter what your business major is—marketing, finance, accounting, HR—you must know how to meet them. That's what this text is about.

We take a look at this discipline called Operations Management. You will learn how to design a product and how to design a process to make it well. You will learn how to recognize a process when you see one. You will learn how to check its health. You will learn how to improve a process—through better forecasting, enhanced capacity management, quality improvements, inventory corrections, supply chain management, and location decisions. You will also learn how to design, monitor, and run projects. You will make use of concepts and numbers to analyze, recommend, and apply.

Some of us may be numbers-challenged. Regardless of your mathematical ability, there's one promise I will make to you—you *will* be pleasantly surprised by how much you can do with your analytical abilities as you progress through this text. The text does not shortchange content. It makes it easy to understand and apply. You will see, understand, and appreciate how Operations Management concepts and tools improve and enable business decisions. Concepts and models have been built step by step and applied step by step to actual business decisions. You will see that stats and math are not things to do and forget—but really cool tools that you can put to immediate use to get bonus-boosting, promotion-worthy business performance gains. And we do not accept the results blindfolded—we interrogate the models we build—testing for robustness and leaks in real-life conditions, questioning how they are of use (or not). The spirit is always to inquire, examine, and understand, not just consume.

Another surprise for you may be the stepping away from the 'sage on stage' language that is typical of textbooks. I have tried to speak to you as I do in the class—normal words, normal voice, and normal everyday language. I hope you like it.

You will find key point summaries and worked out examples at frequent intervals, allowing you to pause the chapter and absorb the learning in 'chunks.' Most of us do not read an entire chapter at one go or learn everything at one go.

Engage with the material and the book will reward you—not just with an 'A' in your college course, but with a competitive edge in interviews and your work life, as well. Now roll up those sleeves and dive into the text!

Preface for Faculty

A brief note for my OM colleagues: My objective was to write a student-friendly, affordable, and sufficiently rigorous introductory level text on OM. The introductory OM course is a requirement in most undergraduate and MBA business programs. It generally covers core operations such as forecasting, inventory, quality, process, supply chain, location/layout, project management, product design, production and capacity planning, and a brief chronological view of OM and how it relates to the strategic goals of a firm. Students generally take this course after having declared a business major. While some students may go on to major in operations, the majority consist of marketing, finance, accounting, and HR majors. The OM course is a requirement, and, hence, initial motivation is fairly low. Further, since OM is not as familiar or as clearly defined as, say, marketing or finance, many students are confused or indifferent about the course. OM texts have not done much to clarify the relationship between studying OM and student careers/prospects in the job market.

As typically taught, the success rate for this course is relatively lower than other non-quantitative courses. The main problem, in our experience, is student inability to connect content to their interests and, perhaps, a fear of Greek letters.

The author regularly teaches introductory OM courses and has extensively modified and extended current OM text material to specifically address these course challenges, with significant success.

The writing, flow, and content is clear, connected, and current. The context is current and relevant. Although you may find the somewhat informal tone of this text quite different from conventional OM texts, the quality of the content is not diluted or compromised. I think many of us have found that a formal tone, perhaps a natural outcome of our training and education, does not come as naturally to our students. In writing this text, I am deliberately writing *to* the student, grad or undergrad, who is taking his/her first (and perhaps last) OM course.

This text brings to you:

a) Thirteen chapters, beginning with an intro to OM chapter, further continuing to work processes and ways to improve work processes, and concluding with location and project management. Each chapter's material is wrapped into four fundamental questions:

- What is it?
- Why is it important?
- How is it done?
- How do we know that we are doing/have done a good job?

b) A comprehensive, yet not overwhelming Instructor's Manual, with

- Test banks for each chapter
- Solutions for test bank questions
- Teaching slides for each chapter with notes for key concepts and computations
- A list of sites that offer quick and inexpensive engagement opportunities with students
- Sites that offer quick treatments of more advanced OM material, should the instructor wish to introduce such in class sessions
- Sample syllabus

c) An author who has worked hands-on several years in industry and brings that experience and perspective to the telling of our discipline in this textbook.

Students buy OM books but do not 'read' them, walking away with little understanding of, or respect for, our discipline. Our introductory courses in OM are our first 'moments of truth' with our students—a capture point for future OM majors and an opportunity to create an abiding interest in our discipline. If you feel that the text does a fair job of addressing OM basics appropriate for an introductory course, please pass around a sample chapter from this text and an equivalent chapter from your current text to students in your introductory OM course. Ask them which of these excites them to the potential and the joy of Operations Management. I look forward to your feedback. Thank you.

Acknowledgments

I begin by placing on record my deep appreciation and gratitude to my friends Professors Will Millhiser and Georghios P. Sphicas. They suffered through my drafts, tested text material in the classroom, and provided invaluable feedback, advice, and encouragement throughout the writing of this book.

My personal thanks go to Leslie M. Bobb, Ph.D., for his gracious giving of time and effort in developing the IM materials for the text, and providing valuable input and advice.

Several reviewers have spent time and knowledge on this text. Their comments and suggestions have contributed immeasurably in developing text content, sequence, problems, and examples.

I sincerely thank, in alphabetical order:

George N. Kenyon	Lamar University
Gurkan Akalin	University of Texas-Arlington
Kathryn M. Zuckweiler	Kearney University of Nebraska
Lancie Affonso	College of Charleston
Laura Meade	Texas Christian University
Mark Jacobs	University of Dayton
Steven Harrod	University of Dayton
Steven Williams	Marian University
Ying Liao	Meredith College

And a sincere thank you to reviewers at the following schools—the text has benefitted immensely from their constructive reviews:

Athens State University
Bowling Green University
Canisius College
Columbus State Community College
Delta State University
Elon University
Florida State College at Jacksonville
Fordham University
Frostburg State University
Georgia College and State University
Illinois Valley Community College

New York Institute of Technology, Old Westbury
Niagara Community College
Oklahoma State University, Stillwater
Robert Morris College, Chicago
Sam Houston State University
South University
Texas A&M University, College Station
University of Akron
University of Louisiana, Lafayette
University of Mississippi
University of Nebraska, Lincoln
University of North Carolina, Greensboro
University of Pittsburgh
University of St. Thomas
University of Texas, Pan American
Valencia Community College

Introduction

1 Operations Management and You

Chapter Take-Aways

- A practical understanding of the purpose and tasks of operations management
- Jobs—the benefit of studying operations management
- How to evaluate operational performance
- What's happening now in operations management

Operations Management and You: A Road Map

Introduction

Welcome to Operations Management! Let's take a look at what it's about.

1.1 What, Exactly, Is Operations Management?

Speaking broadly, the operations function designs, makes, and delivers an organization's products or services. It gathers materials and resources and transforms them into finished goods and services through value-adding conversion activities. Operations management (OM) is the design, management, and improvement of the systems and activities involved in this task.

1.1.1 A Way to Think about Operations

Operations comes from the Latin word 'opus,' meaning work. Operations management is the management of that work—to make it run well and to improve on it. The scope of the operations function of any business can be described through a simple diagram:

Figure 1.1 A Simple Model of Operations

Operations takes in inputs and converts them using resources to make products/services that customers want. The goal is to do so efficiently and effectively, so as to maximize whatever the organization wishes to achieve— profit, low cost, or high customer service levels. A college takes in fresh high school or transfer students (inputs). The students are typically put through a four-year transformation process where they work with faculty, technology, and each other to be converted into polished, knowledgeable, and highly employable output (graduates). A hospital takes in sick patients as inputs. Their examination and treatment by doctors and nurses, medicines, laboratories, and diagnostic and surgical equipment constitutes the transformation process. Healthy patients are released from the hospital as quality-certified finished products. Likewise, in a Ford plant, operations designs the car, sources steel and car parts, designs the manufacturing process, forecasts and sets production targets, schedules worker shifts, monitors and improves quality, and delivers the car to the dealer. It does so efficiently, effectively, and safely, making it possible for Ford to turn a profit from the revenue it gets from the sale of the car.

Although OM plans and strategizes for business success, it differs from marketing, accounting, and other functions in that it also rolls up its sleeves and plunges right into the fray of making and delivering products and services. As a senior operations Northrop Grumman executive stated, "Operations really is the heart of most companies, because the operations department actually gets the job that the company needs to get done, done."[1]

1.1.2 What Operations Managers Do

Every day in its life, a business has to answer that fundamental question posed by all customers—*why* should I choose *you*? Look at the picture below.

Yes, you're right—the business is a boutique. And how does it seem to be responding to that fundamental question posed by all consumers to a business: "*Why should I choose You?*"

Look closer. The business seems to be saying, "*Choose us* because we promise you":

Exclusivity—every dress shown is different
Affordability—a reasonable price
Quality—good fittings and durable colors
Availability—the dress will be there when you want it
Service—friendly expert advice and help
Location—right off the subway and plenty of safe parking

You can see a group of happy, excited women exiting the store—obviously the business fulfilled the promises it made to its customers. Who delivers on these promises? Operations! Every business makes promises to its customers.

Figure 1.2 Why Should I Choose You?

Source: andresr (2014). Group of women shopping. Retrieved from: http://www.istockphoto.com/photo/group-of-women-shopping-41417898?st=1d22a09. Courtesy of iStock.

OM IN PRACTICE

Every Business Makes Promises

Here's a sampling of promises made by well-known companies:

Toyota promises efficiency, safety, longevity, innovation: http://www.toyota.com/productleadership/

Kia promises the "power to surprise" with "exciting and enabling" vehicles: http://www.kia.com/#/about/

Ritz-Carlton promises to be and always be the "gold standard" in luxury hospitality: http://corporate.ritzcarlton.com/

Motel 8 promises consistent delivery of eight features in a guest stay: http://www.super8.com/Super8/control/amenities?variant

But not all promises are kept.

Many retailers, including Amazon and Kohl's, accepted online orders till the last minute during the Christmas 2013 season, promising delivery before Christmas. Packages arrived damaged or late or did not arrive at all. While finger pointing goes on, carriers like FedEx have identified the root causes as faulty labeling, too little time allowed for logistics, and plain old misspeak—packages said to have been shipped were not even handed over to the carrier at the time. Retailer online fulfillment employees were focused on meeting internal shipment rate targets, shifting the problem over to the carriers. UPS and FedEx hiked capacity, rates, and advance notice requirements for 2014.

Lesson: "Don't overpromise or say we do things that we end up not being able to do." And consult operations before making promises.

Operations managers deliver on promises that are made by the business to the customer. In doing so, operations essentially focuses on a single, foremost real-world challenge—variability. Customers do not show up in orderly, well-timed fashion. Neither do they all demand the same work or go to the same location. Workers too, do not work at the same pace or quality level all day or all week. Suppliers do not deliver 100 percent on time, quality, cost, or location. Faced with this variability, operations managers act in four ways.

a) First, by building forecasting systems that attempt to anticipate variability—this, obviously, can never be perfect.

b) Next, they try to control variability by influencing demand patterns (e.g., doctor appointments, happy hours), controlling worker variability (e.g., worker training and incentives), and managing supplier variability (e.g., information sharing, technical assistance, incentives, and penalties).

c) Since forecasting and attempts to control variability typically offer limited results, managers build in excess capacity in the system (labor, machines, raw materials) so that peak demand can be met. This leads to waste at times of low demand and costs the business a lot.

d) Alternatively, managers try to make their operations synch with variability by adding flexibility to work systems. Basically, they convert fixed costs into variable costs. Think of hiring temps, varying worker hours according to demand, training workers to perform different jobs, leasing equipment/hour instead of buying, and buying materials when needed instead of holding inventory. Such actions are not always possible.

Here is an example of what businesses actually expect operations managers to do:

Operations Manager Responsibilities

Here's a description of what a company may require from its operations managers. Not all tasks are required for all operations managers, but the responsibilities listed are quite representative of what an actual operations manager does on the job.

Job Description: Operations Manager JN: 42570 **CACI International** (abbreviated)

Duties and Responsibilities

Working on a leadership team with NGB-ASM, analyzes factors and components of systems and processes to manage interrelationships and facilitate change. Detects inefficiencies or conflicts in systems and processes and helps to identify effective improvements. Facilitates communications between customers, SMEs and technical staff. Ensures efficient operation of Recruit Sustainment Program internal processes.

Specifically:

- Gathers information from users to define work problems and support the design of procedures to resolve problems.
- Analyzes factors and components of systems/processes to recommend and institute changes to increase efficiency.
- Performs functional analysis to document complex process steps, tasks and their inter-relationships.
- Plans studies of work problems and procedures, such as organizational changes, communication, information flow, integrated production methods, or cost analysis.
- Recommends improvements of modifications in sequence of operations, equipment utilization and related matters. Generates recommendations in the form of technical briefings, reports, and other major documents provided to senior level client personnel.
- Writes specifications manuals and user documentation for client or user personnel. Translates user requirements into system specifications, configuration management plans, life cycle management documentation, and integrated logistics support plans and related operational summaries.
- May serve as a client liaison and coordinates with sub-contractors, government personnel, and technical experts.
- Provides guidance and work leadership to less-experienced operations personnel, and may have supervisory responsibilities. May review the work of others and be able to detect errors or needed modifications.
- Participates in special projects as required.

Source: Job originally listed on http://careers.caci.com.

Operations management reaches beyond pure analytics to a practical understanding of the inter-connectedness of activities in an organization and the behavior of the people engaged in those activities. An effective operations manager would display analytical, communication, presentation, and teamwork skills. Employers seek such capabilities, as the following example shows.

Fresh Direct, LLC Careers

Operations Manager—Fresh Foods

New Business Initiatives, Long Island City, New York

The operations manager is responsible for the execution and management of FreshDirect's operations. This role is responsible for both inbound and outbound operations and supporting the policies, goals and objectives of the company, all while ensuring the highest level quality of service to our customers, provided by our associates. This is a newly created role that will offer an outstanding opportunity to be an integral part of FreshDirect's rapidly expanding business.

Essential Functions:

- Direct, coordinate and manage inbound receivables, inventory replenishment, and order fulfillment
- Dispatch deliveries based on FreshDirect process and procedures
- Assist in operational and culture training
- Coordinate with outside vendors on arrival times and establish receiving processes
- Find resolutions for outstanding issues within span of control according to the standards set by the company
- Ensure compliance with food safety, safety compliance and FreshDirect quality policies
- Plan and manage staff schedule while adhering to budgets and/or business needs
- Identify, and help implement, changes related to process improvement opportunities
- Identify and train talent for the department, including coaching, training, and maintaining of standards of continued excellence
- Implement and support a safety first culture with all site associates

Interactions

Supervision Received:

- Plans and carries out work assignments; coordinates work with others as necessary; communicates policies with hourly team. Keeps site manager informed of progress and any roadblocks that need to be addressed.
- Plans, designs, and carries out programs, projects, studies, or other work in conjunction with site manager.

Team Leader Responsibility:

- The operations manager is responsible for ensuring a safety first environment, all the personnel within their shifts, and the execution of the daily operations.

Minimum Qualifications:

- BA/BS in management, logistics, engineering, or a related field
- Several years of inventory, warehousing, and/or inbound–outbound operations experience in addition to four plus (4+) years experience in management roles with increasing responsibilities
- Must have experience with perishable items, fresh foods, and/or merchandise with a short shelf-life

- Previous exposure to, and demonstrated success in, a high-growth business environment
- Must be flexible to work weekends and/or nightshifts
- Must pass FreshDirect's pre-employment testing: background check and drug screening

Knowledge, Skills, and Abilities:

- Knowledge of Microsoft Office, including Outlook, Excel, and Word
- Strong analytical and problem-solving skills
- Effective time management and prioritization skills
- Ability to communicate clearly and concisely (both written and orally) with colleagues at all levels and from various backgrounds
- Active learning, listening, and critical thinking skills to find effective solutions for any problems that may arise
- Proven ability to lead, manage, and motivate during periods of change and disruption
- Ability to counsel and discipline in a style that improves and fosters a positive team environment

Source: http://jobs.jobvite.com/fresh-direct/job/oGOc1fwr, accessed Sept. 26, 2015.

1.1.3 A Brief History of Operations Management

The answer to the question of what operations managers do has evolved over the years. Operations management, in a broad sense, began with the early 1900s scientific management work theories of Frederick W. Taylor (1856–1915). He introduced time studies and the concept of breaking up what was traditionally craftsman work into short, repetitive tasks that could be standardized through observation, measurement, and analysis. Henry Ford was a practitioner of the scientific management principle, partitioning work into standard, repetitive components that raised productivity and made possible the advent of the 'Ford Model T,' the common man's automobile. The mechanistic approach of Taylor was balanced by the human relations school. Professor Elton Mayo (1880–1949) ran the famous 'Hawthorne' experiments at a Western Electric plant (1924–1927) and found that workers, unlike machines, respond positively to personal attention and job enrichment. Later, World War II demanded productivity from limited resources, and several resource-optimization and logic-based approaches to work decisions appeared, such as PERT/CPM (program evaluation and review technique/critical path method) and linear programming. Complex mass production systems grew, with the invention of computers and automated machinery in the 1950s and '60s. Competition and rising customer demands for cost and quality performance in the '70s and '80s stimulated the introduction of manufacturing process improvement practices such as JIT (just-in-time) and TQM (total quality management) in business. The growth of information and web technology in the '90s facilitated management visibility and control of large enterprises and parts of their supply network, birthing the practices of off-shoring, e-commerce, and supply chain management. Today, in the early stages of the 21st century, operations management seeks to build on its accomplishments of innovation, efficiency, quality, and responsiveness by addressing issues of, perhaps, greater significance to the world. Particularly important is the recognition that operational decisions have larger and lingering consequences for the community and the world we inhabit. Businesses today are aware of the need to balance consumption with renewal, such that the resource environment is never depleted to the point that it cannot fully recover.

We shall talk further about the role and tasks of operations management later in the chapter. Let us now try to understand why operations management is important to a business and to you.

KEY POINTS

- Companies have to promise products or services that attract the customer to the business.
- Promised products or services are created through a chain of sequenced tasks that acquire inputs, convert these inputs into a product or service and then deliver such products or services to the customer. This set of tasks is called a work system or work process.
- Operations management is the design, implementation, and running of work processes that transform material, capital, and labor resource inputs into products and services.
- Operations managers design, study, analyze, and improve work processes.

1.2 Why Is Operations Management Important?

With revenue growth disappearing, companies are chasing profits through efficiency and differentiation goals. OM is integral to both objectives.

1.2.1 The Importance of Operations Management to Business

From a business perspective, operations management is a strategic capability; that is, it can impact business performance and profits directly.

Note the leveraging power of operations management. To illustrate:

Suppose, selling price   = $10/unit
          Sales   = 1 unit
     and COGS   = $9/unit (no other costs involved).
Therefore, total earnings = (Sales revenue − COGS)
                          = $10 * 1 unit − $9
                          = $1

Now suppose, operations works with its suppliers and reduces COGS *by* $1 (price and sales remain unchanged).

Therefore, total earnings = $10 * 1 unit − $8
                          = $2

A 100 percent boost in earnings from an 11 percent reduction in cost (from $9 to $8)!

Whereas, consider if cost ($9) and price ($10) remain the same, but marketing efforts boost sales. How much would sales have to increase to improve earnings to the same $2?

          Total earnings   = (sales revenue − COGS)
          Total earnings   = $2

So:

          $2   = ($10 * sales − $9/unit * sales)
               = $1 * sales
Thus: required sales   = 2 units (would be higher in reality, since we have not included the costs of marketing efforts).

Marketing would have to increase sales by *100 percent* (from 1 unit to 2 units), in order to obtain the same financial impact that we can get from just an *11 percent* reduction in operational costs.

Speaking the language of the executive suite:

Return on assets (ROA) = earnings/assets = (revenue − costs)/assets   (Equation 1.1)

Boosting ROA would require increased revenues, lower costs, and/or a reduction in assets. Operations drives all three elements of the ROA model: Revenue, costs, and assets.

Operations management can drive revenues too—here are some examples.

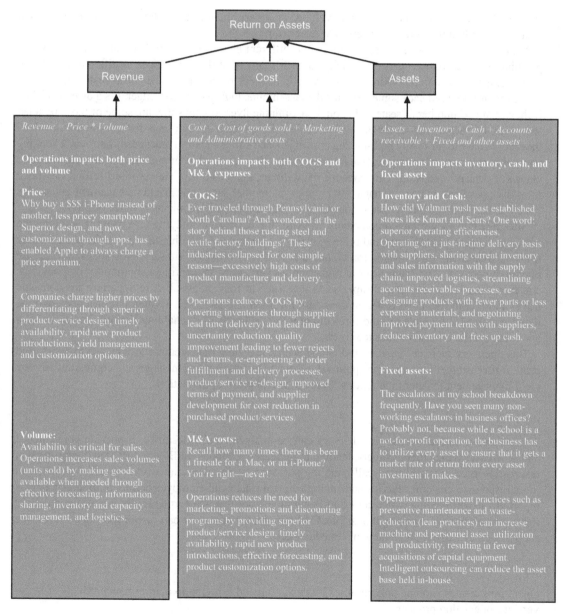

Figure 1.3 How Operations Contributes to ROA

OM IN PRACTICE

How Operations Generates Sales Revenue

Intelligent operations management through yield management, process/product design, and excellence of quality drives sales revenue in difficult business environments.

Yield Management

'Sabre,' the yield management system developed at American Airlines, is thought to have contributed nearly $1.4 billion in a three-year period at American.

Yield management categorizes customers into different classes based on their capacity for advance planning and distributes a part of capacity to each segment at different prices at different times. For example, airlines open up bookings up to a year in advance of the flight. The cheap seats sell out first. However, airlines hold back some seats for the last-minute, high-paying passenger. It's a dicey decision. If they retain 'x' number of seats and enough last-minute flyers do not show up, some of those retained seats may fly vacant—a loss for the airline. If they do not keep enough seats for last-minute travelers, they would have to turn away high-paying passengers and suffer a loss. In practice, airlines track booking patterns in real time, allocating seats to low-fare classes if sales are slow or pulling seats from lower-price classes if demand trends up. This happens many times, and customers are surprised to find low-price fares disappearing one hour to magically reappear at another, later time. Yield management guides this dynamic distribution of seat capacity into different fare classes for optimizing revenue or profit.

Sites like http://www.farecompare.com work for the passenger, studying fare patterns and booking trends to suggest a 'right' time and price to make the booking. According to reports, the cheapest day to fly is Wednesday for domestic travel, and the best day to book is Tuesday. Nowadays, airlines are playing it both ways, releasing seats at higher prices very early on, continuously monitoring bookings, and then selectively releasing cheaper seats just three to four months before departure for domestic travel and four to five months before departure for international travel. Twitter and Facebook and the like are making it possible to send fares directly to customers 24/7, enabling limited time-flash sales and other special events for selected flyers.

Bus operators such as Megabus and BoltBus also use yield management to increase revenues and profit from customer time and price points. Real estate investment and management companies employ yield management to determine rentals for revenue and profit optimization.

Process Design

The process of product or service delivery can be analyzed and redesigned to provide convenience and time/cost savings for customers, leading to increased revenues. JetBlue redesigned the airline seat reservation processes and used call-handling software to distribute the work virtually—resulted in more responsive customer service and savings on real estate and employee commute time. Amazon is reportedly experimenting with trucks outfitted with 3D printers that could rapidly produce and deliver items on their travels—making it possible, for example, to make a car part on the spot for a car service shop or a heart valve for an emergency medical need.

Product Design (and Redesign)

Operations creates revenue opportunities by designing and bringing to market new products or better versions of existing products.

Figure 1.4 Cell Phones Circa 2007–2015
Source: Author.

Excellence in Quality

Many businesses have high costs and higher prices yet continue to draw customers. They offer the highest quality of service and product. The Ritz-Carlton and Four Seasons hotel brands and Rolls Royce Motors are examples of premium category services and products with premium pricing and high cost structures. The Geek Squad (Best Buy) provides superior service, and customers are willing to pay for the reassurance of top quality service.[2]

Operations, therefore, is much more than a cost-cutter—it can be a significant revenue driver and a profit generator.

1.2.2 Why Is Operations Management Important for You?

Operations Management is a *foundational* discipline for a business education. Pedagogically, operations management teaches us how to make smart, sound, and sustainable operational decisions. It will help you understand the basic tasks involved in the design and delivery of services and products to the customer, and that knowledge will help you in any job—finance, accounting, human resources, marketing.

- Auditing that unusual increase in inventory turnover would become easier and more rigorous when you have an insight into the underlying operational reasons.
- A marketing promise to a customer for delivery in 24 hours for a product shipped from 5,000 miles away can be justified if supported by a keen awareness of the operational capabilities of the organization.
- Human resource majors can turn to the forecasting techniques they learned in operations management for staffing planning and recruitment.

An operations background could propel you to a leadership position one day. GM recently appointed Mary Barra as CEO, recognizing her nuts and bolts familiarity with GM operations as executive vice president, supply chain. Apple CEO Tim Cook has an operations background, with stints as director of fulfillment at IBM, and VP corporate materials at Compaq. Mark Hurd, president of Oracle Corp and ex-CEO of Hewlett Packard, used his operations background and savvy to help HP grow revenue from $80 billion to $118.4 billion and more than double its earnings per share. Myron E. Ullman III, recently appointed CEO of J.C. Penney, also has a strong operations background, with a degree in industrial management. Spencer Stuart, a research and consulting organization, reported recently for the second year in a row that operations was found to be among the most common functional backgrounds of CEOs among the S&P 500.[3] Another study found that CEOs with a functional background in operations perform better than CEOs with other functional backgrounds and that recent placements to CEO positions favor candidates with a background in operations.[4]

Operations managers earned a median of $96,430 in 2014, with some earning more than $187,199 per year (Bureau of Labor Statistics). The Bureau of Labor anticipates about 244,000 new jobs in operations management over the next 10 years. Positions in operations management are represented by titles such as:

- Operations analyst
- Six Sigma black belt
- Purchasing manager
- Transportation manager
- Warehousing manager
- Production planner and scheduler
- Project manager
- Business analyst
- Distribution and location planner
- Inventory control manager
- Buyer
- VP-Operations
- Chief Operating Officer (COO)

You can look for jobs on sites such as Monster.com, as well as on professional association sites, such as:

Job Sites and Professional Associations for OM Careers

- The Institute of Supply Management (www.ism.ws)
- APICS—the Association for Operations Management (www.apics.org)
- The Council of Supply Chain Management Professionals (http://cscmp.org)
- International Society of Logistics (SOLE—www.sole.org)
- International Warehouse Logistics Association (www.warehouselogistics.org)
- American Society for Quality (http://www.asq.org)
- American Society of Transportation and Logistics (AST&L)
- The Council of Supply Chain Management (http://cscmp.org/)
- Association for Manufacturing Excellence (http://www.ame.org)

Several of these associations offer professional certifications.

Hires in operations management are made by service enterprises including financial houses, hospitals, banks, airlines, medical, consulting, insurance, restaurants, and the hospitality businesses; by manufacturing organizations such as the automotive, electronics, medical devices, and food industry; and by the nonprofit sector, including public services, government enterprises, NGO's, transportation, and regulatory organizations. Jobs that combine functional expertise and operations expertise with titles such as 'Business support functions consultant specializing in Human Resources' and 'Business support functions consultant specializing in Finance' are emerging in companies such as McKinsey and Goldman Sachs.

1.2.3 Where Does Operations Management Reside in the Firm?

Operations personnel are prominently located in organizational charts, with highly visible titles and major responsibilities. Organizational reporting relationships are generally confidential information, but a few examples can be found:

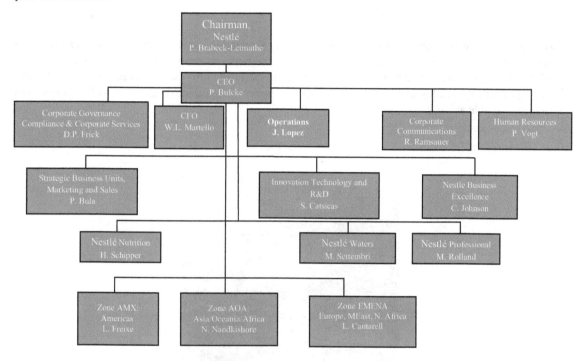

Figure 1.5 Organizational Chart, Nestlé S.A.

Source: *Nestlé S.A.,* accessed Sept. 26, 2015, http://www.nestle.com/AboutUs/Management.

KEY POINTS

- OM is a powerful lever for generating profit. A dollar saved through OM adds a whole dollar to profits.
- Saving opportunities abound in OM because it is involved in activities that typically are highly resource intensive in terms of capital, material, and labor investments.
- Revenue-generation opportunities abound in OM through yield management, price premiums through differentiating with superior product/service design, timely availability, rapid new product introductions, and customization options.
- OM designs, analyzes, and redesigns products and processes to satisfy current and emerging customer, community, and ecological sensibilities. Knowledge of OM helps non-OM people see and exploit similar opportunities.
- OM seeks to fulfill a dual responsibility to the business owner: delivering efficiency and affordability today while innovating to bring the products and services of tomorrow.
- OM seems to be an increasingly effective preparatory route to CEO positions, nowadays.

1.3 How Is It Done?

What are the actual tasks in operations management that transform promises into reality? Let us take a look at the operational tasks required to deliver on an actual promise made by a company to its customers.

1.3.1 The Tasks of Operations Management

A while ago, Walgreens introduced the 'European Beauty Collection,' seven high-end skin-care lines from five countries—France, Spain, Greece, Germany, and Switzerland—at nearly 1,000 of its stores.[5]

What is Walgreens promising its customers? *Choose me*, because I *promise* you a fine collection of exclusive beauty products, readily available, at a competitive price, in an attractive location, with expert service assistance available at hand.

Figure 1.6 Beauty Aisle at Walgreens

Source: Author.

What are the key operations management tasks involved in delivering on Walgreen's promise? Operations would need to:

- Forecast potential demand for the seven skin care lines. Separate forecasts would have to be developed for each line, taking into account possible complementarities and substitutes among the selection. Note the challenge: Historical sales data do not exist, and the products are fashion items with high demand uncertainty, dissimilar to any other product that Walgreens carries and has experience forecasting.
- Identify and select suppliers—recall these are new products, and Walgreens buyers probably have little knowledge of the supply market.
- Ensure quality control—at supplier sites worldwide and along the supply chain. Walgreens would probably initially need to hire external expertise for the job. Finding a toxic chemical like lead in a skin care cream would be a disaster.
- Decide how much to order of each of the seven products at a time, and time its orders to minimize inventory holding and order placement expenses.
- Determine whether and how to transport the products from the point of entry to central warehouses or for direct shipment to its stores
- Determine how much to stock of each product at each store. The challenge is to ensure that supply meets demand without carrying huge stocks. Returns may be difficult, and discounting would diminish brand value.
- Manage a global supply chain—international chains have long and uncertain lead times, with accompanying financial, logistical, foreign exchange, and quality risks. Newer uncertainties that operations needs to manage concern ethics and sustainability. Children cannot be involved in the manufacture or delivery of the products, animals cannot be harmed or affected, and sustainability and compliance concerns would have to be addressed.
- Create a special layout and ambience for the special line, preferably far away from the diaper and snack aisles.
- Recruit/train and schedule personnel who can best represent the product in terms of image and knowledge. In all likelihood, a commission compensation system would be designed for such employees. Hourly paid workers would not be a good fit.

Note that Walgreens is not manufacturing the products, so production tasks are not included. The tasks in operations management are not essentially different between manufacturing and service, but there are some unique traits of each that do affect some operational decisions—we shall revisit this issue at greater length in our section on product and service design (chapters 2 and 3).

1.3.2 Operations Management Strategy

The purpose of the business is often stated explicitly in a 'mission statement.' *Business strategy* describes how the business chooses to compete in its chosen market(s) and supports the mission statement. *Functional strategy* describes how each part of the business sets its own goals and makes choices to support the business strategy. *Functional strategy* is executed through *operational practices*.

Businesses in the same industry may pick very different ways to compete and, resultantly, have very different operations strategies. Walmart's mission is "saving people money," targeted through a business strategy of offering "quality merchandise at the lowest prices." The functional level operations strategy develops aligned cost, quality, and availability goals that, in turn, are achieved through operational practices in focal areas such as supply chain management, logistics, and inventory management. Whole Foods, in contrast, has

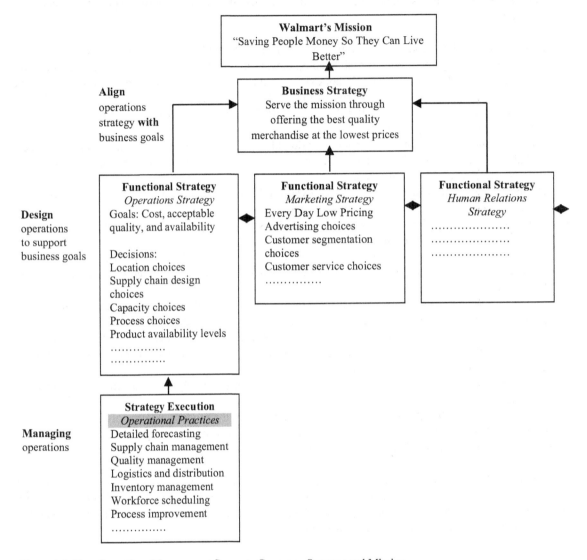

Figure 1.7 How Operations Management Supports Company Strategy and Mission

"Whole Foods, Whole People, Whole Planet" in its mission statement, focusing on the "health, well-being, and healing of both people—customers, Team Members, and business organizations in general—and the planet." Saving people money is obviously not the prime objective here. Whole Foods differentiates through its business strategy that emphasizes quality of product and service to customers, community, and the environment—not quite Walmart. We would expect to see these business goals reflected in Whole Foods' functional operations strategy, actualized through operational practices such as green sourcing, quality audits, and a very selective supplier base with deep ties.

It is difficult to achieve excellence on all performance dimensions—and make an acceptable profit. For example, McDonald's does well on efficiency and cost, but Chipotle does better on quality and innovation. USPS does well in terms of lower prices, but FedEx does better in terms of delivery speed. So competitive advantage needs to be sharply defined and then pursued by designing operations suitably. Note that operational practices and strategies may not keep pace with business strategy changes due to bureaucracy or other reasons. Also, practices and functional strategies may change from time to time in the name of improvement. Any change, though, can be called an improvement only if it helps improve performance on the strategic goals of the business.

KEY POINTS

- OM knowledge helps every decision maker understand the impact of decisions on work systems.
- OM teaches managers to view business in terms of work systems that can be examined, dissected, and put back together for improved performance.
- OM responsibilities are situated at senior organizational levels, enabling it to influence and participate in business strategy formulation as well as execution.
- OM consists of a collection of decisions and tasks that can be sequenced into three sets of actions: aligning, designing functional strategic decisions, and managing operational practices.
- Aligning refers to the act of ensuring that operations management goals support company business strategy.
- Functional strategic decisions refer to foundational decisions in business operations, such as location, capacity planning, product/service design and process choice, supply chain design, and forecasting.
- Operational practices refer to subsequent day-to-day decisions and tasks such as process analysis and management, forecasting short term and medium term, capacity planning, inventory management, quality management, scheduling, supply chain management, and project management.

1.4 Was It Done Right?

Business decision makers maintain focus, speed, and direction by steering with a dashboard of key performance indicators (KPI). Operations employs both strategic and operational dashboards, depending on the decision maker's level in the organization and the depth of information desired. KPIs on a strategic dashboard can be drilled down to connect with underlying KPIs on an operational dashboard. Dashboards can also provide visual comparisons with KPI levels of earlier years. Examples of both types of dashboards are provided below—of course, organizations custom build dashboards to suit their unique reporting and monitoring needs.

1.4.1 Strategic KPI Dashboard

The strategic dashboard tells a disturbing story. The business seems overly focused on efficiency and cost control. Sales are mediocre, but margins are being maintained for now because of cost efficiencies. The future looks dark. Quality and innovation are deteriorating, sales will eventually drop drastically when the new product pipeline dries up, and margins will come under pressure when efficiency gains plateau and the market demands price slashing for aging products.

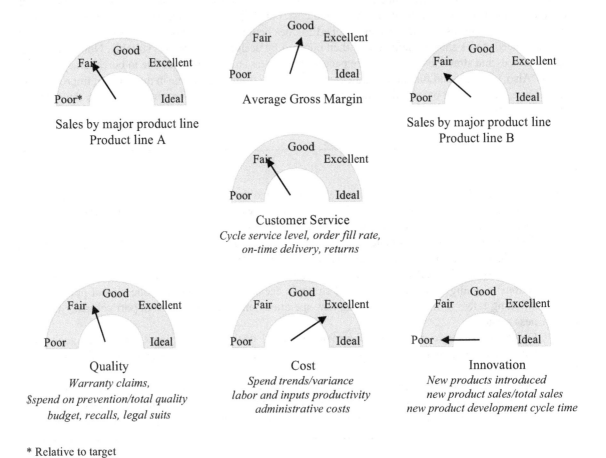

Figure 1.8 Tracking Performance on a Strategic Key Performance Indicators Dashboard

* Relative to target

1.4.2 Operational KPI Dashboard

The operational dashboard provides more detailed insight on the state of affairs in the business. The cost control and efficiency focus is evident from the input costs, inventory holding costs and manufacturing cycle time metrics. The decline in quality is reflected in the poor supplier and internal quality. The worker absenteeism rate reflects employee morale and engagement. The low reading appears to reinforce the lack of strategic attention to anything else but costs. Perhaps most strikingly, the new products prototyped metric shows a dismal 'poor' rating, with major adverse implications for the company's ability to compete on differentiation.

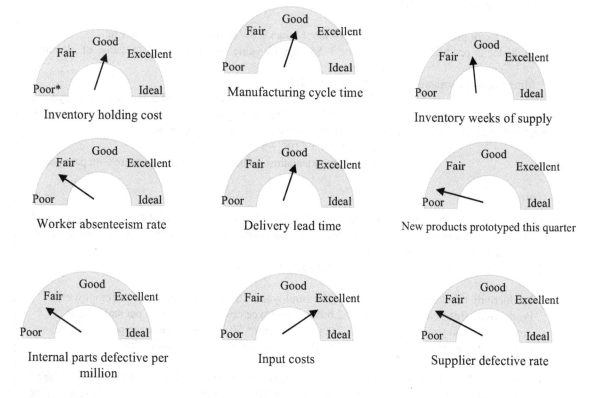

* Relative to target

Figure 1.9 Tracking Performance on an Operational Key Performance Indicators Dashboard

1.4.3 Productivity of Work Systems

Productivity measures the value of the output relative to the value of the input. In computational terms:

Single factor productivity = output/input value of a factor   (Equation 1.2)
Multi-factor productivity = output/input value of selected factors   (Equation 1.3)
Total system productivity = output/total input value of all factors   (Equation 1.4)

Example 1

Output of house cleaning in a motel = 80 rooms in a day; room rate = $50/day
   Inputs: 5 people working 8 hours each in a day at $15/hour; total cleaning and replenishment supplies $100/day; depreciation on cleaning equipment = $75/day;

Using equations 1.2, 1.3 and 1.4:

Single factor productivity = 80 rooms/# labor hours = 80/40 hrs = 2 rooms/labor hr
Multi-factor productivity = 80 rooms * $50/day/($ value of labor hrs) + ($ value of cleaning supplies)
(direct costs/factors only) = $4,000/($600 + $100)
= 5.72 (benchmark against industry figures and compare with past years)

Total system productivity = 80 rooms * $50/day/($ value of labor hrs) + ($ value of cleaning supplies) +
(direct and indirect costs) ($ value of depreciation on cleaning equipment)
= $4,000/($600 + $100 + $75)
= 5.16 (benchmark against industry figures and compare with past years)

Example 2

Revenues for a bank this year are $12 billion ($11 billion last year), while total employee costs are $2 billion ($2.5 billion last year) for a workforce of 10,000 employees (12,000 last year). Some of the work has been outsourced since last year.

The manager of the bank computes bank productivity as follows:

Productivity this year = $12 billion/10,000 employees = $1.2 million revenue per employee
Productivity this year = $12 billion/$2 billion employee costs = $6 revenue per staff dollar
Productivity last year = $11 billion/12,000 employees = $0.92 million revenue per employee
Productivity last year = $11 billion/$2.5 billion = $4.40 revenue per staff dollar

The manager claims a bonus based on the notable improvement in productivity. Is she right in her claim?

No! The single factor productivity measures computed by her do not reflect current reality. Note that a part of the work has been outsourced since last year. The correct approach to measuring productivity would involve a multi-factor computation, requiring outsourcing cost figures (say $0.40 billion):

Multi-factor productivity this year = $12 billion/($2 billion employee costs + $0.40 billion cost of outsourced activities)
= 5.00
Multi-factor productivity last year = $11 billion/$2.5 billion (employee costs – no outsourcing at that time)
= 4.40

The productivity increase is not as high as claimed! It's important to include all relevant inputs and their associated costs to ensure accurate productivity calculations.

Like many measures, productivity metrics can be manipulated in the short run by running a short-staffed operation, for instance, by cutting corners on quality or safety, or by raising output prices (sales volume remains unchanged). Remember, too, that comparisons of productivity using labor hours may be misleading if labor cost differences are not taken into account. A foreign operation in a developing country may use double the labor hours relative to a similar operation in the U.S. but still be competitive because of lower labor costs. Also, besides productivity and quality, other aspects of business performance are equally relevant, including ensuring that what is made is what the market wants. Like with all such measures, one must check trends and benchmark, where possible.

QUICK CHECK

Eight workers working 8-hour days prepare and issue 18 insurance policies/day each, valued at $200/policy. Each worker is paid a salary of $3,000/month (20 working days). They use a total of 4 lbs. of paper (at $1/lb.) each and 3 ink toners/day (at $40/toner). They also each get 3 free beverages in a day as well as a free massage at the end of the day (cost to company $0.10/beverage, $25/massage). Depreciation on computers and beverage machines is $300/day. What is the company's:

a) Labor productivity?
b) Multi-factor productivity?
c) Total system productivity?

Labor productivity	= Output units/labor hr input value = 18 policies a day * 8 workers / 8 workers * 8 hrs
	= 2.25 policies/labor hr
Multi-factor productivity	= 18 policies * 8 workers * $200 per policy / (8 workers * 8 hrs per day * $150/day salary)
(direct costs only)	+ (4 lbs paper * $1 per lb + 3 toners * $40 per toner)
	= 2.96
Total system productivity	= 18 * 8 * $200/(8 * 8 * $150) + (4 * $1 + 3 * $40) + (3 beverages * 8 workers * $0.10
(all costs)	+ 1 massage * 8 workers * $25 per massage + $300 daily depreciation)
	= 2.82

KEY POINTS

- OM identifies and employs dashboards of key performance indicators (KPI) to monitor system operations and their impact on business performance.
- A high-level dashboard can look at trends in sales, gross margins, cost, customer service, quality, and innovation performance.
- More in-depth probes are performed with lower-level dashboards that look at trends in inputs costs, supplier quality, inventory holdings, and delivery lead times.
- Dashboards have current as well as anticipatory value.
- Productivity is a common measure of the efficiency of operational processes.
- Quality, innovation, and time are other metrics that tell us if we are doing a good job.
- Metrics can be manipulated.

1.5 Current Trends in Operations Management

It's a fast-paced world, and operations management is a fast-paced function. Several operations areas are witnessing special attention of late and are seen to have significant potential to contribute to competitive advantage. Among them are supply chain management, service science, lean operations, sustainability, and new technologies in operations. Let's take a quick look at important emerging issues in managing operations in the 21st century.

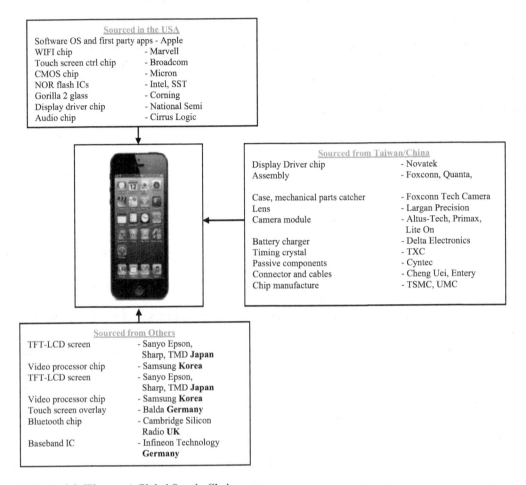

Figure 1.10 Apple's iPhone—A Global Supply Chain

1.5.1 Supply Chain Management (SCM)

Take a look at iPhone's supply chain[6]—imagine the complexity of finding, evaluating, synchronizing, and managing supplier quality, delivery, price, risk, and performance. By the way, what do you think is the costliest part of the phone? (See "The $um of iPhone Parts" in chapter 10.)

US corporations such as Texas Instruments, Fairchild Semiconductor, Avago Technologies and Maxim Integrated have joined Apple's supply base for the newer iPhone series. Current suppliers also include SONY, Toshiba, TDK, and Win from Japan and Taiwan, as well as STMicroelectronics (gyroscope), an Italian-French company.

SCM includes:

- The design of the supply chain—selecting suppliers in different locations that can make and move goods and services in a manner that supports the buying company's competitive edge. A company selling a fairly mature product, say flat screen TVs, would look for cost, efficiency, reliability, and quality in its suppliers, whereas in a growth market such as smart phones, a supply chain would be designed primarily on the criteria of quick delivery and rapid response capability to changes in demand

and features. Cost and efficiency would not be the primary supplier selection criteria (initially)—speed and flexibility is of the essence. And perhaps quality lapses, too, may be forgiven, if relatively minor in nature and corrected quickly.

- The supply chain thus built requires active management including influence, reporting, evaluation, and control mechanisms. The typical tasks of management are complicated by such factors as distance, time, logistical and infrastructural weaknesses, corruption, language differences, and cultural differences towards work quality, time commitments, and ethics. Project management and team management skills become critically important. Information technology enables collaborative planning, communication, visibility, accountability, monitoring, coordination, evaluation, and control of the work of all the companies involved in the task of making and moving goods and services to the ultimate consumer.
- Supply chain design today also needs to satisfy other criteria such as ethics and sustainability.
- Supply base optimization is the intelligent selective whittling of supplier numbers to selective key suppliers in whom investment is made for deep relationships, large volume business, new product development, process improvement, and quality at source certification.

SCM design and management will be discussed in more detail in chapters 10 ("Supply Chain Design") and 11 ("Managing Supply Chains") of the text.

1.5.2 Service Science

Look at the pictures below—mark the dramatic decline in manufacturing employment and the equally dramatic rise in service industry employment.

Currently, over 80 percent of the U.S. GDP (gross domestic product) is service-based (Bureau of Labor Statistics).[7] Operations designs and studies service processes, that is, the work steps or actions required in the preparation and delivery of a service. A service process could constitute the steps that a heart patient goes

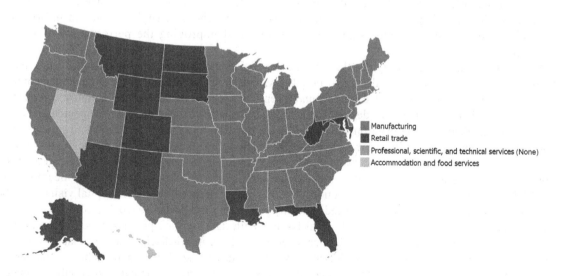

Figure 1.11 Industry-Wise Breakdown—Employment in the U.S., 1990

Source: "Major Industries with Highest Employment, by State 1990," *U.S. Bureau of Labor Statistics*, accessed July 28, 2014, www.bls.gov/opub/ted/2014/ted_20140728.htm.

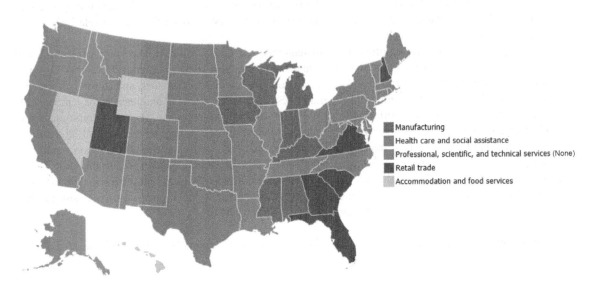

Figure 1.12 Industry-Wise Breakdown—Employment in the U.S., 2013

Source: "Major Industries with Highest Employment, by State 2013," *U.S. Bureau of Labor Statistics*, accessed July 28, 2014, www.bls.gov/opub/ted/2014/ted_20140728.htm.

through in a hospital, the tasks performed in a car wash, or the activities involved in a visit to the hair stylist. Service science (formally called SSME—service science management engineering) is the systematic application of operations management, statistics, psychology, engineering, and information technology to the cause of understanding, analyzing, and improving the performance of service processes.

Service processes are generally people centered or people sensitive and are distinguished from manufacturing operations in terms of degree of tangibility, frequency of and intimacy of customer contact, customer focus, variability in service delivery and reception, and simultaneity of production and consumption. Service science visualizes the desired status of processes as instrumented, inter-connected and intelligent, with applications ranging from smart buildings, cars, highways, and appliances to power grids, apparel, and water grids. To illustrate, companies are working on an at-home health care process that is instrumented with sensors to monitor and capture and send data to centralized collection and analysis points. The process will use data analytics to extract intelligence about health signs from incoming and stored data for emergent and preventive actions. In theory, regular family visits or hospital visits could be replaced with such a process, but people and company pain points can be envisaged, including psychological, security, confidentiality, legal, and social issues. With data, service processes can be monitored, controlled, optimized, and integrated. Service science applies a multi-disciplinary approach to try and provide comprehensive solutions to such issues. We shall study some of these approaches in chapters 2, 3, 4, 6 and 9, on process/product design, managing processes, managing capacity, and quality management, respectively.

1.5.3 Lean Operations

Lean, in its simplest form, means shedding fat and waste reduction. Fat and waste takes a variety of forms—materials, time, space, energy—and occurs because of deficiencies in work system design and operation, including task duplication, bottlenecks, poor quality, badly designed complex or long work pathways, disorganized work environments, unreliable suppliers, and redundancies in product or service design. Operations management provides an array of useful tools for reducing waste and eliminating fat. We shall examine some of the tools of lean operations in the chapters on managing inventory and managing processes (chapters 8 and 4, respectively).

1.5.4 Sustainability

Do not take more than what you can give back. Take only so much, such that enough is left for the provider to survive and regenerate. Ancient cultures practiced sustainability through taboos and customs. Prohibitions on hunting or fishing during spawning season ensured survival of the species and those who depended on it. In ancient times in Asia, prohibiting the felling of perennial fruit-bearing trees species such as the banyan and mahua ensured that their fruit fed animals at times when other trees were barren.

Sustainability can concern energy, water, biodiversity and land use, chemicals, toxins and heavy metals, air pollution, waste management, ozone layer depletion, oceans and fisheries, and deforestation. The sustainability challenge is being met by business in several ways:

*   **Sustainability through analysis and design:**[8]

A sustainability analysis begins with finding out the sources of waste and evaluating the amount and nature of wastes being produced by the business currently.

Key consumption ratios are defined: e.g., ratios of grouped inputs per unit, e.g., power used/unit produced, or ratio of virgin material/recycled material used; water in product/water discharged; and trends. Equipped with this preparatory knowledge, a business can develop a TBL (triple bottom line—Profit, People, and Planet) plan that links specific sustainability projects with goals. Such projects may include waste reduction initiatives, using the 5Rs to identify consumption reduction opportunities: refuse, reduce, reuse, repair, recycle, in order of priority. For example, refusing to use plastic bags would be ideal, reduction of plastic used in a bag would be less so, reusing plastic bags even less so, and so on.

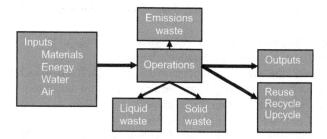

Figure 1.13 Understanding the Sources and Disposal of Wastes

A good example is a bag of chips. We buy a bag of chips, crunch through them in quick-time, and trash the packet, which then remains in the environment for a long time. Frito-Lay studied the issue and came up with a bio-degradable bag.

Biodegradable but Noisy Bag-o-Chips!

Figure 1.14 Frito-Lay Bag-o-Chips.
Source: Author.

What happens to those bags once we shake out that last bit of chip inside? Typically, chips bags are made from nonrenewable materials and just become litter. Frito-Lay took steps:

- Use less, eliminating five billion square inches of packaging by reducing the materials used by 10 percent.
- Use plant-based materials to make the bags—now, 33 percent of every 10 1/2 oz. size SunChips® bag is made with renewable, plant-based materials.
- Introduce the first fully compostable chip bag of its kind, built to decompose in about 14 weeks.

As Frito-Lay says, "So you eat the chips. The earth eats the bag. And we all live in a cleaner world."
NewsFlash: Frito-Lay withdraws biodegradable bags!
What happened? Well, the bags were biodegradable all right, but made a lot of noise when opened and handled. So it's back to the drawing board for Frito-Lay. And the chips will return to the old bags, which are still noisy, but won't wake up the neighbors.
NewsFlash: Frito-Lay makes quieter SunChip Bags!
A newly designed biodegradable Frito-Lay chips bag uses a different adhesive to reduce the noise level to around 70 decibels, on par with ordinary chip bags.
Even the usual plastic bags can be "upcyled" into new products such as a wood substitute that may be used for park benches, landscape decking, boat docks, and the like. For example, Frito-Lay bags have been used to make trash cans sold at Home Depot.

Adapted from: "Our Steps to Reduce, Reuse and Recycle," *Frito Lay,* http://www.fritolay.com/purpose/our-steps.

Figure 1.15 Nature Designs a Product

Source: "BionicAnts," *Festo Americas*, Sept. 26, 2015, https://www.festo.com/net/en_corp/SupportPortal/press.aspx?tab=11&s=t.

Businesses are also looking to nature for sustainability ideas. Biomimicry is an emerging discipline that studies and adapts nature's designs to human applications.[9]

Design principles from ant anatomy and cooperative behavior have been used as a role model by the engineers at Festo Inc., using complex control algorithms. The 'ants' work collaboratively, as in real life, to perform tasks jointly (see Fig 1.15 above). Another design takes inspiration from the way a metacarpal bone in a horse gains structural strength via a hole-based stress-dispersing microstructure. This design principle is applied for saving material and fuel and for increasing the structural robustness of planes, boats, automobiles, and other structures that have holes for wiring or fuel and hydraulic lines.

- **Sustainability through carbon credit offsets:** A carbon offset is a financial instrument—one carbon offset represents the reduction of one metric ton of carbon dioxide or its equivalent in other greenhouse gases. Organizations may purchase carbon offsets in order to comply with legal caps on the total amount of carbon dioxide they are permitted to emit. Individuals can also purchase carbon offsets. Airlines offer passengers the option to pay for individual carbon offsets.
- **Sustainability through supply chain initiatives:** Since materials, inputs and systems are provided by suppliers, the supply chain presents enormous potential for designing and implementing sustainability initiatives. Such initiatives may include supplier rewards, joint process improvement programs, tracking GHG emissions, energy usage, supplier wages, use of sustainable sources, material toxicity, impact of material waste, and usage of recycled materials, as well as requiring 3rd party certification for major suppliers.
- **Sustainability through acquisition:** Coca-Cola acquired Odwalla, a leader in organic beverages, for $181 million and Republic Tea, a leader in organic tea bags, for $43 million. Clorox paid $900 million plus for Burt's Bees, a major producer of natural personal-care products. Colgate-Palmolive spent $100 million to acquire Tom's of Maine, another sustainable brand in natural toothpaste and other personal-care products.

Measuring sustainability performance is a problem. A carbon footprint is "the amount of carbon dioxide released into the atmosphere as a result of the activities of a particular individual, organization, or community."[10] Similarly, water footprints are being estimated by researchers at the University of Twente, the Netherlands.[11] Water scarcity affects over 2.7 billion people for at least one month each year. Meanwhile, it takes 53 gallons of water, on average, to produce just one egg. Recognize, too, that a slice of pizza may take 43 gallons of water on average, while a bar of chocolate uses about 317 gallons of this scarce resource.[12] One problem in computing accurate carbon footprints is that the product usage stage may see more emissions and wastes than the product production and delivery stage—automobiles, for example. To illustrate, Greenpeace claims that devices like Apple's iPad have a larger footprint than would seem going by the size of the product, citing Internet cloud use and subsequent server farm energy demands for "dirty coal power."[13] Companies are also trying to measure sustainability through comprehensive sustainability indices, such as Walmart's sustainability index. Watch this clip for a practical farm-to-fork look at a sliced turkey product and the complexity underlying sustainability efforts in the field.[14]

Is sustainability profitable? The jury's still out on this. Atos Origin and IDC researched 165 European companies such as Rhodia, Ford Europe, Philips Lighting, and Volvo as well as industry associations to answer this question. Their findings suggested that companies with "more mature environmental sustainability programs have a profitability advantage over the industry in general." It's difficult, though, to separate the profits/share price effects of sustainability from other initiatives and firm-specific capabilities. The Dow Jones Sustainability Index tracks performance of companies with significant sustainability initiatives. Certainly, customers do not seem to pay more for sustainability, and, in fact, a recent survey shows that managers considered that 84 percent of their customers would choose lower costs over sustainability.[15]

OM IN PRACTICE

Monozukuri and Toyota

In Japanese '*Mono*' means an object, while '*zukuri*' is the act of making that object. Taken together, the Monozukuri philosophy is the act of making *carefully*, so as to maintain a balance between consumption, depletion, maintenance, and regeneration of production resources.

Toyota subscribes to the Monozukuri tradition in manufacturing, evaluating choices along five criteria: safety, environment, quality, production, and cost (in that order). Toyota considers human effort especially deserving of monozukuri, empowering, engaging, and involving workers to take pride in their work and output. For Toyota, monozukuri rather than regulations and compliance underlie environmental performance. Toyota now outperforms the rest of the industry in terms of the direct emissions measured in tons of CO_2 per vehicle manufactured.

Philips and a Circular Economy

Philips Healthcare's $200 million business of leasing equipment to a hospital, taking it back, and then refurbishing and leasing the same equipment to another customer, is going great guns. The original customer upgrades to a more current technology, while the latter's needs are met with tried out and budget-friendly equipment. Philips designs products that can be upgraded, refurbished, and ultimately recycled, well and easily. In doing so, Philips creates a circular economy, where products can be returned, refurbished and recirculated among customer's that have different profiles in terms of technology maturity, consumer needs, and budgetary constraints. New markets have emerged as a result. Of course, Philips engages with quality guarantees, service support availability, and education to quiet any misgivings about using a refurbished product.

Adapted from: Keivan Zokaei, Hunter Lovins, Andy Wood and Peter Hines, "Recapturing Monozukuri in Toyota's Manufacturing Ethos," *MIT Sloan Review*, March 11,2014; Keivan Zokaei, Hunter Lovins, Andy Wood, and Peter Hines, *Creating a Lean and Green Business System* (Boca Raton, FL: CRC Press, 2013). Thomas Fleming and Markus Zils "Toward a Circular Economy: Philips CEO Frans van Houten," *McKinsey Insights & Publications*, February 2014.

Can sustainability be enforced? Protocols such as Kyoto and recent laws are putting some teeth in the sustainability movement. Companies can continue to expect intense attention from social interest watchdogs.[16] Apps are also emerging to popularize sustainability.[17] Compliance, however, remains the primary reason for investments in sustainability.

KEY POINTS

- Operations management in the 21st century is likely to be much more concerned with environmental and social imperatives, driven by regulatory and social pressure.
- Lean is principally concerned with the reduction of waste in operations.
- Sustainability differs from lean in that it has a moral element and is much larger in scope.
- Sustainability is achieved not just through the reduction of waste in internal and supplier operations but also through the acquisition of sustainable businesses and carbon credit trading to offset sustainability deficits.
- Standardized metrics for evaluating sustainability performance are in the works, including carbon footprinting and sustainability indices.
- Supply chain management is a strong and growing priority action area for businesses, with more value being added by suppliers to company products and services.
- Service science is the application of a multi-disciplinary, data-driven, analytical, and behavioral approach to finding solutions to service problems in a dominantly service economy.

1.5.5 New Technologies in Operations

Manufacturing and service are pursuing the '3i' trinity of becoming fully instrumented, integrated and intelligent—a truly lights-out operation (machines do not need lighting to operate). Back in the 1980s, GM could not get its automation to perform properly, even with the lights on. The robots painted each other, dismembered other robots, smashed cars, and froze movement of materials in the plant.[18] Technology has made remarkable progress since then.

OM IN PRACTICE

Lights Out Factory

Figure 1.16 FANUC Plant

Source: Photo used with permission from FANUC.

"Not only is it lights-out," says a Fanuc vice president, "we turn off the air conditioning and heat too." At Fanuc's plants near Mount Fuji, manufacturing robots can operate unsupervised for as long as 30 days at a time. For the few humans, company kitchen robots cook rice, pack lunch boxes, and wash dishes. "They even wear rubber gloves." Similarly robots are now practically running full-fledged plants and warehouses at Amazon, Tesla, Philips, and many distribution centers.

See current video-cams of robotic manufacturing at http://www.fanuc.co.jp/en/profile/production/index.html and Tesla Motors "Part 1: Behind the Scenes of How the Tesla Model is Made," http://www.youtube.com/watch?v=8_lfxPI5ObM

Adapted from: John Markoff, "Skilled Work, Without the Worker," *New York Times*, Aug. 18, 2012; "Fade To Black: The 1980s Vision of 'Lights-out' Manufacturing, Where Robots Do All the Work, Is a Dream No More," Christopher Null and Brian Caulfield, *Business 2.0 Magazine,* June 1, 2003.

Rapid prototyping, radio frequency identification devices (RFID), computer-aided testing (CAT), computer-aided engineering (CAE), robotics, local area networks (LANS), vision systems and flexible manufacturing centers are considered the 'hard' factors of advanced manufacturing technology. 'Softer' technology areas involve design for manufacturing (DFM), productive/preventive maintenance, JIT, Kanban, concurrent engineering, value analysis/ engineering, and integration of manufacturing systems. Advanced technologies require accompanying changes in work practices, including skill upgrades, teaming, decentralization, operator preventive maintenance, and operator empowerment.[19]

The goal was and still remains for the customer at the end of the supply chain to be able to speak directly to the manufacturing/delivery system of every company in the chain, which will then proceed to procure the inputs and make the product precisely according to the customer's preferences. It's a challenge linking all the various systems, languages and communications platforms among the different functions and business units in a company on a single data and machine control highway, and tougher yet to replicate the same process in all the key members of a supply chain. Besides technological difficulties, a good deal of trust and loosening of control along functional and divisional lines, as also along the supply chain, is called for. Software companies such as SAP and Oracle and automation companies such as Fanuc are working towards such a future.

New technologies in services are also availing of advanced information and machine technologies. Ocado, an online grocer, has developed perhaps the world's best warehouse management system. Located in Hatfield, UK, Ocado combines advanced product storage and movement technologies with information systems to dispatch groceries from a centralized warehouse to 65 percent of UK postal codes.[20] Real time sensing technologies are moving real-time visibility to the front-line, in contrast to today's systems that, as IBM says, call for "trying to cross a street but you can only see how the traffic looked 5 minutes ago."[21]

3D printing is another emerging manufacturing technology on the cusp of mass commercialization. 3D printers contain both design and manufacturing features in one small machine and can today manufacture products using a variety of metals, powders, plastics and biological cells. Hospitals may soon one day be able to manufacture customized human hearts and livers on premises.

OM IN PRACTICE

OREO 3D Printer Makes Customized Flavor Cookies

Figure 1.17 Double-Stuf Oreos

Source: Evan-Amos, "Double-Stuf Oreos, by Nabisco," (Creative Commons [CC] license), via *Wikimedia Commons*, Feb. 19, 2011, http://commons.wikimedia.org/wiki/File%3ADouble-Stuf-Oreos.jpg.

Want an orange flavor Oreo? Simple—we'll just print up a dozen just for you! OREO introduced 3D printer vending machines recently at a tech show in Austin, Texas. The printers turn out "deliciously hyper-personalized and customized snacks"—the flavor to print is based on Twitter (hashtag #eat-thetweet). Production time is under two minutes, and flavors change with Twitter trends.

Adapted from: Garett Sloane, "Oreo Uses Twitter to Make 3D Cookies at SXSW," *Adweek,* March 6, 2014, http://www.adweek.com/news/technology/oreo-uses-twitter-make-3d-cookies-sxsw-156121.

The rapid development and transferability of technology have enabled many smaller companies and countries to leapfrog the intermediate stages of technology evolution. For instance, South Korea created its semi-conductor competency by accessing the best technology available in the world. China has surpassed the United States in a key measure of high tech competitiveness: On the Georgia Institute of Technology's biannual "High-Tech Indicators" scale of one to 100, China's technological standing shot up from 22.5 in 1996 to 82.8 by 2007, compared to the U.S. 2007 score of 76.1. The United States peaked at 95.4 in 1999.[22]

1.6 How to Read the Book

At this point, you may well exercise your fundamental right as a consumer and ask: Why should I choose to read *this* text?

Let me try to answer that. You should choose to read this text, because I promise that:

1   This text is unlike any other text you have probably read on a traditionally technical business subject. Each chapter will take you on an exciting journey into the core of a business and show you how it delivers on promises made to the customer—and does so at a profit.

2   The text will be an easy read, with a clear sequence of topics and simple, yet adequate, explanations of complex subjects.
3   The examples are real and drawn from your world.
4   If you engage the material, the book and course shall reward you. You will be able to apply many insights and tools to your current major and future career.
5   You can help keep the text updated by submitting current examples and new ideas, news, and insights of OM significance and relevance.

How should you read the text?

- Chapters 2 and 3 deal with the core task in operations management—to design and build products/services and the associated work processes to make and deliver them in volume.
- Chapter 4 is about managing a process, once built.
- Chapters 5–9 deal with ways to improve process performance—better forecasting, capacity, inventory, and quality management.
- Chapters 10 and 11 discuss supply chain design and its management. Companies today get many tasks done by suppliers.
- Chapter 12 explains how location decisions are taken by managers, especially important in view of the frequent openings of retail and service outlets.
- Chapter 13 is about managing projects. Unlike processes that are organized for high volume with standardized output, certain products and services are required in low volume for customized use. Work for such products and services is organized as projects, with specific and unique problems and challenges.

Chapters begin with a road map. Within each chapter, the material is wrapped up into four basic issues:

1   What is it?
2   Why is it important?
3   How is it done?
4   How do we know that it was done right?

The flow is punctuated with Key Points summaries after each significant section, and offers business examples and worked out problems.

I hope you liked this opening chapter. I wanted to provide you with a sense of the breadth and scope of operations management. Operations management has to deliver efficiency and affordability today while innovating to bring the products and services of tomorrow. Operations managers have to do so in ways that satisfy customer, community, and ecological sensibilities. It is my genuine hope that this textbook will help you learn and like operations management—well enough to not just understand it yourself but make you want to and be able to use it in your life. Experience the joy of operations, and let me know how you do!

What Have We Learned?

What Is Operations Management?

- Operations represents activities in a business that take inputs of different kinds, works on them to add value, and turns them into goods and services needed by the customer. Operations management concerns the planning and management of such activities.

- At a more basic level, operations management is that part of the business that is responsible for delivering on promises made to the customer.

Why Is It Important?

- Operations managers make a direct contribution to ROA—through increasing revenues, reducing costs, and increasing the productivity of asset-bases.
- Knowledge of OM helps non-OM people see and exploit opportunities to understand and improve the pattern of work in their jobs and functions.
- The number of CEOs with operations management backgrounds are increasing. Jobs in operations are available at all experience levels.

How Is It Done?

- To accomplish company goals, operations managers engage in a series of tasks, including forecasting, location planning, capacity planning, inventory management, supply chain management, quality management, and project management. An important part of the job is to understand and analyze work flows for product and process design and improvement.
- The tasks of operations managers can be organized into a simple framework:

  Aligning: Ensuring that operations goals are in synch with and support larger business goals.
  Designing: Foundational tasks that build business operations, including forecasting, process/product design, capacity planning, and supply chain design.
  Managing: Managing the flow of activities in the day-to-day running of a business, including work process analysis and improvement, managing capacity, supply chain management, inventory management, and managing quality and projects.

Was It Done Right?

- Operations managers design and use high-level dashboards (margins, customer service, quality, and innovation) and lower-level, operational dashboards (inputs costs, supplier quality, inventory holdings, delivery lead times) of key system performance indicators (KPIs).
- Productivity is a common measure of the efficiency of operational processes. Productivity can be measured as single-factor and multi-factor productivity.

Current Trends in Operations Management

- Supply chain management is a continuing and growing theme in operations management, with the supply and customer base stretching over multiple continents—risk, time, cost, and quality are areas of focus.
- Service science, a reflection of the importance of services to most developed economies, attempts to replace gut feel with sensory, data-driven, integrative, and intelligent decision-making systems, using quantitative and qualitative tools.
- Lean operations emphasizes the reduction and elimination of any kind of waste in business processes—using a variety of tools from process analysis to Six Sigma quality.
- Sustainability requires that businesses take only so much, such that enough is left for the provider to survive and regenerate. Means include lean methods for waste reduction, carbon-offsetting, and product, packaging, and process redesign for conserving resources.
- Technology advances provide instrumentation, integration, and intelligence to operations in manufacturing and services.

Key Terms

Inputs: Resources used in making and delivering a product or service. Resources can include workers, raw materials, technologies, land, information, and money.

Transformation of inputs: The actions performed on inputs resources by the company to convert them into sellable products or services.

Output: The final product or service that is sold to the customer.

'Hawthorne' effect: Experiments run during 1924–1927 at a Western Electric plant in Hawthorne found that workers responded positively if they felt that management was paying attention to them—the specific nature of the attention did not seem to matter.

ROA: Return on assets. From the profit and loss statement, subtract cost of goods sold, and selling and general administrative expenses (S&GA) from sales revenues. Divide this sum by the total asset figure that you can get from the balance sheet. The resultant figure is the ROA.

Yield management: A method that slices capacity in terms of market segment and offers those capacities at different times at different prices. Airlines offer lower prices early on for a certain number of seats, while releasing the remaining seats gradually at generally higher prices to higher-paying last minute business/emergency travelers. Prices and seat offerings are changed frequently in response to experienced demand and competitor actions.

Work processes: An ordered series of tasks that transform inputs and deliver a product or service to the customer. Basic work processes are sourcing inputs, production, and order fulfillment. Each, in turn, consists of sub-processes. Order fulfillment, for example, would include customer service and order receiving, warehouse inventory checking, production, shipping, and handling, and billing and accounts receivables.

Process design: The work steps and technologies involved in making and delivering a product or service.

Product design: The specifications of a product—functions, weight, looks, durability, ease of use, cost of making, packaging and so on. Tied intimately to consumer wants and process design. A product could be 'over designed,' containing features that the average consumer may rarely use (e.g., 'reset picture' in MS Word) or that are too expensive or complex to make/deliver with existing manufacturing and delivery processes.

Productivity: Ratio of value of output to value of input.

Supply chain management: A broad term that includes tasks such as qualifying and picking suppliers, monitoring their performance, establishing relationships with suppliers and customers, and directing the actions of all member companies in the supply chain to the needs of the ultimate consumer. A company can have different supply chains for different products and markets.

Service science: The study of service work operations (hotels, hospitals, banking, and insurance).

Lean operations: Improving a work process or a product design by identifying and eliminating wasteful activities and materials.

Sustainability: A method of doing business that uses just enough resources in making, delivering, and using a product, such that sufficient resources are left to regenerate. Also includes ethical considerations.

Carbon credit offset: A financial product that can be purchased by a company to compensate for its own generation of greenhouse gases. One carbon offset represents the reduction of one metric ton of carbon dioxide or equivalent greenhouse gas.

Discussion Questions

1   What is operations management? Respond in one clear and complete sentence of your own.
2   Why would knowledge of operations management basics be of use to:

   a)   A finance major
   b)   An accounting major
   c)   A marketing major
   d)   An HR major?

3   How does operations management affect the financial health of a company? Be brief and use numbers.
4   Develop some examples of aligning, designing and managing tasks and decisions for:

   a)   A school of business
   b)   A bakery
   c)   An airline
   d)   An automobile plant
   e)   A hospital

5   Go to RenttheRunaway.com, a designer dress rental startup. Describe some of the key operational tasks the company has to perform.

   Instructor: Forecasting types and sizes and colors, determining inventories of each type of dress, dry cleaning and repair, logistics, order-fulfillment, maintaining relationships with vendors (i.e. designers) . . .

6   Country differences drive globalization of manufacturing and supply. Find out the difference in comparative labor costs between the U.S. and China/India. Find out how trade balance trends between these economies. What is your read of things to come and what should the U.S. do?

Thought examples—how to estimate the:

1   Productivity of a department store: Sales/sq. foot or sales/store employee?
2   Productivity of a legal office: # of cases filed/# of lawyers (or cost of lawyers)?
3   Productivity of U.S. immigration offices: # of visas issued/# of labor hours (or cost of labor hrs)?
4   Productivity of a Broadway stage company?
5   Productivity of an airline?
6   Productivity of a school of business?

   Sum total of academic productivity + administrative productivity + proportion of graduating students/# of faculty? Can we quantify everything important to a comprehensive measurement of productivity? Is this a complete measure? How about quality, time taken to graduate, retention rate (1- dropout rate), market reception (remember the student who sued her school when she could not find a job on graduating)?

7   Productivity of people in different countries—see http://www.bls.gov/fls/chartbook.htm for international labor productivity comparisons.

Suggested Class Project

Ethics in OM

Many of you will work in global businesses and global supply chains. Somewhere, sometime, you will come across child workers in a business that you are a part of, or that is an important source of competitive advantage to your company. What will you do?

Nearly one in seven children in the world are forced into child labor, some as young as 5 years of age.[23] Look at the two pictures below. List five reasons against and two reasons in support of the use of child labor in business operations. The legal aspect is clear—practically all countries have laws barring the use of child labor—but some do not choose to or are unable to implement the laws.

Figure 1.18 Child Labor

Source: Shanjoy, "Child Labor, Bangladesh," [CC], via *Wikimedia Commons*, http://commons.wikimedia.org/wiki/File%3AChild_labor_Bangladesh.jpg.

Figure 1.19 Child Labor—Heavy Loads

Source: ArmyAmber, "Afghan Girl," [CC], via *Pixabay*, http://pixabay.com/en/girl-afghani-person-alone-child-60732/.

For Instructor

Not all work is bad for children. For example, a child who delivers newspapers before school would learn a lot about responsibility and the value of earned money. But what if the child is not paid or underpaid, or works all the time delivering papers?

Consider, though, if the alternative to work is worse? Starvation, being sold, or the death of siblings who are fed with the child's earnings? Or that competitors are doing it, and the low costs of directly or supplier employed labor enable the company to survive and compete?

UNICEF and ILO suggest the following remedies:

- Increased family incomes
- Education—that helps children learn skills that will help them earn a living
- Social services—that help children and families survive crises, such as disease, or loss of home and shelter
- Family control of fertility—so that families are not burdened by children

Note that none of these are in the realm of a typical manager's responsibility or control in a commercial business.

Service Science Sites

http://www.businessweek.com/technology/content/jan2005/tc20050121_8020.htm
http://www.ibm.com/developerworks/spaces/ssme
http://servtrans.com/blog/category/ssme/
U.S. Bureau of Labor Statistics

Notes

1 Please see this link for additional information on what a business operations manager does: http://money.usnews.com/careers/best-jobs/business-operations-manager, (accessed April 25, 2015).
2 I thank my colleague Corey Hwong for this example.
3 "Leading CEOs: A statistical snapshot of S&P 500 leaders," *Spencer Stuart,* February 2006, http://content.spencerstuart.com/sswebsite/pdf/lib/2005_CEO_Study_JS.pdf.
4 B. Koyuncu, S. Firfiray, B. Clais, and M. Hamori, "CEOs with a Functional Background in Operations: Reviewing Their Performance and Prevalence in the Top Post," *Human Resource Management,* 49(5), 2010, 869–882.
5 Amy Merrick, "Walgreen Pretties Up; European Skin Line, Store Advisers Mark a High-End Shift," *Wall Street Journal* (Eastern edition). New York, N.Y.: Feb. 8, 2007, B.2.
6 "A Surprising Report on How Much of Apple's Top Product is US-Manufactured," *Supply Chain 24/7,* Aug. 12, 2013, http://www.supplychain247.com/article/how_the_iphone_is_made, accessed April 25, 2015; see also http://www.allroadsleadtochina.com/2007/08/15/iphone-made-in-shenzhen.
7 "Largest Industries by State, 1990–2013," *The Economics Daily,* Bureau of Labor Statistics, U.S. Department of Labor, accessed Sept. 26, 2015, http://www.bls.gov/opub/ted/2014/ted_20140728.htm.
8 Adapted from Young, Ian, "Beyond Lean, Toward Green," *Target Volume 25,* 2009, www.AME.org. The complete article is available at http://www.ame.org/sites/default/files/documents/09-25-03Lean_toward_Green.pdf.
9 Read more about this new discipline at "A Biomimicry Primer," *Biomimicry 3.8,* accessed April 25, 2015, http://biomimicry.net/about/biomimicry/a-biomimicry-primer/.
10 "Carbon Footprint Definition," *Oxford Dictionaries,* accessed Sept. 26, http://www.oxforddictionaries.com/definition/english/carbon-footprint.
11 Securing Fresh Water for Everyone, *Water Footprint Network,* accessed April 25, 2015, http://waterfootprint.org/en/.
12 "Water Footprints Concepts and Definitions," *Grace Links,* accessed Sept. 26, 2015, http://www.gracelinks.org/1336/water-footprint-concepts-and-definitions.

13 "iPad, Internet and Climate Change," *Greenpeace*, March 30, 2010, http://www.greenpeace.org/usa/en/news-and-blogs/news/the-ipad-internet-climate-change-100329/.

14 Walmart, "The Secret Life of Sliced Turkey," *YouTube*, accessed April 25, 2015, https://www.youtube.com/watch?feature=player_embedded&v=ABqYqZluvDg.

15 "2013 Executive Survey on Supply Chain Sustainability," Alix Partners, accessed Sept. 26, 2015http://www.alixpartners.com/en/Publications/AllArticles/tabid/635/ArticleType/ArticleView/ArticleID/691/Default.aspx#sthash.qNi7A68j.dpbs.

16 Two examples are Exxon Complaints, www.ExxposeExxon.com, and Making Change at Walmart, http://makingchangeatwalmart.org; both accessed April 25, 2015.

17 An example is "Where's My Water," a free i-app or android app at https://play.google.com/store/apps/details?id=com.disney.WMWLite (accessed April 25, 2015).

18 "When GM's Robots Ran Amok," *The Economist* (US), Aug. 10, 1991, http://www.highbeam.com/doc/1G1–11105558.html.

19 Watch video-cams of rapid prototyping at http://www.youtube.com.

20 See Ocado's website at https://www.ocado.com/webshop/startWebshop.do.

21 "What Is Analytics," *IBM*, accessed April 25, 2015, http://www-01.ibm.com/software/analytics/infographics/what-is-analytics/.

22 Alan L. Porter, Nils C. Newman, J. David Roessner, David M. Johnson, and Xiao-Yin Jin, "International High Tech Competitiveness: Does China Rank #1?" *Technology Analysis and Strategic Management*, Vol. 21, no. 2, 173-193, 2009. Technology Policy and Assessment Center, Georgia Tech, Atlanta GA, USA. http://www.tpac.gatech.edu/sites/default/files/doc/HTI_China1_2008_jun10.pdf. For more about U.S. manufacturing, see "Hi-Tech in US Manufacturing," *Manufacturing News*, http://www.manufacturingnews.com; view a CNN video about how technology used in iPhones helped save a glass company at http://www.cnn.com/video/data/2.0/video/tech/2012/05/09/cm-f500-corning-iphone.cnn.html; hear a podcast at http://www.ncms.org/index.php/multimedia/podcasts/ for a scary yet thought-provoking discussion of manufacturing's significance to the U.S.

23 "Child Labor: Vital Statistics," *UN Resources for Speakers on Global Issues*, accessesd Sept. 26, 2015, http://www.un.org/en/globalissues/briefingpapers/childlabour/vitalstats.shtml.

Part I

Designing Products and Processes

2 Product Design

Note for instructor: Chapters 2 and 3 integrate product design with process and service design in the operational tradition of designing the product or service first before designing the supporting production and delivery process. There is a natural connectivity between product design and process design that students sometimes lose sight of.

Chapter Take-Aways

- The meaning of product, process, and service design
- The relationship between design and performance
- How to design—a product, a process, a service
- Key indicators of design performance
- Key trends in design

Product Design: A Road Map

2.6 Conclusion
   End of chapter
   - What have we learned?
   - Discussion questions
   - Suggested cases

Customer: *"Why should I choose you?"*

Business: *"Because we promise you a product that has been designed and built for your needs, lifestyle, and excitement."*

2.1 What Is Product Design?

"That's cool!" Design evokes the first emotion of excitement between a product and a consumer. Steve Jobs, former CEO of Apple, perhaps the best known example of a company with innovative product design, says "Design is not just what it looks like and feels like. Design is how it works. . . . Design is the fundamental soul of a human-made creation that ends up expressing itself in successive outer layers of the product or service."[1]

From an operations perspective, a good design must fit the needs and ability of everyone who touches the design and product—customer fit, manufacturing fit, worker fit, cost fit, movement fit, storage fit, ergonomic fit, disassembly fit, and remanufacturing/recycling fit. The International Design Excellence Awards (IDEA) recently added ecological, social, and economic responsibility, as well, to their list of design evaluation criteria.

OM IN PRACTICE

IDEA Best Student Designs

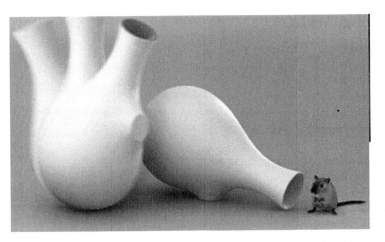

Figure 2.1 OneDown Mousetrap

Source: Photo used with permission by Aakash Dewan, www.aakashdewan.com.

International Design Excellence Award's (IDEA) 2010 competition's best-in-show winner was a One-Down mousetrap that swings upright using a mouse's own weight to keep it confined (designer Aakash Dewan, DSK International School of Design, India). The elegant simplicity of the mousetrap design and the humane treatment of the entrapped mouse appeals to the user. The absence of moving parts facilitates manufacturing, reduces tooling, material, and parts costs, and enhances the reliability of the product.

Adapted from: http://www.fastcompany.com.

KEY POINTS

What Is Design?

Product design has different meanings:

- Affordability, aesthetics, and functionality to the consumer
- Ease of manufacture to the manufacturer and worker
- Emotion and personal engagement to the designer
- Weight and volume to the transporter
- Ease of disassembly/disposal to the recycler
- Environmental and ethical concerns for the community

2.2 Why Is Design Important?

2.2.1 Importance for Businesses

As much as 80 percent of the final cost of making a product is determined by its design. Product design is inextricably woven into the fabric of operations, touching cost aspects such as choice of material, process design, quality standards, layout, worker skills, equipment choice, logistics, and supply chain design.

Design impacts company reputation and revenues. Contrast the brand image of Nike with New Balance; Target with Walmart; Apple with Dell; Jimmy Choo with NineWest. In each case, design has been a core component of brand reputation. Design can brand a user, too—just being seen in a Starbucks in some countries is a status symbol. And it's so easy to turn off that little footer "sent from my iPhone" (or iPad) that goes out with every mail and text—settings/mail/contacts/ . . . but how many of us choose to do so? Perhaps because, within us, is a secret desire to broadcast our 'i-Status' to the world.

Finally, design is important because bad design choices can come back to haunt companies.

OM IN PRACTICE

Ignition Switch Design Leads to Driver Fatalities

GM recalled over 2.5 million cars, including Chevy Cobalts and HHRs, Pontiac G5s, Pursuits, and Solstices and Saturn Ions and Skys (2003 to 2007) because the ignition switch could accidentally shut down the car while it was still being driven. Cars would veer off course and accidents would happen as engines stalled, power brakes and steering failed, and air bags failed to deploy. Ignition switch failures have been associated with at least 169 deaths and many injuries.

The sorry aspect of this tragedy is that it was not a quality or manufacturing defect that led to the ignition switch failure—rather a conscious decision to pick one switch design over another. GM considered two alternative designs while making its choice, a shorter switch or a longer switch.

The shorter switch was reportedly chosen for cost reasons (reportedly $0.57 parts cost)—and did not meet GM's own internal requirements. After experiencing problems with the shorter switch, documents suggest that GM quietly switched to the longer ignition design in later model cars but did not inform dealers or customers of the earlier model cars about the change. If they had, at least eight deaths that occurred in ignition-related accidents in the older cars after that change may have been prevented. Whether GM had enough information about the magnitude and consequences of ignition failures at that point in time is moot. It is also a fact that probability-based risk-cost decisions about the value of human life and the cost of product perfection are made regularly, not just by businesses, but also regulatory agencies such as the FDA, EPA, and the Transportation Department. Consider, too, that if every manufacturer literally had to treat human life as priceless, most products would not be affordable.

Congressional committees crucified the carmaker in several hearings, pointing out that a 57-cent parts cost change/car could have saved several lives and that GM had the knowledge and opportunity to do the right thing. It apparently did not—safety, investigators think, took a backseat to cost. General Motors is facing a significant hit to earnings and reputation as it tries to work its way out of this design problem—so far more than $5.3 billion on a problem authorities say could have been handled for less than a dollar per car.

Adapted from: Associated Press, "General Motors to pay $900 million for faulty ignition switches linked to at least 169 deaths," *The New York Daily News*, Sept. 18, 2015, http://www.nydailynews.com/new-york/gm-pay-900-million-fatal-faulty-ignition-switches-article-1.2365124; Yoel Minkoff, "Deadline Passes for GM Compensation Claims," *Seeking Alpha*, Feb. 2, 2015; Rich Gardella and Talesha Reynolds, "Did GM Reject Safer Ignition Switch Design in 2001 Because of Cost?" *NBC News*, April 16, 2014; Paul Lienert and Marilyn Thompson, "GM Didn't Fix Deadly Ignition Switch Because It Would Have Cost $1 Per Car," *Reuters*, April 2, 2014; Binyamin Appelbaum, "As U.S. Agencies Put More Value on a Life, Businesses Fret," *New York Times*, Feb. 16, 2011.

2.2.2 Importance for You

Designers are drawn from a spectrum of backgrounds—artists, engineers, anthropologists, psychologists, and architects—forming a profession that has intellectual roots and market value. Design will impact your major. As a marketing executive, you would provide critical guidance to product/service/process design considerations, translating the voice of the customer into specific product characteristics and cost parameters. As a finance manager, you would conduct detailed risk and cost-benefit analyses of competing designs and provide capital. As an accountant, you would prepare cost estimates of alternative designs, working with purchasing and design to cost inputs and process costs. In HR, you would identify and provide level of labor skills required to design and make the product and develop appropriate incentive and compensation systems. In operations, you would work closely with design to match design specifications with manufacturing, worker, logistics, and supplier capabilities.

Jobs in Design

Industrial Designer (content abbreviated)
Company: *Trek Bicycle Corporation*
Location: *Madison, Wisconsin*
Posted: *04/21/2014*

Description

As a designer at Trek your purpose is to create great ride experiences. You work together with a world class product development team to provide forward thinking concepts and design direction for bicycles, components, and accessory products. A designer in this position is engaged in rider research, concept planning, design refinement, and production support. The ideal candidate will possess exceptional design, problem solving, communication, and visualization skills, and excel in a multi-functional team culture. Experience with both Solid Works and Adobe systems are highly desired—awesome visual communication skills are a necessity.

Desired Skills

- Awesome at solving complex design problems with elegant solutions.
- Good mechanical/structural aptitude and knowledge of various materials and their associated manufacturing processes.
- Sketches like mad—visual communication and form development skills are critical.
- Proficient in all phases of product development: ideation, sketching, concept development.
- 3D modeling skills and a solid understanding of the manufacturing process.
- Self-motivated and ready to forge their own path as the career develops.
- 2+ years of post-graduate, professional design experience.
- Bachelor's degree/diploma in Industrial Design or Product Design. Proficient in SolidWorks modeling.
- Competency in Adobe Illustrator/Photoshop, Microsoft PowerPoint.
- Digital Sketching—Sketchbook Pro a plus.

   Trek employees enjoy a Great Place to Work. Offerings include onsite fitness center with full equipment and classes, cafeteria with healthy options, medical clinic, mountain bike trails, and a library. Other perks are casual dress, flexibility, great health, wellness, and retirement benefits, and vast opportunities for training and development.

   Designers enjoy employment possibilities in many industries. Carnegie Mellon's graduates in design were picked up by companies such as Apple, Google, Microsoft, IDEO, Second Story, Frog Design, BMW, Glaxo-SmithKline, Microsoft, R/GA Brazil, Siegel + Gale, New Balance, and others.

KEY POINTS

Why Is Design Important?

- Design has been positively associated with sales, profits, stock price, and brand reputation.
- Design lowers costs—cost of components, cost of manufacturing, cost of transportation, cost of quality, the cost of repair and recycling, and the costs of energy and emissions.
- Design impacts every function and business study major.
- Design offers employment potential.

2.3 How to Design?

Can design be taught? From a business perspective, design can be considered a verb representing a process, an approach that can be explicated and replicated in organizations. Surrounding this process are key underlying principles, processes, and a complete tool kit.

2.3.1 Principles of Product Design

Design principles emerge from the development of ideas and the operational feasibility of transforming that idea into a tangible product or service. Marketing research plays an important role too, but we leave that for your marketing course.

Sources of Ideas

How can a business get ideas for new designs? Formal approaches include investing in research and development, engaging consultants (IDEO and such), looking to suppliers, and listening to the customer. Beyond such conventional strategies lie methods that are novel and have surprised designers with their results.

Regular employees are a valuable source of ideas. IBM's 'innovation jam' in 2008, an online crowdsourcing brainstorming session with 60,000 employees worldwide (and contributors from another 1,000 companies), resulted in almost 30,000 posts. Grants, recognition awards, training workshops, sabbaticals in design-rich environments, and time off for tinkering or simply thinking are all initiatives to teach and encourage employees to think creatively. Notable examples of companies that employ such approaches are 3M and Nokia. Experimentation with loose goals, physical layouts, and organizational structures that encourage frequent mixing of unlikely people together are approaches that have been tried successfully in companies. Designing a new car at BMW begins with relocating the entire development cross-functional team to BMW's Research and Innovation Center for periods up to three years. Close proximity among engineers, designers, production, marketing, and sourcing facilitates communication, brings down functional silos, and enables early detection and resolution of design contradictions. The result—a shortened and bug-free design launch.

Some companies are innovating with newer initiatives. Haier, the Chinese appliances company with a nearly 50 percent market share of dorm refrigerators, has a rather unusual approach to incentivize designers. Its product developers are rewarded on the basis of product sales, not design looks or awards won. If a new design exceeds its break-even sales point, the designer earns a bonus from the profits generated. A 'resource passbook' is maintained for the designer, with just two columns—revenue from designed product and product development cost. A negative balance is carried over for adjustment against surpluses from future designs. Care to conjecture about what happens to a designer running a persistent deficit? Probably nothing good, which raises the concern that Haier's system could push a designer to play 'safe,' focusing on incremental design additions instead of experimenting with completely new and therefore riskier designs. Perhaps because of such potential dysfunctionalities of purely quantitative design incentive systems, more qualitative criteria are being considered to develop a more effective incentive system. GE incentivizes innovation by assessing executives for "growth traits" such as "external focus" and "imagination and courage." Other companies evaluate traits such as executive 'risk tolerance.'

Stripping down competitor products (reverse engineering) and mimicking design elements is another source of design ideas, at times resulting in a clone army of a particular product (e.g. smartphones, oval, rounded shaped autos, LCD TVs). Resulting patent wars can ensue though, as seen recently with Samsung and Apple.

Customers can be an important source of ideas, through design competitions (Apple, Nike) and hands-on customization options such as the one offered by Nike ID Studio at Nike Town in New York City (6 East 57th Street). Nike entices customers to become designers at its NIKEiD studio in the store, allowing individuals to customize Nike products from shoes to team jerseys to equipment. Other ideas are fostered by local needs—cell phones designs in China may come with 7.1 stereo sound, dual SIM cards, a functional cigarette holder, and a built-in UV LED for counterfeit money detection. Similarly, cell phones with flashlights have become very popular with truck drivers on India's dimly lighted roads.

Open sourcing, that is, seeking and actively inviting design ideas from outside the organization, is becoming a viable strategy despite security, confidentiality, and control reservations. Threadless.com invites designs from around the world, and the designs chosen by community members are printed and sold. Domino's and Coca Cola designed new pizzas and bottle shapes through social media crowdsourcing. P&G's "connect and develop" initiative solicits design ideas from its supply base (Innovation Expo) and scientific/technical networks, such as NineSigma, that connect scientists with companies. It also created a manager for cultural change to help the P&G old guard accept not-invented-here ideas.

Nature is another source for design ideas. Biomimicry is an emerging discipline that studies and adapts nature's designs to human applications.[2]

OM IN PRACTICE

Nature Provides Surprising Templates for Human Designs

Figure 2.2 Kingfisher

Source: Andreas Trepte, "Common Kingfisher, Alcedo atthis," www.photo-natur.de [CC], Oct. 22, 2013, http://commons. wikimedia.org/wiki/File:Common_Kingfisher_Alcedo_atthis. jpg#/media/File:Common_Kingfisher_Alcedo_atthis.jpg.

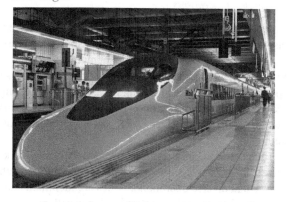

Figure 2.3 Bullet Train

Source: Hisagi, "A 7-car L0 Series Maglev Shinkansen Formation Undergoing Test-running on the Yamanashi Test Track," [CC], https://commons.wikimedia.org/wiki/File:JR_Central_ SCMaglev_L0_Series_Shinkansen_201408081002.jpg.

The Shinkansen Bullet Train, the fastest in the world, travels 200 miles per hour—and made a lot of noise! Loud claps of thunder could be heard for miles around due to changes in air pressure when the train emerged from a tunnel. The train's chief engineer, Eiji Nakatsu, spends time watching birds and recognized the fish-catching kingfisher as a bird that "that travels quickly and smoothly between two very different mediums"—diving from air into water smoothly, with little splash. He designed the nose of the train after the kingfisher's beak, reducing noise significantly. And as a bonus, the nature-inspired streamlined design reduced power usage by 15 percent and increased train speed by 10 percent. Nature teaches great designs to the observant.

Adapted from: "Beak Provides Streamlining: Common Kingfisher," accessed Sept. 28, 2015, http://www. asknature.org/strategy/4c3d00f23cae38c1d23517b6378859ee.

Figure 2.4 Cost of Changes in Product Specification at Different Stages

Adapted from: Steve Hanssen, "Design for Manufacturability," DFM Seminar, San Jose University, San Jose, CA, Sept. 15, 2004.

Design for Operations

Having to change a design at the production stage because of an unforeseen mismatch with equipment, materials, worker skills, or packaging and transportation carries a high cost.

The nature of a design can impact many sources of costs—raw materials, machinery, labor, tooling/jogs/fixtures (what you need before starting production), inspection, and engineering. Complex designs may need special worker training or hiring for assembly and changes in machinery layouts in a plant. Number of orders placed, supplier monitoring/expediting costs, inventory costs, and parts tracking costs all go up when the number of parts in a product increase. Bad-looking products (even if functionally good) would increase marketing and sales costs.

Today, design, engineering, and manufacturing work together to ensure that late, nasty surprises are minimized. Product designers work with engineering, manufacturing, warehousing, logistics, and sustainability to ensure that diverse operational issues are identified and accommodated at the design stage itself. This design principle, broadly called designing for excellence, can be broken down into a number of operations-related product design goals.

- *Design for Manufacturability and Assembly (DFMA)*: DFMA asks the designer to explicitly consider manufacturing ease, safety, productivity, and cost. A design should be capable of being commercially manufactured with minimal changes in equipment, components, work processes, worker training, and suppliers. Unless it's Steve Jobs, who persuaded Corning to invest in a high-risk, radical new design—the iPhone glass. DFMA targets ease of product assembly—the key is simplification, which, ironically, is difficult to do in practice. Parts reduction is key. Assembly is easier done when there are not too many parts to put together, when component shapes allow easy fitting such as snap-together instead of welding, parts and assembly processes are standardized, and the number of steps in product assembly are minimized. Consider Texas Instruments re-design of a part:

BEFORE

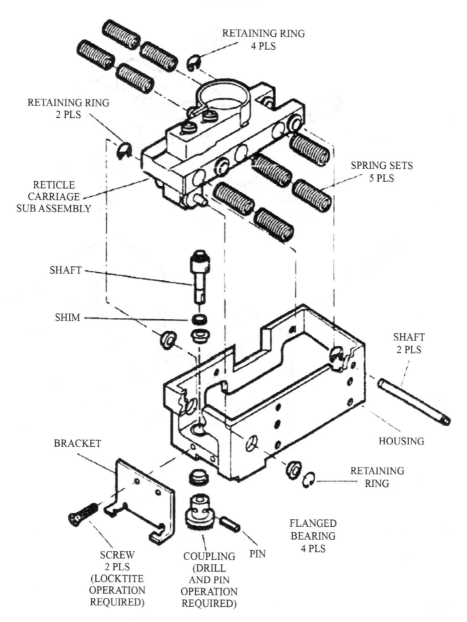

RETAINING RING
4 PLS

RETAINING RING
2 PLS

RETICLE
CARRIAGE
SUB ASSEMBLY

SHAFT

SHIM

SPRING SETS
5 PLS

SHAFT
2 PLS

HOUSING

RETAINING
RING

BRACKET

FLANGED
BEARING
4 PLS

SCREW
2 PLS
(LOCKTITE
OPERATION
REQUIRED)

COUPLING
(DRILL
AND PIN
OPERATION
REQUIRED)

PIN

Figures 2.5a and 2.5b DFM in Texas Instruments

Source: Images used with permission from Michael Guillory, director, WW Corporate Brand Communications, mguillory@ti.com.

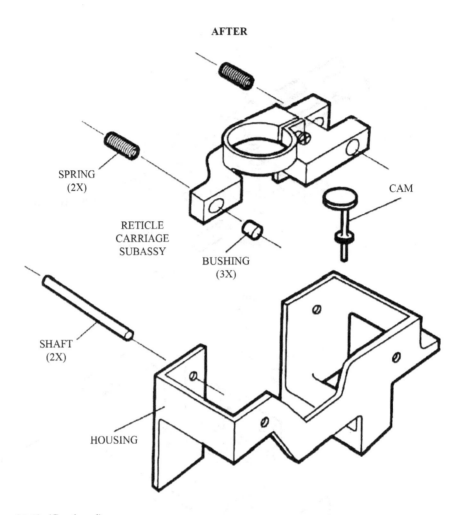

AFTER

SPRING
(2X)

RETICLE
CARRIAGE
SUBASSY

BUSHING
(3X)

CAM

SHAFT
(2X)

HOUSING

Figures 2.5a and 2.5b (Continued)

Table 2.1 Improvement from Product Redesign

Measuring Improvement

	Original	Redesign	Improvement
Assembly time (h)	2.15	0.33	84.7%
Number of different parts	24	8	66.7%
Total number of parts	47	12	74.5%
Total number of operations	58	13	77.6%
Metal fabrication time (h)	12.63	3.65	71.15%
Weight (lb)	0.48	0.26	45.8%

Source: Data used with permission from Michael Guillory, director, WW Corporate Brand Communications, mguillory@ti.com.

The redesign of the reticle resulted significant improvements in terms of cost and time savings.

DFMA[3] forces explicit consideration of manufacturing material and equipment specifications in product design, typically resulting in capital conservation, reduced number of parts, more streamlined processes, and less waste in manufacturing. DFMA also studies the assembly process in great detail, including how every component of the product is to be handled, grasped, and fitted into the product. Line efficiency is assessed using time and cost estimates developed using time studies and standard costing. DFMA software can let designers explore alternatives in materials, parts, and designs and immediately see the associated cost implications. DFMA software allows categorization of parts into 'essential—A' and 'target for designing out—B,' seeking to maximize the following:

Design Efficiency Ratio: [# of A parts/total # of (A + B) parts] * 100

Typical 'B' parts are fasteners, bolts, and screws. A study at Ford identified threaded fasteners as a common culprit in 75 percent of reported assembly line defects.

An over-emphasis on technical performance metrics can lead to dysfunctionalities such as over-engineered products with excessive margins of interior material specifications, reliability, and safety. For example, an office chair designed to accommodate uncommon loads up to 400 pounds increases the cost structure and diverts resources from other features, such as exterior cover material, that may be more visible to the consumer.

Standardization, in particular, reduces variety of formats, parts, and products—reducing time and costs, improving reliability, and facilitating repair. The Health Insurance Portability and Accountability Act of 1996 (HIPAA) requires the standardization of all forms utilized in connection with medical information. All medical bills, lab reports, and hospital records must be formatted in the exact same manner. For products, fears of 'sameness' can be met through design modularization, where modules are combined in different ways to produce products that do not look similar, yet share components and common platforms.

OM IN PRACTICE

Standardization: 22 Centuries Ago

As the first emperor of China (259 B.C. to 210 B.C.), Emperor Qin Shihuangdi, of Terracotta Warriors fame, had to fight a lot of battles. He observed that his archers made their own arrows, and one archer's arrows could not be used in another archer's bow. Emperor Qin standardized arrow length and tip specifications to fit all bows. Standardization improved archery capability immensely, allowing archers to borrow arrows from each other, or from fallen fellow archers, during battle. The emperor also standardized axle widths to fit all wheels to the same ruts in the road, and standardized money, measurement systems, and the written script, helping unite China into a country.

On the other hand, standardization reduces variety—which is bad news, because variety makes a species in nature as well as a product line robust to the spread of infections or defects. Banana disease affecting South America producers has spread quickly because growers have standardized on one specific 'best' banana type. Similarly, a shared ignition switch used by GM led to performance failures across many of its different car models. Exploding Takata-made airbags, similarly shared across multiple auto manufacturers, have led to one of the largest recalls in automotive history—potentially 34 million vehicles in the U.S. and another 7 million worldwide. Cost control encourages designs that use the same part or product across as many applications as possible. Just one failure, then, can quickly become everybody's headache.

Adapted from: Barbara Gotthelf, "The Terra-Cotta Army of Emperor Qin," *Highlights Kids*, https://www.highlight-skids.com/stories/terra-cotta-army-emperor-qin-0; Clifford Atiyeh and Rusty Blackwell, "Massive Takata Airbag Recall: Everything You Need to Know, Including Full List of Affected Vehicles," *Car & Driver*, Sept. 28, 2015; Alice Rawsthorn, "What Is Good Design?" *New York Times*, June 6, 2008.

- *Design for reliability/quality (DFR, DFQ)*: DFQ recognizes that quality begins at the design stage. A complex design with highly sensitive parts may not stand up to user operating conditions. Reliability is measured by the frequency of product failure—for example, how many times does a car fail? Reliability is a function of the number of parts used in the product and the sensitivity of the design to changes in operating conditions (robust design). To illustrate, Russian-built helicopters were preferred by NATO for use in Afghanistan's harsh environment because of the former's reliability and robust design. Although the Russian machines have fewer and less advanced features, their design simplicity plus robustness mean less frequent failures and easier repair relative to the more sophisticated U.S. made machines. Which leads to the well-known KISS principle in design: keep it simple and short! Durability is another aspect of design—expensive products are expected to live long, and a robust design helps. Both reliability and durability encourage longer warranty terms that consumers appreciate, especially for expensive products.
- *Design for logistics (DFL)*: DFL makes designers consider how a product's design can facilitate storage and transportation. Utilizing DFL, companies design and package products to minimize the space required to ship. DFL also concerns packaging, which should be considered while finalizing product design. Packaging must protect the product, be easy to stack and move on pallets and store, save space in transport, be convenient to pick up and carry in a warehouse, and carry some identification technology such as barcodes or RFID tags.
- *Design for service (DFS)*: DFS focuses on the ease of product repair and service. During the 1970s, some cars required lifting the engine with a chain hoist in order to change sparkplugs. Easy access to parts that need regular changing, simple changing tool requirements, and quick change parts design are part of DFS. Repairing a dishwasher now is much easier. Slide out the defective module and slide in a new one. No need to repair or replace individual parts. DFS took a big step forward with power-by-the-hour contracts, where, for example, an airline would pay an engine manufacturer a certain amount of money for every hour the aircraft engine operates. Effectively, it is in the engine manufacturers' interest to design an engine that a) is of high quality (DFQ) and does not need frequent repair and b) is easy to maintain (DFS). Because of this, the manufacturer is incentivized to improve the reliability, serviceability, and cost of the engine design. Additionally, electronic monitoring systems to provide continuous feeds and early warnings on engine health are built into the engine design, improving both safety and maintenance costs.

Product liability and legal requirements are important considerations in design. Manufacturers and operators are liable for product design safety and any damages caused by faulty design or manufacturing. There are numerous examples of product recalls and legal suits, including the 2015 airbag recall and associated legal suits in Honda, Chrysler, and Toyota cars. Manufacturers are also responsible for the implicit warranty imposed by the Uniform Commercial Code (UCC) requiring that products must be fit for the purpose of intended use.

KEY POINTS

The Principles of Product Design

- Design ideas traditionally come from research and development, consultants, suppliers, and customers.
- Companies organize for 'creativity' by open sourcing ideas, developing collaborative spaces and cultures, and designing incentive structures to stimulate design creativity.
- Designers are now looking at nature and employees for inspiration.
- Ease of manufacturing and assembly, reliability, standardization, and environmental considerations are key principles in designing.
- Additional considerations are design life, safety, and legal requirements.

2.3.2 The Product Design Process

Product design is also seen as a process comprised of a series of sequential 'gatekeeper' steps. An idea for a new design emerges; design shapes it into a more formal concept and hands the concept over to marketing. Marketing digs deeper and provides some idea of customer preferences and hands it over to design engineers, who prepare more definitive technical specifications and a mock-up or working prototype, then hand it over to manufacturing engineers. Manufacturing engineering and purchasing examine the design from a manufacturing and supplier fit perspective and hand it over to production; production finally makes the product. Each function acts like a silo, throwing the design over the walls into the next silo. The process takes time, employs narrow functional perspectives, and is inefficient. Faults in design usually surface during actual production runs, and the design gets thrown back over the walls in reverse order until the kinks are smoothened out. Is there a better way?

Why not use cross-functional teams that work at all sequential design process stages, with each function leading the team at a particular stage? Companies have tried this approach successfully and call it concurrent or simultaneous engineering (CE/SE). The design benefits from the value of different perspectives being brought to bear at the early stages of design development, where cost and quality parameters are established. U.S. automotive industries have used SE very successfully over the past decade. CE has recently extended to flexible engineering, where cross-functional teams involving purchasing, design, engineering, manufacturing and packaging, and logistics work at every stage, but stages overlap in time and are recursive—there is a certain amount of waste and conflict in going back and forth among stages, but the flexibility to change a design at a late stage is an important advantage.

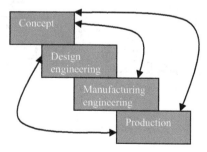

Figure 2.6 The Flexible Engineering Process

Flexible Engineering Approach

Flexible engineering allows late-stage design changes to accommodate ongoing changes in customer preferences, competitive moves, technology changes, and the legal and economic environment. It is made possible through a mixture of modular architectures, rapid prototyping and frequent tests and checks with key customers and suppliers, and using common design platforms with several add-on options.

Let's walk through an imaginary design process to understand the actual tasks involved in, say, designing couches for a furniture manufacturing business:

- *Idea generation*: From employees, customers, technology experts, using focus groups, in-house teams, Delphi forecasting processes, and market prediction (see chapter 5, "Forecasting"). The ideas are assessed by the design team and reduced to a set of prospective design ideas.
- *Concept development*: We often have different understandings of a concept, especially since different functions and different customers speak different languages. To get clarity and consensus, the concept has to become 'real'—a model, a picture, a drawing—something everyone can look at, touch or feel.

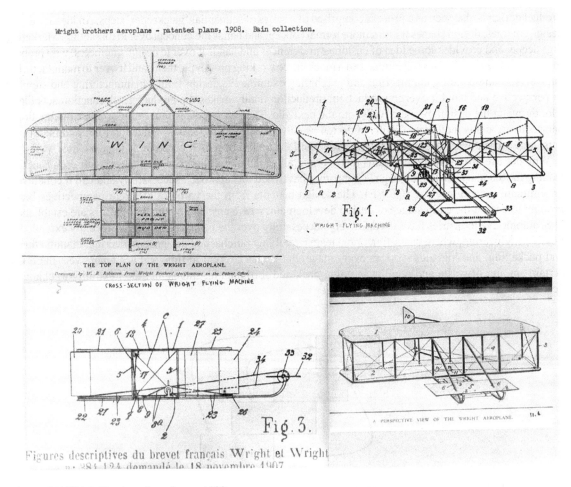

Figure 2.7 Wright Brothers Aeroplane—1908

Source: "Wright Brothers Negatives," *Library of Congress*, accessed Sept. 28, 2015, http://www.loc.gov/pictures/collection/wri/.

Design folks visualize the set of prospective design ideas with quick hand or computer 3D sketches for developing basic mock-ups made of paper, foam, straw, cardboard, and wood. The basic models, also called block models, are shown to customer focus groups. Immediate reactions help identify emotive negative and positive features about the form, shape, and feel of different couch designs. Focus group discussions with internal and external groups identify features of value and validate preliminary designs.

- *Design engineering*: Design engineering builds more detailed prototypes and develops fabric, wood, steel, component, and design specifications and tolerances for the couch designs. These prototypes are built using rapid prototyping technology using 3D imaging and computer-controlled material shaping and fabrication. Design engineering also conducts costing estimates for alternative designs. Preliminary testing rigs are set up, and different design prototypes are tested for functionality, reliability, and durability. Structural analysis using 3D computer aided design technology (CAD) conducts load testing, time between, and time to failure tests, robustness analyses, and other design engineering tests. A few designs are picked for further consideration at the manufacturing engineering stage. Engineering drawings are prepared for the components and product, showing dimensions, tolerance, and finish.
- *Manufacturing engineering* takes over design leadership at this stage and proceeds with detailed manufacturing planning based on the detailed design engineering drawings. Equipment needs and manufacturing process specifications are determined to ensure compatibility between couch design and manufacturing capabilities. Design features are evaluated for ease of manufacturing. For instance, rounded edges are more difficult to fabricate than square edges. A bill of material (BOM) is also developed listing the description and quantities of all components required to make a couch. Manufacturing simulation, using CAD, optimizes product design by predicting performance under different manufacturing conditions as well as simulating the effects of the design on various manufacturing process parameters. Process problems are identified and resolved by changing product design and manufacturing process specifications.

'Make-buy' decisions are made as to which components of the product would be made in-house and which would be made by suppliers. Typically, standardized items are outsourced while complex items are developed in-house or with specialty suppliers. Suppliers are sourced and assessed for technology and flexibility capabilities, necessary for short first production test runs. Volume production is not an important consideration at this time. Suggestions are invited from key suppliers regarding material specifications, costs, and availability. Production verification test runs are made for checking and fine-tuning product quality. Cost estimates are firmed up at this stage. A target cost is established considering what consumers would likely pay for the product. Cost estimates are brought in line with target cost through design simplifications, raw material changes, and manufacturing process changes.

Compliance documentation, documenting testing, and manufacturing process technical files are also developed by engineering in the form of engineering drawings, simulation results, and assembly process flow charts. Tooling required for production is designed and acquired.

- *Production* finally takes over the design for volume manufacturing. Volume suppliers are sourced for long-term contracts. Production documents consist of assembly drawings—an exploded 3D view of the product; assembly flow charts—showing how components flow into sub-systems and into the final products; routing sheets—showing the list of operations involved in making the product; and a work-order—an order to produce a certain quantity at a particular time. Worker training and production schedules are developed.

Volume production usually uncovers more problems with design or process, leading to ECNs (engineering change notices), changes in product design features to improve manufacturability and product performance. ECNs may also be encountered during the earlier phases of design and manufacturing engineering. Tooling requirements are examined and firmed up.

Design at Dyson

"Truly original ideas come to life when people dare to be different. It's a combination of inventive engineering, passion for technology and brave design;
   I want people who haven't done something before and will find a new way of doing it, and that aren't afraid of failure;
   If you always succeed, you're learning nothing. Failure is terribly important."

—James Dyson, British inventor, industrial designer, and founder of the Dyson company

Dyson products have won many design awards as well as many customers around the world. Here are a few working principles that Dyson employs in its pursuit of innovative designs for vacuums and more:

Figure 2.8 Model Dyson DC37

Source: Dina Ilyina, "Dyson 37," [CC] via *Wikimedia Commons*, Nov. 14, 2011, https://commons.wikimedia.org/wiki/File:%D0%9F%D1%8B%D0%BB%D0%B5%D1%81%D0%BE%D1%81_Dyson_DC37.jpg.

Figure 2.9 Dyson Airblade

Source: Nick, "Dyson Airblade hand dryer," [Public domain], via *Wikimedia Commons*, Dec. 10, 2013, https://commons.wikimedia.org/wiki/File:Dyson_Airblade_Transparent_BG.png.

- **Cross-functional knowledge:** Everyone makes a vacuum cleaner on their first day. Hands-on experience with the making and operation of a Dyson imparts more experience and perspective than a dozen meetings or training sessions. Employees take the machine home to further understand how it is used in a home setting. They get to keep it at a heavily discounted price.
- **Informal and open physical environment:** An open office layout at work facilitates communication, idea exchanges and social cohesion. Graphics and engineering form the center. Talk is encouraged—no memos, and no suits and ties.
- **No design divas:** Design is not divorced from engineering—both participate in idea and concept generation as well as in developing engineering specifications and product testing.
- **Hire early and encourage differences:** Dyson hires right out of school to attract and avail fresh mind-sets that can differ and argue but are responsible for designing and developing new products.
- **Respect and pay well:** Dyson's once-a-month group discussion with employees ranges from business matters like marketing issues, management changes, and property purchases to issues such as shift changeovers and pensions. Pay is boosted with attendance bonuses, company-paid insurance and pension, 22 holidays a year, paid sick leave, and early Fridays. Busing to work is free, and employees eat at the company cafeteria.
- **Worker-paced lines:** Dyson's assembly lines are worker paced, allowing great flexibility in changing lines, line capacity, adding new lines, or changing assembly methods. Such flexibility enables the line to accommodate design changes at very short notice.

Finally, Dyson believes in continuous improvement and the value of ownership of design and manufacture. As mentioned by Mahoney (see citation), Dyson believes "Whatever you make should be perfect, as well as exciting and beautiful."

Adapted from: http://www.dyson.com; Patrick Mahoney, "Industrial Design: Design the Dyson Way," *Machine Design*, Aug. 7, 2008, http://machinedesign.com/article/industrial-design-design-the-dyson-way-0807. Also see interview with John Dyson at http://fora.tv/2012/05/01/WIRED_Business_Conference_Inventing_Sucks.

- *The softer aspects of design*: Successful designs start with clear goals and a clear scope—say "design a couch that can seat 3 people"—changing the scope to a 5-people size later on may lead to design delays. A clear understanding of customer requirements facilitates the making of trade-offs between product performance and things like cost, time to market, and project risk. Staffing design projects with the right people is essential—there are thinkers and doers, and sometimes these groups conflict. A good leader draws on distinctive strengths yet maintains a project culture of mutual respect. Leaders also identify their teams/organization's technical capabilities and shortcomings. Knowing when to outsource is important. As suppliers are drawn into product design, the flow of information to and among suppliers needs to be managed and protected. Components and sub-assemblies designed by different suppliers need to fit together and be developed and delivered together. Such design interfaces require extensive information sharing and collaboration to work well. "Volkswagen FAST" initiative, for example, identifies and works with suppliers at the early stages in innovation cycles, aiming to boost both product and process innovation. Suppliers will contribute to preseries development of cars, and production networks will be harmonized to improve global synergies. Finally, cooperation and communication between design and marketing is critical—conflicts have to be resolved early. Once developed, products are also regularly put through value engineering—a thorough analysis to find out if any materials, components, or packaging can be substituted or redesigned to improve performance and/or reduce costs.

2.3.3 Tools for Engineering and Production Design

Designing a product or a process or a service requires a toolbox and the knowledge to pick and use the right tool. Let's open the design toolbox and peek at the tools.

- *CAD*, or computer aided design, uses a mix of hardware and software to develop 3D mechanical designs, run simulations, and prepare tool and molding designs. Products like Autodesk® Inventor® products enable designers to explore, document, exchange and collaborate on designs before they are built without having to build physical mock-ups. For example, an aircraft manufacturer would use CAD to simulate and compute the wind drag on different wing configurations under a variety of operating conditions virtually, without having to build several mock-ups for physical testing. The fashion design industry has adopted CAD to digitize and translate hand sketch specifications, providing virtual views of colors and shapes of apparel designs on virtual models, reducing prototyping and sample development time.
- *Rapid prototyping* technology offers quick development of product prototypes and mock-ups. Earlier, large investments in machinery and software tools made prototyping an expensive task. No longer—set-ups like Techshop have set up design tool centers equipped with lathes, laser cutters, welding equipment, and 3D printers to manufacture prototypes for innovators.
- *CAQC* (computer aided quality control), uses computers to control either analog or digital test techniques for product inspection and testing purposes. Using non-contact sensors, CAQC inspects and evaluates quality without touching the product, leading to quicker, safer, and less expensive quality evaluation. CAQC also enables accelerated life testing, where abnormal use conditions are created and product failure patterns observed under conditions of high stress or extended periods of simulated use.
- *CAM,* or computer aided manufacturing, involves cutting, shaping, forming and welding machine tools that can be loaded with CAD-programmed designs. Machine technology has developed tools that use steel, air pressure, and water to shape metal and other materials to very fine specifications. Such machines are equipped with on-board computers, allowing for direct input of design specifications. Robotics is another form of production technology, now emerging in services fields such as medicine.

OM IN PRACTICE

CAM in Surgery

With two open heart surgeries under his belt, Andy's chances of surviving another one were slim. But the *da Vinci®* Surgical System came to his rescue. The *da Vinci®* surgical robot combines programmable computer and robotic technologies, enabling minimally invasive incisions, better surgeon visualization, accuracy, dexterity, and control, resulting in fewer post-operative problems and quicker patient recovery. Unlike earlier surgeries, Andy's breastbone was not split or spread open for his open heart procedure. The surgeon used the *da Vinci®* system to make a minimally invasive incision on one side of Andy's chest—completing the procedure in quicker time, and saving Andy from days on the hospital bed, and much post-operative pain.

Reputed hospitals including The University of Chicago Medical Center currently use the da Vinci Surgical System for robotic MIS (minimally invasive) procedures.

Figure 2.10 Da Vinci Surgical Robot

Source: Purplrockscissors, "Da Vinci Robot," [CC], via *Wikimedia Commons*, Oct. 12, 2011, https://commons.wikimedia.org/wiki/File:Da_Vinci_Robot.jpg.

Adapted from: http://www.davincisurgery.com; http://www.uchospitals.edu/specialties/heart/patients, (both accessed Sept 28. 2015).

- *FMS*, or flexible manufacturing systems, is a collection of linked supervisory control, automated material handling, and programmable CAM equipment. An FMS enables off-diagonal moves on the product-process matrix discussed earlier, allowing production of a variety of products in small numbers at low cost.
- *CIM*, or computer-integrated manufacturing, integrates design, engineering and manufacturing systems in a plant-wide net, enabled by information technology and computer systems. CIMs may combine several CAD, FMS, and CAQC systems in a plant into an integrated, centrally controlled, low-cost, high-quality, variety-capable super system.
- *Paper Kaizen*, a detailed simulation of manufacturing steps, equipment locations, and process flows, enables testing and optimization of the manufacturing process before equipment investments are made.
- *Target costing* determines the cost goal for a new design, using the following equation:

Target cost for product/service = Estimated market price – Required profit margin

Target costing is conducted at the design and manufacturing engineering stages, since changes at the production stage are expensive, cumbersome, and time consuming. After estimating the target cost, costing decomposes the product target cost into cost targets for key product components. Cross-functional target costing teams, together with key suppliers, distributors, and key customers, work on design specifications, material, and manufacturing processes for cost reduction opportunities. The goal is to bring component costs within target costs limits. Specifications may be changed or materials substituted in order to lower costs. Target costing has assumed greater importance in current times. Caterpillar, manufacturer of branded heavy earth-moving equipment, is battling competitors in high growth markets such as China, who offer three pieces of stripped down versions of CAT equipment for the price of one original CAT machine. The target cost for equipment in China and similar markets places immense cost pressure on established western manufacturers. CAT may consider various options, including designing a new 'lite' line of equipment after a careful review of competitor designs and a selective elimination of unnecessary design refinements/features from its existing models. CAT has to be careful to protect its reputation for innovation, sophistication, reliability, durability, and after-sales service while addressing the conflicting goals of cost reduction and sophistication in design.

KEY POINTS

Design Tools for Engineering and Production

- CAD or computer aided design enables 3D drawings and experimentation with specification changes.
- Rapid prototyping technologies enable inexpensive and quick production of physical prototypes for better tactile and visual assessment and for customer showings.
- CAM, CAQC and other computer-aided manufacturing and testing technologies use programmable equipment to bring precision, speed, and flexibility to manufacturing engineering, production, and testing.
- Target costing sets cost goals for components and finished products by subtracting the desired profit margin from the estimated market price.

2.3.4 Testing the Design

Showtime! It's time to test the design outside the walls of the organization. The more traditional approaches involve focus groups, consumer surveys, and pilot testing in selected markets. Real-time experiments using social media and interactive tools are more recent methods. P&G is working with TwitterMoms, a virtual opinion army of 30,000 tweeting moms with at least 1,000 followers each, for product trials and feedback. The first product design with the TwitterMom seal of approval: a redesigned version of P&G's MicroFiber Twist Mop. A close cousin of social sites is market prediction sites—competing designs can be placed on the sites for market prediction (covered in more detail in chapter 5).

Prototyping for public use is an excellent way to test designs and obtain rich feedback on specific design features. Volunteer patients actually spent nights in the new model patient room at the University Medical Center at Princeton (New Jersey). The room's design was continuously updated with feedback from inhabitants, doctors, nurses, and other personnel. Specific design features were tested: Would having a separate sink near the door encourage more washing of hands? Would patients falls decrease by locating the toilet near the head of the bed, making a shorter trip to the bathroom? Would patient the bed height reduce falls and help weigh a patient in bed? Would two-way cabinets in the room reduce room traffic by allowing housekeeping to resupply the linen and medicines from the hallway? Similar experiments are often seen with retail store layouts and innovations/customer convenience features like TVs and web-linked PCs in doctors' clinics and waiting areas of businesses. The disadvantages are expense and time. More to the point, if customers like it, they will ask for it all the time, and complaints would escalate when older products and facilities continue to be used or when the new features are removed after the experiment.

Prototyping with a finished product can be costly or provide feedback when it's too late/too expensive to make changes to a design. Experimentation with simple, inexpensive prototypes of a design is a quick way to probe market response before committing to a final design and mass production/implementation. This approach has been called 'Pretotyping' by Alberto Savoia, a former Google employee.[4] He calls it "a way to test an idea quickly and inexpensively by creating extremely simplified, mocked or virtual versions of that product, to help validate the premise that 'If we build it, they will use it.'" Savoia also describes it more informally, "Fake it and test it before you make it!" Pretotypes can be made using paper, wood, or digital means and used to gauge the initial level of interest (ILI). ILI's can be tracked continuously using pretotypes with YouTube, Google AdWords, Balsamiq, ProtyperPro, Quirky, and KickStarters. ILI's provide feedback used to create improved iterative versions of the pretotype for repeated testing.

A harsher design testing method is the sink or swim test. Swatch and Seiko make hundreds of watch designs, Sony used to make dozens of varieties of Walkman music players, a restaurant may create hundreds of new recipes, Hearst Magazines introduces multiple magazines every year. The sheer variety and speed of design development for such products makes traditional market research impractical. Companies take a fast and furious approach—introduce multiple designs simultaneously and watch which ones rise to the top. Products are generally variations on a basic design platform, so companies can be nimble with design changes. The money saved on market research is spent on flexible manufacturing equipment and increasing supply chain responsiveness to help mass produce market winners quickly. Strategically, some companies limit supply of 'hot' designs to build hype and brand value in the market.

KEY POINTS

Tools for Design Testing

- Designs are evaluated using market research and social media to solicit and interact with customers and participants on a mass basis.
- Building and testing product prototypes for use by consumers is an effective but expensive way to evaluate design.
- A 'fast and furious' approach to design evaluation calls for building numerous variants on a few common platforms, launching them simultaneously, and waiting to see the designs that sell.

2.4 Have We Done a Good Job?

What is a 'good' design? Musing about that question, Intel's in-house cultural anthropologist, Genevieve Bell, feels that a well-designed product should connect deeply with everyday life; "it has to be so important that you bury people with it."[5] That's a reality in Southeast Asia, where paper and bamboo models of popular designs such as Honda SH150 and Dylan motor scooter designs and SONY designed TV sets are burnt to accompany their (deceased) users to the next life. A designer has her work cut out nowadays—the design should be beautiful, functional, safe, ergonomic, reliable, durable, sustainable, affordable, benefit society, confer status, and connect emotionally with the user. With such tall standards, it is no wonder that 'bad' designs abound. Let's examine some of the ways in which designs could go 'wrong'.

Figure 2.11 Beautiful but Unsafe

Source: Courtesy of Badddesigns.Com; M.J. Darnell, *Bad Human Factors Designs*, 2006, http://www.baddesigns.com/rstdoor.html.

2.4.1 *What Could Go Wrong?*

Design failures are common but hard to predict. Remember, any design introduced by a business must have passed internal evaluation and tests, so deciphering the reasons for rejection by the market is not a simple task. Take a look at a few examples of 'bad' designs, and try to understand why things went wrong:

The door at this restaurant is a beautiful piece of work, but has smashed several unaware noses on the other side of the door. People exiting the restaurant have no visibility of what is on the other side.

Costco's recently introduced tall milk gallon jug does not leave as much empty space on top as conventional milk jugs. The redesign facilitates stacking and saves on pallet space and transport. It has not been a hit with customers, though, judging from social media. Complaints are piling up about spills due to the lack of a spout. From personal experience, I know one almost always spills while pouring—and it is annoying.

Figure 2.12 Cost-Cutting but Dysfunctional

Source: Author.

Why do design flubs happen? Experience and studies suggest a few recurring themes that lead to design flaws. The pressure for fast design development puts pressures on design and engineering. A 'simple' change request may set into motion a long and time-consuming series of events, cascading to design and engineering for specification and cost re-computations, suppliers for negotiating repricing, quality reconfirmations, rescheduled deliveries, costing for developing revised product cost estimates, and so on. Rushed designing could lead to incomplete consideration of design features and their implications for users. Inadequate collaboration and lack of incentives may be two other reasons behind design failures. Businessweek's[6] survey found a lack of coordination as the second-biggest barrier to innovation, noting that the best innovators restructure reporting lines, set aside physical spaces for collaboration, and promote cross-functional participation in projects. Poor design could also stem from hesitancies to depart from established products for fear of not meeting near-term sales and profitability targets; 'not-invented-here' mental models; lack of management follow-through after grand announcements; and the decoupling of incentives from stated goals, quickly revealing the real intentions of leaders to organizational rank and file. Businessweek's survey of innovative companies also cites the difficulty of finding out the 'unmet' needs of the consumer as a major obstacle to the creation of new products— especially if that need cannot be articulated well and there are no actual consumers, since the product does not exist yet. Ethnographic techniques can help here, providing useful insights on latent consumer needs from intelligent observation of people in everyday activities. Observation can identify points of friction or frustration in consumer lives and suggest appropriate product/service remedies. Simple prototypes can also help make latent needs tangible, sometimes asking the consumer to co-produce and evolve the design together.

Cultural issues among disciplines could also affect design quality. Designers and manufacturing may have divorced perceptions of each other's function. Designers may view manufacturing as dull beings, focused on detail, routine, and the rough and tumble of process. Manufacturing, on the other hand, may see designers as pie-in-the sky people who live in an imaginary world and create designs that do not work in the real world. Conflict erupts and design suffers.

The consequences of bad design can go well beyond lost sales or loss of reputation. Legal repercussions could arise. Unlike manufacturing defect cases, which focus on errors that a manufacturer made while actually making the product, design defect cases focus on design flaws in a product. The law applies a cost-benefit analysis in resolving design defect cases, wherein the complainant must identify an alternative practicable design that could have made a product safer. The court then determines whether the presented design alternative is cost-efficient. For example, assume that the fan in a forced air room heater is covered by a guard, but the openings in the guard were an inch wide. During use, the complainant's fingers slip through the openings in the guard cover, and an injury occurs. The plaintiff may file a product design product liability suit arguing that an alternative design with one-quarter inch guard cover openings would have prevented the injury. If the court agrees, it would then decide on whether such an alternative design would be practicable and cost-effective for manufacture.

2.4.2 Measures and Metrics

Design performance has two dimensions—technical success and commercial success; and two questions—how well did *this* design do, and how good are we at designing *in general*? For instance, Nike could ask how well will this particular shoe design do, and, how well are we doing as a company in terms of design performance?

The technical performance of an individual design is assessed through metrics such as design reliability and durability, often measured in stress testing as MTBF (mean time between failures) and MTTF (mean time to failure), respectively. Other metrics include number of engineering change notices (ECNs, fewer the better) in manufacturing, time and cost from concept to production, and product specific ergonomic and safety factors. Some technical design dimensions are hard to measure accurately—the sweetness, balance and body of a wine; the tartness of cheese; the knowledge in a newly minted graduate. Expert panels usually conduct performance tests on such subjective yet important design criteria.

Companies also like to know the technical performance of their design departments in general. General measures of design technical performance include direct measures such as counts of patent filings and approvals and the number of prototypes built (more the better), as well as indirect ones like the number of technical publications reported by R&D personnel.

How well a particular design has done commercially can be evaluated through financial and market-oriented metrics.[7]

- Has the design led to an increase in *financial performance*? Studies have found a significant relationship between design effectiveness and higher returns on sales, returns on assets, net income, and cash flow, and stock performance.
- Has the design resulted in creating a *new market*? An excellent example is the introduction of shampoo in small individual plastic sachets designed by Unilever in India—sachets are inexpensive, easy to store, and let potential consumers test a new product at little expense. Sales of shampoo surged, though an unexpected consequence has been the increased litter from the millions of plastic pouches discarded after use.
- Has the design led to increased *market share* in the existing market? Snapple's repackaged ®Mistic RE energy drink marked its first move from glass to aluminum. The newly designed aluminum bottle reportedly drove a 30 percent increase in Snapple's sales. Whereas

Tropicana's redesign (the one on the right) was recalled quickly when unit sales slumped 20 percent in two months.

Figure 2.13 Tropicana—Old and New Designs

Source: J. Lai, "Tropicana—Old and New," [CC], *flickr*, https://www.flickr.com/photos/jlai321/3123175118/.

* Is the design *sticky*? Stickiness in a design means the design has traction, that the user prefers to remain with the design even when reasonably attractive alternatives present themselves. Reasons could range from emotional attachment and experienced ease of use to high switching costs in terms of time and effort and social peer pressure. Jeep by Chrysler is an iconic sticky design that has continued over the years.

Figure 2.14 Jeep Wrangler

Source: IFCAR, "Jeep Wrangler,"[Public domain], via *Wikimedia Commons*, Oct. 16, 2007, https://commons.wikimedia.org/wiki/File:Jeep-Wrangler.jpg.

An exclusive focus on quantitative measures can inhibit true experimentation and blue sky ideas. People play safe when outcomes are measured with numbers. Managers may also be reluctant to invest in designs that can cannibalize existing cash-generating product lines.

To fire up employees for creative thinking, companies need to measure more than revenues and costs. Personal engagement grows when design has emotional content and a visible impact on the world they live in or the people they care for. Many organizations working with your generation are realizing that social and ecological goals bring excitement, passion, and success to the design and innovation process. Metrics are being updated.

Of all the different metrics, the most valuable metric would be a predictive measure of design success. Rogers provides a useful conceptual tool to respond to that dreaded project make/break question: *Will* this design be a commercial success[8]? The answer to that question, Roger says, depends in significant measure on how the adopter perceives the attributes of the design.

- *Relative advantage*: How is the design superior over current designs in terms of form and functionality?

  What are the advantages of the current iPhone over the previous model?

- *Compatibility*: How compatible is the new design in meeting consumer needs, lifestyle, and values?

  For instance, e-greetings are incompatible with many peoples' values. The personal touch—a phone conversation or a hand signed card—is generally valued more by both sender and recipient than an animated bulk mail.

- *Complexity*: How difficult or challenging or time-consuming is it to understand and use the design?

  You may still see some die-hard professors who have stayed with the decade-old MS Office 2003. It's not worth their effort to learn keys and functions anew for doing the same job. Perhaps less drastic design changes would have reduced the perceived difficulty and prompted more switches to the current product.

- *Trialability*: How easy or practical is it for a user to try out or experiment with the design in a limited way?

  User experimentation with in-process designs could yield valuable insights: Is it used in unanticipated ways? What features are not used? The design is paused while the designers listen and observe as the user experiments with and thinks aloud about the design. Oftentimes, companies offer new consumer products like perfumes and make-up in small trial size bottles or disseminate coupons and free samples to promote trialability. Paint company, Benjamin Moore's site and eyeglass sites like Coastal.com offer virtual try-ons where users can see the effects of using different colors and designs.

- *Observability*: Can we see someone else use the design and use that experience to judge its utility?

  The ability to watch others use the design is particularly valuable when there's uncertainty about the purpose of the design or its utility. Companies conduct live demonstrations or TV/online infomercials to promote observability of new designs. Snuggies, the oversized fleece blanket with sleeves, became a major hit, and Blentec's http://www.willitblend.com site shows strangely addictive clips of its blenders decimating weird items like an iPhone and golf balls to dust.

New designs may fail (80 to 90 percent failure rate) because of technical deficiencies or over-pricing, but inattention to the perceived attributes of design is almost sure to kill product adoption.

KEY POINTS

Have We Done a Good Job?

- Designers overlook design conflicts and deficiencies because of ever-tightening deadlines and inadequate collaboration.
- Technical success in a design is evaluated by reliability, durability, cost, development time, and ergonomic and safety metrics.

- Technical success in design at the organizational level is measured through patent counts, prototype counts, and technical publications.
- Commercial success in design is evaluated through financial, market growth, market share growth, design longevity, green content, and various R&D ratios.
- User adoption of a design is a function of relative advantage over existing designs, compatibility with user lifestyle, design complexity, the opportunity for limited user trials, and the feasibility of observing someone else use the design.

2.5 Current Trends in Design

The most prominent trend is probably the role of sustainability in the design of products and manufacturing and delivery processes. Other trends like convergence in design may be less visible, but active nonetheless. Innovations are also appearing in design tools like netnography, *kansei* design engineering, and 3D printing.

2.5.1 Sustainability in Design

What would products and processes look like if designers considered "all children, all species, for all time," asks William McDonough, designer-in-chief of seven new green cities in China?[9] Designing for the triple bottom line (TBL/3BL), "people, planet, profit," although maybe not in strict order, is the goal of sustainable (environmental) design.

Design for the environment (DFE) can be decomposed into specific design aspects relating to sustainability, such as design for manufacturing, design for environment, and design for recycling and remanufacturing. DFE emphasizes prevention, asking designers to explicitly consider all environmental aspects of a product in all the stages of its life cycle. For example, designers would need to examine the energy and environmental impact of extractive materials like iron ore and coal that could be used directly and indirectly in the manufacture of the product. Similarly, DFE would also look at the energy used in packaging and in transporting inputs and finished product along the supply chain, the energy spent in using the product (e.g., gas for autos), and the ease of recycling or reusing the product after use. A 'green' design implies the use of recycled, low energy footprint, raw materials, a low energy, nonpolluting manufacturing and delivery process, and effective nonpolluting and energy efficient methods of disposal, recycling, or remanufacturing/refurbishing after first use.

Arturo's Osteria & Pizzeria in New Jersey has introduced a 100 percent recycled material, new GreenBox pizza box for pizza delivery—the box has a perforated lid that breaks into four plates. The remainder of the box then folds into a half-size, easily storable container for leftover pizza—Eco Incorporated designed the box.

Figure 2.15 GreenBox

Source: Photo used with permission from Arturo's pizza. Arturo's Osteria & Pizzeria, www.arturosnj.com, 180 Maplewood Ave, Maplewood, NJ 07040.

Nike has a new app called Making that helps designers choose green materials for their designs. Materials are rated out of a possible 50 points, with higher scores indicating a more positive environmental impact. The EPA (Environmental Protection Agency) allows its DfE logo on some 2,000 products that have demonstrated use of the safest ingredients in each class of chemical. However, most consumers may not be willing to pay a significant premium for a DfE certified product or take the trouble to actively search for one. Design for the environment is getting a boost from laws requiring the manufacturer to take back products at the end of their lifespan or when retired for newer products. In Europe, the WEEE Directive mandates that products must be designed for dismantling and recovery, recycling, or reusing between 50 percent and 75 percent of the old equipment on the market, depending on the product category. In the U.S., although not federally mandated, 25 states have passed legislation mandating e-waste recycling. All states except California adopt the producer responsibility approach, whereby the manufacturer pays for recycling.

OM IN PRACTICE

HP's Design for Environment (DfE) Program

Primary DfE goals:

- Energy efficiency—lower the energy requirements for manufacture and use of HP products.
- Materials innovation—reduce input usage and use inputs with lower environmental impact and higher end-of-life value.
- Design for recyclability—design products that facilitate upgrading and/or recycling.

How to achieve DfE goals:

- Include environmental stewards on every design team to identify design changes that may reduce environmental impact throughout the product's life cycle.
- Eliminate the use of harmful chemicals.
- Standardize and reduce variety and quantity of inputs.
- Use molded-in colors and finishes instead of paint, coatings, or plating whenever possible.
- Design product for energy consumption.
- Use fewer and more recycled materials in product packaging.
- Design for disassembly and recyclability.

Actual realization of DfE goals: PCs

Reduction of hazardous materials:

- Plastics greater than 25 grams have no halogenated flame retardants
- No use of polyvinyl chloride (PVC) except for cables
- No use of polybrominated biphenyls (PBBs), polybrominated biphenyl ethers (PBDEs) also known as polybrominated biphenyl oxides (PBDOs)
- No use of ozone depleting substances in product manufacturing

Resource conservation:

- Manuals are printed on elementary chlorine free (EFC) bleached virgin or recycled paper or put on CD-ROM to minimize paper use.

Power consumption:

- Standby mode saves significant power by turning off the display and other components. The current session is stored in RAM, which allows for quick restarts.
- Hibernate mode saves more power than standby mode by saving the current session to disk, then shutting down.

Design for recycling:

- Marking plastic parts weighing more than 25 grams according to ISO 11469 for easier sorting.
- Eliminating glues and adhesives from product construction where feasible.
- Using common fasteners.
- Including snap-in features.
- Plastic and metal are easily separable for easy dismantling and recycling.
- Metallized plastic casings are not used.

Adapted from: "Design for Environment," *HP*, accessed Sept. 28, 2015, http://www8.hp.com/us/en/hp-information/environment/design-for-environment.html#.Vgs9lnldGUk.

2.5.2 Convergence in Design

Long, long ago, when your parents were young, people used land-line phones, played CDs on Walkmans, used a PDA (look it up) for keeping appointments, bought a camera to take pictures, got a paper delivered to the door, and looked up a road atlas for directions. Now think about how you accomplish all those tasks. Probably through a single product—a smartphone. Technology has converged mail, phone, text, broadcast, computer, personal assistant, GPS, camera, alarm, car door opener, teleconferencing, medical assistant, music storage and playback, newspaper, stock market, banking, shopping, and bill and purchases payment into a single device. Convergence is happening in products, technologies, and services. The enabler is intelligent technology and miniaturization. The incentive is the growing trend to multi-task, unencumbered, in a cordless, travel light, lifestyle. People see value in products that have multiple functions—multi-functional furniture, for instance.[10]

Figure 2.16 Multi-Functional Furniture

Source: Photo used with permission from Clei/Resource Furniture, http://www.clei.it/ and http://www.resourcefurniture.com, 969 3rd Ave, New York, NY 10022.

Notice the convertible bed and other multi-functional furniture. It serves multiple purposes with a single product. Probably, if you ask Resource Furniture, maker of such products, it may say that the product design and manufacturing is more complex compared to single-use products. Because the technology to create these pieces is often complex, the time it takes to move from design to engineering to prototype often spans a year or more. And the complexity adds to manufacturing costs.

Convergence in design has some cautions. Users become over-dependent on a single device. A lost or broken device could create a serious problem for a user. And the crowding of complex technologies in small spaces can cause unforeseen problems—the antenna on the iPhone4 was wrapped around the case to conserve space, but users' fingers covered it while holding the device, causing calling and reception issues.

2.5.3 Affordable, Relevant Design

There is a growing interest in affordability in design. Caterpillar and Komatsu are facing extremely competitive price structures in China. Their normal sales pitch based on the 'total cost of ownership' over a 10–20 year period does not work too well in China. The Chinese equipment buyer prefers to buy two 'local' machines at a lower cost, perhaps keeping one on stand-by for breakdowns, and sell both to an inland provinces buyer a few years down the road. With such cost pressures, companies are turning to design to strip away costs yet maintain acceptable quality levels from the perspective of the customer as well as the brand. Honda saw its market share drop more than 60 percent in Vietnam from 1997 to 2002 due to intense competition from Chinese made imitations of Honda motorcycles. Honda engineers were surprised to find that the quality of the Chinese made imitations was not significantly inferior to Honda manufactured products. Instead of persecuting the imitators, Honda struck an alliance with the Chinese manufacturers and designed a new motorcycle, Wave, with Chinese parts and Honda engineering. The huge success of the Wave, however, in turn, spawned imitators of itself! These designs often result in entirely new lower cost products that can be migrated back to economically hard-pressed developed market consumers. Mahindra and Mahindra, an automotive manufacturer in India, has successfully targeted segments in the U.S. market with its small 75 HP or lower capacity, low-priced models built for the Indian market but converted for use in the U.S. Among the design changes—cup holders in the tractor cabin.

Low-cost design innovations extend into services, with payment options such as pay per use and community ownership in schools and villages. An example of a service design that has migrated from Asia to the U.S. is found in the tutoring industry. The business design in the U.S. was based on face-to-face tutor-student sessions priced at $40/hour and higher. Companies like www.tutor.com and TutorVista were among the pioneers of a new low-cost, process design that hired technically and linguistically competent teachers in India and other locations to offer low cost ($99/month), 24/7 no- prior-appointment-required availability tutoring products to the U.S. public.

There is a natural tension between globalization and localization in design. Although iconic designs like Apple and the Coca-Cola bottle are universally admired and purchased, product designs are being increasingly localized for user relevance and product differentiation. The China-based Haier Corporation received frequent breakdown complaints about its washing machines from customers in the southwest regions of China. It was not so with customers from other parts, and engineers were puzzled. Site visits revealed that the customers of washing machines in the agricultural southwest washed not just clothes but also produce like potatoes and veggies in their machines. The dirt clogged the machine. Haier redesigned the machine with an interchangeable washing barrel and wider pipes and solved the problem. Haier also makes extra-large washing machines for accommodating the voluminous robes of Saudi Arabian customers and voltage fluctuation robust machines for power outage-plagued Indian users.

2.5.4 Digital Design and Manufacturing

Often called 'Industrial Internet' or 'Industry 4.0' or the 'Internet of Things, (IOT)' digital design and manufacturing include a variety of digital technologies such as 3D printing, smart cars and appliances, and digitally connected manufacturing equipment. 'Mercedes me' from Daimler tracks the usage and wear of key automotive parts in running cars. The vast trove of recorded and on-the-job data generated by such digitally connected 'things' can be analyzed and used for both product and process improvement.

OM IN PRACTICE

Both President Obama and VP Biden were reportedly "dazzled" when Local Motors printed the 'Strati,' the world's first 3D electric car, right on the floor of the International Auto Show at Detroit—a single-piece product integrating chassis and frame, exterior body, and some interior features. Mechanical, suspension, and electricals were supplied separately. Local Motors plans a "distributed manufacturing" system of 'microfactories.' Each microfactory would have a showroom where customers can design and order their customized cars and accessories; a 'Local Motors Lab' where anyone could use the company's machines to create accessories or apps that improve car performance (and get a royalty); a manufacturing area with heavy-duty printers and 'routers' that smooth finish products; and a warehousing space. The vision is already taking shape, with the first 'micro-factory' coming up in Knoxville, Tennessee, on 10 acres of land.

Figure 2.17 "Strati," World's First 3D Printed Electric Car

Source: Image used with permission from https://localmotors.com.

At a personal level, imagine an Amazon truck pulling into your driveway and asking you what color and precise size would you like those shoes you ordered—and then making it before your very eyes. Amazon has actually filed for a patent for what it calls 'mobile manufacturing centers,' trucks equipped with 3D printers that'll park and print out your order at your curbside. While that particular scenario may take some more time to materialize, 3D printers are printing parts and products on the manufacturing shop floor today. Airbus uses 3D printers to make tools or to make parts that are no longer available. 3D printing can make one integrated part of a highly complex part, such as an aviation fuel nozzle. A nozzle traditionally is made of several different components that have to be made and tested separately and soldered together.

3D printing uses a repetitive layering motion that accumulates into a finished product. Recent printers also employ a faster, fluid, build-up process using a pool of resin—remember how the Terminator 2/3 bad guys/gals regenerated? Customization and convenience are the main advantages. Prototypes can be made quickly, obsolete spare parts made locally, and customized medical products like knee joints and prosthetics can be made with great precision. Mass manufacturing and economies of scale are, however, difficult to achieve with this technology, as yet. Raw materials used are also more expensive—steel powders used in 3D printing are 100 times more expensive than commercial grade. As the technology improves and prices come down, the responsiveness, flexibility, inventory savings, and customization advantages of 3D printing will attract more users in more industries.

Adapted from: Rich McCormick, "Amazon Wants to Fit Trucks with 3D Printers to Speed Up Deliveries," *The Verge*, Feb. 27 2015; Dale Buss, "Local Motors Executive Discusses 3D Printing and the Future of Manufacturing," March 4, 2015, *Chief Executive*, Chiefexecutive.net; http://carbon3d.com.

2.5.5 New Design Tools

Observe how you use a pencil. Catch yourself: a) bringing it to your lips, b) chewing on one end, c) rolling it between your fingers, d) tapping it on your cheek or chin, or e) massaging it up and down your desktop. Your actions are probably unconscious and reflect your emotions of the moment—perhaps an awkward social situation, or a need to concentrate, or a 'wish I wasn't here' feeling, or a 'wish that person would shut-up' desire (stabbing the desktop). The lowly pencil suddenly acquires a psychological profile that essentially shows the emotional uses of the product. The pencil designer can observe such interactions and create a mechanism for articulating and connecting such subliminal feelings with specific design features, like inserting a nontoxic, pleasant-tasting eraser at the end, designing an 'acupuncture' pencil with in-built massage ridges, and such. Kansei engineering is a tool that can help the designer do that.

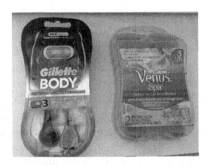

Figure 2.18 His and Hers Kansei Design of Razors

Source: Author.

The consumer's emotional image of a product is called *kansei* in Japanese, and has become the basis of a design tool called 'kansei engineering.'[11] 'Image' words are used to describe the consumer's cognitive perspective and connected to specific design elements. Kansei includes emotion words like 'Free,' 'Simple,' 'Boring,' 'Healthy,' 'Happy,' 'Light-hearted,' 'Stressful,' 'Relaxed,' 'Exciting,' 'Frustrating,' 'Greedy,' 'Intelligent,' 'Safe,' 'Smooth,' 'Lasting,' 'Annoying,' 'Strong,' 'Ethical,' 'Comforting,' 'Young,' and 'Personal.' Analytical tools such as multivariate statistical analysis, rough-sets algorithms, and neural network analysis are employed to construct image-evaluating patterns and link those to design and product styling. Kansei engineering integrates psychological and mathematical methods to translate, link, and incorporate the consumer's image of a product into design reality. Kansei engineering particularly suits the trend towards designing emotional 'experiences' around products. Applications are as diverse as designing a children's playground, a coffee shop, and a pair scissors, or gender-specific razor design and packaging.

Another contemporary design tool is netnography. Do you tweet, or blog, or belong to a bulletin board, a chat room, a discussion group, or use Facebook, subscribe to any feeds, or are a part of an e-forum or rating site on any subject? If so, the choices, opinions, and decisions that you make online with others can be tracked, connected, and analyzed to provide business information on consumer interests, opinions about brands, consumer trends, consumer search, and consumption patterns. Companies like Google or Amazon with their vast access to consumer data favor quick data-driven pattern recognition. Hidden correlations can be uncovered and profiles can be built and tested more rigorously with more traditional, lengthier, hypothesis development and testing approaches.

2.5.6 Patenting Design

The USPTO (United States Patent and Trademark Office) is the official site for patenting designs in the U.S. (http://www.uspto.gov/). Patents are limited in time and have expiry periods. In fields like medicine, where a single patent can be a billion-dollar revenue generator, patent expiry is a closely watched and stock-price-affecting factor. International patents are awarded by the World Intellectual Property Organization (WIPO; http://www.wipo.int /portal/index.html.en), an agency of the United Nations. Europe has a continent-wide patent office—Europe Patent Organization (http://www.epo.org). Domestic patents in countries such as China, India, and Russia are administered by local country patent offices. Intellectual property (IP) laws protect patents in theory, but getting punitive action or a court conviction against an imitator may not be an easy task. The United States placed Russia on its list of countries with the worst IP protection records for the 15th straight year. China and India also feature regularly on the U.S. 'priority watch list.' Here's a quick look at the filing process in the US for when you come up with that novel design for a product or service:

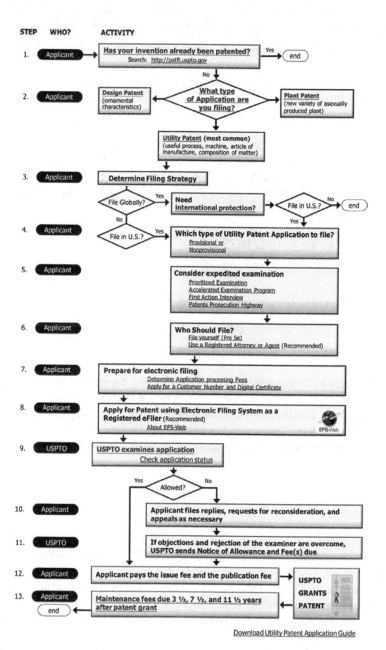

Figure 2.19 Patent Application Process

Source: U.S. Patent and Trademark Office, http://www.uspto.gov.

Patents can be useful in other ways, too:

Figure 2.20 Patent Gets You Out of Jail!

Source: Used with permission from *South China Morning Post*.

That's an advertisement in China offering advice on applying for patents in order to get jail terms commuted. The law in China reportedly allows reductions in prison sentences in return for innovating products. Prisoners buy inventors' designs (illegally) and file applications for product patents, with services beginning at about 6,800 yuan (HK$8,580). Early action is advised—agents remark that "some rich people come to us right after they get into trouble and before they go to jail. It takes a lot of early preparation."[12]

KEY POINTS

Trends in Design

- Sustainability considerations demand that designs fulfill the triple bottom-line—people, planet, and profits.
- Sustainability in design comes from design for manufacturing and assembly, design for environment, design for remanufacturing, and design for recycling.
- Design convergence packs multiple features and technologies on a single platform, for convenience of access and use.
- Low-cost designs are being developed for fast-growth global markets. Lessons learnt are being transferred into core design processes.

- Kansei engineering, a design tool, allows the emotional image of a product to be converted to specific design elements.
- Netnography analysis allows the application of ethnographic techniques for online social and commercial transactions.
- IP protection is provided by patent organizations worldwide, but enforcement is spotty.

2.6 Conclusion

Customer: *"Why should I choose you?"*
Business: *"Because we promise you a product that has been designed and built for your needs, lifestyle, and excitement."*

Design drives sales, costs, and brand reputation. We began the chapter by defining product design and its importance in achieving differentiation and customer satisfaction in today's world. We looked at career opportunities in design. We also examined frameworks and tools that explain how designs are created. Design pitfalls were illustrated in bad designs, and we identified and discussed some notable metrics and emerging trends in design.

I'm sure you have some great ideas about new products or services. Let's do something exciting and real. Sketch out your concept—a short description, a rough image, a picture—and put it to the test. Online feedback is available in plenty. Showcase your idea and design on sites such as AYTM.com, UsabilityHub.com, User-Testing.com or http://zurb.com/apps and get instant 'love it/hate it/ how to improve it' feedback, and numerical reports. Then what? Well, go ahead make those products at the nearest Techshop (techshop.ws/) and rock the world (get your patents first at USPTO.org). Or sell it to a telemarketer like Telebrands.

Made you look! Designers love that reaction. Because if we look, we may buy, and touch, consume, drive, wear, or watch the product or service that we purchased and, perhaps, then buy another one. As Plato once said:

"The beginning is the most important part of the work."

What Have We Learned?

What Is Design?

- Design is a creative activity, grounded at the intersection of art, maths, and engineering.
- Product design is 'industrial design'—the shape, composition, weight, and looks of an industrial product—designed to meet the functional and emotional needs of users, manufacturing, workers, transporters, warehousing, suppliers, repair, remanufacturing and recycling.

Why Is It Important?

- Design drives financial performance through revenue growth in existing and new markets, improvements in safety, and cost reductions through improved material substitution and easier manufacturability, reliability, lower energy consumption needs during manufacturing, miniaturization, and ease of disassembly and recycling.

- Design draws on marketing, operations, finance, accounting, and HR. Marketing identifies and interprets consumer preferences, operations provides engineering, production, and supply base inputs, finance conducts project evaluations and arranges capital, accounting provides cost estimates, and HR provides the labor skills necessary for design and manufacture. Every major will interact with some aspect of design in their job.

How to Design?

- Design ideas can be found from R&D, nature, employees, reverse engineering, and through open sourcing.
- The principles of design include consideration of manufacturability, reliability, standardization, safety, sustainability, and legal compliance.
- The design process begins with idea generation, concept formulation, design engineering, manufacturing engineering, and production. Flexible engineering is a current approach to the product design process, involving design, engineering, and production concurrently in the design process. The process allows flexibility in the design process and improves final product quality.
- Open collaboration between design and marketing is critical to the design process.
- Engineering and production design tools include a variety of computer-aided design, manufacturing, and quality control equipment (CAD, CAM, CAQC) that enable flexibility and speed in developing and testing designs.
- Target costing sets design cost parameters by subtracting the desired profit margin from the potential selling price of the design.
- Design ideas require collaborative spaces and opportunities, employee incentives, and acceptance of external input.
- Designs are evaluated using market research, social media, and consumer/employee interaction with physical mock-ups and prototypes and by using the market to pick from simultaneous launches of multiple variations of a product.

Have We Done a Good Job?

- Technical success metrics include reliability, durability, number of engineering changes, time to develop and make, and ergonomic and safety elements. Expert panels evaluate subjective elements such as smell and taste.
- Commercial success measures include sales growth and market penetration, stock price increase, increase in reputation, and the extent to which the design fulfils 'green' expectations. Metrics include percent sales from new products, ration of new products to R&D investment, and ROI on R&D.
- Too much focus on quantitative design success measures can discourage risk taking and innovation in design.
- Personnel management and incentive policies have to change to accommodate the multi-tasking, rapid feedback, rationale seeking, community/planet health-minded work and life habits of the entering workforce—the millennials.
- Predicting the commercial adoption of a design requires consideration of the relative advantage of the design over existing designs, compatibility with user values, degree of complexity in use, the opportunity for user trials, and the opportunity to observe others use the design.

Current Trends in Design

- Laws and consumer pressure are pushing inclusion of sustainability considerations in design, specifically evaluating design conformity with input, manufacturing and usage energy consumption, remanufacturing and recycling goals.
- Products are being designed to be part of a consumer experience to achieve differentiation goals.
- Design convergence is using miniaturization and innovative forms to cluster different technologies and offer a variety of functionalities on a single product platform.
- Low-cost designs are beginning to interest companies seeking entry in high-growth developing markets. Affordable design and relevant functionalities are the success factors in such markets.
- Design tools like kansei engineering, which translate consumer emotional perceptions of design into design elements, and netnography (observing and analyzing online behavior) are finding increased use.
- Designs are patented at the USPTO and WIPO offices, for U.S. and international patent filing, respectively. Patents are difficult to enforce in some parts of the world.

Discussion Questions

1 A beautiful design? Evaluate, compare, and comment on the design feature of the product shown below.

   Instructor: Easier to hold and use shape. Large cap allows a firm grip for ease of opening. Shape facilitates stocking and stability in use—does not tip over. Large mouth means higher volume flow and quicker consumption. Manufacturing ease?

2 Provide reasons why design would be an important knowledge area for a) a finance major, b) an accounting major, c) a marketing major, d) an HR major.

3 Improve on the current iPhone design. Use DFMA principles and develop comparative before and after design efficiency ratios.

4 Use DFE to critically examine the use of plastic parts in a product.

Figure 2.21 Old Listerine Bottle

Source: VoxEfx, "DIY Lightbox Practice 2," [CC], flickr, April 11, 2008, https://www.flickr.com/photos/vox_efx/2404835357/.

Figure 2.22 New Listerine Bottle

Source: Author.

Suggested Cases

Cradle-to-Cradle Design at Herman Miller: Moving Toward Environmental Sustainability

Deishin Lee, Lionel Bony
Source: HBS Premier Case Collection
21 pages. Publication date: May 30, 2007. Prod. #: 607003-PDF-ENG

Description

"Herman Miller, an office furniture supplier, decided to implement the cradle-to-cradle (C2C) design protocol during the design of its mid-level office chair, Mirra. The C2C protocol was a set of environmentally friendly product development guidelines created by architect William McDonough and chemist Michael Braungart. The essence of this protocol was to eliminate waste and potentially harmful materials by designing the product so that, at the end of its useful life, the raw materials could be fed back into either a technical or biological cycle and used for the same or other purposes. Therefore, materials remained in a closed-loop, eliminating the need for landfill and other toxic forms of disposal such as incineration. The case describes the C2C protocol, the details of how Herman Miller implemented C2C during the design of the Mirra chair, and the impact of the new protocol on their internal processes: design decisions, manufacturing, and supply chain management. The proximate decision point in the case is whether the company should replace the polyvinyl chloride (PVC) material in the arm pads of the Mirra chair. PVC was a highly toxic material to manufacture and dispose of and thus violated the C2C protocol. However, it was the standard material for arm pads and many other parts in the office furniture industry because it was durable, scratch resistant, and inexpensive. To switch to thermoplastic urethane (TPU), a more environmentally friendly material, for the Mirra Chair arm pad required at least modification of a production tool or possibly a completely new tool. In addition, the cost of TPU was higher than PVC. There was also uncertainty about how consistent the quality of the arm pad would be with TPU."

Learning Objective

To show that by scrutinizing processes through an environmental lens, Herman Miller can also improve performance.

Bang & Olufsen: Design Driven Innovation

Daniela Beyersdorfer, Robert D. Austin
Source: Harvard Business School
24 pages. Publication date: Sept. 1, 2006. Prod. #: 607016-PDF-ENG

Description

A successful company, recognized worldwide for exquisite design of consumer electronics products, strives to better integrate software design into its traditional physical product design processes to meet the demands of a post-iPod world. Details the Bang & Olufsen "design driven innovation" process, which works very differently than many companies' product development processes but allows this company to produce very high-profit-margin products that retain their margins for a very long time in an industry in which products come and go very quickly. The case helps students understand processes and practices that support the creation of highly differentiated products. It also deals with issues of change in an already successful context and of managing highly creative staff who are vital to a company's business model.

Learning Objective

To examine the details of product design, development, and production in a company with very differentiated products.

Notes

1 Steve Jobs, *Quotations Page.com*, http://www.quotationspage.com/quote/38348.html and http://www.quotationspage.com/subjects/design/.
2 See "A Biomimicry Primer," *Biomimicry 3.8*, accessed April 28 2015, http://biomimicry.net/about/biomimicry/a-biomimicry-primer/.
3 See a video of this process at "Design for Assembly," *DFMA*, https://www.youtube.com/watch?feature=player_embedded&v=E7_afjJTAok.
4 Alberto Savoia, *Pretotype It: Make Sure You Are Building the Right It, Before You Build It Right* (Mountain View, CA: Self-published on Google drive, 2011, pg 24), https://drive.google.com/file/d/0B0QztbuDlKs_NzBjYWNiOGQtNmQyNi00OWE2LWI2YzktN2Y3YTEzM2VjYTNj/view?pli=1.
5 Michael V. Copeland, "Intel's Cultural Anthropologist," *Fortune*, Sept. 27, 2010.
6 "The World's Most Innovative Companies," *Businessweek,* April 24, 2006.
7 Thomas Lockwood, "Ten Ways to Measure Design's Success," *Bloomberg Businessweek*, Oct. 5, 2009.
8 E. Rogers, *Diffusion of Innovations*, 5th ed. (New York, NY: The Free Press, 2003).
9 William McDonough, "Cradle to Cradle Design," *TED*, April 2007, http://www.ted.com/talks/william_mcdonough_on_cradle_to_cradle_design/transcript?language=en#t-224000.
10 See an example of multi-purpose furniture at http://www.resourcefurniture.com/space-saving-video.
11 For more information on Kansei engineering, read S. Schütte, et al., "Concepts, Methods and Tools in Kansei Engineering," *Theoretical Issues in Ergonomics Science*, no. 5, (2004): 214–232.
12 Adrian Wan, "How to Get Out of Jail Early in China: Buy an Inventor's Idea and Patent It," *South China Morning Post*, Jan. 19, 2015.

3 Process and Service Design

Process and Service Design: A Road Map

Customer: *"Why should I choose you?"*
Business: *"Because we promise that each step of your experience with us and our products will be smooth, trouble-free, and of value to you."*

3.1 What Is Process Design?

After a product is designed, it has to be made. To do that, a production process must be designed. Materials, machinery, and labor are organized in certain ways depending on the product design characteristics, the anticipated production volume, the extent of variety offered on the basic design, and the nature of the skills required in the making of the product. Making wedding dresses, for example, would require a quite different organization of production factors as compared to auto manufacturing. Wedding dresses come in far greater variety and sell in far fewer quantities for a specific design relative to automobiles. The skills required in dress-making may be more labor intensive and specialized, while automobile manufacturing may require standardized repetitive tasks with a large part of the work being done by machines.

In the past, process design would typically either be done after product design or begin at the prototype stage. Currently, marketing strategy, product design, supplier organization, and process design are actioned concurrently and interactively in the development and launch of new product designs. Changes in one affect the others, and the value of a flexible design approach (see chapter 2) becomes evident.

Process design can be product or process focused (oriented). You can find an example of a product-oriented process in assembly lines in car assembly plants, where equipment, workers and material are all located along the path the product flows as it's made. Work stations are built around the conveyer belt path that all car bodies move on during their manufacture. In a product-oriented process, seen in high volume–low variety products, labor and machinery are arranged around the flow of product manufacturing. The product moves mostly linearly through a series of operations performed by labor or machines. It makes sense to use equipment and labor specialized to the product if an operation makes just a few similar products in high volumes. The initial fixed costs would be high, but unit variable costs would be low. The downside to such an arrangement is that the production system becomes relatively inflexible, capable of making only a limited range of products.

In contrast, a process-focused (-oriented) arrangement, typical of low volume–high variety products, is very flexible and can accommodate a variety of products. Labor and machinery are placed in specific locations by task or type, each performing a specific process, with products moving through these centers as and when needed. A hospital emergency room is a good example of a process-oriented design—staffed with versatile ER physicians, nurses specially trained to handle a wide variety of accidents and medical emergencies, general purpose X-ray and diagnostic equipment, and an operating room that can accommodate many different types of 'products.' Process-oriented designs are flexible in terms of the variety of tasks/products that can be handled/made but generally have high variable costs and high idle time. Individual work centers may remain idle at times since not all products need to go through all work centers.

3.2 What Is Service Design?

A service either accompanies the delivery of a tangible product or is itself accompanied by tangible accoutrements. While a hamburger is tangible, the smile and attitude of the server are not; experiencing a movie may be intangible, but the movie theater chairs and air conditioning are not. Services are actions that are part of a package of tangible physical goods and intangible psycho-sensory experiential goods. A pure intangible service may be difficult to find sans any supporting tangible factors. The quality of the result from service actions depends on the quality of the *design* of those actions. Service design plans, constructs, evaluates, relates, and tests service tasks and activities. Consider, for example, what likely happens behind the scene

Before   *After*

Figures 3.1a, b Professorial Looks

Sources: Left: Author. Right: Jerry Avenaim, "Dwayne 'The Rock' Johnson," [CC license], via Wikimedia Commons, https://commons. wikimedia.org/wiki/File:The_ROCK.jpg.

in your professor's office *before* the professor walks in on the first day of class. He has likely spent hours designing the course, mapped out the course objectives and individual tasks and topic modules, prepared and stored homework assignments, tried to anticipate typical first day student questions and concerns, located and checked out the classroom, and placed material on the blackboard or a similar site. And then professors, strange as it may seem, like to look good for the first encounter with their class and try to upgrade themselves, too (see photos above).

Service design is a conceptual exercise that first identifies consumer wants and develops actions to satisfy those wants, making deliberate choices among production factors in that process. Frameworks exist: Kano[1] developed a hierarchy of customer wants, ranging from must-have needs to delighters. Levitt (1972)[2] suggested substituting technology for labor as a means to improve the consistency of product offering together with the use of standardized documented material usage and work procedures. Today, surgeries are being performed by robots, and technology has supplanted labor in many tasks. Another approach focuses on converting the consumer into a factor of production, involving consumers in a variety of production tasks, a situation that we commonly experience in self-serve places and fast food places. A different approach uses design modules to mix and match into specific service designs—much like we pick specific courses to complete a major in college. Yet another approach balances the 3Ts—task, tangibles, and treatment—in different combinations to suit the nature of the service.[3] We shall look at some frameworks in greater detail later in the chapter.

KEY POINTS

What Is Design?

- Process design is the way equipment and labor are organized to make a product or service. There are two principal forms of process design–a product-oriented design and a process-oriented design.
- A product-focused (-oriented) process design is suited to high volume–low variety production made in sequenced steps with dedicated labor and machinery arranged around the flow of product manufacturing steps. Fixed costs are high, but unit variable costs are low. The production system cannot handle much variety. Goal: resource utilization; e.g., car assembly, steel making.
- A process-focused (-oriented) design is suited to low volume–high variety production, where labor and machinery are clustered by type into work centers, and the product goes to a center, if the operation demands. Variable cost and resource idle time are high, but the system can make a variety of products. Goal: customization and product variety; e.g., an E.R., Starbucks.
- Service design is the composition of an offered service package, typically a combination of a tangible product and psycho-sensory goods. Goal: provide customer service with efficiency, automate where feasible, and engage customers in production tasks; e.g., a tangible physical examination and EKG test and a warm greeting at the doctor's office reception.

3.3 How Is It Done?

Process design is more complex to develop than product design but confers more lasting advantage since it is a synthesis of many different elements that are difficult to separate and imitate. Toyota's well-known 'Toyota Production System' manufacturing process design has been widely, but imperfectly, imitated. Even Toyota itself has experienced problems transferring its process design to other manufacturing locations outside Japan, as evident from the well-publicized product design quality/safety issues that beset it during 2009–10.

3.3.1 Process Design

Experts have looked at hundreds of processes and found that machines and labor are organized in five distinct ways—project production, job shop, batch, assembly (worker-paced or machine-paced line), and continuous process. Let's begin by understanding these arrangements of production factors and their rationales.

Project production assembles or manufactures a product that is too large or too fragile to be moved, such as building construction and ship manufacturing. Equipment, material, and labor are transported to the production location to work on the product. The product being made is generally in numbers of one or a few. Such an arrangement is akin to a project and is thus called project production. The project production environment is covered in the project management chapter and hence does not find elaboration here. The other four types of organization are found where the product moves as it's made.

A *job shop* organization is a product-oriented layout with different products moving among different work centers, while the remaining process types are progressive variations of process-oriented systems with increasingly standardized products moving at progressively higher rates through a fixed sequence of work steps. As one goes down the list from job shop to continuous flow, the speed of the flow of product through the steps of the process increases. Also, in a job shop process arrangement, the product travels to the resource. For example, in an ER, all X-ray equipment would be located together in a specific part of the facility, and a patient needing an X-ray would have to travel to the X-ray center. All patients may not need an X-ray, so X-ray equipment/technician utilization rates would vary. The X-ray machines, as also the personnel in an ER, would be versatile and general-purpose—able to handle many different types of emergency cases. Similarly, as students (products), you could consider your school as a job shop, offering a wide variety of majors and courses that are taken selectively and taught by skilled professionals. Volumes can vary dramatically depending on the course and the major. In contrast, resources in all the other types of processes are laid out along the path of the manufacturing flow, which is only possible if the product is fairly standardized.

Batch processes are based on variations on a basic design. For example, all ice creams start with milk, eggs, cream, sweetening, and air—flavors are added later. Ice cream is blended, pasteurized, homogenized, cooled, aged, frozen, and packaged, in that order of manufacturing. Dedicated blending equipment and personnel would be located at the first stage of the process, followed by a similar positioning of resources dedicated to every subsequent stage of manufacture. Running a chocolate flavor batch would be materially no different from running a vanilla flavored batch—but each flavor is run in a separate batch since the blender and pasteurizer would need a quick cleaning between different flavor batches.

Assembly line arrangements are similar in principle—dedicated workers and/or equipment are positioned to follow the natural sequence of product manufacture. A recent distinction is the difference between worker-paced assembly lines and machine-paced line organization. Worker-paced lines are processes where a major part of the manufacturing is performed by hand assembly, and the average pace of manufacturing is effectively determined by how long the worker takes to complete manufacturing tasks. Recall that Ferrari that you will gift your prof after you become rich and famous? It's made in a worker-paced line. Every one of the approximately 6,500 cars Ferrari makes at its Maranello, Italy, plant, is handmade, smoothed, hand finished, and hand checked (http://www.ferrari.com/).

A Ferrari begins as an aluminum-silicon ingot that is melted and cast into an eight- or twelve-cylinder engine block using sand and steel molds. Workers meticulously operate, control, and check the casting process, to achieve precision casting geometries and thicknesses of just 2-3 millimeters.

Engine parts are mechanically milled to millimetric precision in Ferrari's 'green' machining center, using technology and sophisticated craftsmanship.

Each engine is assembled by a single craftsman in the engine assembly area prior to bench testing.

Figure 3.2a Ferrari Symbol

Figure 3.2b Casting Process

Figure 3.2c Mechanical Machining Workshop

In parallel with engine manufacturing, the Ferrari body shell begins to take shape, where traditional manual skills shape aluminum ingots to produce the distinctive lines and shapes of Ferraris. Body paneling, fitting of doors, hood and trunk, and surface quality control are craft tasked, critically dependent on worker expertise and experience.

Figure 3.2d Body Shell Crafting

Figure 3.2e Paint Shop

The shells are assembled and sent to the paint shop for a 360-degree dunk.

Final assembly and testing is done at Ferrari's two-level ergonomic new assembly lines. The line pincers hold the cars at the best height for the worker, allowing free rotation to access the underbody. The general assembly sequence: install pedals and brake lines, fuel tank, steering box, engine, front and rear suspension, cooling systems, bumpers, tires, and, finally, an extensive and comprehensive road test.

Figure 3.2f New Assembly Lines

Figure 3.2g Ferrari 458

Source: All photos by Neil Bridge, www.neilbridge.co.uk. Text adapted from: http://www.ferrari.com, and http://www.enjoythe music.com/milan2002/ferrari; watch the process at https://www.youtube.com/watch?v=XdY7f4EL9SM, "Ferrari Enzo Factory Tour–21 Days."

The final product—a unique combination of technological excellence and the superb craftsmanship of more than 3,000 Ferrari plant workers.

The volumes in assembly lines are greater than in batch, but the variety is lower, making it possible to deploy equipment and workers who specialize in a particular task—like sewing or welding.

Machine-paced assembly lines are similar in volume and variety to worker-paced lines, excepting that machines rather than labor perform the greater part of assembly tasks. This makes the average speed of the line more dependent on machine speed and performance rather than worker speed. The speed of the line is higher, the volumes are higher, and the variety is lower than in a worker-paced line. The pace is more stable than that of a worker-paced line. Most standard high-volume manufacturing processes fall in this category (auto production, chip production). Worker-paced lines are seen mostly in low-labor cost locales in manufacturing businesses like garment assembly or specialized high-end product assembly. A notable difference between worker-paced lines and machine-paced lines is flexibility. A worker-paced assembly line can generally handle changes to volume and specifications relatively quicker because of the innate ability of humans to learn and adjust quickly when required to do so. When Apple did a last-minute redesign of the iPhone's screen, new screens began arriving at the plant near midnight. "A foreman immediately roused 8,000 workers inside the company's dormitories . . . each employee was given a biscuit and a cup of tea . . . and within half an hour started a 12-hour shift fitting glass screens into beveled frames. Within 96 hours, the plant was producing over 10,000 iPhones a day. The speed and flexibility is breathtaking."[4] Not particularly humane, one might say, but nonetheless, the remarkable flexibility of worker-paced lines in China enables Apple to fight and win competitive battles based on rapid changes in specifications and volumes.

A *continuous process* makes very standardized products in very high volumes, like cereals, sugar, steel, bulk chemicals, power plants, and oil refining. Do you like Cheerios? Or Cap'n Crunch? Cereal manufacturing is an example of a continuous flow, highly automated, centrally controlled flow process making extremely high volumes of a standardized product. Automated machines run the line at a relatively fast and fixed pace, with monitoring and control typically performed centrally by a few highly skilled personnel.

Besides the fact that the type of process one adopts is the best fit for specific product volume and variety conditions, process type also affects how we plan production, manage employees, and design our supply chain.

PROCESS TYPE AND ASSOCIATED CHARACTERISTICS

Process Type / Process Feature	Job Shop	Batch Process	Assembly Line	Continuous Flow
Flow of product	Jumbled intermittent →			Linear, fast and uninterrupted
Volume	Low →			High
Variety of products handled/made (flexibility)	High →			Low
Customer involvement	High (design, delivery date) →			Low
R&D investment focus	New product designs, customization →			Reducing costs through process and product design
Fixed costs (equipment)	Low →			High
Type of equipment	General purpose, wide application →			Dedicated, limited purpose
Variable cost	High →			Low
Use of labor	High →			Low
Type of labor	Versatile craftsman →			Skilled technician
Energy use	More machinery (automation) leads to higher energy usage and footprint.			
Waste/idle time	High →			Low
Amount of unfinished inventory in system	High →			Low
Made when?	Made after order is received MTO (made to order) →			Made in advance and held in stock MTS (made to stock)
Management tasks	Hands-off leadership Scheduling jobs Streamlining work w/o annoying expert workers Locating status of individual orders	Removing monotony Motivating workers Balancing work loads Reducing process inventory in-between work stations that work at different speeds		Making full use of equipment Preventive maintenance Not making too much
Supply chain	Responsive/agile →			Efficient, low cost
Competitive advantage	Product made per customer specification →			Low cost, high quality

Figure 3.3 Process Type and Associated Characteristics

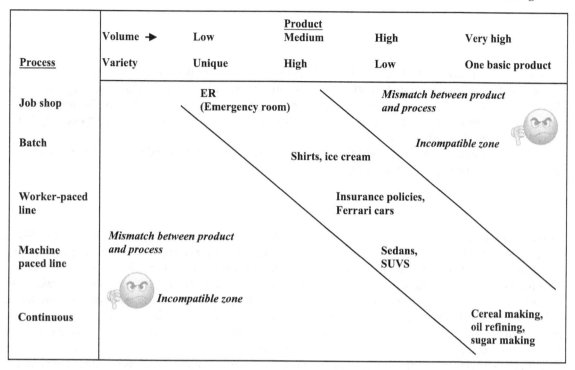

Figure 3.4 Hayes and Wheelwright's Product-Process Matrix (Adapted)

Well, now that we have a good grip on process type, let's discuss the more complex question of how does one combine labor and manufacturing equipment most effectively for a particular product design? Professors Hayes and Wheelwright from Harvard developed a way to look at this issue, matching product to process in a 'product-process matrix'.[5] The matrix identifies the right process for the right product, characterized in terms of volume and product variety. A process designer would be guided by the combinations of product and process depicted in the diagonal of the matrix. Off-diagonal positions would usually lead to inefficiencies in production.

The 'incompatible zones' in the matrix are instances when a mismatch between product and process happens. Think about what would happen if we were to organize labor and equipment in a batch or line or continuous process manner for a hospital ER? We would have to set up dedicated equipment and labor for every type of emergency (patient) that came in. Since an ER sees many different kinds of emergencies (patients) with different frequencies of occurrence, we would have a whole lot of dedicated equipment and labor standing idle for periods of time—very expensive and wasteful! If the market is price-insensitive, the customer will pay the extra cost, but that's usually not a viable option. Therefore, the most effective way to organize resources for an ER is a job shop, with general purpose resources that are located centrally, and accessed by the product (patient) as and when needed. Read Juanita's tale—an application of the matrix to a simple business.

Juanita's Tale

JOB SHOP: HIGH CUSTOMIZATION, VERY LOW VOLUMES OF EACH PRODUCT

Juanita has just opened her first small bakery. She bakes only custom cakes for weddings, consulting extensively with the bride-to-be to make each cake a special, unique product. She is skilled in preparing many different varieties of cakes, and her bakery equipment is capable of baking cakes of many different sizes and types. Some cakes require processing in the icing machine—others do not. Some require processing in the special flavor blender—some do not.

Juanita is operating a job shop production process. It offers her flexibility and customization capabilities, but the cost and time of production are high.

BATCH: MULTIPLE PRODUCTS, SIMILAR PLATFORM, LOW VOLUMES OF EACH PRODUCT

Juanita's cakes are a hot seller in the wedding cake market, and she starts getting more orders. She tries to continue to make the cakes one at a time but soon has a long line of waiting (and complaining) customers. Juanita reads up on OM and realizes she has to switch to a batch process operation. She knows that the generic base for a cake does not change—it's the shape, flavoring and decorations that distinguish one cake from another. She also realizes that because of the increased volume of orders, some types of cakes are being ordered frequently. Juanita begins to group the orders into similar cake categories every two to three days and run a batch of similar cakes at a time. This system proves quicker and less expensive than making each cake one at a time, and, consequently, her customer wait lines gets shorter.

Shifting to a batch production process allows Juanita to reap the efficiency gains of standardization and repetition. Of course, now she can no longer advertise "any cake, the exact way you want it" in the true sense—but there's still a lot of variety and options for the customer. Juanita has narrowed her product mix to enable batch processing.

WORKER-PACED LINE: STANDARDIZED PRODUCTS, HIGH VOLUMES OF EACH PRODUCT

Juanita's cakes now go online, and her Google ads garner national attention. Orders begin to pour in and her batch manufacturing process now cannot cope with the increased volumes—the wait lines begin to grow again. She begins to lose business. Juanita realizes that almost every cake in her product line is being ordered in substantial quantities, many cakes are being repeat ordered and she can, in fact, make some quantities of those cakes beforehand and store them for a day or two for anticipated customers. With growing volumes and predictable orders for some cakes that seem to have become standardized products, Juanita decides to change her batch manufacturing system to a worker-paced line. She hires people who are adept in a particular aspect of cake making and leases equipment that can make the best sellers in larger quantities. Each worker has a specific but complex task to do in the production process—one mixes, another adds flavors, another does the decorations, and so on. The speed of the cake making operation is paced by the speed of the workers, since the cakes still require a lot of individual detail and finish. She continues to make a few cakes for special orders by batch or personally but charges extra.

Juanita's switch to a worker-paced line required significant outlays in terms of hiring and getting new higher capacity equipment. Her gains come from the increased efficiencies of repetitive large scale manufacturing, the ability to make to stock, and the simplicity of managing a line where everybody has a designated job and the product flow is easy to see. The trade-off, of course, is the reduced ability to execute orders for customized cakes. Also, since her workers are cake craftspeople, she has to spend time in developing a managerial style that respects their skills and importance to the business and yet maintains the organizational realities of discipline and structure—not an easy task with those pastry chef divas!

MACHINE-PACED LINE: STANDARDIZED PRODUCTS, HIGH VOLUMES OF EACH PRODUCT

Orders now turn into a flood, and Juanita is falling behind again. She sees that her workers cannot step up the pace anymore without affecting quality and having major dramas at work. Juanita observes that 90 percent of her customers are ordering just a few kinds of cakes and decides to revamp her offerings to a reduced menu of a carefully chosen set of cake sizes and flavors, with many options for the final finishing.

To make it work, Juanita changes her worker-paced line for a faster, machine-paced line. She puts the cake divas at the finishing stage of the process and installs dedicated machinery that can blend, mix, set and bake the standardized product line at a fast pace. She hires skilled workers who can run and maintain the machinery— no cake divas! Her capital costs go up, but her variable costs go down drastically with the faster pace of the line, less variable quality, and the discounts she now negotiates with her input and utility vendors for volume buys. She continues to make to stock and incurs some stocking costs for the cakes she makes and stores for expected orders.

Juanita's managerial tasks change, too. She now has to find ways to motivate workers who do repetitive jobs for long periods of time and do not have any emotional connection with cakes. She also has to make sure that the line is balanced, that is, blending should not make quantities that setting cannot handle, or setting should not make more than baking can handle. There will be some amount of work-in-process inventory, but Juanita wants it to be just enough for a safety stock, just in case one step in the process breaks down suddenly. She also does not want workers to be idle, since expensive machinery costs have to be recouped.

CONTINUOUS FLOW: STANDARDIZED PRODUCT, VERY HIGH VOLUME

Conceivably, Juanita's product market may remain well suited for a machine-paced line. But in the unlikely case that a great majority of her customers prefer a single product, say three-tiered chocolate-anchovy wedding cakes, and her customer base now becomes international with millions of repeat ordering, repeat marrying, choco-anchovy loving customers, Juanita would again run up against volume problems, and customer wait times would increase again.

Juanita's solution is to change her production process to a continuous flow, with extremely large volumes of a single standardized product, three-tiered chocolate-anchovy wedding cake. The cakes come off the line continuously without stopping, are stored in a warehouse, and packed and shipped worldwide.

To accomplish the process change, Juanita sets up the cake divas in a separate custom cake unit, shifts her line workers to shipping and handling, and installs a line of completely automated equipment that makes just choco-anchovy three-tiered wedding cakes from start to finish. She makes just one fresh hire—an expert on the cake making machinery who will monitor, control, and maintain the entire process from a centralized cake-free control center.

Now rich and famous, and having gained some pounds, Juanita appreciates not having to run around massaging diva egos, motivating workers, and balancing workloads. The extremely large volumes and continuous operations bring about drastic reductions in variable costs, some of which Juanita passes to her customers. Competitors cannot afford to match her price and leave the business. On the other hand, the move to continuous flow cost Juanita considerable fixed outlays of equipment and line health monitoring devices. She also pays almost paranoidal attention to ensuring that the machinery does not break down, since the lost production and re-starting time and costs would be considerable. The payback period, the time required to recover the investment on machinery, depends critically on continuous utilization of the equipment. She loses sleep worrying that the choco-anchovy-loving crowd may switch to regular vanilla, and her highly efficient but inflexible and expensive continuous flow equipment may become obsolete.

ANOTHER SITUATION

Well, Juanita's worst fear has come true. Customers have now gone back to asking for cakes that are "the exact way you want it." Juanita is stumped—she cannot make anything else than choco-anchovy in her existing continuous flow process. Luckily, choco-anchovy becomes a favorite flavor for cake dumplings, and a Chinese investor offers to buy her machinery. Juanita can go back to her job shop—but her customers are too used to low prices to pay the high price dictated by a high-cost job shop process. What can Juanita do?

Juanita's situation is really asking for the ideal process, one that could make products in great variety like in a job shop but is also able to extract the efficiencies of high volume manufacturing even at low volumes: in effect, to have the flexibility to be able to cope with whatever volume/variety combination the product market throws at the process, at least for cost and time. Can it be done? Not perfectly, but flexibility could be acquired through the use of computer-based flexible manufacturing technologies like CAM and CAD (computer-aided manufacturing and computer-aided design), basically equipment that can be programmed together to perform a wide variety of jobs at a reasonably efficient (not lowest cost) level. Flexibility can also be improved by cross-training workers in different tasks and by designing a responsive supply chain. The capability to efficiently manufacture a variety of products is called mass customization, and a well-developed mass customization capability can help companies to differentiate by operating successfully in the off-diagonal 'incompatible zones' of the product-process matrix. It is an expensive and difficult task, though. Operations can also be nudged toward successful off-diagonal positions through imaginative layouts of labor and equipment. Is there a way to bring a job shop layout, low-volume structure with similar equipment and labor grouped together, for a product that is made in high volumes? Breaking away from the traditional linear assembly line layout, machines and workers can be arranged in 'U' shaped forms or arranged in cells that combine several assembly tasks into a self-contained 'cellular manufacturing' structure. Duplication of equipment and personnel may happen, but adopters of such structures have experienced improvements of time, productivity and quality.

> *Example:* Consider an industrial laundromat with four washers laid out as shown in 'A' below. Should we move from 'A' to 'B'?

The operators sit together.

Possible benefits of B over A:

- Operators can talk to each other—reduce operator monotony, improve motivation.
- Cross-training each other in machine specific peculiarities (machine 1 makes a funny noise on starting—just kick it hard)—gives them the freedom to schedule machines to individual workers.
- Substituting for one another during breaks—gives them the freedom to schedule their own breaks.
- Being able to work an absent co-worker's machine.
- Learning from each other about 'best' practices at work and machine maintenance—increased productivity.
- Quality checks—being able to look at each other's output and evaluate quality.

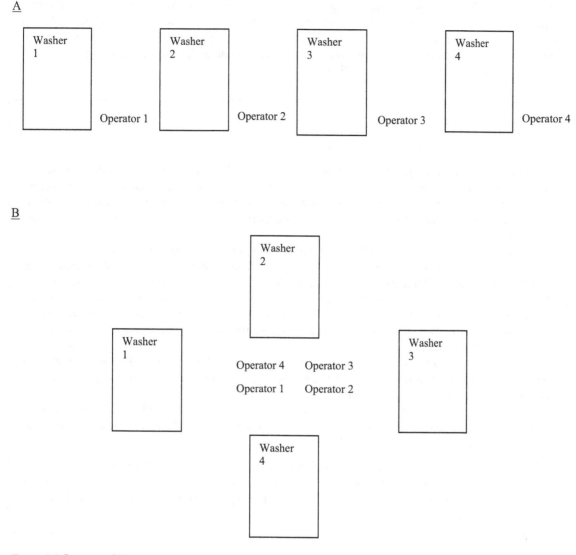

Figure 3.5 Layouts of Washing Machines in Industrial Laundromat

See any disadvantages? Sure: personal conflicts, gossip idle time, may form a union, compare each other's wages, loss of accountability since earlier one operator could be held responsible for a specific machine . . . but the benefits have been seen to outweigh the downsides.

And therein ends Juanita's tale. With mass customization, Juanita gets to eat her cake and have at least part of it, too! She is now in great demand as a consultant and speaker, guiding other business owners with her hard-won experience with changing product markets and changing processes.

Juanita's story holds a lesson for marketing majors, especially, who should note the link between product markets, changes in these markets, and associated manufacturing processes. Business examples are all around us. Corrective eye surgery used to be a special task, low volume, performed in a hospital, in a job shop process—now laser eye clinics have transformed the operation into a high-volume standardized procedure that works practically like a worker-paced line.

OM IN PRACTICE

Pharma Changes Its Manufacturing Habits

Traditionally, pharma companies make drugs in batches, mixing chemicals in vats at different stages at different locations. Not too efficient, true—but who cares when selling margins are high. Generics entered, and cost competition heated up. Pharma woke up to the opportunities to lower production costs and improve quality by changing from batch manufacturing to a continuous manufacturing process.

Novartis's under-construction Swiss plant would see ingredient production flow seamlessly to finished coated pills in one continuous manufacturing process. Since continuous lines need less equipment and less room, costs of building one can be as much as $150 million lower compared to setting up a traditional batch manufacturing process. Quality improves in a continuous process because defects can be caught and corrections made in-process. Batch manufacturing defects can result in entire batches of products being thrown out. Production time falls since the product is made in a continuous flow at one location. Vertex Pharma, for example, expects an estimated 100,000 tablets per hour output from a continuous manufacturing process for its approval-pending cystic-fibrosis drug. The same 100,000 tablets would take about four to six weeks if batch manufactured. J&J and Glaxo are some other pharma companies with continuous manufacturing plants.

Although manufacturing costs are quite small in pharma relative to R&D and marketing costs, every bit of cost reduction adds to the bottom line, especially important for products with expired patents that are subject to fierce cost competition (think Lipitor).

Adapted from: Girish Malhotra of Epcot International, "A Blueprint for Improved Pharma Competitiveness," Sept. 8, 2014, *Contract Pharma*, http://www.contractpharma.com/issues/2014-09-01/view_features/a-blueprint-for-improved-pharma-competitiveness/. Jonathan D. Rockoff, "Drug Making Breaks Away From Its Old Ways," *The Wall Street Journal*, Feb. 8, 2015.

Yet caution needs to be exercised when it comes to investing in highly automated or continuous processes. GM invested billions in the 1980s in highly automated, but limited flexibility, manufacturing technology—the welding robots could weld fast, well, and cheaply, but were limited to a certain range of welds and required large weld volumes to achieve full utilization and recover their investment. The auto market changed, volumes dropped, rapid design changes became the norm, and, suddenly, GM was saddled with an assembly line that could not handle the variety or operate efficiently at the lower individual product volumes demanded by the market. Webvan, an ancestor of Fresh Direct, went bankrupt after investing millions of dollars in highly automated, complex, warehouses in anticipation of volumes that never came.

KEY POINTS

Designing a Process

- Product variety and flow speed dictate the way production resources are arranged.
- Job shop processes group similar equipment and labor into separate work centers. Small numbers of many different products are made, using the work centers selectively. Variable costs are high.
- Batch, worker-paced line, machine-paced line, and continuous processes organize workers and equipment around the steps of natural flow of product manufacturing. Product standardization and production volume increase as process type changes from batch to continuous. Initial fixed costs increase while unit variable costs decrease.
- The product-process matrix uses the above logic to guide a fit between product type and process type. Straying off the diagonal of best fit hurts performance.
- Computer aided design and manufacturing systems can enable assembly-type production efficiencies while maintaining product-mix flexibility and low production volumes close to that of a job shop—the mass customization concept.

3.3.2 Service Design

Services are designed to meet the needs of specific customers or customer segments. Go to a motor vehicle office, and you'll see different counters and procedures for customers with different needs. Similar to the product-process matrix discussed earlier, a matrix also exists for matching service process type to customer type.

We see services being slotted into four broad categories in the 'Service Design Matrix':

- *Service factory*: Same type of service for all customers (low service customization), low customer involvement in backroom operations, variety, high speed, equipment-intensive services such as budget airlines, movie theaters, vending machines, baggage handling, fast food—automated at times, high speed, volume service operations, using low-skilled labor for security, ticketing, greeting, janitorial, etc., purposes.

   Machine utilization and maintenance, worker monotony/absenteeism, and managing demand workloads to avoid overloading equipment and employees are managerial concerns in service factory processes.
- *Service shop*: High customization, high variety, high speed/turnover services such as hospitals, auto repair shops, and traditional restaurants. The high customer interaction and customization require multi-skilled labor. Equipment needs may be high too, with diagnosis and treatment technology dominating.

   Managers pay attention to employee retention, managing demand to fill slack periods, and machine maintenance.

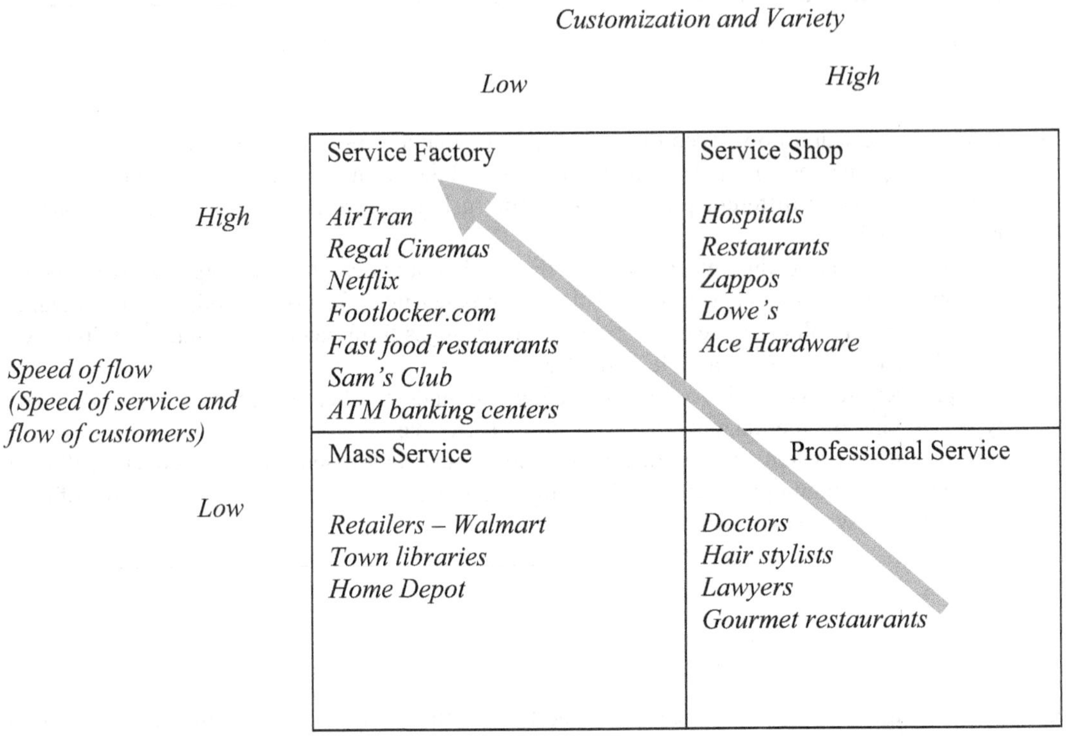

Customization and Variety

Low   High

	Service Factory	Service Shop
High	*AirTran* *Regal Cinemas* *Netflix* *Footlocker.com* *Fast food restaurants* *Sam's Club* *ATM banking centers*	*Hospitals* *Restaurants* *Zappos* *Lowe's* *Ace Hardware*
Low	Mass Service *Retailers – Walmart* *Town libraries* *Home Depot*	Professional Service *Doctors* *Hair stylists* *Lawyers* *Gourmet restaurants*

Speed of flow
(Speed of service and flow of customers)

Figure 3.6 Service Design Matrix

Adapted from: Roger W. Schmenner "Service Businesses and Productivity," *Decision Sciences*, 35.3, (Summer 2004): 333–347.

- *Professional services*: Highly customized, attending to individual customer needs, such as found in general practice doctors and lawyers. Process tasks are very varied. The focus on the customer calls for a high level of labor skills and time spent on customers. The process cannot rely on technology because of the need for human judgment in understanding complex, often not obvious, customer needs. Speed of service is subordinated to understanding and satisfying individual customer needs. Managers of professional services treat their expert employee assets with care, aiming for high morale and maximum utilization.
- *Mass service*: Standardized services in high volumes. The processes are hard to automate because most interactions with customers require a human response. Employees can be trained easily and turnover is high, but high customer contact at the point of sale calls for consistency in service. The speed of the process is dependent on variable human behavior and is thus slower than an automated process. Macy's is an example of a mass service. Managers of mass service processes try to maintain employee morale, reduce employee turnover, and keep the customer happy with the overall transaction experience.

Let's use the matrix.

a) *Where are we?*

It's difficult to slot businesses neatly into the service matrix quadrants, but we can make reasoned and approximate calls.

Old Navy? Little advice on clothes selection, on-the-rack designs, heavy traffic flow, lots of checkout counters. Seems like a mass service.

Saks 5th? "We offer our customers the finest assortment of designer apparel, as well as extraordinary handbags, shoes, jewelry, cosmetics and gifts. The spirit of our current Mission Statement: To inspire customer confidence and style with every Saks shopping experience."[6] Lots of sales associates providing personal attention and advice to customers; designer apparel show spaces—seems like a service shop. Why not a professional service? Well, because the skills required of a sales associate are not very complex or demanding and because the flow of customers is greater than that in, say, a doctor's office.

H&R Block? Standardized services, high volumes, low cost, high speed flow during tax time. A service factory, with basic operations removed from the immediate customer, allowing technology to perform the routine steps in the tax preparation and filing process.

Garren New York at 781 Fifth Avenue, New York? Hair stylists to Madonna, Giselle, and Oprah, a haircut and style with the hair maestro himself, Garren, means a one-personal-hour ($805) consultation. Garren will find the 'right look for you' and offer you a massage on a shiatsu chair during the shampooing and conditioning treatment, accompanied by your choice of 'Garren New York' bottled water or fine teas and espressos/cappuccinos. Heavy customization, expert labor, personal attention and thus slow speed of flow—sounds like a professional service.

b) *Where would we like to be?*

Should Saks 5th move to a more efficient, lower cost, service factory setting (perhaps because of the slow moving economy) or move more towards a professional service boutique offering exclusive expert designer services to clients?

c) *How do we get there?*

Suppose Saks 5th decides to move towards a service factory process: What should it do? It has to replace the human element with technology, reduce costs, and increase process flow. 3D electronic sales associate booths, point of display 3D body scanners for trying out designs? Change store layout to something like IKEA—one way in and one way out and a path laid out that takes you to every department in between entry and exit? Increases flow and efficiency. Automated checkout booths? Employees are kept for tasks like security and customer assistance for checkout and such. Actually, Saks 5th has moved part of its business towards a service factory process—check out Saks5th.com.

What's the best place to be for service business in a general sense? The service matrix diagonal suggests that most service businesses have a tendency to drift towards the low customization–high speed flow 'service factory' quadrant: offer a standardized menu of services, automate operations as much as possible, increase efficiency, increase speed of customer flow, and reduce costs. The drift is evident in several cases. Hernia operations have been standardized into a tightly scripted, repetitive process at Shouldice Hospital, Canada;

corrective eye surgery has moved from general hospitals to Lasik centers; cosmetic treatments are migrating from plastic surgery practices to national franchisee-run laser and Botox spa centers like Dermacare. Most shifts have seen a reduced, standardized and simplified services offerings menu, higher patient volumes, lower costs and procedure prices, and quicker speed of process flow.

The trend towards speed and standardization/simplification can be questioned. Perhaps an 'ideal' service would be one that offers a high degree of customization together with high speed of flow, like Zappos, which automates the routine parts of order placement and fulfillment but offers personalized selection, ordering, changing your mind, and return services to its customers. Similar to mass customization, such combinations of standardized and customized steps in a process or service offering can deliver both cost efficiencies and personal service. Instead of being swift and even, the service delivery flow could be swift and customized.

KEY POINTS

Service Design Matrix

- The Service Design Matrix groups services into four categories, along two axes—speed of service/customer flow and extent of customization/variety.
- Service Factory: High flow, equipment intensive, low variety, low worker skills, standardized services. Managerial focus: employee turnover, machine maintenance.
- Service Shop: High customer interaction, high variety, high flow service, with skilled labor and equipment. Managerial focus: Employee retention and resource utilization.
- Professional Service: Highly customized, high variety, slow flow speed. Complex services cannot be handled by machines and require highly skilled labor. Managerial focus: Maximize utilization of skilled resources, keep skilled resources happy.
- Mass Service: Low customization but high customer contact, labor intensive, with high volumes, but slow flow speed service. Managerial focus: Employee turnover, customer satisfaction.
- The matrix suggests that services drift towards the low-customization, high-speed service factory category over time, in their quest for efficiencies.

Guided by our selected service design combo of customization and speed of flow, let's actually build a service design. We use a structured approach, called the 3Ts service design. The 3Ts framework designs a service using different combinations of tangibles, task, and treatment.[7] Our client wishes to develop a nail salon—and we shall use the 3Ts framework to design the business.

3.3.3 Designing a Nail Salon with the 3Ts Framework

The first step is to understand how the salon proposes to answer the customer's basic question: Why should I choose YOU? The chief concern of customers is the spotty quality of service in the nail makeover market. We promise consistent and reliable quality care for each client; we also promise to minimize waiting and keep a reasonable speed of flow. It is clear, however, that we do not wish to compete on the basis of speed of service—not a 'nails done fast' promise.

With reliability and consistency of service as the goal of our service design, we use the 3T framework as the building bricks of the design. Tangible, task, and treatment comprise the 3Ts. *Tangibles* consist of elements that can be experienced through the five senses—touch, hear, see, smell, and taste—in a nail salon; these might be the arrangement of customer couches in the reception, lighting, music, candle scents, complimentary cookies, and such.

OM IN PRACTICE

Starbucks Service Design Using Tangibles

Ever wondered why you seem drawn to Starbucks—besides that enticing coffee aroma, of course?

Starbucks attracts through meticulous attention to store design, beginning with its welcoming tactile "handshake" doors with vertical logos. Once inside, notice how customer flow is directed towards the back of the store—not by a hanging 'Order here' sign, but cleverly placed back store lighting that draws attention to the back. We naturally walk towards the bright lights and, in doing so, a) see all those other good looking folks sipping coffee happily, confirming our feelings about Starbucks as a vibrant, happening place; b) can see and pick available seating, and c) get a chance to see and drool over all those treats in the displays. Everything at the counter is placed below customer eye level, so that we can make eye contact with our barista. A little ledge runs all along the counter, creating a space between those tall coffee machines and customers, so that we don't instinctively step back. And finally, there are those colorful little Starbucks packs and goodies placed strategically near the doors, so that the last image we carry as we exit is actually a reinforcement of the Starbucks experience.

Probably everything that Starbucks has designed has worked well, except probably its van design.

Figure 3.7 Coffee Store Design

Source: Spuadlmn, "HK Mongkok Grand Tower Mall Interior Starbucks Coffee Shop," [CC], via *Wikimedia Commons*, http://commons.wikimedia.org/wiki/File%3AHK_Mongkok_Grand_Tower_mall_interior_Starbucks_Coffee_shop.JPG.

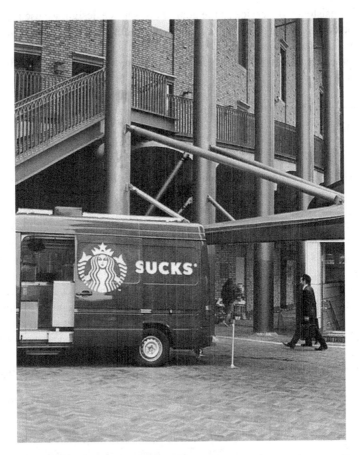

Figure 3.8 An Inadvertent Design

Source: Heuristicus, "Starbucks Van," [CC], *Flickr*, Oct. 13, 2012.

Text adapted from: Starbucks.com; "Five Design Tricks Starbucks Uses to Seduce You," *Bloomberg* (video), May 2014, http://www.bloomberg.com/video/five-design-tricks-starbucks-uses-to-seduce-you-y3lVAVItSRSvVRPm3vt43Q.html

Task comprises the process—the steps and actions required to accomplish the service, such as greeting and seating customers, keeping them occupied/entertained during wait times, the manicure steps, possible sales pitch for products, payment collection, and saying goodbyes. *Treatment* consists of the softer side of service, empathy, attitude, smiles, listening, and consideration for people.

- Which T should form the foundation of the service design? Since reliability of service is the main goal, task forms the foundation. Years of studies of service businesses have reported that reliability is best accomplished through careful scripting and rehearsal of the tasks involved in service delivery. First, we need to identity the nature and extent of tasks our salon should provide. Shostack's (1987) framework provides a structure.

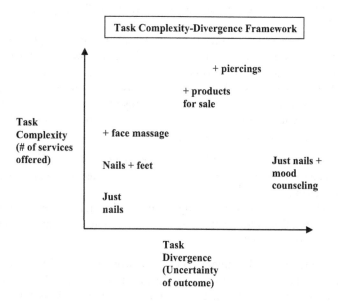

Task Complexity-Divergence Framework

Task Complexity (# of services offered)

+ piercings

+ products for sale

+ face massage

Nails + feet

Just nails + mood counseling

Just nails

Task Divergence (Uncertainty of outcome)

Figure 3.9 Balancing Task Complexity and Task Divergence

Adapted from: *G. Lynn Shostack, 1987, "Service positioning through structural change," Journal of Marketing, January 1987, Vol. 51(1), 34(10)*

Adding service tasks would no doubt increase revenue, but, at some point, the sheer size of our service menu may blur our identity as a nail salon, confuse the customer, force workers to do very different tasks, dilute quality, and cause us to lose focus on our primary service. As we have learned, adding steps to a process lowers overall reliability. We do not wish to appear as a stripped-down nail salon either, so a good sense of what the customer desires, employee competence, and the extent of managerial monitoring and control resources available would go into determining a 'good' level of task complexity for our nail salon. Quite separate from the consideration of task complexity is the issue of task divergence. Consider the outcome of a nail treatment—the procedure and materials are fairly routinized, salon employees are well trained in such tasks, and it is possible to deliver a fairly competent quality of service most of the time. But add mood counseling to the package and we are suddenly faced with much more uncertainty—salon employees are not trained counselors, and the customers' psychological needs are much more difficult to decipher and treat than their nails. What if the customer turns suicidal, or violent, or angry during the service? There's a far greater chance of a dissatisfied customer with a nonstandard offering like mood counseling. So even though the service package is a relatively low complexity 'just nails + mood counseling' offering, it is a package with a high level of divergence. Adding complexity need not add to task divergence. Adding a routine face massage to a basic nail + feet treatment adds to task complexity but does not increase task divergence. But adding products for sale or offering piercings would increase task divergence since the salon has no control over the quality of the product and piercings may cause medical (and legal) problems. Tasks that add excessive divergence to the service design have to be considered carefully in terms of their necessity to the business and its customers.

- Once the tasks are chosen, practice sessions and dry runs are conducted to ensure that everyone in the process understands, experiences and becomes familiar with steps involved in service delivery. But with all the training and practice sessions in the world, tired workers and stressed customers make task performance difficult at times. So we use the other two T's, tangibles and treatment, to support the foundation 'T'—task.

- Using tangibles to support task: Intelligent use of tangibles can help prevent or recover from task failures. Often, tangibles are used for fail-proofing tasks (*poka-yoke* in Japanese)—such as the height bars at amusement parks that help keep younger children off high rides; an escalator becomes a staircase in a power failure; the on-line form does not let us move on to the address line until we fill in the name line first. Our nail salon could use indented trays to visually remind employees to keep tools in place, auto-cut off switches to prevent that foot bath from reaching scalding temperature, or a checklist under the reception desk to help employees remember what to say:

  Tired-looking customer walks in: "Hello! Looking good today—can we offer you a nice long foot soak?"
  Rushed-looking office worker: "Hi there! You seem to be in a hurry—we have our first-class lunch time package ready for you!"
  Task failure recoveries using tangibles can range from offering hot cookies for long waits to free service for myopic manicures. But a bloody finger would require more consequential remedies. Can you think of any (that won't bankrupt us)?

- Using treatment to support task: Treatment begins with hiring people with the right attitude and extends to reminding employees to apologize for long waits or minor slip-ups. Southwest Airlines handles task failures such as flight delays by imaginative treatment—games such as 'guess the flight attendants' weight' to 'who has the most holes in their socks?' People like genuineness, a sincere apology, and to see visible efforts to make the failure more tolerable.

  Treatment is also used to support and motivate employees in the performance of tasks. A small business owner, unable to offer big bonuses, would personally wash the employee of the month's car.
  Our nail salon can train people in manicures, but not in treatment. It is easy to spot a fake smile or apology. Making the right hires is therefore critical for our business. Because it is easy to fake a personality for a short time such as during a job interview, companies actively but discreetly look for appropriate for-the-job personalities in unconventional settings such as bars and parties.

Summing up, the 3Ts framework enables us to identify the distinctive appeal of the business, match our promise to the principal 'T,' and use the remaining two Ts to support the design. If our promise to the customer changes, for example, now offering an upscale luxury experience, the Ts would need rebalancing, with perhaps more attention to tangibles like décor and ambience. Indeed, if the ambience and appeal are contemporary and relevant, says McDonald's president, Don Thompson, "the food tastes better."[8]

KEY POINTS

Service Design—the 3Ts Framework

- Tangibles consist of physical layout and space elements as well as sensory elements that can be seen, smelled, heard, tasted, or touched.
- Task consists of the jobs required to perform and deliver the service.
- Treatment consists of psycho-social elements such as empathy, attitude, and consideration.
- The designer positions one of the Ts as the center point of the service design and supports it with the other two Ts.
- The selection of the foundational T depends on the service performance priorities of the business.

3.3.4 The Behavioral Aspects of Service Design

Unlike manufacturing processes, where the customer is not personally involved in the making or delivery of the product, service processes often engage the consumer of the service as a co-producer. Even if the service is part tangible, like a burger, customers take over the delivery and post-usage process—they take the food to their table, clean up the tables, and remove the waste when done. Human involvement demands consideration of human psychology. Here are some tips to 'psych-proof' a service design:

- Which one of these scenarios appeal more to you?

A	*B*
Exam 1: 79 percent	Exam 1: 95 percent
Exam 2: 85 percent	Exam 2: 85 percent
Exam 3: 95 percent	Exam 3: 79 percent
Overall: 86.33 percent	Overall: 86.33 percent

  Most people would pick 'A' over 'B'—we have a natural desire to see improvement
  Lesson: People are psychologically wired to like improvement. A slow start may not hurt the process if customers experience improvements towards the finish. Pace the service design such that customers can see and experience improvement as they proceed through the tasks of the service.

- If asked to remember a vivid service experience, most people tend to recall service failures or painful moments in the service process. Do not position a point of pain towards the end of the service process—that'll be the last memory customers will carry about their experience and your business. If pain is inevitable, try to make the final step or final few seconds relatively pain free. Doctors are taught to leave the needle in for a few seconds after delivering the injection—it doesn't hurt at that point, and that's the last memory patients carry away about the entire unpleasant experience. A similar rationale underlies the balloon/lollipop giveaway after an injection. Similarly, think about your last memory of a trip to McDonalds/Burger King/Wendy's or similar fast food places. It's probably trying to dump the food remnants and paper wrappings and glasses into a smelly trash receptacle with one hand, while trying to hold the lid of the receptacle open with the other. McDonalds is experimenting with new trash bins, re-designed to shield the customer from that final memory of unsightly waste and unpleasant smells.

  Lesson: Pain has a long memory. Position steps that involve pain, such as payment, vaccinations, filling out forms, etc., at one time, towards the early part of the process. The customer will go through the hassle early on and hopefully forget it as things improve.
  Corollary: Locate pleasurable experiences towards the end of the service process. Sprinkle small doses of pleasure throughout the process to provide many memories of moments of pleasure for users.

- Waiting for a train or bus in a deserted station at dead of night, five minutes can seem like half an hour. On the other hand, a couple of hours watching a movie or a Monday night football game (or reading this chapter) goes by in a flash! Where did the time go?

  Lesson: Experienced time is not linear time. It stretches or contracts based on conditions. Use tangibles or treatment to speed up experienced time in difficult conditions. Divert customers by engaging them in activities. Segment pleasure into smaller pieces—e.g., introduce a small refreshment time out in between showing of a movie.

- Unpleasant experiences are not the prerogative of customers only—employees experience stress and pain in difficult situations, too. Customer interface points can become unpleasant work locations, particularly in the mornings and evenings, before and after work hours. People are in a hurry in the mornings and tired and grumpy after returning from work.

  Sometimes an employee may feel pain at a point that provides pleasure for the customer. Nail salons often seat manicures near large glass windows looking out at the street. Customers like the outside view, and the street-visible 'show' attracts street traffic walk-ins. However, most employees hate that location. Imagine being put behind a glass window for eight to ten hours a day with strange eyes on you every moment. A worker compared the experience to being inside a cage in a zoo!

  Lesson: Pain affects everybody! Identify potential points of friction in the tasks of the service design. Place trained, psychologically able employees in such positions. Reward and rotate personnel in such positions.

- We like control over what affects us. Being able to choose between sugar, *Splenda,* or honey for our coffee makes us feel good. Giving students a choice of dates for an exam seems to improve mood and attitude. The availability of choice, and the power to choose, appears to please customers.

  Lesson: Control empowers and reassures. Provide customers with real or perceived control over some tasks in the service design. The choice of a left or right arm for taking an injection, a choice of dates and times in making an appointment, a choice of table to sit at in a restaurant, a choice of delivery dates for furniture delivery, and a choice of elevator music all satisfy the psychological need for control. The designer bright colored seats at JetBlue's lounge at JFK International Airport in New York can be moved around by travelers—something as simple as not being forced to sit at a designated place gives people a sense of control—an unusual feeling in airline travel. Employees also like to be afforded some freedom in their choices in work, such as being asked to choose among different work times in a work schedule.

KEY POINTS

Service Design—Behavioral Aspects

- Start well and let the customer experience improvement during the steps of service delivery.
- Pain has a long memory—administer it early, and not often.
- Finish with a pleasurable experience.
- Time lengthens in moments of waiting or stress and contracts during moments of pleasure.
- Employees can feel pain, too. Reward and rotate personnel at stressful points in the service design.
- People like control over what happens to them. The freedom to exercise a choice, however minor, provides a sense of control and increases both provider and customer satisfaction.

3.3.5 Tools for Process Design

Companies use simulation and charting to design production and service processes. Simulation technologies provide a dynamic view of a process, enabling experimentation with changes in task design, sequence, and combinations under a variety of task conditions. Simulations have been used to model complex processes such as the U.K. government's tax receivable management system, identifying peak periods and simulating cost-benefit analyses of staff required to reduce those peaks, and opportunities for automation and outsourcing in Johns Hopkins organ transplant process flow.

Models of processes begin by flowcharting the steps in the process, showing key tasks, task inter-relationships and sequence, participants, and material flows. Universal flow chart symbols are used to depict basic tasks, such as transportation, delay, and inspection. A simple flow chart of our nail salon is drawn below. The symbols are self-explanatory:

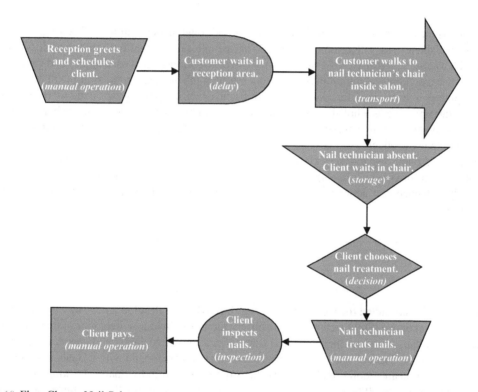

Figure 3.10 Flow Chart—Nail Salon

* Storage means being kept waiting without any communication or cues. Delay is informed storage, where the client is told or can understand the cause of the delay and may have some idea/cues about how long it may be.

A more sophisticated version of the flow chart is the service blueprint, which adds details on customer-server interactions, identifies tasks that are carried out outside the sight of the customer (for possible centralization or outsourcing), highlights potentially high friction or high failure tasks, and provides time estimates for tasks. Softwares such as *SIMUL8 Corporation, SmartDraw* and *BreezeTree* offer easy-to-use tools for flowcharting and simulation—most have a free trial feature. Process mapping is described in more detail in chapter 4, "Managing Processes."

3.3.6 Tools for Service Design

The market contains valuable tacit information and insights. Surveys, focus groups, and interviews, in online, phone, or face-to-face format, are popular tools for tapping customer and market ideas and preferences. Translating the voice of the market into design ideas and concepts can be done using a variety of tools: We focus on four tools: ethnography, conjoint analysis, quality function deployment (QFD), and Kano's framework. All these tools have one goal—to listen to the customer and translate the customers' voice into product or service design features.

Ethnography: Yogi Berra—"You Can Observe a Lot Just by Watching"

Ethnography is the systematic observation of behavior and usage patterns in natural settings. "*Genchi Genbutsu,*" as the Japanese say: "Go look, go see." What people say is often not what they do. If we wish to understand how a student really uses a smartphone—favorite features, most used apps, hand grasp, frequency of use, use of bandwidth—we could invite him to a research lab and ask or tag along with him and observe as he uses phones in everyday life, connecting with friends, mailing/posting pics and video, and using apps. Doing the latter will give us a holistic view of his behavior in his world, a picture far richer and deeper than what could be obtained from a survey or focus group session, perhaps even offering insights on new ways that users find to use products.

Since deep and unobtrusive observation is involved, trained ethnographers have to be employed (look at anthropology departments in schools). Even so, trained observers may misinterpret observed behavior or inadvertently influence user actions. The results are interpreted with help from psychology, sociology, and market research.

OM IN PRACTICE

Examples of Ethnography in Design

Bank of America consulted the well-known design firm IDEO to develop a new way to induce people to open bank accounts. IDEO's ethnographic observation of individuals' behavior in financial settings showed individuals round-up their financial transactions for convenience and speed. Eureka! A new product, 'Keep the Change,' was created that rounds-up purchases made with a Bank of America Visa debit card to the nearest dollar and transfers the difference from individuals' checking accounts into their savings accounts. BOA matched the round-ups at 100 percent for the first three months and at 5 percent thereafter. The product was a resounding success in attracting new checking and savings accounts.

3M observed customers increasingly writing notes and memos on laptops and phones—Post-its were in danger! 3M also observed that people were taking lots of digital pictures but would fumble in drawers to find the few pics they printed out and wanted to show people. 3M's observations of consumer actions led to the creation of Post-it Picture Paper, photo paper coated with adhesive for sticking pictures to wall cubicles for display. "We listened carefully to what consumers didn't say and observed what they did," said Jack Truong, vice-president of 3M's office supply division.

Nokia phones sell especially well in rural areas of developing markets. Nokia's ethnographic study of how literacy-challenged people deal with numbers and letters in a hot dusty climate led to the creation of icons on phones, durable dust-proof and moisture-resistant covers and handles, and radios and flashlights on phones.

Adapted from: J. Forlizzi, *How Robotic Products Become Social Products: An Ethnographic Study of Cleaning in the Home*, Proceedings of HRI07, New York, NY: ACM Press, 2007, 129–136; Pete Abilla, "Doing ethnographic and observational research," July 7, 2006, http://www.shmula.com/shmula-on-ethnography-and-product-design/144/#ixzz0zEkg7fYz; "The World's Most Innovative Companies," *Bloomberg Businessweek*, April 24, 2006.

Conjoint analysis: Should we put in an L-shaped single unit couch or two separate couches in our nail salon reception area? Install a 70-inch 3D TV or provide customers with iPads with web hook-up? Offer free cookies and a beverage, or offer a more substantial but subsidized quick breakfast/lunch snack option? Display our services menu and prices on the TV, or leave it to the stylists for a less direct sales approach? What would consumers prefer? Which combination of features would consumers prefer? Conjoint analysis evaluates the perceived utility of alternative sets of product or service design features and attributes from the consumers' perspective, and estimates how consumers react to changes in product/service features and price. A list of features and product attributes is drawn up, different levels of the attributes are specified, combinations of attributes at different levels are developed, consumers express preferences for particular attribute combination choice sets, and that data is used to develop a regression-based consumer utility model that shows how each attribute contributes to consumer utility. For example:

a) Attributes and Levels for Hair Salon Reception Design

Furniture	*Entertainment*	*Menu*	*Services Display*
L-shaped couch	3D TV	Free cookies & coffee	On TV
Individual chairs	Individual iPads	Quick b'fast/lunch ($2)	Told by stylist

b) Combination Choice Sets

#1	L-shaped couch	3D TV	Free cookies & coffee	On TV
#2	L-shaped couch	3D TV	Free cookies & coffee	Told by stylist
#3	L-shaped couch	3D TV	Quick b'fast/lunch	On TV
#4	L-shaped couch	3d TV	Quick b'fast/lunch	Told by stylist

. . .

#16 . . ., and so on, for a total of 16 possible choice set combinations

c) Choice Set Ranking

Please rank your preference of choice sets

Combination #	*Rank*
#1	
#2	
#3	

. . .

#16

Based on the consumer data, a consumer utility model would be developed. The model would estimate the relative utility of each attribute to the customer using statistical analysis and can be used to predict consumers' utility, potential profits and market share for a new design.

QFD: "*Hin-shitsu Ki-no Ten-kai*" meaning, literally, 'quality function deployment,' is a design technique developed in Japan. QFD builds a series of matrices, called 'houses,' that translate the consumer's voice into design, engineering, and manufacturing language. The mapping employs a conversion sequence that considers consumer priorities and competitor comparisons, identifies how technical features satisfy customer wants, and develops targets for technical features that satisfy customer wants in desired areas.

The first 'house,' called the 'house of quality,' captures and translates consumer desires into technical requirement priorities in product design or service attributes (elaborated in the Statistical Tables section of the book).

Kano's framework: How can we set apart our nail salon from the competition in terms of design features? Using the QFD or conjoint analysis tells us what the customer wants and how to incorporate these wants into a product or service design. To meet these wants, could we identify those features that our salon must absolutely have, or features that we can calibrate selectively, depending on customer and market conditions? What about features that can address unarticulated wants? A framework developed by Professor Noriaki Kano at Tokyo Rika University provides a structured way of thinking about the role of design features in improving customer satisfaction.

Dissatisfiers are must-haves that represent the cost of entry in the product market. Such features must be present in the product or service 100 percent. Anything less than 100 percent would result in a visibly dissatisfied customer who would likely walk away and bad mouth the product to everyone. The presence of a dissatisfier does not increase customer satisfaction; however, its absence leads to a deterioration of customer satisfaction. Examples could be a charger supplied with a cell phone; ABS brakes in a car; access to the school's mail or Blackboard system; a PC and projection equipment in a classroom; confidentiality in a doctor; parking space in a department of motor vehicles office. In our nail salon, an example of a dissatisfier may be clean washcloths or tools—anything else than 100 percent clean may drive customers away in disgust. Not offering basic services such as manicures, pedicures, polish changes, acrylics, wraps, and basic nail art may evoke the same reaction.

Satisfiers are features that generate customer satisfaction in proportion to the degree to which they are present in the product or service. The more the customer gets, the greater the increase in customer satisfaction.

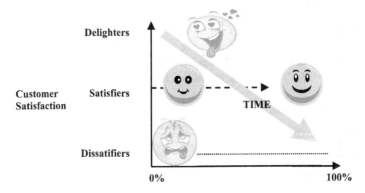

Figure 3.11 Kano's Framework

Adapted from: Noriaki Kano, "Nobuhiku Seraku, Fumio Takahashi, Shinichi Tsuji," ("Attractive Quality and Must-be Quality"), *Journal of the Japanese Society for Quality Control*, 14 (2) (April 1984): 39–48; and Ernest R. Cadotte and Norman Turgeon, "Dissatisfiers and Satisfiers: Suggestions from Consumer Complaints and Compliments," *Journal of Consumer Satisfaction, Dissatisfaction, and Complaining Behavior*, 1 (1988): 74–79.

Increased capacity, lower cost, and higher reliability are typical satisfiers: examples include features like free cell phone minutes and texts, gas mileage, and more pixels in a camera. However, the relationship between a satisfier and customer satisfaction is seldom linear—continuously increasing the level of a satisfier would result in a slowing rate of increase in satisfaction levels. For our nail salon, a satisfier feature could be a two-for-one deal, extended open hours, or a larger reception area.

Delighters are differentiators, clearly and definitively distinguishing a product from its peers. Delighters fulfill unstated, often unfelt needs, and their presence absolutely delights the consumer! The key element of a delighter is *surprise* (not money or cost). Examples: taking a bouquet of flowers home (or a six-pack, ladies) for no particular reason; a couple of reusable, take-away aluminum water bottles in a hotel room; a restaurant settling the parking ticket for a customer at dinner; an upscale gourmet grocery store sometimes supplying a chef with purchased groceries; a professor canceling an exam suddenly (not!). Regularity robs the element of surprise, converting a delighter into a satisfier and, eventually, a must-have dissatisfier. In the context of our nail salon, a delighter may be an offer to take and send a picture of the client, freshly and perfectly manicured, to Facebook, or to a significant other, or a random rose to a customer at the end of a visit, or delighting a client with a 'no charge this time' surprise at random times of the day or week.

A delighter may also emerge from a novel solution to a problem. Altshuller, a Russian scientist, did not like the use of brainstorming as a solution generator because of its random and uncertain nature. He developed the well-known TRIZ approach to problem-solving that focuses on the process of generating creative solutions to contradictions.[9] Altshuller and, later, his disciples, studied millions of patents over the past 60 years to develop a 'Matrix of Contradictions' with 39 system design features, such as speed, weight, and accuracy of measurement, improvements in one often conflicting with improvements in another. They also developed a set of 40 inventive principles to resolve the contradictions. For example, principle 13, 'The other way round,' prescribes the following in part:

a) "Invert the action(s) used to solve the problem (e.g., instead of cooling an object, heat it).

- To loosen stuck parts, cool the inner part instead of heating the outer part.

b) Make movable parts (or the external environment) fixed, and fixed parts movable.

- Rotate the part instead of the tool.
- Moving sidewalk with standing people
- Treadmill (for walking or running in place)

c) Turn the object (or process) 'upside down'.

- Turn an assembly upside down to insert fasteners (especially screws).
- Empty grain from containers (ship or railroad) by inverting them."

There are some other aspects to Kano's framework. Note the downward-pointing arrow in Kano's framework. It represents the natural maturation, replication, and standardization tendency of products and service features and rising human expectations with time. Delighters become satisfiers, and satisfiers become dissatisfiers as technology grows, competitive initiatives increase, and customers become more sophisticated.

Kano's elements of customer satisfaction have to be present in intelligent measure in a product. A hotel may offer many satisfiers such as free airport transportation, a lower room rate, and free in-room wireless access but suffer poor ratings because of ignoring dissatisfiers like lack of clean bed linen and bathrooms and quiet air-conditioners. Failed product designs often suffer from such omissions, particularly since the customer is unlikely to explicitly ask for a dissatisfier at the start of service. Unexpected inter-relationships among dissatisfiers and among satisfiers could also affect customer satisfaction. In fine hotels, guests have high expectations of service. A hotel maid inquiring several times a day about service needs would be a satisfier, but one that conflicts with the (unspoken) need of the guest to remain undisturbed. Similarly, a satisfier in a car could be increased pickup and engine acceleration; however, that would negate the satisfier of lower cost, since a bigger engine would increase the cost of the car.

Kano's model could be related at a behavioral level to Maslow's hierarchy of needs, as well as Herzberg's theory of motivation. Dissatisfiers could manifest as Maslow's physiological or Herzberg's lower order hygiene needs, such as safety and hunger, while satisfiers and delighters could correspond to the higher order needs.

KEY POINTS

Tools for Idea Generation and Concept Formulation

- Ethnography is the observation and interpretation of user actions and behavior to cue into design ideas of practical value to users.
- Conjoint analysis uses statistical analysis of user choices of design features to evaluate the contribution of design features to customer utility.
- The 'House of Quality' identifies consumer priorities, conducts competitor comparisons, relates technical features to customer wants, and develops targets for technical features.
- Kano's framework stimulates design innovations by examining how design features affect customer satisfaction. 'Dissatisfiers' are 'must-have' features; 'satisfiers' are 'more is good' features; and 'delighters' are features that surprise and delight the user.

3.4 Trends in Service and Process Design

Some interesting trends are emerging in service and process design.

3.4.1 Designing an Experience

Stop for a moment, and try to recall the various places and times you bought a Coke or Pepsi? Here are some images to jog your memory:

Designing an experience with Coca-Cola

Figure 3.12a Coca-Cola at a Store

Value = price

Source: Pete, "191214 Buy It In Bottles" [CC], via *Flickr*, Dec. 19, 2014, https://www.flickr.com/photos/comedynose/15871418768/in/photostream/; Atlantis_C,11.

Figure 3.12b Coca-Cola from a Vending Machine

Value = convenience of location + size

Source: "Vending Machines, Coca-Cola," [CC], via *Pixabay*, http://pixabay.com/en/vending-machines-coca-cola-276171/.

Figure 3.12c Coca-Cola at McDonald's

Value = service in glass/cup + option to sit down

Source: itsusmanmirza, "McDonald's Grand Chicken Special Art," [CC], via *Deviant Art*, Sept. 9, 2014, http://fav.me/d7yjnmm; stevepb.

Figure 3.12d Coca-Cola at a Dining Restaurant

Value = service + ambience

Source: stevepb, "Coca-Cola," [CC], via *Pixabay*, Sept. 26, 2014, http://pixabay.com/en/coca-cola-cold-drink-soft-drink-462776.

You may have drunk Coca-Cola out of a two-liter bottle or a vended can, at a fast food place, a dining restaurant, or at a beach resort. The value of that drink differed markedly depending on the circumstances of purchase. A retail-store-bought two-liter Coke is just the basic product—but it becomes an experience when you're sipping an ice-cold Coca-Cola on the rocks in a crystal glass, sitting on a beach chair, looking at the azure blue seas of the Bermudas. That memory, the sensations at that moment in time, would last for a long time. Wrapping up the basic product within a carefully staged design experience transforms a drink into a memorable experience.

Experiences generate revenues. To achieve stickiness, product designs are evolving to move products into authentic experiences—not just for experiential products like theater and music and hotels but also for more mundane items like coffee and autos. Picking up a BMW from the auto manufacturer's Spartanburg, SC, plant, is much more than a handshake and a long ride. BMW has designed a memorable "Driving Experience" at its BMW Performance Center, with fully paid stays at the Marriott, gourmet meals, and driving memories to last.

Designers should understand how the elements of the experience relate to the basic product. Take a basic food product like a hamburger. We know that people eat with their eyes first, so colors, cleanliness, and neatness are important parts of the eating experience. More interestingly, a recent study found that foods taste less salty and sugary as noise levels increase. Diners were also more likely to like the taste when they also liked the music being played.[10] A side of Taylor Swift with that burger, anyone?

Experience engineering skills are drawn from design, engineering, marketing, and anthropology. But they're expensive to design and hard to implement without sacrificing speed and efficiency at some point—the argument that it is the customer experience that drives sales has to be vigorously and unambiguously accepted by top management. Experiences can also become stale quickly when the novelty factor wears off. Constant updating and redesigns are necessary to attract and maintain customer experience. And experiences are fragile designs with intensive interactions and prone to human failures. Experience designs can also become unaffordable in tough economic times. Being without a job, or being in fear of losing one, makes that Cinnamon Dolce Latte experience at Starbucks very much an optional part of our mornings.

3.4.2 Substituting Technology for Employees in Process Design

A recent MIT-Harvard 'Race Against the Machine' conference concluded that technology is replacing mid-level professional and mid-level manual labor, effectively decimating middle management. In the past, machines used to replace humans for dangerous, dirty, or monotonous tasks. Processes today are using technology to replace labor in jobs like bank tellers and airline check-in agents and in routine tasks in accountancy and actuarial science. Automated scan tunnel checkout counters are being tested in stores that can scan 60 items a minute with a read rate of 98.5 percent vs. having a cashier or customer do it. Even a contract manufacturer like Foxconn plans to install one million robots to replace low (but rising) cost China labor and improve efficiency. The total capital-labor ratio in industries has been steadily rising since 1990 (Bureau of Labor Statistics), with substitutions of labor with investments in equipment and information technology growing even faster. Here's a look at some new work tools and technologies that we may see in the factories and workplaces of the future:

OM IN PRACTICE

Bionic Work Technologies in the Factory of the Future

Bionic Ants may replace workers and lumbering pieces for heavy machinery in the workplaces of the future. Festo Inc. BionicANTs communicate and collaborate to handle work tasks. Algorithms work with radio modules, a Cortex M4 communications processor and Piezoelectric actuators to move each ant's six legs and the pincer jaws in its head. The ants use a 3D stereo camera and a sensor. "Tasks that are now managed by a central master computer will be taken over by the components in future," Festo predicts.

Figure 3.13 BionicANTS 1

Figure 3.14 BionicANTS 2

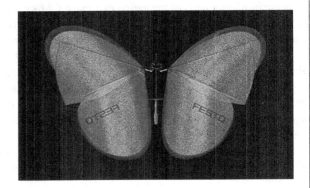

Figure 3.15 eMotion Butterflies 1

Figure 3.16 eMotion Butterflies 2

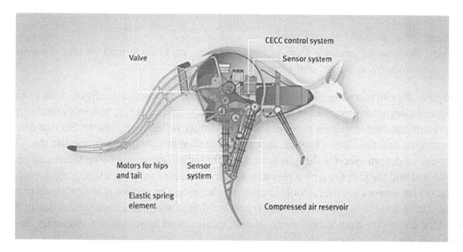

Figure 3.17 Bionic Kangaroo 1

Figure 3.18 Bionic Kangaroo 2

"eMotion butterflies" provide a glimpse of how the "intelligent networking system creates a guidance and monitoring system, which could be used in the networked factory of the future."

The "Bionic Kangaroo" can leap over tall buildings in a single bound or at least carry and deliver tools and materials quickly, safely, and efficiently where needed. No need for miles of transportation conveyors or tracks.

Source: Photos and text used with permission from www.festo.com, https://www.festo.com/cms/en_corp/9617.htm and https://www.festo.com/cms/en_corp/10924.htm.

3.5 Conclusion

Customer: *"Why should I choose you?"*
Business: *"Because we promise that each step of your experience with us and our products will be smooth, trouble-free, and of value to you."*

Process design is the organization of the factors of production in various configurations to manufacture a product design. We organize processes in five types: project, job shop, batch, assembly, and continuous flow, each configuration matched to make a particular mix of product variety and volume. Service design integrates tangibles, treatment, and task into a service package for customer consumption. We use the 3Ts framework to develop a service design. Service designs have a psychological dimension—remember to place your pain points early on and end the process with a pleasure activity. Process mapping, ethnography, conjoint analysis, QFD, and Kano's framework are useful tools in designing a process or service. Current trends in service design package products as service 'experiences,' seeking to build emotional and experiential ties to the consumer. Design provides competitive advantage through cost, quality, and attachment. Companies that design well generally do very well.

What Have We Learned?

What Is Process and Service Design?

- Process design is the organization and physical layout of the factors of production to best produce a product or a service.
- Service design is the organization of product and experience into a service package, using technology, co-production with consumers, and customization with modules of options.

How to Design?

- Process designs organize machinery and labor in five principal ways: job shop, batch, worker-paced line, machine-paced line, and continuous process. Fixed costs, volume, and flow speed increases as process moves from job shop to continuous, as variable costs, customer involvement, variety, and flexibility decline.
- The product-process matrix matches process to product, with low-volume, high-variety production being organized in a job shop format and higher volume, lower variety production being organized in batch, line, and continuous flow layouts. Mismatches between production conditions and process type result in inefficient performance.
- Service designs are matched to market conditions using the Service Design Matrix. Service factories represent high flow, low customization service characteristics, such as in cinema theaters, and equipment utilization and worker turnover as the main concerns. Service shops are high customer interaction services like hospitals and Zappos, with equipment investments and multi-skilled labor—worker retention and process equipment maintenance require management's attention. Professional services such as doctors and hair stylists function in high customization, slow speed mode, with high-cost employee utilization being a primary goal. Mass services are high flow speed, high customer contact businesses like department stores. Labor is cheap, but turnover is high.
- The service matrix diagonal suggests that service businesses have a tendency to drift towards the low customization-high speed flow 'service factory' quadrant—offering a standardized menu of

services and automating operations as much as possible to increase efficiency and speed of customer flow.

- The 3Ts framework guides the design of a service in terms of relative attention to tangibles, tasks, and treatment. Tangibles are physical products, symbols, signage, and ambience-related elements. Tasks are the basic work steps required to deliver the service. Treatment concerns the psycho-social realm, emphasizing consideration, empathy, and emotional aspects of service delivery. Choose one T as appropriate to service design goals, and use the other two T's to prevent failures in the foundational T, as also to recover from such failures.
- The behavioral aspects of service designs demand visible improvement in customer experiences as the delivery process progresses. Pain has a long memory—administer it early, and not often, and finish with a pleasurable experience. Time is not linear in service delivery, seeming longer in stressful or idle conditions and shorter when experiencing pleasure. Reward and rotate personnel at stressful points in the service design. Provide customers and employees some amount of control over their decisions and the actions being performed by/on them.
- Ethnography is a design tool involving observing human behavior in practical working conditions and providing useful insights for design ideas.
- Conjoint analysis is a design tool that estimates which combination of features consumers prefer in terms of relative utility
- The House of Quality, a component of QFD, constructs a matrix that translates the voice of the customer into technical requirements, allowing comparisons with competitors and explicit consideration of the effects of technical design features on consumer desires and preferences.
- Kano's framework is a design tool that classifies design features into consumer 'must-have' dissatisfiers, 'more is good' satisfiers, and surprise delighter categories. Delighters provide the greatest impetus to customer satisfaction and competitive advantage.
- Flowcharts and service blueprints are process design tools that describe the nature, sequence, times, and utility of key work tasks in a process.

Current Trends in Design

- Products are being designed to be part of a consumer experience to achieve differentiation goals.
- Labor-capital ratios have been steadily declining in the U.S., indicating a gradual but consistent move towards automating labor tasks.

Discussion Questions

1 How can you use the Product-Process Matrix in your own life? Look at the tasks you regularly do during your workday. Do you currently use a "job shop" approach for any, where you should really be using a batch or assembly line process?

2 a) Visit a McDonald's/Wendy's/Burger King.
  b) Develop a flowchart of the order-fulfillment process, including both customer and restaurant perspectives.
  c) Identify tangibles, tasks and treatment in the service design—which seems to be the dominant 'T'? How are the other T's supporting the principal T?

3 Use the 3T framework to develop a service design for a barbershop. Map the process design using flowcharts.

4   Think of two good examples of products for each process type in the product-process matrix. Explain what would likely happen if there is a mismatch.
5   Think of two good examples of service businesses for each service type in the service design matrix. Explain what would likely happen if there is a mismatch. Name a service that seems to be moving 'up the diagonal.'

Can you think of an additional quadrant in the matrix?

Suggested Case

Call Center Design for Lion Financial Services

J. Michael Harrison, Yuval Nov

Publication Date:	**Product number:**
Oct 16, 2003	OIT29-PDF-ENG
Discipline:	**Length:**
Operations Management	21p
Source:	
Stanford Graduate School of Business	

Description

Andy Carr, the founder of a small consulting firm that specializes in telephone call-centers, is completing an analysis of call center operations for Lion Financial Services (LFS). LFS operates three call centers that collectively employ 170 agents and handle 30,000 calls per week. Agents are organized into different "pools" according to their training and experience; complicated rules are used for routing calls among the three centers and their constituent pools. Carr's analysis and recommendations touch upon a variety of issues: capacity requirements, including the mix of agents by skill category; training programs, promotion ladders, and the definition of agent pools; call routing protocols; potential benefits of physical consolidation; and most prominently, the degree of call "scripting" that is appropriate in designing the LFS work system. Carr believes that by developing a small number of "call blueprints," training agents in their use, and measuring adherence to the blueprints in call-monitoring programs, LFS can improve the quality of service it delivers and reduce the experience and educational levels required of its call-center agents. Concerns are raised about the creation of a factory-like atmosphere.

Learning Objective

To explore operational issues in the call-center industry—particularly decisions about work system design.

Notes

1 Noriaki Kano, Nobuhiku Seraku, Fumio Takahashi, Shinichi Tsuji, "Attractive Quality and Must-be Quality," *Journal of the Japanese Society for Quality Control,* 14(2) (April 1984): 39–48.

2 T. Levitt, "Production Line Approach to Service," *Harvard Business Review,* 50(5) (September–October 1972): 41–52.

3 D. M. Stewart, "Piecing Together Service Quality: A Framework for Robust Service," *Production and Operations Management,* 12(2) (2003): 246–265

4 C. Duhigg and K. Bradsher, "How the U.S. Lost Out on iPhone Work," *New York Times,* Jan. 21, 2012.

5 R. H. Hayes and S. C. Wheelwright, "Link Manufacturing Process and Product Life Cycles," *Harvard Business Review* (January–February 1979): 133–140.

6 "A Saks 5th Promise," *Saks 5th,* accessed Sept. 28, 2015, http://www.careersatsaks.com/AboutUs.aspx.

7 D. M. Stewart, "Piecing Together Service Quality: A Framework for Robust Service," *Production and Operations Management,* 12(2) (2003): 246–265

8 Ben Paynter, "Super Style Me," *Fast Company,* October 2010.

9 Genrich Altshuller, *Creativity as an Exact Science.* (New York, NY: Gordon & Breach, 1984). Also see Karen Tate and Ellen Domb, http://www.triz-journal.com/archives/1997/07/b/index.html.

10 A. T. Woods, E. Poliakoff, D. M. Lloyd, J. Kuenzel, R. Hodson, H. Gonda, J. Batchelor, G. B. Dijksterhuis, A. Thomas, "Effect of Background Noise on Food Perception," *Food Quality and Preference* (2010), doi: 10.1016/j.foodqual.2010.07.003.

Part II

Managing Processes

4 Managing Processes

Chapter Take-Aways

- How to identify a process
- Ways to measure process health
- Ways to analyze a process
- Ways to improve a process

Managing Processes: A Road Map

Customer: *"Why should I choose you?"*
Business: *"Because we promise that you shall find it convenient, cost effective, transparent, and comfortable to transact with us."*

4.1 What Is Process Management?

Recently, I ordered a camel hair blazer from a national men's clothier. It came, and it's awesome—even a professor looks good in it. Yet the hoops the company made me jump through, including a series of mails, wrong addresses, mixed-up credit card numbers, and calling 800 numbers with 20-minute holds, have made it practically certain that I will not be a repeat customer. Did the business have an order fulfillment process—you bet! The site informed me about how to place an order, what happens to it, who to contact, and when to expect delivery. Somehow, somewhere, the actual process failed. Process failure, though, is not a problem that is owned by this clothier. After a business designs a process of standardized work steps to accomplish a task, it runs it—and inevitably runs into problems. Customers come up with new ways to use and misuse the process, demand outstrips process capacity, employees develop workarounds to meet unanticipated situations, and new technologies make established ways of work outmoded. Consistency of output suffers. Who's responsible? Yes, we managers! It's our job to monitor work, quality and output, our job to maintain oversight on what employees are doing, and our job to keep a close ear on customer satisfaction with the process and its outcomes. In short, it is our job to manage the process. But let's recall our memories of chapter 3, and refresh our understanding of what exactly is a process.

4.1.2 What Is a Process?

A process consists of an *organized* sequence of *repeatable, standardized* work steps. Units are run through it repeatedly to deliver output of consistent quality and value in significant volume. It has measurable objectives, is initiated by a customer or a business event, and generally involves multiple functions and organizations. Managing a process involves planning, organizing, staffing, leading, controlling, analyzing and improving process activities. Process management is usually unsuitable for one-of-a-kind outputs since there is no opportunity or reason to study, standardize, and organize work steps for a job that is unlikely to occur soon again. In other words, where there is no process, there's obviously no need for process analysis and management. However, even special customized transactions may have certain work steps that are shared with other transactions—such as common admission and discharge steps for patients undergoing different paths of treatment in a hospital. Such common, repetitive activities that are shared by units being processed quite separately otherwise can be analyzed, improved, standardized, and managed.

We can think of a process as the middle box in a simple input-output model of any business. The middle is a black box that consumes capital and labor resources to convert inputs into outputs. A restaurant process transforms raw produce into cooked and served dishes, using grills, fryers, ovens, chefs, and work staff. A cardiac clinic transforms ill patient input into diagnosed and treated patient output via the use of medical devices and medical personnel. Process management takes the black box apart in order to understand it, monitor it, measure its performance, and figure out how to improve it.

Figure 4.1 Input-Output Model of a Process

Procurement Process

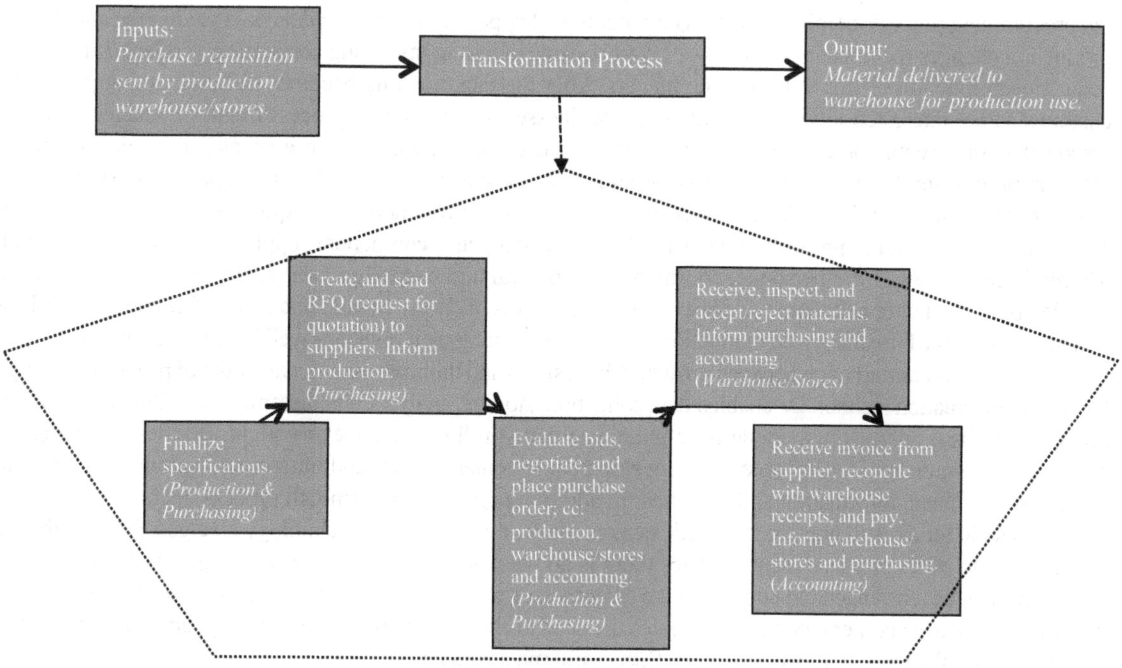

Inputs:
Purchase requisition sent by production/warehouse/stores.

Transformation Process

Output:
Material delivered to warehouse for production use.

Create and send RFQ (request for quotation) to suppliers. Inform production.
(Purchasing)

Receive, inspect, and accept/reject materials. Inform purchasing and accounting
(Warehouse/Stores)

Finalize specifications.
(Production & Purchasing)

Evaluate bids, negotiate, and place purchase order; cc: production, warehouse/stores and accounting.
(Production & Purchasing)

Receive invoice from supplier, reconcile with warehouse receipts, and pay. Inform warehouse/stores and purchasing.
(Accounting)

Figure 4.2 Core Business Processes

Viewed at a high level, businesses use three fundamental operational processes—procurement, production, and fulfillment. The complexity and content of these processes vary greatly among companies, but they do represent the core work systems in a business organization. Let's peek into a black box:

As we see below in Fig 4.2, the input for the *procurement* process typically is a purchase request for some material or service from another part of the business. The procurement process itself consists of a series of inter-related tasks that begins with discussions on material/service specifications and concludes with receipt of materials and payment to the vendor. We note that the procurement process involves different functions and departments such as purchasing, production, warehousing, shipping/receiving, and accounting.

Similarly, the *production* process consists of inputs in the form of materials and components from the warehouse/stores, a production process that consists of input transformation, assembly, inspection, testing, and packaging, and outputs in the form of final products.

The third core business process is the *order fulfillment* process, which consists of inputs represented by customer orders received by sales and a process that includes preparing shipment from available inventory by the warehouse or placing a production order, shipping, invoicing, and receiving returns and payment from the customer. The output is a completed, accepted, and paid-for customer order. The three processes intersect with each other, and each has its own sub-processes.

4.1.3　What Is Management of a Process?

As we saw, processes require information sharing and coordination across functions. Who owns a process? For the procurement process, nominally purchasing, but what happens if accounting delays in paying the supplier, or production changes specifications midway, or warehousing delays in informing accounting of rejects? If a failure occurs, each function claims to have done its part. After the fact, tracking becomes difficult, and anyways the customer is not interested in internal failures. So businesses are appointing process owners/managers who are responsible for the entire process. Process managers design, communicate, oversee, evaluate, and initiate improvements in process inputs, operations, work flows and methods so as to deliver value to the process customer.

In a small business, Bob in sales can walk over to Nancy in the warehouse for a quick discussion on an urgent customer order. Ahmad in production picks up the phone and gets a component supply problem sorted out with Minnie in purchasing. Inter-personnel coordination is natural and easy. However, as the business grows, each function becomes larger and more complex. There are now lots of 'Bobs' in sales and lots of 'Minnies' in purchasing. People become bureaucratized in functional silos, performing their own jobs well but in isolation. Businesses seek to bridge this contradiction between growth-driven silos and the cross-functional nature of processes through the use of information technology-enabled data collection, storage, analysis, and dissemination. But, as your mom no doubt realizes, giving you a phone is no guarantee that you'll call home every night. Besides providing the means for communication, companies also develop people-centered inter- and intra-organizational incentives to share and coordinate information and activities. In addition to maintaining smooth process operation, managers are responsible for questioning process work steps in view of customer and technology changes. Perhaps there's a better way to perform a work step. Perhaps there is no need now to perform that work step at all. Perhaps the work steps can be rearranged to better serve the customer, or reduce costs, or improve employee morale. Perhaps the changes made in another process have created the need to change our process. Eternal vigilance and continuous improvement is the price of process success. Successful managers pay it.

KEY POINTS

- A process is a sequence of *inter-related*, *repeatable*, *standardized* work steps, typically cutting across functions and companies, designed to *repeatedly* deliver *consistent output* of value in *volume*.
- Process management applies measures and IT and human incentives to study and speed up the flow of goods/services of value and quality through the process.
- Since processes are distributed among many functions, some companies have appointed process owners who are responsible for the smooth functioning and improvement of the process as a whole.

4.2　Why Is Process Management Important?

Process managers can bring important benefits to their companies. In your work, too, you can learn to look at work from a process view and make impressive improvements.

4.2.1　Importance for Businesses

As a business scales up, ad hoc actions and individual practices have to be replaced by processes. The reasons are efficiency and consistency. Customers can buy a Big Mac at McDonald's pretty much anywhere in the world and find that it has the same look, taste, and ingredients. McDonald's has developed a process for sourcing and storing ingredients and a process for cooking, making, selling, and serving. These processes are standardized across restaurants and broken down into standardized individual steps. New workers can get up to speed in just a day or two. Measurement and comparisons of performance become easier with common and standardized definitions and sequences of work steps. Compliance becomes easier, too, with consistency in definitions, measurement, and reporting. A business-wide process perspective also allows more complete risk assessment and protection. Processes naturally impact financials. Look at the effect of work steps in the procurement process on a balance sheet:

Table 4.1 How Process Steps Impact Financials

Process Work Step	Effect on Balance Sheet
Finalize specifications of purchase requisition	None
Create and send RFQ	None
Evaluate bids, negotiate and place order	None
Receive, inspect, and accept materials	Inventory goes up
Receive invoice from supplier	Accounts payable goes up
Pay supplier	Cash assets go down Accounts payable goes down

4.2.2 Importance for You

How does she do it? Nicole captains the school swimming team, is seen in the gym every day, rocks all the weekend parties on campus, *and* gets straight A's! Well, maybe we can get Nicole to describe and map out her work process for succeeding so spectacularly in college. And maybe you can consult Nicole, identify where you are lacking, and draw up a future process map of how to get to where you wish to be. Process management will equip you with the tools and methods to do so. Process management will also equip you with a broad perspective of the nature and interrelationship of work across an organization and its supply chain. Understanding how your major forms a part of or is impacted by different business processes will help you a) understand your own responsibilities in work life, b) understand the core activities in the business and c) use this knowledge to stand out from the crowd by proposing and leading process improvement initiatives.

Businesses are always looking for systematic and sustainable ways to cut costs and improve customer service. Here's a typical job.

Process Improvement Analyst—Major Telecom Company

Essential Duties and Responsibilities

Supports all process improvement projects on site.
Communicates ongoing project performance with management.

Participates in the planning and development of client-facing presentations with supporting tools/ documentation as required.

Supports ongoing process improvement training and implementation.

Provides process mapping and other related process documentation as required.

Maintains reports that enable the management of continuous performance improvement and operational excellence onsite.

Supports departmental improvements, i.e., tools, templates, processes.

Job Specifications

- Six Sigma White Belt training/certification highly desirable
- Experience in process improvement methodology
- Experience leading teams
- Experience in project management methodology
- Experience in call center industry
- Knowledge of Microsoft Windows applications (Word, Excel, PowerPoint, Outlook)
- Knowledge of Visio highly desirable

4.3 How Are Processes Managed?

Three roles are prominent in a business process: process owner, line manager, and process worker. The process owner designs the process, aligns it with business goals, sets key process monitoring and performance metrics, communicates and helps implement designed work steps, analyzes process performance, and develops process improvement programs. The view is process-wide, spanning functional areas and points of contact with other business processes. Line managers ensure that the process workers who report to them are trained and equipped with the tools and resources needed for their jobs. They evaluate and provide feedback and guidance to workers about performance and how that performance relates to process performance. Line managers naturally pay more attention to their own functional areas of responsibility but nonetheless are charged with maintaining a process view of operations. The process owner nudges them with helpful information and direction. The actual workers in the process are supposed to understand and benchmark their own performance against prescribed parameters. Workers, with their hands-on experience, are a vital source of ideas on work improvement. Companies create incentives to encourage workers to own their work and make improvements to it. Some companies allow workers to stop production if they find a defect in the process.

Against this backdrop, let us look at what you may have to do as a process manager.

4.3.1 Setting Process, Line Manager, and Worker Goals

Too often, business-level goals lose meaning in the translation to process goals and sub-goals. Our job as process managers is to cascade the translation of business goals to process goals and sub-goals and monitor that they are being pursued. For example, if a new business goal is to gain efficiencies, the procurement process goal may be to reduce administrative and material costs by 10 percent; the process sub-goals may require a 15 percent savings from the commodity purchasing group, 8 percent from the special alloys purchasing group, and so on. Similarly, these sub-goals will generate specific activities for workers in that process, including negotiations with suppliers of specific items, migrating purchases of select commodities to an e-bidding format, reduced time to order, target inspection times, and target invoice processing times. It's likely that we would have to re-examine and redesign the procurement process (and its sub-processes) to achieve these goals. Once redesigned, the process itself and its components represent 'best practice,' but of the moment. The 'best' way to do a task is not set in stone—rather it represents the best practice of the day, as defined, accepted, and replicated by all involved. Forward-thinking companies encourage and incentivize worker-led formal experiments to devise better ways to work. When such is found, and can be standardized and replicated, it replaces the earlier 'best practice' for that task for accomplishing that goal. Conversely, if a particular work step or task is found to be adding little value to the customer or company, it can be eliminated from the process.

4.3.2 Evaluating Process Flows

Just as we breathe, a process must flow. In process flow evaluation language, the 'unit of analysis' is what flows through the process—such as a student lining up at the bookstore to find and buy a text, or an online application for renewing a car's registration, or a car body that is being worked on in an assembly line. A flow unit is usually framed in terms of the output of the process. For example, a car could be a unit of analysis in a process. We ask how many cars flowed out of that manufacturing process in a period of time. In a ride, the flow unit would be the rider, not the worker or the seats in the ride. The flow unit in almost all business processes could be converted into a unit of money, say a dollar.

QUICK CHECK

What would be the best choice for a unit of analysis for a bookstore, for business process analysis purposes?

a) Number of books sold
b) Number of workers
c) A dollar
d) Number of customers

Answer: A dollar, since books come in different types and selling prices—however, all the different books that flow through (are stocked and sold) the store can all be converted into a common unit—a dollar.

Number of customers can be a unit of flow, if the purpose is customer service or layout or capacity improvement—but a dollar better represents the financial impact of those customers on store performance.

Workers do not flow through the process—they are a fixed resource.

Questions about flow arise. Supposing we're interested in service performance. How much time does it take, on average, for a student to find and buy a text in a bookstore? How many students, on average, go through the bookstore in, say, an hour? How many students, on average, are inside the bookstore at any given time? The corresponding metrics are: average flow rate, average flow time, and average inventory. Let's define these metrics:

> *Average flow time*: The average time it takes one unit to move from the beginning to the end of the process, e.g., 5 minutes/unit.
> Flow time includes wait time at steps or between steps, as well as time spent on transportation or movement between work steps. This measure is similar to 'makespan,' a measure used in manufacturing that estimates the time difference between the start and finish of a sequence of jobs or tasks.
> *Average flow rate*: The average number of units that the process is delivering as output, per unit of time, e.g., 10 units/hour.
> *Average inventory*: The average number of units that are inside the process at any time.

We must remember that these metrics are averages. Variability around these averages can be measured in terms of standard deviation or preferably the coefficient of variation (standard deviation/mean) measure. Processes cope with variability through demand management, safety inventory, safety capacity, or temporary increases to capacity, as discussed in the chapters on inventory management, capacity planning, and capacity management. Variability impacts process times much more at higher capacity utilization rates, and thus the need for these countermeasures typically grows as capacity utilization increases.

Flow time, flow rate, and average inventory are interrelated, of course. Shorter flow times may lead to increased flow rates or reduced average inventory. How do we get numbers for these three metrics? We could observe the process directly or use Little's law (which we shall explain shortly).

Using direct observation, we get the average flow time in a series of steps:

1   Identify the beginning and end of the process and the unit of analysis.
2   Take/track x number of random samples over a period of time, each sample consisting of y arriving units at the beginning of the process; x and y are estimated from statistical formulas.
3   Observe and record how long it takes each unit in a sample to go through the process.
4   Compute the average time it took a sample to go through the process (total time taken by units in a sample/# of units in the sample).
5   Repeat step 3 and 4 for all the x number of samples taken over that period of time.
6   Compute the average of the x sample average times, i.e., the average of the averages. Average flow time = the average time it takes for a unit to go through the process.

We can measure the average flow rate and average inventory much in the same manner:

1   Randomly pick several different times of the day(s)/week(s) for observation, e.g., observe for an hour-long period, picked randomly twice a day, over x random days during the next two weeks.
2   Each day represents a sample. The sample size is say, two observations (one hour period each) per day. The number of samples is x days.
3   Compute and record the number of units that come out of the process for each of those two hour-long observation periods, beginning any particular day. Add and divide by 2 = average number of units that came out of the process for that sample day.
4   Repeat for all the x days, and record the average number of units/hour that come out of the process for each sample day.
5   Average the average number of output units/hr. across the x sample days = average flow rate/hr.

To make it a bit clearer:

Table 4.2 Average Flow Rate from Direct Observation

Sample #	Day	First hourly observation	Second hourly observation	Sample average flow rate
1	Monday	3 units output	2 units output	5 units/2 hrs = 2.5 units/hr.
2	Wednesday	3	4	3.5 units/hr
3	Thursday	5	2	3.5 units/hr
4	Monday	3	1	2 units/hr
5	Tuesday	6	3	4.5 units/hr
6	Friday	4	2	3 units/hr
			Grand average	19/6 = 3.17 units/hr Average flow rate/hr

Our sample *size* is 2 (observations/day), and the *number* of samples is six (days).

The average inventory is found by counting the beginning and ending inventory at various times [recall average inventory = (beginning inventory + ending inventory)/2], computing an average figure for each time, and drawing up an average of the average inventory figures thus calculated. For example, we walk in at the beginning and end of, say, each of seven different days of the month. The morning of day 1 we count 3 units at different locations in the process. As the close of business on day 1, we count just 1 unit inside the process. The average inventory for day 1 would be (3 + 1)/2 = 2 units [(beginning inventory + ending inventory)/2]. If our average inventory for each of the seven days of that month amounts to 2, 4, 5, 6, 10, 4, and 4 units respectively, our 'average inventory' would be 35/7 = 5 units. That does not mean we shall see 5 units inside the process when we randomly walk in during any month. It means that if we walk in at various times and count inventory, then the average of those figures would be 5 units over an extended number of walk-ins.

Little's law: The second approach is to employ Little's law, which states that:

$$\text{Average inventory} = \text{average flow rate} * \text{average flow time} \qquad \text{(Equation 4.1)}$$

Little's law can find out the third metric when the other two are provided. Remember, though, that it provides an *average* for all the metrics, so what prevails at any given time would likely differ from the average. It does not matter that one customer took two hours while another took 45 minutes, or that 10 customers were inside the process one day and 25 another day. The process is evaluated on the basis of averages. Of course, if the deviations are large and frequent and nonrandom, it may be better to compute averages on a seasonal basis. The average inventory, flow rate, and flow times for a general practitioner's clinic, for example, would certainly merit separate estimations at least twice in a year—flu season and outside flu season. To use Little's law, the process must be stable, that is, the average inflow rate would be equal to the average outflow rate. Average inventory will be stable. A process is stable *only* when the *average* rate of arrival or demand rate (e.g., an average of four customers an hour) is *equal to or lower* than the process or service capacity (e.g., five customers/hour). Little's law can be useful:

QUICK CHECK

1   We count 50 students inside the bookstore at 10 a.m. on Monday morning and 70 students at 5 p.m. the same day. The Monday of the following week, we similarly count 30 students at 10 a.m. and 60 students at 5 p.m. What is the average inventory of students in the bookstore?

Average inventory 1st day = (beginning inventory 50 + ending inventory 70)/2 = 60 students
Average inventory 2nd day = (30 + 60)/2 = 45 students
Average inventory over that 2-week period = (average inventory 1st count + average inventory 2nd count)/# of days

$$= (60 + 45)/2 = 52.5 \text{ (or 53 students)}$$

2   The college cafeteria is always busy on weekdays, serving an average of 500 students an hour. The average student spends 40 minutes in the cafeteria on weekdays. How many students are in the cafeteria on average?

Unit of analysis: A student
Average inventory   = average flow rate * average flow time
                         = 500 * 0.67 hr
                         = 334 students, approximately

3   The cafeteria carries an average inventory of 20 gallons of olive oil (to fry stuff). It uses about 15 gallons a day. How long does a gallon of oil stay in inventory?

Unit of analysis: A gallon of oil
20 = 15 * average flow time
Average flow time = 1.33 of a day (which is good since olive oil turns rancid when kept for long)

4   The college admissions office has about 200 applications in various stages of processing, on average. It wishes to communicate a decision to the candidate in 30 days on average. How many applications would the process have to complete/day, on average?

Unit of analysis: An application
200 = Average flow rate * 30
Average flow rate = 200/30 = 6.67 = about 7 applications a day

How many full time employee hours (FTE) would it need to achieve this (7/apps a day) goal? Assume one application requires 4 hours of work over all processing steps, and 1 employee = 8 work hours.
work hrs needed/day = 7 apps * 4 hrs each = 28 work hrs
28 work hrs/8 hrs per FTE = 3.5 FTEs, that is, hire 4 full-time employees, or hire 3 and add some overtime.

Let's think larger. How would you compare the efficiency of Walmart vs. Target? Well, we cannot access their internal records or observe their workings in detail. Little's law can help. We can visualize Walmart and Target as business processes. Walmart takes in a unit, stores it, and sells it. The units are disparate, ranging from groceries to TVs, so we convert every product that these retailers sell into dollar terms. In that case, what moves through their processes is money, and one unit of money is one dollar. The unit of analysis thus is a dollar. We can estimate the time it takes for Walmart and Target to process one dollar through their business, that is, estimate the average flow time for a dollar. Consider the income statement and balance sheets for the year 2013 for Walmart and Target. Record the following:

From 2013 year-end balance sheets (*all numbers in thousands*):

Average inventory Walmart (Jan. 31, 2013 to Jan. 31, 2014)	= (Beginning inventory + ending inventory)/2 = (inventory Jan. 31, 2013 + inventory Jan. 31, 2014)/2 = ($43,803,000 + $44,858,000)/2 = $44,330,500
Average inventory Target (Feb. 2. 2013 to Feb. 1, 2014)	= (inventory Feb. 2, 2013 + inventory Feb. 1, 2014)/2 = ($7,903,000 + $8,766,000)/2 = $8,334,500

From year-end income statement (in thousands):

Cost of goods sold Walmart (cost of revenue)	= $358,069,000 (for year ending Jan. 31, 2014)
Cost of goods sold Target (cost of revenue)	= $51,160,000 (for year ending Feb. 1, 2014)

Now the unit of analysis is $1, so the:

Average inventory	= Average inventory in $ (Balance sheet)
Average flow rate	= Total # of $ that flowed through the process in a year = Sales revenue
	= Sales revenue valued at cost (to maintain consistency, since inventory is valued at cost)
	= Cost of goods sold (COGS)

Little's law:

Average inventory	= average flow rate * average flow time, or
Average flow time	= average inventory/average flow rate

Thus,
Walmart:

Average flow time	= $44,330,500/ $358,069,000 (in a year) = 0.1238 of a year
	= 0.1238 * 365
	= 45.19 days for one dollar to flow through the process of buying, stocking at store, and selling (compared to 39.96 days in 2010— has deteriorated)

Target:

Average flow time	= $8,334,500/ $51,160,000(in a year) = 0.163 of a year
	= 59.46 days (compared to 58.97 days in 2010—not a significant change)

From a process efficiency perspective, Walmart is beating Target hands down, selling its goods quicker and turning over its inventory more frequently. However, Walmart flow times are increasing (bad news), while Target's is quite stable. Of course, we need to compare the flow times over a number of years for a more reliable comparison.

There are other metrics used to evaluate process performance, such as productivity (see chapter 1), yield (see chapter 6), and capacity utilization.

Labor productivity = output/input = # of units made/labor hours   (Equation 4.2)

Multi-factor productivity = output in \$/(\$cost of labor + \$cost of materials + \$cost of overhead)   (Equation 4.3)

Yield = # of good units/total # of units that flow through the process/day or week or month or year = # of good units/average flow rate   (Equation 4.4)

A yield of, say, 90 percent means that, on average, 10 percent of the output would be defective (not that every tenth unit will be a defective unit). We *can* get a bad run of several defective units at a time, but the number of defectives will be 10 percent of the total # of units processed over an extended period.

Capacity utilization = # of units that flow through the process/process capacity = flow rate/process capacity   (Equation 4.5)

Process capacity is the effective capacity of a work step or process that can be sustained under *normal* working conditions. Theoretical capacity is the ideal capacity, when all waste and obstacles have been removed from work—it is an abstract concept and practically impossible to observe. Companies track the above metrics across the years and benchmark against competition. To improve on these process metrics, we need to improve the process itself. The first step in doing so is to map a process into its different work steps.

KEY POINTS

- A process manager interprets business goals in terms of process goals and an aligned series of subordinate sub-goals for the sub-processes and work steps involved in the processes, respectively.
- Workers are incentivized and provided resources and guidance to experiment with improvements. When a better way to perform a work step is found, it is analyzed, standardized, and replicated. When a step is found to be redundant or of low value, it is dropped from the process.
- Having plenty of process goals without a corresponding emphasis on sub-process work step goals suggests misalignment and inadequacies in implementation.
- Average flow time (FT), average flow rate (FR) and average inventory are three metrics that measure process health.
- Little's law states that: Average inventory = average FT * average FR.
- Productivity, yield, and capacity utilization are other process health metrics.

4.3.3 Process Analysis and Improvement

A few years ago, we were leaving a friend's party on Labor Day. It was pretty late, our 4-year-old was sleepy, and we were tired. I got into our van, and my wife put our kid into his car seat at the back and shut the sliding door. A piercing scream split the night air—the sliding door had slammed over our 4-year-old's fingers! He was in agony, and so were we. We rushed to the nearest ER. Here's what happened next:

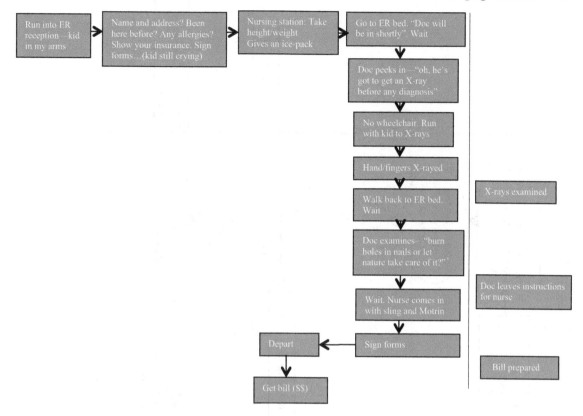

Figure 4.3 Flow Diagram—A Night at the ER

* To relieve the pressure of congealed blood on underlying nerves

We just made a flow diagram of my night at that ER process. Can I call it a process? Yes, because hand and arm injuries of this sort are fairly common and high volume in ERs and are handled in a pretty standardized sequence of steps. What is the unit of analysis? The patient (information such as doc instructions to the nurse, and documents such as the X-ray report are also units of flow, if that is of interest). What is the flow diagram telling us? Quite a lot, actually, some of it unsaid.

- Identifies major work activity steps in the process and their sequence.
- Identifies steps that are decoupled (not visible/directly experienced) by the patient (customer), i.e., X-rays examination, doctor leaving instructions for the nurse, bill preparation.
- Suggests steps customer perceives as addressing immediate need: pain relief, doctor exam.
- Suggests steps critical to ER: Allergy checks, X-rays, doc exam.
- Suggests important (frequency and consequence) points of possible failure: Error in entering allergy information, X-rays taking and reading errors, doc exam error.
- Suggests potential points of friction: usually high stress steps, such as reception, where patient and employee interface for nonmedical tasks. Employees can be trained, incentivized, and rotated at such steps.

What it does not tell us—times, distances, and costs, and bottleneck location (maximum wait?). Let's add some of those elements and convert the flow diagram into a process flowchart. The billing step is excluded.

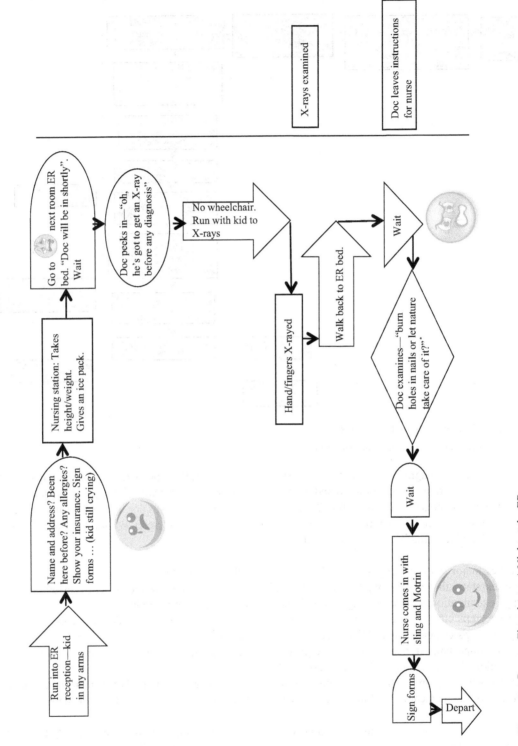

Figure 4.4 Process Flowchart—A Night at the ER

Note that our overriding objective was to get some fast pain relief for our suffering child—everything else was secondary at that moment. In process language, any activity that provided pain relief to our kid was a 'value-added' step. The remaining activities were not perceived to add any value (to us). Here are the estimated times and distances involved for our ER visit:

Table 4.3 Common Flowchart Symbols

Description	Activity	Flowchart Symbol	Time	Distance traveled (feet)
Running into ER reception.	Transportation.	⇒	1 min from the ER parking lot	200
Waiting at reception and answering questions.	Delay: Purpose of visit was to obtain pain relief. Pain relief delayed by this step.	D	20 minutes	
Nursing station. Check height/weight, essential signs.	*Operation.* Got ice-pack—some pain relief.	▭	20 minutes	
Wait at ER bed.	Delay.	D	10 minutes	
Doc parts bed curtains and peeks in—"get an X-ray."	Inspection (am tempted to call it delay, but the words of a doc provide some psychological comfort).	○	2 minutes	
No wheelchair guy. Run with kid to X-ray.	Transportation.	⇒	2 minutes	300
X-rays taken. Two retakes because hand was shaking bad.	Inspection.	○	25 minutes	
Walk back to ER bed.	Transportation.	⇒	2 minutes	300
Wait in ER bed. Feel totally forgotten—no information/intimation of when doc will come, or what'll happen next. Feel we have been stored like a sack of potatoes in a dark stockroom.	Storage.	▽	25 minutes	

(Continued)

Table 4.3 (Continued)

Description	Activity	Flowchart Symbol	Time	Distance traveled (feet)
Doc comes in and examines our kid. We tell him not to burn any holes in his nails. Give pain meds and let him heal.	Decision.		5 minutes	
Wait for nurse to arrive with meds	Delay		20 minutes	
Nurse comes in and gives Motrin and puts his arm in a sling.	*Operation* = real pain relief at last!		3 minutes	
Sign more forms.	Delay (in departure).		10 minutes	
Departure – walk back to ER parking lot.	Transportation.		3 minutes	200
	TOTAL		*148 min = 2¾ hrs 14 steps*	*1,000 feet*

Of the almost three hours we spent in the ER, the value added steps, where our kid got physical respite from his pain, accounted for only 23 minutes (less if we take out the height/weight measurements at the nursing station), representing just under *16 percent* of those 148 minutes spent in the ER. The major pain-relieving step (Motrin) can near the very end of the process! The value-added work steps comprised just two steps (nursing station and doc exam) out of the 14 steps in the process (just *14 percent* of the process steps). Now there must have been some good reasons for the other 12 steps, but surely all of them were not strictly necessary or a prerequisite to our child getting some immediate succor from his pain. Or were they? It depends on who is beholding the process. We can draw a process flowchart more detailed but similar to the one above that shows where and what value is added (or not added) in the entire process. That value identifying chart is called a value stream map, indicating value added (or not) at every step of the process, stretching across internal functions to external parties in the supply chain (such as radiologists on contract).

The first cut at drawing a process flowchart should always be from the customer's perspective. All businesses must first wear the customer's hat and walk, or 'gemba,' as the Japanese say, in his or her shoes to experience the process directly. Taking a *gemba* helps surface and understand the feelings of customers (and workers) as *they* experience the steps in the process—emotions can be depicted on the flowchart appropriately, as shown (can also be done for employee emotions in high-stress locations). Including additional perspectives, such as that of the producer/legal/safety/other process constituents and interactions with the customer, can be done later and mapped onto the first flowchart to align customer and producer goals and points of view. This is done through a more complex flowchart called a service blueprint, which lies beyond the scope of this introductory text. Flowcharts can also be developed for multiple, parallel processes which are generally shown as separate 'swim lanes' with convergence at specified points. The work steps that are decoupled from the customer could be viewed as a separate process(es) that parallels the main process flow and intersects it some point. In our ER example, the X-rays reading step is decoupled from the main flow. The reasons may vary from keeping the patient from distracting the radiologist to outsourcing X-rays readings to a central location for reasons of economy and quality (centralized offices gain experience reading thousands of X-rays). The X-rays reading step may consist of several activities in itself that form a separate process such as transfer of films to the radiologist, recording, examination and interpretation, re-work requests (additional X-rays), report writing, and possible discussions between the radiologist and the attending ER doctor. The customer-experienced process and the X-ray reading process could be depicted in two separate lanes that touch each other at some point.

Now, let's bring our attention back to the ER process flowchart. How can we improve the process? First, define the customer and what the customer perceives as 'value.' Then challenge every step and the tasks in it. Identify waste. Review and re-organize work steps to eliminate waste and focus on delivering value to the customer as quickly as possible. Involve and incentivize process personnel and customers to conduct this analysis and implement solutions under the guidance of a process analysis expert. The goal is to provide value to the customer as *quickly* as possible. Any work step or task within a work step that delays the customer from receiving value is subject to review and possible elimination, or moved to other, later, locations in the process. Let's pick the reception work step in our ER process flowchart as an example.

Define the Customer

1   *Who* is the customer at reception? The patient, or the doctor, or the legal counsel of the hospital? In some situations, hospital personnel may consider their employer or the health insurance provider as their customer rather than the patient.
2   *What* does the customer need? Are those needs being met? Value for us at that ER was immediate pain relief. For other customers of the process, it may have been due diligence in record keeping, medical-related information such as allergies to meds, protocol to avoid lawsuits, and such. There is a belief that patients do not know what is really wrong with them and, therefore, what they really need. Be that as it may, patients do suffer from the symptoms of the underlying disease/ailment, and those symptoms have to be addressed as early as medically possible.

Challenge Every Step

3   *What* is being done? Reception consisted of Q&A's on patient history, parent history, demographics, some medical questions, and social security and insurance questions. Why are all those questions necessary? Does it satisfy the customer's need?
4   *When* is it being done? Before the patient enters ER. Why at that time? Can some of the Q&A be done later at the time of checkout, when more forms are being signed anyway? ERs are law bound to provide stabilizing care to all patients, regardless of whether they can pay or not. What would be the harm if the insurance questions are postponed till a later time? Can some of the questions be asked/answered online en route to the ER, just like ambulances are in contact with ER before they reach the hospital?
5   *Where* is it being done? Is it the right place? Is reception the right place to collect all that information? Why can't everything but medically necessary information be collected during the process while the patient is waiting for service or towards the end of the process, when discharge papers are presented for patient signature?

6   *Who* is doing it? Why that person? An RN (registered nurse) was manning reception. She was probably overqualified for the position, seeing that no medical examination or tests were performed at reception. A clerk could easily perform the same job, if legally permissible.

7   *How long* does it take? Why? Is time wasted on transportation or waiting? Some ERs have now set up monitors that show expected waiting times at the reception or outside the hospital. Monitors are also placed at process locations where patients generally wait for significant periods of time.

8   *How* is it being done? Can it be done better with improved methods or new technology? Some ERs are now using self-use kiosks like the airport ticket machines for noncritical patients to enter symptoms, demographic information, and medical history in the ER foyer. The data are immediately reviewed by the nursing station, and cases with dangerous symptoms can be triaged.

Identify Waste

9   It's easy to cut workers to reduce costs—but it's more enduring and rewarding to cut waste. Waste is simply that which does not add value to the patient or other legitimate constituents of the ER process. Every work step and its constituent tasks are examined for waste—waste that hides in the workspace. We focus on removing waste in any form—time, physical exertion, movement, attention, money, emotions, and talent—involving elimination of entire work steps or the streamlining of specific tasks carried out within a work step. A process can have many types of waste. *TIMWOODS*, an acronym based on based on a list of *mudas* (waste) created by Toyota's chief engineer, Taiichi Ohno, identifies the important ones. A perfect process will have no waste. Most processes will have at least one or more of the wastes listed below:

T—Transfers and transportation
I—Inventory of stored parts, products, or waiting customers
M—Motion, such as bending, stretching, leaning, lifting, twisting
W—Waiting for parts, people, information, instructions, tools, or machines (delay)
O—Overproduction or making more than current demand
O—Over-processing, i.e., tighter than required tolerances and standards, using higher grade material than necessary, redundant work steps
D—Defects including re-work, scrap, returns, wrong documentation, wrong/inadequate treatment, errors in meds administration
S—Skills, specifically underutilization of personnel capabilities, or delegating tasks without adequate training.

Even with our admittedly simple analysis of the ER process, some wastes are evident—wasted transportation, patient waits, waits for information, and under-utilization of employee skills. Process analysis using TIMWOODS can result in major outcomes. A cable installer found that its technicians could do three jobs a day instead of two if they prepared the day before, during the last hour of the afternoon, when too little time remained to begin a new job.

Review and Reorganize

10   We next prioritize and eliminate identified wastes as well as non-value-added steps/tasks within steps using a systematic procedure such as SAMD. Again, the objective is to locate and perform the value-adding steps as early as possible in the process.

*S*ubtract steps/remove reasons for steps. For instance, we could discuss if a standard protocol for crushed fingers and similar injuries could have the nursing station direct the patient for an X-ray before the doc exam. There would be just one doc exam in that case, and the 'Doc parts bed curtains and peeks in—"get an X-ray"—step' will be eliminated.

*A*dd steps together, combining tasks, expanding activity scope. Leveraging the RN at reception for performing the nursing station duties is a case in point. Add additional steps if current steps are lacking in delivering customer needs.

*M*ultiply and leverage resource investments across multiple steps. Issuing iPads to docs and nurses would reduce waits for information, reports, and instructions at several points in the ER process. This would cut down patient waits. Information can be added locally and stored at a central point for easy access and updating.

*D*ivide by splitting activities into high resource/low resource sub-processes or high priority/regular customers to save money and focus attention on cases that need special attention. Most ERs perform triage on arrivals but may not have enough choice of processes. Our visit, for example, fell into a common hand/limb injury category—not life threatening—but certainly requiring more immediate pain alleviation attention than, say, for a patient with the flu. We should have been high priority initially and then moved to a regular care path.

SAMD actions essentially stabilize the process by reducing uncertainty through work step and sequence rationalization, enhanced communication, and patient flow monitoring. ERs could also take limited actions to reduce variance in patient demand, such as diversion to other hospitals and advertising current ER times.

We conduct a similar analysis on every work step in the ER process, suggesting remedies for the elimination of waste. Treat waste like a product—identify, describe, classify, and standardize it across the business so that everyone knows what it is and can take action. After the waste removal exercise, the remaining work steps are arranged into a smooth tight flow, minimizing inventory and wait times.

Execute and Replicate

11 The first step in execution is to show personnel how the proposed changes will improve their work lives and help patients. Successfully doing a small demo project on a part of the ER—with well-publicized before and after facts—is much better than talking about it. Once interest is piqued, begin honest discussions, and soon people will get reasons to start talking and thinking about chronic problems.

12 Find change leaders in the organization and set teams for creating future 'maps' of key processes.

13 Introduce incentives for participation and suggestions, allowing time from work for training in process analysis tools and methods. Put a documentation and learning structure in place, and facilitate and reward systematic shared experimentation on job design and process issues.

14 Build on successes, breed excitement in the air, and generate a passion for improvement. Do more projects, keeping strong critics out of the team. Publicize success widely. Reward both success *and* failure. Again, publicize widely. People will soon begin to embrace a culture of Kaizen.

Kai—Change   Zen—good

Figure 4.5 **Kaizen**

15 Standardize and replicate in other parts of the business and its supply chain. The best way to do a task is not how a superstar does it. It is the 'best replicable practice'—a way of doing a task that can be replicated, such that every qualified worker can learn to do it the same way and achieve the same outcome. As workers gain from experience and training, 'best replicable practice' resets to higher performance outcomes. The improvement can be accelerated by pairing experts with regular personnel. Standardization is achieved in various ways, from setting standard practices to providing standard tools, layouts, and equipment and scripting of process tasks. Limiting the service menu also helps.

16 Go back to the beginning and ask—who is the customer and are her/his needs being met? Keep that movement and momentum going!

OM IN PRACTICE

Flow Time Reduction in ERs

ERs are a hospital's face to the world and a growing source of criticism and dis-satisfaction. Let us take a high-level view of an ER as a typical Input-Transformation-Output model.

ER input includes emergency care, urgent care, and safety net patients. Visits have been increasing in all three categories. Reasons range from the use of ER for nonurgent care to hospital closures, after-hours ailments, difficulties in making physician appointments in time, and the desire to have tests and other procedures done in a single location. Longer life spans mean people experience more chronic diseases like heart problems, pulmonary disorders, and kidney failures. Increasingly expensive medicines mean more patients not taking their pills in time (noncompliance). Episodic flare-ups result in both avoidable and justified ER visits.

ER transformation includes triage, initial evaluation, diagnostic testing, and treatment. It is commonly measured by average flow time—the average time taken by a patient to be treated and moved out of the ER. The problem, especially with urban ERs, is not so much variability in demand—they are almost always crowded—but the growing variety in input. ERs are providing more resource-intensive care. The increase in the input of patients with chronic and complex ailments, including difficult mental illnesses, who cannot use private doctors, increases unit average treatment and flow time and absorbs a disproportionate amount of limited expensive resources. Patients are also kept for observation at ERs (not regular wards) to identify those who may need inpatient admission. Teaching hospitals train residents, who have been seen to order more tests and process patients slower relative to regular staff. The number of specialists on call for ERs is also declining. Specialists today have more lucrative work opportunities at specialty hospitals and outpatient surgery centers. A higher-risk ER environment also deters malpractice-wary specialists from signing on for ER on-call duty. To sum up, a combination of increasing input complexity and capacity constraints has resulted in significantly longer flow times at ERs.

ER output constitutes patients who have been discharged or routed to inpatient admissions or another hospital. Such discharges and transfers are often stalled, and patients bunch up within the ER itself. Culpability lies with factors such as lack of available inpatient beds, especially in intensive care unit (ICU) and telemetry beds, and nurse shortages for available hospital beds. Sometimes ERs may provide additional services, with the anticipation that follow-up care will not be available. Also, failure to obtain post-ER follow-up care may lead to repeat visits, affecting ER input as well as output. In sum, a variety of factors slow down ER patient discharges, which in turn impacts flow time adversely.

Some Solutions

Adding capacity is an expensive proposition and may not speed up flow times. Albert Einstein Medical Center in Philadelphia, PA, doubled its ER capacity but still had to turn away patients because of bottlenecks in other sections of the hospital.

Demand management in ER is a difficult option with variable input and overcrowding. Forecasting can help prepare for specific types of input demand. Input from events such as traffic accidents and heart attacks can be forecasted to an extent using statistical models.

Process innovations such as zone nursing are being tried out. Nurses are assigned to specific zones to minimize the distance and time required to treat multiple patients. Some ERs try to reduce discharge waiting times by rescheduling physicians' discharge rounds when input increases. Other flow time reduction initiatives include fast tracking noncritical patients to less critical levels of care, streamlining ER patient registration, and dedicated labs for ER. ER flow time is also being reduced by streamlining patient flow in other departments of the hospital. A 'bed czar' monitors the flow of patients throughout the hospital, signaling capacity availability through 'traffic light systems.' Hospital units use the information to coordinate operations. A green light at a unit signals capacity utilization of 85 percent or below so that patients can be sent there by ER. If capacity utilization tips over 85 percent, the unit signals yellow, still accepting patients, but warning other units of an incipient capacity shortfall. A yellow that turns to orange indicates utilization just below capacity. Available resources are rushed to the unit. Red signals that the unit is running flat out and cannot accept new patients. Efforts are focused on moving patients out of the unit to other units and adding resources to increase capacity at the moment. Other initiatives target flow times by expediting bed vacating turnover. Such practices include abandoning whole unit room and bed cleaning schedules in favor of housekeeping SWAT teams that refresh individual beds as soon as patients are discharged; maintaining discharge lounges where patients can complete documentation, receive discharge instructions and wait for their rides (without occupying an inpatient bed). ER also competes for time and material/personnel resources with elective surgeries in other hospital units. Better coordination and scheduling can help smoothen out demand for elective surgeries that are, by nature, more forecastable and controllable than ER surgeries.

Studies have found scattered adoption of such initiatives in hospitals partly because the brunt of the slow flow time problem is experienced by ERs. Inpatients are generally covered by insurance, and scheduled elective surgeries are significant profit centers. ERs treat many uninsured/under-insured patients and cannot compete. ER flow time improvements may also disrupt more profitable elective surgery schedules and allow more loss-making cases to enter as inpatients.

Adapted from: D. Delia and J. Cantor, "Emergency Department Utilization and Capacity," *Center for State Health Policy*, Rutgers University, Robert Woods Johnson Foundation, 2009.

At the end of the day, process improvement simply means cutting down the time in all the business processes involved between receiving an order and the time we receive payment from the customer. Let's regroup and review what we have learned in process analysis so far.

KEY POINTS

- A flow diagram of a process shows major work steps, identifies steps that are decoupled, steps of importance to the customer, and possible points of failure and friction between workers and customers.
- A process flowchart uses standard symbols to provide time and information on where and what value is added along the process. It evaluates the entire process in terms of what % of the time and work steps really added value as perceived by the customer.
- Every work step in the process flowchart is examined for value added worth for the primary customer and meeting his/her needs.
- Every work step is examined to identify waste. TIMWOODS is a useful guide to identifying types of waste.
- Any step that does not add value or includes waste is either removed or re-designed or relocated to other, subsequent, locations in the process. SAMD provides a template for this activity.
- Better ways of completing process work steps are developed, primarily through worker initiative/ input. Such improvements should be capable of being replicated and performed/learned by average workers.
- After process redesign, implementation begins with worker incentives, training, documentation, tool support, and other resources. Rewards and penalties both work towards steering and sustaining change in behavior and actions. The redesigned process is replicated in other parts of the company and its supply chain, as needed.
- The redesigned process is reanalyzed to find further improvement opportunities.

So far, we have engaged in a largely qualitative discussion of process analysis and improvement. Let's do it now with numbers. Consider the following flow diagram of a simplified process at an urgent care medical clinic:

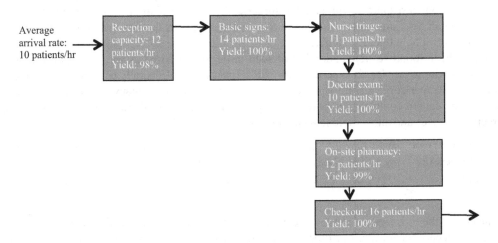

Figure 4.6 Flow Diagram of an Urgent Care Clinic

a) What is the average flow rate of the clinic?
b) What is the capacity of the process under normal operating conditions?
c) What is the capacity utilization of the process?
d) What is the implied capacity utilization of the process?
e) Where is the bottleneck in the process?
f) What is the yield of the process?
g) What is the effect of re-work on the process?
h) Where would I like to work in the process (if all jobs are equally rewarding)?

Let's respond:

a) The average flow rate of the process is 10 patients/hour.
b) The effective capacity of the process is 10 patients/hour. It cannot process more than that on a sustained basis since the doctor cannot examine more than 10 patients/hour on average. Patients bunch up the most just before the doctor exam step and flow out at 10 patients/hour, on average, from the exam step. The capacity of a work step is the sum of the individual server service rates—for instance, if reception has 2 workers, each with an average service rate of 6 patients/hour and working independently, the capacity of that work step will be 12 patients/hour. The average flow rate *cannot exceed* the process capacity but *can be lower* than the latter. If the patient arrival rate falls to 2 patients/hour, the flow rate would be 2 patients/hour, much below the process capacity of 10 patients/hour. In such a case, we say that we have an 'external' bottleneck, or the process is 'demand constrained.' This would not be an internal capacity problem.
c) Process capacity utilization = average flow rate/process capacity = 10 patients per hr/10 patients per hr = 100% The capacity utilization of any work step or the process as a whole cannot exceed 100 percent on a sustainable basis, since flow rate cannot be greater than capacity.

   Note that lines may still form in the clinic at any work step (longest at the bottleneck) and at any given point in time. Remember, we are dealing with averages here. We could have a sudden influx of patients at any particular hour (arrival rate can change), and/or a staff member may be stuck with a difficult patient or may be a bit too under the weather to be able to work at 100 percent at any particular time (service rate may change). However, the good news is that actual arrival rate may also dip below the average arrival rate, and the actual service rate may also increase above the average service rate, at times, giving the clinic opportunity to work the lines down. Lines will form and show a pattern of increase and decrease. They will eventually dissolve, and the average exit rate will match the average arrival rate. The urgent care clinic is a stable process since the average arrival rate is not higher than the average process capacity—on average, 10 patients arrive per hour and 10 patients would exit/hour. If the average arrival rate were higher than the process capacity, while the number in line may vary at times, the overall trend would be upwards—an infinite line, if allowed to form. This would be an unstable system.

d) The *implied* capacity utilization of the process is a measure that estimates the rate at which the process (bottleneck) *would* have to work *if* it had to fulfill all of the demand that is arriving at the beginning of the process. In our case:

   Implied capacity utilization = actual arriving demand at start of process/process capacity
   = Average 10 patients per hr/average 10 patients per hr
   = 100%

e)   In a process, the bottleneck is the resource with the highest implied capacity utilization. That resource, in this clinic, is the doctor:

Implied capacity utilization of doctor = average demand (arrival rate) at that resource/
capacity of the resource
= 10 patients per hr from nurse triage#/
10 patients/hr doctor capacity
= 100%

#: Note that 10 patients/hr actually flow through nurse triage (flow rate), even though it can handle 11 patients/hr (capacity). 10 patients/hr arrive at the clinic. Reception and basic signs have enough capacity to process an average arrival rate of 10 patients/hr.

Every other resource (reception/basic signs/nurse triage/pharmacy/checkout) operates at an implied capacity utilization rate of less than 100 percent. For example,

Implied capacity utilization of reception = 10 per hr arrival rate/12 per hr capacity
= 83.33%

The bottleneck is the doctor, the weakest link(s) in the process. So the doctor, the bottleneck resource, would have to work at 100 percent capacity utilization in order to process all the 10 entering patients/hour, on average.

Can there be more than one bottleneck? Not in the above process, but theoretically, yes. Two work steps or resources could have had the same (highest) capacity utilization. Can there be a bottleneck if the resource is working at less than 100 percent implied capacity utilization? Yes, it would be that resource(s) that is the highest capacity utilized resource(s) in that process. It would be a *potential* bottleneck—the step or resource in the process that would fail *first* when demand increases.

f)   For our clinic example,

• The yield at reception is 98 percent. (0.98): 98 out of 100 incoming patients, on average, would be processed correctly by reception. All 100 patients, though, would pass on to the next step, 'basic signs.'

• Basic signs would find out that 2 patients of the incoming 100 are 'defective' and would therefore process just the 98 'good' units. Basic signs has a yield of 100 percent, so all 98 good arriving units would be processed correctly. The two 'defective' patients are not treated by basic signs but are not thrown out either. They are passed on to the next step, together with the correctly processed 98 patients.

• All the 100 patients would thus go on to nurse triage (yield 100 percent), which again will note and correctly process all the 98 incoming good patients only. All 100 patients go on to the next step, doctor exam.

• Doctor exam has a yield of 100 percent, so all 98 good patients are processed correctly, and all 100 patients flow on to the next stage, on-site pharmacy. Note that the doctor still has to spend time identifying and placating the 'defective' units.

• On-site pharmacy has a yield of 99 percent. It finds and treats 98 good patients of the total 100 arriving patients coming in from doctor exam; 99 percent of those 98 patients (= 97 patients) will be processed correctly. All 100 patients (97 good + 3 defective) will go on to checkout.

- Checkout gets 97 good patients and 3 'defective' patients from on-site pharmacy. The yield at checkout is 100%, so it processes all 97 good patients correctly. It does not treat the 3 defective units. All 100 patients then exit the system.

   Overall then, the urgent care clinic correctly processes 97 of every 100 arriving patients, on average. The process yield would thus be 97/100 = 97 percent. Note that this is an unrealistically high figure, since it assumes that 4 out of 6 work steps process everything correctly (yield = 100 percent) all the time. Such perfection is not even found in robots!

A quicker way to obtain the process yield would be to compute the following:

Process yield = yield of work step#1 * yield of work step#2 * . . . yield of work step#6
$$= 0.98 * 1.00 * 1.00 * 1.00 * 0.99 * 1.00$$
$$= 0.97$$

   The process yield is the product of the yields of the individual work steps.
   The average process flow rate would be 100 patients/10 hour day, but only 97 of the 100 patients who actually flow through the system would be classified as 'good' exiting units.

g) The effect of re-work on the process would depend on whether capacity is available at the bottleneck (or any other location with a capacity utilization of 100 percent). Say patients arrive at 2/hour, and there is a need for a patient to return to the doctor for another exam after going to the pharmacy. The doctor exam work step would have enough spare capacity to accommodate the re-work. The flow rate would remain undiminished, although variable costs may increase. Scrap is treated as a special form of re-work since replacement units have to be made. This is not applicable to the clinic since it has no fixed 'production' target, as such. In a production scenario, though, where a specific number of 'good' units must be made, scrap must be replaced with good units, going through all the steps that the scrapped unit went through. For that reason, the earlier we detect and scrap defectives, the less the waste.

h) Looking at the capacity utilization of all the six work activities, the step with the lowest capacity utilization is the final step, checkout. The average number of patients going through that step is 10/hour, while it can process 16 patients/hour. The capacity utilization is about 62.5 percent (10/16), leaving me with enough time to catch up on my reading and tweet with friends and family. The worst place to work at, from a free-time perspective, would be the bottleneck with waiting lines, cranky patients, and overworked doctors.

   Let's now apply lessons learned to find the bottleneck(s) in a more complex process—one that processes multiple products with different work step routes. We would need to compute the implied capacity utilization of all work steps—the bottleneck would be the step with the highest capacity utilization. Let's take the case of an insurance company that receives applications for auto, home, and commercial property insurance. Not all applications go through all work steps.
   The following parameters characterize the process:

- An average of 20 auto, 10 home and 2 commercial property applications arrive at station A per hour;
- All 3 types of applications take the same time to process (flow time) at any particular workstation
- Flow times for different workstations has been estimated—(as shown in table below)

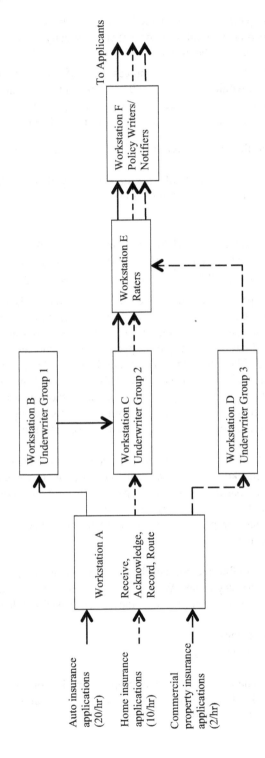

Figure 4.7 Flow Diagram of an Insurance Application Handling Process

Table 4.4 Finding the Bottleneck

Workstation	# of workers	Flow time/ app	Available capacity	Demand on station. Average # of apps/hr			Total demand/hr	Actual capacity utilization	Implied capacity utilization
				Auto	Home	Property			
A	2	3 min/app	40 apps/hr (2 * 20 apps/hr)	20	10	2	32	80% (32/40)	80% (32/40)
B	4	10 min/app	24 apps/hr (4 * 6 apps/hr)	20	0	0	20	83.33% (20/24)	83.33%
C	3	6 min/app	30 apps/hr	20	10	2	32	100%	106.67% (32/30)
D	2	10 min/app	12 apps/hr	20	10	2	32	100%[i,iii]	266.67%[ii] (32/12)

- # of workers in different workstations is given (as shown in Table 4.4). Within a workstation, a worker handles an application independently. For example, at workstation A, the flow time is given as 3 minutes/ application = 20 applications/hour by each worker. The capacity of that station = 2 workers *20 applications/hour = 40 applications/hour.
- Capacity utilization = demand/capacity

Where is the bottleneck(s)?

i)   D cannot process demand exceeding 12 applications/hour, since its capacity is limited to 12 applications/ hour. Capacity utilization cannot exceed 100 percent.

ii) Implied capacity utilization can exceed 100 percent, since we consider the demand that station would theoretically face rather than the demand it actually is processing at the moment. Thus D's implied capacity utilization = 32 apps per hour theoretical demand/12 apps per hour capacity = 266.67 percent.

iii) At D, total theoretical demand is 32 applications/hour. But if station C is actually processing only 30 applications/hour (100 percent capacity utilization), D would in reality receive just 30 applications/hour from C, which is still more than its capacity of 12 applications/hour—so capacity utilization = 100 percent.

An implied capacity utilization greater than 100 percent does not automatically make the workstation a bottleneck. The bottleneck with the *highest* implied capacity utilization is the bottleneck. Workstation D is the bottleneck in this process. A line does form just in front of C, because it is facing a demand of 32 applications/hour against capacity of 30 applications/hour, but a much longer line will form in front of D, the bottleneck. D is facing an actual demand of 30 applications/hour flowing from C, but can process just 12 applications/ hour. The process capacity is thus 12 applications/hour (capacity of bottleneck). If we expand D's capacity to, say, 32 applications/hour, it no longer remains a bottleneck. Of course, then the bottleneck shifts to C.

In the example above, different types of applications are assumed to take the same time to process at a particular workstation. More likely, different types of applications would take different amounts of time to process (flow time) at a workstation. It's simple to accommodate this fact in our analysis—we compute available capacity in terms of available minutes rather than number of applications/hour. To illustrate, say at Workstation A: Auto applications take 3 minutes/application, home applications take 2 minutes/application and property applications take 6 minutes/application, all average flow times.

Table 4.5 Computation with Capacity and Demand in Minutes

Workstation	# of workers	Available capacity	Demand on station. Average # of apps/hr			Total demand	Actual capacity utilization	Implied capacity utilization
			Auto	*Home*	*Property*			
A	2	120 min in an hour (60 min/worker * 2 workers)	60 min (20 apps/hr * 3 min/app)	20 min (10 apps * 2 min/app)	12 min (2 apps * 6 min/app)	92 min	76.67% (92/120)	76.67%

Note that the capacity utilization for A has changed from the initial figure of 80 percent in Table 4.4, since we are now considering different flow times for different application types at workstation A. We can do the same computations for the other stations if we are provided the flow times for different types of applications for those respective stations.

An entire system of process analysis and improvement has been built around the concept of bottlenecks. It is called the 'theory of constraints' or TOC, developed by the late Dr. Eli Goldratt. Just as blood flow is impaired when it reaches a blockage or choke point, process flow is impaired when it reaches a bottleneck. TOC attributes bottlenecks to internal (workstation capacity), market (external, i.e., demand on workstations), and policy (such as limitations on overtime) constraints. It directs resources to identify and resolve such constraints in order to eliminate bottlenecks in the process.

Applying TOC to our insurance application handling process above, we would:

1   *Identify* the process bottleneck(s): workstation D (table above)
2   *Exploit* the bottleneck: Ensure that the bottleneck point does not stay idle. Bottleneck capacity defines process capacity, and we wish to maximize capacity utilization at the bottleneck. In our example (table above), the bottleneck capacity utilization is already at 100 percent.
3   *Subordinate* all decisions to step 2 above: All other workstations should work to ensure that the bottleneck runs smoothly and does not have to slow down or wait for any other step. This includes making sure that workstation D has enough demand (it has) and that everything the workstation needs to operate at full capacity is provided (delivered meals, office chair massages and haircuts, computer time).
4   *Elevate* the bottleneck: To expand capacity at the bottleneck, we could add workers or add/replace equipment at the bottleneck, expand its operating hours, subcontract or outsource capacity, reduce stoppages and breakdowns at that point, or move some bottleneck work to other workstations by cross-training workers.
5   Prevent inertia from settling in: Don't relax. As we relieve bottleneck D, workstation C becomes a bottleneck, requiring attention. Bottlenecks keep shifting between external and internal locations as process improvement progresses, requiring continual monitoring and corrective actions. *Also*, people snap back to old ways if incentives and worker involvement are not maintained until the new process is well established.

Process Improvement with Numbers

Process improvements have to be shown with numbers. Let's do a process redesign with before and after measurements. An insurance company issues complex corporate insurance policies that are highly profitable as well as small business policies that are simpler, but much less profitable. The complex/simple mix is currently 20/80, respectively. Assume that it currently processes both types of applications together. A flow diagram of its existing process for evaluating and approving applications looked as follows:

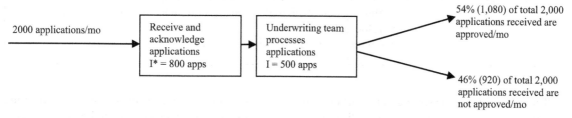

Figure 4.8 Insurance Application Processing

I* = average inventory at that work station (from observation)

Let's figure out the average time it took to process an application in this process, in order to understand a) how long customers had to wait to hear a decision about their application and b) how long the insurance company itself had to wait before an application turns into possible revenue. The process is stable, meaning that the inflow and outflow of applications is equal, that is, the flow rate of the process is 2,000 applications/month. We use Little's law to compute the average flow time:

Little's law
Average inventory = average flow rate * average flow time
I = FR * FT
Or, average flow time = average inventory/average flow rate = I/FR

Existing Process

Workstation	Average inventory	Average flow rate	Average flow time
Receiving	800 apps	2,000 apps/mo (1 mo = 20 working days)	Using Little's law: FT = I/FR = 800/2,000 = 0.40 mo = 8 working days/app
Underwriting	500 apps	2,000 apps/mo	0.25 mo = 5 working days/app

Total Process Flow time is a weighted average of the flow times of all workstations:

Workstation	Average flow time	Volume processed	Proportion of total volume	Weighted average flow time
Receiving	8 days	2,000 apps/mo	100% (1.00)	1.00 * 8 = 8 days
Underwriting	5 working days	2,000 apps/mo	100% (1.00)	1.00 * 5 = 5 days
				13 days

Thus, average process flow time = 13 working days/app
Another way:

Average process flow time = sum of average inventory in process/average flow rate
  = 800 apps (at receiving) + 500 apps (at underwriting)/2,000 apps
  = 1,300/2,000
  = 0.65 mo/app = 13 working days/app

Thus, the current process makes the customer wait for about 13 working days, on average, from the time the insurance company receives her application. Customers are unhappy, and a redesigned process is introduced. The company wishes to confirm that it has actually reduced flow time for applications, especially for the complex applications that generate significant revenue. The redesigned process splits the underwriting workstation into two separate workstations, each dedicated to complex and simple application categories.

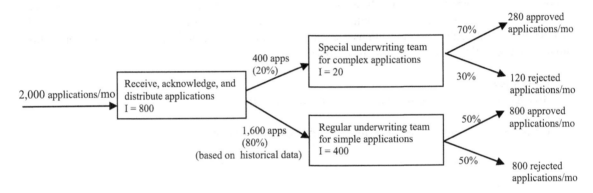

Figure 4.9 Redesigned Process for Insurance Application Processing

Redesigned Process

Workstation	Average inventory	Average flow rate	Average flow time
Receiving	800 apps	2,000 apps/mo	8 working days/app
Special Underwriting	20 apps	400 apps/mo (20% of 2,000 apps inflow)	20/400 = 0.05 mo, that is, 1 working day/app
Regular Underwriting	400 apps	1,600 apps/mo (80% of 2,000 apps in flow)	5 working days/app

So:
  Average flow time for complex applications = 8 days at receiving + 1 day at underwriting = *9 days*
  Average flow time for simple applications = 8 days at receiving + 5 days at underwriting = *13 days*

Total process flow time is a weighted average of the flow times of all workstations:

Workstation	Average flow time	Volume processed	Proportion of total volume	Weighted average flow time
Receiving	8 days	2,000 apps/mo	100% (1.00)	1.00 * 8 = 8 days
Special underwriting	1 day	400 apps/mo	20% (0.20)	0.20 * 1 = 0.20 days
Regular underwriting	5 day	1,600 apps/mo	80% (0.80) 0.80	$* 5 = \dfrac{4\,days}{12.20\,days}$

Thus, average process flow time = 12.20 working days/app
Another way:

Average process flow time = Sum of average inventory in process/average flow rate
= [800 apps (at receiving) + 20 apps (at complex underwriting) +
400 apps (at regular underwriting)]/2,000 apps
= 1,220/2,000
= 0.61 mo/app = 12.20 working days/app

We notice that the average time to process the insurance company's premium customer, the complex application, has been reduced to 9 days in the redesigned process vs. 13 days in the old process. A definite improvement! The company now wishes to know how long it takes on average to process applications that are eventually approved, since only approved applications generate revenue.

The average flow time for all approved applications is a weighted average of the flow times for complex and simple applications. The weights are derived from the proportion of total approved applications processed at each underwriting station. Note from figure 4.9 that a total of 1,080 applications (280 from special underwriting team and 800 from regular underwriting team) are eventually approved out of the total 2,000 applications that flow through the process every month (920 are rejected).

Average flow time
for all approved apps = (a) Proportion of total approved apps processed by the special
underwriting station * flow time for complex apps
+
(b) Proportion of total approved apps processed by the regular
underwriting station * flow time for simple apps

(a) Proportion of total approved apps processed by the special underwriting station
= # of apps approved at special underwriting station/total # of approved apps
= 280/1,080 apps
= 0.26

(b) Proportion of total approved apps processed by the regular underwriting station
   = # of apps approved at regular underwriting station/total # of approved apps
   = 800/1,080 apps
   = 0.74

From earlier:
Average flow time for complex apps = 9 days
Average flow time for simple apps = 13 days
Therefore:
Average flow time
for all approved apps = (0.26 * 9 days) + (0.74 * 13 days)
   = 2.34 + 9.62
   = *11.96 days*

Commensurately:
Average flow time
for all rejected apps = (0.13 * 9 days) + (0.87 * 13 days)
   = 1.17 + 11.31
   = *12.48 days*

Summing up, the redesigned process provides the following advantages over the old process

Table 4.6 Results from Process Design Improvement

	Old Process	*Redesigned Process*	*Improvement*
Average flow time/app	13 days	12.20 days	6.15%
Average flow time/app for all complex apps	13 days	9 days	30.76%
Average flow time/app for simple apps	13 days	13 days	Stable
Average flow time/app for all approved apps	13 days	11.96 days	8%
Average flow time/app for all rejected apps	13 days	12.48 days	2%

The insurance company processes its most profitable customers, complex applications, much quicker in the redesigned process and is able to approve applications (which generate revenue) in 8 percent less time.

KEY POINTS

- Process capacity is the maximum number of units that can be made or serviced by the process per hour/day/week . . . in normal working conditions. It is equal to the capacity of the bottleneck(s). Work step capacity is the maximum number of units that can be processed at that work activity station per hour/day/week. . . . . in normal working conditions.
- A bottleneck(s) in a process is the work step(s) that has the higher implied capacity utilization. There can be more than one bottleneck in a process, all working at the same implied capacity utilization.

- Flow time is the average time taken by a unit to go through the process. Flow rate is the average number of units that actually pass out of a process per unit of time (hour/day/week . . .).
- Flow rate cannot be greater than process capacity.
- Process capacity utilization = process flow rate/process capacity (bottleneck capacity).
- Process work step capacity utilization = flow rate at the work step/work step capacity.
- Work step yield = # of good units that came out of that work step per hour/day/week etc. . . .
  Flow rate = (total # of units that came out of the process per hour/day/week).
  Process yield = yield of work step #1 * yield of work step #2 * . . . yield of the last work step.
  Process yield generally diminishes as the number of work steps in a process increase.
- In processes with multiple types of units going through different workstations, the bottleneck(s) is the work step(s) with the highest implied capacity utilization. An implied capacity utilization greater than 100 percent does not automatically make the workstation a bottleneck—look for the maximum figure.
- The theory of constraints (TOC) channels attention and resources to managing the bottleneck. All decisions must be made in the context of achieving full capacity utilization of the bottleneck (since it dictates process capacity) and expanding its capacity.

4.4 Was It Done Right?

Professor Satya Chakravorty of Kennesaw State asks an interesting question.[1] What do weight-loss plans and process-improvement programs have in common? No surprise for getting it right—in both cases, adopters are gung-ho at the beginning but fall off after some time. In fact, Chakravorty goes on to say, 60 percent of process improvement initiatives, such as Six Sigma, ultimately fail, even after experiencing early successes. Why does that happen, and what we can do to be a part of the other successful 40 percent?

4.4.1 Warning Signs

The list below is not exhaustive, but keep an eye out for the following warning signs of deteriorating process management conditions:

- *Shadow processes*: When the prescribed way does not seem to work, employees develop work routines around formal processes and create 'shadow processes.' These shadow processes may likely be 'better' than the existing process but remain low profile.
- *Not enough failures*: Process improvement leaders would have their bonus and promotion tied to performance. It is entirely rational, though not right, to ignore failures and highlight successes. A slew of success stories without any acknowledged failures should raise red flags.
- *Too many metrics*: Excessive KPIs (key performance indicators) confuse and paralyze. Inconsistencies among process workers on process performance priorities or how the process is doing signal confusion.
- *Too many belts*: A proliferation of black belts and green belts (certifications of process improvement training) may be good news. On the other hand, it is not impossible that some workers have obtained process improvement skills certification by mostly hitting the books and completing courses. There may just not be enough projects to go around for intensive hands-on application of

book learning, creating process zealots who can talk the talk but cannot walk it. The lack of a standardized body of knowledge and multiple accreditation agencies complicate assessment of real worth.

* *Worker decline in engagement*: Disinterest among workers after an initial enthusiastic start may point to failures in training, guidance, feedback, or a lack of connection of process KPIs (key performance indicators) to reward systems.

* *Senior management decline in interest*: Your process leader talks with passion about process change and outcomes but fails to connect process improvement outcomes to actual market and business results. Senior managers do not deny local or internal outcomes such as reduced flow time and improved quality but demand to see their impact on customer metrics and financials. Transforming the organization is all right, but where's the money?

4.4.2 Why Things Go Wrong

Based on studies and accounts of involved managers and employees, there are some obvious and not so obvious reasons for process improvement initiatives that have gone awry:

1. *Will my job be safe?*

Am I process improving myself or my fellow workers out of our jobs? Companies should do their best to provide an assurance that no one will be fired as a consequence of process improvement initiatives. Transfers to other jobs, yes; transfers to other offices, maybe; at worst, transfers to the outsourcing firm. The alternative has to be presented clearly, too—no process improvement means loss of competitiveness, and everyone may lose their jobs, or someone else makes that decision. Also, process personnel gain confidence in their ability to make the process competitive and, thereby, make their jobs more secure.

2. *What do I gain?*

Besides the negative reinforcement of worrying about keeping my job, how else will my efforts matter in my evaluation/compensation/penalization scheme? I'll buy in if I can see the link between my compensation or quality of work life and improvements to the process. If you wish me to recount the specials of the day to diners all day, make it so that there is an incentive for me to do that consistently and with enthusiasm. Incentives to examine or re-examine processes can be indirect, too. O'Neill, Alcoa's CEO till 2000, surprised observers by his insistence on a full explanation and a solution from senior management for every accident on the job. Promotions and penalties were tied to this simple rule. What happened was insightful. To understand why accidents happen, senior managers had to understand job processes intimately—which led to discussions with workers—which led to ideas for improving operations. In other words, in trying to understand reasons for accidents and develop remedies, Alcoa improved its operating processes and quintupled its profits.[2]

3. *How am I doing?*

Feedback, guidance, and encouragement keep me on track. I lose traction and confidence if no one tells me whether my actions are actually improving process performance and what I need to do to correct course. All diet programs deliver continuous support and encouragement to retain participant interest and prevent backsliding. Controls may also be useful. Effective controls are designed to be immediate, visible, and sufficiently painful to remind the guilty about their lapses. A gym mails members' spouses when they notice a break in normal rhythms or frequent absences.

4. *It's too confusing and/or risky.*

A typical call center tracks 'after call work time' (ACW—time allowed to finish work relating to a call), auxiliary time on breaks, average call handling time, calls per hour, quality, sales through service, and demonstrations of company values, among other metrics, and compares these against weekly or monthly minimums and targets. Then, every so often, metrics are added or removed or re-weighted. The plethora of process performance KPIs creates a confusing, shifting, high-stress work environment and is one reason for the relatively high turnover in call centers. Unintended consequences can result from metrics. If a service person is measured by flow time alone, it creates an incentive to pass on the more difficult customers to other stations. Similarly, employees can be overwhelmed with information—asking people at work to read and follow 500 page change manuals, a revised production planning system, and a new HR manual all at once is a recipe for failure. Change has to be introduced in measured doses.

Process analysis and improvement also calls for a certain competence with statistical and mathematical concepts. Will I be exposed? I cannot learn stats or math at my age. What happens if they find out? Training takes away some of the fear and so does seeing examples of workers of similar age and background successfully tackle process analysis. If Bob could do it, anyone can!

5. *Is it for real?*

It's the flavor of the month—will go away. I'll fake it till it goes away. The strongest signal to the contrary is visible and sustained resource spending on training and applications along with aligned reward systems. If management moves on from one hot buzzword to another, employees are quick to catch on. They pretend to play. Managers move on in a year or two. I can outlast the new manager and her newfangled ideas.

6. *I can't keep up!*

I did it—got good benefits—but now day-to-day work tugs me away from process improvement tasks. One way companies deal with this issue is to set aside paid time off for meetings and training sessions. Offering quick cash rewards for accepted suggestions on process improvements is another strategy. More significantly, an improved process should make some of those 'day-to-day' jobs redundant—if not, it's time to take a look at whether the targeted improvements have actually been implemented and accepted.

7. *Gains have petered out.*

Low hanging gains have been plucked, and diminishing returns have set in. It's becoming more difficult to find and make improvements, and there is no additional incentive to compensate for the increased effort required. It is at this stage that senior management needs to step in and provide encouragement and resources to keep spirits and initiative alive. A process expert is also valuable at such times for providing new ideas, new tools, and new leadership to the process improvement team.

8. *The process improvement 'expert' is gone!*

The king is dead—let's hunker down and wait for the next one. Projects should not die with leaders. When a process leader departs prematurely, frequently, on-going initiatives are revisited and challenged by management. Coattail hangers-on clamber off the wagon quickly, unwilling to put in the political and personal effort to keep things going. The lonely few soldier on in a spiral of slowly dying initiatives, lacking fresh direction, guidance, and support. Process improvement experts should be kept on in permanent roles with distinct career paths and succession plans. A word of caution, though—process initiatives can create their own bureaucracies, so regular assessment of returns on investment is recommended.

9. *Global supply chains.*

Companies depend on supply chains for product cost reduction, quality, timely delivery, and new ideas. Hard as it is to involve and engage people within one's own company, aligning and involving external businesses in process improvement presents a difficult yet necessary-to-meet challenge. Companies that are engaging their external partners in supply chain process improvement initiatives have a few lessons to tell. Cultural and economic differences make it difficult for a supply chain to understand why some things are essential to do locally when not required or expected by local laws or norms. Process alignment becomes complicated when the 'why' question cannot be fully or satisfactorily answered. Successful companies also bear part of supplier costs for tools, training, and rewards required for process change and do not jettison suppliers every year for lower cost ones. Engaging consultants with a global footprint helps since their local staff can provide valuable tacit information and advice on various regional/national issues and help coordinate process changes across multiple continents.

10. *Don't always follow the process.*

Sometimes it's as important to *not* follow the process—especially when customer interactions are involved. My utility sent a technician to check out my furnace. While he was there, a three-way light switch failed suddenly. The proper procedure was to call the utility and schedule another appointment. Instead, the tech inspected the switch and resolved the problem. Processes are important for maintaining efficiency and consistency when a business scales, but don't let blind insistence on process harm your business! This doesn't mean, though, that workers should be able to get back to old habits or create workarounds to avoid work. Management should make it difficult for individuals to develop workarounds. Studies show that when processes are definitive, people accept them to avoid feeling psychologically discomfited over a change that they know they cannot alter.[3] But bendable rules may encourage revolt.

Although process improvement and replication is structured and systematic in approach and content, the element of excitement should never be allowed to die down. Passion is contagious. Management must develop a passion for improvement, seen and voiced every day, for every task and every person. Process improvement should become a de facto way of work, and bonuses and recognitions should be tied to participation and performance. Celebrations of even small successes must be loud and heard. The failure or success of any single initiative is immaterial. A deeper culture of continuous improvement takes root. Those who do not buy in must feel the effects—no bonuses, no promotions, no pats on the back.

KEY POINTS

- Underground, informal processes, no failures, excessive metrics or certifications, and worker or management decline in interest are some warning signs of poor process management.
- Fears of job loss have to be handled with positive encouragement.
- Performance feedback, guidance, and positive reinforcement are necessary for workers trying out new ways of working. Rewards have to be tied in to participation in process improvement initiatives as well as performance.
- Visible commitment of resources, providing time off for training, learning, and work analysis, are conducive to maintaining interest in process improvement initiatives.
- The presence and guidance of process leaders is particularly necessary when easy gains have been achieved and diminishing returns have set it.

4.5 Trends in Process Management

Information technology from IBM, SAP, and Oracle coupled with consultants from companies such as Accenture and McKinsey have re-engineering business processes using process analysis and technology, wringing out cost and the last bit of waste. Now businesses are asking—what else can you do? Providers advice on M&As (merger and acquisitions), conducting due diligence on behalf of their clients on the health of processes in the target company, identifying areas for improvement and recommending pre- and post-M&A actions. Due diligence on supplier processes can be done similarly.

Technology has allowed a process to be decoupled and its parts distributed among different locations around the world, picking the best people and sites for particular steps for optimizing process time, cost, and quality performance. So the risk analysis function may be in New York, but the supporting IT structure may be in India, while the trading desks are in London. Companies have to monitor, analyze, and improve their risk analysis process and/or other processes across disparate work cultures, time zones, languages, and functions. Coordinating such efforts is an enormous task even with technology, calling for intimate knowledge of local regimes and their business and legal idiosyncrasies. Consultants in the business re-engineering business are increasingly expanding their global footprint, anticipating and following client parceling of process parts internationally.

Digital technology and the 'internet of things' has added to existing operational data available to companies from shop-floor and maintenance logs, equipment-performance data, and supplier evaluation reports. Current data technology enables this dispersed data to be collected, analyzed, and applied for finding hidden bottlenecks, operational rigidities, and problem areas. Data mining and analytical/statistical methods such as Monte Carlo simulation, neural net modeling analysis, and value-in-use modeling are used to identify critical variables, understand interactions, identify bottlenecks, and estimate probabilities of occurrence of failures. Such methods help identify specific equipment and process steps in need of attention, optimize production and maintenance schedules, and guide experiments with lower cost materials. Social technologies such as Skype, Facebook, and Twitter have also been found useful. Early warnings of supplier problems, political risks, labor issues, and safety violations can be gleaned. Teams begin to self-form since information about needs and matching capabilities becomes more widespread and accessible. Companies using social technologies for processes now include IT, legal, pharma, retailing, transportation, health, and financial sectors.

Process performance metrics have increased in number and complexity. It's no longer sufficient to evaluate a process on efficiency or quality. New concerns about safety, ethics, and sustainability have added to the assessment task. McDonald's workers in 19 cities have recently filed a labor complaint over burns from grills and fry lamps, lack of safety gear, and other workplace hazards. Workers complained of being burned while cleaning grills that are required to be kept on. Other complaints speak of inadequate training for operating hot fryers, falls on wet floors, and allegedly being told to apply mustard on burns![4] They allege that these safety problems are caused by persistent understaffing and employees being pressured to work quicker—the consequences of a performance system that tracks sales and staffing metrics.[5] In other industries, the scoreboard has become more granular and deep. For example, hospitals track patient volumes, net revenue, and hospital profit margins. These margins may even be monitored for decisions on a daily basis. Narayana Hrudayalaya in India, specializing in heart surgery with mortality rates and costs lower than leading U.S. hospitals, examines profit and loss statements (P&L) on a daily basis. Doing so, the hospital explains, allows them to determine the extent of price concessions it can offer the next day to needy patients. Every patient is assessed and coded for severity of condition, with scores for clinical outcomes and the costs involved in individual patient care. Flow time metrics are being developed at the patient-level for individual work steps, such as time to draw blood from a patient and the time from the arrival of a post-surgery patient in the intensive-care to the point when the patient can function without a ventilator. Such granularity enables focus on specific work steps and locates where improvement is most needed.

Process management principles developed in manufacturing are finding their way into services. One such principle is to match the resource to the job, avoiding allocation of more expensive resources to a job that can be done by less expensive means. Nurse practitioners can address many routine illnesses and examinations, leaving the more expensive MD to focus on more complex cases. Companies are also establishing different process paths for different levels of customers, providing personalized treatment to VIP customers. Similarly, a particular work step may be divided into a subtask requiring expert talent and another sub-task that can be handled by cheaper labor. When our bathroom faucet at home began to run hot water instead of cold (after I had performed a few exploratory surgeries to fix a leak), the master plumber I called asked very detailed questions over the phone. He conducted a virtual diagnosis of the problem and dispatched his less expensive apprentice to actually fix the faucet.

4.5.1 *Efficiency vs. Innovation*

An issue that has been troubling many in business for some time now is the perceived incompatibility of process improvement with innovation in the firm. Process improvement connotes discipline, focus, reduction of waste and variance, and established best practice routines. Innovation speaks to blue-sky thinking, experimentation, tolerance of uncertainty and waste, and constant questioning of routine. There is a natural tension between process efficiency and innovation. So while 3M worries "whether the relentless emphasis on efficiency has made 3M a less creative company?" a deeper concern is that the organizational adoption of Six Sigma filters meant that "more predictable, incremental work took precedence over blue-sky research."[6] One school of thought recommends "ambidextrous organizations" that comprise tightly internally coupled sub-units yet remain loosely coupled with each other. These sub-units are highly differentiated, with some designed for blue-sky initiatives and others for incremental improvement purposes. Process efficiency interventions are kept away from the former.

KEY POINTS

Trends in Process Management

- Companies are seeking assistance from process re-engineering experts for due diligence on process health and performance in M&As.
- Global process engineering companies are leveraging their global presence and experience to offer advice about local opportunities, challenges, and resources to companies entering new markets.
- Process metrics have become more detailed and granular, offering deeper insights on process performance.
- IT has enabled companies to distribute a process in separate pieces on a best practice or best-personnel-for-the-job basis. Process improvement in such fragmented processes requires extraordinary technical and behavioral resources for coordination, integration, and implementation of new procedures.
- Concerns exist about the effects of too much emphasis on speed and efficiency in business processes on creativity and innovation.

4.6 Conclusion

Customer: *"Why should I choose you?"*
Business: *"Because we promise that you shall find it convenient, cost effective, transparent, and comfortable to transact with us."*

Processes organize volume work in standard, replicable ways to transform inputs into outputs. Process management dissects these work systems to assess, compare and improve their efficiency and enhance the quality of outcomes. To do so, process managers use evaluation metrics such as flow time, flow rate, and yield. Every process has a bottleneck(s) resource, the one with the highest implied capacity utilization. The capacity of a process is limited to the capacity of its bottleneck(s). For that reason, relaxing the bottleneck will increase process capacity. Processes are further examined using flow diagrams and process flowcharts, which help understand the major work steps in a process, how they interrelate, and which steps add value. Process analysis examines and challenges every step in a process from the point of view of its reason for existence, its contribution to value, the waste it generates, and its potential for improvement. Managers try to reduce waste and add value by eliminating, combining, dividing and repositioning work steps in a process. Steps that are particularly prone to errors of consequence are fool-proofed with poka-yokes. After the waste and non-value-added steps are eliminated and value-adding steps are possibly added, the resulting steps are put together in a tight sequence. The new process runs with a minimum of inventory, friction, and wait times, maximizing flow times and yield across the process. Process management techniques are well established in manufacturing. Services present new opportunities of great value. If you learn to become a process doctor, you'll find plenty of patients calling on you for your expertise. Good luck!

What Have We Learned?

What Is Process Management?

- A process is a collection of interrelated and standardized work steps that are located in different functions and companies in a supply chain. It is run repeatedly to deliver output of value in significant volume.
- Most companies have three fundamental processes: order fulfillment, production, and procurement.
- Managing a process requires measurement, analysis, and implementation actions. The metrics are typically efficiency oriented.
- Since processes are distributed among many functions, some companies have appointed process owners who are responsible for the smooth functioning and improvement of the process as a whole.

Why Is It Important?

- Process management replaces local practice with a set of standard, documented best work practices and systems with an enterprise-wide performance perspective.
- Compliance regulations and risk analysis demand standardization and active management of processes.
- Process management identifies and eliminates waste and non-value-added work steps from processes, making them more efficient, speedy, and defect free.
- Process management aligns and integrates functional systems, metrics, and goals with overall business goals.

How Is It Done?

- Business goals are translated into cascading process level, functional, and work step level goals.
- Existing processes are checked for vital signs, such as flow time, flow rate, average inventory, and yield.

  Average flow time: The average time it takes one unit to move from the beginning to the end of the process, e.g., 5 minutes/unit

  Average flow rate: The average number of units that the process is delivering as output, per unit of time, e.g., 10 units/hour.

  Average inventory: The average number of units that are inside the process at any time.

  Yield: Number of good units/total number of units that flow through the process per day or week or month or year.

- Little's law can be applied to find flow times (or average inventory/flow rate) for processes in a variety of operations, including company-level comparisons of efficiency among different companies.

  *Average inventory = average flow rate * average flow time*

- Processes are analyzed for improvement using process-mapping techniques, including flow diagrams and process flowcharts.
- Mapping and analysis should first be done from the customer's perspective.
- Every work step in the process flowchart is examined for value-added worth for the primary customer in meeting his/her needs.
- Every work step is examined to identify waste.
- Any step that does not add value or includes waste is either removed or redesigned or relocated to other, subsequent, locations in the process.
- Improved work practices are developed through worker initiative and input. Such improvements should be capable of being replicated and performed/learned by average workers.
- Implementation of redesigned processes requires worker incentives, training, documentation and tool support, and other resources. Rewards and penalties both work towards steering and sustaining change in behavior and actions. The redesigned process is replicated in other parts of the company and its supply chain, as needed.
- The capacity of a process is constrained to the capacity of its bottleneck.
- The bottleneck in a process is the work step with the highest implied capacity utilization. There can be multiple bottlenecks with identical implied capacity utilizations.
- Process capacity utilization = flow rate/capacity
- The theory of constraints (TOC) attributes bottlenecks to internal, market (external), and policy (such as limitations on overtime) constraints. It directs resources to the full utilization and relaxation of bottlenecks in the process.

Was It Done Right?

- Signs of poor process management can range from no reports of failures to the existence of parallel informal processes.
- Fears of job loss must be handled.
- Behavior changes are managed with both positive and negative reinforcement. Both participation and performance are linked to compensation.
- Process leadership and guidance is particularly necessary to sustain efforts when easy gains have been achieved and diminishing returns have set it.

Trends in Process Management

- Companies are using process management consultants for due diligence in supplier and other company processes.
- IT and behavioral science advances enable process improvement initiatives for processes that are fragmented across different parts of the world.
- Companies are trying to reconcile the incompatibilities between efficiency-focused process improvement initiatives and new product or service innovation.

Discussion Questions

1   In a busy motor vehicles office, the average process flow time = 15 minutes/customer; therefore, the average process flow rate would be equal to 4 customer/hour. Is that likely? Why or why not?

2   If you had a choice between making direct observations of flow rate, flow time, or average inventory, which two variables would you normally pick to observe? Why?

3   Would Little's law work for a process that experiences large swings in flow rate, flow time or inventory?

   Answer: Yes, Little's law is for the long-term—the average, which accommodates variations.

4   During peak hours, students get onto a school's first floor escalator at 30 students/minute in order to reach the second floor elevators to higher floors. There are 100 students travelling on the escalator, on average. How long is their journey on the escalator, on average?

   Answer: I=FR * FT; FR = 30 students/minute; inventory = 100 students; therefore, FT = 100/30 = 3.33 min

5   Explain how the work steps of the order fulfillment process affect the balance sheet and statement of accounts?

   Answer: Work step of sending goods to the customer in an order fulfillment process would increase sales revenue as well as COGS in the Income Statement, while depleting inventory and increasing accounts receivables in the balance sheet. When the customer makes payment, accounts receivable decline while cash assets increase in value.

6   You often hear statements such as "I'm working at 150 percent." Could that be true? Could process capacity utilization exceed 100 percent?

   Answer: For a short time, yes. Sustained—no, if quality is being maintained.

7   Increasing the capacity of the bottleneck work step in a process by 50 percent would usually increase process capacity by 50 percent. True or false? Why?

   Answer: No, because, typically, another bottleneck springs up somewhere else and constrains process capacity.

8   Adding more parts/steps to a process/product generally results in lower yields. Is this a correct statement? Please provide reasoning.

   Answer: Yes, because total process yield is a multiplicative function: Yield of process = yield of step A * yield of step B * yield of step C * . . .

9   Does flow time reduction always reflect process improvement?

Answer: No—FT reduction is not all good—e.g., hurried haircut, nails. Longer Starbucks lines mean more time to drool and eventually buy that piece of double-layered rich chocolate cake that's been seducing you for the past five minutes—buy me, eat me!

End of Chapter Problems

1   A hotel takes in 500 guests/day on average (it has capacity to house and serve 600). The average length of stay is 2 days. What is the average flow rate and average flow time?

Answer: It is a stable process (average arrival rate is lower than capacity). FR = 500 guests/day; FT = 2 days

2   Cars at a car wash come out of the car wash at an average rate of 5 cars/minute. Cars are arriving at an average rate of 5 cars/minute. Will there be any wait line at the arrival step?

Answer: Yes, because arrival and processing are both variable. Cars may arrive in a bunch at lunch time. Also, all cars do not spend equal time at or are not processed by all work steps—e.g., just wash service or full service with wax and undercarriage work.

3   The average number of people in the inventory in the lost/replacement driver license line is 20. It takes the DMV 10 minutes on average to process a customer. What is the average flow rate?

Answer:
I = FR * FT; 20 = FR * 10; therefore, FR = 2 customers/minute

4   The state tax office audits handles 300,000 complaints, on average, in a year. Critics allege that the department is inefficient, given that an average of 60,000 untouched complains exist at any given time (confirmed from an official audit of the tax office). The office claims that they resolve a complaint, on average, in less than a month. Is that true? Provide reasoning.

Answer:
Average inventory I = 60,000; flow rate FR = 300,000 complaints/yr (we assume a stable system).
Thus, average flow time, FT = I/FR = 60,000/300,000 = 0.2 yr = 2.4 months > than 1 month. The Tax Office's claim is not correct.

5   TaxCut Inc., a small but established taxation firm, finds increasing demand for its services but is apprehensive that it may not be able to deliver on its promises to its clients. As usual, you (OM Inc.) are called to analyze, diagnose and fix the problem.

Here are the facts, as dug out by you.

Five kinds of clients come to TaxCut Inc. in the following numbers, on average:

Type A: New clients, personal	10 clients/month
Type B: New clients, business	5 clients/month
Type C: Old clients, personal	30 clients/month
Type D: Old clients, business	50 clients/month
Type E: International clients	5 clients/month

Five work steps are involved in processing clients. Each type of client needs a different amount of time at the 5 work steps.

Client	Reception	(CPA) Meet client	(Trainee CPA) Q&A session	(CPA) Review draft return	(Trainee CPA) Correct and Submit
A	10 minutes	20 minutes	90 minutes	10 minutes	30 minutes
B	10	60	180	80	50
C	5	0	30	8	20
D	10	15	150	60	40
E	15	80	250	100	80

Reception works 8-hour days, 25 days a month. The CPA and her apprentice, the trainee CPA, each work 10-hour days, 25 days a month.

a)   Find the bottleneck, current or potential. What is his/her current implied utilization?

A suggested template is provided below to facilitate analysis.

Labor	Available capacity total minutes/mo	Client A demand	Client B demand	Client C demand	Client D demand	Client E demand	Total demand	Implied capacity utilization
Reception	12,000	10 min* 10 clients = 100 min	50 min	150	500	75	875	875/12,000 = 7% rounded off
CPA	15,000	(20+10)min * 10 clients = 300	700	240	3,750	900	5,890	39%
Trainee CPA	15,000	1,200	1,150	1,500	9,500	1,650	15,000	100%

b)   Is TaxCut Inc. likely turning away clients? Yes (but why?)
c)   How would you improve the process (assume no money to hire anyone)?

Answer:
Many options: a) CPA handles some returns herself (type D); b) Train reception to handle some 'easy' old customer returns; c) Place some Q&A online for clients to prefill before appointment, thus lowering demand on firm resources.

Suggested Class Projects

a)   Visit your main computer lab on campus and compute the average flow time, flow rate, and inventory from direct observation, following procedures outlined in this chapter. Apply Little's law to see if your observations match up to the Little's law numbers. Do you see notable differences? If so, explain why.

b)   From your analysis above, develop some process improvement ideas. Apply the methods outlined in the chapter.

  For the next three questions, go to https://rehabstudio.com/projects/whole-foods-of-the-future.

c)   How does the new product (apple-watch) change the shopping process?

d)   How does the new product change the shop layout?

e)   What implications do these changes have for speed of order fulfillment, inventory holdings, re-order frequencies, worker training and other store operations?

Suggested Cases

Toshiba: Ome Works: Harvard Business School case
Marzana Insurance: HBS case
National Cranberry: HBS case

Notes

1 Satya S. Chakravorty, "Where Process-Improvement Projects Go Wrong," *Wall Street Journal Online,* Jan. 25, 2010.
2 Charles Duhigg, *The Power of Habit: Why We Do What We Do in Life and Business,* (New York: Random House, 2012).
3 Kristin Laurin, Aaron C. Kay, and Gavan J. Fitzsimons, "Reactance versus Rationalization: Divergent Responses to Policies that Constrain Freedom," *Psychological Science,* 23(2) (2012): 205–209.
4 Jana Kasperkevic, "McDonald's Workers Told to Treat Burns with Condiments, Survey Shows," *The Guardian,* March 16, 2015.
5 Candice Choi, "McDonald's Workers Detail Burns, Job Hazards in Complaints," Associated Press, March 16, 2015.
6 Brian Hindo, "3M: Struggle between Efficiency and Creativity," *Businessweek,* Sept. 14, 2007.

Part III

Improving Process Performance

5 Business Forecasting

Forecasting: A Road Map

5.6 Conclusion

End of chapter

- What have we learned?
- Discussion questions
- End of chapter problems
- Suggested class projects
- Suggested cases

Customer: *"Why should I choose you?"*
Business: *"Because we promise to anticipate your needs."*

5.1 What Is Business Forecasting?

Business forecasting is the systematic application of human experience, human responses, human judgment, and historical data to develop a tangible, probabilistic statement about future events and trends. The statement could be specific to the future value of a particular variable(s) of business interest, e.g., the forecasted price of steel next July, with 75 percent probability. Business forecasting is not fortune telling. Fortune tellers believe they have the gift to 'see' the future. Forecasters use data and experience to make reasoned anticipations of the future. Forecasting is not estimation. Estimation is most often conducted for things that exist, without probabilities. Forecasting looks into the state of the future. Preparing a project estimate is different from forecasting the chances of being awarded that project. We forecast, not estimate, snow tomorrow.

Where does forecasting belong in an organization? The Journal of Business Forecasting[1] reports that forecasting is moving from finance and marketing to the Supply Chain/Operations function. Let's now take a look at some specific reasons for using business forecasts.

5.2 Why Is Forecasting Important?

Some time ago, Everbank USA offered a five-year gold CD that guarantees 100 percent return of capital while offering an upside potential of a maximum 50 percent return. Obviously, Everbank would have had to forecast the trend in gold value over the five-year period of the CD, to a) ensure that they do not make a loss, and b) ensure that they make a decent profit on the product. And, of course, Everbank's customers would have had to evaluate the attractiveness of the offer, both in terms of risk and return. Why would you invest in Everbank's CD, which limits you to a 50 percent return, albeit providing principal protection? What if the price of gold skyrockets another 300 percent in five years? How probable is that event, relative to the risk of a decline in gold price in five years? As we can see, without reasonably reliable forecasts, neither Everbank nor its customers would have a logical basis for making business decisions. Forecasting is a critical capability for a business, and, for that matter, an important part of reaching personal decisions that involve a consideration of the future.

5.2.1 Importance for Businesses

Merger and acquisition decisions are influenced by forecasts of the economy, stock markets, borrowing costs, and cash flows. Forecasts of interest rates and stock market behavior inform the choice of raising capital through short-term notes, bonds, or preferred or common stock. Similarly, labor cost and wage contract decisions are impacted by inflation forecasts, while capacity or marketing decisions are affected by forecasts of demand and economic growth. Sourcing decisions are influenced by forecasts of commodity and input prices, which in turn are influenced by forecasts of demand, supply constraints, weather, inflation, and economic growth.

A forecast tells us what the future may look like. If the future appears attractive, we can try to accelerate its emergence; if not, we can try to stop, stall, or change it. The most valuable forecast may be one that we stop from coming true. A forecasted slump in product demand may be preventively handled with intelligent product and price management. We can also change our business model to meet what cannot be averted. As a case in point, life expectation in the U.S. is increasing significantly.[2] So, on a slightly morbid but business-like note, how should the CEO of a funeral business respond to the forecast? More people living longer *is* bad news for funeral parlors—and the trend cannot be stopped or slowed in any legitimate manner! So funeral parlors are changing their business model to cope with the effects of a declining death rate. FuneralOne makes tribute DVDs that mourners seek as keepsakes, enables real time webcasts for remote attendance, and makes a Vid Tombstone that plays a 10 minute loop of the departed soul.[3]

5.2.2 Importance for You

According to the World Future Society, "The single most critical skill for the 21st century" is foresight.[4] Forecasting provides foresight with a degree of measurable error. Major corporations spend millions of dollars on methods to forecast events and trends that may affect business plans. You can learn how to utilize some of these methods to make a difference in your studies, your career, and your life.

Work as a Forecaster for Nintendo!

Forecast & Inventory Analyst (1000000022) Nintendo of America Inc.

Description of Duties (abbreviated)

- Analyzes and prepares retailer sell-through and inventory data to form the basis for the market item forecasts.
- Analyzes and recommends on product needs based on analysis of the completed forecasts.
- Maintains the preliminary Item Forecasts for purchase order requirements
- Maintains forecast variance reporting to monitor forecast accuracy
- Collects and maintains core data requirements for monthly sales forecast
- Establishes and leverages historical promotion data to predict and model future promotional success
- Collaborates with CPFR/Sales Admin on product forecast results between Business Planning and those teams
- Supports account analysis functions to improve inventory level planning and maximize the Nintendo business
- Collaborates and monitors with NOCL and Latin America regarding product performance, forecast tracking

---

Summary of Requirements

- Two to three years of related experience
- Proficient in spreadsheet and database applications (Excel, Word, Business Objects)
- Ability to analyze business environment, understand market dynamics and develop business recommendations based on market activity
- Strong statistical analysis skills and ability to create forecast models

Required Education

- Undergraduate degree in Business, Economics, Marketing, or related field, or equivalent

---

Typical jobs in forecasting include titles such as forecast analyst, product forecasting planner, manager—risk analytics and forecasting, and demand planner. Entry, or near entry level openings, offer a $60,000 to $80,000 range in compensation. The Institute of Business Forecasting and Planning hosts job openings in forecasting on its site.[5]

KEY POINTS

- Business forecasting is a probabilistic statement about the state of the future based on a systematic synthesis of data, experience, and judgment.
- Besides operations and sales planning, forecasts are useful for financing (future interest rates), procurement (future material prices and shortages), labor wages agreements (future inflation rate), hiring (future personnel needs), acquisitions, and other decisions.
- The ultimate utility of a forecast lies in our response to it—we can try to accelerate, slow down, or change the forecasted future, as needed, while positioning the business suitably.

5.3 How to Make a Forecast?

Your boss tells you, "Please prepare a demand forecast for product X." Here's a step-by-step process to get you started:

5.3.1 The Process of Forecasting

- *Form a team:*

Include:

- A senior management supporter/champion, to provide resources, and interpret decisions to top management.
- Information technology and operations research/analytical, to collect, clean, organize, analyze ,and maintain data.

- Operations/supply chain and key suppliers, for purchasing, shipping, inventory control, and material planning input.
- Accounting, for accuracy in costing and adherence to accounting norms.
- Sales and marketing and key customers, for input on demand.

- *Ask: What is the desired forecasting level, and what is the purpose of the forecast?*

What we wish to forecast has a bearing on the choice of forecasting method. While it may be possible to use historical data to forecast that skirts sell more than jeans in the summer, forecasting which color will be in fashion next year requires more judgment than data. We can forecast at a deep level, such as an individual item (like a specific song on iTunes), or at higher levels such as categories (a song category—R&B/Hip-Hop), aggregate (Billboard 100), or industry (online vs. CD sales). We can also breakdown forecasts by region, channels of distribution, and customers segments. The deeper the level, the greater the volatility of demand, and the larger the forecast error. The added money and effort required to reduce forecast error is contingent on the purpose of the forecast. A large error in a demand forecast used for projecting future cash flows may have serious consequences for the business. However, that same error may not matter that much if the forecast is used for workforce planning.

- *Ask: What's the time period for the forecast?*

Forecast error amplifies the further out into the future we go. Using historical data-based forecasting methods works for a short- to medium-time horizon. Call centers use historical calling patterns data to develop hourly forecasts for staffing shifts and determining their need for personnel. Long-term forecasts rely extensively on experience and judgment.

- *Identify, collect, clean, and analyze data.*

If running a data-based forecast, know your key drivers for the variables you wish to forecast. To forecast domestic sales for a steel manufacturer, key drivers of steel demand have to be identified. These may include steel imports, competitor pricing and capacity, housing and infrastructure construction, auto manufacturing, and the availability and pricing of steel substitutes. Historical data on these demand drivers and steel sales for the company can be collected from existing company databases, from secondary sources (Conference Board, Bureau of Commerce), and from interviews and surveys with industry, key suppliers, and key customers. The data is screened for errors and missing data and reorganized into a workable format. Analytical methods are then applied to examine the relationship between these drivers and domestic steel sales for that company. The future values of the drivers themselves are forecasted. These forecasted values are used for developing a forecast for steel sales using the relationship patterns found from the analysis.

- *Refine the forecast.*

Usually, a mixture of data-based methods is employed to develop an initial forecast, which is then run through human experience and knowledge filters. Use people from different functions such as marketing, sales, production, and finance to review the data-based forecast, prepare a consensus data-based baseline forecast, and overlay judgment on the baseline forecast as necessary.

- *Sell the forecast.*

If users cannot understand the forecast or feel threatened by the forecast (e.g., hey, this low-demand forecast could mean I may be laid-off!), it is quite likely that the forecast will not be used. The best way to mitigate such problems is to actively seek out organizational opinion makers and engage employees in the forecasting process from the initial step. Impress on them that working with the forecast may make it possible to take anticipatory action to influence future events or reduce the negative effects of such events.

- *Measure performance and correct.*

Mechanisms to consistently track forecasts against actual demand should be developed and institutionalized. Actuals for orders (ordered items and quantities), shipments, order backlogs, supply receipts, and inventory should be available in units and dollars, in usable format, and for specified time periods (week/month). Consensus and feedback meetings with forecast users should be prescheduled at regular intervals for communicating errors and taking corrective action. Quick and regular feedback has been shown to cure overconfidence/underconfidence tendencies in forecasting.

Two pieces of practical advice: a) Begin with a small forecasting project that has high demonstration effect potential, and b) introduce changes gradually. Other suggestions: Present visual displays; identify participants with forecast override authority (and work with them); and develop a plan to identify and react *quickly* to significant deviations of actuals from forecasts. Use the RACI approach: who's responsible (R), accountable (A), consulted (C), and just informed (I).

5.3.2 Forecasting Approaches

Can you forecast the proportion of A's in a course you're currently taking? How would you approach this task? Your first thought probably is to see if reliable data is available for your instructor's grading distribution for the past few years. You may also narrow your data search to match the particular semester, class time, and the size of the class. Additionally, you may consult with friends and ex-students, as well as garrulous profs, to obtain opinions about the 'hard/soft' grader question. Further, you may wish to look at student evaluations of instructor teaching performance that may be available at school and on professor rating sites. You may choose to weight these inputs differently and synthesize them with your knowledge about your classmates' performance in past courses of similar difficulty (if obtainable) and their course load this semester (again, if obtainable). The final forecast would likely represent a data-based foundational forecast refined with qualitative information from multiple sources. Such is the case with businesses, too. But if A's are awarded intermittently, or randomly, or at very long intervals, forecasting with any reasonable accuracy would be a difficult task.

We don't need to and, in some cases, realistically cannot develop good forecasts for every product or item. Applying Pareto's 80/20[6] principle generally turns up a substantial number of products that are of low importance, i.e., low sales or profit contributors. A small proportion of items emerge as truly important.

Quadrants I and IV contain high volatility items, products with intermittent, irregular demand. Generally speaking, high volatility items with high coefficients of variation (standard deviation/mean >1.0) are extremely difficult to forecast unless detectable patterns exist in the data. If such items are of high importance, we can effectively manage them using other options, such as finding suppliers with quick delivery times, incentivizing the customer to wait or order regularly, better communications with users, product standardization, and inventory pooling.[7] We could also keep some inventory (more if the item is inexpensive) to meet sudden spurts in

	High Volatility	Lower Volatility
High Importance	High volatility – high importance Very difficult to forecast. Make other arrangements (preferably), or use judgment and experience. I	Low volatility – high importance Easier to forecast and high importance. Develop and use data-based forecasts. II
Low Importance	High volatility – low importance Do not forecast, except for special cases. IV	Low volatility – low importance Develop and use forecasts only if cost-benefit analysis suggests so. III

Figure 5.1 To Forecast or Not

demand (safety stock). Qualitative forecasting methods may also be of some use. An example of a high volatility-high importance item could be rare AB-type blood, which exists in less than 1 percent of the U.S. population. For high volatility-low importance items, we do not spend resources developing forecasts. We also do not keep much stock, since stock-outs should not normally cause much harm.

Quadrants II and III include lower volatility SKUs (stock keeping units, that is, every unique item being carried) that are receptive to forecasting. Data-driven forecasting is recommended for high importance items. If resources are available and cannot be used gainfully elsewhere (high volatility-high importance items, for example), forecasts can be developed for low importance items, too.

KEY POINTS

- Forecasting is a formal process, with clear actionable steps.
- Forecasting accuracy declines with the level of detail required and the length of the time horizon.
- High volatility-intermittent demand items are difficult to forecast using data and should be managed using a mix of short lead times, safety stock, pooling, demand management, and other coping mechanisms.
- Historical data-driven forecasts are useful for the short and medium terms. Qualitative forecasts are not based on data analysis and are more suited for the longer term.

We can take two broad approaches in our choice of primary forecasting method, qualitative or quantitative. Qualitative means having to do with judgment, and, usually, an absence of reliable historical data. Quantitative refers to various data-based methods, where reliable and accessible historical data exist for forecasting purposes. Quite often, data-based method forecasts are refined using qualitative approaches.

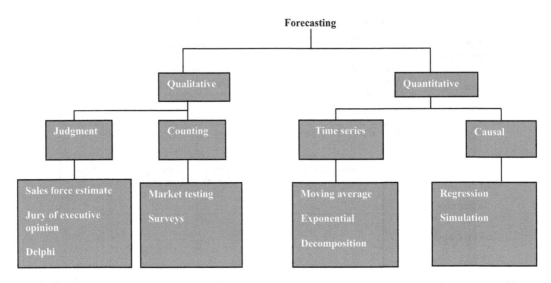

Figure 5.2 Forecasting Approaches, Categories, and Methods

Among the approaches shown above, time series techniques are most commonly used for business forecasting.[8] Let's examine each group of methods in turn.

5.3.3 Qualitative forecasting

Forecasting without performing data analysis can be done in a number of ways, most of which you would recognize as fairly intuitive and frequently seen, as described below:

Judgment

The sales force estimate technique takes input from the sales force. Using this technique, a district sales manager for a pharmaceutical company would ask her sales representatives in the various territories comprising the district to forecast sales of a product. The forecasts she receives would then be overlaid with her judgment and accumulated into a forecast for the entire district. The advantages are clear: Those on the frontline have frequent and direct exposure to the actual consumer and direct knowledge of competitor moves on the ground. Sales people tend, however, to understate forecasts because they well know that their numbers would be inputs in setting future sales targets. A good manager recognizes this factor and compensates with her own experience and judgment. A manager could also ask for a range of forecasts, representing pessimistic, optimistic, and most likely scenarios and ask the sales person to later clarify if his scenario forecasts are very wide apart.

The jury of executive opinion logic is that many eyes improve accuracy. To illustrate, marketing, operations, purchasing, accounting, finance, and selected key suppliers and customers would meet and trade perspectives on the future, eventually arriving at a consensus judgment. However, as we see sometimes in class presentations or discussions, a strong personality (or an influential function such as marketing) may push through its

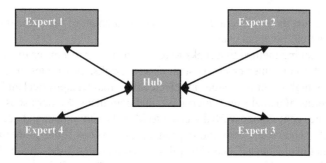

Figure 5.3 The Delphi Method

own world view on the decision-making body. We could make the process anonymous. Opinions could be recorded anonymously, discussed, and finally voted on by the group without author identifiers.

The Delphi method, named after the Greek oracle at Delphi, lends itself to forecasts for long-term emerging phenomena or revolutionary technologies. In these cases, neither the sales force, nor the customer, nor the company has adequate information or market/product experience to develop a forecast. For example, the market for tissue engineering (growing human organs) is potentially huge, but the technology is still in a formative stage. Using a Delphi, we would collect a few recognized authorities from top research labs around the world and ask these experts to develop individual forecasts of the likely development trajectory for the technology.

Each scientist would send a forecast to the hub (us). We would simply list all the forecasts and send the list back to each scientist. At this point, they would become aware that other scientists are involved in the exercise. In the small world of cutting edge technology, the stars of the field may know about each other, but the Delphi method makes it difficult for a participant to associate a specific forecast with a specific author. The participants would look at the other forecasts and resend a set of second-round individual forecasts to the hub. We develop those into another summation for further circulation. The process goes on until we, the hub, call a stop. Either a consensus has been reached, or we feel that further agreement among the expert forecasters is improbable. The Delphi method can be time consuming and expensive but is often the only credible resort available for developing forecasts for emergent events, technologies, or concepts. Software to guide us through the procedure is available.[9] The forecasts for new, little-known, long-term subjects have been found to be generally more accurate using Delphi than forecasts using traditional group forecasting or combined judgment.[10]

Forecasting, particularly in smaller businesses, may simply be an extension of what happened yesterday or today. This approach, labeled 'naïve extrapolation,' works in high inertia environments such as consumer staples like milk and bread. So, if a grocery sold 500 gallons of 2 percent milk on a weekend, it would expect to sell about the same quantity next weekend, too. In a sense, this approach uses data. Unlike some other textbooks, we do not, however, categorize it as a quantitative approach, since the data is just extrapolated for the immediate term without any analysis of trends, events, or influence factors. Naïve extrapolation is most useful when used as a baseline forecast for comparing the incremental worth of other, more expensive, methods and is also perfectly acceptable for highly stable markets.

Another judgment-based approach uses role playing to simulate how and what decisions could be made in the future. Role players engage in realistic interactions with other role players, and their decisions during the role-plays are used to guide forecast development.

Counting

Counting techniques do just that—make a decision based on a count of the number of positive, negative, or 'don't know' responses from potential users.

Market testing is a counting method that seeks to record customer responses to a new or modified product or concept, especially for consumer products such as soft drinks, chocolates, and cereals. Prototypes are developed and placed in high visibility venues in selected pilot markets, physical and online. Consumer reactions are recorded in terms of actual sales, interviews, and comments. Modern sensing technologies such as eye-tracking technologies capture non-verbal signals to identify and understand cues about how consumers visually and cognitively perceive and respond to products and events. If the count of buys is significant, the product goes on for a national launch. Coca-Cola pilot-tested its state-of-the-art vending machines that allow consumers to mix and match different flavored drinks (Fanta-Cherry Coke, anyone?) in Atlanta-area and Southern California restaurants.

A newer approach is virtual market testing. A virtual version of the product is posted, and customer preferences are recorded and used to forecast the potential market. The garment and food industries now conduct virtual market research of different new product designs with designs posted online and actual responses noted. In an interesting experiment, designer Ora Ito designed and posted a variety of imaginary products, including a faux Vuitton backpack and non-existent Swatch watch collections, online. The response was overwhelming, with shoppers besieging Vuitton stores with calls and visits in search of the elusive backpack.[11]

Figure 5.4 Coca-Cola's New Vending Machine

Source: MBRS Stooge, "Coca-Cola Freestyle Machine," [CC], via *Wikimedia Commons*, https://upload.wikimedia.org/wikipedia/commons/a/a9/Coca_Cola_Freestyle.JPG.

Figure 5.5 Ito's Faux Creations[12]

The brands did not sue Ito—they gave him a job! And ironically, a factory in China actually began making illegal copies (of a non-existent product)! Ito is now a global name in 'simplexity' design.

In fact, a lack of interest by counterfeiters in a new product can be bad news! Reports suggest that Samsung should worry about the future of its new 'Smartwatch,' since counterfeiters couldn't seem to care less.

Surveys represent another counting approach. Surveys can be designed for consumer or industrial targets. Consumer surveys are designed for consumer products such as shampoos and soap, while industrial surveys are targeted at institutional users/buyers of industrial products, such as video-conferencing systems. Compared to industrial surveys, consumer surveys are far larger, less reliable, and typically more time consuming and expensive to administer. Market forecasts for new products are often done through surveys. All surveys suffer from a major flaw: Will people do what they say they'll do?

Preparing a Sales Forecast Using Survey Data

Real Men Inc. wishes to estimate potential sales for its new retro-design hand-made, replaceable blade, gunmetal steel razor. It describes the product and sends pictures of a prototype to men between 50 and 70 years of age, asking them if they would buy the product (at a given price) if available. The size of the potential market for this premium priced product is about 3 million high-income, nostalgia-affected possible users.

The results of the survey come back:

Total number of respondents: 25,000, broken down as follows:

'Definitely buy'	*'Likely buy'*	*Don't know*	*Likely not buy*	*Definitely not buy*
3,000	6,000	9,000	4,000	3,000

What are the forecasted sales for the new product?

a)	Proportion of 'Definitely buy'	= 3,000/25,000 = 0.12 (purchase intent)
b)	Proportion of 'Likely buy'	= 6,000/25,000 = 0.24 (purchase intent)
c)	Size of market	= 3 million possibles
d)	Sales volume forecast	= PI * market size = (0.12 + 0.24) * 3 million
		= 1.08 million users

However, the real sales volume would be lower. Why? Because purchase intent (PI) does not always translate into purchase action. Research suggests that more than half of the people who say they will 'definitely buy' don't. And the proportion of 'likely buy' people who actually buy is even lower.

Let's assume that the probability of actual buy is as follows:
50 percent of 'definitely buy' respondents will actually buy, and
30 percent of 'likely buy' respondents will actually buy

In that case, our adjusted purchase intent numbers would be:

0.50 * PI of 'Definitely buy'	= 0.50 * 0.12 = 0.060, and
0.30 * PI of 'Likely buy'	= 0.30 * 0.24 = 0.072

Using the adjusted PIs,

Sales volume forecast	= (0.060 + 0.072) * 3 million
	= 0.396 million users

A far cry from the 1.08 million users forecasted using the unadjusted PIs.

One more refinement. Real Men Inc.'s marketing campaign may not reach all the 3 million potential users. Suppose 2 million potential users are exposed to the marketing campaign and become aware of the product. Thus:

Proportion of users aware of the product	= 2 million/3 million = 0.667 (market awareness)
Therefore:	
Revised sales volume forecast	= Market size * market awareness * sum of adjusted PIs
	= 3 million * 0.667 * (0.060 + 0.072)
	= 0.264 million users

How exactly companies adjust PIs and estimate market awareness is proprietary information. Models have been developed by MIT and others. A better, if more expensive, way to predict actual buying behavior is to run a real experiment with mock-up markets with real shelves and real competitive products (and perhaps vary prices, too).

Survey problems are also found in sampling methods. The sample may not be completely random or may not be representative of the general population. A low response rate may lead to non-respondent bias, where only respondents with specific characteristics respond, such as angry customers. Moreover, issues can arise from the survey questions themselves, which may be ambiguous or interpreted in several different ways. Asking similar questions at different parts of the survey and reconfirming responses through follow-up phone calls or mails are remedies for some of the above-mentioned problems. Survey data can be analyzed in different ways, ranging from simple counts and proportions to more sophisticated statistical methods. Surveys can now be developed and hosted relatively inexpensively on many sites such as "questionpro.com" and "SurveyMonkey.com," or conducted by market research firms.

A qualitative technique commonly employed for new product forecasting is forecasting by *analogy*. Experts identify and describe analogous products, rate their similarity to the current product, and draw on their experience with analogous products to develop forecasts for the current product. It is harder, though, to forecast the sales stages in the life cycle of a new product using analogies. The method relies on the similarity of the forecasted item with the items that are being used as analogies and is subjective.

KEY POINTS

- Synthesizing forecasts from the sales force (sales composite method) offers ground-level information, but salespeople can deliberately under-state forecasts if the forecasts are used for setting sales targets.
- Asking different functional managers to reach a forecast consensus (jury of executive opinion) queries multiple perspectives but may suffer from a 'dominant' personality effect.
- The Delphi technique asks a set of experts for their opinion about an entirely new product or concept, for which no prototype or data exists—can be slow or inconclusive.
- Market testing, a counting approach, observes and counts consumer responses to product/concept placement in selected pilot markets as a decision aid for a larger launch.
- Consumer surveys are used for obtaining consumer opinion on a large scale for a consumer product or idea. Industrial surveys are used to query industry buyers for industrial products.
- Surveys cannot tell whether respondents may actually do what they say they will do.
- Naïve forecasting simply assumes that tomorrow would be the same as today and can be used for benchmarking the accuracy of more sophisticated methods.

5.3.4 Forecasting with Data: Moving Average and Exponential Smoothing

Quantitative, data-based demand forecasts employ trends and factors that influence demand such as historical sales, seasonal patterns, historical impact of marketing promotions, and consumer income levels. The models can be used to develop historical forecasts to test their accuracy against actual past demand. Over time, market intelligence and experience hone such models.

Time Series Analysis

Time series analysis is popular with businesses. It does not seek to understand *why* events occur, but when— forecasts are a function of time. For example, we can look at historical data about temperature and forecast

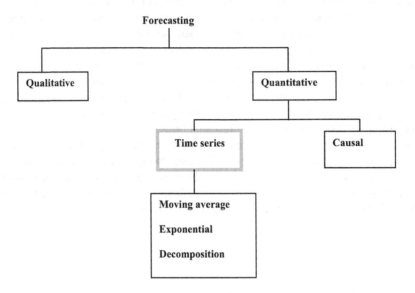

Figure 5.6 Quantitative Forecasting—Categories and Methods

that the air temperature will drop 20 degrees Fahrenheit between 4 p.m. and 10 p.m. We do not have to explain why (the sun goes down) if the business does not need to know the reason. Time series analysis is composed of several techniques:

- Moving averages: The forecast is a computed average of the past few periods' actual data.
- Exponential smoothing: A special type of moving average where the effects of previous periods declines exponentially.
- Time series decomposition: Breaking down data streams into discernible trends and seasonal/cyclical patterns.
- Box-Jenkins: A complex autoregressive moving average ARIMA model, not in the scope of this text.

Let us illustrate some of these methods using a small hypothetical dataset of student registration for 'Smart-Apps Development 101' over the last five semesters:

'Registration for Smart-Apps Development 101'

Semester		Actual registration
Spring	1	2,000
Fall	1	5,700
Spring	2	6,000
Fall	2	5,900
Spring	3	8,000
Fall	**3**	**To forecast**

Moving Average

Computing a moving average (MA) forecast calls for a decision on two important issues:

1   The number of periods to take into consideration, and
2   The weights to attach to each period of data considered

Semester		Computing a Simple Moving Average Forecast		
		Actual	*5-period*	*3-period*
		registration	*MAForecast**	*MAForecast***
Spring	1	2,000		
Fall	1	5,700		
Spring	2	6,000		
Fall	2	5,900		
Spring	3	8,000		
Fall	**3**		**5,520***	**6,633****

* Take preceding 5-period data/5 = (SP 1 to SP 3)/5 = (2,000 + 5,700 + 6,000 + 5,900 + 8,000)/5
(forecast for Fall 3) = 5,520

** Take preceding 3-period data/3 = (SP 2 to SP 3)/3 = (6,000 + 5,900 + 8,000)/3
(forecast for Fall 3) = 6,633 (approx.)

The calculation, as you see, is easy. The challenge in a moving average forecast is the choice of how many past periods of data to include in making the forecast. Look at the above dataset. Why do periods of extraordinarily high (Spring 3) or low (Spring 1) numbers (outliers) suddenly appear in the data? Note that the demand in Spring 3 is an unusually high 8,000 registrations—let's investigate. We find that a one-time cancellation of a similar course at a neighboring school caused many more students to enroll for 'Smart-Apps Development 101'during Spring 3. The cancellation of the course at the other school was a random event and happened suddenly with no prior warning or any possibility of being anticipated. It is not an event that we would expect to happen regularly. Thus we would wish the (random) data for Spring 3 to be *excluded* when preparing a forecast for a normal Fall 3 period. On the other hand, the high registration in Spring 3 could represent a permanent change in the business environment, such as the permanent elimination of that course from the curriculum of the other school. We would, therefore, expect higher enrollments at our school to continue for Fall 3. In that case, we would wish to *include* the data for Spring 3 to build our forecast for Fall 3. Analogous arguments could be raised for the low data (2,000) period of Spring 1. Whatever the decision, we could, of course, include or exclude the data for Spring 3 or Spring 1 manually, but it is easier to let our choice of the number of data periods do the task. A shorter 3-period moving average would *not* include the Spring 1 data, and thus let the Spring 3 number substantively affect the forecast for Fall 3. A longer 5-period moving average would include both Spring 1 and Spring 3 period data, allowing these outliers to offset each other.

Generally speaking, if we find that events underlying outlier data points in our market are truly random, we could expect a similar number of high and low outliers to occur over time. Such outliers would cancel each other out if we include a sufficiently long number of data periods in the moving average computation. In contrast, if we find that large changes in our historical data represent true turning points in the market, reflective of real, continuing change in the market, we would choose a shorter moving average time period. Setting a shorter moving average period implies that the probability of outliers canceling out each other is lower, that is, we *do* wish outliers to affect our forecast. In brief, we opt for shorter periods of data when we feel that the data history does not contain much randomness. We opt for longer periods of data when we believe that sharp changes in the data are primarily a result of random events.

We can also skip periods in a moving average forecast. For example, fall registrations may appear more closely related to other fall registrations, rather than spring registrations. In that case, we could skip the spring data altogether and compute a forecast for Fall 4 using, say, a 3-period moving average of actual data for Fall 1, Fall 2, and Fall 3 (when available).

The other issue in forecasting with moving averages is the importance or weight we attach to a period of data. The above periods of data were identically weighted for computing the simple moving average forecasts. However, the school registrar may observe from her experience that data from one semester removed from the current period is more reflective of the next semester, that is, Fall 2, rather than Spring 3, is more indicative of Fall 3. In that case, one may weight the periods differently. For instance, a 3-period weighted moving average for Fall 3 might be weighted .10 (SP 2), .70 (FA 2) and .20 (SP 3), as shown below.

Semester	Computing a Weighted Moving Average Forecast		
	Actual registration	Subjective weights	3-period weighted MAForecast
Spring 1	2,000	–	
Fall 1	5,700	–	
Spring 2	6,000	.10	
Fall 2	5,900	.70	
Spring 3	8,000	.20	
		1.00	
Fall 3			**6,330***

*3-period weighted moving average forecast for Fall 2010 = $\sum$(weight for period) (actual demand for period)
= 0.10(6,000) + 0.70(5,900) + 0.20(8,000) = 6,330

These weights are purely imaginary but do represent the perceived greater importance of Fall 2 numbers in forecasting Fall 3.

Weights are subjective (based on judgment), so it is advisable to set them by consensus and leave an audit trail for future forecasters. Also note that the above method of computing a weighted moving average by multiplying the period data with their corresponding weights works only if the weights sum up to 1.00 (try to make it so). If not so, and for any other sum of weights including 10, 100, or any other number, an additional step is needed where we divide the total weighted actual demand by the sum of the individual period weights:

Semester	Computing a Weighted Moving Average Forecast Using Any Weighting Values		
	Actual	*Subjective*	*3-period weighted*
	registration	*weights*	*MAForecast*
Spring 1	2,000	–	
Fall 1	5,700	–	
Spring 2	6,000	20 (imaginary numbers)	
Fall 2	5,900	140	
Spring 3	8,000	40	
		200	
Fall 3	**?**	(sum of weights)	**6,330** * (same result as with sum of weights = 1.00)

*3-period weighted MA forecast for Fall 3 = ∑(wt for period)(Actual demand for period)/sum of wts.
= [20(6,000) + 140(5,900) + 40(8,000)]/200 = 1,266,000/200
= **6,330**

Single Exponential Smoothing

Single exponential smoothing is a form of weighted moving average that takes the weighted average of past data, giving proportionately lower weights to progressively older periods of data. The exponential smoothing method takes the current period actual data into account, offering the opportunity to continuously review the relevance of current market data for forecasts.

$$F_{t+1} = \alpha D_t + (1 - \alpha) F_t,$$ (Equation 5.1)

where:

F_{t+1} = forecast for tomorrow

D_t = actual demand recorded today

F_t = demand that was forecasted for today

α = alpha, a weight that ranges between 0 and 1.00, also called a 'smoothing constant.'

Observe that setting $\alpha = 0$ would imply that our forecast for tomorrow would be identical to our forecast for today (F_t), while fixing $\alpha = 1.00$ would make our forecast identical to the actual demand experienced today. In the former case, we would implicitly ignore actual current market demand. In the latter case, we would disregard any forecast we may have made about today's demand.

In a way, setting α is akin to determining the relative importance of current market demand for the next period—if today's actual demand was an outlier driven by random events, we would set α at a low value. If, however, we believe that today's actual demand, outlier or not, is reflective of true, sustainable, changes in the market, α would be set at a correspondingly high figure. A surge in umbrella sales one day in June due to an unexpected rain shower should not be considered typical for sales during the normally sunny days of June. Therefore, α for forecasting tomorrow's umbrella sales (the rain shower is long gone) would be set low—we ignore the random event-driven outlier demand that happened today. But what if today's umbrella sales were high because our brand new website attracted large online orders from Southeast Asia (where monsoon season is beginning)? In that case, our forecast would take these conditions into account and fix α at a suitably high value. A new web presence, and rain during June in Southeast Asia, are sustainable events that are expected to continue on a regular basis.

Continuing with our course registration data set, an exponential forecast for Fall 3 given two alternative alphas, say, 0.2 and 0.6, would be computed as follows:

Semester	Single Exponential Smoothing		
	Actual	*Forecasted*	*Forecasted*
	registration	*registration (α = .20)*	*registration (α = .60)*
Spring 1	2,000	–	–
Fall 1	5,700	–	–
Spring 2	6,000	–	–
Fall 2	5,900	–	–
Spring 3	8,000	–	–
Fall 3		**To forecast**	**To forecast**

Using an alpha of 0.2:

$F_{t+1} = \alpha D_t + (1 - \alpha) F_t$,   where F_{t+1} = forecasted registration for tomorrow; t = today = Sp3
D_t = today's actual registration;
F_t = What we had forecasted for registration today;

So:

$F_{Fall\,3} = 0.2\,(D_{Sp\,3}) + 0.8\,(F_{Sp3})$

$= 0.2\,(8,000) + 0.8\,(F_{Sp3})$

But we don't have any forecast for Spring 3, so to find it:

$F_{Sp3} = 0.2\,(D_{Fall\,2}) + 0.8\,(F_{Fall\,2})$

$= 0.2\,(5,900) + 0.8\,(F_{Fall\,2})$

Well, we are not provided the forecast for Fall 2 either, so:

$F_{Fall\,2} = 0.2\,(D_{Sp\,2}) + 0.8\,(F_{Sp2})$

And so on . . . until we arrive at the first period of our historical data, Spring 1, which does not have a forecast, either. We assume a number, say equal to the actual demand in Spring 1, which was 2,000, as a starter forecast—any other number close to demand would do, too—since the weight of that number would diminish exponentially in subsequent period forecasts.

Now that we have a concocted forecast (2,000) for period Spring 1, we can go back in time and compute what our forecast would have been for Fall 1:

Single Exponential Smoothing (continued)

$$F_{Fall\ 1} = 0.2\ (D_{Sp\ 1}) + 0.8\ (F_{Sp\ 1})$$
$$= 0.2(2,000) + 0.8(2,000)$$
$$= 2,000$$

With this forecast for Fall 1, we can similarly go back in time and compute what our forecast would have been for Spring 2;

$$F_{Sp\ 2} = 0.2\ (D_{Fall\ 1}) + 0.8\ (F_{Fall\ 1})$$
$$= 0.2(5,700) + 0.8(2,000)$$
$$= 2,740,\ \text{and}$$

Similarly,

$$F_{Fall\ 2} = 0.2\ (D_{Sp\ 2}) + 0.8\ (F_{Sp\ 2})$$
$$= 0.2(6,000) + 0.8(2,740)$$
$$= 3,392,\ \text{and}$$

$$F_{Sp\ 3} = 0.2\ (D_{Fall\ 2}) + 0.8\ (F_{Fall\ 2})$$
$$= 0.2(5,900) + 0.8(3,392)$$
$$= 3,894$$

Having gone back in time to develop forecasts for all historical periods till today, that is, Spring 3, we are now ready to prepare a forecast for tomorrow, Fall 3.

$$F_{Fall\ 3} = 0.2\ (D_{Sp\ 3}) + 0.8\ (F_{Sp\ 3})$$
$$= 0.2(8,000) + 0.8\ (3,894)$$
$$= 4,715$$

In a similar fashion, we use the provided alpha of 0.60 to generate a series of historical forecasts for the data periods. The computed forecasts for the past periods, as well as for Fall 3, appear below:

Semester	Computed Forecasts		
	Actual	*Forecast*	*Forecast*
	registration	*α: 0.2*	*α: 0.6*
Spring 1	2,000	2,000	2,000
Fall 1	5,700	2,000	2,000
Spring 2	6,000	2,740	4,220
Fall 2	5,900	3,392	5,288
Spring 3	8,000	3,894	5,655
Fall 3		**4,715**	**7,062**

In practice, one would generate forecasts with a variety of alphas and pick the one that provides the lowest error, on average. Businesses generally do not use extreme alpha values. If the forecast consistently varies widely from actuals, higher alpha values are recommended. Too frequent use of high alpha values may signal the presence of a trend in the data, a situation that is better handled by other methods.[13] Single exponential smoothing is relatively easy to operate once set up, with just one data entry for actual demand for the current period.

You may have noticed that our data set has an upward trend. It is deliberately designed to be so in order to draw your attention to an important shortcoming of all average-based forecasting methods. The downside of any average-based forecast is that the forecast would necessarily lag real-time changes in the data, since averages smoothen the fluctuations in the raw data. Thus, moving averages or other averages-based methods such as single exponential smoothing are not the ideal techniques for data with a strong trend because, like all averages, they lag real time. There are exponential models that can incorporate trend and seasonality in the data, but these are not described here since trend and seasonality are better handled by time series decomposition, as described later in the chapter.

5.3.5 Measuring Forecast Accuracy

Which Fall 3 forecast should we adopt for planning purposes? Should we organize resources for the forecasted 4,715 registrations (α =0.2), or for the forecasted 7,062 registrations (α = 0.6)? This determination requires a comparison of the relative accuracy of the two forecasts, measured as error:

Forecast error = actual minus forecast
(Look in the 'formulas' section at the end of the chapter for examples on computing error measures.)

A negative forecast error implies that the forecast was greater than the actual, termed over-forecasting. A positive forecast error implies that the forecast was lower than the actual, termed under-forecasting.

Forecast accuracy % = (100 − % forecast error) = [100 − (forecast error/actual)*100]
Cumulative forecast error (CFE) = sum of all errors.
Average (mean) error = CFE/number of periods

Forecast directionality is called forecast bias. A perfectly unbiased forecaster or forecasting method is one that provides an average forecast error of zero. For example:

Month	Actual demand	Forecaster A	Forecaster B	Error A	Error B
January	100	80	110	20	(−)10
February	90	85	75	5	15
March	105	110	107	(−)5	(−)2
April	95	105	98	(−)10	(−)3
Average	97.50	95.00	97.5	10	0

Forecaster B, with an average forecast error of zero, is a perfectly unbiased forecaster. Practically speaking, forecasts almost always carry bias—the one with the lower average error would be the less biased one. A negative bias (error) means that we are over-forecasting, since 'error = actual − forecast.' A positive bias (error) means that we are under-forecasting. The effects of bias depend on which situation a business thinks it can manage better: if more customers actually show up than forecasted (positive bias; loss of sales and goodwill) or fewer customers turn up than forecasted (negative bias; additional costs for wasted resources).

Mean squared error (MSE) = Square each error for each period and compute the mean across periods. (See 'error computations' for the exponential smoothing example below.)

MSE, by squaring error, provides a quick eye-ball look at individual period errors, highlighting periods of error highs or lows. It also makes the errors absolute by eliminating their signs and thus avoids a situation where a poor forecaster cannot be distinguished from a better one. Think of it this way—a forecaster with small errors would have a small average error. Yet, another forecaster, one who makes bad forecasts but with large positive and negative swings, may end up with the same average error. The large positive and negative errors would offset one another. MSE prevents that by squaring the errors into absolute values.

Root mean square error (RMSE) = √MSE ≈ (approximately equals) standard deviation of the error.
   Mean absolute percentage error (MAPE) = Convert individual period error into absolute value, divide by actual demand for that period, and multiply by 100. Sum up the resultant percentage figures across all periods and compute the mean. (See 'error computations' for the exponential smoothing example below.)

MAPE is a relative form of error, telling us that the error in the forecast was x% above or below the actual demand, on average. It provides a sense of perspective on the error. For example, a forecast error of 100 when actual demand is 200 (MAPE = 50 percent) is significant, but a forecast error of 100 when actual demand is 10,000 (MAPE = 1 percent) is trivial. MAPE does not indicate bias, that is, whether the forecast was higher or lower than actual demand, on average. MAPE is the *only* error metric that can be used to compare the magnitude of errors across different datasets. *MAPE can be greater than 100 percent.* Also, if there are zero values in the actuals column, there will be a division by zero, and MAPE may be undefined.

Mean absolute deviation (MAD) = Take absolute values of error and compute the mean absolute error across periods. (See computations for the exponential smoothing example later in chapter.)

MAD tells us that actual demand was 'x' units above or below the forecast, on average. MAD does not indicate error bias. MAD also allows a statistical underpinning to error statements. One standard deviation ≈ 1.25 * MAD, and we can calculate confidence intervals around the mean error using the numerical value of MAD obtained from the data.

We now take our computed exponential forecasts for all the historical periods and measure the degree of error for the two competing, α: 0.2 and α: 0.6 based forecasts, as shown below.

Semester	Error Computations Using α:0.2 and α:0.6										
	Actual	Forecast	Forecast	Error	Error	SE*	SE*	APE**	APE**	AD***	AD
	Regis.	α: 0.2	α: 0.6	α:0.2	α: 0.6	α: 0.2	α: 0.6	α: 0.2	α: 0.6	α: 0.2	α: 0.6
Spring 1	2,000	2,000	2,000	0	0	0	0	0%	0%	0	0
Fall 1	5,700	2,000	2,000	3,700	3,700	1,369	1,369	65%**	65%	3,700	3,700
Spring 2	6,000	2,740	4,220	3,260	1,780	1,063	317	54%	30%	3,260	1,780
Fall 2	5,900	3,392	5,288	2,508	612	629	38	43%	10%	2,508	612
Spring 3	8,000	3,894	5,655	4,106	2,345	1,686	550	51%	29%	4,106	2,345
		MEAN	ERROR	2,715	1,688	949	455	43%	27%	2,715	1,688

	Forecast	Forecast
	α:0.2	α: 0.6
Fall 3	**4,715**	**7,062**

All figures are rounded off;

Error = actual registration minus forecast

---

* SE = Squared error in 0000's;** APE = absolute % error = (absolute error/Actual) * 100 = e.g. Fall 1 at α:0.2 = (3,700/5,700) * 100 ≈ 65%

*** AD = Absolute deviation = |Error|

Summing up and computing the errors:

Error type	α:0.2	α: 0.6	Formula	
CFE	13,574	8,437	(Sum of error column)	Note that negatives, if present in the error column, would offset the positives
Average error	2,715	1,688	(CFE/n)	n=5 periods. Positive, so on average, forecasts are lower than actual.
MSE*		949	455	(Sum of SE column/n)	Note Fall 2 error is low; Spring 3 error is high—ask why?
* in (0000's)				
MAPE	43%	27%	(Sum of APE column/n)	That is, the error in the forecast was 43% (or 27%) above or below the actual demand, on average
MAD	2,715	1,688	(Sum of AD column/n)	That is, actual demand was 2,715 (or 1,688 units) above or below the forecast, on average. In this case, MAD is *identical to the average error*, since no negative errors are present, and thus *absolute error values are identical to error values.*

An α of 0.6 generates a forecast with errors lower than that with an alpha of 0.2. Therefore, we recommend preparing for 7,062 registrations, the α 0.6 forecast for Fall 3.

But hold on, how *sure* are we about that recommendation? You can anticipate that question from your boss or client every time you present a forecast. We can use the qualities of MAD to respond. Our MAD for an alpha 0.6 forecast was 1,688, indicating that actual demand has been, on average, 1,688 units higher or lower than the forecasts. Also note that 1 standard deviation (σ) is $\approx 1.25 * $ MAD, and that our mean (average) error was 1,688. In *this* case, mean error is identical to MAD since all errors were positive, and thus the absolute values of an error would be identical to its non-absolute value. Mean absolute deviation would therefore, not differ from mean error. Assuming errors are normally distributed,

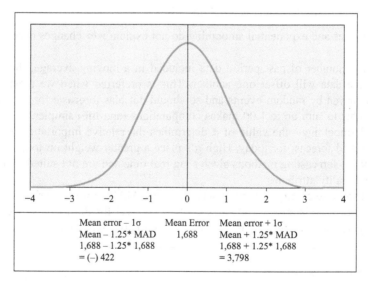

Mean error − 1σ	Mean Error	Mean error + 1σ
Mean − 1.25* MAD	1,688	Mean + 1.25* MAD
1,688 − 1.25* 1,688		1,688 + 1.25* 1,688
= (−) 422		= 3,798

Figure 5.7 Normally Distributed Errors

The forecast error would thus vary between (−)422 and 3,798, 68.3 percent of the time (± 1 standard deviation). In other words, we can forecast with 68.3 percent confidence that the actual demand for Fall 3 would range between 6,640 (forecasted 7,062 minus 422) and 10,860 (7,062 plus 3,798). That's a wide spread, but the best we can do given the alphas we were handed. We can expand the confidence level to 95.4 percent (±2 σ), or 99.7 percent (±3 σ), but that would, of course, expand the range, too. The trade-off is between a greater confidence level and a tighter range. MAD can also be used to create a tracking signal and control charts that let us look at error behavior over a period of time.

A good forecasting method aims to a) minimize bias (average error) and b) minimize MAPE or MSE. It is possible that minimizing MAPE or MSE may not provide an unbiased forecast—and we may be willing to tolerate a little bias in the interest of accuracy. It is also possible that a minimum MAPE may not mean a minimum MSE. The MSE can shoot up because of a single large error. A large single period error can skew the MSE figure, since the method squares each period's error (and then calculates the average squared error). MAPE uses absolute error values and avoids this problem.

While presenting, use at least one measure each for bias, magnitude, and confidence level. People are conditioned to ask for the mean, so provide the average error. Note whether it's positive or negative and point out the bias present in the forecast. For magnitude, provide MAPE, readily understood, since it presents error as a percentage of actuals. Use MAD to furnish a statistical basis to the forecast. Compare the error associated with your forecasting method to the error being experienced with the forecasting method in current use, or the error that would be associated with a naïve extrapolation approach. Use Theil's U statistic to see how our chosen techniques compare to the low cost simple naive forecasting method. Theil's U Stat = standard error of the model/standard error of the naive model. U Stats below 1.00 indicate model superiority over the naive approach in terms of magnitude of error. Use the results to evaluate the *incremental* benefit from your forecast (include the additional costs of your method).

KEY POINTS

Moving Averages and Single Exponential Smoothing

- Moving averages and exponential smoothing do not explain *why* changes occur in what is being forecasted.
- The more the number of past period data included in a moving average, the more likely that outliers in the data will offset one another. This is preferred when we reasonably know that outliers are driven by random events and so should not bias forecasts for normal periods.
- Setting weights to sum up to 1.00 makes computations (and life) simpler.
- Exponential smoothing—the value of α determines the relative importance of today's demand vs. what we had forecast for today. High α's place a greater weight on today's demand.
- Averages-based forecasting methods always lag real time and are not suited to data with marked trend or seasonality attributes.
- Forecast errors: Use average error for detecting bias, MAPE for comparing error magnitude as a percentage of actuals, and MAD for a confidence level for the forecast. Compute Theil's U stat to compare the error relative to the error from a naive approach.

5.3.6 *Forecasting with Data: Time Series Decomposition*

Time series decomposition:

Our familiar registration data set has been changed in order to perform time series decomposition.

Semester		Actual Number of Registrations
Spring	1	3,000
Fall	1	4,000
Spring	2	3,200
Fall	2	4,300
Spring	3	3,900
Fall	3	5,000
Spring	4	3,800
Fall	4	5,600
Spring	5	4,000
Fall	5	5,900
(10 periods of data)		

Do you see any pattern in the data set above? Time series decomposition breaks down raw data into trend, seasonal, and cyclical components, to the extent that such are present. A trend can be identified by simply using regression to model demand as a function of time—using Excel charts, the raw data scatter plot suggests an upward trend in our data.

There seems to be a trend as well as seasonality in the data. An Excel regression run on the data (Tools/ Data Analysis/Regression) to extract the trend element yields the following model:

*# of registrations/semester = 3,013 + 228 * Semester#* (figures are rounded off).

The gradient of the fitted line is 228, indicating that registration rises on average by 228 units as a semester goes by (trend).

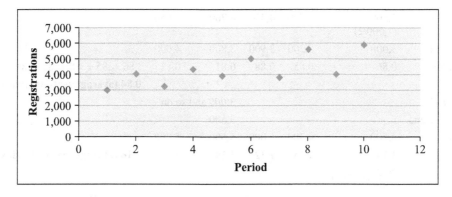

Figure 5.8 Scatter Plot Raw Demand Data

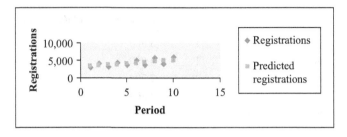

Figure 5.9 Trend in Data: Period Line Fit Plot

When data repeats an up or down pattern at regular intervals, seasonality exists. The scatter plot of original demand shown in figure 5.8 suggests the presence of seasonality (and trend) in the data. We can decompose and account for seasonality using a simple proportion method or with more complex regression methods.

Simple Proportion

This method adjusts for *seasonality only*. The seasonal factor is first computed for every season for each year as a ratio: the demand for each season/the average period demand. The average period demand in a particular year is the total demand for that year divided by the number of seasons. For example, total demand in Academic Year 1 (Spring + Fall) was 3,000 + 4,000 = 7,000; the average period demand = 7,000/2 = 3,500; and thus the seasonal index for Spring 1 = 3,000/3,500 = 0.86. We re-arrange our data set above in order to compute the average seasonal indices for Spring and Fall:

Years	Computing a Seasonal Index					
	1	2	3	4	5	
Total demand per year	7,000	7,500	8,900	9,400	9,900	
Average period demand	3,500 (7,000/2)	3,750	4,450	4,700	4,950	
Spring demand	3,000	3,200	3,900	3,800	4,000	
Seasonal index	0.86	0.85	0.88	0.81	0.81	(.86 + .85 + .88 + .81 + .81)/5 = 0.84
						0.84 (average seasonal index for spring)
Period demand				*3,000* and so on		
Avg. period demand				3,500		
Fall demand	4,000	4,300	5,000	5,600	5,900	
Seasonal index	1.14	1.15	1.12	1.19	1.19	**1.16 (average seasonal index for fall)**
	$\frac{4000}{3500}$ and so on					

Supposing we are handed a forecast for a total of 11,000 registrations for the entire year 6, spring and fall. This forecast can be broken down into a seasonally adjusted forecast.

Seasonally Adjusted Forecast for 11,000 Total Registrations

	Total forecast for Year 6	Average period demand	Average seasonal index	Year 6 seasonally adjusted forecast
Spring 6	—	5,500 (11,000/2)	* 0.84 (from above)	= **4,620**
Fall 6	—	5,500	* 1.16	= **6,380**
	11,000			11,000

We multiply the average period demand by the average seasonal index to arrive at the seasonally adjusted forecast. The simple proportion method results in a forecast of 4,620 registrations for Spring 6 and 6,380 registrations for Fall 6, after adjusting for seasonality.

Regression

A more rigorous approach that accounts for both trend and seasonality is the least squares regression method, using a multiplicative approach:

Forecast = trend * seasonal

An alternative is the additive approach:

Forecast = trend + seasonal

The multiplicative approach is more rational since the seasonal variation would increase as the data trends, such that the larger the trend forecast, the greater its seasonal variation.

The regression method consists of five steps:

1   Compute the average seasonal index (repeating the simple proportion approach)

Years	Compute Average Seasonal Index					
	1	2	3	4	5	
Total demand per year	7,000	7,500	8,900	9,400	9,900	
Average period demand	3,500 (7,000/2)	3,750	4,450	4,700	4,950	
Spring demand	3,000	3,200	3,900	3,800	4,000	
Seasonal index	0.86	0.85	0.88	0.81	0.81	(.86+.85+.88+.81+.81)/5 = 0.84
						0.84 (average seasonal index for Spring)
Period demand	*3,000* and so on					
	....					
Avg. period demand	3,500					

(Continued)

(Continued)

Years	Compute Average Seasonal Index					
	1	2	3	4	5	
Fall demand	4,000	4,300	5,000	5,600	5,900	
Seasonal index	1.14	1.15	1.12	1.19	1.19	**1.16 (average seasonal index for Fall)**
	4,000 and so on _____					
	―――――――					
	3,500					

2   De-seasonalize the data by dividing the raw demand for each period by the average seasonal index, as shown in the table below (all figures rounded off):

Year	1	2	3	4	5	Average Seasonal Index
Spring demand	3,000	3,200	3,900	3,800	4,000	**0.84**
De-seasonalized demand	3,571 (3,000/0.84)	3,810	4,643	4,524	4,762	(seasonality had depressed demand to the extent of 84%, so figures increase once seasonality has been removed: e.g., Spring demand notes that 3,000 is 84% of 3,571)
Fall demand	4,000	4,300	5,000	5,600	5,900	**1.16**
De-seasonalized demand	3,448 (4,000/1.16)	3,707	4,310	4,828	5,086	(seasonality had inflated demand to the extent of 116%, so figures decrease once seasonality has been removed: e.g., Fall demand note that 4,000 is 116% of 3,448)

3   Build a regression model (least squares line) using the de-seasonalized data to account for the trend component of the data.

De-seasonalized demand	
Spring 1	3,571
Fall 1	3,448
Spring 2	3,810
Fall 2	3,707
Spring 3	4,643
Fall 3	4,310
Spring 4	4,524
Fall 4	4,828
Spring 5	4,762
Fall 5	5,086

Note how the de-seasonalization smoothes the data pattern.

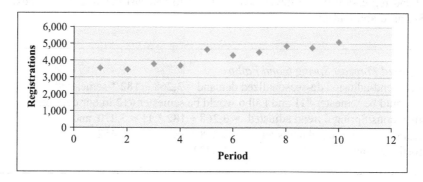

Figure 5.10 Scatter Plot De-seasonalized Demand

Contrast with the original data with seasonality:

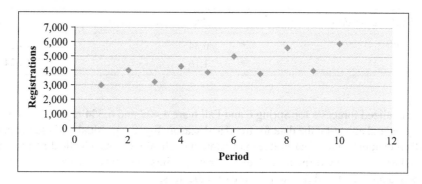

Figure 5.11 Scatter Plot Original Demand (Raw Data)

Developing a linear regression model with the de-seasonalized demand data, picking semester period as the independent variable and de-seasonalized demand as the dependent variable, we obtain:

Forecasted trend adjusted de-seasonalized demand = 3,268 + 182*semester#

Note the trend component (182) in the above model.

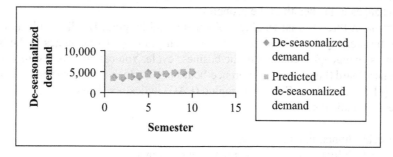

Figure 5.12 Forecast with De-seasonalized Demand

4   Use the trend regression model developed in step 3 to forecast demand for the next two semesters, that is, Spring 6 and Fall 6:

Trend-adjusted Forecast Spring 6 and Fall 6
Forecasted trend-adjusted de-seasonalized demand = 3,268 + 182 * semester#
Spring 6 would be semester #11 and Fall 6 would be semester #12 in our dataset:
# of registrations/Spring 6 trend adjusted = 3,268 + 182 * 11 = 5,270, and
# of registrations/Fall 6 trend adjusted   = 3,268 + 182 * 12 = 5,452
    Total for year   = 10,722

---

5   Seasonalize the forecast by multiplying the de-seasonalized forecasts with the related average seasonal indices.

	Trend forecast de-seasonalized		*Average seasonal index*		*Seasonalized forecast*
Spring 6	5,270	*	0.84	=	**4,427**
Fall 6	5,452	*	1.16	=	**6,324**

The final seasonalized forecasts for Spring 6 and Fall 6 are 4,427 and 6,324 registrations, respectively.

After identifying and adjusting the data for trend and seasonality, the residual variation could be attributed in part to cyclical elements. Our dataset does not contain cyclical patterns. Cyclical patterns vary in length and duration and are extremely difficult to detect. Turning points in cycles, such as seen in business cycles, are best understood and identified through the use of indicators.

Using Indicators

We spent a week searching for a stainless steel oven on Google. Little did we know that economists from the Federal Reserve and other banks may be using our (and others') Google search data to forecast the state of economy. Studies have found that search volumes on Google for certain products correlate with and can be used as indicators of business cycle behavior.[14] Indicators are things whose demand/sales/occurrence correlate strongly with changes in the health of the economy.

Indicators come in three forms: leading, coincident, and lagging. Leading indicators change *ahead* of changes in the business cycle, coincident indicators change *along with* changes in the business cycle, and lagging indicators change *after* changes in the business cycle. You can look up examples of such indicators at The Conference Board (http://www.conference-board.org/), which maintains and interprets economic indices of leading (LEI), coincident (CEI), and lagging (LAG) indicators. The Conference Board's LEI currently consists of these ten indicators:

*   Average weekly hours, manufacturing
*   Average weekly initial claims for unemployment insurance
*   Manufacturers' new orders, consumer goods, and materials

- ISM® New Orders Index
- Manufacturers' new orders, nondefense capital goods excluding aircraft orders
- Building permits, new private housing units
- Stock prices, 500 common stocks
- Leading Credit Index™
- Interest rate spread, 10-year Treasury bonds less federal funds
- Average consumer expectations for business conditions

Not all indicators in an index move consistently at a point in time. For example, the Conference Board LEI for the U.S. increased slightly in August 2015, with large positive contributions from the yield spread and building permits more than offsetting the large negative contributions from initial unemployment claims and the ISM® new orders index.

As the Board reports in its September 18, 2015, release, two of the ten indicators that make up The Conference Board LEI for the U.S. increased significantly, helping to offset negative contributions from initial unemployment claims and the ISM® new orders index. Overall, in the six-month period ending August 2015, the leading economic index increased 2.3 percent (about a 4.7 percent annual rate), an improvement from its growth of 2.0 percent (about a 4.1 percent annual rate) over the previous six months. The strengths among the leading indicators remain more widespread than the weaknesses. The board feels that "The U.S. LEI suggests economic growth will remain moderate into the New Year, with little reason to expect growth to pick up substantially."[15] We'll see.

Note that changes in indicators may not always reflect changes in economic cycles. Indicators based on purchases and inventories may rise for non-cyclic reasons, such as businesses stockpiling in anticipation of a port strike.

Some Unusual Indicators

Alan Greenspan, ex-Federal Reserve chief, mentions men's underwear sales as a leading indicator! Data suggest that underwear is among the first things men stop buying when a recession looms, and by the same token, replenish once the recession shows signs of improvement.[16] Women seem less inclined to wear old undergarments with holes. Men wear tighter underwear, too, during recessions, preferring briefs over baggy boxers (figure out that one on your own). Bad times are also reflected in more conservative wear, so conversely, seeing more plunging necklines and higher hemlines on the street should signify economic recovery. Other indicators of the presence of tough times are a rise in product returns of high-price discretionary items and purchase patterns of staples that show bunching up at month's beginning (welfare checks and stamps are often issued at the beginning of the month).

After the trend, seasonal, and cyclical components of a data set are understood, the variation that still remains is simply classified as 'random,' that which we cannot explain or anticipate. For a manager, the important thing is to identify and track the key economic indicators for his/her business. Walmart, for instance, may track consumer expectations and the unemployment rate to try to anticipate turning points in the retail business cycle. It will likely use government-published data to track such indicators. Recently, though, Google and other online search sources are becoming important, since relevant data is available in almost real time to business, while the Department of Commerce data lags by more than a month.

With all this analysis, the record for economists forecasting recessions is rather poor:

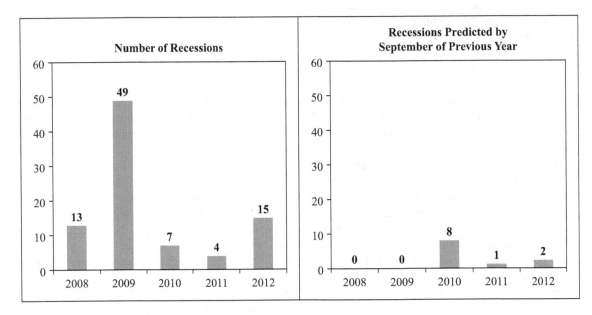

Figure 5.13 Track Record—Forecasting Recession

Source: Used with permission from Hites Ahir and Prakash Loungani, "Fail Again? Fail Better? Forecasts by Economists During the Great Recession," *George Washington University Research Program in Forecasting Seminar*, Jan. 30, 2014.

Forecasts made in September 2007 missed all of the sixty-two recessions around the world during 2008 and 2009. Their forecast of two recessions in 2012 also came up woefully short of the fifteen that actually happened. Of interest is that forecasts are revised each month to reflect current data—but apparently not by enough. Perhaps the data available is not adequate, or there is a natural reluctance to avoid being seen as a doomsayer, or experts are just slow to accept that they could be so wrong.[17]

KEY POINTS

Time Series Decomposition

- Time series decomposition does not explain the underlying reasons for changes in forecasted variables.
- Raw data is decomposed into trend, seasonal, cyclical, and random components.
- Trends are consistent upwards or downwards slopes in the data – best detected by data plots and modeled as the slope of a regression line.
- Seasonality manifests in the dips or crests in the data seen at fixed intervals every year—best detected by data plots and modeled through the construction of seasonal indices.

- Trend and seasonality can be captured and accommodated in forecasts using regression.
- Cyclicality refers to the rise and dips in the data that happen at irregular intervals and span across many years—typically business cycles—best detected by indicators and (imperfectly) modeled with econometric models (outside scope of text).
- Leading indicators change *prior* to changes in a business cycle. Coincident indicators change *with* changes in a business cycle. Lagging indicators change *after* changes in a business cycle.

5.3.7 Forecasting with Data: Causal Methods

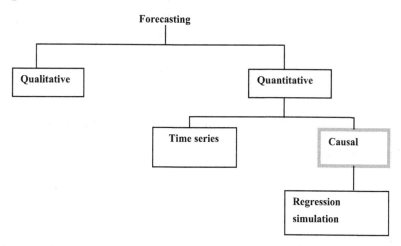

Figure 5.14 Forecasting—Causal Models

Causal analysis is not required for every forecast, just for those forecasts where understanding *why* events change is important for a business. Causality in business is difficult to prove with data but can be argued using logic. For that reason, every causal model must begin with a sound theory, and the soundness of the theory must be discussed extensively with experts. Only then should data collection, analysis, and model building begin.

A Sound Theory?

A study in a remote island concluded that body lice is the cause of good health. Researchers studied the inhabitants of the island and found that sick people did not have body lice, while healthy people did—ergo, lice is necessary for good health. Assuming that the data collection and analysis were performed properly, does this logic hold? Of course not! It was soon found out that a third unconsidered factor, body temperature, explained the apparent causal relationship. Sick people usually develop fever, which caused body lice to flee their host for cooler climes (people without fever). Healthier (cooler) bodies attracted lice, while sick (hotter, in the medical sense) bodies repelled lice. The observed data relationship between body lice and health was a spurious correlation and not a causal association. The lesson here is not to confuse correlation for causation and consequently mis-specify a model.

Among causal methods, regression is a common choice for business forecasting. Consider sales forecasting and the many factors that potentially cause changes in sales. One theory is that changes in sales, the dependent variable, are caused primarily by pricing and advertising decisions, both independent variables. Does it sound like a credible theory? Past studies and experience certainly seem to say so. Given a sound theory, we collect historical data on sales, price and advertising, and develop a multiple regression model for forecasting sales.

Sales $	Price $	Advertising $
12	10	20
10	12	14
14	9	16
52	6	60
25	8	28
36	7	38
55	5	65

Using Excel (Tools/Data Analysis/Regression), we develop the following regression model:

Sales = 15.80 − 1.49 * price + 0.74 * advertising

QUICK CHECK

(−) 1.49 is the unstandardized regression coefficient for price, i.e., one unit increase/reduction in price would reduce/increase sales by 1.49 units on average, provided advertising levels are kept constant. Similarly, one unit increase/reduction in advertising would increase/reduce sales by 0.74 units on average, provided price is kept constant.

Using the above model to forecast sales at a price level of $11, advertisement remaining constant at $15:

Forecasted sales = 15.80 − 1.49 * 11 + 0.74 * 15 = 10.51 units

Can this model be trusted for broader application? Let's simplify the output table from our Excel regression analysis—the outputs from other stats packages are similar.

We employ a basic and quick four-step process to interpret the output:

1   Look at the R square: The explanatory power of the model represented by the 'R square' of 0.987968 indicates that variations in price and advertising, taken together, explain 98.7968 percent of the variation of sales around mean sales.

2   Look at the 'Significance F': The 'Significance F' figure of 0.000145 indicates a confidence level of 99.9855% (1 minus Sig. F) for the model as a whole. A 'Significance F' number ≤ 0.05, corresponding

SUMMARY OUTPUT

Regression Statistics	
Multiple R	0.99396583
R Square	0.98796807
Adjusted R Square	0.9819521
Standard Error	2.5400185
Observations	7

ANOVA

	df	SS	MS	F	Significance F
Regression	2	2119.050367	1059.552	164.22434	0.000144767
Residual	4	25.80677586	6.451694		
Total	6	2144.857143			

	Coefficients	Standard Error	t Stat	p-value	Lower 95%	Upper 95%	Lower 95.0%	Upper 95.0%
Intercept	15.7968572	12.6134679	1.2523802	0.278657899	-19.22374402	50.8174584	-19.223744	50.8174584
Price $	-1.4937486	1.057772986	-1.4121637	0.230758227	-4.430597204	1.443100054	-4.4305972	1.443100054
Advt .$	0.74093638	0.122294904	6.0586039	0.003746548	0.401391295	1.080481472	0.401391295	1.080481472

Figure 5.15 Regression Output from Excel

to a confidence level of 95 percent or greater $(1 - \text{Sig. F})$ is considered necessary for models in business. Statistically, the F-test posits H0: the regression coefficients = 0, vs. H1: at least one of the regression coefficients $\neq 0$.

3 Look at the 'coefficients': The regression coefficients of price and advertising, $(-)1.49$ and 0.74 (rounded off), provide the average explanatory power of price and advertising on changes in sales. These are not trivial in that a $ increase/reduction in price is associated with an average 1.49 unit reduction/increase in sales; and similarly, a $ increase/reduction in advertising is associated with an average 0.74 unit increase/reduction in sales.

4 Look at the 'p-value': The p-value is interpreted similar to the 'Significance F,' and should be ≤ 0.05, corresponding to a confidence level of 95 percent or above. Statistically, the p-value provides the p-value result for the test H0: the regression coefficient = 0, vs. H1: the regression coefficient $\neq 0$.

The p-value for advertising reads as 0.003747, well under the stipulated 0.05 standard, indicating a confidence level of 99.6253 percent (1 minus p-value). However, the p-value for price is 0.230758, much above the required 0.05 mark, indicating a confidence level of only 76.69242 percent (1 minus p-value).[18] Since a 95 percent minimum confidence level is generally prescribed for business models, the statistical validity of price as an independent variable is rejected. Price has no place as a predictor in our regression model.

We should remove price from the model and re-run the regression using just advertising as an independent variable. Try it, and you will see that the results actually show an improvement.

QUICK CHECK

Running a regression on a retailer's dataset results in the following model:

Sales = 4 + 7income − 5distance from downtown

R^2: 0.78; Significance of F: 0.04; *p*-value for b_1: 0.04; *p*-value for b2: 0.09

Evaluate the above model.

Step 1: R^2 is 0.78, meaning 78 percent of the variation in sales is explained by changes in income and distance from downtown, together. This is a strong relationship, useful for decision making.

Step 2: Significance of F is 0.04, meaning that we are 96 percent (1 − Sig of F) confident about the statistical significance of our conclusion at Step 1 above. This is higher than the norm of 95 percent in business.

Step 3: The coefficient for income is 7, meaning that a unit increase (decrease) in income results in a 7-unit increase (decrease) in sales, on average, keeping distance from downtown unchanged. Similarly, a unit increase (decrease) in distance from downtown results in a 5-unit decrease (increase) in sales, on average, keeping income unchanged. Note the negative relationship for distance from downtown. These are strong relationships, useful for decision making.

Step 4: The *p*-value for b_1 is 0.04, meaning that we are 96 percent confident (1 − *p*-value) about the statistical significance of the coefficient for income. However, we are only 91 percent confident (1 − 0.09) in the case of b_2, the coefficient for distance from downtown.

Conclusion: Reject the model. It fails at step 4. Re-run without distance from downtown as a predictor variable.

Any causal model should *first be plotted* with data. A relationship has to be visually seen, if possible, because statistical properties can be deceptive.

Data Set 1		Data Set 2	
y	*x*	*y*	*x*
64	100	49	64
49	64	36	64
64	169	60	64
81	81	80	64
64	120	70	64
100	195	50	64
49	36	30	64
16	17	150	361
121	145	30	64
25	50	63	64
36	25	48	64

The regressions and plots look like this:

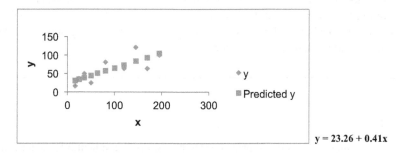

$$y = 23.26 + 0.41x$$

Figure 5.16 Regression and Plot For Dataset 1

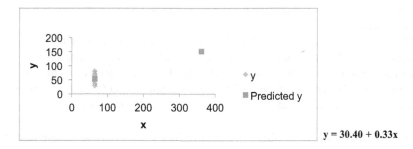

$$y = 30.40 + 0.33x$$

Figure 5.17 Regression and Plot For Dataset 2

Obviously, there is no relationship between *x* and *y* in Dataset 2. Yet, the regression models for both data sets look similar. Dataset 2 is not a viable candidate for regression analysis or for any other causal model.

Beyond initial plotting, the usual cautions apply. Make sure you have: clean and reliable historical data with outliers identified and removed; a linear relationship between the independent variables and the dependent variable; non-correlated and normally distributed error terms; and non-random values of the independent variables. It is unwise to extrapolate beyond the historical data range. For example, if a historical price data range lies between \$5 and \$12, do not try to forecast sales for a price greater than (e.g., \$13) or less than (e.g., \$4) the range limits, as we do not know the relationship between sales and price for any value outside of the range of the historical independent variable data. Sometimes 'weird' results emerge. For example:

Sales = 15.80 + 1.49*price – 0.74*advertising.

Could you spot what's 'weird' in the above model? You're right—it shows that a dollar increase in price would *increase* sales by 1.49 units on average, while a dollar increase in advertising would *reduce* sales by 0.74 units. Such cases may occur because of multi-collinearity, a situation where there is a high degree of correlation between two independent variables, i.e., they proxy each other. The solution is to identify such inter-correlated independent variables (Tools/Data Analysis/Correlations in Excel) and remove one variable out of the offending pair(s) based on variable reliability, data collection cost, or other criteria. Sometimes, causal factors cannot be measured directly. For instance, soda sales are likely to be causally affected by consumer thirst, but how does one measure and record reliable data for 'thirst'? One can look for a proxy, such as outside temperature, but, obviously, thirst is associated with many other factors. Finally. regression can also handle non-linear relationships, either by transforming variables (using log, square root) into linear form, or by developing non-linear models (quadratic, cubic).

OM IN PRACTICE

Regression in the Life Insurance Business

Life insurance companies run blood and urine tests to assess applicant health for determining premium and eligibility for insurance. It takes time and money, requiring sending nurses to applicant homes, specimen transportation, lab analysis, and doctor reads. Some insurance companies are investigating whether they can do away with lab tests and instead draw a picture of the applicant's health by looking at demographic attributes and behavior, such as online shopping, magazine subscriptions, leisure activities, and information from social media sites.

Aviva PLC (U.S.) hired Deloitte Consulting to run similar data on 60,000 applicants and found that a predictive regression model mimicked the conclusions drawn by the traditional lab test evaluation method.

Such health forecasting techniques using available applicant data can replace the tradition probe and poke methods of today. The cost of running a data model is estimated at $5 per applicant, a vast reduction from the estimated $125 it takes an insurance company to conduct lab tests on applicants at this time.

Adapted from: Leslie Scism and Mark Maremont, "Insurers Test Data Profiles to Identify Risky Clients," *Wall Street Journal*, Nov. 19, 2010.

Both qualitative and quantitative methods of forecasting are in use in business. Taco Bell saved more than $40 million over four years on employee scheduling, using moving average-based forecasts of customer arrival times every 15 minutes. NBC-Universal (NBCU) used Delphi and related methods to forecast demand for TV commercial time and use the forecasts to outperform competition in pricing decisions. Hard Rock Café takes point-of-sale demand data to forecast sales on a daily and hourly basis, uses regression to forecast effects of changes in menu prices on item demand, and uses moving averages forecasts to set sales targets.

KEY POINTS

Causal Models

- Causality in business cannot be proven. All causal models must begin with a good theory about why x correlates with y.
- In multiple regression modeling, look at R square, Significance F, independent variable regression coefficients and their p-values to evaluate the soundness of a regression model.
- Higher R squares denote greater explanatory power; higher regression coefficients denote a stronger association between the dependent variable and the independent variable(s).

- Sig. F denotes the statistical validity of the model; *p*-values denote the statistical validity of the regression coefficients. Both should be ≤ 0.05, corresponding to a confidence level of 95 percent or greater.
- Do not extrapolate regression forecasts using data beyond historical data boundaries; do not use highly inter-correlated independent variables.

5.3.8 Guidelines: What to Use and When

In order to forecast sales for a brand, say, Colgate's Total toothpaste, forecasts would be developed for each type (SKU) of Total brand toothpaste by sales volume, market share, and selling price. The SKU level forecasts would be assembled into an aggregate forecast for the brand, which, some studies suggest, generally produces better results compared to a top-down approach.[19] A top-down approach would forecast total sales for all type of Total toothpaste first and then break it down into individual toothpaste type. The table below elaborates some applications of different forecasting methods.

Table 5.1 Applications of Forecasting Methods

Applications of Forecasting Methods

Forecasting what	Forecasting level	Primary forecasting approach	Relative accuracy and comments
Parts usage	SKU individual product	Quantitative:*	Accuracy: Good
Production scheduling	Short term	Moving average	
Employee scheduling e.g., Taco Bell forecasting staffing requirement for lunch time on Mondays		Exponential smoothing	Not advisable for data with strong trends or seasonality Cost: Low
Purchasing quantities	SKU groups	Quantitative:	Accuracy: Fair
Production planning	Product categories	Time series decomposition	
Sales planning	Medium term	Causal modeling	Identifies trends
Plant leasing			and seasonality
e.g., Krispy Kreme using regression to forecast seasonality in on-premise/off-premise sales, and forecasting sales for new location			Cost: High
Plant or supply chain capacity	Consumption	Qualitative:	Accuracy: Fair-poor
	Total demand/sales	Judgmental	
Location decisions	Long term	Counting	
New technologies		Delphi	Cost: High
e.g., nano-technology products high fashion apparel			

* Assuming reliable historical data is available

Forecasts from different techniques for the same time periods can be combined into some form of simple or weighted average. We should also include qualitative information about market happenings. Menu Foods (since bought by Simmons Pet Food) was forced to recall 60 million containers of 'cut and gravy' style food in 2007 because of contamination. You can bet that competitors such as P&G and Del Monte took note and raised their own sales forecasts.

OM IN PRACTICE

How Intuit Does It

Intuit, the well-known tax software company, has an extremely seasonal business. To forecast well in a high-volatility business, Intuit has designed a multi-method approach to producing forecasts.

- All data for forecasting uses is first cleaned and adjusted for outliers.
- Exponential smoothing, time series decomposition, and regression models are used for volume forecasting.
- Delphi models are used for new products lacking historical data.
- A minimum of five years of data is used to develop monthly seasonality indices using time series decomposition. Estimates, from marketing projections, on sales and associated contacts are then factored in these months. These monthly volumes are then decomposed into weekly and daily volume estimates that are used for staffing and scheduling purposes.
- Simulation models do scenario analysis for maximum customer service delay time, impact of different forecasts, backlog resolution speed, and other key performance items.

Intuit's system has produced remarkable improvements. In recent years, forecasts, frozen every 60 days, have come in within 10 percent of actual volumes, leading to improved workforce management scheduling and tactical operations. Reliable forecast together with flexible capacity plans and simulation analysis help avoid last-minute crises, and provide alternative ways to maintain operational effectiveness.

Adapted from: Sanjay Ramanujan and Andréa Fisher, "Forecasting & Planning in an Extremely Seasonal Business—Intuit's Experience," *The Journal Of Business Forecasting*, Fall 2006, 11–16.

Typically, for the same demand forecast, operations would like metrics in terms of units; sales may need metrics in terms of brand or SKUs and dollars per customer segment; and finance may ask for a translation in terms of periodic cash flows. All metrics should be visible to all functions to show how different parts of an organization view the same forecast.

5.3.9 Measuring Forecasting Accuracy of Forecasters

Forecasters can be rated on their past performance: Consider two forecasters projecting sales for the same new item. Their past forecasting performance on previously introduced new products is known and can be incorporated in their current forecasts, for deriving an expected value for the forecast.

Name	Item	Previous forecast performance			Average A/F ratio	New forecast	Weighted new forecast
		Forecast	Actual	Actual/forecast ratio			
Yasmin	A	1,500	2,000	2,000/1,500 = 1.34	**1.14**	1,100	1,100*1.14 = **1,254**
	B	2,000	2,200	2,200/2,000 = 1.10	(1.34 + 1.10 + 0.97)/3		
	C	3,100	3,000	3,000/3,100 = 0.97			
		....	....				
Josh	A	1,500	1,300	1,300/1,800 = 0.72	**0.97**	900	900*0.97 = **873**
	B	2,000	1,900	1,900/2,000 = 0.95	(0.72 + 0.95 + 1.24)/3		
	C	3,100	2,500	3,100/2,500 = 1.24			
		....	....				
		....	.....	**Expected forecast = (1,254 + 873)/(1.14 + 0.97) = 1,008**			

Similar approaches may consider the average individual forecaster error, the standard deviation of the A/F ratio, or many other related ways to measure forecaster performance over time.

KEY POINTS

What to Use and When?

- Quantitative forecasting using historical data is suited for the short to medium term.
- Moving averages and exponential smoothing are appropriate for short-time horizons, for data without pronounced trend, seasonality, or cyclicality.
- Time series decomposition and regression are suited for the short to medium term and can accommodate trend and seasonality in the data.
- Longer term forecasting is almost always better done with qualitative methods, sometimes combined with quantitative forecasts for data that can be extrapolated, such as demographic trends.
- Combining forecasts in some manner (average, weighted average) may result in more accuracy. Relative individual forecaster capability can be evaluated using historical performance, and forecasts can be weighted accordingly.

5.3.10 Behavioral Considerations in Forecasting

Self-interest may bias forecasts. Understating a forecast can lower expectations, setting up an easy target to beat in the future. Overstating a forecast can bring immediate rewards in the form of share price increases and bonuses. Functions have personalities, too. Operations and supply chain err on the side of over-forecasting in order to avoid running out of resources and/or achieve production or purchasing economies of scale. Salespeople play down their forecasts, since sales target quotas are often based on forecasts. Marketing may over-forecast if advertising budgets are tied to forecasts. And as the 2008–2009 financial catastrophe showed, finance can grossly over-forecast earnings and prospects when stock prices and bonuses are at stake. Sales forecasts are usually not as quantitatively oriented, as, say, finance or operations. Sales focuses on the sales target, and does not consider forecasting as its principal job. In contrast, planning and forecasting are quantitative, employ a longer time horizon, and treat forecasting as the main job. Accounting would be conservative by training, comfortable with numbers, and sensitive to the costs of over-forecasting. One way to combat functional bias is to organize functions on a process basis, giving process ownership to an accountable and authority equipped position such as vice president for supply chain management or similar integrative titles. Another approach that companies such as Lucent have taken is to embed forecasting experts in their sales force.

OM IN PRACTICE

Forecasting at Heinz

Everyone in the company had a forecast! Even while using the same baseline forecast, different functions at Heinz developed different forecasts. When forecasts went wrong, everyone had an explanation.

Heinz overhauled their forecasting process, using bottom-up forecasting at a much lower item level. Item-wise forecasts per channel-fiscal month/quarter/year were first aggregated into a segment-channel-fiscal month/quarter/year and then into a forecast by brand-channel-fiscal month/quarter/year.

Marketing, sales, and finance benefited from gaining visibility on the item/segment and channel/market drivers of growth and decline. The item level of detail also provided weekly solutions for supply chain planning. A one-number forecast system developed to replace the earlier multiple function forecasts.

The one-number forecast system enabled different functions to base their plans on the same assumptions and information. For instance, budgeting became easier as the same demand forecast drove marketing, sales, production, inventory, transit/warehousing, manufacturing/co-packing, and finance plans. It became easier to share impact assessments of promotions and special events. Potential problems concerning suppliers and capacity surfaced earlier.

The president of the company demanded truth in forecasting. Over delivering on targets and commitments "would no longer be received with the same kind of enthusiasm as before."

Adapted from: Sara Park, "One-Number Forecasting: Heinz's Experience and Learning," *The Journal Of Business Forecasting*, 29, Spring 2008.

5.4 Was It Done Right?

The sales manager presents her forecast. Manufacturing ignores her numbers and prepares production plans based on last year's production/sales. Warehousing has different product descriptions than sales—Das Portable Generator 4000 is recorded in their database as Portable Generator 4000 Das—and reports the item as unsold, affecting its forecast quantity. Senior management massages the sales forecast to match analyst expectations. Actual sales turn out to be quite different from all of the above. Customer complaints grow, and we see excess and aging inventory (and no one has a good idea why). Frequent marketing promotion and discounting programs are run. Shipping and purchasing make frequent use of air or express shipments. If you see any similarities with your own organization, forecasting is *not* being done right.

Figure 5.18 Forecast For Online Classes

5.4.1 What Could Go Wrong?

Actually, this 1934 forecast of online study was not far off, especially when it comes to forecasting student attitudes to morning classes. But consider these forecasts:

A 30,000 DOW by 2000 end (this forecaster has not come out of hiding yet!)

640 MB ought to be good for everybody (guess who?).[20]

Why do such massive mistakes happen? New products or technologies, over-attachment to the status quo or expectations, and extrapolating into the far future are common culprits. Such errors are understandable and, at times, the result of individual 'expert' opinion. But companies, with their substantial resources and experience pool, also suffer from major forecasting failures. Some do not know the difference between a plan and a forecast—a plan is essentially an intention, while a forecast is an intelligent and rational anticipation of the future. To illustrate:

The sales manager plans to set the sales target 20 percent over this year's sales—an intention of action.

vs.

The sales manager forecasts the sales next year to be 20 percent over this year's sales—a reasoned expectation, based on information, analysis, and judgment.

Hopefully, the former is based on the latter. It is a dangerous situation when the sales manager mistakes her plan for a forecast. The lack of an actual forecast makes the sales manager unaware of the potential impact of future events on sales—new competitors coming in, key salespeople turnover, pricing moves, internal production and supply constraints, laws allowing freer imports of the products. And so the plan turns into dust when next year comes around. A plan, to be effective, prerequires a careful consideration of future possibilities. Similarly, listing the number and amount of parts required to make a product is not forecasting—it is planning. Forecasting is anticipating the number of product orders that will be received or anticipating the future availability and prices of parts in the supply market. Another frequent error is to mistake sales for demand. Consider the following scenarios:

1   # customers who asked for the product   = 3 = demand
    # of pieces in stock and sold to customer = 3 = sales
    Sales = demand

2   # of customers who asked for product   = 3 = demand
    # of pieces in stock and sold to customer = 2 = sales
    Sales < demand

3   # of customers who asked for product   = 3 = demand
    # of pieces in stock   = 5
    # of pieces sold from stock   = 3 = sales
    Sales = demand

Sales can *never* be greater than demand. Scenario #2 is a dangerous situation because most companies do not or cannot track the number of customers turned away. Think about the difficulty of tracking missed orders for the hundreds and thousands of SKUs in a busy store like Macy's. A special incentive system has to be put in place for the customer to report an 'item-not-found' event, as well as for the busy sales associates to record a 'customer turned away' event. If not, and sales have been consistently lower than demand, the forecast would implicitly mistake sales for demand and under-forecast that item(s) real market demand. Online companies such as Lands' End can track abandonments more easily but may not know the reasons.

An important issue in forecasting is the existence of very low probability events, or what are popularly now called 'black swans.' A black swan had not been seen in nature in the Western world—ergo, it did not exist. However, just because one has not seen a black swan does not mean that it does not exist. One was eventually spotted in Australia. If someone were to spot a black swan, therefore, it would be an extremely rare, previously unobserved, and highly impactful event.[21]

OM IN PRACTICE

A Black Swan Event in the Airline Industry

"There has never been anything like this" according to Lufthansa, the German airline. The eruption of the 'Eyjafjallajökull' volcano in Iceland in 2010 spread a huge cloud of fine particles of glass and rock across Europe. Thousands of flights were cancelled, and passengers were stranded for days in airports around the world.

Figure 5.19 'Eyjafjallajökull' Volcano Eruption

Although volcanic eruptions are not rare, 'Eyjafjallajökull' was an unprecedented, not seen in a lifetime, experience. Eruptions of this nature are extremely rare, previously unobserved, and highly impactful—qualifying the event as a probable 'Black Swan.'

Source: Bjarki Sigursveinsson, "The 2010 eruption at Eyjafjallajökull in Southern Iceland," [CC], via *Wikimedia Commons*, April 17, 2010, http://commons.wikimedia.org/wiki/File%3AEyjafjallaj%C3%B6kull_17-4-2010.jpg.

Forecasting black swans is an extremely challenging task, if it can be done by any measure at all. Distribution tails are where black swans happen, with positive or negative consequences.

Labeling the x-axis as frequency of occurrence, the further away we go from the center, the less probable but larger the loss or gain relative to the 'average.' In the 2007–8 market crash, deviations to the extent of mean minus 24 standard deviations were encountered.[22] In other words, events happened that were not supposed to happen in millions of lifetimes—an extreme fat tail event. The magnitude 9.0 Richter scale earthquake that devastated Japan's northern shoreline on March 11, 2011, was another black swan event. The sea walls surrounding the coastal towns were not built to withstand a 9.0 scale quake triggered tsunami. Neither did the designers of the stricken Fukushima Daiichi nuclear plant anticipate that a tsunami could short out the power to cooling systems in the nuclear reactors, leading to a core meltdown and widespread radioactive

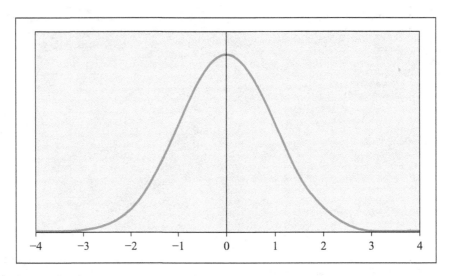

Figure 5.20 Finding Black Swans in Tails

contamination. Given such catastrophic consequences, can black swan events be forecasted with any accuracy? Perhaps one can try, with wider bell curves with fatter tails, incorporating more extreme values in the tails.[23] Other actions include attaching higher probabilities to extreme events, considering longer periods of historical data to better define 'extreme' and conducting war games to scenario analyze the nature and consequences of possible black swans. Can one buy insurance against black swans? Some companies are now bundling catastrophic risks and pushing these products to pension funds and other investors. Apparently, the lessons of the subprime mortgage collapse have not endured well.

Given our dire warnings of how forecasts could be grossly wrong, here are a few remedies:

- Agile suppliers—a supply chain capable of efficiently changing specifications or volumes in response to sudden changes in the market reduces the need for forecasting accuracy.
- Short and reliable supplier delivery times—reduce the need for forecasting accuracy, since replenishments can be made quickly and consistently.
- Holding a safety-stock buffer inventory of important materials—reduces the need for forecast accuracy.
- Reduce product variety—increases forecasting accuracy.
- Use shorter time horizon—longer time horizons reduce forecast accuracy.
- Forecast at the group level—more accurate than individual item level forecasts.
- Get closer to the end customer—the further the business is away from the end consumer, the more volatile the experienced demand and the lower the forecast accuracy at that position.
- Aggregate or combine the results of different forecasting approaches—usually improves forecast accuracy.
- Do demand management—promotions, discounts, and sales can smooth seasonality and improve forecasting accuracy. Do not do demand management in a stable demand market, since promotions can disrupt stable demand patterns and reduce forecasting accuracy.
- Buying insurance to cover losses or developing disaster plans for extreme events—reduces the need for forecast accuracy.

5.5 Current Trends in Forecasting

Collaborative planning, forecasting and replenishment (CPFR), a growing phenomenon in supply chain forecasting, combines information and intelligence across firms in a supply chain to forecast and plan to meet customer demand. CPFR is enabled by information technology and good relationships. Collaborative forecasting is an important component of sales and operations planning (S&OP), where sales and operations collaborate on forecasts and action plans. Vendor managed inventory (VMI), where the supplier stores and manages inventory at customer sites in retail and manufacturing, and collaborative replenishment programs (CRP) in grocery, are similar to CPFR.

Crowd forecasting, also called market prediction, is a relatively recent technique for business forecasting. Market prediction provides a forum that gathers mostly tacit, qualitative and disparate information, aggregating individual opinion into a crowd forecast. A prediction market builds a trading site with a virtual stock that reflects an event with a dichotomous outcome—yes or no. Traders bet on the probability of either of those outcomes becoming reality. A virtual stock generally carries a price range of 0 to 100, with higher market prices corresponding to a higher probability of that event coming true. Participants trade with real money. Market prediction helps HP forecast microchip prices and enables Microsoft to anticipate the number of bugs in new software applications. HP's market prediction-generated forecasts on revenues and operating profits turned out to be 40 percent more accurate than the company's official forecast.[24] It should be understood that market prediction is not a means to make events happen. Markets do not actually take ownership or wish to assume responsibility for a project or activity—they just comment on the likelihood of it happening. You can try your hand at market prediction at http://www.biz.uiowa.edu/iem. Other sites such as Intrade have shut down since regulatory guidelines in the U.S. now restrict the trading of 'event futures' for real money.

Data mining is a forecasting technique enabled by improvements in information technology that allows the collection, storage, and organization of vast amounts of data, over 80 percent of which may come from unstructured sources like tweets, posts, and emails.[25] The data are then mined by sophisticated statistical and non-statistical techniques for answers to questions like "Which customers are most likely to defect to competition in the next 90 days?"

How Companies Use Data Mining for Forecasting

With the right algorithms, very specific forecasts such as this may emerge: "19 year olds purchase Xbox 360 when a store runs a promotion that offers 3 games free with the purchase of a console."[26]

P&G uses data mining to analyze online shopping data, identifying complementary connections such as between Pantene shampoo and Olay moisturizer, to better forecast and boost sales revenue.[27]

So does Amazon for its U.S. patented "anticipatory package shipping" method (US patent# US008615473) where it will deliver *before* the customer has even placed his order based on data mining of customer search history, wish lists, and other behavior.

Target Stores forecast pregnancy based on sales/search records (surprising a young mom-to-be's parent in the process). Postpartum depression is being forecast by looking at how many times pregnant women use words like "I" and "me" in posts on social media.[28]

However, we only get to hear the success stories; companies do not publicize actual forecast error encountered when forecasting for their entire customer base.

Data collection is a sensitive aspect of such techniques. Methods like data 'scraping' that (silently) harvest online conversations and collect personal details from discussion boards and chat rooms through bots are coming under fire.[29] Yet the search for new data mining methods continues. Kaggle.com offered a $3 million prize for the best way to forecast patients who will be admitted into a hospital next year, using historical claims data.

OM IN PRACTICE

Music Meets Algorithm

Forecasting what will top the charts in the music world is an art. But an algorithm claims to have introduced science to the challenge of forecasting hits. Mike McCready's Music Xray has successfully forecasted the success of artistic products like Norah Jones and Maroon 5 before they became well known. His algorithm analyzes the musical structure of a song and compares it to tunes of the past for evaluating its 'hit' potential. To date, Music Xray forecasts of song success have enabled 5,000 artistes to sign contracts. Similarly, Epagogix has built up a reputation for scientific forecasting of box office returns for movies. It stunned Hollywood by successfully forecasting six out of nine hits just by analyzing film scripts. Algorithms are now being used to forecast matters ranging from a football game to intelligence forecasts on the probable decisions of foreign regimes. As Professor Bueno de Mesquita tells, his algorithms that dissect data for the CIA do not have any ego or biases or personalities that typically constrain objectivity in human intelligence analysts.

Adapted from: Christopher Steiner, "Automate This: How Algorithms Came to Rule Our World,". (Penguin Books, NY, 2012).

One problem with data mining is that correlation and not causation underlies connections. One could forecast ice cream sales by the number of forest fires (both are stimulated by hot weather), but that's clearly not a causal relationship! The lack of theory as to *why* things associate can lead to misplaced forecasts when the underlying causes change. A few years ago, Google found a correlation between online searches about flu and flu spread. Using that knowledge, they famously beat the CDC (Centers for Disease Control and Prevention) in developing a forecast for the spread of flu in the country. A study reports, though, that later 'Google Flu

Trends' forecasts were off by almost a factor of two.[30] Google did not know *why* the search terms were connected with the spread of flu. One explanation of the flu trends forecasting failure in later years is that increased awareness of flu in the public led to increased internet searches by people who were healthy (who did not eventually catch the flu). As such, the correlation between the number of searches and the number of actual cases weakened significantly. Google forecasts were presumably still running based on the earlier (stronger) correlation. Also, Google overfitted the model by including unrelated phenomena that tend to show search spikes at the same time as flu spikes, such as baseball high school season.

Finally, since many of you may be working globally in your careers, some awareness of popular 'informal' forecasting approaches may be useful. Users are usually small enterprises in developing economies. For example, 10–10–10 (Oct 10, 2010) had been predicted by numerologists as an exceptionally lucky number. One immediate effect of this prediction was a tremendous rush among people planning to get married on that date, preferably at 10:10 a.m. Businesses like wedding planners, caterers, marriage reception halls, honeymoon cruises, and the like do not have to believe in numerology. They could, however, make advance preparations to take advantage of their customers' belief in such forecasts. Rationality can take many forms in different lands and cultures. Selling and executing a modern technique-based forecast calls for an understanding of the influence of such beliefs on user and customer actions.

KEY POINTS

Current Trends in Forecasting

- Market prediction provides a structure for participants to buy and sell stocks representing event occurrence probability.
- Companies are finding forecasts using market prediction comparable or superior to conventional forecasting methods
- Data mining, using computing power and sophisticated analytical methods, enables the discovery of otherwise hidden relationships among variables of interest.

5.6 Conclusion

Customer: *"Why should I choose you?"*
Business: *"Because we promise to anticipate your needs."*

In the end, a business forecast will be wrong. Recognize that surprises wait around the next corner—supply chain and logistics glitches, disasters, quality issues, labor problems, competition actions, and market changes can disrupt the best of forecasts. Realistically, we seek to improve consistently rather than pursue unattainable 100 percent accuracy. A process that monitors mistakes and identifies and tries to correct/learn from reasons for major mistakes is essential. We should be honest and quick about communicating forecast errors to the entire organization and its supply chain so that suitable risk management strategies such as hedging, buffering, and risk-pooling can be developed and applied. Even though business forecasting is an uncertain endeavor, forecasting has utility. It reduces the set of options for decision making and offers guidance using history, experience, and knowledge as markers. Done well, it can reduce uncertainty and stimulate preemptive actions.

What Have We Learned?

What Is Forecasting?

- Business forecasting uses human experience, human responses, human judgment, and historical data to develop a probabilistic statement about future events and trends. A forecast states the future value of a particular variable(s) of business interest.

Why Is It Important?

- Demand forecasts are used for marketing and operational decisions and drive other forecasts, interest rate forecasts are used in financing decisions, inflation forecasts are used for labor and supply contracts, and commodity price forecasts are used in purchasing decisions.
- Offers the opportunity to act proactively. The most valuable forecast may be one that we stop from coming true.
- Forecasting offers jobs: forecast analyst, product forecasting planner, manager—risk analytics and forecasting.

How Is It Done?

- Process: Form a multi-functional team, invite key customers and suppliers, determine the purpose of the forecast, determine the level of forecasting and the time horizon, identify variables of interest, collect and clean data on such variables, choose a suitable forecasting method, sell the forecast, monitor and improve.
- Know your key drivers for what you wish to forecast—not every product or business depends on the same set of factors.
- Prioritize items for forecasting attention in order of importance to the business—focus forecasting resources on high priority, forecastable items.
- Intermittent demand, high uncertainty items are very difficult to forecast—use qualitative forecasting methods, together with coping strategies such as making products after receipt of orders, demand smoothing through customer incentives, shortened supply lead times, product standardization, and inventory pooling.
- Qualitative forecasts do not use/possess historical data and are suited for longer time period forecasts.
- Judgment-based qualitative forecasting approaches include:

  Sales force estimates that solicit and aggregate forecasts from sales people—who are closest to the customer—but who may also deliberately under-forecast in order to surprise on the 'upside' the next period.

  Jury of executive opinion synthesizes forecasts from senior executives in different functions—allows the balancing of a variety of perspectives—but may actually represent the judgment of one dominant function or personality (the bully effect).

  The Delphi method, suited to long time horizon forecasts of just emerging products or technologies, consults a group of experts iteratively—allows anonymity—but can be expensive and inconclusive (if expert judgments remain far apart).

Naïve extrapolation simply extends the immediate present into the immediate future, without any data analysis—useful in very stable markets and as a baseline method for evaluating other techniques—but is too simple for most forecasting conditions.

- Counting based qualitative forecasting approaches include:

Market testing of new products in selected pilot markets, actual or virtual— positive/negative/neutral responses are counted to create a forecast for the larger market— useful if market is representative— but people can change their minds later.
Surveys seek consumer opinion about a product or service. They allow collection of information from a large number of respondents—but may suffer from biases in sample selection, and the possibility of responders interpreting questions differently or changing their minds later.

- Quantitative forecasts use historical data, and are suited for shorter time period forecasts.
- Time series quantitative forecasting approaches include:

Moving averages, with forecasts being developed as a simple or weighted average of preceding period data—not for data with strong trends. Longer period-based moving averages remove the influence of outliers, while a shorter period base allows more opportunity for outliers and immediate data to influence forecasts.
Single exponential smoothing picks different values of a weight, alpha, to develop a forecast. A high alpha places more value on today's actual demand, while a low alpha places more value on what we had forecast would happen today. Simple to develop and maintain, but not suited for strong trend or seasonality conditions.
Time series decomposition breaks down raw data into trend, seasonal and cyclical components, easiest detected through data charting. Trends are consistent up or down movements over time—explicated through regression. Seasonality is a regular pattern in the data that occurs at fixed times during the year—explicated through seasonal indices. Cyclical movements refer to business cycles that occur at irregular intervals over multiple-year spans—difficult to explicate, but indicators have utility. Leading indicators change before, coincident indicators change simultaneously, and lagging indicators change after changes in the business cycle.

- Causal quantitative techniques include regression, where causal influences (independent variables) on the forecast variable (dependent variable) are theorized and tested with data. In regression:

R square represents the proportion of change in the dependent variable that is explained by changes in the independent variables, taken together.
$(1 - \text{Significance F})$ represents the confidence level of the model—the significance of F figure should be ≤ 0.05, corresponding to a confidence level of 95 percent or greater.
The regression coefficient (b_1 b_2) of an independent variable represents the magnitude and direction of the change in the dependent variable for a unit change in the independent variable.
The *p*-value of the regression coefficients represents their confidence level—should be should be ≤ 0.05, corresponding to a confidence level of 95 percent or greater.

- Do not confuse correlation with causality.
- Moving averages and exponential smoothing are more appropriate for short-term forecasting, while time series decomposition and regression can be used for medium-term forecasting, too.

- Forecasts from different techniques for the same time bucket can be combined into some form of simple or weighted average.
- Forecast error = actual minus forecast.
- Commonly used measures of error:

  MAPE: Mean absolute % error, e.g. actual demand was X% above or below our forecast, on average

  Average error: e.g., (−)4.7, indicates that our demand is lower by 4.7 units than our forecast, on average. Averages can be misleading if there is significant variance in the data.

  RMSE: Root mean square error, approximately equal to the standard deviation of the error.

  MAD: Mean absolute deviation, 1.25 MAD is approximately equal to 1 standard deviation. MAD enables building a confidence interval around the forecast.

- Behavioral factors such as ignoring data that conflicts with held opinion, and the tendencies of different organizational functions to over- or under-forecast, bias forecasts.

Was It the Right Forecast?

- Do not confuse sales with demand. Sales may be less than demand but not realized as such because systems for tracking customers turned away are not present.
- 'Black swans' are extremely rare, previously unobserved, highly impactful events. Wider bell curves with fatter tails, incorporating more extreme values in the tails, may be of some utility in preparing for black swans. Even so, the precise nature of the next black swan is never known.
- Early warning signals could range from an increasing frequency of expedited shipments, aging inventory, an absence of incentives for using forecasts, forecasting being consigned to a single point in the organization, little change in forecasting methods over time, and a general lack of trust in forecasts.
- Use the same demand forecast for all the functional areas of the business, translated into units relevant to the function—e.g., units shipped for logistics, sales revenue for finance, units sold for marketing.
- Short and reliable supplier delivery times—reduce the need for forecasting accuracy, since replenishments can be made quickly and consistently.
- Holding a safety-stock buffer inventory of important materials—reduces the need for forecast accuracy.
- Buying insurance to cover losses, or developing disaster plans for extreme events—reduces the need for forecast accuracy.

Current Trends in Forecasting

- CPFR in the supply chain is becoming practical and executable with advances in information and analytical technologies.
- Market prediction develops a trading market where participants can buy and sell shares of a stock representing a yes/no 'bet.' The price of the stock (≥ 0 and ≤ 100) is designed to reflect the probability of the bet coming true (yes).
- Data mining searches data repositories for relationships that can help forecast complementary, intricate, and not so obvious connections between variables of interest.

Key Formulas/Equations

Period	Actual demand (imaginary)	Weights (imaginary)
1	10	
2	12	.30
3	11	.20
4	15	.50
5		

<u>Moving average</u>: (Sum of) $\sum$data for specified # of past periods)/(# of periods specified)
So, 3 months moving average forecast for period 5   = (12+11+15)/3 = 12.67

<u>Weighted moving average</u>: Sum of (period wt * period data) for specified # of periods.
Make sure sum of weights = 1.
So, 3 months weighted moving average forecast for period 5   = (.30)(12) + (.20)(11) + (.50)(15)
$$= 13.3$$

<u>Exponential smoothing</u>: $F_{t+1} = \alpha D_t + (1 - \alpha) F_t$, where:
F_{t+1} = forecast for tomorrow
D_t = actual demand recorded today
F_t = demand that was forecasted for today
α = alpha, a weight that ranges between 0 and 1.00, also called a 'smoothing constant'

Period	demand data (imaginary)	Forecast (using a start value of 10) $\alpha = 0.20$ (given)
1	10	10
2	15	
3		

$F_2 = (\alpha)D_1 + (1 - \alpha) F_1$
$F_2 = 0.20 (10) + (1 - 0.20)(10)$
$F_2 = 2.00 + 8.00$
$F_2 = 10$

So,
$F_3 = (\alpha)D_2 + (1 - \alpha) F_2$
$F_3 = 0.2 (15) + (1 - 0.20)(10)$
$F_3 = 3.00 + 8$
$F_3 = 11$

Errors:
Error = actual − forecast
Under-forecasting: When forecast < actual
Over-forecasting: When forecast > actual

i) Cumulative forecast error (CFE): Cumulative sum of errors (negative and positives offset)

Period	Actual demand (imaginary)	Forecast (imaginary)	Error
1	10	10	0
2	12	13	(–)1
3	11	10	1
4	15	12	3

$CFE = 0 + (–)1 + 1 + 3 = 3$

Average error = CFE/# of periods = 3/4 = 0.75

Period	Actual demand (imaginary)	Forecast (imaginary)	Error	Error^2	Absolute error	Absolute percentage error
1	10	10	0	0	0	0%
2	12	13	(–)1	1	1	8.33%
3	11	10	1	1	1	9.09%
4	15	12	3	9	3	20%

ii) Mean squared error (MSE):

= [(error for period 1)^2 + (error for period 2)^2 + (error for period 3)^2 + (error for period 4)^2]/# of periods
= (0 + 1 + 1 + 9)/4
= 2.75

iii) Root mean squared error (RMSE)

= $\sqrt{MSE}$
= $\sqrt{2.75}$
= 1.66

iv) Mean absolute percentage error

= [(absolute error for period 1/actual demand) * 100 + (absolute error for period 2/actual demand) * 100 + (absolute error for period 4/actual demand) * 100 + (absolute error for period 4/actual demand) * 100]/# of periods
= [(0/10) * 100 + (1/12) * 100 + (1/11) * 100 + (3/15) * 100]/4
= [0 + 8.33 + 9.09 + 20]/4
= 9.36

v) Mean absolute deviation (MAD)

= [(absolute error for period 1) + (absolute error for period 2) + (absolute error for period 4) + (absolute error for period 4)]/# of periods
= [0 + 1 + 1 + 3]/4
= 1.25

Regression:
$y = a + b_1x_1 + b_2x_2 + b_3x_3 + \ldots\ldots b_jx_j$
Where:
Y = dependent variable
$x_1, x_2, x_3 \ldots x_j$ are independent variables that affect the dependent variable
$b_1/b_2/b_3 \ldots b_j$ are regression coefficients indicating the average effect of one unit change in the independent variables on the dependent variable

Discussion Questions

1   A monthly forecast is prepared using sales historical data with a time horizon of a year. Corporate production plans its production plans for different plants based on the forecast. The plants get orders from different warehouses independent of the production plan provided to them. The warehouses, in the meantime, develop their own bi-weekly forecasts based on inventory and shipping history and place weekly orders on the plants. Separate production schedulers at each plant handle the corporate production plan and the orders received from the warehouses. Communications and adjustments inside the plants happen through sporadic meetings, mails, texts, and phone calls. What problems do you see with the above situation?

   Answer: There is potential for a lot of confusion in forecasting and production planning. Plants see different demands for the same products—one from corporate production planning, another from the warehouses, and separate production schedules from the two production schedulers at the plant. Forecasting and planning is not synchronized between corporate, warehouse, and plants. The time horizon for forecasting, planning, and order placement varies. Multiple warehouses order independently on any plant of their choice without consulting with each other or corporate. Within-plant communication and synchronization mechanisms are ad hoc and error prone. It's quite likely that inventory safety stocks build up as individual departments try to cope with the complexities of the situation.

2   Mismatches between supply and demand in the medical profession affect health systems, with both shortages and excess supply of doctors reported in different regions. Since it takes a long time to manufacture the product (doctor) and there is much variety in the product mix (medical specializations), forecasting supply is difficult at any level of detail. Similarly, demand for different medical specializations changes over time with changes in demographics, technologies, health habits, insurance policies, medicines, and medical procedures. It is thus very difficult to reconcile potential supply with potential demand over an eight to ten year time horizon, the time it generally takes for a doctor to be 'made.' Develop a comprehensive set of recommendations to achieve a better balance between the demand and supply of medical doctors.

   Answer: Build a team of planners comprising of practicing doctors, medical technology firms, insurance agencies, patients, and hospitals. Assess the demand, soliciting input from doctors in the field and experts in the field of medical technology, planners at insurance agencies and hospitals, and the census bureau. Forecast at the *aggregate group* level, accumulating similar specialties under groups, as done in hospitals and insurance agencies (internal medicine, radiology, ENT). Evaluate the relationship between demand for each group and the specific variables that *correlate* with changes in demand, based on past history and expert opinion. Establish credible models of *cause and effect*. Employ regression or similar techniques to build forecasting models for the near term. Run simulation models with different levels of independent variables. Use Delphi, with experts representing key demand influencing variables to forecast long-term demand. Run scenario analysis. Assess the supply next for each medical group, using historical data and dropout rates from medical schools, retirement rates for doctors using medical graduation dates, number of nurse practitioners/physician assistants graduating in the future, compensation rates for different specialties and other variables that can influence supply. Since the supply lead time period is eight to ten years, qualitative forecasting methods are recommended, supported by causal modeling for the near term. Develop coping mechanisms for the inevitable gap between demand and supply, through a variety of policies: allowing doctors to change specialties in mid-career with a short but intense skills re-orientation programs (flexibility), permit medical students to change specialties until late in their career (postponement), incorporate more specialization coverage in the basic medical training (feature standardization), offer incentives to graduates in short supply, typically lower paying disciplines (smoothen supply), import doctors, export patients (medical outsourcing), and look at standardizing basic medical procedures to enable increased use of nurse practitioners and physician assistants (task standardization and substitution).

3   You notice that the sales forecasts you are receiving from your subordinate are very accurate. The product is in great demand, and you pay bonus depending on forecast accuracy. Is your subordinate a forecasting genius?

Answer: Likely not! Since the product sells well, your subordinate is simply constraining forecasted sales to anticipated supply based on the capacity of your production system. It is a classic case of treating supply as demand.

4   Name two possible drawbacks of (besides the ones mentioned in the text):

   a)   Judgment methods
   b)   Counting methods
   c)   Moving averages
   d)   Exponential smoothing
   e)   Time series decomposition
   f)   Regression

5   Give two reasons why forecasting might be useful for a finance major, a marketing major, an accounting major, and a HR major.

6   Give two examples of industries that have seasonal sales. Give two disadvantages and one advantage of seasonality in sales.

7   Give one example each of a product/technology that would be best suited for:

   a)   Naïve forecasting (e.g., milk)
   b)   Delphi forecasting
   c)   Jury of executive opinion forecasting
   d)   Moving average forecasting
   e)   Causal forecasting

End of Chapter Problems

1   Joe says his method results in an 'unbiased' forecast of demand—what does he mean?

   a)   Each period forecast is exactly equal to the actual demand.
   b)   The average of all period forecast errors is equal to zero.
   c)   There are an equal number of positive and negative forecast errors over the periods.

Answer: b

2   MAPE could be a better method of computing forecast error as compared to MSE because:

   a)   A single large error in a particular period would be magnified when squared in MSE and thus result in a large MSE number, whereas MAPE does not square errors
   b)   MAPE provides an unbiased forecast
   c)   MAPE is easier to compute
   d)   None of the above

Answer: a

3   Would any time series forecasting method result in a forecast that is lower than any of the historical data points used in developing the forecast?

a)   Yes
b)   No

Answer: b

4

Period	demand
1	12
2	14
3	10
4	14
5	18
6	13
7	17
8	18
9	14
10	16
11	12

a)   Do you see any trend or seasonality in the above data? Plot to find out.
b)   Beginning period 5 and ending period 12, forecast demand using a 4-period simple moving average. Plot your moving average forecast.

Answer: e.g. a 4-period simple moving average forecast for period 5 would be:

Average of [(demand in period 1) + (demand in period 2) + (demand in period 3) + (demand in period 4)] = 12.50;

Similarly, for period 6:

Average of [(demand in period 2) + (demand in period 3) + (demand in period 4) + (demand in period 5)] = 14.00; and so on . . .

c)   From period 5 till period 12, forecast demand using a 4-year weighted moving average with weights 0.2, 0.3 and 0.5 (0.5 for most recent year). Plot your weighted moving average forecast.

Answer: e.g., a 4-period simple moving average forecast for period 5 would be:

Average of [(demand in period 1) + (demand in period 2) + (demand in period 3) + (demand in period 4)] = 12.50;

Similarly, for period 6:

Average of [(demand in period 2) + (demand in period 3) + (demand in period 4) + (demand in period 5)] = 14.00; and so on . . .

d)   Does a simple moving average or a weighted moving average seem to provide the more accurate forecast? Compute MSE and MAPE to arrive at your answer.

e)   Which method provided a lower bias forecast?

5   Analyze the data from the Boston Red Sox at http://boston.redsox.mlb.com/bos/history/year_by_year_results.jsp

a)   Forecast the percent of winning games for the Red Sox Nation in 2010, using a 3-year and 6-year simple moving average.

b)   Plot both forecasts against actual historical wins. Which forecast appears more accurate?

c)   What is the correlation between team attendance and the percentage of wins/year?

d)   Should we develop a causal regression model? If so, which of the two variables, team attendance or percentage of wins, would you pick as the predictor (independent) variable and which as the dependent variable? Describe the theory behind your choice.

6   The New York Yankees are well known for the biggest payroll in baseball. Other teams complain about not being able to match the financial power of the Yankees. Does payroll make a difference to performance? Analyze the data on the performance and payroll of all 30 baseball teams in 2014. Can you build a credible regression model to examine the theory that pay drives team performance in baseball?

Performance: http://espn.go.com/mlb/standings/_/season/2014/dir/desc
Payroll: http://deadspin.com/2014-payrolls-and-salaries-for-every-mlb-team-1551868969

Suggested Class Projects

a)   Forecast unemployment/employment rates for the next two years (great data is available from the Bureau of Commerce).

b)   Forecast where the economic cycle will be for Home Depot in the next six months using indicators (use indicators from Conference Board).

c)   Forecast the proportion of the class that will earn A's, earn B's, earn grades lower than a B.

d)   Use a market prediction site (Iowa Electronic Markets) to forecast the outcome of an election. The election must close for that event before the course ends (so as to assess the accuracy of the market prediction).

Suggested Cases

Forecasting the Adoption of E-Books

The Bass forecasting model may be dropped since it is outside the scope of the text, unless the instructor wishes otherwise.

Description

Gives students an opportunity to understand the challenges inherent in forecasting the demand for a new technology embedded in an old product (books).

Learning Objective

To understand the many factors that impact forecasting for a new product.

Description

In its eight quarters of operation, Google's internally developed prediction market has delivered accurate and decisive predictions about future events of interest to the company. Google must now determine how to increase participation in the market and how to best use its predictions.

Learning Objective

To illustrate how market prediction and IT synergize for delivering improved forecasts.

Carol Prahinski, Eric Olsen

Description

The newly promoted inventory manager wonders if there is an easier, more reliable means of forecasting sales demand. Currently, forecasts are based on the plant manager's, sales/marketing manager's, and inventory manager's knowledge of industry trends, competitive strategies, and sales history. The inventory manager must decide if using statistical forecasting methods would ease the forecasting process and make the forecasts more reliable. Students are exposed to different forecasting techniques, including executive opinion, linear regression, and time series. The data characteristics include seasonality, trend, and random fluctuations.

Learning Objective

To provide an introduction to demand forecasting. Students are expected to understand the strengths and weaknesses of various forecasting methods and tools, the managerial implications of alternative forecasting methods, and to recognize the difficulty in developing and maintaining accurate forecasting systems.

Samuel E. Bodily

Description

This is a Darden case study.

The manager of a large downtown hotel has to decide whether to accept 60 additional reservations or not. If she accepts, she will be overbooked and face certain costs if all the people holding reservations show up. The manager must forecast, based on historical data, how many of the people holding reservations will show up, and then decide, after taking into account the cost involved, whether to take the additional bookings. The case can be used in a class on seasonality and exponential smoothing in time series forecasting.

Learning Objective

The case is intended to introduce the concept of seasonality into time series forecasting. Here it is a seven-day season, although seasonality is often associated with the 12 months of the year. The student is expected to de-seasonalize the data, extrapolate the series, and then reseasonalize the forecast. Exponential smoothing may be used to extrapolate the data; however, a five-period ahead forecast is needed.

Notes

1 L. J. Chaman, "Benchmarking Forecasting Processes," *The Journal Of Business Forecasting*, Winter 2007–8: 9–23.
2 "Life Expectancy Increases," *U.S. Census Bureau*, accessed Sept. 30, 2015, http://www.census.gov/compendia/statab/2011/tables/11s0103.pdf.
3 See http://www.funeralone.com/life/tributevideos.htm.
4 World Future Society, http://www.wfs.org/forecasts/index.html
5 "Jobs in Forecasting," *The Institute of Business Forecasting and Planning*, http://www.ibf.org.
6 Vilfredo Pareto, an economist, found in 1906 that 80 percent of the land in Italy was owned by 20 percent of its population. Hence, Pareto's generalized 80/20 principle—e.g., 80 percent of our sales comes from just 20 percent of the total types of products we make, that is, out of many, very few things are truly important—the Pareto principle.
7 Inventory pooling: Centralized stocking and distribution of a product to multiple markets, such that a sudden surge in demand in one market is likely to be offset by a simultaneous decline of demand in another market, thus smoothing overall demand. Further elaborated in chapter 11, "Managing Supply Chains."
8 "Answers to Your Forecasting Questions," *The Journal Of Business Forecasting*, Spring 2009, Vol. 28 Issue 1, pg.3.
9 See 'forecastingprinciples.com.'
10 G. Rowe and G. Wright, "Expert Opinions in Forecasting Role of the Delphi Technique," in J. S. Armstrong (Ed.) *Principles of Forecasting* (Norwell, MA: Kluwer Academic Publishers, 2001) 125–144.
11 Rachel Tiplady, "From Faux To Fortune," *Businessweek*, Nov. 14, 2005: 112–113)
12 http://www.ora-ito.com/profile/about/. Asked for permission May 2nd and May 20th 2015
13 An optimum alpha can be found for a historical data-set using SOLVER in Excel or a similar program.
14 Aki Ito and Alisa Odenheimer, "What is Your Central Bank Googling?" *Bloomberg Businessweek*, Aug. 13-26, 2012: 13–14.
15 Ataman Ozyildirim, the director of Business Cycles and Growth Research at The Conference Board, quoted in "Global Business Cycle Indicators," *The Conference Board*, updated August 2015, https://www.conference-board.org/data/bcicountry.cfm?cid=1); "The Conference Board Leading Economic Indicators for the United States," *The Conference Board*, August 2015, https://www.conference-board.org/pdf_free/press/US%20LEI%20-%20Tech%20Notes%20Sep%2018%202015.pdf.
16 "Underwear Sales Increase, Suggesting A Rebounding Economy," *Huffington Post*, Oct. 10, 2012, http://www.huffingtonpost.com/2012/10/09/underwear-sales-growth-economy_n_1952214.html.
17 Hites Ahir and Prakash Loungani, " 'There Will Be Growth in the Spring': How Well do Economists Predict Turning Points?" *Vox*, April 14, 2014, http://www.voxeu.org.
18 Remember the *p*-value from Stats 101? With a *p*-value of 5 percent (or 0.05), there is only a 5 percent chance that results you are seeing would have come up in a random distribution, so you can say with a 95 percent probability of being correct that the variable is having some effect, assuming your model is specified correctly.
    The *95 percent confidence interval* means that you can be 95 percent confident that the real, underlying value of the coefficient that you are estimating falls somewhere in that 95 percent confidence interval, so if the interval does not contain 0, your *p*-value will be .05 or less.
19 D. G. MacGregor, "Decomposition for Judgmental Forecasting and Estimation," in *Principles of Forecasting*, ed. J. S. Armstrong (Norwell, MA: Kluwer Academic Publishers, 2001).
20 Bill Gates, 1981.
21 Nassim Nicholas Taleb, *The Black Swan: The Impact of the Highly Improbable*, (New York: Random House, 2007); see prologue.
22 Joe Nocera, "Risk Mismanagement," *New York Times Magazine*, Jan. 2, 2009.
23 Instructor may wish to expand on Cauchy and Pareto-Levy rates of exponential decay.
24 Erick Schonfeld, "What Works: The Wisdom of the Corporate Crowd," *Business 2.0*, September 2006: 47–49.
25 "Smarter Technology for a Smarter Planet," IBM 2012.
26 Tom Kozenski, "Algorithms in Forecasting," *APICS Extra*, Vol 3, no. 10, Oct 30. 2008.
27 "Tech Executives Stop Cutting and Get Strategic," *Fortune*, June 8, 2010, tech.fortune.cnn.com/2010/06/08/tech-executives-stop-cutting-and-get-strategic.
28 Eduardo Porter, "Tech Leaps, Job Losses and Rising Inequality," *New York Times*, April 15, 2014.
29 Julia Angwin and Steve Stecklow, " 'Scrapers' Dig Deep for Data on Web," *Wall Street Journal*, Oct. 12, 2010.
30 Tim Harford, "Big Data: Are We Making a Big Mistake?" *FT Magazine*, March 28, 2014.

6 Capacity Planning

Chapter Take-Aways

- Types of capacity
- Computing capacity
- Estimating and meeting capacity needs
- Key indicators of capacity planning performance
- Sustainability and capacity planning
- Service capacity planning
- Sustainability and capacity planning

Capacity Planning: A Road Map

6.6 Conclusion

   End of chapter

   - What have we learned?
   - Discussion questions
   - End of chapter problems
   - Suggested class projects
   - Suggested case

Customer: *"Why should I choose you?"*

Business: *"Because we promise we'll be prepared with adequate resources to be able to meet your needs, in time."*

6.1 What Is Capacity Planning?

Capacity is the maximum amount of output that a system can produce, with existing resources, in a given time period. Capacity is a *potential* statement, since we may not chose to use the system to its maximum extent. Capacity planning is the act of anticipating and arranging for capacity needs to provide satisfactory service levels to the consumer, at a profit. Let us illustrate the concept of capacity planning with a practical example. Your family owns a bakery downtown, where traffic has increased significantly lately with more offices and residential rentals moving in. Business is up and, in fact, on some days customers leave because your bakery runs out of products during rush hours, or cannot serve people in a timely fashion. In other words, you run out of production or serving capacity at certain times of the day. How would you plan to meet the situation?

Should you expand the capacity of the bakery? If so, why? Do you expect the market growth to continue? What if a competitor comes in? What if tastes change, with people moving to healthier food options? Does your family have the inclination, and the necessary managerial skills and time to manage a larger bakery? Should you instead try to shift peak demand to other times of the day, through price promotions and off-peak discounts? How difficult would it be to downsize if the expected increase in demand does not materialize?

If you do decide to expand the capacity of the bakery, how would you go about it? Should you expand enough to be able to meet average demand or meet demand peaks? Should you expand by adding more ovens, or more employees, or both? If the added investment is significant, your break-even point will rise. Or should you do neither, and simply outsource the baking for rush times? Should you lease or buy the ovens? Should you ask your employees to work overtime, instead of hiring new workers?

How would you pace the expansion? Should you complete the planned expansion at one go, saving money and saving the cost of repeated disruptions to the business? Or should you expand in an incremental fashion, a little at a time, waiting for demand to materialize, before sinking money in new assets?

Where should you expand? At your current location or a few blocks away? Or would you rather meet increased demand through take-out and delivery, instead of adding new space?

As you can see, these issues require a lot of decisions. Capacity planning provides a systematic approach to making these decisions. The goal of capacity planning is to minimize the discrepancy between demand and capacity in a revenue-effective, cost-effective, quality-effective, and safety-effective manner.

Capacity planning is often confused with capacity management. Capacity planning is a strategic task that involves the future: future development and acquisition of capacity in order to meet future market needs. Capacity management is a tactical activity in the present moment, primarily focused on the efficient utilization of capacity and short term actions to increase capacity scalability and flexibility to meet current demand. In brief, considered from any angle, capacity planning is a complex yet necessary part of running a business. Before we take a look at how it's done, let's take a deeper look at the notion of capacity.

6.1.1 Types of Capacity

Capacity is the upper limit of a system's ability to make, store, deliver, or receive products or services at a point in time. Next time you enter the classroom, look at the notice on the wall. It probably says something like, "Maximum capacity 80 people." Remember registering for a class and being waitlisted, because it was full? Recall that occasion when the doctor was fully booked but squeezed you in anyway? Or being put on wait for that 'next available representative' at your credit card customer service center? Well, all these situations concern capacity, or more precisely, running up against capacity limits. Capacity could be an issue of physical space like a classroom or a warehouse or a truckload, an issue of time or personnel like a doctor's workday hours, an issue of machine or technology like the overloaded bandwidth of a cell phone carrier, or an issue of manufacturing or raw material capacity that leads to problems such as the delivery delays for practically every iPhone version launch.

Capacity can be measured in many ways. For instance, the capacity of an airplane can be measured in terms of seats in the plane for different travel classes.

Figure 6.1 Capacity in Cabin Class in an Airplane

Source: SuperJet International, "SSJ100 for Interjet – Interiors" [CC], via *Wikimedia Commons,* June 5, 2013, http://commons.wikimedia. org/wiki/File%3ASSJ100_for_Interjet_-_Interiors_(9016257074).jpg.

When a business has a standard product to sell, capacity can be measured in terms of finished product or service output. In fact, airlines often measure overall capacity in terms of available seats miles (ASM) per year, one ASM being one seat available for one passenger for one mile of travel. On the other hand, an operation with a large variety of products to sell or process such as a hospital emergency room (ER) cannot state capacity in terms of a standard finished product. An ER cannot measure capacity in terms of patients/year since patients arrive with widely different conditions and any one patient may take much longer to treat than another. Hence, for an ER, capacity has to be stated in terms of the available input resources, such as number of ER doctors or amount of doctor time available, number of beds, and similar patient-impacting resources. A few measures of capacity are shown below:

Table 6.1 Capacity Metrics in Terms of Inputs and Outputs

Type of operation	Capacity measured in terms of outputs (normal operating conditions)	Capacity measured in terms of inputs (normal operating conditions)
Hospital maternity ward	Babies delivered per year Moms discharged per year	# of beds available/year Available doctor or nurse hours/year # of expectant mothers admitted/year
College	# of graduating students/year	Available faculty hours/year Available classroom space # students admitted/year
Car manufacturer	# of cars made/type/year	Labor hours available/year Equipment hours available/year

6.1.2 The Dimensions of Capacity

Design or peak or theoretical capacity is the maximum output capacity possible, usually sustainable for a short period of time. A Porsche would not last very long if driven flat out all the time. Your capacity to study peaks just before an exam—imagine being asked to study that hard all year long! Peak capacity is often achieved by overworking the resource (overtime) or by deploying additional resources on a short term-basis (temps, outsourcing). Operating at or near design capacity can be very expensive and lead to other problems, such as drops in quality and lower employee morale.

Effective capacity, rated capacity, or the best operating capacity level is the capacity of the resource under normal, sustainable operating conditions. What is 'normal' is typically specified or informally understood in a business, considering the realities of equipment maintenance, human maintenance (lunch breaks, water cooler breaks), and operational issues such as scheduling and balancing operations. Effective or rated capacity is also the capacity that is immediately available for use. There's also the concept of potential capacity, which is the capacity that can be made available in the near future. Effective capacity is lower than design capacity.

Capacity has other dimensions, too, such as range and response. Range represents the ability to ramp the output up or down during operations, while response is the ease and cost of making those changes. Making informed decisions among such alternatives requires intelligent capacity planning on the part of businesses.

6.1.3 Capacity Utilization

Capacity utilization is the amount of design capacity that is utilized on average in fulfilling demand. Capacity utilization cannot exceed design capacity:

$$\text{Capacity Utilization \%} = \frac{\text{Actual average output or extent of resource use} * 100}{\text{Design capacity (maximum capacity of resource)}}$$

Efficiency is the amount of effective capacity that is utilized on average in fulfilling demand:

$$\text{Efficiency \%} = \frac{\text{Actual average output or extent of resource use} * 100}{\text{Effective capacity (capacity of resource under normal working conditions)}}$$

A pizza place can make 50 pies/hour with normal staffing, normal inventory levels of ingredients, and normal oven running. Its effective capacity is thus 50 pies/hour.

It can step up the output rate to 60 pies/hour (while maintaining quality) for a short time by adding temps, skipping worker breaks, and forgoing scheduled oven maintenance. Its design capacity is thus 60 pies/hour.

On every day of the week, except Fridays, pizzas are made @40 pies/hour on average. Fridays, pizzas are flying out of the place, with output rising to 60 pies/hour at certain hours. More cannot be made even if demand exceeds that figure. Other times on Fridays, pie making slows down. The average output over the week, including Fridays, is 45 pies/hour. Thus:

$$\text{Capacity Utilization} = \frac{\text{Actual output on average}}{\text{Design capacity}} = \frac{45}{60} * 100 = 75\%$$

$$\text{Efficiency \%} = \frac{\text{Actual output on average}}{\text{Effective capacity}} = \frac{45}{50} * 100 = 90\%$$

A high efficiency percentage ratio is not necessarily good news if the effective capacity has been significantly lowered relative to design capacity on account of shoddy maintenance, poor quality, or worker mismanagement. An overall system capacity utilization of 75 percent to 80 percent is considered reasonable and sustainable in a healthy manufacturing economy. Utilization in services may be lower because of variability in customer arrivals, customer needs, and employee mood and energy levels.

Bringing effective capacity closer to design capacity is the real goal, through improved worker scheduling, machine scheduling and maintenance, raw material availability, and worker training. Increasing design capacity involves identifying the constraining factor(s) in the system that limits capacity (bottleneck) and adding capacity to that point(s). In the pizza example from above, the design capacity of 60 pies/hour may be a limitation imposed by the size of the oven, the bottleneck. The oven is being fully utilized in making 60 pies/hour, so the only way to increase design capacity is to add another oven. Of course, as soon as we do so, another

Figure 6.2 Capacity Utilization in Cabin Class

Source: Ma1974 "Airplane Interior," [CC], via *Flickr*, Jan. 4, 2007, https://www.flickr.com/photos/ma1974/344683989/in/photostream/.

bottleneck may emerge in the form of worker availability or other factors of production, and the new design capacity would reflect that limitation. Usually, the bottleneck is the most expensive resource in the production system—one that we do not wish to have in excess and that we wish to utilize as much as possible in order to recoup our investment quicker. A doctor in a medical practice is a good example, being the most expensive resource and therefore targeted for maximum utilization through heavy patient bookings. Highly paid doctors (and machinery) have high break-even volumes and are not hired (purchased) unless enough demand exists to ensure that they are worked hard.

1. Industrial production, capacity, and utilization

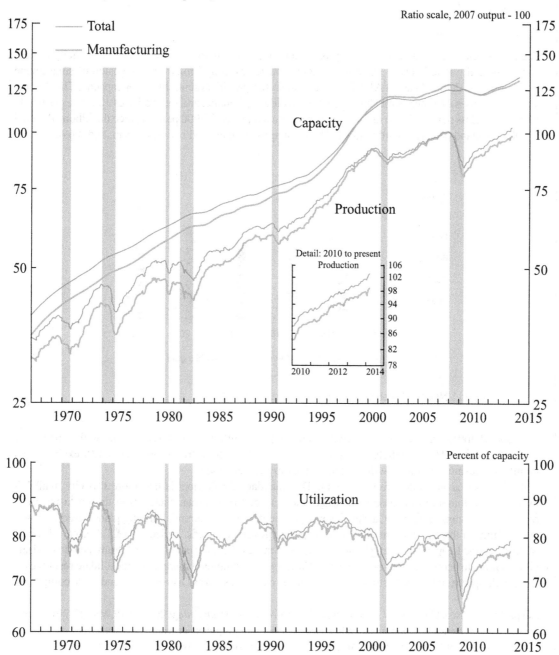

Figure 6.3 Industrial Capacity Utilization in the U.S.

Source: Federal Reserve.

OM IN PRACTICE

Capacity Crunch for Cell Phone Carriers

The bottleneck in the cell phone industry is carrier spectrum (airwave space) capacity. Capacity utilization in the cell phone industry has run up against carrier capacity limits. The explosion of smartphone technology and demand has set AT&T, Verizon, and other providers scrambling for capacity. The iPhone, for instance, uses 24 times as much spectrum as an older cell phone, and the iPad uses 122 times as much. AT&T's wireless data traffic on its network has grown a reported 20,000 percent since the iPhone debuted in 2007. Demand peaks are hard to meet: The most apps are launched between 7 p.m. and 8 p.m.

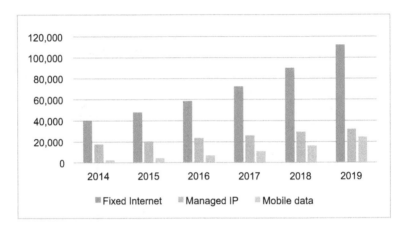

Figure 6.4 Cisco VNI Global Mobile Data Traffic Forecast, 2014–2019

Global IP traffic in 2014 stands at 59.9 exabytes per month. CISCO forecasts that will nearly triple by 2019 to reach 168.4 exabytes per month, while Consumer IP traffic will reach 138 exabytes per month and business IP traffic will exceed 29.6 exabytes per month.

4G high speed networks are being built. The quandary for carriers is that more capacity availability pushes customers to increase their usage rate, and cell phone manufacturers to design faster, more capacity-consuming products. Carriers have experimented with differential pricing plans based on usage rate and time of the day. They have imposed caps and governed speeds. Verizon, AT&T, Sprint, T-Mobile, MetroPCS, and Leap are investing billions to squeeze more efficiency out of the spectrum they do hold and billions more to acquire or rent new capacity. Carriers have attempted mergers to consolidate resources—and sought spectrum from industries that have unused capacity, such as Dish Network and cable companies.

Adapted from: Cisco, *Cisco Visual Networking Index: Forecast and Methodology*, 2014–2019, May 27, 2015, http://www.cisco.com/c/en/us/solutions/collateral/service-provider/ip-ngn-ip-next-generation-network/white_paper_c11-481360.html; David Goldman, "Sorry, America: Your Wireless Airwaves Are Full," *CNN Money*, Feb 21, 2012; Roger Cheng, "Verizon to Curb Highest Data Users," *Wall Street Journal*, Feb. 4, 2011; Greg Bensinger, "AT&T's Switch from Unlimited Plans May Set the Tone for U.S. Carriers," *Bloomberg Businessweek*, July 5–11, 2010.

6.2 Why Is Capacity Planning Important?

Capacity planning in business is necessary primarily in order to possess adequate capacity to be able to meet expected customer demand and make a profit.

6.2.1 *Importance for Businesses*

Should a business plan to meet 100 percent of anticipated demand at all times, that is, meet peak demand whenever it happens? In that case, some amount of capacity would be wasted during nonpeak demand hours. Or should the capacity plan aim to meet average demand or, perhaps, 90 percent of the anticipated peak demand level? Each choice would have to consider the costs of capacity development, the uncertainty associated with the demand forecast, and, particularly, the cost of not being able to satisfy all the customers all of the time. United Airlines's capacity planning illustrates an interesting strategy. Even as passenger demand improved as the economy revived, United continued to lower its flying capacity. The result? Increased occupancy rates (capacity utilization and efficiency) in flights and higher profits. The danger was that seat unavailability, fewer flight choices, and crowded aisles might have pushed passengers to other airlines. However, seeing costs go down, other major airlines like Delta soon followed suit. United now plans to add new capacity, but at a rate that lags the GDP growth rate.[1] Capacity planning also involves reductions in capacity along the supply chain. The closure of the Bender Shipbuilding and Repair Co. in Mobile, AL, not only cut capacity in the shipbuilding industry but also affected suppliers of customized ship repair parts such as metal valves.[2] Faced with a loss of a major customer, suppliers had no choice but to reduce capacity themselves.

Some companies may also use capacity planning in a strategic role. Excess capacity is deliberately kept to serve as a warning to competitors to stay away, since the business signals that it can potentially ramp-up and out-compete entry stage rivals on the basis of economies of scale.

OM IN PRACTICE

Capacity Changes in U.S. Auto Manufacturing

U.S. businesses have been on a capacity shedding drive since the economic downturn of 2008–2009. The government records a capacity reduction only when that capacity has been completely removed or dismantled. Things are looking up, though. A look at the chart below (Y axis is '# of autos in million') shows the decline and revival of the North American auto industry.

Hyundai and Kia's U.S. plants in Georgia and Alabama are running flat-out at unsustainable rates of 125–130 percent. Hyundai Motor Co.'s chairman Chung Mong-koo earlier froze capacity expansion, troubled by the quality issues that he saw Toyota grapple with during the latter's aggressive global capacity expansion in the 2000s. Now, he may have no choice. Hyundai and its affiliate Kia Motors Corp. are again looking to invest in new manufacturing capacity—in Alabama—to make cross-overs. To meet anticipated demand, Volkswagen announced plans to build a new North American plant while Honda Motor Co. and Mazda Motor Corp. also are building new plants in Mexico. Nissan Motor Co.'s new plant in Mexico is already churning out cars. Honda, Ford Motor Co., Toyota Motor Corp., and General Motors Co. are all expanding capacity at their existing plants in the U.S. and Canada, adding shifts and pursuing efficiencies.

The danger lurks in the possible glut in global production capacity. Globally, Fiat and Peugeot Citroën SA and GM's Opel are still struggling with underutilized plants. China is capping the number

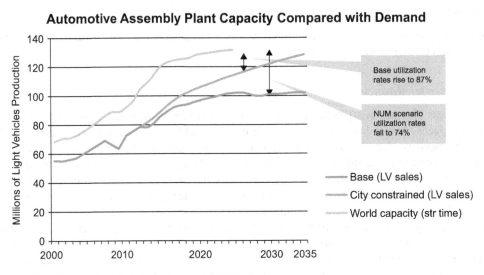

Figure 6.5 North American Auto Industry Capacity Changes

Source: With permission from author, Phil Gott (senior director, long-range planning, IHS Automotive), "A Look at the Parc Down the Road," IHS, December 2013, https://www.ihs.com/newsletter/automotive/dec-2013/parc-road.html.

of cars on city streets. Historically, car makers make strong profits at near 100 percent capacity utilization, but suffer losses as utilization dips below 80 percent. Inventory piles up and discounting damages margins. Top auto executives will be watching demand, capacity, and sales numbers carefully.

Adapted from: Alisa Priddle, "Hyundai Eyes Second Plant in Alabama," *Detroit Free Press*, March 11, 2015, *Wall Street Journal*, Jan. 14, 2014; Hyunjoo Jin and Norihiko Shirouzu, "After Two-year Pause, Hyundai Motor Poised to Add New Capacity," Seoul/Beijing, *Reuters*, Feb. 10, 2014.

6.2.2 Importance for You

Capacity planners are required in all businesses, including manufacturing and services. Goldman Sachs requires capacity planning as part of its trading strategy, moving and housing physical inventories of commodities like aluminum at warehouses sites;[3] Morgan Stanley had more oil stored in tankers at one time than Chevron; JP Morgan Chase created capacity by leasing a supertanker for storing heating oil, selling it later for an estimated return of more than 50 percent.[4] An advertised position is reproduced below.

CAPACITY PLANNING ANALYST (ABBREVIATED VERSION)

Zappos Merchandising Inc. Is looking for Capacity Planning Analyst!

Why join us? Our unique culture has made Zappos.com, Inc. and its subsidiaries one of FORTUNE's 100 Best. . . . Oh, and one more thing! Cover letters are cool, but do you know what's even cooler?! Show us who you are with a cover letter VIDEO! You will be able to upload one when applying for this position. (Video cover letters are not required, but if you wanna do one, we wanna see it!)

Position Summary

This Capacity Planning Analyst position is responsible for creating and maintaining weekly forecasts associated with sales, returns, and receipts in dollars and units for multiple business segments and product types.

Responsibilities

- Gather, generate, analyze, and validate weekly data from key business functional teams to plan and implement weekly statistical forecast reports.
- Continuously improve forecasting techniques, method, and approach, establishing and utilizing best practices. Evolve and maintain standard work for demand planning processes and procedures.
- Involved in capacity planning and supply chain process, including weekly and monthly meetings, to review forecasts and inventory goals and make strategic recommendations that optimize short-term and long-term profitability.
- Complete additional demand planning and sales analysis projects within scope and schedule as assigned.
- Interact with buying, planning, and finance to understand demand forecast drivers.
- Work closely with logistics, warehouse operations, and capacity teams to achieve established goals and expectations.

Requirements (abbreviated)

- 2+ years experience in forecasting and forecasting methods with an understanding of their financial and operational impacts. Knowledge of SAP, Oracle, and/or other ERP systems.
- Advanced Excel experience to include building complex pivot tables.
- S&OP, supply chain, and capacity management experience preferred.
- Bachelor's degree or equivalent (4+ years of industry experience) is preferred.

Adapted from: http://zappos.applytothisjob.com.

Typical jobs in capacity planning include titles such as capacity planner, planning analyst, and forecasting planner.

KEY POINTS

- Capacity planning develops alternative ways of providing capacity to minimize the discrepancy between anticipated demand and capacity, for revenue, cost, quality, and/or safety performance goals.
- Design or peak capacity is the maximum output capacity possible, usually sustainable for a short period of time. Effective capacity or the best operating capacity level is the capacity of the resource under normal operating conditions.
- Capacity utilization is the amount of design capacity that is utilized on average in fulfilling demand.
- Efficiency is the amount of effective capacity that is utilized on average in fulfilling demand.
- High levels of capacity utilization are required of expensive capacity.

6.3 How Is Capacity Planning Done?

Who does capacity planning in an organization? Professionals with titles such as 'capacity analysts' or 'planning analysts,' with input from sales and marketing, as well as finance, sourcing, and production. Capacity planners are distinct from schedulers and operations managers who manage day-to-day capacity issues at lower tactical organizational levels. Capacity planning has a significant forecasting and planning content and employs a strategic future outlook.

6.3.1 Determinants of Capacity Planning

Capacity plans utilize the factors of production (land, labor, capital). We are talking about facilities, inputs, work processes, workers, and supply chains. In particular, the potential to expand capacity is affected by many factors. Facility design, the size of the equipment we buy, and where we choose to place it determine size, flow, quality, and working environment. Flow and capacity are also improved by standardizing products and services. Work design as well as worker motivation and training affect productivity and quality. Reliable and responsive suppliers provide timely inputs for capacity utilization at buyer plants. Other determinants include external influences such as union and government regulations on safety, job flexibility, and environment.

From a financial perspective, capacity planning decisions depend on product/service accounting performance (contribution margin) since margins represent the opportunity costs of having too little capacity. A few guidelines:

- Higher margins lead firms to invest in higher capacity, even with low capacity utilization expectations. So a luxury brand like Salvatore Ferragamo may well keep a few more designers and manufacturing resources than strictly required because of the large profits they would forgo if a rare but sudden surge in demand cannot be met in time.
- Lower margins products or services benefit from additional capacity only when capacity utilization is already high.
- Higher demand uncertainty also promotes capacity investment. Studies show that costs increase in proportion to capacity utilization as demand uncertainty increases.[5] Therefore, it may be cost-effective to keep capacity in excess of expected demand (thus keeping capacity utilization low) when demand is highly uncertain and profit margins are high.

Having the capacity to be able to meet uncertain demand is important for other reasons, too. Hospitals like to minimize their 'turn-away probability,' the probability that patients would have to be turned away due to capacity shortfalls. For example, in 2004, Stanford University teaching hospital was operating at peak capacity utilization but still had to turn away more than 40 children a month for lack of surgical floor space and medical capacity. The effects on hospital employee morale and children's health were disturbing.[6]

6.3.2 The Five Questions of Capacity Planning

How does one begin a capacity plan? There are five basic questions that every capable capacity planner asks:

- *Why*? Reasons for capacity planning.
- *How much*? Estimate capacity required relative to future demand.
- *What type*? Sources of capacity; tools for evaluating relative advantages of different sources.
- *When*? Wait for demand to become visible or act in advance?
- *Where*? Physically locating capacity.

Why Change Capacity?

All capacity planning should start with the basic question: Why? Is the business a new start-up? Has anything happened to cause us to re-examine our capacity (or capacity utilization level) to serve customers? For some companies, capacity planning is a regular feature; nonetheless, it is desirable to understand *why* such planning is being undertaken. Does the existing business anticipate market growth or a decline? Is capacity required to serve a new market or enable product availability for a new product launch? Has new productivity or quality-enhancing technology or new equipment made it necessary to refresh existing capacity? Is the business reacting to competitor actions, or perhaps preempting competitive moves by using capacity availability as a strategic warning to newcomer entry? A lack of clarity could lead a business to make inappropriate decisions on capacity planning.

A number of reasons can cause a business to decide not to add capacity or even reduce capacity: infrequent demand increases, an expected change in industry technology, a shrinking industry market, customers who are prepared to wait, or the high costs of adding capacity. A hotel will not add rooms for a game that brings in an influx of fans for just a few days in a year. And a utility would not want to add capacity to its old coal-burning plants, considering the emergence of new power generation technologies.

How Much Capacity Is Required?

Resolving 'how much' begins with a forecast of demand, both long and medium term, which is then converted into labor and capital capacity requirements. Demand is then converted into capacity requirements by accumulating product-wise forecasts into equipment and labor requirements, whose availability is then projected over the relevant time period. The capacity requirement we compute is generally inflated by a cushion factor called the 'capacity cushion.' The extent of the cushion greatly depends on the degree of variability and unpredictability of the forecasted demand. Let's calculate the 'how much capacity needed' question with two worked-out examples.

How Much? A Service Example

A bank operates 16-hour, 7 a.m.–11 p.m. days. It averages 2,000 customers every day, and automatic teller stations take an average of 3 minutes/customer. The bank wishes to keep a capacity cushion of 15 percent to accommodate uncertainties in customer arrival rates.

Teller station capacity needed = 3 minutes/customer * 2,000 customers/day = 6,000 minutes/day
Capacity of one teller station = (16 hours * 60 minutes) less maintenance 60 minutes = 900 minutes/day
Therefore, number of teller stations required at 100% utilization = 6.66
Considering the 15% capacity cushion requirement, 6.66 should represent 85% of the total capacity (X). So,
6.66 = 85% of total capacity
6.66 = .85 * X
X = 6.66/.85 = 7.84 (6.66 is 85% of 7.84) = 8 teller stations
The teller station capacity required = total number of automatic teller stations required = **8 teller stations**

How Much? A Manufacturing Example

A bakery plans to introduce two new two varieties of Danish: dark chocolate mojito and rum'n'vanilla, raised-center and flat-center. Raised-centers and flat-centers are made in different specialized ovens run by specially trained ex-bartenders.

a)   *Expected half-year forecasts* for the two products have been developed from past demand data. We assume that the uncertainly level (variance of the forecasted demand) is low.

Month	1	2	3	4	5	6
Dark chocolate mojito						
Raised-center (pieces)	500	900	1,000	1,800	2,000	2,200
Flat-center	1,000	1,400	2,000	1,500	3,000	3,200
Rum'n'vanilla						
Raised-center	550	900	950	900	1,000	1,200
Flat-center	1,000	900	1,200	1,400	1,000	2,500

b)   Product line aggregated forecasts:

Month	1	2	3	4	5	6
Raised-centers	1,050	1,800	1,950	2,700	3,000	3,400
Flat-centers	2,000	2,300	3,200	2,900	4,000	5,700

c)   Compute capacity requirements:

Oven capacity for making raised-centers is 500 pieces per month per oven, while that for making flat-centers is 2,000 pieces per month per oven. Each oven requires two operators—one to mix ingredients and one to set up and monitor the baking process. Therefore:

Raised-centers

Minimum oven capacity needed	$= \dfrac{1,050 \text{ pieces}}{500}$	= 2.1 raised-center ovens
Minimum labor capacity needed		= 4 workers @ 2 workers/oven
Maximum oven capacity needed for any one month	$= \dfrac{3,400 \text{ pieces}}{500}$	**= 6.8 (7) raised-center ovens**
Maximum labor capacity needed		**= 14 workers**

Flat-centers

Minimum oven capacity needed	$= \dfrac{2,000 \text{ pieces}}{2,000}$	= 1 flat-center oven
Minimum labor capacity needed		= 2 workers @ 2 workers/oven
Maximum oven capacity needed for any one month	$= \dfrac{5,700 \text{ pieces}}{2,000}$	**= 2.85 (3) flat-center ovens**
Maximum labor capacity needed		**= 6 workers**

How much capacity do we need? We need 7 raised-center ovens, 3 flat-center ovens and a total of between 6 and 20 workers, depending on the month. There would be a small capacity cushion. Exactly how the business proposes to acquire the required capacity is an issue that we will consider when we look at capacity types and evaluation later in the chapter.

The computed capacity requirement is matched with existing capacity to generate an estimate of net capacity requirement.

QUICK CHECK

Companies are increasingly turning to robots for manufacturing. A startup wants to estimate how many robots it needs to satisfy demand for its products. Product demand forecasts and processing time estimates are as follows:

Product	Monthly demand forecast	Making time hours/piece	Total machine time required.
A	500 pieces	2 hrs	1,000 hrs (500 pieces*2 hrs each)
B	800 pieces	1 hr	800 hrs
			GT: 1,800 hrs required

A robot can work 2 shifts of 8 hours each, 30 days a month, with time off for maintenance and coding changes. How many robots should the company install?

(Answer: Production capacity/robot = 2 shifts * 8 hrs each * 30 days = 480 hrs/mo.

Total robot time required = 1,800/mo. Therefore, # of robots needed = 1,800/480 = 3.75 = 4 robots

---

Capacity planning does not always seek to match demand with capacity, that is, 100 percent capacity utilization is not always the aim, even when capacity has to be invested in fixed and valuable assets (permanent). Firehouses and hospital emergency rooms generally like to keep a low average utilization goal. That's so in order to keep enough capacity cushion to meet the sudden emergencies that can quickly drive up demand. The consequences for a capacity shortfall could be devastating to a seriously sick patient or the owner of a burning house. Fine retail stores like Saks Fifth Avenue and Nordstrom may not like to keep their customers waiting and thus opt to keep a capacity cushion of permanent associates to meet occasions of peak demand. A large part of that capacity may not be used at other times. Predictable demand allows businesses to plan for higher capacity utilization goals. Options to increase capacity on a variable and timely basis (temps/outsourcing) also enable higher capacity utilization through closer matching of capacity with demand. High capacity utilization requires careful attention to avoid deteriorations in product and service quality and customer satisfaction. In a sense, high utilization lowers the capacity cushion and helps surface defects and inefficiencies in processes and methods, but these deficiencies have to be addressed quickly in order to avoid hurting customers. Capacity utilization could also be high for goods that the customer is prepared to wait for and orders in advance. An example is the 6.5-liter V12 five-mode seven-speed gearbox Lamborghini Veneno Roadster, which at $4.5 million can buy almost two of the second most expensive production sportscar in the world, the Bugatti Veyron 16.4 Super Sport/Grand Sports. Just nine Venenos are reportedly being made, while the Bugatti's production is also reported to be capped at 150 pieces.

Figure 6.6 Bugatti Veyron 16.4

Source: M93, "Bugatti Veyron 16.4," [CC], via *Wikimedia Commons*, April 5, 2012, http://commons.wikimedia.org/wiki/ File%3ABugatti_Veyron_16.4_%E2%80%93_Frontansicht_(1)%2C_5._April_2012%2C_D%C3%BCsseldorf.jpg.

Figure 6.7 Lamborghini Veneno

Source: Clément Bucco-Lechat, "Geneva MotorShow 2013—Lamborghini Veneno," [CC], via *Wikimedia Commons*, March 6, 2013, http://commons.wikimedia.org/wiki/File%3AGeneva_MotorShow_2013_-_Lamborghini_Veneno_1.jpg.

Strategic intention dictates capacity planning, too—capacity may be deliberately limited and utilization increased to promote an image of exclusivity or quality. The sight of people lined up outside a restaurant, a club, or a Broadway play carries positive connotations for the business.

Capacity may not match demand for economic reasons. The relationship between capacity utilization and costs is not linear. Costs initially decline with an increase in production owing to learning curve and economies of scale effects, including volume discounts from suppliers and the spread of total fixed costs over a larger number of units. The cost decline, though, typically hits a wall at some point and begins to rise again. As capacity increases and utilization begins to approach a physical limit, sudden shortages of inputs occur, breakdowns of equipment, workers and supply increase, bureaucracy expands, coordination difficulties increase, space becomes crowded, tempers flare, quality suffers, and the system cannot absorb sudden fluctuations well. Consequently, costs begin to go up and business performance deteriorates. There is an optimum production point for most business where the total cost/unit is at a minimum—MES, or the minimum efficient scale of production, also called the best operating level in services. In classical economics, the minimum efficient scale is defined as the lowest production point at which long-run total average costs are minimized. That 'optimal' production point often remains an elusive quantity in view of the difficulty of estimating costs and cost behavior of factors such as increased bureaucracy or coordination. Break-even analysis, as described in the location chapter (chapter 12), can identify a mathematical optimum break-even point where total costs are at a minimum but that presupposes precise knowledge about costs and the cost-production relationship. Short product life cycles encourage smaller than MES capacity since expected revenues over a short life cycle may not allow payback of MES investments. Large and expensive capacity investments in industries such as steel and semi-conductor manufacturing are being replaced with much smaller capacity, low cost minifabs and mini-steel mills.

KEY POINTS

Key Steps in Capacity Planning

- The motivation for capacity expansion or reduction must be clearly understood—demand, competition, economies of scale, vertical integration, etc.
- Higher margins and high costs of stock-outs lead to higher capacity, even with low capacity utilization expectations. Low margins benefit from capacity expansion only when capacity utilization is high.
- Costs increase in proportion to capacity utilization as demand uncertainty increases. Higher demand uncertainty promotes capacity investment in order to avoid high levels of utilization.
- Planning for net capacity needs starts with the conversion of demand into resource capacity forecasts. Capacity cushions are added considering the degree of demand and resource supply uncertainty.
- A capacity gap analysis identifies net capacity requirements. Planned capacity may differ from expected demand, for reasons of production cost minimization (MES), short product life cycles, or an intentional short supply strategy.

What Type of Capacity?

Assuming that the business does decide to add capacity, there are many alternative ways to do so. These approaches are generally employed in some combination to suit the needs of the business.

Sources of Capacity

- *Acquiring equipment and labor*

  Capacity needs can be filled by adding new technology and labor to bottleneck points in the system. New technology can replace labor-intensive processes and materially change business models. For example, online banking and ATMs have expanded the geographical reach of many regional banks and smoothed demand over longer hours. In-house capacity is also freed up—customers transact at the ATM, making withdrawals, transfers, and deposits, instead of with the teller. Flexible technologies like computer-aided design and manufacturing (CAD, CAM) and complete flexible manufacturing systems (FMS) offer scalability and range while adding capacity. These are typically more expensive to procure and run than dedicated equipment that offers more efficiency, albeit for a limited number of jobs. The use of temporary workers and employee overtime can also be options, particularly attractive in an uncertain economy.

However, safety, quality, and productivity may suffer with overtime or temporary workers, regular employees may experience overtime fatigue or fear job take-over by temps, and temps may feel demoralized by the contrast in compensation and benefits relative to full-timers. Leasing is the temp version of buying equipment. JetBlue, for instance, deferred taking delivery of six new Airbus A-320's, instead opting to lease seven used A-320s aircrafts.[7] The benefits of leasing equipment, flexibility and a lower risk of obsolescence, have to be weighed against the benefits of buying new or used equipment. The latter usually offers lower total costs and the advantages of owning assets (to use as loan collateral, etc.).

- *Outsourcing*

Outsourcing to contractors or manufacturers with excess capacity is a common approach for meeting peaks in demand. The business runs a steady state capacity and maintains a stable of sub-contractors to boost capacity at peak times. The variable costs of doing so may be higher or lower compared to internal production, but the savings in fixed costs and risk exposure are generally significant. Coordination costs, quality inspection, sub-contractor opportunism, and loss of managerial control are the key disadvantages experienced with this approach. Capacity can also be borrowed from another firm for both production and maintenance purposes. Under-utilized capacity can be used in strategic collaborations—Uber is a prime example. Pininfarina, the well known design, product and process engineering, and niche auto manufacturer, lends design and manufacturing capacity to Alfa Romeo, Ford, Mitsubishi, and Volvo. In the same context, townships are increasingly seeking opportunities to share excess fire, trash, and other utility-related capacities with/from other townships. Vessel capacity sharing agreements are common in the shipping industry in which a number of container positions ('slots') are reserved on particular vessels for another shipper. Yet sharing capacity is not without risk—control over operations becomes diluted, competitors may steal intellectual property, and suppliers may leak confidential information to other customers. Perhaps the greatest constraint to pooling or sharing capacity is the very human fear of becoming redundant and losing one's job.

- *Increases in business productivity*

Process re-engineering can increase productivity and capacity without adding resources. Process re-engineering breaks down and examines the steps of basic business processes like order fulfillment, material sourcing and storage, and accounts payable. Each activity is then examined for waste, employing the lens of *TIMWOODS*,[8] covering *T*ransportation of people and material; *I*nventory; *M*otions of bending, turning, reaching, and lifting; *W*aiting for parts, information, instructions, or equipment; *O*ver-production; *O*ver-processing to tighter standards than required; *D*efects of material, product, or documentation; and the use of over-*S*killed or under-*S*killed capabilities for the job. Job tasks are removed, combined, or split as necessary to eliminate waste, and the remaining activities are tightly integrated for a smooth flow, eliminating inventory and waiting time. Worker training and motivation, changing work space organization and sequence, realigning supervisors to suit worker personalities, preventive maintenance of equipment, and in-house equipment customization can aid in adding capacity without substantial cost. Identification and elimination of bottlenecks by reallocating personnel or equipment from other noncritical tasks would also increase system capacity without significant expenditure. Cross-training employees adds to capacity flexibility.

- *Product Redesign*

Manufacturers redesign and standardize products and parts to better fit equipment or worker conditions (design for manufacturability: DFM). Why don't all cars have gas caps on the same side? It would certainly make manufacturing less complex and increase productivity at both supplier and car assembly points—of course, the flip side is that only one side of a gas pump may find use in gas stations. Restaurants often use the same gravy stock to prepare different dishes, saving on both labor and the costs involved in making and storing different stocks. Component or tool standardization does not necessarily endanger variety—we use the same twenty-six letters of the English alphabet to form a practically infinite variety of words.

- *Managing demand*

    When capacity cannot be expanded, a business can try to change demand patterns. Pricing is a powerful means to achieve this end. Demand management works best when the following conditions are present: Demand is variable and unpredictable, capacity is fixed, capacity is perishable, and customers are willing to pay different prices or forgo degrees of convenience for using capacity at different times. Toll roads, hair salons, doctor clinics, hotels, cruise lines, 'happy hour' bars, car rentals, and airlines use variable pricing on limited chunks of capacity to move customers to off-peak times. High pricing can also be used to shed low margin customers and bring demand down profitably to match available capacity. New markets can be created, as well, with new product and service offerings for off-season periods—the coffee vendor down the street utilizes capacity year around, changing over to iced coffee during the peak summer months when regular coffee sales drop.

Faced with the many capacity planning alternatives described above, a manager has to make a choice. Which approach(es) should he/she adopt? Break-even analysis, cash flow analysis, and decision tree analysis are the major evaluation tools in the capacity planning toolbox.

Tools for Evaluating Capacity Sources

- *Break-even analysis (BEA)*

    BEA in capacity planning considers the cost of providing capacity and identifies the amount of production capacity required to turn a profit. A business breaks even at the point where total sales = total costs. BEA compares the break-even points of different types of capacity addition alternatives based on the different costs of such alternative. Remember, the revenues and costs are estimated, assumed to grow linearly, and have not yet been actually experienced. Normal linear relationships between cost and capacity may suddenly change into exponential increases, at what some call '*the knee of the curve point*,' as capacity expansion approaches a physical limit. BEA also assumes synchronous cash inflows and outflows.

Evaluating Capacity Planning Alternatives for Lady RA-RA

Lady RA-RA's capacity planning analyst wishes to find out what minimum level of capacity is required in order to turn a profit for a new concert tour proposal. Capacity is measured in terms of number of concerts performed. He figures that the total upfront, nonrefundable fixed costs involved in staging the entire tour (advance orders for dresses, wigs, and hats, and township preapprovals, venue booking, stage, utility, audience and traffic control) amount to about $200,000. The variable costs add up to $18,000 per concert, chiefly for performance-related labor activities. Each concert is kept to the same audience capacity, priced identically, and is expected to sell-out, grossing $22,000 per concert.

Alternatively, Lady RA-RA could get some well-deserved R&R and outsource the concerts to her very popular stand-in, Lady ra-ra. The fixed costs would remain the same at $200,000, but expected revenues would decline to $16,000/concert. The variable costs would also decline to $13,000/concert. The capacity planner wished to know the minimum number of concerts that either Lady RA-RA or her stand-in would have to do in order to begin earning a profit.

Recapping:
Fixed (sunk) cost irrespective of # of concerts = $200,000

If Lady RA-RA performs:

Total costs for any given # of concerts = fixed costs + variable costs/concert * # of concerts
= $200,000 + $18,000 * # of concerts

Total revenue for any given # of concerts = revenue/concert * # of concerts
= $22,000 * # of concerts

BEP is the # of concerts at which total revenue = total costs
So: $22,000 * # of concerts = $200,000 + $18,000 * # of concerts

Solving for # of concerts $= \dfrac{\$200,000}{(\$22,000 - 18,000)} = 50$ concerts

BEP (quantity) = 50 concerts
BEP (in revenue $) = 50 concerts * $22,000/concert = $1,100,000

The formulas are:

BEP (quantity) $= \dfrac{\text{Fixed cost}}{\text{Revenue/unit} - \text{Variable cost/unit} \left(\text{i.e. Unit Contribution Margin}\right)}$

BEP (in revenue $) $= \dfrac{\text{Fixed cost}}{\text{Unit Contribution Margin}} \times \text{Revenue/unit}$

So Lady RA-RA will break even at 50 concerts and start making a profit from the 51st concert onwards. She has to figure out if she has the health and stamina to perform at 50+ concerts (required capacity), or alternatively outsource the tour to her understudy.

If Lady ra-ra performs:

Total costs for any given # of concerts = fixed costs + variable costs/concert * # of concerts
= $200,000 + $13,000 * # of concerts

Total revenue for any given # of concerts = revenue/concert * # of concerts
= $16,000 * # of concerts

Solving for # of concerts at BEP $= \dfrac{\$200,000}{\$3,000} = 66.66 = 67$ concerts

So Lady ra-ra will break even at 67 concerts and start making a profit from the 68th concert onwards.

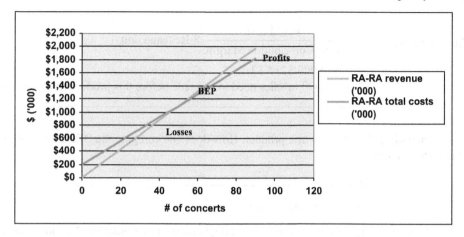

Figure 6.8 Lady RA-RA Break-Even Analysis

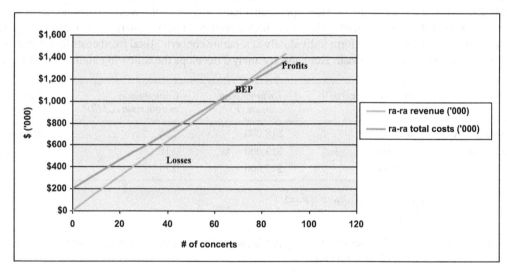

Figure 6.9 Lady ra-ra Break-Even Analysis

QUICK CHECK

NYC Bagels is considering adding food fad 'cronuts' to its product line. This new addition, though, would need a special forming machine that costs $50,000. Variable costs are $1/cronut, which will be priced at $3 each. What is the break-even point for this project—in terms of both cronuts and dollar revenue?

Answer: BEP (quantity) $= \dfrac{\text{Fixed cost}}{\text{Revenue/unit} - \text{Variable cost/unit} \ (\text{i.e. Unit Contribution Margin})}$

$= \$50,000/(\$3 - \$1)$

$= 25,000$ pieces

Profits would begin after 25,000 cronuts are sold.

$$\text{BEP (in revenue \$)} = \frac{\text{Fixed cost}}{\text{Unit Contribution Margin}} \times \text{Revenue/unit}$$

$$= (\$50{,}000/\$2) * \$3$$

$$= \$75{,}000 \text{ in sales need to be made before this product turns a profit}$$

Businesses generally sell more than one product. How does one compute the BEP for a multiple-product business? Let's take a look.

Lady RA-RA Inc.—A Multiple Product BEA

Lady RA-RA, awed by the capacity planning exercise, becomes more businesslike and forms a corporation together with Lady ra-ra and the well-known rapper Z-J. The business now has three products: Lady RA-RA, Lady ra-ra, and Z-J. They approach a bank to finance the working capital needs of the new corporation. The bankers wish to know the break-even point of the enterprise in terms of required revenue dollars. The artistes perform individually at separate concerts. Total fixed costs for the corporation are estimated at $220,000/year. Her capacity analyst develops the following additional estimates:

Artiste	Revenue/concert(P)	Variable cost/ concert (V)	Contribution margin ratio (CMR)*	Forecasted demand/yr
Lady RA-RA	$ 22,000	$18,000	0.18	80 concerts
Lady ra-ra	$ 16,000	$13,000	0.19	70 concerts
Rapper Z-J	$ 22,000	$17,000	0.23	77 concerts

$$*\text{CMR} = \frac{\text{Unit Contribution margin}}{\text{Revenue/unit}} = \frac{(P-V)}{P}$$

Finding the BEP for a business with many products involves weighting each product's contribution ratio with its proportion of total revenue.

Artiste	Annual revenue	Proportion of total revenue	CMR	Revenue weighted CMR
Lady RA-RA	$1,760,000*	0.38	0.18	0.38 * 0.18 = 0.07
Lady ra-ra	$1,120,000	0.25	0.19	0.25 * 0.19 = 0.05
Rapper Z-J	$\dfrac{\$1{,}694{,}000}{\$4{,}574{,}000}$	0.37	0.23	$0.37*0.23 = \dfrac{0.09}{0.21}$

* Forecasted demand/yr * revenue/concert

$$\text{BEP ($ revenue)} = \frac{\text{Total Fixed cost}}{\text{Total weighted CMR}} = \frac{\$220{,}000}{0.21} = \$1{,}047{,}619$$

The new corporation shall have to generate $1,047,619 in sales revenue per year ($87,302, approximately monthly) to break even. The bankers ask for a marketing plan and revenue estimates.

- *Cash Flow Analysis*

Cash flow analysis converts anticipated cash outflows and inflows into present value and computes their difference as the net present value (NPV) of a particular approach. All relevant revenues and costs through the life cycle of each alternative are considered, including capital and operating costs, periodic upgrades, disposal costs, and salvage values. NPV considers all cash flows to occur at the end of the period (week/month/year) and assumes a specific interest rate that stays stable for the entire period of time being considered.

Lady RA-RA: An NPV Analysis

Lady RA-RA is actively considering outsourcing her concert career to Lady ra-ra and going in for a PhD in her new love, operations management. But she wants to run some numbers first to see how she and Lady ra-ra relatively stack up in terms of concert earnings. She can count on 80 concerts/year if she performs herself and 70 concerts/year if her understudy performs in her stead, for now. But she knows that fame is fickle and can count on no more than five more years of (declining) concert demand. She does not want to reduce ticket prices at any time. She also knows that a dollar earned now is worth more than a dollar earned later. Lady RA-RA instructs her capacity planner to come up with some numbers that consider the time value of money.

NPV is an ideal tool for this situation. The estimates for fixed ($200,000) and variable costs ($18,000, Lady RA-RA; $13,000, Lady ra-ra), and revenues ($22,000/concert, Lady RA-RA; $16,000, Lady ra-ra) remain the same. An interest rate of 5 percent is used. The capacity planner gets paid an extra $20,000 right now for all the additional work he is being asked to do.

Lady RA-RA

Year	# of concerts	Cash receipts	Cash outflow	Net cash inflow	Present value factor @5%*	Present value of net cash inflow
1	80	$22,000 * 80 = $1,760,000	$200,000 + (80*$18,000) = $1,640,000	$120,000	.952	$114,240
2	60	$22,000 * 60 = $1,320,000	$200,000 + (60*$18,000) = $1,280,000	$40,000	.907	$36,280
3	56	$1,232,000	$1,208,000	$24,000	.864	$20,736
4	52	$1,144,000	$1,136,000	$8,000	.823	$6,584
5	50	$1,100,000	$1,100,000	$0	.784	$0
						$177,840
				Minus capacity planner's bonus		$20,000
				NET PRESENT VALUE (NPV)		$157,840

---

* From present value table (see below)

Similarly, table PV factor using an interest rate of 5%   = PV factor @5% * $40,000
= 0.907 * $40,000
= $36,280

$$\text{Present value } (PV) = \frac{\text{Future value}}{(1 + \text{interest rate})^{\text{# of years}}}$$

e.g., PV of \$40,000 net cash inflow in year 2 = $\dfrac{\$40,000}{(1 + .05)^2}$ = \$36,281.18

Specimen Present Value Table

Period	1%	2%	3%	4%	5%	6%	7%	8%	9%	10%
1	0.990	0.980	0.971	0.962	0.952	0.943	0.935	0.926	0.917	0.909
2	0.980	0.961	0.943	0.925	0.907	0.890	0.873	0.857	0.842	0.826
3	0.971	0.942	0.915	0.889	0.864	0.840	0.816	0.794	0.772	0.751
4	0.961	0.924	0.888	0.855	0.823	0.792	0.763	0.735	0.708	0.683
5	0.951	0.906	0.863	0.822	0.784	0.747	0.713	0.681	0.650	0.621
6	0.942	0.888	0.837	0.790	0.746	0.705	0.666	0.630	0.596	0.564
7	0.933	0.871	0.813	0.760	0.711	0.665	0.623	0.583	0.547	0.513
8	0.923	0.853	0.789	0.731	0.677	0.627	0.582	0.540	0.502	0.467
9	0.914	0.837	0.766	0.703	0.645	0.592	0.544	0.500	0.460	0.424
10	0.905	0.820	0.744	0.676	0.614	0.558	0.508	0.463	0.422	0.386

Lady ra-ra

Year	# of concerts	Cash receipts	Cash outflow	Net cash inflow	Present value factor @5%*	Present value of net cash inflow
1	70	\$16,000 * 70 = \$1,120,000	\$200,000 + (70*\$13,000) = \$1,110,000	\$10,000	.952	\$9,520
2	70	\$16,000 * 70 = \$1,120,000	\$200,000 + (70*\$13,000) = \$1,110,000	\$10,000	.907	\$9,070
3	68	\$1,088,000	\$1,084,000	\$4,000	.864	\$3,456
4	68	\$1,088,000	\$1,084,000	\$4,000	.823	\$3,292
5	67	\$1,072,000	\$1,071,000	\$1,000	.784	$\dfrac{\$784}{\$26,122}$
				Minus capacity planner's bonus		\$20,000
				NET PRESENT VALUE (NPV)		\$6,122

Looking at the difference in the NPV figures, Lady RA-RA decides to continue to provide capacity using her own performances.

Cautions with NPV: Actual interest rates may turn out to be different from the assumed interest rate; different interest rates may need to be used for benefits and cost; cash inflows and outflows may not happen at the same time; cash flows are assumed to occur at the end (not beginning) of a period. For these reasons, it is recommended to run several NPV scenarios considering future best case, most likely case, and worst case figures for all important variables.

Other cash flow methods can also be used for evaluating capacity planning alternatives, notably, the internal rate of return (IRR) method and the payback period. The IRR approach identifies a rate of return that equates the initial cost with the present value of future returns. If the IRR is greater than the project's cost of capital, or hurdle rate, the project will add value for the company. The payback period simply estimates the number of years it would take to recover the invested amount—it ignores the time value of money and is therefore appropriate for short-term planning horizons only. Another approach is the benefit-cost analysis (BCA), useful for evaluating alternatives with different outcome benefits. BCA accounts for all life-cycle benefits and life-cycle costs, irrespective of nature, computing a benefit-cost ratio (BCR) for each alternative. In practice, BCR is expressed as a ratio of NPV evaluated over the alternative's service life to the present value of the initial expenditure. It may be difficult to monetize all costs or benefits in this approach.

- *Decision Tree Analysis*

  A decision tree quantifies the expected value of capacity planning alternatives, providing a structured way to analyze alternative capacity-related decisions. Decision points are represented by squares (nodes), decision alternatives are represented by branches, and oval nodes represent expected values of probabilistic outcomes. By now, you may be weary of Lady RA-RA's capacity-planning issues, so let's use another example where capacity is often a problem: campus parking lots. Here's the situation:

Decision alternatives:	Undertake a large expansion now or go smaller, with an option for further expansion in four years.
Demand:	Probability of parking demand being high is 0.60 and being low is 0.40.
Lifetime profits:	Large expansion, $280,000 with high parking demand; $60,000 if demand is low. Smaller expansion, $95,000 with low demand; $265,000 if high demand occurs and option to further expand is exercised in year 4; $95,000 if high demand occurs but said option is not exercised (unlikely decision). Draw the decision tree branches first from left to right, and then compute the expected values from right to left.

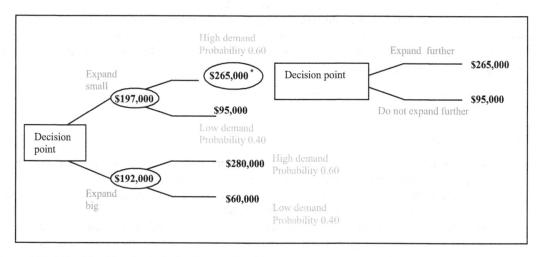

Figure 6.10 A Decision Tree Analysis for Capacity Decisions

* The node of $265,000 is the expected value of the node leading to further expansion/no further expansion, since a rational decision maker would typically like to expand when faced with evidence of expanding demand.

As we see, expanding in stages would provide a higher expected value of $197,000. The expected values at the oval nodes are computed as follows:

Expected value of 'expand small'   = 0.60 * $265,000 + 0.40 * $95,000 = $197,000

($197,000)

Expected value of 'expand large'   = 0.60 * $280,000 + 0.40 * $60,000 = $192,000

($192,000)

Since the difference in expected values associated with the two capacity planning alternatives is not very large, other factors such as cost escalation and availability of construction resources at a later time, risk of competition in the future, and the time value of cash flows should also be considered while picking an alternative.

Optimization, simulation, and some advanced decision analysis methods are also available for evaluating capacity planning alternatives but lie outside the scope of this text.

In terms of what to use and when, a simple application guideline can be developed:

Table 6.2 Matching Methods with Conditions

Probabilistic outcomes with uncertainty	*High time value of money*	*Stable market and costs*
Use decision tree method	Use NPV method	Use break-even analysis
Use simulation methods	Use IRR method	Use payback period method

Combinatorial approaches would add insight and rigor to the evaluation.

Besides quantitative evaluation, a qualitative assessment of alternatives is equally important in capacity planning. The capacity of the business to take on risk, the availability of capital, the life cycle stage of the market, the impact on employees, and community/government reactions and laws are a few important qualitative aspects to consider in capacity alternatives evaluation.

KEY POINTS

Key Steps in Capacity Planning (Continued)

Fixed alternatives: Capital investments and permanent hires, process and product re-design initiatives, preferred when demand is predictable and growing.

Variable alternatives: Use of temps, overtime, outsourcing, and capacity sharing, preferred in situations of high demand volatility and uncertainty.

Demand management alternative: Shifting demand peaks to off-peak periods through marketing promotions, off-season buying discounts, variable pricing, and complementary products.

Evaluating alternatives:

BEA: Finds the break-even point of capacity utilization for a capacity plan. Cautions—assumes linearity in the cost-production relationship, assumes linearity of revenue growth, and assumes simultaneity in cash inflows and outflows. Suitable for stable cost and price environments.

NPV: Finds out if the capacity plan would turn a profit in terms of the net difference between current investment and the present values of future cash flows. Cautions—interest rate used to discount future flows to present value may change, flows are deterministic. Suitable for investments with a long time horizon.

Decision tree analysis: Provides expected pay-offs from different alternatives under conditions of probabilistic demand. Suitable for conditions of probabilistic demand and differential pay-offs from different alternatives.

When to Change Capacity?

A capacity gap analysis should also identify the times when such capacity requires adding or removing. One should also consider the time it takes to implement the capacity change, which may range from a simple hiring to bringing an entire new plant into operation Another way to answer the question of when to make capacity changes relates to the alignment of capacity to demand. Three alternative strategies, expansionist, chase, and level, are generally seen in industry.

Expansionist strategy: Aggressive expansions that lead demand characterize the expansionist approach, often seen in retail businesses, examples being Starbucks, Dunkin' Donuts, Gap, and Kohl's. This approach benefits from being pro-active to demand changes and being first to market. If the expansion is large, economies of scale may also be availed. Downsides include the possibility of excess capacity, downsizing costs and loss of reputation, risks of technology change, and the need for capital in advance of demand. Expansion in anticipation of demand is also seen in industries with long capacity expansion lead times such as in automobile or steel manufacturing. An expansionist strategy can also serve as a strategic warning to would-be competitors to stay away from that market. Expanded capacity can also be deployed to steal market share from lower capacity competitors through economies-of-scale-based lower prices.

Chase strategy: A more conservative approach is capacity chases demand. Capacity changes are not made until after demand is seen and understood and typically occur in measured, incremental steps after demand becomes visible. Some amount of overtime, additional working days in a week, switching personnel among different jobs, and the use of temps are experienced in peak demand periods. Businesses in slow growth or highly uncertain markets favor a chase strategy, especially when the cost of adding permanent capacity is high. Honda's Odyssey plant in Alabama began with an investment of $400 million only compared to the $1 billion plants of its competitors. Capacity was added gradually as demand was seen to grow.

The risks of adding capacity after demand develops are obvious: being preempted by competitors, running out of products, losing the opportunity to be first to market, or coming in too late to re-coup lost market share, and the organizational disruption caused by frequent capacity changes. Also, if the capacity increments are small, the business loses potential economies of scale. On the other hand, the more conservative chase approach to adding capacity reduces risk exposure to market downs, staggers the need for capital, and increases opportunities to refresh capacity with newer technologies. Keeping supply limited can also enhance the market cachet of a product.

Level strategy: A business chooses to keep a relatively fixed level of capacity, straddling demand, in a sense. There are periods with matched supply and demand but also periods of shortages or excess capacity. The level strategy is practical in market conditions where the customer is prepared to wait and where the costs of hiring, terminating, or re-hiring employees are high. It promotes the benefits of stability of employment and operations. In low demand periods, employees may be scheduled for training and development or encouraged to take their annual leaves, and major plant maintenance could be scheduled. Efforts focus on demand management, using advance bookings, pricing, advertising, and complementary products to try to smoothen demand to fit the fixed supply of capacity. Level strategies with fixed capacity are most often seen with expensive professional services, such as the legal or medical field.

A fourth approach, one not seen that often, is a *match strategy*, essentially a compromise between the chase lag and expansionist lead strategies. With match strategy, the idea is to incrementally increase capacity simultaneously with increases in demand. This approach can work only with very short capacity implementation lead times, ready availability of capital, and market research capabilities adept in anticipating and tracking market changes, and where small investments in capacity are organizationally and technically feasible. Overtime, use of temps, and sub-contracting find use in this strategy. Some restaurants follow a match strategy, curtaining off parts of the facility when demand falls and opening up closed sections when demand increases.

Businesses are not limited to any one of the above approaches, often using some hybrid to suit their particular circumstances. The choice is sometimes out of their hands depending on whether customers choose to wait or not wait for products or service.

KEY POINTS

Key Steps in Capacity Planning

An *expansionist* strategy adds capacity in anticipation of demand growth, benefits from first mover advantage and economies of scale. Risky except in markets with predictable growth and stable technology.

A *chase* strategy avoids market decline risks by adding capacity after demand growth becomes evident, but may cost lost customers and the organizational inconvenience of repeated capacity additions. Works best if capacity is expensive and demand is unpredictable.

A *level* strategy keeps capacity fixed. Customers may wait if capacity is not available. Typically seen with expensive capacity in specialized products/high cost professional services. Appointments systems, price discounts, and variable pricing are some ways companies try to spread demand so as to create an even utilization of capacity.

A *match* strategy aims to adjust capacity in synch with demand, possible only when capacity can be rapidly expanded or reduced. Retailers, bars, and restaurants avail of freely available temp labor to call in workers when needed.

Where to Add Capacity?

Capacity planning targets specific locations. Where to add capacity may be a strategic decision. A site with a relatively low growth market could see capacity additions in order to warn competitors to stay away from other, more valuable markets, or lock out competitors from further expansion, or signal a company's interest in staying in a community.

Capacity may be added to suppliers in regions far removed from product markets and producing plants in order to boost supply chain capacity, as witnessed by China's rapid tie-ups/acquisitions of mining and oil production sites in Africa, Brazil, Australia, and elsewhere. Market considerations, of course, play an important role. Capacity planning for a call center network would consider the location of customers not for distance considerations, but for language, time difference, and cultural factors. Government regulations impact capacity planning decisions. Australia's proposal to impose a 40 percent tax on mining company profits caused mining businesses to pause expansion plans there—the proposal has since been withdrawn and replaced by a much milder rate of tax, with many commodities put on the tax exempt list.

OM IN PRACTICE

Capacity Planning in the Bottled Water Industry

For bottled spring water companies, the summer season sees water supply capacity at its lowest, while demand is at its peak. Since demand cannot be manipulated, that is, postponed to another time or satisfied with substitutes, managing supply capacity is the only option. Springs are full with fresh melting snows in the spring but dry up during summer. Droughts affect water availability. Finding new springs is an expensive and multi-year process requiring extensive searching and compliance with regulatory laws.

Capacity options include expanding internal bottling capacity for making and storing bottles of water ahead of summer demand or buying capacity from other sources. The capacity bottleneck is the availability of water in the summer. In-house capacity is expensive and difficult to downsize. Equipment and labor would be idle during summer when water supply falls. Labor could be temporary, but equipment would be idle during summer when water supply falls. Making and storing inventory means inventory costs and additional storage space. Outsourced capacity is higher cost, requires long term contracts, and high cost transportation since water is a heavy product.

The capacity problem is complex, with multiple factors including production capacity, the cost of new springs and facilities, spring water availability, the cost of transporting water, the cost of carrying inventory, and the cost of distribution space. Solutions are provided with quantitative modeling tools, possibly combining elements of outsourcing, expansion of internal production, storage and distribution capacity, and serving certain premium market segments at higher service levels than others.

KEY POINTS

A typical capacity planning process follows a well-defined sequence:

- *Why?* Examine business situation to forecast future market growth (or decline).
- *How much?* Assess existing capacity, with clearly defined capacity metrics. Determine capacity required to fill the gap.
- *What type?* Identify alternative approaches to match supply with demand. Assess the alternatives.
- *When?* Estimate market risk, lead times, and gestation periods for appropriate timing/sequencing of capacity addition projects.
- *Where?* Identify locations of capacity change initiatives.
- Update demand forecast and capacity availability at regular intervals.

6.4 Was It Done Right?

In capacity planning, the worst times are when a business is forced to shed capacity. Families lose livelihoods, local businesses lose customers, schools lose funding, and local community activities like Little League baseball lose sponsors. While a business shut-down may be on account of economic or competitive factors beyond its immediate control, those reasons do not absolve the business from the responsibility to undertake care in capacity planning. If a closure is imminent, capacity planning would include the timing and execution of shutdowns, including graduated worker attrition strategies, equipment transfers/auctions, proper advance communication to employees, job retraining options, help with securing unemployment benefits, and placement assistance to laid-off workers.

6.4.1 What Could Go Wrong?

Dec. 25, 2013, saw a lot of disappointed people. Orders on online retailers like Amazon were not being delivered in time. UPS was unable to make thousands of deliveries on time due to a sudden increase in last-minute online orders. UPS boosted labor hiring at the last minute, but the capacity bottleneck proved to be inadequate cargo aircraft. UPS financials took a hit. Under-capacity, however, can be corrected more easily than over-capacity. If there's evidence that a profitable market exists, resources can be acquired and investments can be made. While some amount of over-capacity may be desirable as a safety cushion, excess capacity comes with high maintenance and exit costs. The auto and air-travel industries are currently experiencing the pains of over-capacity.

OM IN PRACTICE

How Businesses Cope with Over-capacity

Faced with over-capacity, airlines are taking out airplanes from service on a temporary and long-term basis. The over-capacity is being stored in the deserts of the US southwest, whose arid climate and open land makes it an ideal location for storing airplanes.

Figure 6.11 Planes Stored in the Desert

Source: Alan Radecki. "Mojave Airport: Airliner Storage Area," [CC], via *Wikimedia Commons*, Nov. 18, 2003, http://commons.wikimedia.org/wiki/File%3AMhv-031118-area3-31cr-8.jpg.

Over-capacity has led to several coping strategies.

Plant closures—Ford Europe shuttered its Genk, Belgium, plant at the end of 2014 following plant closures at Southampton and Dagenham, England, in 2013. The goal is to bring overall Europe manufacturing to 80 percent of capacity—a prerequisite to profits. Ford and General Motors Holden shut down their manufacturing operations in Australia.

ArcelorMittal closed or idled several of its steel-making plants due to continued weakness in the European construction market. Conversely, Caterpillar, buoyed by reconstruction demand in tsunami-stricken Japan and mining and construction demand in Asia, is going on a capacity addition binge—building a new 1.2 million square foot facility at Athens, GA, for making mini-excavators and small track-type tractors, a new mining truck factory in Indonesia, a small engine plant in India, and a wheel loader plant in China, while expanding its hydraulic cylinder manufacturing capacity in South Carolina, forest products facility in LaGrange, GA, and off-road truck making capacity in Tosno, Russia. However, this capacity expansion may run into problems with the recent downtrends in commodity prices and mining/construction activities.

Capacity sharing—GM announced a purchasing and joint vehicle development agreement with Peugeot, France, with co-manufactured cars slated to hit the road by 2016. Nissan Motor Co. and its partner, Renault SA, recently completed a capacity-sharing agreement with Germany's Daimler AG, under which Daimler's commercial vehicles will be produced at a Renault plant in France. Nissan CEO Carlos Ghosn said he plans to manufacture Daimler cars at Nissan's plant.

Capacity shifting—Automakers are shifting capacity to emerging markets such as China, Mexico, and Thailand, where cheap labor can be exploited, and new markets tapped. GM plans to increase production capacity in China by 65 percent by 2020, investing $12 billion in China between this year and 2017, while shedding 1,100 workers at its Gusan, South Korea, plant. Hyundai Motor Co plans to build its fourth plant in China for about 1 trillion won ($926.48 million) and start production in early 2016. Nissan and Renault are expanding the production capacity of their joint venture plant in India by one-third, while Honda Motors is building a new plant with a 120,000 unit/year capacity at San Paulo, Brazil.

Adapted from: Staff, "Caterpillar Plans Expansion in LaGrange," *Atlanta Business Chronicle*, Feb. 12, 2015; "GM Boosting China Production Capacity to 5 Million," *The Associated Press*, April 20, 2014; Christopher Freeburn, "GM Stock—General Motors May Make 1,100 Job Cuts in South Korea," *InvestorPlace*, Jan. 24, 2014; Dave Guilford, "Ford of Europe Works Its Way Back," *Automotive News*, March 10, 2014; "Hyundai Motor Eyes Major Expansion with New Plant in China," *Reuters*, March 26, 2014; "CAT Christens New Ga. Manufacturing Plant," *Manufacturing Net*, Nov. 11, 2013; Taro Konoya, "Auto Industry Under Capacity—New Alliances, Emerging Markets Seen As Possible Solutions," *The Daily Yomiuri*, April 20, 2010; Trefis Team, "Caterpillar Ramps Up Capacity On Strong Backlog," *Dow Jones Newswires*, March 22, 2012.

Drops in demand are not the only reason for such over-capacity situations. Over-capacity can develop in several ways, some almost unnoticed. Reasons include capacity jumps in large chunks, chasing economies of scale, increasing MES levels, long gestation periods, and changes in production or delivery technology. Other drivers could include high exit costs, over-optimistic demand forecasts, a desire to establish a company presence brand in new markets or intimidate competition, managerial risk profiles, excess idle capital, early mover benefits, government incentives, and employment pressures. At a more micro level, capacity planning can suffer from neglect because of management preoccupation with everyday firefighting, inadequate documentation of existing capacity, lack of forecasting resources and incentives, use of inappropriate capacity measures, and frequent changes in company strategy.

On the other hand, capacity shortfalls are also experienced, especially when businesses are caught off-guard by sudden increases in demand, such as happened recently with some electronic products, when demand overran the supplier capacity for touchscreens and memory chips. Another pitfall in capacity planning is the failure to consider quality standards in capacity computations. Consider the following example.

Experience shows a loss in step yield of 10 percent in a production process with six sequential steps, that is, on average, 10 percent of the output at every step would be defective (does not mean that 1 out of every 10 pieces of output would be defective—defectives happen at random). What should be the production capacity of the process if a total of 100 'good' products are required at the end of the process?

Capacity required of an 'n' step process $= $ # of good units desired/
$$(1 - \text{yield loss of step\# 1}) * (1 - \text{yield loss of step\# 2})$$
$$* (1 - \text{yield loss of step\# n})$$

Capacity required of a 6-step process $= \dfrac{100}{(1-.10)^6} = \dfrac{100}{0.531} = 189 \text{ units}$

That is, the process should be capable of processing a total of 189 units in order to emerge with a 100 good units at the end.

6.4.2 Indicators of Capacity Planning Performance

KPIs (key performance indicators) of successful capacity planning would include both efficiency and customer-facing metrics. Efficiency is measured through evaluation of changes in productivity and capacity utilization. Customer-oriented measures would include metrics such as customer order fill rate (percent of items in an order fulfilled in time), and cycle service level (percent of orders fulfilled completely in time, on average). The traditional KPI of capacity planning was capacity availability—get enough capacity and utilize it fully to meet demand. Current capacity planning KPIs also recognize quality, inventories, and lead times as performance dimensions, all of which are adversely affected as capacity utilization gets closer to 100 percent. Capacity planners and line managers need to explicitly consider such trade-offs in seeking high levels of capacity utilization for greater output.

Poor capacity planning may also be reflected in:

- Unbudgeted increase in employee overtime
- Unbudgeted increase in use of temps
- Number of orders turned away for lack of timely capacity
- Number of stock-outs in peak demand periods
- Excess inventory and no one knows exactly why
- High proportion of aging inventory
- Frequent use of air shipments or other form of expedited shipping
- Rise in workplace accidents (due to consistently high utilization)
- Rise in machine breakdowns beyond normal patterns.

> **KEY POINTS**
>
> **Was It Done Right?**
>
> - Under-capacity may be a good problem to have relative to over-capacity.
> - Over-capacity leads to plant closures, capacity sharing ,and capacity shifting to other higher demand locations.
> - Poor quality yield may result in under-capacity because of low production of 'good' units.
> - Both efficiency-based and customer-facing metrics are required.
> - High levels of capacity utilization may require trade-offs between output and quality, productivity and cycle time goals.

6.5 Current Trends in Capacity Planning

Sustainability and the use of simulation and real options are emergent trends in capacity planning. Services present special challenges in capacity planning, and both demand and capacity tools have been developed to meet the capacity planning needs of service businesses.

6.5.1 Sustainable Capacity Planning

Businesses today are aware of the triple bottom line (TBL/3BL), 'people, planet, profit.' Sustainable capacity planning is a holistic planning process that seeks to match capacity to anticipated demand in a manner that adheres to these larger goals. Every unit of capacity is analyzed for an energy footprint projection. Energy is viewed as a distinct resource for capacity planners for specific measurement, analysis, forecasting, and use. For example, Sweden is examining methods to introduce sustainability in auto manufacturing capacity. The paint shop in an auto plant is the single largest consumer of energy, water, and chemicals, and a significant producer of emissions and waste in an auto manufacturing plant. A Swedish initiative by Volvo and Saab Auto found that "approximately 80% of the water and 40% of energy consumption at the vehicle manufacturer comes from the ovens, air ventilation and heating bath systems in a paint shop. More than 2/3 of the water consumption comes from the pretreatment process."[9] A Swedish auto research group is actively looking at technologies in ventilation including recirculation, cascading, heat exchanging, low energy- and water-consuming pretreatment processes, oven redesigns and energy-efficient heating technology, and solvent-free paints processes for a targeted energy consumption reduction of 50 percent and zero water consumption. The reuse of surplus energy from one process for use in another is also being examined.

One of the newer approaches to sustainable capacity planning is virtualization, the modeling of virtualized operations to estimate energy footprints and other attributes of a capacity plan prior to acquisition, implementation, and deployment. To build a model, data is collected on existing systems and a baseline established for important capacity-related and performance output factors. Virtual models are developed, and their capacity and resource consumption are evaluated against the baseline data and baseline performance. Virtual models find application in capacity planning in many environments. A recent study developed a generic simulation model of hospital capacity planning during a bioterrorist attack, relating characteristics of the hospitals to various stages of exposure and providing policy recommendations.[10]

6.5.2 Real Options Approach to Capacity Planning

Let's assume AT&T Wireless is planning to expand its capacity. It may use net present value analysis to compare the discounted future cash flows expected from a capacity investment with the cash investment required today. However, there may be some value is being able to postpone the investment until market demand becomes more visible. Similarly, businesses using offshore production capacity face exchange rate and demand uncertainties. Such businesses may benefit from maintaining both domestic and overseas capacities, keeping an option to switch production as currency fluctuations and demand surges dictate. The value of the option grows in proportion to the increase in exchange rate or demand uncertainty. Using a real options approach allows us to quantify the value of having an option to wait compared to not having such an option. A real option is a right, but not an obligation, to:

- Postponement option: A call option to delay the start of a project. The exercise price is the money invested to get the project started.
- Termination option: A put option to terminate a project. The exercise price could be a penalty or forfeited deposit for originally anticipated work.
- Expand option: A call option to expand a project. The exercise price is the additional investment required to enable project expansion.

Option values are formally computed using the Black-Scholes model from finance together with other methods such as decision tree analytics and simulation. Real options analysis requires a deep knowledge of business operations, market behavior, competition, and business strategy to enable a well-specified simulation model that includes all key factors and develops realistic ranges of values for modeling uncertainty. The timing and price of an option exercise are not as readily apparent in real options relative to financial options, leading management to make decisions on the basis of judgment.

6.5.3 Capacity Planning for Services

Companies like Zappos have been built on the ability to quickly respond to customer wishes and needs. Doing so requires capacity availability at all times—in terms of people, equipment, bandwidth, and supply chains. Customers do not think about how much capacity planning has gone into developing Zappos's rapid response online order taking and fulfillment system. Customers do not care why a site goes down or a transaction or return is delayed. But Zappos has to plan and install a system that has the capacity to deliver even when thousands of customers may be using the system at the same time. Services capacity planning is particularly complicated by the nature of services—services can be intangible and perishable. Services are also customized and delivered for quick consumption (like movie watching). The same customer may demand different qualities of service depending on mood, want, and need—e.g., quick service at lunch but leisurely dinners. Humans typically deliver services, meaning that human behavior, attitude, and state of mind affect the quality and variability of the service. The human factor in services also means that consistently high levels of capacity utilization cause more quality problems in services relative to manufacturing. Both capacity and demand require active management in the delivery of services. Substantial capacity safety cushions may be tolerated because of reputation, or need (fire stations). Capacity may be limited as a deliberate 'product hype' building strategy, frequently seen with new toys and electronic devices around the holidays. The difficulties of the supply-demand balancing act are managed through a combination of capacity management options (CMOs) and demand management options (DMOs).

Table 6.3 Capacity and Demand Management Options

Capacity management options	Demand management options
Hiring and firing staff	Booking in advance
Worker scheduling	Overbooking/underbooking at different prices—yield/revenue management
Use of temps	
Worker furloughs	Complementary services (stools at a bar for waiting dinner customers)
Worker overtime	
Worker idle time	Substitute unavailable services with services of lower cost/higher quality
Cross-train workers	
Introduce time-saving technologies	Timely information sharing with customer
Change process steps to eliminate waste of time and resources	Marketing promotions
Outsource/lease capacity from another business	Volume order discounts
Co-own capacity with another business	
Share own capacity with another business	
Involve customers in service preparation/delivery	
Make customers wait	
Tolerate loss of customers	

Adapted from: K. J. Klassen and T. R. Rohleder, "Demand and Capacity Management Decisions in Services: How They Impact on One Another," *International Journal of Operations & Production Management*, 22(5) (2002): 527–548.

Of these, yield (also called revenue management) has perhaps contributed the most to service profitability, especially in airlines and hotels. Yield management slices up capacity among different customer segments and prices these for profit maximization. It is quite possible for a low paying sure-shot customer to be turned away in the (quantified) hope of getting a higher paying customer later for the same service. Yield or revenue management is more strictly a matter of capacity management rather than long-term capacity planning and is treated in more detail in the capacity management chapter (chapter 7).

KEY POINTS

Current Trends in Capacity Planning

- Sustainable capacity planning performance goals are based on the triple bottom line 'people, planet, profit.'
- Energy is viewed as a resource, and energy consumption and emission footprints are estimated for every capacity resource.
- Simulation and virtual modeling are cost-effective tools for sustainable capacity planning.
- Real options in capacity planning offers the opportunity (not obligation) to exercise choices to stop, delay or expand capacity at different project time points.
- Capacity planning in services employs a mix of capacity management (overtime, temps use, outsourcing) and demand management (yield management, marketing promotions) options.

6.6 Conclusion

Customer: *"Why should I choose you?"*
Business: *"Because we promise we'll be prepared with adequate resources to be able to meet your needs, in time."*

The ideas and methods discussed in the chapter will help you fulfill that promise. Capacity planning is an exercise that enables businesses to go beyond the basic issue of simply trying to match supply with demand. It asks *why*, determining the reason for adding or shedding capacity. Capacity planning could mean planning not to meet demand in full or shifting demand to meet capacity; or keeping excess capacity to avoid the dysfunctionalities of high utilization rates. It asks *how much*, forcing discipline in forecasting and scenario analysis. It asks *what type*, including options to outsource, use temps, lease not buy, re-engineer or redesign, or manage demand, together with the tools to evaluate these capacity-sourcing alternatives. It asks *when*, demanding an explicit assessment of the risks and advantages of keeping capacity level, or changing capacity ahead of, behind, or simultaneously with changes in demand. And, finally, capacity planning asks *where*, choosing whether to locate capacity near existing business locations, existing customers, suppliers, raw material locations, emerging markets, or locations determined by political and strategic factors.

Today, capacity planning extends across the supply chain, exponentially increasing the inherent complexity, risk, and scope of the exercise. The five decisions of capacity planning—why, how much, what type, when and where—are important at every stage of the supply chain, since capacity planning in supply markets would ultimately affect responsiveness at the retail level to the end consumer demand.

What Have We Learned?

What Is Capacity Planning?

- Capacity planning is the acquisition and development of capacity to meet anticipated user demand. Capacity planning does not always target 100 percent fulfillment of user demand or 100 percent utilization of available capacity.

  The goal of capacity planning is to minimize the discrepancy between demand and capacity in a cost-effective, revenue-effective, quality-effective, and safety-effective manner.

- Capacity is the upper limit of a system's ability to make, store, deliver, or receive products or services at a point in time.

  Design or peak capacity is the maximum output capacity possible, usually sustainable for a short period of time.

  Effective capacity or the best operating capacity level is the capacity of the resource under normal operating conditions

  Fixed capacity represents investments in assets that cannot be reversed easily such as land, equipment, and permanent hires (or classroom capacity by law).

  Variable capacity represents investments that can be recovered or changed relatively easily, such as outsourcing contracts, personnel overtime, and temp hiring.

- With standard products, capacity can be measured in terms of finished product or service output, e.g. number of cars/year; number of pizzas/day, number of rooms.

With multiple products, capacity can be measured in terms of input resource availability, e.g. number of ER doctors available per shift, number of beds.

- Capacity utilization is the amount of design capacity that is utilized on average in fulfilling demand. Capacity utilization cannot exceed design capacity:

$$\text{Capacity Utilization \%} = \frac{\text{Actual average output or extent of resource use}}{\text{Design capacity}} * 100$$

Efficiency is the amount of effective capacity that is utilized on average in fulfilling demand:

$$\text{Efficiency \%} = \frac{\text{Actual average output or extent of resource use}}{\text{Effective capacity}} * 100$$

A high efficiency ratio is not necessarily good news if the effective capacity is low relative to design capacity on account of poor maintenance, poor quality, or worker mismanagement. A high utilization ratio may also increase costs exponentially under conditions of high uncertainty.

Why Is It Important?

- Excess capacity results in waste and expense—for example, the estimated cost of an empty hospital bed is $65,694.

  Capacity shortages can result in lost customers, poor quality, and loss of reputation and goodwill.

- Capacity planning can be used for strategic advantage, e.g., using scale economies to reduce prices and raise entry costs for potential entrants.
- There are jobs in capacity planning—capacity planner, capacity analyst. Even financial firms like Goldman Sachs and Morgan Stanley are now taking delivery of physical products as part of their trading strategy and require capacity planning for product transportation, storage, and sale.

How Is It Done?

- A capacity planner works with facilities, products/services, work processes, workers, and supply chains. High product margins encourage higher investments in capacity. Unions and government regulations on safety, job flexibility, and environment are also key determinants.
- The five questions of capacity planning:

  Why?
  What is the perceived need for capacity planning? New markets, new suppliers, greater uncertainties in demand or supply, competitor moves, new production, or logistical/warehousing technologies?

  How much?
  Product-wise demand forecasts are converted into forecasted equipment and labor resource requirements. The computed requirement of labor and capital is inflated by a capacity cushion, appropriate to the uncertainty of the operating environment. A capacity gap analysis reveals the net difference between computed capacity requirement and existing resource capacity. Planned capacity may not match demand. Large capacity cushions are preferred in conditions of high demand uncertainty and high shortage

consequences, e.g., firehouses and hospital emergency rooms. Capacity may be deliberately kept at levels lower than demand to create exclusivity and hype (luxury goods, fine restaurants). The company's MES, or minimum efficient scale of production, could also limit capacity investments. MES represents the optimum production point where the total cost/unit is at a minimum.

What type?

Capacity plans develop alternative strategies to align supply with demand. Short product life cycles and high levels of demand uncertainty discourage investments in fixed capacity. Outsourcing, overtime, training workers to perform multiple jobs, and the use of temps are preferred forms of variable capacity in such environments. Managing demand through marketing promotions, differential pricing for specific market segments, volume pricing discounts, and the use of complementary or substitute products is another alternative. Break-even analysis (BEA), discounted cash flow analysis, and decision tree analysis are tools used for evaluating capacity planning alternatives. BEA is a graphical tool that finds the break-even point of capacity at which total revenues become equal to total costs. BEA is suited to stable conditions. Discounted cash flow analysis typically computes the net present value (NPV) of an investment alternative by subtracting the present value of future cash flows from the value of currently made investment. NPV uses a selected interest rate factor to covert future dollars into current value dollars. NPV is suited to projects with a substantive future life. Decision tree analysis decomposes a decision into what-if lines of action with specific event probabilities that culminate in expected payout outcomes. Decision tree analysis is suited to analyzing uncertainties in choice of action under probabilistic conditions.

When?

An expansionist strategy involves expanding capacity ahead of anticipated demand; suited to high benefit from first-to-market stable demand and stable technology environments and capacity investments that have long gestation periods. Losses accrue if expected demand does not materialize. A chase strategy involves capacity expansion after demand becomes visible, with capacity changes occurring incrementally, in stages. Slow growth, high uncertainty, and high investment characterize a chase strategy environment. Risks include being preempted by competitors, running out of products, losing first-to-market gains, disruptions from frequent capacity changes, and loss of potential economies of scale. A level strategy involves maintaining a fixed level of capacity for relatively long periods. Level strategies are suited to markets where the customer is prepared to wait (risky) and where capacity costs and capacity utilization are high; e.g., doctors in a clinic. A match strategy involves matching capacity changes to changes in demand in a near simultaneous manner. This approach can work only when frequent small investments in capacity at short notice are organizationally, financially, and technically feasible.

Where?

Factors that influence capacity location are market proximity, raw material proximity, operating and delivery costs, competitive strategy, and asset lock-in opportunities.

Was It Done Right?

- Over-capacity can creep up through technology obsolescence, chasing MES goals, high exit costs, over-optimistic demand expectations, availability of idle capital or labor, and pressures to maintain employment.

- Capacity surges may affect product quality adversely, especially when fed by mandated overtime or consistently high levels of equipment utilization. The 'yield' of an activity indicates the proportion of good units produced by that activity relative to the total number of units processed.
- Capacity plans become more realistic when those providing or using capacity are involved in the planning process.
- The modern view of capacity planning recognizes that efficiencies, quality, inventories, and lead times are adversely affected as capacity utilization gets closer to 100 percent. Managers may have to make choices among different performance parameters at different levels of capacity availability and utilization.
- Early warning signals could range from unbudgeted increase in employee overtime, unplanned use of temps, order rejections/delays, increasing stock-outs, excess inventory without good reason, or a rise in workplace accidents and machine breakdowns.

Current Trends in Capacity Planning

- Sustainable capacity planning adheres to the triple bottom line of 'people, planet, profit.' Every resource and every unit of capacity is analyzed for an energy footprint projection.
- Virtualization enables the modeling of operations to estimate energy footprints and other attributes of a capacity plan *prior* to implementation and deployment.
- A real option represents the right, but not an obligation, to exercise a choice in the future, such as options to postpone the start, abandon mid-way, or expand at a later time, with specific exercise prices. Real options analysis enables a cost-benefit analysis of designing options into a capacity plan.
- Capacity planning in services requires a combination of capacity management options (CMOs) and demand management options (DMO) decisions.
- Yield management reserves capacity among different customer segments and prices these capacities differently for profit maximization.

Discussion Questions

1 Suggest input and output measures for capacity for a dentist, a theater, a restaurant, Walmart, Amtrak rail, and a business school.
2 The U.S. postal service is experiencing a dramatic drop in letters being mailed. USPS capacity was built for an era when writing letters was the popular way to communicate. Examine and expound on the capacity-planning alternatives available to USPS at this time.
3 High capacity utilization of expensive resources is desirable in capacity plans. Imagine you are the dean of your college and would like to maximize capacity utilization of faculty. Discuss the different aspects of this policy.
4 Think of two good examples of products/services for expansionist, chase, level, and match capacity planning approaches. Explain the reasons underlying your choice of examples.
5 Write a short memo to your boss explaining the advantages and risks of BEA, NPV and decision tree analysis.
6 Provide one reason why capacity planning would be an important knowledge area for a) a finance major, b) an accounting major, c) a marketing major, and d) an HR major.
7 One of the most common and frustrating experiences in school is getting an elevator to make it to a class in time. Consider the elevators in your school and their utilization at various times. Did the building elevator planners use an expansionist, chase, level, or match capacity planning strategy? What would you have done and why?

End of Chapter Problems

1   Rich, the manager of Quick Oil Change, is getting a few complaints from customers about service delays. The technicians complain about being short-staffed. Rich wishes to get some operational numbers on capacity utilization. The design capacity (maximum possible) of the oil change shop is 300 autos per day. The effective capacity (sustained output under normal conditions) is 260 autos/day. On average, the shop completes 240 oil changes/day. Compute the efficiency and capacity utilization of the shop. Could there be any truth to the technicians' complaints of being short-handed? Why or why not?

Answer:

Efficiency%   = actual output/effective capacity   = (240/260) * 100 = 92.3%
Capacity utilization = actual output/design capacity   = (240/300) * 100 = 80%

There appears to be adequate capacity (capacity utilization is 80%, efficiency is 92.3%)—assuming demand is even.

2   The department of management at the 'Let's Do It' school of business is planning to retire its old copy machines and lease new state-of-the-art copiers instead. The office manager, Linda, needs to know how many copiers should be leased. The copiers are used by three distinct groups in the department—faculty for small print jobs of academic papers and the occasional mid-term; office support staff for large print jobs of exams, bulk mailings, and circulars; and authorized students for small print jobs and the occasional sneaked-in book chapter copy (desist—it's illegal!). She forecasts the following demand:

Demand source	Average total weekly demand	Average processing time/ unit (on new copier)	Total processing time
Faculty	300 copy jobs	6 min/copy job	1,800 min/week
Staff	700 copy jobs	10 min/copy job	7,000 min/week
Students	100 copy jobs	5 min/copy job	500 min/week

The department runs an 8-hour day, 5 days a week, 45 weeks in a year. How many copiers should Linda lease?

Answer:
Total capacity need = 9,300 min/week * 45 weeks/year = 418,500 min = 6,975 hours
Total capacity available/copier = 8 hours/day * 5 days a week * 45 weeks/yr = 1,800 hour/yr

So Linda would have to lease out 6,975/1,800 = 3.88 = 4 new copiers.

3   A technology consulting firm is proud to report 70 percent utilization of its billable employees currently standing at 800 people worldwide. The firm bases 60 percent of its people outside the U.S. in low-cost locations. In the year 2010, the firm generated $70 million in fees. Assume 5 days per week and 50 weeks per year[11]:

i)   What is the firm's average daily productivity per person?

Answer: Average daily productivity = output/daily input per person
Output = annual fees
= $70,000,000
Daily input per person = number of billable person days
= number of people * percentage utilized * number of billable days in a year

= 800 * 0.7 * 5 * 50
= 140,000 person-days
Average daily productivity = $70,000,000/140,000
= $500 per person-day.

ii) If the firm's utilization were to improve to 85 percent in the year 2011, how much fees would they generate, assuming the same average daily productivity per person?

Answer: At 85% utilization, the firm-wide aggregate billable days = 800 * 0.85 * 5 * 50
= 170,000 person-days
Estimated fees for year 2011 @ 85% utilization = 170,000 * $500
= **$85 million**

iii) If the average daily billing rate in the U.S. is $800 per person, what is the non-U.S. contribution to the year 2010 revenues?

Answer: Year 2010 revenue = $70,000,000
Total billable days = 140,000 person-days
Non-U.S. contribution = 0.6 * 140,000 person-days
= 84,000 person-days
Therefore, U.S. contribution = 56,000 person-days
U.S. contribution to 2010 revenues = $800 * 56,000
=$44,800,000
Therefore, **non-U.S. contribution** = $70,000,000 − $44,800,000
= **$25,200,000**
Average daily rate @ low cost location = $300 per person-day

4   A bank staffs four tellers between 9 a.m. and 3 p.m. Both the branch manager and the investment specialist operate as tellers during the peak operating hour between noon and 1 p.m. Over a one-month period, they have observed an average of 5 minutes to serve each customer and only 2 minutes per customer during the peak operating hour. They also observe that their average throughput is 100 customers during the peak hour and 60 per hour at other times during the day.

i)   What is the capacity utilization of the branch during the peak hour?

Answer: Capacity utilization = capacity used/available capacity
Reference capacity model below
Approach 1: Capacity is computed in units of resource-time; i.e., 'teller-minutes.'
Total resources available during peak hour (noon to 1 p.m.) = 4 tellers + branch manager + investment specialist = 6
Available capacity during the peak hour = 6 * 60 minutes
= 360 teller-minutes
Capacity used = number of customers served * average teller time per customer
= 100 * 2
= 200 teller-minutes
Therefore, capacity utilization = 200/360
= **55.56%**
Approach 2: Capacity is computed in units of output; i.e., customers served
Available capacity during the peak hour = number of customers that can be served
= maximum number of customers that can be served per teller * number of tellers
= (60/2) * 6

= 180 customers
Therefore, capacity utilization = number of customers served/available capacity
= 100/180
= **55.56%**

ii) What is the average daily capacity utilization of the branch?

Answer: Daily capacity utilization = capacity used/available capacity for the business day
Using Approach 2:
Capacity used per day = number of customers served during off-peak hours +
number of customers served during the peak hour
= 60 customers/hr * 5 hrs + 100
= 400 customers per day
Available daily capacity = available capacity during off-peak hours +
available capacity during the peak hour
= {(60/5) customers/hr/branch resource * 6 branch resources * 5 hrs} +
{(60/2) customers/teller * 6 tellers}
= 540 customers per day
Average daily utilization of the branch = 400/540
= **74.1%**

iii) How can the branch improve the peak hour capacity utilization by at least 20%?

Answer: Current peak hour capacity utilization = 55.56%
Target peak hour capacity utilization = 66.67%
In order to achieve the target utilization, either (a) decrease available capacity or (b) increase capacity used, i.e., increase customer throughput.
The branch does not have control over the customer arrivals. Hence, let us try to reduce available capacity during the peak hour. Let the branch manager receive customers and help streamline the service.
This will provide for **5 tellers during the peak hour**.
Hence, new available capacity = 5 * 60
= 300 teller-minutes
New capacity utilization = 200/300
= **66.67% Target achieved**

5   A group of doctors are considering setting up a photon radiation center for treatment of various cancers and growths. The fixed cost to set up a center is very high—about $150 million. It costs, on average, $5,000/patient for an entire treatment. Medicare pays about $30,000 on average per patient for an entire treatment. How many patients would the photon radiation center need in order to break even?

Answer: Let the # of patients be = x
Total cost   = fixed cost + variable cost
                = $150,000,000 + x * $5000

Total revenue = # of patients * revenue/patient
                = x * $30,000

At break-even:
Total revenue = total cost
$30,000x = $150,000,000 + $5,000x$

Solving for x;

$x = \$150,000,000/\$25,000 = 6,000$ patients

The break-even point for the planned center would be 6,000 patients. The center would begin turning a profit after the 6,000th patient.

6 Referring to the above question, the doctors now have a breakdown in terms of patient type as well as associated demand forecasts, costs, and reimbursements. What would be the break-even point in terms of revenue?

Patient type	Revenue/ patient	Unit variable cost	CMR*	Forecasted demand
Prostate growth	$25,000	$4,000	0.84	2,000
Nervous system	$35,000	$10,000	0.71	1,000
Others	$20,000	$3,000	0.85	1,500

$$*CMR = \frac{\text{Unit Contribution margin}}{\text{Revenue/unit}} = \frac{(\text{Revenue/patient} - \text{Unit Variable cost})}{\text{Revenue/patient}}$$

Patient type	Annual revenue	Proportion of total revenue	CMR	Revenue weighted CMR
Prostate growth	$50,000,000*	0.44	0.84	0.44 * 0.84 = 0.37
Nervous system	$35,000,000	0.30	0.71	0.30 * 0.71 = 0.21
Others	$30,000,000 $115,000,000	0.26	0.85	0.26 * 0.85 = 0.22 0.80

* *Forecasted demand * revenue/patient*

$$\text{BEP (\$ revenue)} = \frac{\text{Total Fixed cost}}{\text{Total weighted CMR}} = \frac{\$150,000,000}{0.80} = \$187,500,000$$

Answer: The new corporation shall have to generate $187,500,000 in sales revenue to break even. Following the 'proportion of total revenue' from the table above (44 percent, 30 percent and 26 percent for prostate, nervous system and others patient types, respectively), this $187.5 million of sales would consist of $82.5 million from prostate patients, $56.24 million from nervous system patients, and $48.76 million from others. We can also divide these dollar numbers by the patient type revenue to obtain an estimate of number of patients required in each category, e.g., 3,300 prostate patients ($82.5 million/$25,000 per prostate patient).

7 A pizza place is considering adding another oven (a bottleneck). The owner estimates that, after considering expansion costs, a profit of $100,000 is possible if demand surges—the chances of the latter happening is 40 percent. Conversely, she anticipates a loss of $10,000 if demand dips (chances 30 percent). If demand remains the same, she expects a profit of $60,000. If no expansion is made, the corresponding profits with the same demand probabilities are $50,000, $40,000, and $30,000, for 'high,' 'no change,' and 'low' demand scenarios, respectively. Develop and use a decision tree to help the pizza place owner make a decision.

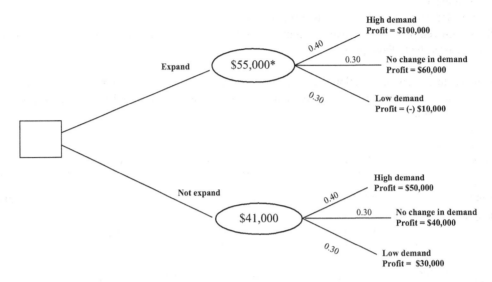

Figure 6.12 Problem 7 Decision Tree

* The expected value at the nodes are computed as follows. For example,
'Expand' node = 0.40 * $100,000 + 0.30 * $60,000 + 0.30 * (−) $10,000 = $55,000

Answer: Pick expand. Advise the owner, though, that she should have the financial ability to withstand the loss of $10,000 (or perhaps even a bit more—it's an estimate, after all) if demand does actually decline from its current level (30 percent chance).

Suggested Class Projects

a) Prepare a capacity plan for the commercial shipping industry for the year 2012 (data available from Federal Reserve Board).
b) Prepare a capacity plan for electricity using both capacity management and demand management options for the Con Edison utility company for New York City. Remember demand surges in the summer.
c) For hospitals, surge capacity is the availability of beds to treat a sudden surge of patients, typically in an epidemic or disaster. The Health Services and Resources Administration (HRSA) has set a surge capacity standard of 500 beds immediately available for every million people living in an area (Agency for Healthcare Research and Quality, 2004).[12] The number of empty staffed beds and available equipment like mechanical ventilators and decontamination showers often fails to meet this standard.

Provide some suggestions on how to increase capacity in hospitals to meet sudden surges in patients.
Suggestions:
It is prohibitively expensive to maintain large amounts of excess capacity at all times. A patient surge will require hospitals to add capacity by a variety of measures:

•   Creating additional patient treatment areas. This may involve placing beds or stretchers into cafeterias and conference rooms or the use of specialized tents and mobile facilities that can be placed near the hospital building.

- Some inventory of equipment such as mechanical ventilators and decontamination showers could be kept.
- Existing care patterns can be changed, including postponing elective procedures and redirecting patients seeking nonurgent care. Ordinarily, hospitals give priority to the most critical patients first, but in a disaster, the focus changes to maximizing the number of lives saved at the cost of not 'doing everything possible' to save an individual life. Triage systems for disasters need to be developed.
- Reverse triage systems are also possible, when some patients can be discharged early to accommodate incoming disaster victims. Existing patients would need to be categorized into risk categories depending on their ability to tolerate early discharge.

Suggested Case

Shouldice Hospital[13]

Description

A hospital specializing in hernia operations is considering whether and how to expand the reach of its services.

Learning Objective

To teach in service management, management of operations, and business strategy courses.

Notes

1 "United Plans To Add Capacity After Years Of Scaling Down," *Trefis*, Nov. 26, 2013, http://www.trefis.com/stock/ual/articles/216920/united-plans-to-add-capacity-after-years-of-scaling-down/2013-11-26.
2 Justin Lahart, "Auction Highlights a Drop in US Capacity," *Wall Street Journal*, May 17, 2010: B1, http://www.wsj.com/articles/SB10001424052748704414504575244741639539902.
3 David Kocieniewski, "A Shuffle of Aluminum, but to Banks, Pure Gold," *The New York Times*, July 20, 2013.
4 Peter Robison, A. Loder, and A. Bjerga, "Amber Waves of Pain," *Bloomberg Businessweek*, July 26–Aug.1, 2010: 56.
5 R. Balakrishnan and N. S. Soderstrom, "The Cost of System Congestion: Evidence from the Healthcare Sector," *Journal of Management Accounting Research*, 12 (2000): 97–114
6 "These kids are by far the sickest kids in California," said a medical director at the hospital; from J. Morrissey, "Stretching the Limits," *Modern Healthcare*, 34(39), 2004, 46–48, 50.
7 Lori Ranson, "Interview: JetBlue Chief Executive, Dave Barger," *Airline Business*, July 23, 2010.
8 "8 Wastes of Lean: TIMWOODS," *Six Sigma*, http://www.isixsigma.com/dictionary/8-wastes-of-lean/
9 From the January 2010 R&D program proposal to secure competitive vehicle and powertrain production in Sweden: Anders Carlsson, Volvo Cars; Sven Hjelm, Björn Holmgren, Scania; Lennart Malmsköld, Saab Automobile; Magnus Granström, Johan Svenningstorp, AB Volvo; Anna Wik, FKG, "2020 Sustainable Manufacturing Systems Capable of Producing Innovative Environmentally Friendly and Safe Products," Swedish Automotive Manufacturing R&D Cluster, 2010. The 2013 version of the report is available at: http://www.produktionskluster.se/dokument/omg/Sustainable_Manufacturing_Systems_RD_Program_Fitfth_Edition_130517.pdf accessed Oct. 1, 2015.
10 Jomon Aliyas Paul and Govind Hariharan of Kennesaw State University, "Emergency Response/Homeland Security: Bioterrorist Disaster Planning," conference session in Proceedings of the 39th conference, *Winter Simulation: 40 Years! The Best Is Yet to Come*, Winter Simulation Conference Archive, Washington, D.C. (2007): 1139–1147.
11 Questions 3 and 4 courtesy of Mr. Prakash Rao of Baruch College, Accenture, and Ernst & Young; used with permission.
12 "National Healthcare Quality Report 2004," *AHRQ*, accessed Oct. 1, 2015, http://archive.ahrq.gov/qual/nhqr04/nhqr04.htm.
13 *Harvard Business Review*.

7 Managing Capacity

Chapter Take-Aways

- How is capacity managed?
- Yield management applications and benefits
- Scheduling
- Understanding how to analyze and manage waiting lines
- Performance measures

Managing Capacity: A Road Map

Customer: *"Why should I choose you?"*
Business: *"Because we promise that we shall serve your needs without long waits or exorbitant charges."*

7.1   What Is Capacity Management?

In response to concern about growing utilization of hospital emergency departments (ED), the New Jersey Department of Health and Senior Services (NJDHSS) commissioned the study "Emergency Department Utilization and Surge Capacity in New Jersey," conducted by the Rutgers Center for State Health Policy (CSHP). The study found that the hospital sector in New Jersey experienced declines in capacity (maintained beds) and inpatient utilization (inpatient days) from 1998 to 2005. Annual occupancy rates at the state and regional levels were around 70 percent during this time. However, these annual occupancy figures were misleading. Hospitals experienced recurring peaks and troughs of occupancy. On more than 75 percent of the days in 2003 through 2005, the state had less than 500 empty staffed beds available per million residents, which is a surge capacity benchmark developed by the federal Health Resources and Services Administration. Part of the reason is that since 1995, more than seventeen general care hospitals have closed in New Jersey. This has created additional stress on available capacity, most visible in the emergency department. In response, hospitals are trying to manage capacity better, notably through two strategies: managing demand and managing resources. Patients cannot be told when to fall sick, but hospitals try to influence incoming demand through ambulance diversions, where patients are diverted to other centers if they cannot be accommodated. Internally, hospitals run initiatives for better management of resources, through improved work flows, better real-time information on patient flows, removal of siloes among departments, and using scheduling to better match work force and equipment capacity with demand fluctuations. Together, the management of demand and resources constitute the two broad content areas of capacity management.

Capacity is the maximum amount of output that a system can produce with existing resources in a sustained manner over a given time period. Capacity management is a tactical activity in the present moment, primarily focused on the intelligent utilization of capacity and short-term actions to increase capacity scalability and flexibility to meet current demand. We focus on two broad themes in capacity management: managing demand and managing resources.

7.1.1   Managing Capacity with Demand Management

When capacity cannot be easily expanded or reduced, we can try to shift demand to meet available capacity at a point in time(s), principally through pricing differentials. To do this, managers must understand the price sensitivity of their markets. The Holland Tunnel from New Jersey to New York City has a fixed capacity. It is overwhelmed at opposite ends on weekday mornings and evenings, respectively, when traffic flows into and out of the city. The tunnel authorities have created a slab of different toll rates (inbound to NYC only) at different times of the day and week to try to move a portion of the morning rush to periods of lower utilization. It has helped, though the price elasticity of demand seems to be rather low for tunnel travelers, perhaps a reflection of inflexibility in work hour timing. Similarly, hotels, trains, golf courses, and airlines use variable pricing on limited chunks of capacity to try move customers to off- peak times. Premiums are charged at times of peak capacity utilization. Pricing can be used effectively to wean out low-profit customers during peak capacity utilization times and bring demand down to match available capacity.

We shall look at techniques of allocating fixed capacity to different customers differentiated by timing and price elasticity, such as yield management, to understand how it's done.

7.1.2 Managing Capacity with Resource Management

When the resources that provide capacity are fixed, they should not be wasted. There are methods that seek to allocate fixed capacity most efficiently to demand such as production and workforce scheduling. Scheduling seeks the most effective use of capacity to satisfy specific goals, such as customer satisfaction, speed of work flow, and employee satisfaction. Operations management offers scheduling techniques for various situations.

OM IN PRACTICE

Boston Medical Center changed its surgery scheduling to try to reduce variability in their surgery loads and increase overall operating room capacity utilization. The variability was caused by a) emergency surgeries that disrupted scheduled elective surgeries and b) allocating blocks of operating room time to individual surgeons. Usually, surgeons would be allocated blocks of time in an operating room each week and would schedule patients into these blocks as required. The hospital rescheduled part of the scheduled load of elective surgeries from the weekdays to Friday through Sunday. The revised schedule had the surgeons coordinating with schedulers to allocate operating rooms for elective surgeries on an as-required basis. With the changes to the scheduling, the ensuing five-month period saw 159 emergency surgeries (compared to 157 during the same period in the past year), with just two elective surgeries disrupted (compared to 334 during the same period in the past year). The results suggested that disruptions could be handled by keeping a single operation room in reserve for emergencies. The scheduling changes were considered very successful, albeit requiring considerable cooperation from surgeons, who had to depart from the traditional way of scheduling elective surgeries.

Adapted from: Derek DeLia, PhD, Rutgers Center for State Health Policy, "Hospital Capacity, Patient Flow, and Emergency Department Use in New Jersey," a report to the New Jersey Department of Health and Senior Services, September 2007.

Process management can increase capacity by redesigning work flows, simplifying work, cross-training workers, and identifying and managing constraint points in a system. We examine this at length in the next chapter. Additionally, techniques such as queuing theory rearrange resources to achieve lower wait times and increase system efficiencies in meeting demand. There are businesses like car rentals when the business does not have control over demand and available capacity fluctuates in a particular location. Capacity management in such situations requires both demand and resource management techniques.

7.2 Why Is Capacity Management Important?

Many retail businesses see their best sales during the holiday season. What if a worker suddenly falls sick a couple of days before Christmas, or lengthy lines of customers begin to form, or a customer comes in with a large last-minute order? How can we handle such events? Capacity management offers solutions: Develop a new schedule around the remaining workers, apply waiting-line techniques, and use scheduling priority rules, respectively. We discuss these approaches later in the chapter.

7.2.1 Importance for Businesses

Capacity issues can hamstring a business. Production capacity issues can prevent shipments arriving on time. Storage and distribution capacity issues can affect inventory costs and customer service levels. Supplier capacity issues can starve production or warehousing. Logistics capacity issues can impact every node of the supply network, disrupting inward and outward flows. Returns capacity issues can result in stockpiles of obsolete inventory and large write-offs. Human capacity issues can hurt production and other business activities. An aging workforce and declining enrollment in technical studies caused a shortfall of available engineers in Germany. Porsche and BMW are vying to find enough engineering capacity to design and make their cars.

Capacity management in such areas develops ways to deal with demand surprises and the constraints imposed by capacity-creating resources, such as space, machinery, inventory, and skilled labor. Capacity management can also be a powerful source of competitive advantage. Yield management parses capacity into separate pricing segments, aiming to maximize profits or revenues. Bus companies such as Megabus and BoltBus running selective $1 fares have challenged established companies in the bus and rail industry. Cell phone providers are actively using yield management techniques like pricing and limited broadband access to smoothen data demand on their networks. Businesses from call centers to retailers are using waiting line theory to predict customer waiting times and rearrange capacity and demand to manage wait times.

7.2.2 Importance for You

Capacity management impacts all majors. *Finance and accounting* skills are critical to yield management, for instance, in estimating revenues, costs, capital, and inventory needs in a dynamic operational environment. *Marketing* majors would find dynamic pricing a vital tool to increase revenue and capture market share. *HR* could help understand the effects of different scheduling rules on personnel motivation and behavior and facilitate employee receptivity to new work systems. Work process re-engineering projects cut across functions to achieve improvements in flows and quality.

Capacity management jobs can be found in many kinds of businesses.

Manager—Special Projects—Capacity Management

Boston, MA, USA | Diversified Global Property and Casualty Insurer

    Industry: Insurance
    Position Type: Full-Time
    Functions: Business Development, General Management
    Experience: 5–7 years

Job Description

Qualifications:

- Bachelor's degree or equivalent training required; focused study in areas like operations management, supply chain management, and process design a plus.
- Master's degree and CPCU a plus.

- Minimum of 5–10 years relevant work experience required; experience within the P&C industry and claims operations a plus.
- Proven track record of project management, execution, and problem-solving skills.
- Must have very strong communication skills and presentation-building ability

Responsibilities:

- Conceptualizes immediate and long-range needs of the APD operation with respect to strategic goals and translates these goals into comprehensive projects with defined objectives and outcomes.
- Collaborates with the field to collect data, map critical processes, and evaluate claims strategic initiatives for assigned area. Summarizes results, identifies opportunities for efficiencies and improvements, makes recommendations and communicates key messages to senior management.
- Negotiates project objectives and direction with product manager, field managers, and information technology teams; develops measurable targets with assistance from analytics teams to track progress of project.
- Prepares presentation and report outs for senior managers regarding project status and keeps senior managers informed of project direction and re-negotiates direction as necessary.
- Models demand and assess the optimal balance of staffing, productivity, inventory, and caseloads within each job family based on a thorough understanding of work effort for each stage in the claim lifecycle.
- Thinks strategically and identifies segmentation, channeling, and process opportunities that will help optimize capacity management. The optimal operating levels should reduce loss costs while maximizing the customer experience.
- Collaborate with the innovation and technology teams to identify areas of the value stream to introduce more automation and technology to minimize manual intervention and rework, while improving the customer experience.

Source: Ivy Exec, accessed Oct. 2, 2015, https://www.ivyexec.com/professionals/jobs/job/2855448?funnel=true &ref=BY2012J&promo=BY2012J.

Capacity management will help you think and act on your toes to job situations where you may have to decide whether to open another checkout line, or add another teller, or prioritize a late order, or make customer wait lines move (or seem to move) quicker. It is knowledge that will serve you well.

KEY POINTS

- Capacity management is the tactical task of matching demand at the moment to capacity available at the moment.
- Doing so may require influencing demand patterns through pricing and user incentives.

- Capacity is allocated using yield management and scheduling techniques.
- Capacity can be changed by reorganizing work processes.
- Capacity management decisions involve and affect marketing, finance, HR, and other functions in an organization.

7.3 How Is Capacity Managed?

We look at three scenarios—fixed capacity and flexible demand as in hotel rooms and airlines; fixed capacity and inflexible demand, as in an emergency room where demand cannot be easily shifted; and variable demand with waiting lines, as may happen in a bank front office or the food truck vendor located outside your college. Flexible means that which can be influenced. Variable means that which is uncertain and cannot be easily influenced or forecasted well.

7.3.1 Fixed Capacity and Flexible Demand

Businesses with inelastic capacity and price-elastic demand can allocate capacity using a technique known as yield management, also called revenue management. Yield management enables fixed-capacity businesses to realize optimum revenue, particularly from perishable inventory. Fixed capacity is often time dependent. Every second of underutilized capacity on Verizon's wireless network represents a wasted second of nonmonetized capacity for the wireless carrier. It is not unreasonable to assume that unused capacity could be used if priced appropriately or that high demand periods can be priced at a premium for increased revenues. Yield represents the extent to which capacity is being utilized in achieving full revenue-generating potential. Yield managers will work on capacity and pricing issues simultaneously to maximize revenue across different customer segments.

Yield = actual revenue/potential revenue (*Do not confuse this with 'yield' in process management or quality, which measures the ratio of # of good units made to total # of units made*)

Where:

Actual revenue   = actual capacity used * actual price
Potential revenue   = total capacity * maximum price

Maximizing yield does not mean maximizing capacity utilization. For example, in a 100-room inn:

Actual revenue booked at full capacity: 100 rooms * $50/night = $5,000

But:

Potential revenue of 100 rooms * $80 full price = $8,000
Thus, yield = 5,000/8,000 = 62.5% at full capacity utilization

It is unlikely that all 100 rooms would be booked at the full price of $80, but we could bump up the yield by experimenting with different rates for different portions of capacity. For example:

> 80 rooms * $50 = $4,000
> Remaining 20 rooms * $80 = $1,600
> Total revenue = $5,600
> Yield = 5,600/8,000 = 70%, so an improvement.
> Yield management can:

a) Determine the number of overbookings to accept over and above full capacity.
b) Use dynamic pricing and dynamic capacity allocations for different customer segments.

College admissions use yield management for the former purpose. Industries such as hotels and airlines use yield management for both purposes.

Yield management works when certain conditions are present:

- Fixed capacity: Capacity is relatively inelastic and cannot be easily expanded or reduced. Think of a flight or a hotel with x number of seats or rooms.
- Capacity splitting: Capacity can be split for allocation among different customer segments.
- Flexible demand: Demand is not fixed and varies. Demand is price-elastic.
- Different customer segments: Demand can be segmented into price- and time-sensitive categories, such as business customers and leisure customers.
- Advance sales: Capacity can be sold in advance, and customer segments exist to buy in advance.
- Cancellations are refunded: Customers are typically issued full or partial refunds for cancelled orders/ bookings/no-shows or are not charged at all.
- There is no legal restraint on differential pricing, such as the anti-price discrimination Robinson-Patman Act of 1936 that discourages differential pricing for manufactured products.
- High fixed costs, low variable costs: Capital intensive assets such as airplanes, hotels, movie halls.
- No salvage value for unsold inventory—perishable inventory.
- The costs of no-shows (wasted capacity) and stockouts (no capacity available—customer with confirmed booking turned away) are computable and real. Busy people like doctors, for example, often enjoy the break provided by a no-show or spend that time constructively on other tasks like checking lab reports, completing documentation, conferring with colleagues and such. No-shows, in such conditions, do not translate into a total loss of doctor/medical fees.

To make yield management work well, companies need certain capabilities:

- Accurate, real-time, reliable, and comprehensive system-wide information systems for demand, pricing, and capacity.
- Ability to quickly analyze emerging demand data and emerging cancellation data or no-shows (customer does not formally cancel but just does not show up).
- Ability to generate forecasts of demand and no-shows (cancellations).
- Analytical capabilities to compute offer prices dynamically.
- Ability to communicate dynamic pricing to market in real time.

There are some problems:

- Need economies of scale to defray cost of implementation and operation.
- Customer may see differential pricing as 'unfair.'
- Makes it difficult to advertise 'best price,' since price keeps changing so often.
- Customers may manipulate system.

Organizations locate yield management in different functions in a company. Its importance sometimes places it in marketing. Other times, yield management is placed under finance in view of its impact on profits. Companies that rely heavily on yield management have chief revenue officers with oversight on all revenue generating centers such as sales, pricing, new product development, and marketing activities.

Yield Management for Overbooking

We look in detail at the use of yield management in overbooking decisions. Companies that offer advance sales, such as hotels and airlines, experience last-minute customer cancellations or customers simply not turning up (no-shows). Overbooking makes sense, considering that rooms and departures would go empty otherwise. Customers typically cannot be charged for cancellations or can only be charged partially. Also, there may not be many repeat offenders, so it may not be possible to isolate and manage such customers separately. The key question in overbooking is, of course, how much should one overbook? Too much, and we have angry customers Instagramming instantly or singing bad things about us on YouTube. Too little, and losses from bookings that do not show up pile up because of last minute empty rooms or flight seats. Let us see how we can best make this decision for a hotel.

OVERBOOKING ON THE BASIS OF EXPECTED NUMBER OF NO-SHOWS

If we have a record of past last-minute cancellations or no-shows, we could find the expected value of such events and simply overbook by that amount. The table below provides a probability of no-shows based on the 'no-shows' history over the past one year (not shown).

As the below table indicates, we can overbook by about 8 guests, the expected value of no-shows based on previous history. Do you see what's wrong with this approach? You're correct! We are not considering costs at all. What if the cost to the hotel of turning away a guest with a confirmed booking is zero? We can then safely overbook 17 guests every day, being the maximum number of no-shows we have experienced in our data (column 1 in table below). Or overbook even more since there is no cost to overbooking, just in case future no-shows exceed 17 customers. We can overbook by as many guests as practical (lobby size constraint) in order to be 100 percent sure that we have enough traffic to fill all our rooms. There is, after all, no cost in turning away a guest with a confirmed booking. More realistically, hotels that have to turn away confirmed guests usually walk them over to another hotel, bear the difference in room charges, if any, and perhaps compensate the guest with a free night for the inconvenience. So there is usually a substantial cost to overbooking, which may be significantly more than the cost of an unanticipated room vacancy from a no show. If so, common sense then says we should be restrained in our overbooking policy, just in case we do not get enough no-shows to accommodate the number of guests we have overbooked. As we can see, looking at expected values or historical averages of no-shows does not provide much guidance on the number of overbookings we should make until relevant costs are considered. It is only when the costs of no-shows and overbooking are about equal that an average or expected value figure alone could work as a basis for overbooking decisions.

Table 7.1 Probability of No-Shows

# *of no-shows* last year	*Probability of* this 'no-show'(NS) (confirmed bookings do not show up)
0 (all confirmed bookings showed up)	0.05
	Assume we found that in 18 days of the past 365 days of data, there were no cancellations, and all our bookings showed up.
	That is zero no-shows happened 18 times in the past 365 days of data.
	Thus, probability of 0 no-shows = 18/365 = 0.05
1 (1 confirmed booking did not show up)	0.05
2	0.10
	Assume we found 2 no-shows occurred 36 times in the past 365 days of data.
	36/365 = 0.10
3	0.05
4	0.05
5	0.05
6	0.05
7	0.05
8	0.05
9	0.05
10	0.05
11	0.10
12	0.05
13	0.05
14	0.05
15	0.05
16	0.05
17	0.05
	1.00

Expected # of no-shows = $\sum$ (0 no-shows *.05) + (1 no-shows * 0.05) + (2 * 0.10) + . . . (17 * 0.05)
= 8.30 no-shows

EXPECTED COST ANALYSIS

We build an expected cost analysis table based on the costs of overbooking and no-shows for our hotel. The goal is to identify and recommend an overbooking number that will minimize costs. Given:

C_o = cost of 'overage' = cost of wasted capacity (empty rooms) = cost of no show = $40.00;
C_s = cost of 'stockout' = cost of running out of capacity (had to turn away confirmed booking) = cost of overbooking = $60.00
OB = # overbooked; NS = number of no-shows

Table 7.2 Expected Cost Table

$C_o = \$40$ $C_s = \$60$	Probability of no-shows (historical	If we overbook by:									
No-shows	data table 1)	0	1	2	3	4	5	6	7	8	9
0	0.05	$0[i]	60[iv]	120[vi]	180	240	300	360	420	480	540
1	0.05	40[ii]	0	60	120	180	240	300	360	420	480
2	0.1	80[iii]	40[v]	0	60	120	180	240	300	360	420
3	0.05	120	80	40	0	60	120	180	240	300	360
4	0.05	160	120	80	40	0	60	120	180	240	300
5	0.05	200	160	120	80	40	0	60	120	180	240
6	0.05	240	200	160	120	80	40	0	60	120	180
7	0.05	280	240	200	160	120	80	40	0	60	120
8	0.05	320	280	240	200	160	120	80	40	0	60
9	0.05	360	320	280	240	200	160	120	80	40	0
10	0.05	400	360	320	280	240	200	160	120	80	40
11	0.1	440	400	360	320	280	240	200	160	120	80
12	0.05	480	440	400	360	320	280	240	200	160	120
13	0.05	520	480	440	400	360	320	280	240	200	160
14	0.05	560	520	480	440	400	360	320	280	240	200
15	0.05	600	560	520	480	440	400	360	320	280	240
16	0.05	640	600	560	520	480	440	400	360	320	280
17	0.05	680	640	600	560	520	480	440	400	360	320
Expected Cost $		332	297	267	247	232	222	**217**	**217**	222	232

i   Overbooked 0 guests, 0 no-shows

    Cost = 0

ii   Overbooked 0 guest, 1 no show

    Cost = C_o = $40. Cost of empty room (wasted capacity)

iii   Overbooked 0 guests. 2 no-shows

    Cost = $C_o * 2$ = $40 * 2 = $80

iv   Overbooked 1 guest, 0 no-shows

    Cost = C_s = $60 = cost of turning away guest who was overbooked (running out of capacity)

v   Overbooked 1 guest, 2 no-shows

    Cost = $C_o * 1$ empty room = $40

vi   Overbooked 2 guests, 0 no-shows

Cost = C_s = $60 * 2 = $120

We have not shown computations beyond 9 overbookings, since clearly overbooking either 6 or 7 guests results in the lowest expected cost of $217. An advantage with the expected cost table method is that we can change C_s, the cost of stockout, for different levels of stockouts. With an overbooking of 1 and 0 no-shows, we estimate that it will cost us $60 to walk the one turned away guest to another hotel. Well, if we overbook by, say, 17, and no-shows turn out to be 0, we would probably not be able to walk every one of those 17 turned away guests for $60 a piece. We may run out of $60 alternate accommodations after some time and have to pay for higher priced rooms in other hotels, which means that C_s is greater than $60 for some of those 17 overbooked guests, and the average C_s for the 17 overbooked guests would be greater than $60.

MARGINAL COST ANALYSIS

We continue overbooking till the point where we still expect to make a profit or not make a loss. That is, we keep overbooking as long as the expected revenue from adding the next unit of overbooking is greater than or equal to expected loss from adding the next unit of overbooking.

Our recommended overbooking point is found by the following formula, called the newsvendor model:
$C_s/(C_o + C_s) \leq$ P(no-shows $\geq$ overbookings), or equivalently,
P(NS $\geq$ OB) $\geq C_s/(C_o + C_s)$, where:

C_o = average cost of overage = cost of wasted capacity = cost of no show = $40;
C_s = average cost of stockout = cost of running out of capacity = cost of overbooking = $60;
OB = # overbooked; NS = number of no-shows

For our hotel:

The critical ratio, $C_s/(C_o + C_s)$ = $60/($40 + $60) = 0.60, or
$0.60 \leq$ P(NS $\geq$OB), or, equivalently,
P(NS $\geq$ OB) $\geq$ 0.60

From the table below (an extension of table 7.1), find that overbooking quantity 'OB' (column 3) such that the probability of 'no-shows' being equal to or greater than 'overbookings':

P(NS $\geq$ OB) is at or greater than 0.60.

To do that, first look at column 4 of the table below to identify that P(NS $\geq$ OB) value that is equal to or immediately greater than the critical ratio 0.60. We have a match at 0.60, corresponding to an overbooking quantity OB of 7 guests (see column 3). The recommended overbooking quantity of 7 tallies with our expected cost-analysis recommendation. The next higher overbooking figure is 6 at an P(NS $\geq$ OB) of 0.65.

If we find that that the historical data of no-shows in our hotel is approximately normally distributed, we can use the critical ratio $C_s/(C_o + C_s)$ of 0.60 to find the recommended number of overbookings.

Table 7.3 Record of No-Shows

# of no-shows last year	Probability of this 'no show'(NS)	If we overbook by this qty 'OB'	Then the probability of 'no-shows' being equal to or > 'OB,' i.e., P(NS ≥ OB), would be
0	0.05 Assume we found 0 'no show' days 18 times in the past 365 days of data	0	$P(NS = 0) + P(NS > 0)$ $= 0.05 + \sum [P(NS = 1) + P(NS = 2) + P(NS = 3) + P(NS = 4) + \ldots + P(NS = 17)]$
		Using col 2 of this table,	$= 0.05 + \sum [P(NS = 1) = 0.05 + P(NS = 2) = 0.10$ $+ P(NS = 3) = 0.05 + P(NS = 4) = 0.05 + \ldots$ $+ P(NS = 17) = 0.05]$ $= 0.05 + 0.95$ $= 1.00$
1	0.05	1	$P(NS = 1) + P(NS > 1)$ $= 0.05 + 0.90$ $= 0.95$
2	0.10 (36/365; 2 no-shows occurred 36 times in the the past 365 days of data)	2	$P(NS = 2) + P(NS > 2)$ $= 0.10 + 0.80$ $= 0.90$
3	0.05	3	0.80
4	0.05	4	0.75
5	0.05	5	0.70
6	0.05	6	0.65
7	0.05	7	**0.60**
8	0.05	8	0.55
9	0.05	9	0.50
10	0.05	10	0.45
11	0.10	11	0.40
12	0.05	12	0.30
13	0.05	13	0.25
14	0.05	14	0.20
15	0.05	15	0.15
16	0.05	16	0.10
17	0.05 ‾‾‾‾ 1.00	17	0.05

For example, the mean (expected value) and standard distribution of our no show data (table 7.1 or table 7.3 above) is 8.30 and 5.29 respectively. For normally distributed data, then:

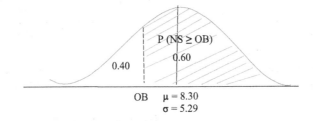

P (NS ≥ OB)

0.60

0.40

OB $\mu = 8.30$
      $\sigma = 5.29$

Figure 7.1 Distribution of No-Shows

Critical ratio = 0.60
Corresponding z value = (−)0.25
$Q = \mu - 0.25* \sigma = 8.3 - 0.25*5.29 = 6.98$, rounded off to a recommended *7* overbookings.

So the recommended overbooking quantity with the data normally distributed would be 7 (or 6 if you round down). We observe that the recommended overbooking quantity is lower than the average # of no-shows (8.30). Why is it so? Note that the cost of a stock-out, C_s ($60/guest) is higher than the cost of a room that is left empty, C_o ($40). It's more expensive ($60/turned away guest) to overbook than run the risk of not filling a room ($40/room). As such, we tend to overbook a fewer number than the average number of no-shows. When the cost of stockout is not precisely known, an estimate works in terms of a factor of how much more stockouts cost relative to cost of no-shows (easier to specify), e.g., if C_s costs, say, twice as much as no-shows, then:

$$C_s/(C_o + C_s) = 2/1 + 2 = 0.66$$

We next discuss the use of yield management for making capacity allocations to different customer segments.

Capacity Allocations Using Yield Management

Restaurants sometimes say "Sorry, we're full," to a casual tourist but will cheerfully welcome and seat an old customer. Airlines reduce available seats for leisure travelers while using those seats for hoped for higher-paying business travelers. The goal is to maximize revenue. If variable cost is small, almost the entire revenue can be thought of as marginal profit.

- *FCFS*: First come, first served is the simplest way to use up capacity. However, the business will usually have to turn away some later-arriving higher rate guests because capacity has been locked up earlier by lower rate customers.
- *Protection fences*: We set a protection level to 'fence off' a specific capacity number for use by a specific rate or fare. For example, a hotel may wish to know how many rooms to set aside for higher paying guests for a certain date. Too much, and it may lead to empty rooms, Too little, and it may

have to refuse higher rate customers. Of course, if the higher rate bookings look good or exceed the rooms reserved for that class early on, the protection level can certainly be expanded by moving more lower rate rooms into the higher rate category. But higher rate guests typically arrive at the last moment and cannot be accommodated because the remaining rooms have been already sold out to lower rate guests. The newsvendor model can help determine the optimal protection level for the higher rate category, specifically the expected marginal seat revenue (EMSR) approach developed by Belobaba of MIT.[1]

The cost of setting too little high rate capacity = C_s. We blocked too few rooms at the higher rate. Since the remaining rooms were available at a lower rate, all were booked much in advance by leisure customers. We had to turn down bookings from higher rate but late-booking guests (that we would have been able to take, if only we had set aside a larger number of rooms for the high rate guests). As such,

C_s = *difference between high rate and low rate.*

The cost of setting too much high rate capacity = C_o. Because we fenced off too many rooms at the higher rate, we had to refuse lower rate bookings, anticipating late-in-the-day higher rate bookings. Unfortunately, that late higher rate demand did not materialize, and no last-minute low paying bookings turned up, either. In hope of a bigger prize, we passed over the chance of booking revenue from a lower rate guest. Thus,

C_o = *cost of missed low rate guest = low rate*

The newsvendor approach would recommend an optimal 'protection level,' i.e., an optimal number of rooms to reserve for high rate guests, that maximizes revenues (and minimizes costs).

If the protection level of 8 rooms at the higher rate that we fixed above is indeed an optimum, doing so would maximize revenue. Let's check if that is so.

Total # of rooms in hotel = 30
Low rate = $40/room
Assume that we could have booked all 30 rooms at the low rate,
Total Revenue = 30 rooms * $40/room = $1,200

We set a protection level of 8 rooms at the higher rate, but how many of those 8 rooms do we expect to book on average (at the higher rate)? The loss function table (see Statistical Tables) for a Poisson distribution provides an expected 'lost sales' figure for every level of demand 'Q' (labeled 'S' in the table). For a high rate demand distribution with a mean of 7 and a 'Q' of 8, the loss function from the table is 0.64173, that is, we expect to have to turn away 0.64173 high rate guests. That is, we can expect to book:

Mean high rate demand – expected lost sales = 7 – 0.64173 = 6.36 rooms at the high rate.
Thus,

Total revenue	= expected booking of high rate rooms * high rate + (total rooms – # of rooms reserved at high rate) * Low rate
(8-room protection)	= 6.366 rooms * $130/room + (30 – 8) rooms * $40/room
	= $1,707.58

Our boutique hotel has a total of 30 rooms. We need to find an optimal number of rooms to reserve for our higher rate guests for the coming March 1st. Available data suggests a Poisson distributed demand forecast of high rate guests for March 1st (we generated this assuming a historical λ (mean) of 7 higher rate guests. Use a Poisson Distribution Function Table—see Statistical Tables at the back of this book). We assume that all low rate bookings requests are received earlier than high rate booking requests.

Forecasted demand 'd'	Probability of 'd'	If we reserve # of rooms 'Q'	Prob of demand being equal to or < 'Q', i.e., $P(d \leq Q)$, would be
0	0.0009	0	0.0009
			$P(d=0) + P(d<0) = 0.0009 + 0$
1	0.0064	1	0.0073
			$P(d=1) + P(d<1) = 0.0064 + 0.0009$
2	0.0223	2	0.0296
3	0.0521	3	0.0817
4	0.0912	4	0.1720
5	0.1277	5	0.3006
6	0.1490	6	0.4496
7	0.1490	7	0.5986
8	0.1304	**8**	**0.7290**
9	0.1014	9	0.8304
10	0.0710	10	0.9014
11	0.0452	11	0.9466
12	0.0264	12	0.9730
13	0.0142	13	0.9872
14	0.0071	14	0.9943
15	0.0033	15	0.9976
16	0.0015	16	0.9991

Assume C_o = \$40 and C_s = \$90 (low rate = \$40, high rate = \$130).
Thus,
Critical Ratio = $C_s/(C_o + C_s)$ = 90/130 = 0.69, and from the newsvendor model,

$C_s/(C_o + C_s) \leq P(d \leq Q)$, equivalently,

$P(d \leq Q) \geq C_s/(C_o + C_s)$, or

$P(d \leq Q) \geq 0.69$

Looking at col 4, $P(d \leq Q)$, we pick the higher probability corresponding to 0.69, which is 0.7290. Col 3 tells us that we have to reserve 8 rooms at the higher rate for March 1st.

Figure 7.2 Overbooking in a Hotel

By setting a protection level of 8 rooms at the high rate, we expect to gain $507.58 ($1,707.58 − $1,200). What if we reserved 9 rooms at the high rate instead? The loss function for a 'Q' of 9, with a mean demand of 7, is 0.37082 from the Poisson loss function table. That is, we can expect to book:

7 − 0.37082	= 6.63 rooms at the high rate, and
Total revenue	= expected booking of high rate rooms * high rate + (total rooms − # of rooms reserved at high rate) * low rate
(9-room protection)	= 6.63 rooms * $130/room + (30 − 9) rooms * $40/room
	= $1,701.90 (is < $1,707.58 we expect from our recommended 8-room protection level)

What if we set the protection level to 7 rooms instead? The loss function is 1.04302, so, the expected number of bookings is:

7 − 1.04302	= 5.96 rooms at the high rate, and
Total revenue	= 5.96 rooms * $130/room + (30 − 7) rooms * $40/room
	(7-room protection)
	= $1,694.80 (is < $1707.58 we expect from our recommended 8-room protection level)

Our computed optimum protection level of 8 rooms at the high rate is indeed revenue maximizing (and cost minimizing).

Dynamic Capacity and Pricing Management

My friend was invited to a wedding and told about a special room rate for the wedding party. On a whim, he checked before booking and found a cheaper rate at the same hotel for the same period. Hotels regularly shift capacity by re-pricing rooms to suit higher or lower paying guest segments. Such businesses 'fence off' capacity for desired customers through pricing decisions. They wait and then relax the fences to accommodate other customer classes if the former's response does not use up that protected capacity in time. Dynamic capacity management and pricing requires monitoring and forecasting demand at different rate levels on a continuous basis. Operations researchers working with IT specialists and marketing personnel have developed sophisticated algorithms to manage dynamic capacity and pricing for many fare categories, group bookings, and fencing and unfencing of unsold capacity. Witness the last-minute bargain flash sales by hotels and airlines and their consolidators. Since such models confer millions of dollars in profits, they are, of course, kept confidential. Besides analyzing petabytes of booking data, users of such systems also monitor competitor actions, weather, and special events. Necessarily, some fine tuning still takes place at the human level. Industries like car rentals present complex problems such as variable capacity dependent on customer returns and no-shows, and use yield management for dynamic capacity, pricing, and overbooking decisions.

7.3.2 Fixed Capacity and Inflexible Demand

Capacity management in services is generally handled by a mix of demand and capacity management. Appointments, reservations, posted schedules, and wait lines are examples of how variations in demand are smoothened. Similarly, capacity can be flexed using temporary and part-time workers, multi-skilled workers, and on-call personnel. But what happens when demand cannot be easily managed and capacity cannot be easily changed? Patients come into the ER at all times and generally cannot be refused. It is difficult to forecast hourly demand, although forecasts can be developed in terms of peak and off-peak loads. Capacity in an ER cannot be readily or significantly enhanced since expert personnel are required. When demand cannot be managed and capacity is limited, capacity must be managed to meet demand. Workforce scheduling becomes a way to manage capacity. Here's a technique that has been used to manage workforce capacity, observing constraints of consecutive days off.[2]

Technicians in a pharmacy have to get two consecutive days off in a week. We wish to manage capacity most efficiently while observing this rule. There are 10 full time technicians. Demand is variable (see Table 7.3).

Forecast the demand for the days of the week and translate in terms of capacity required (number of workers).

Day	Mon	Tues	Wed	Thur	Fri	Sat	Sun
Workers required	7	5	8	8	7	5	2

1   Compute the weekly workforce needs for each pair of consecutive days (except Sun–Mon) and pick the pair with the lowest capacity need.

	Mon	Tues	Wed	Thur	Fri	Sat	Sun
	7	5	8	8	7	5	2

Schedule Harry to work from Mon–Fri, with Sat and Sun off.

2   With Harry working M–Fri, the weekly workforce capacity requirement need now looks like this:

	Mon	Tues	Wed	Thur	Fri	Sat	Sun
	6	4	7	7	6	5	2

Pick the pair of consecutive days with the lowest capacity–turns out to be Sat and Sun again.
Schedule Lateesha to work from Mon–Fri, with Sat and Sun off.

3   With Harry and Lateesha working Mon–Fri and taking Sat and Sun off, the capacity needs now are:

	Mon	Tues	Wed	Thur	Fri	Sat	Sun
	5	3	6	6	5	5	2

Schedule Dave to work from Mon–Fri, with Sat and Sun off.

4   Taking Harry, Lateesha, and Dave working Mon–Fri, with Sat and Sun off, we need:

	Mon	Tues	Wed	Thur	Fri	Sat	Sun
	4	2	5	5	4	5	2

Rafael can take either Sun–Mon or Mon–Tues off. He chooses not to work on Mon and Tues.

5

	Mon	Tues	Wed	Thur	Fri	Sat	Sun
	4	2	4	4	3	4	1

Schedule Mikhail to work from Mon–Fri, with Sat and Sun off.

6

	Mon	Tues	Wed	Thur	Fri	Sat	Sun
	3	1	3	3	2	4	1

We ask Neil to pick and he opts to take off Mon–Tues and work Wed–Sun.

7

	Mon	Tues	Wed	Thur	Fri	Sat	Sun
	3	1	2	2	1	3	0

Schedule Hui Zhong to work from Mon–Fri, with Sat and Sun off.

8

	Mon	Tues	Wed	Thur	Fri	Sat	Sun
	2	0	1	1	0	3	0

Luke chooses to take Th and Fri off, and work from Sat–Wed.

9

	Mon	Tues	Wed	Thur	Fri	Sat	Sun
	1	0	0	1	0	2	0

Josh takes Tues and Wed off and works Thur–on.

10

	Mon	Tues	Wed	Thur	Fri	Sat	Sun
	0	0	0	0	0	1	0

From the several choices available, Anita chooses to holiday on Tues and Wed.

Figure 7.3 Scheduling in a Pharmacy

Here's what the pharmacy techs see when the final schedule is posted:

Table 7.4 Technician Work Schedule

Worker	Mon	Tues	Wed	Thur	Fri	Sat	Sun
Harry	✓	✓	✓	✓	✓	Off	Off
Lateesha	✓	✓	✓	✓	✓	Off	Off
Dave	✓	✓	✓	✓	✓	Off	Off
Rafael	Off	Off	✓	✓	✓	✓	✓
Mikhail	✓	✓	✓	✓	✓	Off	Off
Neil	Off	Off	✓	✓	✓	✓	✓
Hui-Zhong	✓	✓	✓	✓	✓	Off	Off
Luke	✓	✓	✓	Off	Off	✓	✓
Josh	✓	Off	Off	✓	✓	✓	✓
Anita	✓	✓	✓	Off	Off	✓	✓
Capacity	8	7	9	8	8	5	5
Demand	7	5	8	8	7	5	2
Surplus	1	2	1	0	1	0	3

The above roster can be posted, and workers are given the option to ask for changes based on seniority or other criteria or exchange schedules with schedule-specified days off. We assume that all technicians can do the job equally well. We notice that we have surplus capacity five days of the week and that demand does not exceed eight workers on any day of the week. It may be possible to operate the pharmacy with fewer technicians if maximizing capacity is the goal and the personnel are flexible in terms of days off and overtime. On the other hand, pharmacies located inside or near hospitals or disaster-prone areas may just need that extra capacity for emergencies.

The above heuristic is not the only solution, given the excess capacity. Also, we can add more factors, such as de-linking Sunday and Monday because they are part of two different weeks, and incorporate the impact of specific employee issues such as workers who are taking college courses or those with special family responsibilities. In some jobs, such as air controllers, a person cannot be on duty for more than 30 minutes at a time, with 30-minute intervals scheduled in-between work periods. Shift scheduling presents a variety of situations—six on, six off, that is, work three consecutive days and nights and then take three days off; four off, four on; split shifts, as in restaurants where work is scheduled for morning lunch hours and evening dinner hours; and firefighter 'California roll' 24-on, 24-off shifts. Most times, employees desire consistency in shifts. Being moved around different shifts frequently has been seen to cause health and motivation issues.

Work Schedule Stress*

> **From:** noname wife
> **To:** info@arcweb.org
> **Subject:** Employee hours

Maybe you can help me. I am the spouse of a XXXX Assistant Manager. The store this person works at converted to working 24 hours. XXXX expects my spouse to work varying shifts that span the entire 24 hour day in just under two to three months.

Specifically, my spouse will work 11 hour shifts that vary from working days to midnights in a rotation of only two months or so. This is a very distressing situation for our family, not to mention the health and productivity of my spouse. I find it very hard to fathom that a company the size of XXXX would not know of the destructive nature this type of schedule plays on their own productivity—meaning that their own managers are always sleep deprived and not thinking with their most productive minds. Not to mention the stress they have to deal with when trying to sleep during the day when their spouses and children are home. Have you ever tried to keep a 4-month-old from crying because you didn't want to wake your spouse up? My question is this, "Can XXXX use its human resources appropriately by hiring a single 'night-time' manager to work the overnight shifts?"

Please post this as an open forum for any response from other spouses, and even experts in the medical and psychological fields that can provide empirical proof that this type of schedule is destructive to the human condition.

*An actual post from an online site. Company names and personal identities deleted for confidentiality.

An initial schedule is always a work in progress, with emerging constraints and demand shifts necessitating changes with time. Adjustments are now facilitated by technologies such as mobile apps that provide real-time access to workers and schedulers alike. Businesses like 24-hour call centers, casinos, restaurants, police stations, and colleges now use powerful scheduling software that can accommodate multiple constraints in developing schedules for machines, people, classes, and exams. Ask your dean's office about who does the scheduling of classrooms in your college—you may get a peek at some very interesting approaches to resolving scheduling conflicts in a real environment.

KEY POINTS

- When capacity is fixed and demand can be influenced, yield management offers revenue-enhancing capacity-demand matching through optimal overbooking decisions.
- Yield management requires inelastic capacity, customer segmentation by price and time, advance sales, and low variable costs.
- Overbooking on the basis of average number of no-shows fails to consider the difference in stockout and excess capacity costs.
- Overbooking using expected cost analysis computes the number of overbookings that lead to the lowest expected total cost.
- Overbooking using the newsvendor model prescribes accepting bookings as long as we still expect to add to revenue.
- The expected marginal seat revenue technique suggests recommended revenue maximizing protection levels for higher priced capacity
- When capacity or demand are relatively inelastic, scheduling methods help match capacity to demand, considering system constraints

7.3.3 Variable Demand and Waiting Lines

The checkout line has not moved in the past five minutes. Should I hop over to the end of the other, shorter, line? But what if the other line is short because people are intentionally avoiding that line? Does it suffer from a slow cashier? Or is it that the other line is simply moving faster? Forget it—I'll just dump this item and swing by later. Or better still, order it online for store pick-up—no, wait—that may mean standing in line again. Let's bypass the store altogether and get it UPS, USPS, or Fed-Ex. From the perspective of the store manager, it is bad news any way you look at it.

Waiting lines build up for three reasons: inadequate capacity, variability in demand arrival rates or service times, and high utilization. Capacity could be less than demand at all times, such as seems to be the cases in busy doctor's offices and visa sections in U.S. consulates worldwide. Or it could be that capacity is lacking to accommodate seasonal demand peaks at predictable times, such as evening peaks at pharmacy drive-ins. If so, we can anticipate the lines and plan ahead on how to manage them by using demand management or better scheduling, or adding temporary capacity, or other means. But lines form even when there is adequate capacity to handle total workload. It's just that we do not seem to have capacity when it is needed. And we cannot precisely forecast when it'll be needed. Employees sometimes have no customers to serve, while stressing out in 'It's crazy here' situations at other times, and lines form even when capacity is under-utilized. Demand and capacity never seem to match at the same moment in time. High utilization rates mean that customers wait at peak times, and the wait grows exponentially as capacity utilization increases. In this section, we examine the issue of matching capacity to variable demand by a) predicting waiting line times and b) discussing various remedies for waiting lines. We assume a stable system where server capacity is higher than or equal to the average arrival rate (if not, lines will continue to trend up without end).

Predicting Waiting Line Times

Single transaction step, single file waiting lines come in two familiar forms:

Single file single server system, *where customers line up in a single queue and are served by one server*:

Single file multiple server system, *where customers line up in a single queue, but are served by multiple servers:*

Figure 7.4 **Server Systems**

Some businesses operate with a single server at times, like times when there is a single car wash bay, a single checkout lane at a store, or a single window open at the drive-in at McDonald's. Other times, you may see a single line leading to multiple counters, as in a movie theater or a store checkout. We consider a single line, first come-first served line discipline for both single and multiple server systems to keep it simple. For the same reason, we do not consider multiple-phase systems that require the customer to pass through a sequence of server transactions.

SINGLE FILE SINGLE SERVER SYSTEM

Let us first analyze a single server waiting line consisting of one queue, one server, and unlimited customers using the basic M/M/1 queuing model.[3] We assume that the waiting line has no limit, that line discipline is first come, first served, and that customers do not abandon or refuse to join the line. These are the essential formulae—assuming a Poisson arrival rate and exponential service time:

Single File, Single Server System

The average rate at which customers arrive = λ (lambda) per hour
Average arrival rate (λ) is Poisson distributed
Average time between arrivals = $1/\lambda$ (inter-arrival time)
The average rate at which customers are served = μ (mu) per hour
Average service rate is exponentially distributed
Number of servers, M (= 1, in this case)

W_q: average time spent waiting in line	$= \lambda/[\mu(\mu - \lambda)]$	(Equation 7.1)
L_q: average # of customers in line	$= W_q * \lambda$ $= \lambda^2/[\mu(\mu - \lambda)]$	(Equation 7.2)
Average # of customers in the system (waiting + being serviced)	$= \lambda/\mu - \lambda$	(Equation 7.3)
Average time a customer spends in the system (waiting + being serviced)	$= 1/(\mu - \lambda)$	(Equation 7.4)
Capacity utilization of server(s)	$= \lambda/M\mu$ (M is the # of servers)	(Equation 7.5)
Probability of zero customers in system	$= 1 - (\lambda/\mu)$	(Equation 7.6)
Probability of less than n *customers in system*	$= 1 - (\lambda/\mu)n$	(Equation 7.7)
Service rate necessary to fulfil desired 'customer waits in line on average time' μ	$= [L_q + \sqrt{\{(L_q)^2 + 4L_q\}}]/2W_q$	(Equation 7.8)

The DMV is not happy and asks to know how many more servers need to be added to lower the average time spent waiting in line—which brings us to the multiple server system.

SINGLE FILE MULTIPLE SERVER SYSTEM

The DMV wishes to cut down the average time spent waiting in line to 2 minutes or less. How many servers would it need? All other parameters remain the same. The average arrival rate is less than server capacity

---

<u>Basic Single Server waiting line M/M/1 queuing model</u>

We wish to predict wait times at the registration renewal counter at the local DMV office. We collect data on arrivals and service rates and estimate that:

The average rate at which customers arrive λ (lambda) per hour = 10 customers
The average rate at which customers are served μ (mu) = 12 customers served per hour.
Number of servers, M, = 1, in this case

We assume that the average arrival rate (λ) is Poisson distributed;
Thus the average time between arrivals ($1/\lambda$ = inter-arrival times) are exponentially distributed;
We assume that the average service time/customer ($1/\mu$) is exponentially distributed.

Would a line form considering that the average # of customers served per hour is higher than the average # customers arriving per hour?

W_q:*With a single server, average time spent waiting in line* $= \lambda/[\mu(\mu - \lambda)]$
$\qquad\qquad\qquad\qquad\qquad\qquad\qquad\qquad = 10/[12(12 - 10)]$
$\qquad\qquad\qquad\qquad\qquad\qquad\qquad\qquad = 0.4167$ hrs = 25 minutes

As the arrival rate, λ, approaches the service rate μ, the average time spent waiting increases.

L_q: *Average # of customers in line* $\qquad\qquad = W_q * \lambda = \lambda^2/[\mu(\mu - \lambda)]$
$\qquad\qquad\qquad\qquad\qquad\qquad\qquad\qquad\qquad = 4.17$ customers

Average time a customer spends waiting + being serviced $= 1/(\mu - \lambda)$
$\qquad\qquad\qquad\qquad\qquad\qquad\qquad\qquad\qquad\qquad\qquad = 30$ minutes

Capacity utilization of server $= \lambda/M\mu = 10/(1*12) = 83.34\%$

Probability of 'n' customers in system $= (1 - \lambda/\mu)(\lambda/\mu)^n$
Probability of say 5 customers in system $= (1 - .8334)(10/12)^5 = (0.1666)(0.4018) = 0.0669 = 6.69\%$

<u>Insight</u>: Lines can form even when the average customer arrival rate is <u>lower</u> than the average service rate. The reason being variability in both arrival and service rates.

Figure 7.5 M/M/1 Queuing Model

(average service rate * # of servers). We assume that all servers work at the same average service rate. The essential formulae are shown below:

L_q: *average # of customers in line* $\qquad = P_0 * [\{\lambda\mu \, (\lambda/\mu)^{M(\# \, of \, servers)}\} / (M - 1)!^4 \, (M\mu - \lambda)^2]$ (Equation 7.9)

P_0: *probability of zero customers in system* $\qquad = \left[\sum_{n=0}^{M-1} \dfrac{\left(\dfrac{\lambda}{\mu}\right)^n}{n!} + \dfrac{\left(\dfrac{\lambda}{\mu}\right)^M}{M!\left(1 - \dfrac{\lambda}{M\mu}\right)} \right]^{-1}$ (Equation 7.10)

W_q: *average time spent waiting in line* $= 1/(M\mu - \lambda)$ (Equation 7.11)

<u>Multiple Server waiting line M/M/C queuing model</u>

The average rate at which customers arrive λ (lambda) per hour = 10 customers
# of servers M = ?
The average rate at which customers are served μ (mu) = 12 customers served per hour/server.
Desired average time spent waiting in line (W_q) = 2 min or less = 0.0334 hr or less

Given:
Average # of customers in line (L_q) = W_q * λ

Therefore, L_q = 0.0334 * 10 = 0.334 customers or fewer would be in line (on average)

Utilization, $r = \lambda / \mu$ = 10/12 = 0.8334

Use Table "Infinite source values for L_q and P_0 given λ / μ and M" (located in the Statistical Tables section of this book)
For a table r of 0.85 (rounded from 0.8334), and a table L_q of 0.187 (look for $\leq$ desired L_q of 0.334),

M = 2 and
P_0, the probability of 0 customers in the system is .404.

Thus the DMV requires a total of two servers in order to reduce the average time spent waiting in line from 25 minutes to 2 minutes or less.

Capacity utilization of 2 server system = $\lambda / M(\mu)$ = 10/2(12) = 0.4167 = 41.67%

Insight: Capacity and waiting time are *not* linearly related. That's good news! Adding one more server cuts down waiting time from 25 min to less than 2 minutes. The downside is that capacity utilization goes down from about 83% to 42% - the servers will have plenty more free times in the day. Managers should look at ways to use that free capacity, when available, productively.

Figure 7.6 M/M/C Queuing Model

There are waiting line calculators available online that can provide quick results, including useful products at http://www.supositorio.com/rcalc/rcalclite.htm; http://highered.mheducation.com/sites/ 0077814606/ student_view0/waiting_line_model_templates.html.

Fortunately, a table exists to save us from the lengthier calculations. It provides L_q and P_0 for given values of utilization (λ/μ) and *M* (# of servers).

A capacity utilization of 41.67 percent implies that a) the each server is servicing customers 41.67 percent of the time; b) that on average 41.67 percent of servers are servicing, while 58.33 percent of servers are idle; and c) that at any given time there is a 0.4167 probability that any randomly observed server is servicing a customer.

Assumptions such as the first come, first served line discipline, the unlimited line length, the nature of arrival and service rate distributions, and no customer reneging (abandoning line) or balking (deciding not to enter the line at all) have been relaxed in various extensions of the basic waiting line models. In hospital ERs, for example, cases are triaged into priority categories such as heart attacks, severe injuries, broken bones, and flu and fever. Patients are first assigned to a category and then processed first come, first served within their own category. New arrivals in a more important category have precedence over earlier arrivals in less important categories.

WHEN AVERAGE ARRIVAL RATE EXCEEDS AVERAGE SERVICE RATE

When the average arrival rate exceeds the capacity of the system (bottleneck capacity), we have an unstable process, where waiting lines can theoretically stretch to infinity. The line will shorten at times due to slow arrivals or faster service rates at some particular times, but the length of the queue will show an increasing trend overall. In real life, of course, such processes will either begin to turn away arrivals when the waiting line becomes unmanageable or have to shut down because of customer chaos. It's akin to a large hose gushing water into a bucket with a small hole in it. The bucket begins to fill up and overflow. We stop pouring water, and the water level begins to go down gradually. A doctor's office is a good example of an unstable system. Patients nearly always have to wait, and appointments are deliberately overbooked to keep capacity utilization as close to 100 percent as possible. So patients accumulate in the wait areas and grumble. The appointments, though, end at a certain time of the day, and that gives the doctor a chance to work her way through the waiting line of patients. In such unstable systems, the early comer is processed quickly, but how quickly will the line grow, and how long would a patient arriving at a particular point have to wait?

a) *How quickly will the line grow?*

Assume patients arrive on average at 5 patients/hr while the doctor's capacity is just 3 patients/hr on average.

Line growth rate = arrival rate − capacity (Equation 7.12)

Thus, line growth rate = 5 − 3 = 2 patient/hr

b) *How many patients would be waiting after a certain period of time?*

After Y hours of opening, the # of patients waiting is:

Length of waiting line at time Y = Y * line growth rate (Equation 7.13)

So after, say, 4 hours, the # of patients waiting will be = 4 * 2 = 8 patients

c) *How long would a patient coming in at a specific time have to wait?*

Supposing a patient comes in, say, 4 hours after opening. How long will it take until he is seen and serviced? Remember, 20 arrivals will come in 4 hrs at 5 patients/hr arrival rate.

Total time required to service X # of arrivals after opening = X/capacity (Equation 7.14)

So, time required to service all 20 arrivals = 20 patients/3 patients/hr = 6.67 hrs
So, wait + service time for patient who came in 4 hours *after* clinic opening,
  = (6.67 hrs − 4 hrs) = **2.67 hrs**
Putting it together into a formula for convenience:

Wait + service time for patient = (# of arrivals up to time Y hrs/capacity) − Y hrs; (Equation 7.15)
  arriving at time Y hrs

Now, '# of arrivals up to time Y hrs' = arrival rate/hr * Y hrs
So, rearranging (7.14):

Wait + service time for individual   = [(arrival rate * Y hrs)/capacity] − Y hrs;
  arriving at time Y hrs
Consolidating Y on RHS:

*Wait + service time for individual   = Y hrs * [(arrival rate/capacity) − 1]* (Equation 7.16)
arriving at time Y hrs

Applying (7.15) to the doctor's clinic example:

Total time (wait + service) required to service patient who comes in at time 4 hours after opening

$$= 4 \ [(5/3) - 1] = \textbf{2.67 hrs}$$

Another Way

The patient coming in at time Y hours after opening will have to wait until everyone in front of him in line is served.

Line growth rate   = arrival − capacity
Thus, line growth rate = 5 − 3 = 2 patients/hr

After Y hours, the # of patients waiting is:

*Length of waiting line at time Y = Y * line growth rate*

So after, say, 4 hours opening, the # of patients still waiting to be seen will be = 4 * 2 = 8 patients

Supposing a patient comes in 4 hours after opening. There are 7 patients in line when that patient comes in.

Time required to complete service on X # of patients in line = X/capacity
Thus, time required to complete service on the 7 patients already in line = 7/3 = 2.34 hrs

So that patient coming in after 4 hrs of opening will be seen *after* 2.34 hrs and will take *another* 0.33 hrs to be examined and exit the clinic.

Total wait + service time for that last patient = time required to clear X # of patients in front of line + service time for last patient

$$= (X/\text{capacity}) + \text{service time for one patient}$$

Thus, for that last patient:

Total time in system = 2.33 hrs (7 patients ahead in line/3 patients per hr) + 0.34 hrs (@3patients/hr)
= **2.67 hrs**

Remedies for Waiting Lines

Remedies have to target capacity, variability, and capacity utilization, the usual suspects for waiting lines. Besides adding servers, stores like Apple have tried to add capacity or move capacity closer to the customer using iPhones to ring up purchases where the customer happens to stand in the store. Expansion of sales to online channels has also helped reduce waiting line length and, hence, wait times. Lowe's and Home Depot have added mobile checkouts. Self-checkout lanes can be seen in many stores. Other stores like Old Navy deploy 'line busters' when lines get beyond a certain length, employees who prescan shoppers' purchases before they reach the cashier. Waiting times can also be reduced by a) reducing arrival variability and b) reducing service time variability. Capacity utilization can be reduced by smoothing demand spikes or by adding capacity when needed. When further wait time reductions are not possible, managers can use a host of interesting psychological insights developed by keen observers of wait line behavior. There are various ways to influence perceptions of the length of wait times and customer attitudes and behavior in lines.

ACTUAL REDUCTION OF WAIT TIMES

Reducing arrival variability is key. We can try to move demand to when capacity is available. Appointment systems can help smooth over demand for the server, reduce periods of excessively high utilization, and thus reduce waiting lines. However, they may not per se reduce total waiting time for the customer. Appointments do not help patients reduce the months they need to wait to get to see a busy doctor. Incentives to use capacity at specific times also help reduce waiting times. Early bird specials and off season/times discounts on rates for hotels and tolls and such are useful strategies for de-seasonalizing demand. Random variation is harder to reduce, so some capacity has to be kept in reserve for emergencies if the consequences of having to make the customer wait are dire for the customer or for the business.

Reducing service time variability is another lever to push. Employee training helps, as does frequent rotation in high stress positions (CVS pharmacy counter at 6 p.m.; hospital reception). Having alternative scripts that employees can study and use in different situations removes the need to spend time developing impromptu responses to customer idiosyncrasies or internal issues. Restaurant hosts have scripts stuck on their side of the desk: "Welcome to . . . . . . ! Sure hope you got a hungry crew today—would you like a child seat?" is a standard scripted greeting to a family with kids. "Welcome to . . . . . . ! Would you like our business lunch today?" to a busy office worker dropping in for lunch. Call centers have developed extensive scripts to train and guide personnel in handling a variety of customer requests in a set amount of time. Providing servers with proper diagnostic and work tools and including regular feedback on performance are some other ways. Businesses also redesign work flows to reduce and stabilize busy server task times—a subject that is tackled in our chapter on managing processes (chapter 4). Certain tasks could possibly be moved from a server to be done by the customer to reduce stress on bottleneck server points. Self-service lines, stowing away your tray after eating in a student cafeteria, and iPads on restaurant tables instead of waiters taking orders are some commonly seen examples. Less expensive capacity (where easier tasks/routine customers are diverted to) can also be added to reduce/balance load on high utilization servers.

Line balancing is another strategy to reducing wait times. It is a concept adapted from factory production lines, where the product (customer) has to pass through a series of workstations (servers) in order to become finished output. If these workstations are unbalanced, that is, do different tasks with different times, some will be idle while others will be overloaded. The idea of line balancing is to take away tasks from overloaded stations and distribute them to underworked stations, thus increasing capacity for the entire process. Line balancing could be considered as a capacity-enhancing technique for services where the customer has to go through multiple interdependent steps to accomplish a goal. Other production innovations such as organizing all work into single, full-service cells can also increase capacity and reduce wait lines. In a cellular manufacturing scenario, an expert server(s) can service all the jobs that the customer needs done at a single window, removing the need to move the customer through an assembly line-like multi-phase process. Both line balancing and cellular manufacturing concepts require multi-skilled servers who can take over at least part of each other's work functions.

PSYCHOLOGICAL INSIGHTS

Since waiting in line is an experience, perceptions matter. If we cannot actually reduce waiting time itself, we can try to alter wait perceptions. Let's take a look at some psychological insights on how to do so gathered through studies and observations of waiting lines.

- *Fill their wait times*: Having something to do makes time seem to go quicker. Mirrors, magazines, TVs, computer tablets, and smartphone-equipped wait areas are common nowadays. Walt Disney Co. store employees are trained to entertain customers with Disney trivia while they are in line. Once customers reach the cashier, Disney employees switch to focus on efficiency, not entertaining. Activities such as prescanning and filling in forms or simply moving from one room to another 'starts' the process psychologically, removing the perception of waiting for the task to start. A small raffle while waiting helps to entertain and push customers to stay on. Waiting in groups has been shown to reduce wait-time perceptions compared to individual waits. Reasons vary from being more informed from a diversity of sources and varied opinion, an opportunity to vent against a common enemy, and a chance to socialize.

- *Give them control*: Choice gives a semblance of control, and control leads to positive perceptions of waiting times. Choice of music in elevators, multiple screen shot TVs with remotes, and some level of participation in the process do not cost much but may keep them involved and interested. The principle of exercising choice is nowhere better illustrated than in the researched fact that people like separate lines for each server, although a single-file line multiple-server system actually moves people faster. In multiple-file lines, an entire line may be stuck because of a random incident like a price check, whereas in a single-file line such random incidents will hold up just a few servers, leaving the rest open to the remaining customers in line. We choose to ignore that truth, perhaps because the subliminal control we enjoy by exercising our (superior) intelligence, sight, and intuition to choose the 'best' line has been experienced by all of us. No matter that the line we finally pick turns out to be the slowest one!

- *Communicate often*: In a study, two groups of university students were told to register for a course with the understanding that there would be some delay in processing their applications. One group was informed about the length of the delay while the other was kept in the dark. The outcome—communicating the delay information did not change students' perceived waiting time, but they felt more in control and less unhappy about the delay. For long delays, however, the psychological value of communication diminishes. Even so, frequent communication provides an opportunity for customers to vent at someone in authority and get answers. Organizations are cognizant of the value of communicating. Johnson County in Kansas allows customers to join the waiting line by text, phone, going online, or just walking into the office and texts waiting customers with alerts when it's their turn. Customers can attend to other errands without worrying about missing their place in line or missing their turn to be served. MedWaitTime, an app for mobile devices, communicates with color-coded status updates on the time to wait for a doctor. A green signals 0 or short wait times, yellow signifies a moderate wait, while red warns of major delays. The app performs for both individual doctors and hospital ERs. Users can also read medical articles and obtain more specific wait times.

- *Change physical layout*: Managers can change the layout of the waiting environment to improve perceptions of wait times. Disneyland designed snake lines to ensure that customers are not able to observe the entire length of that really long line! Restaurants split up lines into different locations, such as wait lounges and bars, to convey the same impression of small wait lines. Limos have been used at times to seat waiting customers.

- *Observe social justice norms:* Social injustice in waiting is moving up someone in the line without clear and just cause—any violation of the 'first come, first served' line discipline causes unrest. In face-to-face situations, it may be wise to physically shield high-priority customers from the line of sight of us common folks waiting in line. Side doors work. Visible evidence that such VIP customers are actually paying more also helps smooth ruffled feathers, though a certain level of resentment remains. Being rich, however, may not buy you a spot in the line for services such as hospital waits or waiting to get into church for Christmas Mass.

- *Conceal:* Hide away nonserving employees out of customer sight. Waiting customers get infuriated when they see employees prioritizing other work (phone calls, talking to superiors, doing 'something' at their PC) and not attending to the customer.

- *Time of the day*: Time is not linear. A 10-minute wait at a deserted subway station at 2 a.m. at night will feel much longer than a similar wait at 2 p.m. in the afternoon. An hour of doing homework seems an eternity, but that hour flies fast when watching *The Walking Dead*. People rushing to work may be crankier with delays than usual. Businesses should recognize the context of waiting situations and place more resources during times when stress is high in wait lines. We also know that wait times have a tipping point. Studies suggest that customers may abandon a 10-minute waiting time line after the first two or three minutes if they feel it's not moving quickly enough. Men seem to abandon lines quicker than women. Similarly, express service lanes are appreciated by simple/routine need customers. A fitting room in a department store can easily have a separate line for customers who have just one or two dresses to try on.

- *Employee factors:* Time passes quicker with a good-looking or friendly server. Wait times may also seem less onerous if the server has a special expertise. Middle-aged women may be slower but handle breakable objects with more TLC. On the other hand, young cashiers may not look too closely at coupon expiry dates.

Finally, some wait line positives: Businesses sometimes *want* longer wait times. If Starbucks runs me out in two minutes, when will I have the time to drool over those Danishes or eventually succumb to the lure of that chocolate éclair? Also, longer wait times can be equated with quality—those long lines at a movie or restaurant must be evidence that people find them of more fun or value.

KEY POINTS

- Waiting lines form even when the average customer arrival rate is lower than the service rate.
- Nonseasonal uncertainties in demand and uncertainty in service times cause mismatches between demand and capacity.
- Given an average arrival and service rate, the single service single-file M/M/1 queuing model can predict the average time spent waiting in line, average number of customers in line, and the probability of x # of customers in line.

- The M/M/c queuing model can predict the same outcomes for a single-file multiple-server line, allowing managers to estimate the additional capacity needed to cut down wait times.
- Capacity and waiting time are not linearly related. Adding capacity reduces waiting time by a disproportionately greater amount.
- Appointments and incentives can help reduce seasonality in demand.
- Employee training and process redesign can help reduce variability in service times.
- Customer involvement, frequent communication, layout changes, and cognizance of contextual factors can affect customer psychological perceptions of waiting time length and quality of time spent in waiting.

7.4 Was It Done Right?

So how well are we managing capacity? We look at measures that businesses use and follow up with some incidents of when it was not done right and a script for the right way to conduct capacity.

7.4.1 Performance Measures

Using a balanced approach, we consider internal, customer-facing, and financial measures of capacity management performance. Internal measures include metrics such as:

- Percent reduction in production and procurement cycle time
- Reduction in panic buying
- Capacity forecast performance
- Percent productivity improvement
- Percent reduction in labor idle time
- Percent reductions in re-work and scrap rate
- Percent process monitored for capacity planning and management
- Percent change in capacity adjustments events
- Percent reduction in delivery delays
- Percent reduction in inventory levels

Customer-facing measures consider metrics such as:

- Order fulfillment cycle time
- Percent reduction in number of customer complaints due to delivery delays
- Percent reduction in waiting times
- Percent increase in customer satisfaction.

Financial measures could include:

- Variance in planned capacity expenditures
- Cost of underutilized capacity.

Companies build a comprehensive scorecard, weighting dimensions and metrics differently to reflect strategic priorities.

7.4.2 What Could Go Wrong?

Capacity in the crowded South America-China commodity shipping lanes jumped quantum-fold with the 2011 introduction of the Vale Brasil, the longest cargo carrier ever built, intended to carry iron ore to China. Yet, six months into sailing, it did not carry a single ton of iron ore to China. Fierce opposition from Chinese ship owners apprehensive of further reductions in freight rates and rumblings from Chinese steel makers worried about ceding delivery and pricing control over an important part of their supply chain were to blame. It seems like a capacity-management error by Vale, the world's largest iron ore miner, to have deployed this kind of capacity without getting a concomitant demand commitment from their principal buyer. Vale also, perhaps, underestimated the reactions of Chinese ship owners. Capacity changes can occur because of changes in weather, product mix, and equipment, process re-designs, and changes in labor availability. The 2011 floods in Thailand largely spared Seagate's disk drive facilities but practically destroyed more than 100 component suppliers in the region. In turn, disk drive shortages crippled computer makers, some of whom reportedly paid premiums to book Seagate's 2012 capacity. Which brings us to another caution in capacity management—consider carefully before paying for capacity in pursuit of higher volume demand—there is the risk that capacity could turn out to cost more than the realized incremental profits from that increased demand.

Nikita was proud of the online order fulfillment system her team had developed for the company. In fact, it was so successful that the marketing head decided to offer the in-house system to customers for their own use, telling them to just plug it in and run. No one bothered to inform Nikita. In a matter of weeks, the system collapsed, its capacity burnt out by loads several times greater than design-load specifications. Order receipt and fulfillment times shot up, deliveries got mixed up, and angry customers found their own operations compromised. Foolish customers, maybe, but the bigger blunder was made by the production and marketing chiefs in not involving Nikita in capacity management decisions. Companies that manage excess capacity well can see significant gains. Amazon Web Services grew out of Amazon's excess server capacity sale to third-parties that required computing capacity for their own operations.

Following a systematic process helps prevent such mishaps. For any capacity management decision, a good point of departure is to define the components of the production and delivery system, including supplier and internal capacity consisting of buildings, machines, and labor. The capacity of each component should be estimated using direct measurement or verified statements. Then, the demand for each component should be estimated for every context and time, and the capacity requirements computed. A gap analysis will reveal variances from the computed needs, and action can be taken to apply capacity management techniques to achieve a closer match between the requirement of the moment and available capacity. In all these, capacity planners and line managers should be actively involved.

Customer feelings and a sense of fair play are important determinants of yield management success. Coca-Cola experimented with a dynamic pricing vending machine that would increase prices with an increase in temperature. Consumers did not like it. How would you like it if colleges charged more per credit hour if you registered later (although within the last date of registration)? Or, conversely, gave a discount to students at the last moment for courses that did not fill up? What else could go wrong?

What if demand falls suddenly?

- Close facilities, reduce capacity, offer capacity sharing to other companies.
- Shift capacity to growth markets.
- Use capacity for maintenance/product or process, innovation/training, and development/quality and safety improvement initiatives.
- Provide more capacity to existing demand, e.g., allow ticketed passengers to use more than one seat.
- Increase advertising, or sharpen advertising focus on important customer segments.
- Lower prices—but it's difficult to raise prices once lowered, and customers may 'game' the system expecting last-minute price discounts.

What if demand increases suddenly?

- Offer customers incentives to wait
- Identify and address principal points of pain—make wait times less onerous, rotate employees in high-friction, stressful customer-interface positions.
- Involve customer in product/service delivery process—create some capacity by using customers (pay for inconvenience, if necessary).
- Reduce variety of products/services and offer major products/services—variety increases demands on capacity.
- Hype product/service as a 'hot,' hard-to-find offering—increase prices, if feasible.
- If product/service quantities or offerings have to be curtailed, inform customers ahead of time, explain basis of rationing, and inform estimated time for resumption of normal service.
- Develop recovery systems to address service failures—apologies, personal calls, future discounts.

KEY POINTS

- Capacity management performance can be assessed using weighted combinations of internal, customer-oriented, and financial measures.
- Capacity management is critically dependent on customer commitments and natural factors.
- Sudden declines in demand can be met with facility closures/slowdowns, using excess capacity for other productive purposes, and providing freebies to loyal customers.
- Sudden increases in demand can be met by incentivizing customers to wait, reducing product variety, hiking prices, and using customers to create capacity, if possible.

7.5 Trends in Capacity Management

The revenue- and profit-generating power of capacity management models has encouraged migration to other industries and areas. Capacity management intersects with capacity planning, inventory, marketing, logistics, and supply chain management, bringing in a much wider and comprehensive array of factors and considerations in the broad context of synchronizing supply with demand.

Capacity management has migrated beyond its traditional confines of hotels, airlines, and factories. Businesses today face demand uncertainty, multiple distribution channels, and regulatory pressures that prohibit blatant price discrimination. Capacity management offers ways to segment and price capacity using time or other acceptable discrimination criteria. Capacity management models have helped distributors resolve promotion-design and negotiated contracts across multiple and competing SKUs and channels. Banks use capacity management techniques to price customer segments for making and determining dynamic interest rates. Companies in cable and other industries set attractive entry pricing points that later escalate into more expensive plans. Revenue management helps define markets and design tailored contracts for specific markets. Hospitals employ capacity management methods to cope effectively with uncertain demand and service times in ER and other locations.

Capacity management has also found new players to integrate with—supply chain management being one. Revenue management complements the supply focus on cost and delivery with a demand perspective that maximizes revenue, given cost and capacity constraints. Capacity management suggests and coordinates pricing, discounting, and capacity allocation among competing and complementing sales and distribution channels with different price and delivery elasticities. Data mining insights on demand behavior are combined with capacity management techniques that tag price and capacity to observed patterns for revenue and profit gains. Another new partner is customer relations and marketing. Yield management techniques are being married with customer relations management to make offers not just on the basis of price but also other attributes desired by a customer. Instead of discriminating on the basis of low and high payers, imagine hotels being able to design room deals for one customer at a time based on a unique offering matching a hotel's rooms, amenities, and location to the unique expectations of one customer. If a guest plays tennis, likes outdoors activities, and enjoys Thai food, hotels will be able to design a room offer with those specific amenities attached. Availability of data repositories and data mining tools make such customization feasible.

The complexity and sophistication of capacity management models has grown tremendously with increases in computing and data storage capacity and with the benefit of experience in increasingly different industry environments. For example, the original revenue management model for hotels and airlines was developed around single bookings. In 2007, Marriott began using a 'Group Price Optimizer,' booking an additional $46 million in profit. The optimizer helps sales teams by forecasting the probability of winning a bid at different price points. State of the art IT capacity management models now have the ability to split requirements/arrivals into hundreds or thousands of multiple small packets that are simultaneously matched with and sent to small packets of capacity available at that moment at architecturally different locations. The work is fragmented and done in different places and then coalesced back into a whole output. Imagine my hitting the 'save' key to save this chapter in the cloud. The doc would be fragmented into pieces and saved in little bits and pieces in multiple servers. When I wish to retrieve the document, those pieces are stitched back into a whole and sent back to my computer. An example is Napster, which uses idle processor time from participating CPUs to process uploads and downloads of large files. Such file transfers, processed by servers located across the Internet, could take some time; ultra-fast responses may not matter as much in some cases.

Capacity management is not just numbers and models—innovative managers create novel solutions to capacity issues. Consider the case of excess production in a bakery. Normally, a donut shop may choose to discard unsold donuts after a certain number of hours on the shelf. An imaginative manager developed a creative marketing solution. Why not give away the excess donuts on a random basis to loyal customers? The element of a surprise 'bonus' has been seen to be very effective in driving customer satisfaction. On example of such a program is 'MyPanera,' which promises "The more you visit, the more surprises you can get (just when you least expect them)!" If, in doing so, Panera reduces its excess production, it's getting two birds with one stone! Bars do it all the time with happy hour offers, but businesses with volatile demand sometimes cannot anticipate capacity excesses ahead of time. Current technologies can help. A nail salon with a suddenly cancelled appointment can send out a deal of the hour invite through apps like Groupon Now or LivingSocial's daily deals mobile app. Limiting such offers to a specific time period or specific amount/value is necessary to avoid being overwhelmed by responders.

OM IN PRACTICE

LiquidSpace

Like airline seats or a restaurant, an empty office or desk space in an office represents unused capacity and wasted rent paid for that office or desk space capacity.

LiquidSpace lists unused or underused office and meeting space, where listers can set prices and duration by the hour, day, month, or other periods. LiquidSpace offers a central database of available office space, takes reservations, processes payments and allows opportunities for ad hoc rentals and leases. Its offerings range from rates per day for a desk to monthly leases, mostly for suites.

LiquidSpace's goal is to convert available space into cash. Byproducts may be peak office demand reduction, shortened commutes, and possibly fewer new office buildings. Like OpenTable, the restaurant reservation system, Airbnb, the facilitator of peer-to-peer room and apartment rentals, and Zipcar, the car-sharing service, LiquidSpace ultimately aims to match demand at the moment to capacity available at the moment. It will be no surprise to see LiquidSpace eventually utilize more sophisticated yield-management techniques that will vary price to match needs to office spaces before they expire, much like hotel rooms or airline seats on a flight.

Adapted from: G.F., "Yield management, Lofty goals," Babbage: Science and Technology (blog), *Economist*, Feb. 28, 2012, http://www.economist.com/blogs/babbage/2012/02/yield-management.

Think of all the PCs in the school cafeteria that are idle outside meal hours—why not use that excess/idle capacity to process work for other departments in the school or even outside businesses during idle time? And how about the coffee discarded for fresh coffee every couple of hours at places like 7-Eleven, Hess, and Dunkin' Donuts shops? Why not randomly give away coffee to customers that have a loyalty card like a Hess card, if practical?

KEY POINTS

Trends in Capacity Management

- Capacity management techniques have found nontraditional applications in areas such finance, telecom, and hospitals.
- Companies are integrating capacity management with supply chain management, sales, and distribution.
- Businesses are developing creative nonquantitative solutions to capacity issues.

7.6 Conclusion

Customer: *"Why should I choose you?"*
Business: *"Because we promise that we shall serve your needs without long waits or exorbitant charges."*

What you have learnt about capacity management in these pages will help you deliver on that promise. Capacity management is about the ability to match demand at the moment with capacity at that moment. When we see idle employees, we need to remember that there are times when capacity may sit idle waiting for demand. We need to find ways to utilize it. We can also expect to see waiting lines even though we think we have adequate capacity. Demand variability outstrips capacity availability at the time, and waiting lines form. We recall that capacity management teaches us ways to reduce waiting lines and reduce grief for those who have to wait in line. When we face uncertainty in both demand and capacity, we can use techniques such as demand management, systematic overbooking, dynamic yield management, and the dynamic pricing of capacity. Meeting demand will be your responsibility in practically any managerial job—your knowledge of capacity management will help you do so effectively and efficiently.

What Have We Learned?

What Is Capacity Management?

- Capacity management is the tactical task of matching demand at the moment to capacity available at the moment.
- Demand can be managed through pricing and user incentives.
- Capacity can be managed using yield management and scheduling methods.
- Capacity can be changed by reorganizing work processes.

Why Is It Important?

- Companies have to manage capacity in various forms: supplier capacity, production capacity, logistics capacity, distribution capacity, returns capacity, and human capacity. To the extent that capacity falls short or exceeds immediate demand, revenues and profits may be affected adversely.
- Capacity management decisions are inter-functional in scope, affecting marketing, finance, HR, and other functions in an organization. All majors will benefit from an understanding of how the challenges of managing capacity affect operations in their own functions.

How Is It Done?

- Fixed capacity, flexible demand businesses such as hotels can use yield management to optimize overbooking decisions.
- Yield management requires inelastic capacity, customer segmentation by price and time, advance sales, and low variable costs.
- Yield management is useful in determining how much capacity to fence off at higher prices, in order to maximize revenue.
- Fixed capacity, inflexible demand businesses can use scheduling techniques to match capacity with demand at least cost or inconvenience.
- Variable demand and inflexible capacity leads to waiting lines.
- Waiting lines may form even when capacity exceeds demand, on average.
- Adding one unit of server capacity will reduce waiting time by more than a unit.
- M/M/1 queuing models provide wait-line descriptive analysis for single-file, single-server waiting lines. M/M/c models do the same for single-file, multiple-server waiting lines
- Waiting times can be reduced by reducing demand seasonality through appointments and incentives and by reducing service time variability through employee training and process redesign.
- Perceptions of waiting time can be positively influenced by customer involvement, frequent communication, layout changes, and cognizance of contextual factors.

Was It Done Right?

- Capacity management performance can be assessed using weighted combinations of internal, customer oriented and financial measures.
- Sudden declines in demand can be met with facilities closure/slowdowns, using excess capacity for other productive purposes, and providing freebies to loyal customers.
- Sudden increases in demand can be met by incentivizing customers to wait, reducing product variety, hiking prices, and using customers to create capacity.

Trends in Capacity Management

- Capacity management techniques have migrated to businesses such as finance, telecom, and hospitals.
- Capacity management finds a natural integration with supply chain management, sales, and distribution.
- Managers can develop creative nonquantitative solutions to capacity issues.

Discussion Questions

1 Why shouldn't we take the average or expected number of no-shows as the overbooking quantity?
2 Can rooms go empty with an overbooking solution? Why or why not?
3 When would our overbooking figure be lower than the average no show figure?
4 Amtrak typically does not overbook as much as an airline—why not? No-shows are as many, if not more, compared to airlines.
5 Supposing a hotel sets a protection level of 50 rooms for its higher paying business customers. It then learns that competition down the road has reduced their business traveler room rates. Having little choice, the hotel decides to reduce its own business traveler rates to match competitor rates. What effect would this typically have on the size of the earlier set 50-room protection level?
6 From a waiting line perspective, would you rather have two servers in two different rooms or both in one room?
7 From a waiting line perspective, would you rather have two servers each capable of handling five customers an hour or just one very experienced sever who can handle 10 customers an hour?
8 Discuss contexts where a single-file line would be considered inappropriate.
9 Do waiting lines form for online buys?
10 Name three ways that you would incorporate psychological palliatives to waiting lines in a cafeteria checkout.
11 Provide three situations where the line discipline of first come, first served would not be appropriate. How would you convince the line to tolerate the violation of the FCFS discipline?
12 Provide a situation where customer arrival rate would be constant.
13 Provide a situation where the service time would be constant
14 Does placing self-service kiosks in airports really help move traffic faster?

> *Answer:* Yes, because even though self-serve passengers have slower service times compared to experienced airline agents, the number of kiosks installed is more than the number of agent stations replaced. That is, the number of servers goes up even though the average service time per server goes down. So total capacity increases.

End of Chapter Problems

1 Facing a downturn, Hooter Air decides to offer advance booking specials at $90, one-way, on its popular NYC-Miami flight. There are plenty of ticket buyers at this price. Past promotions suggest that the distribution of no-shows for advance specials is normally distributed (mean 7, standard deviation 3). The plane has a total capacity of 100 seats. How many overbookings should Hooter Air do for the flight? It costs Hooter Air $50 in coupons to placate bumped (having to turn away confirmed) passengers.

> *Answer:* Using the newsvendor model:
> $P(NS \geq OB) \geq C_s/(C_o + C_s)$, where:
> C_o = average cost of overage = cost of wasted capacity = cost of no show = $90;
> C_s = average cost of stockout = cost of running out of capacity = cost of overbooking = $50;

OB = # overbooked; NS = number of no-shows
P(NS≥OB) ≥ 50 /(90 + 50) = 0.36; corresponding z value = 0.36
Q (# of overbookings) = μ + 0.25 * σ = 7 + 0.25 * 3 = 7.75 = rounded up to 8 overbookings
So make 100 + 8 = 108 bookings for the 100 seat flight.

2   Hooter Air decides to play safer and overbooks by 6 passengers only. What is the probability of bumping passengers?

Answer: Since 106 passengers are booked for a 100-seat flight, bumping will happen only if the number of no-shows is 5 or less. Distribution of no-shows is normally distributed (mean 7, standard deviation 3).

Computing z = $(x - \mu)/ \sigma$ = (5 − 7)/3 = −0.67, corresponding to an area of 0.2514 from the Z table, means that there is about a 25 percent chance the number of no-shows will be 5 or fewer, that is, there is about a 25 percent chance of having to bump passengers.

3   Early morning commuters stop by to pick up a latte and muffin at DDonuts. The average arrival rate is 12 customers per hour. That early in the morning, it's just the shop owner, who takes an average of 4 minutes to serve a customer. Assume that arrivals are Poisson distributed while the service time is are exponentially distributed.

a)   What is the average number of customers being served at any time?
b)   What is the average number of customers waiting in line?
c)   What is the average time customers spend in the shop?
d)   What is the probability of 8 customers being in the shop?
e)   The owner wishes to cut down the system wait time to an average of 10 minutes or less, from the current 20 minutes. How many servers need to be there in the mornings?

Answers: Single server, single line system.

a)   Arrival rate λ = 12/hr; service rate μ = 15/hr (1/min)
(Utilization) average # of customers being served = λ/μ = 12/15 = 0.80 customers.
A capacity utilization of 0.80 implies that a) each server is servicing customers 80% of the time; that on average 80% of servers are servicing, while 20% of servers are idle; and c) that at any given time there is a 0.80 probability that any randomly observed server is servicing a customer.

b)   Average # of customers in line L_q = $\lambda^2/[\mu(\mu - \lambda)]$ = 144/[15(15 − 12)] = 3.2 customers

c)   Average *time* a customer spends waiting + being serviced= $1/(\mu - \lambda)$ = 1/(15 − 12) = 0.33 hrs = 20 minutes, approximately.

d)   Probability of 8 customers in the shop
Probability of *n* customers in system = $(1 - (\lambda/\mu)) (\lambda/\mu)n$
= (1 − 12/15) (12/15)8 = (0.2)(0.168) = 0.0336

e)   Desired average time spent waiting in line (W_q) = 10 min or less = 0.1667 hr or less

Thus, desired average # of customers in line (L_q) = $W_q * \lambda$ = 0.1667 * 12 = 1.999

Utilization = $r = \lambda/\mu$ = 12/15 = 0.80

From table *"Infinite source values for L_q and P_0 given λ/μ and M"* (located in the Statistical Tables section of this book), for a table *r* of 0.80 and a table L_q of 0.152 (look for table L_q ≤ desired L_q of 1.999), M = 2 servers. Note from the table that P_0 (probability of zero customers waiting) = 42.9%, which means substantial idle time for the servers.

4   A movie theater intends to open a ticket counter for evening shows at a local college cafeteria. On average, 18 ticket buyers come in per hour. The ticket counter can process 1 ticket buyer every 3 minutes on average. What would be the:

a)   Average # of customers in line?
b)   Average time a customer spends in line?
c)   Server idle time?
d)   Probability of 10 customers in the system?

   Answers:

a)   Arrival rate λ = 18/hr; service rate μ = 1 customer/3 min = 20/hr
     Average # of customer in line $L_q = \lambda^2/[\mu(\mu - \lambda)] = 324/[20(20 - 18)] = 8.1$ customers
b) W_q: average time spent waiting in line = $\lambda/[\mu(\mu - \lambda)] = 18/[20(20 - 18)] = 0.45$ hr
c)   Utilization = λ/μ = 18/20 = 0.90 customers.
     Server idle time = 10% on average
d)   Probability of '10' customers in system = $(1 - (\lambda/\mu))\ (\lambda/\mu)n = (1 - (18/20))\ (18/20)^{10} = (0.10)$
     (0.349)
     = 0.0349

5   Reception at a popular restaurant reflects an unstable system with an average arrival rate of 3 guests/minute and an average service rate of 1 guest/minute. What is the:

a)   Line growth rate?
b)   Length of waiting line 30 minutes after opening?
c)   Total processing time (wait + service time) for a guest who came in at 1 hour after opening?

   Answers:

a)   Line growth rate = arrival rate − capacity
     = 3 − 1 = 2 guest/min
b)   Length of waiting line at time $Y = Y$ * line growth rate
     = 30 min * 2 = 60 guests
c)   Wait + service time for individual arriving at time $Y = Y$ * [(arrival rate/capacity) − 1]
     = 60 min * [(3/1) − 1] = 120 min

6   Customers arrive at drive in window at the local fast food place at an average rate of 12 per hour, following a Poisson distribution. The server at the window can service an average of 14 cars per hour, with service times described by an exponential distribution. The manager asks you to help him figure out:

a)   Average utilization.
b)   Average time a customer spends in line waiting to place an order.
c)   Average number of customers waiting in line.
d)   The probability of having more than 4 customers in the system

7   Refer to question no. 6. The manager adds another server, each capable of handling 15 cars per hour (they help each other). The arrival rate increases to 13 cars per hour. What is the:

a)   Average utilization.
b)   Average time a customer spends in line waiting to place an order.
c)   Average number of customers waiting in line.
d)   The probability of having more than 4 customers in the system.

Suggested Class Projects

a) Visit your local hospital's ER and observe the waiting line system. Describe the system in terms of number of lines, servers, line discipline, and the average wait times. Suggest at least two remedies to improve wait times.

b) Visit your local Rite-Aid or CVS or Walgreens. Observe the waiting lines at the pharmaceutical counter during peak and off-peak hours. Compute estimates of average arrival rates and observed average service time. Then, a) make recommendations for adding a server (show effect on waiting line and wait times) and b) make other suggestions to address the waiting time.

Suggested Cases

1   Harvard Business School Publishing: Online exercise (#4386): Multiple Server queues: Students analyze how different variables affect patient waiting times in a hospital, exploring trade-offs between cost, patient experience and clinical quality.

2   Ivey: Yield Management at American Airlines

P. Fraser Johnson, Robert Klassen, John S. Haywood-Farmer
Product Number: 9B00D003, 01/29/2002

American Airlines is a widely cited leader in the development and implementation of yield management practices. This case is based on a training exercise used at American Airlines to introduce managers to their yield management system. The case is designed for use in a service management elective course or in a service operations course and is intended to expose students to yield management by giving them hands-on experience managing bookings for a flight. The game takes approximately 50 minutes to play, leaving approximately 30 minutes for class discussion.

Notes

1   Peter Belobaba, "Application of a Probabilistic Decision Model to Airline Seat Inventory Control," *Operations Research*, 37 no. 2 (1989): 183–197.

2   R. Tibrewala, D. Phillippe and J. Brown, "Optimal Scheduling of Two Consecutive Idle Periods," *Management Science* 19 (1972): 71–75.

3   M stands for Markovian.
M/M/c convention: M = Poisson arrival distribution; /M = negative exponential service time distribution; /c = number of channels/servers. M/M/1: Poisson arrival, negative exponential service times, one server.

4   Recall '!' means factorial, e.g., 4! is 'four factorial' = $4 \times 3 \times 2 \times 1 = 24$

8 Managing Inventory

Chapter Take-Aways

- Types of inventory
- How to count inventory?
- Costs of keeping inventory
- How to prioritize?
- How much to order?
- When to order?
- Levers to reduce inventory

Managing Inventory: A Road Map

8.6 Conclusion
   End of chapter
   - What have we learned?
   - Discussion questions
   - End of chapter problems
   - Suggested class projects
   - Suggested cases

Customer: *"Why should I choose you?"*
Business: *"Because we promise that we will have what you need, when and where you need it."*

8.1 What Is Inventory Management?

8.1.1 What Is Inventory?

Inventory is a product or service that we *could* make, acquire, perform, or provide *after* the customer asks for it but choose to make/acquire and *store now* in anticipation of the customer asking for it. By definition, raw materials like steel and car parts in an auto plant waiting to be turned into cars are inventory, and semi-finished cars waiting for the next operation can be inventory. Of course, cars in the shipping lot or cars being transported on trains/trailers, as well as cars on dealer lots, are also inventory. Similarly, the 'Help' section of Amazon is also inventory, consisting of information on frequently asked questions that is collected and stored in anticipation of the customer asking for it. We run the risk that the customer may not ask for it at all or that the inventory may spoil or become obsolete. Yet, such risks clearly cannot make a business eliminate inventory altogether. Dominos must have a stock of cheese and dough, while that closest-to-your-classroom vending machine better not run out of Doritos!

8.1.2 What Is Inventory Management?

Why does a business carry inventory? The underlying reason is uncertainty. Uncertainty about future demand, about prices, about availability and replenishment supply times, about loss of production when a worker falls sick, about the quality of goods, about what the customer may think if she sees a lot of empty shelf space in a store, and so on. Inventory is an insurance premium we pay to protect us against the effects of uncertainties. To the extent that uncertainty can be reduced, the need for inventory diminishes. Effective inventory management targets reducing inventory levels through the application of inventory models, as well as through more broad-based approaches to reduce uncertainties of demand and supply.

Inventory management is a data-driven approach to making intelligent cost and customer service-driven decisions on what is to be stored; how much is to be stored; where it is to be stored and for how long; how to price and allow customers access to the inventory; and when to replenish inventory stock. The goal, in most cases, is to generate revenue by avoiding or minimizing stock-outs (running out of goods when the customer wants them) while keeping costs at a reasonable level.

While managing inventory is a critical task in large firms, smaller sized operations are especially vulnerable to inventory risks because of the 'bus' factor.[1] Jimmy's been around for years in a small but expanding retail store. Jimmy knows everything. A customer wants that blue dress with white edging—no problem, Jimmy knows exactly where it is—the third rack in the fifth row in the stockroom. Jimmy's got the entire inventory stock, location, and ordering patterns imprinted in his mind. And every morning Jimmy's boss gets up with a prayer on her lips—please God, don't let Jimmy get hit by a bus today! Because if Jimmy became unavailable all of a sudden, the business has no inventory management system to take his place.

8.1.3 Types of Inventory

Physical inventory generally exists in three forms. For example, inventory for FoxConn, China, the assembler of electronics for HP, Apple, and others, may consist of:

- Pipeline or raw material inventory: raw materials or components that are being transported for assembly into a finished product at FoxConn, such as smartphone touchscreens on a ship coming from Korea.
- Work-in-process inventory: iPhones in various stages of assembly at FoxConn; for example, some units waiting to be installed with touchscreens and some units that are being fitted with batteries.
- Finished goods inventory: finished iPhones, packaged and ready for shipment at Foxconn or being held for shipment at a distribution center.

Sometimes inventory is also described in terms of why it has been acquired.

- *Cycle* inventory builds up because large lot purchases in excess of current demand are made at a time in order to avail of price discounts or transportation economies. Shoppers you see at Sam's Club and Costco could be building up cycle inventory.
- *Seasonal* inventory builds up because that product is perhaps only available during a specific time of the year, like mangoes and apples. Juice makers must buy all they can during the fruit season for use throughout the year, or when demand peaks at certain times, but capacity cannot be flexed. Campbell soups are made and stored throughout the year to fulfill demand peaks in the winter. Winter production capacity is limited and cannot be expanded easily.
- *Decoupling* inventory is generated when inventory is built up deliberately in order to buffer (decouple) the work of one workstation from another that is feeding it. If operator B is dependent on operator A for supplies, B suffers if A is absent or slows down work for any reason. But keeping a small stock of operator A made supplies in-between A and B would buffer B from the uncertainty in A's production. Parents almost always keep a buffer inventory of a meal or two in the freezer, just in case teen Josh gets hungry if they are unexpectedly not around to provide the usual meal.

Then there's also *perishable* inventory, items that tend to spoil or become obsolete quickly. Fish, produce, flowers, and daily newspapers are some examples of perishable inventory. Perishable inventory requires special managing, often requiring climate-controlled storage and transportation, and well-designed forecasting, sales promotion, and disposal systems.

There's also *virtual inventory*, physical entities that are converted, digitalized, and stored—such as paper medical records to e-records, books to disks, and product drawings into computer drawings.

Inventory can be classified in terms of location, form, or reason for acquisition, but sometimes a greater challenge is to find it, first.

8.1.4 Where Is Our Inventory?

Every item in inventory should have an identity, and we should know where it is. Let's tackle the last part first—knowing where our inventory is. Have you ever thought about the plight of your local Kroger/Walmart/ShopRite store manager when it comes to tracking inventory? Consider: a tired store cashier sees a customer approaching with a dozen each of strawberry and blueberry yogurt. After a 10-hour shift, he is in no mood to swipe every item. He proceeds to ring up all two dozen yogurts as strawberry yogurt (hopefully all yogurt flavors are identically priced). That tired store cashier's action may wreak havoc in the inventory system. Specifically, the stock of both strawberry and blueberry yogurt was actually reduced by a dozen. The inventory system however, thinks that two dozen strawberry yogurts have left the store and subtracts that quantity from its inventory record of strawberry yogurt. It then finds that the remaining inventory has fallen below a pre-set inventory re-order level for that item and places a fresh order. Result—fresh supplies coming in of strawberry yogurt although there's enough stock in the store. The blueberry yogurt, in the meantime, has left the store undetected. The computer thinks it still has that stock on the shelf and does not place an order, even though the actual remaining stock has fallen to zero. Blueberry yogurt just became 'phantom inventory'—inventory that resides in the store's inventory system but does not exist for the customer. The system stock may not be corrected until an employee finds out that the shelf is empty of blueberry yogurt. Customers will walk in for blueberry yogurt, not find any, and leave—most will not bother to inform the manager. The store may have inadvertently provided an opportunity for that customer to walk away to a competitor's store—which may be cleaner, with more product variety, better looking cashiers, and better customer service! Phantom inventory develops because of both employee and customer actions—theft, misplacement of items, incorrect cashier scanning, or incomplete scanning of goods coming into the store. Big disorganized store backrooms and incentive systems that penalize store managers for stock-outs but not excess inventory also contribute to the problem. Businesses attack the phantom inventory problem in many ways, including quicker worker rotation to avoid fatigue at cash counters, incentives to both customers and employees to report seen shortages, better security, and checkout systems with minimal human involvement.

Shopping for shoes, we ask the salesperson if he has our size only to see him disappear into the stockroom. After an eternity of waiting, the answer is often "We are out of your size." Soon, with the help of a technology called RFID, shoes will self-report their location. RFID (radio frequency identification devices) provides a way to query and track the physical location of products. RFID systems consist of small chips (tags) to be placed inside a product/package, together with chip scanner guns and readers, and software that can receive and emit signals to the chip. A barcode will tell you it's *a* box of Cap'n Crunch, but not *which* box, whereas an RFID on a box can identify an individual box of Cap'n Crunch and track it all the way from the Quaker Oats Company loading dock to the store shelf—answering questions ranging from "Where exactly is that particular box now?" and "What's the expiry date on that box sitting on that top shelf?" to "Let's find out where that box is since there is a recall notice out for that lot."

Providing an identity to everything in stock enables tracking and location. A unique item (product) in stock is identified by its stock keeping unit number (SKU), which we see as a barcode on an item. So, for instance, a men's jacket in grey, size medium, single breasted, sold across Men's Wearhouse stores would have a different SKU number than the same jacket in a brown color at the same stores. SKU numbers are developed by companies for their own in-house use. UPC codes are different. A UPC code is a standard code that is obtained/provided by the manufacturer of the product. Macy's and Saks Fifth, for example, would have different SKU numbers for the same UPC-coded Coach purse, frustrating shoppers who are trying to price shop that brown Coach Ali bag across different company store sites. Smart UPC codes can now raise flags for expired foods, tell the ambient temperature, identify which store is seeing the most coupons being redeemed, and enable passers-by to check out the menu in a restaurant by simply waving their smartphone over a Quick Response (QR) code posted outside.

For manufacturers and assemblers, it's not enough to just track pallet or product lot numbers—tracking has to extend to the level of sub-assemblies and components that go into the product. Besides real time visibility on inventory location, information on attributes such as country of origin, serial number and vendor lot number is useful for identifying culprits in case of product recalls.

Proper slotting also helps in identifying inventory location. Slotting is placing fast-moving and important items closer to shipping docks and in more visible and accessible locations in the warehouse. It also places complementary items that are typically ordered together in adjacent slots. In well-managed inventory systems,

What a UPC code means

The Uniform Code Council (UCC), now called GSI US, provides the first 6 digits of a UPC as a manufacturer identification number for an annual fee. The first digit, 6, in the UPC replicated here, represents the type of product. The manufacturer identification number, 39382 in the image, tells us the identity and location of the manufacturer.

The next five digits, 00039, represent the item number, a unique code that an UPC coordinator, employed by the manufacturer, assigns to each product type. That series of numbers is not used for any other type of product and is retired when the parent product is not made any more.

The last number of the UPC code, 3, acts as a check digit, computed as follows:

1. Sum up the value of all of the digits at odd locations in the UPC code.
   $6 + 9 + 8 + 0 + 0 + 9 = 32$

2. Multiply the result by 3.
   $32 * 3 = 96$

3. Sum up the value of all of the digits at even locations in the UPC code.

4. $3 + 3 + 2 + 0 + 3 = 11$

5. Add the result to step '2' above.
   $96 + 11 = 107$

6. The check digit is that digit, which, when added to the number in step '5' above, makes the resultant number a multiple of 10.
   $107 + 3 = 110$ (a multiple of 10)

The check digit is thus 3. The scanner conducts this check, and on finding a check digit different from 3, signals an error and asks for a re-scan. *Would you like to know what UPC code 639382000393 represents? Go to* http://www.upcdatabase.com/itemform.asp *to find out.*

Figure 8.1 What a UPC Code Means

Source: "Item Record," accessed Oct. 3, 2015, http://www.upcdatabase.com/itemform.asp.

slotting is a daily activity– putting if off to once a quarter or annually compounds the work and the willingness to do it accurately.

KEY POINTS

- Inventory is a product or service that we *could* make, acquire, perform, or provide *after* the customer asks for it but choose to make/acquire now at some cost and *store* in anticipation of the customer asking for it.
- Inventory can be described in terms of form, that is, finished goods, work-in-process, or in the pipeline being transported, or in terms of reason for holding such as cycle and decoupling inventory.
- Inventory management is a data-driven approach to making intelligent cost and customer service-driven decisions on what is to be stored; how much is to be stored; where it is to be stored and for how long; how to price and allow customers access to the inventory; and when to replenish inventory stock.
- Phantom inventory is created when physical stock does not match computer stock, for reasons ranging from pilferage to misplacement and cashier errors. It is especially problematic when the records show inventory present but actual physical stock is zero, since customers will walk away. RFID and other technologies make it easier to locate and match physical inventory with records.

8.2 Why Is Managing Inventory Important?

Inventory management can contribute substantially to corporate performance and profits.

8.2.1 Importance for Businesses

Careful analysis of sales, stock-outs, and customer fulfillment rates is required to tread the fine line between carrying excessive quantities or too many SKUs, and not having enough to satisfy the customer. It's also a matter of carrying the right products. Walmart lost $3 billion in 2013 sales due to out-of-stock merchandise, while its inventory grew at a faster rate than its sales.[2] Substantial money can be unlocked from inventory by moving and selling it quicker, that is, increasing the inventory turnover ratio.

Inventory Performance—A tale of two companies

Lowe's (#s in '000)	Year ending 2013	2012	2011
Cost of revenue	$34,941,000	$33,194,000	$32,858,000
Inventory	$9,127,000	$8,600,000	$8,355,000
Average inventory $	$8,863,500*	$8,477,500	(beginning inventory for 2011 not accessed)
Inventory turnover	3.94**	3.92	–

*Average inventory over 12 months of 2013 = (beginning inventory in 2013 + ending inventory in 2013)/2
= (ending inventory in 2012 + ending inventory in 2013)/2
= ($8,600,000 + $ 9,127,000)/2 = $8,863,500

**Inventory turnover = cost of revenue/average inventory = $34,941,000/8,863,500 = 3.94

Home Depot (#s in '000)	Year ending 2013	2012	2011
Cost of revenue	$51,422,000	$48,912,000	$46,133,000
Inventory	$11,057,000	$10,710,000	$10,325,000
Average inventory $	$10,883,500	$10,517,500	–
Inventory turnover	4.73	4.65	–

Average inventory at Lowe's at 2013 Inventory Turnover ratio of 3.94 = $ 8,863,500

If Lowe's had matched Home Depot's Inventory Turnover ratio of 4.73 in 2013:

Average inventory at Lowe's would have been	= cost of revenue/inventory turnover
	= $ 34,941,000/4.73
	= $7,387,103.50
Potential inventory savings to Lowe's if it could match Home Depot's inventory turnover ratio of 4.73	= ($8,863,500 − $7,387,103.50)
	= $ 1,476,396.50 (in '000)

8.2.2 Importance for You

Inventory management jobs range from inventory specialists in retail to inventory planners and controllers in manufacturing. Marketing majors are perhaps most directly affected by inventory management decisions because of the immediate impact of any change in inventory holdings on customer service levels. Any business major, for that matter, will gain from an understanding of how inventory decisions ramify through multiple functions in an organization and how inventory is managed to optimize customer service at affordable risk and cost.

Manager, Sales Operations (Replenishment Inventory) Estee Lauder, New York

Major Responsibilities: This position is responsible for supporting the ED of Inventory Planning/ Sales Operations with reports, analysis and replenishment projects. There will be a strong focus on the monitoring of service level, out-of-stock, low stock status and SKU contribution analysis. You will need to have the ability to provide analytical insight into the decision making process by adding perspective and value to business planning

   Accountabilities: * Replenishment Quik View Dashboard * Monitor POS service * WOS * Identify key inventory metrics * Review Potential Lost Sales, factory out-of-stocks, and impacts to service levels * Monitor cannibalization due to a new launch, identify ordering pattern when SKUs move to basic over a defined period of time * Tracks weekly ROQ in OTS system and orders passed

- Order Writing file * Builds fiscal file & maintains file enhancements needed + Distribution (closed & new doors) + BI reporting + Carry over reports * Collects & prepares monthly file with planner updates
- Data and analysis * Ad hoc reporting & analysis
- List Maintenance: * Must have/Omit Lists + Work with the launch team as SKUs convert from launch status to basic status

---

- SKU Management/Ranking reports: analyze SKU contribution sell in & sell thru * Report on MOB trends as it relates to inventory needs * Report on cannibalization * Replenishment OH inventory measurement analysis + Provide insights on trends by calling out certain patterns Ex: cannibalization due to a new launch, identify chronic OOS & trends + Analyze category level trends & OH/ordering patterns
- Next Generation * Report on retail sales growth * Category MOB
- RTV's/DIF's & Consumer returns * Record & track RTV's * Collect & analyze return categories data on new products * Collect & analyze returns data by account * Provide insights on analysis * Estimated WOS/ phase outs
- GWP/Passport * Allocate program in passport by account * Track GWP shipments * Track & provide retail sales recap * data collection and analytics on AUS/Step up programs * Provide timely and accurate data analysis for promotion evaluation

Qualifications: * College or University degree required * 5 years previous work experience in retail, inventory planning, sales analysis preferred * Strong analytical skills * Highly focused and organized * Self-starter and the ability to work independently * High level of computer skills including Microsoft Office (Excel). Knowledge of SAP a plus * Ability to balance multiple priorities

Organization: Clinique
Primary Location: Americas-United States-New York-New York
Schedule: Full-time
Shift: 1st (Day) Shift
Job Type: Standard
Req ID: 152698

Source: "Global Jobs," *Estee Lauder*, accessed Oct. 3, 2015, http://elcompanies.jobs/new-york-ny/manager-sales-operations-replenishment-inventory/01566417D69F4AD88073A4FA1993330D/job/?vs=27.

KEY POINTS

- Inventory represents locked up capital.
- Higher inventory turnover will lead to lower inventory levels and cash savings.
- Inventory decisions affect marketing, finance, accounting and other functions in an organization.

8.3 How Can We Best Manage Our Inventory?

We can understand inventory management as a process, with defined and linked steps:

- Count our inventory, in terms of SKUs and SKU quantities.
- Assess current performance in managing inventory.
- Identify and estimate the costs of carrying inventory.
- Identify and prioritize important SKUs.

- Understand current inventory policies and their underlying costs and determinants.
- Estimate the relative costs and benefits of applying inventory management techniques.
- Implement plans to improve inventory management plans, with before and after performance measurements and actions to identify other inventory-reduction operational levers.

8.3.1 How Much Do We Have? Ways to Count Inventory

Cycle counting calls for counting all SKUs (stock keeping units) over the year, following a schedule such that all items are counted at least once a year. One count means physically counting how many units we carry of one specific item (SKU) at a specific point in time. Important items are counted more frequently. Cycle counters (usually employees) perform counts of SKUs and record the information. This count is then checked for discrepancies based on existing inventory records. A tolerance level is used to see how much above or below the actual count is compared to what is on record. This tolerance level is low for fast-moving items and higher for slower-moving items. When a count is taken that falls outside of the tolerance level, we try to understand the root cause of the error, such as pilferage, percent of products misplaced, percent of products not accounted for at receipt, and so on. Cycle counting thus not only identifies discrepancies but also helps repair the process that accounted for the inaccurate information. It is quicker and more accurate to conduct a cycle count when there are fewer items and pieces to count, i.e., just before it is time to re-order, or perhaps just after a sale.

Cycle Counting Inventory

There are 10,000 *A* (high importance) items that must each be counted 6 times each per year.
There are 15,000 *B* (medium importance) items that must each be counted 3 times each per year.
There are 25,000 *C* (low importance) items that must each be counted 2 times per year.

A items are counted (10,000 * 6) 60,000 times per year.
B items are counted (15,000 * 3) 45,000 times per year.
C items are counted (25,000 * 2) 50,000 times per year.

   Therefore, there are a total of 155,000 counts to be made each year, or about 596 counts of different individual items per working day (155,000/260 working days). Personnel have to be organized accordingly. *Quick question: How many A items counted/day? (Answer: 231, approximately)*

With experience, cycle counters can generally count 100 to 130 items per hour. Counters can also check for damage, hygiene, and storage temperature. After all, when one is physically counting inventory, it is easy to identify that shelf needing repair or hear that cooler making weird end-of-life noises.[3]

8.3.2 Inventory Performance Measures

To measure cost or efficiency, companies and analysts use three primary metrics:

1   *Average aggregate inventory*: A measure of how much we carry on average, any given day, over a specific time period. The lower the figure, the better.

Item	Beginning inventory on Jan. 1	Ending inventory on Dec. 31	Average inventory
Raw materials	$1,000	$950	($1,000+$950)/2 = $975
Work-in-progress	$2,000	$1,500	= $1,750
Finished goods	$600	$800	= $700
			Average aggregate inventory = $3,425

This metric does not mean that we will find $3,425 worth of inventory in the facility on any given day of the year. Rather, it means that if we count inventory at different points in the year and then total up the dollar value of those counts and divide that by the number of times we have counted, the resulting figure would be close to $3,425, in the long run. A beginning and end of year averaging, as shown above, works fine with stable inventory flows. However, when inventory levels contract or expand widely at different periods, the most accurate average would be obtained from adding daily inventory over the year and dividing that figure by 365. Less cumbersome is using weekly inventory or monthly inventory, in order of preference (and dividing by 52 or 12, as the case may be). Also note that inventory is valued at cost basis. The basis of costing (FIFO/LIFO) would affect inventory costing as well as the COGS value. If we can lower aggregate average inventory safely, money locked up in inventory is freed up.

2   *Average days of inventory on hand* (also called days of supply): A measure of how many days of production or sales our average aggregate inventory would support if we did not add more. Simply stated, how many days' sales or production does our inventory represent?

Average sales days of inventory on hand = average aggregate inventory/sales
(on cost basis)   = Average aggregate inventory/cost of   (Equation 8.1)
                                                         goods sold (COGS)

Suppose annual sales = 15,000 pieces
Suppose cost = $5 per piece
Thus, annual COGS = 15,000 pieces * $5 cost/piece   = $75,000
Suppose the average aggregate inventory   = $25,000
Sales days of inventory on hand = 25,000/75,000   = 1/3 (of a year, since COGS is annual)
                                                                                    = 1/3 * 365
                                                                                    = 122 days approximately
                                                                                    = 17.43 weeks approximately (122/7)

Again, the lower the figure, the better. Some companies prefer to use dollar sales instead of COGS in the denominator, but frequent selling price changes can invalidate the measure's worth. Generally, customers with single suppliers or faraway supply sources carry more days of inventory. Even sophisticated buyers like Apple can get blindsided by events like the Japan earthquake in 2011 that disrupted the supply of Nand flash memories and special resins for the iPad2.

3   *Inventory turnover*: A measure of how frequently a firm flushes inventory through its system.

Inventory turnover = COGS/average aggregate inventory   (Equation 8.2)
Suppose COGS = $75,000 and average aggregate inventory = $25,000
Inventory turnover = $75,000/$25,000 = 3 turns a year

Flow time = average aggregate inventory/flow rate (Little's law from "Managing Processes," chapter 4)
          = average aggregate inventory/COGS
          = $25,000/$75,000 = 1/3 of a year
(Note the equivalence between flow time and days of inventory on hand).
So if a unit of inventory takes an average of 1/3 of a year to zip through the system, that unit will be replaced 3 times a year, approximately.
Thus, inventory turnover = (1/flow time) times a year = (1)/(1/3) = 3 turns a year

---

A turnover rate of three turns per year is an average figure for all of inventory held. Fast-moving items would turn much more often, while slow-moving items might turn just once or twice a year. This may create shortages of individual items. Stores typically aggregate similar products into categories for purposes of setting inventory turnover targets. For example, Reese's peanut butter cups may be selling fast, but other items in the candy category may be slow sellers, leading to lower inventory turnover expectations and a lower turnover target for the candy category. The ordering intervals for the candy category are longer because of the lower inventory turnover target. Resultantly, the store may have a large inventory of the slow sellers in this category but may run out of the fast moving Reese's peanut butter cups. So the paradox is that while inventory in aggregate may be going up (because many things are not selling fast enough), there may be shortages of specific items that sell faster. It is difficult for a store to keep on top of inventory changes in individual items, considering that it may carry thousands or hundreds of thousands of individual goods. Speeding up inventory turnover generates more cash for the company since profit is made with each inventory turn, that is, every time inventory is converted into final product and sold (for a profit).

Given, current inventory turnover = 5 turns/year; COGS = 100,000 units ∗ $40 unit cost = $400,000
Now, inventory turnover = COGS/average aggregate inventory
Therefore, average aggregate inventory = COGS/inventory turnover = $400,000/5 = $80,000
Suppose the company improves inventory turnover to 7 turns/year. COGS remains $400,000.
Therefore, average aggregate inventory = $400,000/7 = $57,142, compared to the $80,000 carried earlier, that is, a reduction of 28.6 percent in cash investment in inventory. Add to that the reduced space required, lower insurance, taxes, etc., and the savings increase. The company can spend the saved money on other, better, money-making opportunities, such as R&D, expansion, or paying down debt.

Note, however, that as inventory turnover increases, costs of placing repeated orders to replenish inventory, frequent inspections, lost economies of scale in purchasing, and logistic costs all go up too. The capital savings and higher returns from higher turnover must be weighed alongside these increased costs that higher inventory turnover may bring.

So far, we have looked at internal efficiency measures of inventory performance, but going excessively lean can damage customer service levels. The following three metrics can tell us how well a company is fulfilling customer demand.

4 *Average cycle service level* (CSL): Measures the percent of times that 100 percent of customer demand has been satisfied, on average. For any given day or individual transaction, CSL is an attribute measure, that is, we either met all our demand or could not for a given order or day. CSL would accordingly be either 0 percent or 100 percent.

	Day 1	*Day 2*	*Day 3*	*Day 4*	*Day 5*
Demand	100	120	110	90	100
Supplied	100	100	110	90	90
Day-wise CSL	100%	0%	100%	100%	0%
Average CSL over Day 1 to Day 5 = (100% + 0% + 100% + 100% + 0%)/5 = 60%					

Average CSL averages those zeroes and 100 percent CSLs over multiple periods/transactions.

Expected CSL is an estimate of the percent of times that 100 percent of customer demand will be satisfied over time given a pattern of future demand and a given stock level (see worked out example for expected CSL and expected fill rate below).

5 *Average fill rate*: Measures the percent of customer demand met, on average. Fill rate is a continuous measure, ranging from 0 percent to 100 percent for any day or individual transaction. Average rill rate is the simple average of the fill rates for each day/transaction. Naturally, higher levels of inventory would lead to higher levels of CSL and fill rate. Instead of using these metrics as rear-view mirrors to check past performance, a company can compute *expected* CSL and fill rates for what-if scenarios with different demand forecasts and different proposed stocking levels.

A newsvendor forecasts *three* alternative demand scenarios, with probabilities, for tomorrow. What expected CSL and fill rate could she expect if she decides to buy and stock *80 papers* for tomorrow?

Forecasted Demand	80 papers	or 90 papers	or 100 papers
Probability of demand being	80 = 20%	90 = 30%	100 = 50%
If she plans to stock 80 papers (planned inventory),			
And, if demand turns out to be	*80 papers*	or 90 papers	or 100 papers
Then CSL:	100% (80 served out of 80)	0% (80 served out of 90)	0% (80 served out of 100)
Expected CSL	0.20 * 100% (20% chance of demand being 80, so 20% chance of CSL being 100%)	+ 0.30 * 0%	+ 0.50 * 0% Expected CSL = *20%*
Fill Rate	100% (80 served out of 80)	88.89% (80 served out of 90)	80% (80 served out of 100)
Expected fill rate	0.20 * 100% +	0.30 * 88.89% +	0.50 * 80% Thus, Expected fill rate = 86.67%

What would be the expected CSL and fill rate if she stocks 100 papers? You're right, a 100 percent for each metric, but then there's the possibility that our newsvendor would be left with some unsold papers. The ideal strategy for her would be to make a decision on how many papers to stock after comparing the costs of customers turned away (profit + goodwill lost) against the costs of unsold stock (cost of the paper to her) across different stocking levels and different forecasted demand levels. But that's another model. More relevant here is the question "Why use CSL at all?" The fill rate obviously paints a much rosier picture. Well, consider a hospital blood bank, where not being able to satisfy demand in full could lead to fatal consequences. It makes much more sense to use CSL there, tracking whether we are meeting 100 percent (or close) of the demand or not, consistently. That is, we target a very high average CSL. Fill rate is friendly to more normal business situations, where the consequences of not being able to meet demand in full are not as catastrophic. Note though, that even a fill rate of 86.67 percent means that about 13.33 percent of customer demand is not being met in time, on average, and that might be very bad news if your most important customer happens to randomly fall in that 13.33 percent not-supplied category. Lesson: watch CSL and fill rate for premium customers very carefully.

6   *Inventory elasticity*: This metric tracks quarter to quarter changes in inventory drivers—lead time, sales, sales uncertainty, gross margin—and corresponding changes in inventory level in those quarters. Elasticity measures a change in inventory associated with a 1 percent change in such factors. Walmart, for example, is not the leanest of retailers but adjusts its inventory quickly to changes in demand relative to Kmart.[4] Typically, the rate of growth of inventory should lag the rate of growth of sales—if that doesn't happen, profitability dips and share price may suffer.

Summing up, companies and financial analysts utilize metrics that capture inventory management performance in terms of internal efficiency, customer satisfaction, and responsiveness in managing inventory. Other metrics may look at safety and time, such as inventory-handling safety violations and item pick time in the warehouse. Metrics are often tracked over time for identifying trends and other patterns.

Internal efficiency metrics	Customer satisfaction metrics	Responsiveness to changes in demand/ lead time/ uncertainty/margins
Average aggregate inventory	CSL (Cycle service level)	Inventory elasticity
Average days of inventory on hand	Fill rate	
Inventory turnover		

While not their sole focus, lowering inventory costs is a prime performance goal and bonus driver for most inventory managers. Let's look at some of these costs in the next section

KEY POINTS

- Cycle counting follows a schedule such that the quantity of every SKU in inventory is counted at least once a year.
- Generally, declining average aggregate inventory and average days of inventory on hand ratios indicate improving inventory management performance. An increase in inventory turnover is also good news.

- If every customer has been satisfied in full, the CSL for that day is 100, otherwise zero. Compute average CSL by adding up the individual day CSLs (0 *or* 100) and dividing by the # of days. Use CSL for situations where running out has dire consequences.
- If 3 of 4 customers have been satisfied, the fill rate for that day is 75 percent. Compute average fill rate by adding up the individual day fill rates (0 to 100) and dividing by the number of days.

8.3.3 The Costs of Holding Inventory

Let's say we wish to store cases of bottled water for later sale. What would it cost us?

- Obviously, the cost of purchasing the bottled water itself, or rather the cost of borrowing the capital to fund the purchase.
- The opportunity cost of investing that capital in inventory, that is, the additional return we might expect to make if we had invested elsewhere at a similar risk level.
- The cost of leasing space to store the bottled water.
- If self-owned space, the cost of leasing a comparable space.
- Cost of utilities, such as power and gas, to keep the water cool.
- Warehouse property taxes, if any.
- Cost of security.
- Cost of insuring inventory, equipment, and structures against fire, theft, and hazards.
- Cost of warehouse maintenance supplies, such as equipment maintenance, cleaning supplies, and minor repair items.
- Cost of obsolescence or natural deterioration of stored materials, if any. Consumer tastes may change to flavored or vitamin water. Also water, if stored long in plastic bottles, begins to smell of plastic.
- Cost of labor to move around, inspect and count inventory.

We follow a basic rule in identifying what is or is not an inventory holding cost. Any cost that can reasonably be expected to *go up or down with a change in inventory* would classify as an inventory holding cost. By that token, would depreciation on warehouse equipment such as air-conditioning, humidity controllers, forklifts, and office computers be a part of the cost of holding inventory? No! The reason is that these equipment are already installed in the warehouse and will continue to be depreciated even if there's not a single item of inventory in the warehouse. Depreciation of capital equipment does not stop or vary with inventory level. In contrast, the cost of utilities and security may well decline with lower amounts of stored goods, occupying less space and requiring less power and fewer security cameras.

Estimating the Cost of Keeping It on the Shelf

There's a way to estimate the extent to which a company tries to charge you for its poor inventory decisions, in effect passing on the inventory holding costs of an ill-forecasted or bulk volume purchased item to you.

Holding cost of an electronic item such as a LED TV is fairly high (high value, obsolescence cost, etc.), say, 40 percent of the cost of the TV per year of storage.

> You see that 75-inch set beckon every time you have visited the store in the past 3 months—so it has been sitting there for the past 3 months at least. The set is priced at $2,000. How much of that is holding cost?
>
> Assume a profit margin of 10 percent.[5]
>
> Thus COGS = $1,818 approx. (adding a 10 percent margin on that works out to $2,000 selling price)
>
> Holding cost 40 percent of $1,818 = about $727 per year
>
> It has been stored on the shelf for 3 months (minimum),
>
> Thus, holding cost for 3 months = ($727/12 mo) * 3 mo = $182 approximately—also called unit holding cost.
>
> Ask the store to reduce the price by $182, at least. Why should you pay for the cost of the time that TV sat gathering dust on that retailer's shelf?

There are other, more subtle, costs of holding inventory. Holding inventory may increase waste and reduce the motivation to uncover the root causes of defects, since a bad part or product can simply be replaced by a good one from inventory. Inventory also delays the detection of problems. Consider:

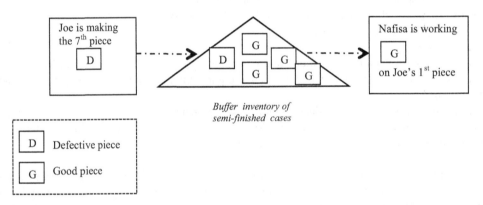

Figure 8.2 Is Buffer Inventory Evil?

Joe's work is inspected and finished by Nafisa. There's a buffer inventory of five pieces already made by Joe that is waiting for Nafisa's attention. If Nafisa makes one piece/minute, how long would it take her to find out and inform Joe that he has started to make defective pieces? Nafisa will eventually find that defective piece in the buffer inventory, but only after she goes through five good pieces (takes five minutes), that is, in the sixth minute. During those six minutes, Joe will go on making defective pieces. Ironically, that buffer inventory of five pieces, supposed to protect Nafisa from sudden absences or machine breakdowns at Joe's station, is actually delaying detection of quality issues in a part of the system. If that buffer inventory was instead just one piece, Nafisa would have been able to find that defective piece in the second minute, and Joe would not have made so many defective pieces.

Excessive inventory also causes confusion and disorganization, with scattered items filling up and cluttering work space. Fill up those empty spaces with flower pots if need be—inventory has a way of expanding to fill space available. Inventory may also discourage innovation. Much like moms and dads, managers hesitate to discard 'perfectly good stuff,' preferring to delay new products until old components have been used up in existing products. Manufacturers selling excess inventory at discounted prices can also create conflict with their retailers and other sales channels.

Table 8.1 Costs of Holding Inventory

Direct costs of holding inventory	Indirect costs of holding inventory

Financial costs:
    Opportunity cost of capital locked up in inventory
    Interest paid on capital
    Opportunity cost of space used for storage (if self-owned)
	Risks:
	    Risk of product obsolescence
	    Risk of product deterioration and pilferage
	    Risk of market price deterioration of inventory

Services costs:
    Leasing
    Utilities
    Security
    Taxes
    Labor
    Insurance
    Maintenance and repair
	Waste:
	    Encourages waste and discourages attention to
	    quality improvement
	    Clutter and disorganization
	    Excess inventory encourages discounting and
	        administratively expensive promotions

	Innovation:
	    Discourages introduction of new products and
	        the use of new components in existing products

Now that we understand the costs and benefits of holding inventory, let's look at how we can try to strike that balance between customer service and cost containment. But companies carry hundreds of thousands of SKUs, and we cannot analyze everything. So we need to first identify the VIPs (very important products) in our inventory and begin managing them first.

What Are the Really Important Items in Our Inventory?

Some years ago, my much better half used to work at Macy's, not the flagship Herald Square store in New York City, but a smaller, suburban Macy's. That store carried bedsheets, offering them in four different sizes, six colors and four thread counts. Let's suppose these bedsheets came from three different suppliers. How many different kinds of bedsheets (SKUs—stock keeping units) were being carried by that (small) Macy's?

4 sizes * 6 colors * 4 thread counts * 3 suppliers = 288 SKUs!

Bedsheets are just one item type in Macy's bed and bath department, which, in turn, is just one department among shoes, beauty, home décor, and many other departments. We're looking at tens of thousands of individual SKUs carried in that one store! How can we begin to sort out what's important from what's not? Some well-tried principles of prioritization can help.

The ABC method: Entails separating stock into three categories: High importance (A), medium importance (B) and low importance (C). 'Importance' is usually assessed using individual SKU sales revenues.

Recall Pareto's 80/20 rule? The Pareto pattern of the highest contribution coming from a minority of stocked items has been found to be true in practice. The inventory management guidelines for these items are:

- A items—close monitoring of usage, stocks, re-orders, and supplier health, accurate record keeping, and easy access location;
- B items—less tightly monitored and controlled, with good record keeping;
- C items—minimal monitoring and wider latitude in record keeping accuracy.

ABC analysis is conventionally based on the total dollar sales of an item, not its individual selling price or rate of turnover. An A class item need not necessarily be a fast moving item. A C category item could be a fast moving SKU but carry a low unit selling price. ABC analysis can also be carried out using other criteria besides SKU sales revenue to evaluate item importance, such as a SKU's contribution to total profits from sales.

Here's an example of an ABC analysis for a woman's apparel discount store that carries 15 different kinds of apparel (SKUs). SKUs have been already sorted in descending order of sales revenue:

Item	Unit sales	Unit sales in $	Cumulative sales ($)	Cumulative sales as % of total sales
Jeans	4,000 * $10 each	40,000	40,000	40% ($40,000/$100,000)
Tops	8,000 * $3 each	24,000	64,000 (jeans + tops)	64%
Skirts	2,000 * $8 each	16,000	80,000	80%
(*A* ITEMS)		$80,000		
Camis	250 * $20 each	5,000	85,000	85%
Gloves	600 * $8 each	4,800	89,800	89.8%
Scarves	1,000*$3 each	3,000	92,800	92.8%
Tanks	120 * $10 each	1,200	94,000	94%
Jackets	5 * $200 each	1,000	95,000	95%
(*B* ITEMS)		$15,000		
Bracelets	210 * $4 each	840	95,840	95.84%
Tunics	20 * $40 each	800	96,640	96.54%
Tees	110 * $7 each	770	97,410	97.41%
Snuggies	30 * $25 each	750	98,160	98.16%
Watches	2 * $332 each	664	98,824	98.83%
Polos	40 * $15 each	600	99,424	99.42%
Blouses	32 * $18 each	576	$100,000	100%
(*C* ITEMS)		$5,000		
Grand Total Items = 15	Grand Total sales = ∑ Unit Sales = $100,000			

Just 3 items, that is 20 percent of the 15 items in stock, are A items, accounting for 80 percent of total sales. Another 5 items, that is, 33.33 percent of the total items in stock, are B items, accounting for 15 percent of total sales. The remaining 7 items, that is, 46.67 percent of the total items, are C items, accounting for just 5 percent of the sales. We need to question the reasons for carrying so many C items in stock.

FSN analysis: SKUs are classified into 'fast-moving,' 'slow-moving,' or 'nonmoving' items, clocked by individual SKU turnover rate criteria set by the company. In high technology or trend industries like consumer electronics and fashion retail, we would call slow and nonmoving items 'SLOBS'—slow-moving and obsolete inventory. Fast-moving items are stored in high visibility, easy access locations in the warehouse, with accurate and regular record keeping and timely re-ordering. We identify slow-moving items and introduce incentives to speed up turnover. We identify nonmoving items for possible disposal, since they occupy valuable space and incur holding costs. A fast-moving (slow-moving) SKU can become a slow-moving (fast-moving) SKU, depending on circumstance. For instance, recently, Walmart found that large packs of basic items like diapers, baby food, and cereal sold quickly at the beginning of the month, while smaller packs sold well at month end. They discovered that recessionary times have forced families into living from month to month paydays, with little money left towards the end of the month. Also, more families are now on food stamps, which are typically issued at the beginning of the month.

VED analysis: We classify our stock into 'vital,' 'essential,' and 'desirable' SKUs. The criterion for placing an item into a particular category is the estimated cost of a stock-out of that item. For instance, blood and anesthetic would be 'vital' items for a hospital. Bandages would not, since sheets and other cloth could be torn up in an emergency—making it an essential item, a major inconvenience, but not a life-threatening event if a stock-out occurs. In contrast, a hospital running out of beverages or flowers in the gift shop is a minor inconvenience in this context, and such SKUs would be called 'desirable' items in a VED analysis. We would keep meticulous receipt and consumption records of vital items, making sure that enough suppliers are available, and keep some insurance inventory. Essential items also qualify for attention, but the situation can be managed if we experience a stock-out for a short period of time.

Substitutability approaches: Would you react differently if you did not find your favorite shampoo on the shop shelf, as compared to not finding a can of that Planter's peanuts you were looking for? Observations show that customers react to stock-outs in one of five ways:

- Buy a substitute product of the same brand
- Buy the same item but of a different brand
- Come back and buy the desired brand another day
- Don't buy the item at all
- Or in the most damaging scenario, walk out and buy the item at another store

How likely *are* you to substitute your Dove shampoo with a Nivea product? Perhaps not as readily as you would, say, substitute Planters peanuts with Planters cashews. Cosmetics have been found to have the least substitutability, while salted snacks enjoy far less brand or product loyalty. Cosmetics SKUs, then, would be the VIPs of inventory for your retailer, watched and tracked closely to avoid stock-outs and placed at easy to spot and reach locations.

Other criteria may also define SKU importance. Price is one—high price items may be tagged for frequent cycle counting, and withdrawals from inventory may need signoffs from senior personnel. Some products, although low priced, have profitable rub-off effects. A supermarket firm found that shoppers who buy a low volume, low margin product like silver polish tend to spend more than $200 buying other items per shopping trip. So it makes sense to make sure to not run out of silver polish for those stores. Inventory can also be categorized into scarce (S), difficult to get (D), and easy to get (E) SKUs based on consideration of lead times, availability, and uncertainty in supply. Sometimes, particular SKUs define a business's core identity in the eyes of the customer. LL Bean keeps slow-moving items such as jackknifes in stock to maintain its image and reputation as an 'outdoor' company.

Table 8.2 **What to Use Where**

Prioritization method	Primary objective	Typical Setting
ABC	Prioritize attention on basis of sales revenue	Retail stores
FSN: fast moving, slow moving, nonmoving	Prioritize attention on basis of frequency of SKU issues/usage from inventory	Warehouses, retail (for shelf position)
VED: vital, essential and desirable	Prioritize attention on basis of consequence of an SKU's stock-out	Hospitals, aircraft and production equipment maintenance.
Substitution approaches	Identify SKUs with no substitutes or that complement sales of other products and ensure availability	Retail, manufacturers that offer options (Dell)

We can mix methods as needed. If an ABC analysis results in too many A items to cover with existing resources, an FSN analysis on the A items would further sharpen our focus on those A items that move faster.

Once important SKUs are identified, two basic inventory management questions arise: how much to buy and when to buy. We use inventory models to guide us in these decisions.

How Much to Buy (at a Time)?

While we would naturally tend to buy more of what we find important, a specific number or order size recommendation would be more useful. Help is available.

Recurring order policies—flat ordering: For SKUs in a certain product category, shops often resort to flat ordering, that is, recurrently buy a certain quantity for all the SKUs in that product category based on average consumption. To illustrate:

SKU	Past Weekly Sales (cases)					
	Wk1	*Wk2*	*Wk3*	*Wk4*	*Wk5*	*Average weekly sales*
Apple jam	100	120	80	90	110	100 cases
Strawberry jam	50	150	170	130	300	160 cases

Supposing the flat ordering policy was to order three weeks of average weekly sales for each SKU, that is, 3 * 100 cases/week = 300 cases of apple, and 3*160 cases/week = 480 cases of strawberry jam. Simple rule, but do you see a problem? Yes, you're right! Strawberry jam has much more variance in sales than apple jam, and that 480 cases we ordered of strawberry jam would likely run out quicker than the 300 cases on order for apple jam. Following a flat ordering policy does not take into account individual SKU variance in sales. Additionally, suppose strawberry jam carries a higher profit margin than apple jam. We should carry more weeks of average demand of strawberry jam just for that reason because we do not wish to run out. Lesson: Do not apply the same flat ordering policy to all SKUs in a product category. Identify SKUs whose historical sales patterns show high variance and order more weeks of average sales for those SKUs.

Did you notice that the word demand does not appear anywhere in the above discussion? A word of caution: Do not confuse sales with demand. Recording sales may not mean that we're recording demand. Consider the following scenario:

Stock = 300 cases					
	Scenario 1		*Scenario 2*		*Scenario 3*
If demand turns out to be:	300 cases	or	250 cases	or	350 cases
Sales	300 cases		250 cases		300 cases
Therefore,	sales = demand		sales = demand		sales < demand

It's the third scenario that merits attention. Stores like Macy's and Walmart, with hundreds of thousands of SKUs, will find it virtually impossible to accurately track the number of customers that walk away for lack of stock. It is convenient to assume that recorded sales are representative of actual demand, but that conclusion may be misleading and dangerous. In scenario 3, if the actual sales figure of 300 cases is taken as actual demand, we would build the next period's demand forecast on that mistaken notion. If next period's actual demand turns out to be 400 cases, we may have to turn away even more customers next time (*but having sold out our stock, would pat ourselves on the back for 'forecasting' demand so accurately*). It is easy to confuse sales with demand, especially if sales occur at a place that is removed from the sight of demand planners and the latter cannot see customers walking away because of stock-outs.

Lot for lot order policy: Order exactly as much as required to replenish what has been used—the trouble is that variable supplier lead times may lead to stock-outs.

Fixed order quantities: A specific quantity for all orders for that item—determined by factors such as supplier-imposed minimum order quantity requirements or the need to make up full truck or full container loads. Inventory may build up with such policies.

The EOQ model: The EOQ (economic order quantity) also results in a fixed order quantity but explicitly considers the cost of placing orders and the cost of carrying inventory. We all make withdrawals from ATMs. How can we do so efficiently? Withdrawal may trigger fees, while money withdrawn does not earn interest. So if we decide to withdraw, say, $100 each ATM visit, instead of, say, $1,000, more money stays in the account longer, earning more interest. Yet, our ATM charges a fee for each withdrawal. So if we make lots of small $100 withdrawals, we'll visit the ATM more often and pay more in ATM fees, as compared to larger $1,000 withdrawals. How much should we withdraw so as to strike an optimal balance between ATM fees and lost interest? The EOQ (economic order quantity) model answers the question.

We have a bank account with a certain sum of money deposited. Our weekly expenses amount to $100, spent evenly throughout the month. We begin our weeks with Q units, say $100, in our pocket—that's the inventory we are carrying (a unit is $1). We run out of money at the end of the week, that is, our inventory touches zero. We go to the ATM and make a withdrawal of another $100, so our inventory goes back to Q ($100). That $100 would last us for another week, and so on. The figure below shows the cycle of consumption and receipt that happens every week. The ATM charges $2 per withdrawal. We call the fee the ordering cost—the cost of placing an order for cash from the ATM. Note that this ordering cost does not change with the amount withdrawn. The bank pays 3 percent annual interest on money that is not withdrawn and remains with the bank. This is the opportunity cost of withdrawing money and represents the holding cost of inventory, in this case. In this static world, nothing changes. But are those $100 withdrawals the best amount to withdraw? Are we working the system to keep our costs at the lowest possible level? Let's begin by figuring out what our current system costs us.

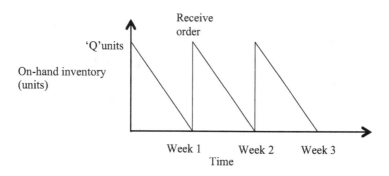

Figure 8.3 The EOQ Sawtooth*

*Sawtooth: Because the on-hand inventory drop and rise pattern looks like the sharp teeth of a saw (I like to think of it as sabre tooth!).

# of orders (ATM withdrawals)/week = 1; Cost of each withdrawal = $2;
  Total ordering cost per year = 52 orders (withdrawals) * $2/withdrawal = $104
  # of units received as inventory/week = $100;
  Note from figure 8.3 that the beginning inventory is always Q units, since order receipts at the beginning of the week is always Q units. We are, in effect, ordering Q units every inventory cycle period and receiving those Q units at the start of each cycle. The ending inventory at the close of a particular cycle is always zero.
  Thus, average inventory   = (inventory at beginning of week + ending inventory)/2
                            = ($100 + $0)/2 = $50
  Cost of holding one unit ($1) of inventory per year   = forgone interest @ 3%/yr
                                                        = 0.03 * $1 = $.03/year
  Total holding cost per year   = average inventory * cost of holding one unit for a year
                                  = $50 * $0.03 = $1.50
  Thus, *total cost* = total ordering cost + total holding cost = $104 + $1.50 = $105.50/year

Can we reduce the total cost? We can see that both total holding and total ordering cost depends on the size of the order. If we place larger orders, the number of times we need to use the ATM would go down—hence, total ordering cost declines. With larger orders, though, the amount of foregone interest increases—hence, total holding cost goes up. Basically juxtaposing two opposing costs, holding cost and ordering cost, the EOQ recommends a specific order quantity that minimizes the sum of the ordering and holding costs. We have discussed the nature of holding costs earlier. Ordering cost in a company would include the administrative costs of placing and expediting an order, such as purchasing clerical wages, cost of phone calls/faxes, travel to the supplier to expedite late supplies, and other variable costs that change with an increase or decrease in the number of orders placed. These costs do not vary by order size and do not include the cost of the item being ordered.
  Graphically,

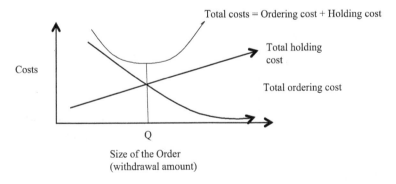

Figure 8.4 Costs and Order Size

The minimum point of the total cost curve is what EOQ targets. That minimum cost point sits directly above the intersection of ordering cost and holding cost. So we could find that economic order quantity, the EOQ that minimizes total cost by writing an equation for the intersection point:

Total ordering cost (TOC) = total holding cost (THC)
TOC = # of orders placed ∗ cost of placing an order S
Now, # of orders placed = annual consumption D/order size = D/Q
Thus $TOC = D/Q * S$

THC = average inventory held ∗ cost of holding 1 unit for a year
Now, average inventory = (inventory at beginning of week + ending inventory)/2
Note from figure 8.3, that the beginning inventory is always Q units, since order receipts at the beginning of the week is always Q units, whereas the ending inventory at the close of a particular cycle is always zero.
Therefore, average inventory = $(Q + 0)/2 = Q/2$
Cost of holding 1 unit for a year = $\$H$
*Thus, THC = (Q/2) * H*

Now, at the minimum total cost point, TOC = THC
Thus $(D/Q) * S = Q/2 * H$ (i)
At the minimum total cost point, the order quantity Q would be the economic order quantity (EOQ):
We solve for Q (i.e., EOQ). Cross-multiplying (i) we get
$2 * D * S = Q^2 * H$
Or, $Q^2 * H = 2 * D * S$
Or, $Q = \sqrt{[(2 * D * S)/H]}$

That is, *EOQ = $\sqrt{[(2 * D * S)/H]}$* (Equation 8.3)

 where D = demand/consumption for a year (or a specific period); S = cost of placing an order; H = cost of holding one unit in inventory for a year (or for the same specific period as demand).
 [1]More elegantly, TC = TOC + THC = $(D/Q) * S + (Q/2) * H$.
We wish to find the minimum point on the TC curve.
$\delta TC/\delta Q = (-)1Q^{-2} * D * S + H/2 = 0$;
$Q^2 * H - 2D * S = 0$;
Q or EOQ = $\sqrt{[(2 * D * S)/H]}$

Applying the above formulas to our ATM decision from earlier,

D = \$100/week = \$,5200/year; S = \$2; H = .03∗\$1 = \$.03/year
Thus, EOQ = $\sqrt{(2 * D * S)/H}$ = $\sqrt{(2* 5,200 * \$2)/\$.03/yr}$ = \$832.66
The most economical ATM withdrawal amount would be \$832.66 at a time.
The total # of withdrawals per year = D/EOQ = \$5,200/\$832.66 = 7 withdrawals per year, approximately.

Therefore, we make a withdrawal = 52 weeks/7 = every 7.42 weeks.

Let's compare the total cost of adopting this EOQ policy with the total cost of our earlier policy of withdrawing $100 at a time.

Total cost of earlier policy = $105.50 per year (from earlier computation)

Total cost of following EOQ policy = Total ordering cost + total holding cost

$$= D/Q * S + Q/2 * H, \text{ where } Q \text{ is the EOQ}$$
$$= (\$5,200/\$832.66) * \$2 + (\$832.66/2) * \$.03/yr$$
$$= \$12.48 + \$12.49 \text{ (note, TOC} = \text{THC, as should be for an EOQ policy)}$$
$$= \$24.97 \text{ per year}$$

Savings $= \$105.50 - \$24.97 = \$80.53/year$

We have reduced our cost by more than 76 percent! Start planning that Hawaii vacation! In a company with hundreds or thousands of *A* or *B* category items, imagine the total cost savings when we compute and apply EOQs to all those SKUs.

The traditional EOQ model was born in an assumed world of known and stable holding and ordering costs, constant demand, 100 percent delivery of order quantity at a time, constant supply lead time, no shortages, and no quantity price discounts. Even so, it has practical value in setting a golden standard for optimal ordering quantity conditions that companies could aspire to and also use for benchmarking. Besides, the EOQ model is fairly robust to errors in cost or demand estimation. Since the total cost curve is quite flat bottomed (see figure 8.4), straying away a little from the true EOQ would not cost us much. Also since we take the square root, the effect of small errors in demand or cost estimation get minimized. For significant changes, of course, one must re-compute. For example, as demand increases, the EOQ increases, too, but at a slower rate.

Say demand = 10, S = $2/order and H = 20% of $20 (COGS)

$$EOQ = \sqrt{(2 * D * S)/H} = 3.163$$

Now assume demand goes up to 20, other factors remaining constant

$$EOQ = \sqrt{(2 * D * S)/H} = 4.47$$

So while demand went up by 100 percent, EOQ went up by about 41 percent only. The total cost of the EOQ (total ordering cost + total holding cost) increases, too, but again at a slower rate than demand. At low demand levels, though, EOQ total costs may become significant relative to the cost of the product. In fact, the cost of ordering and holding a product may turn out to be more than the profit margin from that product! And it makes no sense to carry that product in the store, at least from a profit contribution perspective. The strategic lesson here is that one must take active measures to maintain and increase demand in order to minimize EOQ costs in relation to COGS and associated profit margin.

There are some practical problems with adopting an EOQ ordering policy. Small businesses may not be able to afford to order EOQ quantities or may have no room to store such quantities. Seasonal items would need separate EOQs for each season, since consumption would not be constant throughout the year. Truckers/ shippers may charge more to ship in EOQ lots since such quantities may not make up a full truck or container load. Suppliers, too, may refuse EOQ-size orders if such are below prescribed minimum order quantities.

The EOQ formulation itself has undergone many extensions, each seeking to relax an underlying assumption. EOQs have been developed for groups of SKUs, for volume discounts (EOQ with price breaks—see appendix), back-orders (assuming the customer will wait in a shortage), and staggered receipts. A similar model called the economic production quantity has been developed to determine the optimal production quantity for a manufacturer. These model modifications lie beyond the scope of our introductory text.

KEY POINTS

- Use caution when using sales to proxy demand. Demand may be greater than sales, and such instances are seldom tracked in retail.
- A flat order policy may use an ordering rule for recurring orders, say order three weeks of average weekly demand for all SKUs in a product category. Individual SKU demand variability is not considered, leading to possible stock-outs.
- The EOQ model considers two opposing costs, holding cost and ordering cost, and recommends a specific (recurring) order quantity that minimizes the sum of these costs. May be difficult to actually place orders in EOQ quantities because of lack of capital, supplier minimum order quantity constraints, warehouse space, or excessive risk burdens.
- High stock-out costs relative to leftovers costs lead to recommendations for larger orders and vice-versa. Availability of substitute products lowers the cost of stock-outs.

8.3.4 When to Buy or Replenish?

How often should we buy? If we buy using the EOQ approach, dividing the period demand by the EOQ order quantity would tell us how often, e.g., 1,000 pieces annual demand/EOQ of 200 pieces/order = 5 orders per year = 365/5 = order every 73 days. But this approach works only for a constant rate of use/demand market and a constant supply lead time. With uncertain demand/usage and unstable lead times, it is obviously impossible to recommend a specific date or time interval for placing orders. What we can do is set up a warning system that tells us that it is time to buy. It does so by considering the extent of the uncertainty surrounding demand and supply lead time, our CSL standard, and the length of the lead time itself.

When to buy—the ROP model: More traditionally known as the 'continuous review system,' the ROP (re-order point) model sets a re-order point for an SKU. It then continuously reviews the inventory position for the SKU, noting each withdrawal and receipt, and triggers an order as soon as the inventory position falls to the pre-set re-order point. The model tells us that it is the time to buy but not how much to buy. The order quantity could be the EOQ or be based on other reasons. The heart of the ROP model is the decision about where to set the re-order point, in terms of inventory position. Imagine a stockroom filled ceiling high with inventory. We draw a line on the wall and call it the re-order point. As the inventory in the stockroom keeps falling with usage, the inventory position would eventually hit that re-order line on the wall. We place an order as soon as that happens. Now, if we set that re-order point high up on the stockroom wall, orders will be triggered quickly since the inventory position would not have to decline much to hit that re-order point. We shall carry a large amount of average inventory (expensive), and won't stock out much (high CSL). If we set it low, though, the frequency of ordering would decline since the inventory position in the stockroom would have to fall much further in order to hit that re-order line on the wall. In this case, our average inventory position would be lower (less expensive) since we wait longer between replenishments, but we'll also run out more often (lower CSL). Setting the re-order point thus involves a trade-off between the cost of carrying stock and the desire to offer high CSLs, made complicated by the varying nature of demand and lead time. Let's examine how best to manage this trade-off.

A hospital stocks drug eluting stents used for emergency heart surgeries that typically cost in excess of a $1,000/piece. Under pressure to cut costs, we have been charged to lower the inventory of this expensive and vital item without jeopardizing patient safety. Let us examine this challenge in different operational conditions:

1   *Constant and known demand and lead time*

Suppose we know we shall need exactly 10 stents for patients every day. We have an old and reliable supplier who delivers the stents in three days, rain or shine. Where should our re-order point be? Thirty stents, of course! Just when our inventory position falls to 30 stents, we place an order. That order is delivered exactly at the end of the third day. Our need for the 10 stents/day * 3 days = 30 stents, over the three days of lead time, is met from the stock of 30 stents that we had when we placed the order. Our stock falls to zero at the end of the third day, but fresh supplies come in just then. We re-order again when our inventory position falls down again to the ROP level of 30 stents, and so on. Fixing the ROP in this situation is a no-brainer.

2   *Uncertain demand but constant lead time*

Being more realistic, we understand that demand cannot be constant or known always. Faced with an uncertain number of patients requiring the stents, we examine past demand history. Demand during the order lead time periods of three days, while varying, appears to be normally distributed, with a mean (μ) of 24 stents and a standard deviation of demand (σ_{dLT}) of two stents during the lead time period. Luckily, we still have our old and reliable supplier who does not stray from her three days lead time commitment. What should our ROP quantity be in this situation? Well, what happens if we decide to set the ROP at an inventory position of 24 stents, multiplying our average consumption level of eight stents a day by the three days lead time? No problem, as long as the number of patients does not exceed a total of 24 over the three days of lead time, but there's no guarantee about that. What are the chances of receiving more than 24 patients over the three days when we are waiting for fresh supplies?

As Figure 8.5 shows, 50 percent! If we set our ROP level at 24 stents, we shall not have enough stents for our patients 50 percent of the time. That is not acceptable. So we need to keep a safety stock (SS) for those times when demand during those three days of lead time may surpass 24 stents. The question is how much?

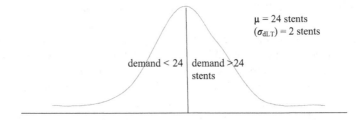

Figure 8.5 Distribution of Past Demand for Stents over Earlier Lead Time Periods (of Three Days Each)

That depends on two things: the degree of uncertainty of demand over the three-day lead time period and the cycle service level (CSL) we set for ourselves (recall that lead time, the third influence on SS, is known and constant in this case). In consultation with our doctors and administrators, we set the desired expected CSL as 95 percent; that is, 95 percent of the time, we shall have enough stents to meet all our patient demand during the three-day lead time period. We make arrangements with sister hospitals to help us out during the remaining 5 percent of the time, when we shall have to turn away patients.

ROP	= Average demand ($\bar{d}$) during lead time + safety stock (provides 50% coverage) + (additional 45% coverage) = 95% coverage
	= 24 stents over the 3 days lead time + safety stock (SS)
SS	= f(standard deviation of demand during the lead time period, CSL)
	= (σ_{dLT}) $*$ z value corresponding to the desired CSL value (95%)
	= 2 $*$ 1.65 (z value from Z table corresponding to CSL value of 0.9500)
	= 3.3
Thus:	
ROP	= $\bar{d}$ $*$ lead time + SS
	= 24 stents + 3.3 = 27.3 = 28 stents approximately
	(50% coverage) + (45% coverage) = 95% CSL of the 3-day lead time period demand

We set our ROP at 28 stents, with an expected CSL coverage of (slightly more than) 95 percent. Every time our inventory position drops to 28 stents, an order is issued. We anticipate that those 28 stents remaining in inventory shall be enough to meet demand during the three days we wait till we receive fresh supplies. That anticipation will be met 95 percent of the time.

Now records of specific demand during past order lead time periods are not usually kept, but data is typically and readily available for daily demand. Using that data, we can derive average daily demand and standard deviation of demand numbers for the entire demand data. We assume that daily demand is normally distributed. We can compute an ROP this way, too:

Say, the daily demand for the stents ($\bar{d}$) = 8/day, and standard deviation of daily demand (σ_d) = 1.16.

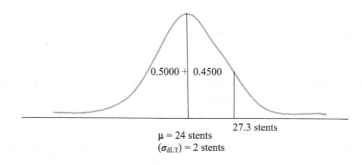

Figure 8.6 Setting ROP for 95 Percent CSL

The standard deviation of daily demand can be converted into the standard deviation of lead time (LT) period demand, using the following formula:

$\sigma_{dLT} = \sigma_d \sqrt{LT}$

Then ROP $= \bar{d} *$ lead time $+ z$ value corresponding to CSL $* \sigma_{dLT}$ (Equation 8.4)

$= \bar{d} *$ lead time $+ z$ value corresponding to CSL $* \sigma_d \sqrt{LT}$

$= 8*3$ days of lead time $+ 1.65$ (z value from CSL of 95%) $* 1.16\sqrt{3}$ days

$= 24 + 3.32 = 27.32 = 28$ stents, approximately

Solution: Read off the z value corresponding to CSL of 95% (i.e., 0.9500) from the Normal Distribution table, or

use Excel to find out the z value corresponding to CSL = NORM.S.INV(0.95)

$= 1.65$

Conversely:

If we knew the z value (in this case 1.65), then the corresponding CSL = NORM.S.DIST(1.65,TRUE) = 0.95

Here's a question your boss may ask when you proudly present that ROP recommendation. An ROP of 28 stents at a CSL of 95 percent means that we shall be able to meet all demand 95 percent of the time, which, in turn, means that we shall have to turn away at least one patient, 5 percent of the time. But just *how many* patients?

$E(n) = E(z)\sigma_{dLT}$,

Where, $E(n)$ = expected number of units short per order cycle

$E(z)$ = standardized number of units short, using a normal distribution service and normal loss function (see Statistical Tables)

σ_{dLT} = standard deviation of lead time period demand

So, for our example, CSL = 95% = 0.9500, $\sigma_{dLT} = 2$

$E(z)$ for a CSL of 0.9500 from the table = 1.64

Thus, $E(n) = 1.64 * 2 = 3.28$ units

We can expect to run short by about four units during any three-day lead time cycle, on average. We'll have to turn away four patients during a three-day lead time cycle, on average.

3   *Uncertain lead time but constant demand*

Another curve ball—let demand be constant now, and let lead time vary. Imagine that we always have more patients than we can admit, common in urban area hospitals. In that case, we are always at full capacity and daily demand = our fixed capacity = a fixed number, 'd.' To cut costs on those stents, we negotiated with an overseas supplier. However, the supplier is not very reliable. The quality has been spotty, leading to some returns and replacements (thus increasing lead times), and the supply times for initial shipments has been fluctuating significantly. The average lead time ($\overline{LT}$) is five days, with a standard deviation of lead time (σ_{LT}) of 4 days. Our constant daily demand is, say, 8 stents/day, and we keep our CSL at 95 percent. Let's see how our ROP changes under these conditions. The formula is:

ROP = demand during average lead time + safety stock (Equation 8.5)

= fixed demand/day * average lead time + z * standard deviation of lead time demand

= $d * \overline{LT} + z * d * \sigma_{LT}$

= 8 * 5 days + 1.65 * 8 * 4

= 40 stents + 52.80 stents

= 93 stents, approximately.

The sharp increase in the ROP over the earlier ROP of 28 stents is due to the longer lead time and the high uncertainty of the lead time. We would do well to look for another supplier, unless the prices we negotiated are low enough to compensate for the additional safety stock that we'll have to carry.

There is another scenario where both daily demand and lead time may vary. The logic for setting an ROP in such conditions remains unchanged. We take the average demand during the average lead time and add a safety stock. The safety stock takes the average lead time and the average daily demand and squares the standard deviations of demand and lead time to obtain their variances for summing and square-rooting. The formula is:

$$ROP = \overline{d} * \overline{LT} + z \left[\sqrt{(\overline{LT}\,\sigma^2_d + \overline{d}^2\,\sigma^2_{LT})}\right]$$ (Equation 8.6)

All models assume that demand and lead time are independent.

The ROP approach allows us to monitor our inventory on a continuous basis and avoid nasty stock-out surprises. It works best for *A* category (ABC analysis) items and for 'vital' (VED) items, where stock-outs can lead to serious losses in revenues or catastrophic consequences.

A practical form of the ROP policy is often seen in the two-bin policy. Imagine a storefront shelf stocked with blue jeans and another shelf for the same jeans in the backroom. The number of jeans on the backroom shelf equals the computed ROP amount at a given CSL, that is, will be enough to cover average demand for the lead time period and act as a safety stock. As soon as the storefront shelf is out of jeans, an order is placed. The ROP quantity in the backroom is brought out to the front and should last until fresh supplies come in.

When to buy—the fixed period/periodic review system: Some businesses find it convenient to inspect their inventory and schedule their ordering for an SKU or a group of similar SKUs at fixed intervals, say, every Monday of the week or the 15th of every month. They place an order large enough to hopefully meet demand till the date of the next inventory check and order and also to meet the expected demand during the lead time *of the next order*. Three things determine the size of the order:

- The length of the time interval between inventory reviews and order placements
- The length of time it takes to receive supplies (lead time)
- The level of uncertainty of demand or lead time.

The system works as follows.[6] We determine how often to review our inventory in terms of a fixed interval of time between reviews. We compute a fixed target inventory position (TIP in units) for the SKU. Each time we walk into the stockroom to review the inventory, we check to see how far down the current inventory position (IP = on-hand physical units inclusive of safety stock + scheduled receipts, if any, from earlier orders – backorders, if any) has fallen from the fixed TIP. We immediately place an order for a quantity such that the current IP at the time of review + the current order placed after checking the current IP together bring up the IP position to the TIP. That is:

Current IP at time of review + current order quantity = fixed TIP in units; that is,
Current order quantity = fixed TIP in units – current IP at time of review.

The TIP itself is fixed such that current IP at the time of review + the current order placed after checking the current IP should be sufficient to last us until the time we place the next order at the time of the next review (duration *P*) *and* receive it physically (duration *L*), i.e., period (*P* + *L*), also called the protection interval. The period between reviews (*P*) is fixed and known. So is the lead time for order delivery (*L*), *irrespective* of the size of the order.

Graphically,

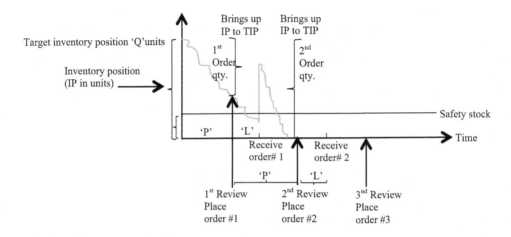

Figure 8.7 When to Order—The Periodic Review System

Let's walk through the above figure. We begin at period zero. The period between reviews is fixed, and orders are placed at the time of review. The TIP has been fixed to meet expected consumption till the time of the first review *and* expected consumption during the lead time period (*L*) of (future) order #1. We walk in on the day of the first review and look at our IP. Finding it lower than our fixed TIP, we place order #1, for a quantity that brings up the IP to the TIP. That TIP, again, is supposed to be enough to cover consumption till the time of the second review plus consumption during the lead time of (future) order #2. Order #1 takes *L* lead time to be received. At the time of accepting delivery, we note that we have significant safety stock in hand. Our fixed TIP at time zero was thus large enough to satisfy expected demand during the time interval (*P* + *L*) at a chosen CSL value (and have some safety stock left over). On receipt of order #1, our IP goes up, but not up to the TIP, because some inventory has been consumed during order #1's lead time period. Inventory continues to be consumed until we come to the time of the second review. In fact, we exhausted our safety stock and ran out sometime *before* we even came in for the second review, a danger that exists in that black box period between reviews when no one is checking stock. Recall the times we have gone to a vending machine and found it stocked out of our favorite snack. Well, the vendor does not know that, and it won't be replenished until the time of the next scheduled review. The premature stock-out means that the TIP we fixed was inadequate to cover consumption till the time of the second review (time interval *P* after first review), *let alone* the expected additional consumption during the lead time period (*L*) of our (future) order #2. This happened because we had underestimated the rate of consumption between the first and second review periods. We will have to re-compute and re-fix our TIP, taking the rise in the rate of consumption into account for all future periods (*P* + *L*). Thus, when we place order #2 at the time of the second review, we would order enough to bring up the then-IP to our re-fixed TIP. Our re-fixed TIP would be for a quantity that should meet expected consumption till the time of the third review (*P*) *plus* expected consumption till supplies from the *third* order come (in time *L*). The core challenge here is to fix and maintain the TIP at an appropriate level, such that we can cover expected demand during the total protection period (*P* + *L*) at a chosen level of fulfillment (CSL). The time between reviews remains fixed, but the order quantity changes. Order #2 in Figure 8.7 is larger than order #1, because the inventory position has fallen further, and more needs to be ordered to bring up the IP to the TIP. The TIP or periodic review model is also colloquially known as the 'order up to model.'[7]

A hotel orders miniature shampoos for guest bathrooms on a periodic basis. Based on convenience, it decides to review its stockroom inventory of these shampoos every 2 weeks. The shampoo supplier takes 10 days to supply an order. The hotel observes average daily demand for the shampoos as 35 a day, with a standard deviation of 5 shampoos. It wishes to maintain an average CSL of 95 percent for this product. What is the TIP? We assume that demand during the (*P* + *L*) protection interval is normally distributed.

$\bar{d}$ = 35; σ_d = 5; CSL = 95% = *z* of 1.65; *L* = 10 days, *P* = 2 weeks = 14 days

TIP   = Expected demand during (*P* + *L*) period + safety stock   (Equation 8.7)
      (Provides 50% coverage) + (additional 45% coverage) = 95% CSL
      = $\bar{d}$ * (*P* + *L*) days + *z* (σ_d)$\sqrt{(P + L)}$ days
      = 35 * (14+10) + 1.65 (5)$\sqrt{(14 + 10)}$
      = 840 + 40.42
      = 880.42
TIP   = 881, approximately

IP = On-hand inventory (including safety stock) + scheduled receipts today − backorders
Where: On-hand inventory   = actual units physically present
         Scheduled receipts   = number of units we expect to receive now (today) from the supplier against old orders
         Backorders   = units that we could not supply in the last (*P* + *L*) cycle to our own customers/users against their last orders/requisitions, and had promised to supply from fresh stock, as soon as received.

Now suppose at this review, the inventory position (IP) is found to be as follows:
   Current IP = 200 + 150 − 50 = 300 bottles.
How much should we order this time? We should order enough to raise the IP to the TIP point. So we order:
   Current order size = TIP − current IP = 881 − 300 = 581 bottles
The 581 bottles when received, taken together with the current IP of 300 bottles, should be enough to meet expected demand during the next 24 days (*P* + *L*) period, 95 percent of the time.
   We can easily see that the next order at the next review period may be different. The TIP remains unchanged, but the then-current IP would likely be different, so the order quantity (TIP − current IP) would be different. We can play around with the period between reviews *P*, lead time period *L*, standard deviation of demand, and the desired CSL to see the effects of how robust the TIP is to changes in these variables.

The periodic review model can be developed to cover uncertainty in supplier lead times, too. It finds common use in fixed capacity operations such as gas stations and vending machine routes. The TIP is such cases is pre-fixed (size of gas tanks/vending machine shelf space), so finding re-order quantities becomes a simple matter of subtracting the current inventory position from a constant TIP. Sometimes the question is "How often should we review and replenish?"—that is, what should our 'P' be, given average demand, standard deviation, lead time, a pre-determined TIP, and a preferred CSL?

$$\text{TIP} = \bar{d} * (P + L) + z\,(\sigma_d)\sqrt{(P + L)} \qquad\qquad (\text{Equation 8.8})$$

Solving for P,

$P \text{ (period between reviews)} = [2\bar{d}\,(\text{TIP} - \bar{d}L) + z^2\sigma_d^2 \pm z\,\sigma_d\sqrt{\{(4\text{TIP}*\bar{d}) + (z^2\sigma_d^2)\}}] / 2\bar{d}^2$

$P = [2\bar{d}\,(\text{TIP}) + z^2\sigma_d^2 \pm z\,\sigma_d\sqrt{\{(4\text{TIP}*\bar{d}) + (z^2\sigma_d^2)\}}] / 2\bar{d}^2 - L \qquad (\text{Equation 8.9})$

In a quadratic form, the equation has exactly one positive and one negative solution. We ignore the negative root solution since it has no meaning.

When should we use the ROP (continuous) vs. the periodic model? Let's consider the pros and cons of each.

Model	Advantages	Disadvantages
ROP	Inventory is reviewed continuously, so use for *A* category items and some fast moving/high revenue generating *B* items.	Cost of continuous monitoring. Not possible for businesses with thousands of SKUs, like retail stores. ROPs for different items from same supplier can be triggered at different times, preventing item grouping in one order for cost savings.
Periodic	Inventory reviewed periodically, so use for some slower moving *B* and for *C* category items. Can fix same review intervals for groups of items from same supplier, allowing bulk ordering with lower ordering, shipping, and packing costs and possible price discounts.	No visibility on inventory movements during period between reviews, so must carry higher safety stock compared to ROP. Consumes significant inventory review and purchasing resources around review (order) dates.

Companies also use hybrid models, most common of which is the (*s,S*) or min-max model. *S* denotes the TIP, while *s* denotes the ROP level. When during an inventory review the inventory position is found to be at or below *s* (ROP or minimum), an order is issued to bring up the inventory position to *S* (TIP or maximum). The frequency of ordering, in this case, is lower than in a regular periodic review system, where no ROP exists and an order is usually placed at every review period to bring up the inventory position to some *S* level. IKEA is known to use such a 'min-max' model that sets a reorder point as well as specifies the maximum amount to order once the ROP is tripped by a fall in inventory. The min/max setting is based on the number of products that will be sold from the reserve stack of bins in a single day or two-day period. Point-of-sale (POS) data is used to forecast sales for the next few days, while warehouse management system data provides information on receipts from suppliers and other IKEA warehouses. Actual sales are regularly matched against forecasted sales, and the logistics manager goes directly to the pallet and bin inventory for a physical count when significant discrepancies are seen.[8]

When to buy—JIT: JIT says do not keep inventory but to order 'just in time' to meet demand as it emerges. Popularized by Taiichi Ohno at Toyota, the just-in-time (JIT) philosophy has one basic goal—to unearth and remove waste in business operations. Inventory, according to Taiichi Ohno of Toyota, is waste, or '*Muda*' in Japanese. A broader view is that waste is anything that adds a cost that the customer is not willing to pay for. JIT orders and receives just at the time of need, with the goal of removing inventory altogether from the system. This helps identify and bring urgency to solving system problems, such as malfunctioning machines or spotty quality raw materials. Having inventory provides a safety buffer that makes people complacent.

KEY POINTS

- Annual demand/EOQ = # of orders placed/year. Under constant demand and constant lead time conditions, dividing 365 days by the number of orders per year would provide the ordering frequency.
- The continuous review model signals when it's time to re-order by setting a re-order point (ROP) in terms of the inventory position. The inventory position is monitored continuously, and when it falls to the ROP, an order is triggered. The ROP is fixed such that when the ROP-triggered order is placed, enough inventory remains to a) meet average consumption till fresh supplies are received and b) provide a safety stock to accommodate the effects of demand and/or lead time variability during the lead time period.
- The fixed period model reviews the inventory position at pre-determined intervals. Orders are placed at the time of review(s) to bring up the existing inventory position to a set target inventory position (TIP). The TIP is fixed such that it covers expected demand till the time of the next order (placed at time of next review), plus expected demand during the lead time of that order.
- JIT simply calls for placing orders or manufacturing at the time of need, with the objective of eliminating inventory altogether. Hidden problems surface (for resolution) when the protective cover of inventory is removed.

8.4 Was It Done Right?

The response from company executives when asked this question about their inventory management system is often a frustrated "Not really!" Why?

- *Models vs. reality*: Large gaps may develop between operational parameters existing when a model was developed and current reality. For example, a change in interest rates would change holding costs in an EOQ model, but users may not be aware of such nuances. ROP or TIP in a replenishment model usually employ normal distributed demand and lead time assumptions. Yet demand may not follow a normal distribution, especially with highly variable daily demand. On removing seasonality, trend, and special events such as promotions and disasters, the data plot of daily demand is typically right skewed. Since demand is never zero, the left tail behaves somewhat, but the right tail can extend to extreme values that a normal distribution may not anticipate. Models using a normal distribution may thus experience stock-outs more frequently than anticipated. Variable lead times may form a right-skewed distribution, too, the lower limit being zero while the upper limits could be much larger than in an assumed normal distribution.

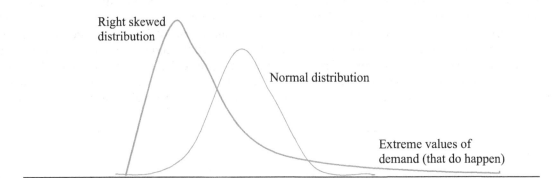

Figure 8.8 Distribution Of Highly Variable Daily Demand

Even when demand is normally distributed, the mean and standard deviation may vary by season. In the toys business, for example, an ROP that corresponds to two weeks demand in May might cover just two days of demand in November and December. ROPs or TIPs for such seasonal products must be changed every season to reflect the changes in average demand and the standard deviation of demand. Similarly, for peak vendor ordering periods, ROPs and TIPs must reflect changes in average lead times and standard deviations of lead time.

Reality may also appear in the form of constrained capital resources, limited risk-taking capability (follow ROP, but what if tastes change?), and physical limits. A bakery with a single production line cannot bake doughnuts and chocolate cake together, so if the ROP for both products happens to fall at the same time, one ROP must necessarily be ignored. One solution is to develop a list of items that require work at the same equipment/workcenter and monitor their ROP strike date status. When an item's ROP strike date appears to clash with another's, the item closest to its ROP strike point could be made a few days ahead of its ROP strike date, other things being equal.

Natural disasters: When disasters like the 2011 Japan earthquake, tsunamis, nuclear leaks, brownouts, and floods in Thailand hit, inventory shortages developed quickly in supply chains that are already lean and low-fat, like those of Honda, Toyota, and Dell. It would be prohibitively expensive to increase safety stock size to cover such risks. Geographers are now providing companies with heatmaps identifying disaster prone locations, which companies can use to diversify their supply sources geographically to spread the risk.

KEY POINTS

- Models using normal distribution assumptions may not represent situations with highly variable daily demand that are characterized by right-skewed distributions.
- Models have to be consistent with the operational realities of capital, space, risk tolerance, and production line and resource constraints in order to realize practical application.
- Catastrophic events cannot be reasonably incorporated in working models. JIT run supply lines are especially vulnerable to disruptions.

8.5 Current Trends in Managing Inventory

Supply chains stretched over multiple continents, proliferating sales channels, increasing product variety, and a demanding consumer create challenges that have inventory management executives on their toes. Let's look at some current and emerging challenges:

8.5.1 Omnichannel Inventory

Customers are ordering later, using different methods and channels. Industrial products supplier Grainger, reports that plant managers are now placing orders on-line after the first shift, close to Grainger's cutoff time for next-day delivery, creating inventory picking and delivery issues for the latter. Orders, in general, are being placed in many different ways: mobile, phones, e-walls like Tesco's Tokyo subway virtual store locations, kiosks, and such. Orders are being fulfilled in as many different ways. Amazon ships from its rapidly expanding fulfillment center network and also directly from warehouses of major suppliers like P&G. Local deliveries are being made to designated password-protected lockers at local retail stores such as 7-Eleven for customers to pick up, with cab and drone deliveries on the horizon. Inventory is being positioned closer to the customer. In fact, the average length of a long haul for truckload carriers has fallen from 700 to 800 miles per load to 500 or so in recent years.[9] Pure omnichannel fulfillment simply means that technology and processes are in place to fulfill customer orders from one pool of inventory irrespective of how such orders are placed (online, phone, stores, virtual catalogues). One pool does not mean building a gigantic warehouse servicing all orders but rather linking real-time inventory held in warehouses, retail stores, ships, planes, rail, trucks, and supplier premises together into a digital, readily visible, and accessible system. Once a product is queried by a customer, that system should be able to pinpoint the most suitable fulfillment source quickly and accurately. Order picking, packing, and logistical resources should be available to service that order from that physical inventory location. If such a system does not exist, separate inventories have to be kept by order placement and delivery channel, leading to costly duplication of inventories, facilities, and activities: ordering fulfillment, the cost and time of picking individual items for individual orders, coordinating shipping of different items on the same order from different locations, loss of scale economies in shipment, configuring systems to accept online returns in stores, real-time order tracking demands by the customer . . . and the list goes on. For many retailers, the tendency is to push the problem down to their suppliers by having them drop ship (ship directly to customer) online orders for their products. Currently, a large part of supply chain investments are investments in online systems, although the revenue from online sales is just about 7 percent today for traditional retailers— and most are *not* making money on their online sales. For most, again, just estimating the true cost of online fulfillment is a challenge. Estimating and collecting inventory, fulfillment, logistics, and returns costs is a difficult task, confounded further by the many information and planning systems that typically exist within a company yet do not/cannot talk with each other—let alone talk to suppliers, distributors, or customers. To handle the increasing complexity, technologies such as distributed order management (DOM) are being employed to capture orders from multiple channels and identify SKUs for direct factory to customer dropshipments. DOM is currently grappling with the concept of 'most profitable fulfill'—identifying the most profitable way to fill an order given all of the potential distribution points and transportation options. Other solutions like multi-echelon inventory optimization (MEIO) software suggest optimal inventory levels and safety stock at different points in the entire supply chain for a chosen level of customer service. Inventory will be intelligently accumulated on shipping docks, roads, rail, ports and ships, customs and inspection warehouses, transshipment points, distribution centers, and wholesaler/retailer locations. The problem with MEIO is that the location that is picked to carry more inventory may not be too happy about it. ERP and SCM system providers like IBM, SAP, and Oracle are working actively to offer truly intelligent integrated supply chain management systems.

Omnichannel at Macy's

In recent years, much of Macy's same-store sales gains have come from online purchases. Confronted with changing consumer ordering habits and fulfillment options and the competitive challenge posed by Amazon and the like, Macy's has embarked on a well-thought-out and successful transition to omnichannel retailing. So what does it do?

- Visibility: Macy's has installed 40,000 Internet compatible in-store terminals that allow a search for a size or color across all of its 840 stores and two dozen fulfillment centers. RFID (radio frequency identification devices) technologies are now permeating down to the SKU level. Macy's has already seen success with RFID in its shoe salon, with improved tracking and increased sales. Mobile apps reports, instead of paper, allow store floor teams to react in real time to developments. In-store mobile apps direct lost customers to where they wish to go in the store (handy at Macy's humungous flagship Herald Square New York City store) and also provide product location data and description and prices, both in store and online.
- Fulfillment: Macy's is building standalone fulfillment centers as well as mini-DCs (distribution centers) attached to stores—the latest is the Tulsa Fulfillment Center, a 1.3 million square foot facility in Oklahoma. It is hiring more temporary workers in the holiday season to fulfill online orders exclusively. It blocks off time before its stores open to fill the bulk of the online orders and sets aside areas within a store to keep online items for pickup or delivery.
- Employees: Macy's 30,000 sales associates have new tools to "think and act omnichannel,"—selling customers merchandise that may not be in the store and offering alternate products to customers making returns. A customer cannot find her size in that new spring skirt collection. No problem—an associate can quickly use the web-enabled store terminals to search Macy's entire system and have the skirt located and delivered to the customer's house the next day.
- Testing: Online is a favorite place to test for extended sizes—if sales take off, the item/sizes are then placed in regular stores. Fresh designs and unique collections can also be virtually exhibited and evaluated for consumer interest and sales potential at relatively little expense and time.
- Logistics: Same-day or even same-hour delivery from physical stores is becoming a reality. Macy's is "working with a few in different markets trying to test different ways of doing this." Macy's is estimated to have 500-plus Macy's stores fulfilling online orders, with same-day or even same-hour delivery as an ultimate goal.
- Payment: Mobile POS handhelds are being introduced that will let sales associates check out customers on the floor without having to locate and stand in line at a check out register. Google 'tap and go' payments and Apple Pay mobile payments will work, too.

Macy's is also using digital technology for marketing purposes so it can have a 360-degree view of customer shopping habits and coordinate merchandising strategies across multiple channels. Digital kiosks, digital mannequins, virtual fitting rooms, mobile apps, i-beacons and mobile in-store navigation are other digital initiatives that are being tested online and at selected physical stores.

Adapted from: Craig Smith, "A Feature on Multichannel at Macy's About Macy's," *Retail Innovation*, accessed Oct. 1, 2015, http://retail-innovation.com/a-feature-on-multichannel-at-macys/; Erin Lynch, "Macy's Addresses Omnichannel and Same-day Delivery," *Multichannel Merchant*, Feb. 26, 2014, http://multichannelmerchant.com/crosschannel/macys-2014-focus-omnichannel-day-delivery-26022014/; Dan Moskowitz, "Macy's: America's Omnichannel Store," *The Motley Fool,* Jan. 18, 2014. http://www.fool.com/investing/general/2014/01/18/macys-americas-omnichannel-store.aspx.

Companies are learning.

8.5.2 Product Returns Inventory

With record sales right after Black Friday and Cyber Monday come record returns. Some reasons are super discounts that encourage impulsive unneeded purchases and a super easy return system. Easy price comparison and price alert apps also prompt returns and re-buys at another place at a cheaper price. Despite clear and firm returns policies, re-stocking fees, manuals with prominent 'contact manufacturer first, do not return to store' labels, setting up on-site FAQs, and providing easy access to competent technical support, returns do happen. There are third party vendors who manage returns from receiving to inspection and sorting, repackaging, repair, re-labeling, recycling and disposal through proprietary private auction exchanges. Such vendors may also provide returns data analysis insights such as returns breakdown by product manufacturer, store and SKU, customer profiles (suspect customers can be barred from making further returns), and reasons for returns.

OM IN PRACTICE

Estée Lauder's Return System

Estée Lauder, the international cosmetics company, used to dump $60 million of their product returns from retailers into landfills each year. Frustrated with the recurring loss, the company invested $1.3 million in scanners and an intelligent data gathering and analysis system. The new system provided intelligence on the causes of returns, what was being returned, and other useful data to facilitate returns management. In the first year of system installation, the company experienced a 150 percent increase in redistribution of its returns, a $475,000 reduction in labor costs, a 10 percent increase in returns re-utilization, and lowered inventory levels resulting from being able to place products back into the market more quickly.

8.5.3 Sustainability in Inventory Management

We do not normally visualize inventory as a pile of elemental energy, carbon costs, fuel, and water. Yet that is what it is. If we can reduce inventory, we reduce our consumption of all of those resources. When inventory does not exist, resources to make it are not consumed, space to hold it is no longer required, energy to store it in good condition is not required, and labor and equipment to monitor and move it around are not required. Eliminating or reducing inventory certainly has a far greater impact on resource use than changes made to a warehouse shelving layout, adding insulation and solar power panels, replacing fuel forklifts with electric ones, or using optimizers to utilize every inch of warehouse and truck loading space. Lean and JIT have a direct relationship with sustainability. The added energy costs of multiple deliveries in JIT are negligible compared to the energy conserved by not making more than what is needed at the moment.

Reducing Inventory—The Levers to Push

The cost of capital (interest rates) is very low nowadays, and one could mount an argument for keeping and using inventory as a competitive weapon for quick order fulfillment. It may be a viable strategy but seems suited for overly delivery-sensitive standardized items, where the customer is likely to abandon the buy or refuse late delivery. Even so, the cost of holding inventory includes a lot more than just interest cost, as we have learned earlier. Actually, reducing inventory without affecting customer service is the name of the game.

Walmart carried on average about 46 days of sales (valued at COGS) in inventory in 2014, while Target, a competitor, carried about 63 days of sales.[10] Home Depot's days of sales in inventory in the same period was about 76 days, compared to Lowe's at 89 days. Precisely why such differences exist between companies in the same industry cannot be answered without being privy to confidential information, but there are some powerful levers that managers can push to attack the root drivers of inventory.

Demand Management Levers

Better forecasting: Probabilistic forecasting of demand that tells of the chances of an extremely large or small order recurring improves forecast value. Forecast accuracy also increases when initial forecasts are fine-tuned by liasing with other functions and supply/demand markets to bring in information—special events planned, new competitors emerging soon, new competing/complementary product introductions, imminent changes in government regulations, and such. Grouping of SKUs by attribute and forecasting by product complementarity adds accuracy. In high flood season, the demand for items like flashlights, sand bags, and batteries, generators, and orange high visibility vests will be inter-correlated and higher than in normal times. Customer service and safety stock levels are set for each unique group, not for the individual item.

Pricing: Discounting to move inventory is a regular feature in grocery, retail, appliance, and auto sales. On the other hand, pricing also helps to reduce demand to match available inventory. Charging high when customers line up is done by hotels, airlines, and concerts; Broadway shows do so all the time.

Pooling: Pooling (consolidating—also discussed in chapter 11, "Managing Supply Chains") distribution centers or warehouses can lower demand uncertainty faced by the seller. Third- or fourth-party logistics (3PL or 4PL) providers also pool parts on behalf of manufacturers. Inventory levels are reduced when several companies use common parts from such pools. Similarly, companies can form common pools amongst themselves. Airlines, for example, operate common pools of spare parts for their fairly standardized fleets (Boeing 737 series, Airbus 320 family) at central locations. Pooling benefits accrue since demand is distributed among many markets (airline fleets), while procurement/storage costs are shared. Virtual pooling is also possible. Netflix, for example, has all its distribution centers scan returned DVDs into a central database. A distribution center receiving an order proceeds to access the central database and finds the physical locations of the ordered DVD. The DVD is mailed out to the customer from the closest available source.

Product variety: A typical grocery store may carry more than 50,000 SKUs. Trader Joe's carries about 4,000. The restricted variety pays off in terms of quicker customer decisions, simpler forecasting, limited inventory, quicker and more reliable inventory counting and shelf stocking, and higher inventory turnover. Trader Joe's sells about 10 varieties of peanut butter compared to the 40 types generally found in a supermarket. If both stores sell 80 jars a week, Trader Joe's may sell an average of eight of each SKU, while the supermarket might sell an average of only two of each SKU. With high turnover on a smaller number of SKUs, Trader Joe's can purchase large quantities of a SKU and obtain volume discounts.

Product design: We sell vacuums in two types (dry vac and wet vac), three sizes, five colors, two technologies (conventional and wind tunnel), and made by four suppliers.

We have 2 types * 3 sizes * 5 colors * 2 technologies * 4 suppliers = 240 SKUs.

Those different vacuum SKUs we sell can be designed to share components within their own brand/make, perhaps common internal parts that the customer usually does not see. Doing so will not reduce the number of SKUs we carry but would certainly reduce the inventory of components and replacement parts/accessories that the vacuum manufacturers need to use and hold in inventory. Perhaps a vacuum can be designed to offer both wet and dry clean in a single machine, thus reducing complexity and inventory at the retail SKU level.

Virtual inventory: Physical inventory is converted to e-inventory. Patient files in medical practices are now being converted into e-files. Movies, magazines, books, and music are digitized and delivered virtually over the net.

Substitution: Offering customers substitutions (with an incentive) also helps reduce inventory. Take a red rose instead of a currently unavailable white one? We'll give you a discount and vouch for the quality. That discount helps when we are running low on white roses and wish to push the pile of red roses we have in inventory.

Planned scarcity: I liked the blue-striped dress shirt so much that I went back to the Jos. A. Bank store a couple of weeks later to pick up one more. I was out of luck—that entire line of shirts was gone and would not return. The idea is to keep styles fresh in order to keep shoppers interested and take away styles quickly. The buyer becomes apprehensive of missing out and buys immediately. This policy of planned scarcity has retailers buying in smaller quantities, freshening mix more frequently, and consequently keeping lower inventories. If something sells exceptionally well, quick replenishment arrangements can bring in more inventory in time. Basic items for a men's apparel retailer, like white shirts and khakis, are stocked all year around.

OM IN PRACTICE

Lululemon, of yoga pants fame, thrives on strategic scarcity, a deliberate policy of keeping low inventories. Keeping items scarce means pushing customers to buy it now rather than wait. Colors and seasonal collections are refreshed in three, six or 12-week life cycles. Although Wall Street has commented on the impact of lost sales owing to shortages of hot items, Lululemon has been able to sell 95 percent of its inventory at full price. They do keep core items like black yoga pants in stock round the year but do not discount. Prices are considerably higher than other retailer prices. Their return policy is strict and limited.

Strategic scarcity is a risky act to do or follow, but if done well, it obviously pays off in terms of increased revenue, lower inventory, and reduced costs. It requires close attention to customer tastes and preferences in order to make products that are desirable and hence kept scarce. Lulu used to keep folding tables in the middle of the store so that associates could overhear customer complaints/comments. Now they are collecting digital profile data, too.

Adapted from: Kim Bhasin, "Lululemon To Collect Customer Data, After Years of Avoiding It," *Huffington Post*, June 12, 2014; Dana Mattioli, "Lululemon's Secret Sauce," *Wall Street Journal*, March 22, 2012.

Supply Management Levers

Lead time reduction: Lead time is the time elapsed between receipt of an order and the delivery of that order. Any reduction in lead time involves reduction in two factors—order fulfillment time and/or order delivery time. A faster order fulfillment process—production, distribution, picking, packing, and positioning on the loading dock—would cut down on lead time. So would quicker logistics. Reducing the order fulfillment time may also allow an extension of the order receipt time and, hence, increased revenue. For example, a company may have a policy that all orders received till 5 p.m. will be delivered the next day. A shorter order fulfillment time would allow the company to extend its order receipt window—maybe now accept orders till 7 p.m. for next day execution. The company could also trade-off the same reduction in order fulfillment time for increased delivery time, getting logistical economies without any increase in lead time.

A shorter lead time, of course, enables lower inventories. Tesco, the European retailer giant, scrapped its 'F&F Couture' premium clothing line after slow sales left large inventories of apparel discounted at more than 80 percent. At the same time, Zara Clothes Group, also in Europe, reported a profit jump. The difference in performance lay in the speed of receiving, deciphering, and reacting to market signals. Unlike many apparel makers sourcing from China, Zara has a short and agile supply chain based mainly in Spain, Portugal, and Morocco with almost real time store-to-production communication systems. It costs more to operate the supply chain and make apparel, relative to outsourcing to lower cost sources like China. But Zara can react quickly to new trends. It can wait to see what customers are actually buying instead of having to pre-order on forecasts and suffer from shiploads of unsold inventories. In fact, recently added (and very successful) online ordering customer options have shortened the time to spot new trends. Social media enables everyone to see and rate what's trending on runaways and blogs, and Zara can get it from runaway to retail shop quicker than anyone else. Stores like GAP and others can become dated in their offerings because of their much slower response and lead times. Zara stocks less and updates collections quickly. Failed designs do not accumulate, and short replenishment lead times enable quick ramp up of supplies of hot sellers, which Zara sells at full price.[11] Lead time reduction also means retailers are more confident carrying less inventory because they know they can get a hot-selling item replenished quickly. This reduces the temptation to place large orders at a time—and then not place any for a long time, as unsold inventory builds up. Elimination of such artificial feast-or-famine lumpiness in ordering allows distribution centers and producers to plan better and reduce inventory at their own levels. Less inventory frees up space in retailer store shelves, which allows more variety on display. A less crowded stockroom can also be redeployed for fulfilling online orders.

All such benefits have to be weighed against the cost of lead time reduction, especially in retail. Amazon and others' one-day fulfillment drive in some cities cut its margins because of loss of economies of scale in production, warehousing, distribution, and delivery. In an effort to reduce costs and reduce lead times, technologies such as 3D printing are being considered—parts/products can be made close to customer locations without keeping large stocks at centralized DCs (distribution centers).

Lead time uncertainty: Reducing the standard deviation of lead time would usually reduce average inventory at a greater rate than reducing lead time, especially if lead time variability is high. Actionable areas include collaboration with suppliers in sharing sales data and preparing joint forecasts, selection of reliable 3/4PL logistics and intermediate warehousing and customs clearance providers, buying closer to home, and building trust so that unpleasant events such as a brewing labor strike at a key supplier's plant are communicated freely.

Supply chain nodes: Reducing the number of hand-over points in a supply chain reduces inventory transfer, inspection, and accumulation. Fewer interruptions makes for smoother materials flow, reducing supply lead times as well as lead time variability. In some industries, third parties take full responsibility for manufacturing and logistics, thus effectively reducing inventory worries for the buyer—consider Li & Fung, who orchestrate a mainly Asia-based network of thousands of designers, suppliers, assemblers, and transporters for major brands in apparel.

Virtual inventories: In the virtual inventory system, a company takes orders but does not own inventory itself. Rather, the supply source drop-ships products directly to customers. Amazon has just introduced a new system in India, Amazon *KiranaNow*, that lets thousands of local grocers ('kiranas') upload their inventory on Amazon's site. Shoppers can browse and pick products online, and deliveries will be made using the local kirana's own resources, Amazon's logistics, or third party logistics, the same day. Of course, the one day delivery promise pales before Taiwan's five-hour delivery. Momo Shop will deliver Kleenex or an HTC smartphone to your door in 12 hours—no shipping charges—while ASAP promises deliveries in five hours.

The virtual-inventory model suits perishable items because of the direct shipment from manufacturer to customer. Also, with direct shipments, bulky products like TVs and furniture do not have to be double- or triple-handled at multiple distribution and transshipment centers, thus reducing cost, time, and risk of damage. Companies like Amazon are in the forefront of integrating the cyber and physical aspects of inventory, with data warehouses *and* physical warehouses. Amazon's 2012 acquisition of Kiva, maker of warehouse robots, and its recent deliveries to customers through lockers located at 7-Eleven and similar stores, are designed to reduce its 9 percent (of revenues) order fulfillment costs.

Besides the above initiatives, organizational reporting and decision-making structure affect speed of response of inventory decisions to changes in demand and lead times. Clear lines of responsibility, accountability and swift decision making characterize companies like Zara. So are well-maintained and updated IT systems, together with trust and good relationships across the supply chain that ensure rapid and accurate information flows both from and to suppliers and demand markets. Information comes from many sources nowadays, including social media, which some senior managers may not be completely comfortable with—technology unfamiliarity breeds confusion, mistrust, and delayed reactions.

KEY POINTS

- Globalization extends and complicates supply and distribution networks, leading to inventory accumulation at multiple points. Companies cope by adopting advanced tracking and modeling technology and process improvements.
- Product returns are now large enough to merit dedicated systems that receive, sort and stage, process, analyze, and support returns to inventory. Such systems could be owned and managed by third parties.
- The biggest contributor to sustainability is to not make another unit—inventory reduction makes this possible.
- Managers reduce inventory through demand management levers such as forecasting, pricing, pooling, product variety reduction, component sharing across products, product/component substitution, and planned scarcity.
- Supply management levers help reduce inventory through lead time length and variability reduction, simplified supply chains, and an organizational culture of trust, open communications, and quick decision making.

8.6 Conclusion

Customer: *"Why should I choose you?"*
Business: *"Because we promise that we will have what you need, when and where you need it."*

Keeping that promise is a challenge in these tight times. What we need to figure out is how to reduce inventory levels and costs without affecting customer service adversely. In doing so, we need to balance three costs in achieving a targeted customer service level—the cost of holding inventory, the cost (and probability) of a stock-out, and the administrative cost of placing an order on a supplier. We have examined various ways and techniques that help us achieve such a balance.

Remember, your growth as a manager would principally depend on your ability to cut costs and gain revenues. Managing inventory intelligently is part of how you may do so. Good luck, and let me know if you come across any especially interesting inventory problems. I'll be happy to chat.

What Have We Learned?

What Is Inventory Management?

- Inventory is a product or service that we *could* make, acquire, perform, or provide *after* the customer asks for it but choose to make/acquire now at some cost and *store* in anticipation of the customer asking for it.
- Inventory can be described in terms of form, that is, finished goods, work-in-process, or in the pipeline being transported, or in terms of reason for holding, such as cycle and decoupling inventory.
- Inventory management is a data-driven approach to making intelligent cost and customer service driven decisions on what is to be stored; how much is to be stored; where it is to be stored and for how long; how to price and allow customers access to the inventory; and when to replenish inventory stock.
- Phantom inventory is created when physical stock does not match computer stock, for reasons ranging from pilferage to misplacement and cashier errors. It is especially problematic when the records show inventory present, but actual physical stock is zero, since customers will walk away. RFID and other technologies make it easier to locate and match physical inventory with records.

Why Is It Important?

- Increasing inventory turnover leads to reduced inventory levels and frees up capital.
- Inventory decisions affect other functions in a company, marketing, finance, and accounting being the primary areas affected.

How Is It Done?

- Cycle counting allows a physical count of all items in inventory in stages, with important items being counted more frequently than other items.
- Inventory measures tell us how well we are doing. Lower average aggregate inventory and average days of inventory on hand ratios is good news. A higher inventory turnover ratio is good news.
- CSL (cycle service level) is *either* 100 or 0, depending on whether 100 percent of customer demand for all customers has been met or not. Fill rate measures the percent of customers satisfied and can range *between* 100 percent and 0 percent.

- The direct costs of holding inventory include a) financial costs such as interest costs and opportunity costs and b) service costs such as utilities, taxes, and insurance.
- The indirect costs of holding inventory include a) risks such as obsolescence and price devaluation, b) waste such as discounting and quality complacency, and c) adverse effects on innovation and product redesign.
- SKU prioritization for management attention uses sales revenues (ABC), turnover rate (FSN), consequence of stock-out (VED) and substitution possibility as criteria for assessing SKU importance. Pareto's 80/20 rule applies, leading to a relatively small number of SKUs being classified as high importance items.
- Two core questions are asked of every high/medium importance SKU. "How much to order?" and "When to order?"

How Much to Order?

- For recurring orders, the question of how much to order is determined by using a flat order policy or the EOQ model. The flat ordering policy may state that we order three weeks of average weekly demand for all SKUs in a product category. Individual SKU demand variability is not considered, leading to possible stock-outs.
- The EOQ model considers two opposing costs, holding cost and ordering cost, and recommends a specific (recurring) order quantity that minimizes the sum of these costs.
- High stock-out costs relative to leftovers cost encourage larger orders, and vice-versa. Availability of substitute products lowers the cost of stock-outs.

When to Order?

- Annual demand/EOQ = # of orders placed per year. Under constant demand and constant lead time conditions, dividing 365 days by the number of orders per year would provide the ordering frequency.
- The continuous review model signals when it's time to re-order by setting a re-order point (ROP). The inventory position is monitored continuously, and when it falls to the ROP, an order is triggered. The ROP is fixed such that when the ROP-triggered order is placed, enough inventory remains to a) meet average consumption till fresh supplies are received and b) maintain a safety stock for demand and/ or lead time variability.
- The fixed period model reviews the inventory position at pre-determined intervals. Orders are placed at the time of review(s) to bring up the existing inventory position to a set target inventory position (TIP). The TIP is fixed such that it covers expected demand till the time of the next review and order plus expected demand during the lead time of that order.
- JIT simply calls for placing orders at the time of need, with the objective of eliminating inventory altogether. Hidden problems surface (for resolution) when the protective cover of inventory is removed.

Was It Done Right?

- Highly variable daily demand is generally characterized by right-skewed distributions—using normal distribution assumptions would likely lead to increased stock-outs.
- Acceptance and implementation of inventory models depends on the operational realities of capital availability, access to storage space, risk tolerance, and production line and resource constraints.
- Catastrophic events cannot be reasonably incorporated in working models. JIT-run supply lines are especially vulnerable to disruptions.

- Globalization adds nodes, transfer points, and risks to supply and distribution networks, leading to inventory accumulation at multiple points. Companies use advanced tracking and modeling technology and process improvements to manage complexity.
- Product returns now warrant dedicated systems that receive, sort and stage, process, analyze, and support returns to inventory. Such systems could be owned and managed by third parties.
- The biggest contributor to sustainability is to not make another unit—inventory reduction makes this possible.
- High CSLs require disproportionately higher levels of inventory.

Levers for inventory reduction

- Managers reduce inventory through demand management levers such as forecasting, pricing, pooling, product variety reduction, component sharing across products, product/component substitution, and planned scarcity.
- Supply management levers help reduce inventory through lead time length and variability reduction, simplified supply chains, and an organizational culture of trust, open communications, and quick decision making.

Key Formulas/Equations

Average inventory: (Beginning inventory + ending inventory)/2

Average aggregate inventory: Sum of average inventories of different SKUs

Average sales days of inventory on hand: Average aggregate inventory/COGS

Inventory turnover: COGS/average aggregate inventory

: 1/flow time

Average CSL: Sum of individual period CSLs/# of periods

Expected CSL: Sum of (probability of CSL*CSL for scenario 1 + probability of CSL*CSL for scenario 2 + probability of CSL*CSL for scenario Z)

Average rill rate: Sum of individual period rill rates / # of periods

Total ordering cost = D/'Q' * S, where D = annual demand, Q = order qty., S = average cost of placing an order

Total holding cost = ('Q'/2) * H, where H = cost of holding one piece of an item in inventory for a year

Total cost = total ordering cost + total holding cost = D/'Q' * S + 'Q'/2 * H

Economic order 1uantity = $\sqrt{[(2*D*S)/H]}$

Re-order point (ROP) formulas:

a) Constant lead time, variable demand

ROP = $\bar{d}$ * LT + SS, where $\bar{d}$ = average daily demand, LT = lead time, SS = safety stock

SS = σ_d $\sqrt{LT}$ * z value corresponding to the desired CSL value, where σ_d = standard deviation of demand

ROP = $\bar{d}$ * LT + (σ_d $\sqrt{LT}$) * z value corresponding to the desired CSL value

b) *Variable lead time, constant demand*

ROP = d * $\overline{LT}$ + z * d*σ_{LT}, where LT = lead time, d = daily demand, σLT = standard deviation of lead time

---

c) *Variable lead time, variable demand*

$$\text{ROP} = \bar{d} * \overline{LT} + z\,[\surd(\overline{LT}\,\sigma^2_d + \bar{d}^2\,\sigma^2_{LT})]$$

Inventory position (IP) = on-hand inventory (including safety stock) + scheduled receipts today − backorders

Target inventory position (TIP) = expected demand during $(P + L)$ period + safety stock

$$= \bar{d} * (P + L) \text{ days} + z\,(\sigma_d)\surd(P + L) \text{ days}$$

Where, $\bar{d}$ = average daily demand, P = period between reviews, L = lead time, z = z value corresponding to the desired CSL value, σ_d = standard deviation of demand

Current order size = TIP − current IP

Discussion Questions

1

Figure 8.9 Inventory Trinity

Consider and explain how a change in one of these three factors—sales, inventory, and profit margin—could affect the other two.

For instructor: Some scenarios: Increase in sales has a long-term positive effect on inventory holdings. Increase in profit margin could mean an increase in selling price, reducing sales, and reducing inventory in the long run. But a strategic decision to increase inventory could also drive down margins if demand does not respond, because of eventual markdowns. Important thing is to explore and provide reasonable rationales for possible interactions.

2   EOQ questions:

a) What happens to EOQ if interest rate goes up (down)?

Answer: Most immediately, holding costs go up and EOQ declines.

b) How can you use EOQ in conditions of seasonal demand or trending demand?

Answer: One approach is to compute separate EOQs for each season.

c) How could you reduce the order quantity and yet maintain EOQ order policy and cost-minimization benefits?

Answer: By first reducing ordering costs.

d) How is holding cost estimated for a product whose value goes up with storage, e.g., wine?

Answer: Unit holding cost/period remains unchanged since the cost of the item remains the same—we use item cost and not selling price in EOQ.

e)   How does JIT affect EOQ?

Answer: JIT does not use EOQ—it orders as much as is needed at the moment. Also, when we implement 'Lean,' we actually work to reduce order costs (cheaper equipment setup, more efficient workers) allowing us to shift the order cost line down and to the left, lowering total cost and reducing the EOQ. With this shift, we can expect to order more often but in smaller quantities Assume annual demand remains fixed.

f)   Could an arbitrary increase in EOQ affect demand?

Answer: EOQ does not consider its effects on demand. Higher order quantities lead to higher inventory levels, improving CSL and product visibility. Sales may increase.

3   ROP/TIP questions:

a)   What happens to ROP recommendations for a variety of SKUs, if you have just one production line and each SKU requires to be run in individual production lots?

Answer: Probably cannot use models because ROPs for several SKUs can be triggered at the same time.

b)   How to reduce ROP?

Answer: Price cuts, uncertainty reduction, LT reduction, demand management.

c)   How to reduce TIP?

Answer: Shorten review intervals, reduce lead time and lead time variability, reduce demand variability.

End of Chapter Problems

1   Sales of hot dogs at the corner of 24th and Lexington Avenue follow the following patterns: 10 percent of the days, 80 are sold; 20 percent of the days, 90 are sold; and the remaining days, 100 are sold. If 80 are stocked each day by the vendor, what demand fill rate is the vendor targeting?

Demand	*80*	*90 100*
Probability	*.10*	*.20 .70*
If we stock 80		
Expected. fill rate	*(80/80)*.1 +*	*(80/90)*.2 + (80/100)* .7= 83.78%*

2   Regarding question 1, how much should be stocked to have a fill rate of 98 percent?

Answer: With a stock of 80, we get a fill rate of 83.78%.

With a stock of 90, we get:
$(80/80) * .1 + (90/90) * .2 + (90/100) * 0.7 = .9300$
So we need to stock more than 90, say x (and $x > 90$)
$(80/80) * .1 + (90/90) * .2 + (x/100) * 0.7 = .9800$ (target fill rate)
$x = 97.14$ or 98 hot dogs
If we are limited to ordering a specific order quantity of 80/90/100 only, then we'll have to order 100 hot dogs, obtaining a fill rate of 100 percent.

3   A restaurant sells 2,000 quarter-pounders each week. They carry an average 100 pounds of meat, costing $3.00/lb.

   a)   What is the inventory turnover?
   b)   On average how many days of supply are covered?

   Answer:

   a)   2,000 quarter-pounders   = 2,000 * 0.25 lbs of meat each = 500 lbs of meat
        Inventory turnover   = $cost of goods sold/$average aggregate inventory value
        $cost of goods sold   = $1,500 (500 lbs @$3/pound)
        $average aggregate inventory value = $300 (average aggregate inventory 100 pounds @ $3/pound)
        Inventory turnover   = 1,500/300 = 5 turns a week
   b)   Days of supply = (average aggregate inventory value/cost of goods sold/week)
        Days of supply of meat = 300/1,500 = 0.20 of a week = 1.40 days (@7 days/week)
        On average, they sell 500 lbs. of meat/week;
        Therefore, 1.40 days of supply = 100 lbs of meat = 400 burgers (@0.25 lb/burger)

4   A company reported $40,000,000 in sales last year. At the end of last year, it also held $20,000,000 of inventory. COGS is $2,000/unit, and the selling price is $5,000/unit. The average holding cost is 25 percent.

   a)   What is the inventory turnover?
   b)   How many turns does it make in a year?
   c)   Based on the parameters given above, what, in absolute terms, is the per-unit inventory cost for a product that costs $1,000? (Hint: it's the actual cost, based on the annual inventory holding cost, spent on holding that unit on the shelf for a specific duration of time—related to inventory turnover.)

   Answer:

   a)   How fast does the company turn its inventory?
        Take $1 as the unit of analysis
        Avg. inventory = $20,000,000
        Sales = $40,000,000; selling price = $5,000/unit
        Thus, # of units sold = 40,000,000/5,000 = 8,000 units
        Cost of producing 1 unit = $2,000
        Thus, COGS/yr = 8,000 units * $2,000/unit = $16,000,000 = flow rate/year
   b)   Avg. inventory = flow rate * flow time
        $20,000,000 = $16,000,000 * FT
        FT = 1.25 of a year (i.e. $1 takes 1 1/4 of a year to speed through the system)
        # of times we can turn over that $ in a year = 1 year/FT = 0.8 times a year
   c)   A unit stays in our system for 1 1/4 of a year (FT) on average.
        Cost of carrying a unit for 1 full year = 25% of the cost of the unit
        Unit cost = $1,000
        Cost of carrying unit for 1 full year = $250
        Thus, unit inventory cost = 250 * 1.25 = $312.50 approx. or 31.25% ($312.50 of $1,000)

5   A firm has been ordering a certain item 600 units at a time. The firm estimates that holding cost is $2 per unit per year and that annual demand is 1,800 units per year. The assumptions of the basic EOQ model are thought to apply. For what value of ordering cost would their ordering action (600 units per order) be economically optimal (i.e., the order quantity of 600 units/order be the EOQ)?

$EOQ = \sqrt{2 * D * S}/H$, where:
D = annual demand in units
S = cost of placing 1 order
H = cost of holding 1 unit of that item in inventory for 1 year

Answer: We are required to work out the ordering cost (cost/order) in this instance that corresponds to an EOQ of 600 units.

Thus, $EOQ = \sqrt{2 * D * S}/H$
Or $600 = \sqrt{[(2(1,800) * S)/2]}$
Thus, $360,000 = [2(1,800) * S]/2$
Thus, $S = 360,000/1,800 = \$200$/order

6   Annual demand for the Ferrari laptop at Circuit Town is D = 1,000 units. Ordering cost (S) = $400/order, each laptop costs $600, and holding costs ($H$) are 4 percent of the cost/unit/month.

a)   How much should be ordered in each replenishment lot (order)?
b)   What is the number of orders per year?
c)   What is the total cost of this ordering policy (total ordering cost + total holding cost)?

Answer:

a) $EOQ = \sqrt{2 * D * S}/H = \sqrt{2 * 1,000/yr * 400}/0.04 * 600 * 12$ mo = 53 units, approximately.
b)   # of orders/yr. = D/EOQ = 1,000/53 = 18.86 = 19 orders/yr approx
c)   Total cost of ordering policy = total ordering cost (TOC) + total holding cost (THC)

TOC = # orders/yr * cost of placing 1 order + average inventory * cost of holding 1 unit/yr
= 19 * $400 ($S$) + 53/2 (EOQ/2) * 0.04*600*12 (H)
= $15,232.00

7   What is the average flow time for a laptop, using data from the question above?

Answer: Using Little's law, average inventory = flow time * flow rate
Flow rate = # of laptops that flow through the store in a year = annual demand = D
Flow time = average inventory/FR = (EOQ/2)/D = EOQ/2D = 53/2 * 1000 = 0.0265 of a yr
= 0.0265 * 365 days = 9.67 days
Average time it takes for a laptop to move through the system and get sold.

8   Dr. 90210 estimates demand for silicone at 50 lbs./week, with a standard deviation of five lbs. Patients can turn (or fail to become) hot if turned away, so the good doctor can accept a stock-out risk of no more than 3 percent. Lead time from the supplier, No Leaks Inc., is stable at four weeks. Assume that demand during lead time is normally distributed. Answer questions a) through c) below.

a)   What value of Z is appropriate (hint: expected CSL = 1 − stock-out risk)?
Expected CSL = 1 − .03 = 97%; Z corresponding to 0.9700 = 1.89

b) How much safety stock should be held?
Safety stock = Z * standard deviation of demand * ($\sqrt{}$lead time)
SS = 1.89(5)($\sqrt{4}$) = 18.90 lbs
c) What's the reorder point (ROP)?
ROP = (average weekly demand rate * lead time) + safety stock
ROP = 50 * 4 + 18.90 = 218.90 lbs.

9   A firm manages an important SKU on a continuous review basis. Demand averages 200 units per day with a standard deviation of 60 units per day, and lead time is stable at 15 days. If the firm sets the re-order point to 3,200 units, what is the implied cycle-service level?

Answer:
ROP = (average demand rate * lead time) + safety stock
SS = Z * standard deviation of demand * ($\sqrt{}$lead time)
So:
3,200 = (200 * 15) + Z (60)($\sqrt{15}$)
Solving for Z,
Z = 0.86
CSL (area under the normal curve) corresponding to a Z of 0.86 = 0.8051 = 80.51%

10   West Side Confectioners employs a periodic system for baking flour with the following system parameters:

Annual demand = 140,000 pounds; # of weeks in a year = 52
Standard deviation of weekly demand = 1,260 pounds
(L) Supplier lead time = 1 week; cycle service level = 95%
(P) Period between reviews = 2 weeks
TIP = average weekly demand * ($P + L$) + safety stock;
Safety stock = Z * standard deviation of weekly demand * $\sqrt{(P + L)}$

How many pounds of flour should be *ordered* if the review is being conducted now? They currently have 2,000 pounds of flour in stock with no incoming shipments and no backorders.

Answer:

TIP	= Average weekly demand * ($P + L$) + safety stock
	= (140,000/52) * (2 + 1) + SS
Safety stock	= Z corresponding to a CSL of 95% * Std Dev of weekly demand * $\sqrt{(P + L)}$
	= 1.65 * 1,260 * $\sqrt{(2 + 1)}$
	= 3,600.93
TIP	= (140,000/52) * (2 + 1) + 3,600.93
	= 11,677.85 pounds
Order quantity	= TIP − current inventory position
	= 11,677.85 − 2,000
	= 9,677.85 pounds = 9,678 pounds rounded up

11   An airline with the new suite-with-personal-shower class provides perfumes in its showers, but only if a suite is booked. The mean demand for perfumes is 20/day, with a standard deviation of 5. The

lead time is five days, while the average ordering cost is $2/order. A bottle of perfume costs $30 and the average holding cost is 20 percent/year. Assume 365 working days in a year.

a)   Recommend an EOQ.
b)   Recommend a ROP for a 98 percent CSL.

Answer:

a) $EOQ = \sqrt{(2 * D * S)/H} = \sqrt{(2 * 20 * 365 * 2)/0.20} * 30 = 69.76 = 70$ bottles
b) ROP = average demand during lead time + SS

Average demand during $LT = 20$/day $* 5$ days $= 100$ bottles
$SS = z$ value corresponding to 98% CSL $* \sigma_d \sqrt{LT}$
$= 2.05 * 5\sqrt{5} = 22.91 = 23$ bottles
$ROP = 100 + 23 = 123$ bottles for 98% coverage.

Suggested Class Projects

1   Recall that your university health clinic ran out of flu shots in some flu seasons. Conversely, its flu vaccine inventories were barely depleted in other seasons. What would be an appropriate inventory-ordering policy for a product such as a flu vaccine? Consult your health clinic about desired customer service level needs, the nature and magnitude of demand and lead times, and the estimated costs of ordering and holding inventory. Note that vaccines are a perishable item. Also remember that the public and federal, state, and medical agencies are suffering from a severe resource crunch.

2   Go to a retail store like Forever 21 or Zara and a store like Macy's a few times—examine the apparel and note how long a design stays on the rack. Develop estimates of inventory turnover and contrast among the stores. Check the financials (if public) and build overall estimates of inventory turnover from the financials.

Suggested Cases

Ralph and Inventory Management

Description

During discussions, Ralph, our hospital stockroom manager gestures proudly at the ceiling-high stocked warehouse and states that he has never had to turn away any request for any item. In other words, he is providing his users 100 percent CSL (cycle service level). We ask him what the average lead times are for the most-used meds, and he responds, "within three days for most items." He then goes quiet, as the implications of what he has just said sink in—why keep so much inventory of everything when replenishments are only three days away? Well, he says defensively, after a pregnant pause, "As I said, I have never had to turn any user away, and you don't know how wildly variable demand can be in a hospital." Sure, we think, but not so variable as to call for a warehouse full of med items! Let's help Ralph out.

Detailed workout with numbers in instructor's manual.

Blanchard Importing, Harvard Business Pub.

Description

Evaluating inventory models and their applicability in an actual business with system constraints.

Notes

1 I thank Mr. Richard Merian for providing this example as well as details about TEU's case during a guest lecture.
2 Paula Rosenblum, "How Walmart Could Solve Its Inventory Problem And Improve Earnings," *Forbes*, May 22, 2014, http://www.forbes.com/sites/paularosenblum/2014/05/22/walmart-could-solve-its-inventory-problem-and-improve-earnings/.
3 Check out http://www.youtube.com/watch?v=JiXLY-D3m08&feature=player_detailpage for an interesting example of inventory counting.
4 Sergey Rumyantsev and Serguei Netessine, "Should Inventory Policy Be Lean or Responsive? Evidence for US Public Companies," Social Science Resource Network, Sept. 3, 2007, SSRN: http://ssrn.com/abstract=2319834.
5 Erica Ogg, "Who Needs a 92-inch TV? Mitsubishi, the Guys Who Make It," *CNET*, June 21, 2011. http://www.cnet.com/au/news/who-needs-a-92-inch-tv-mitsubishi-the-guys-who-make-it/#!.
6 I thank my colleague, Professor George Sphicas, for bringing needed clarity to the matter.
7 Note: The above approach using TIP and IP as the focal points (instead of the order quantity) is a bit different from the traditional:

    Order placed = usage during protection interval ($P + L$)

    The traditional approach may create confusion for students, arising from the fact that the lead-time overlaps a portion of the review period. For example, at the time of the second review, another order would be placed, and the order quantity should cover the protection interval, which would be = (period between second and third reviews + LT for order placed at the time of the third review). However, the order that was placed at the time of the first review already considered the LT for second order (which overlaps part of the period between the second and third reviews). Students point out that the protection interval that the second review period order covers should not "recount" the lead time for the second review order, i.e., the correct interval of time to cover for the second order should be = (period between second and third reviews + LT for third review order − LT for second review order) or simply = (the period between the second and third reviews if the LT assumed constant).
8 Clara Lu, "How Does IKEA's Inventory Management Supply Chain Strategy Really Work?" *Supply Chain 24/7*, Oct. 28, 2014, http://www.supplychain247.com/article/how_does_ikeas_inventory_management_supply_chain_strategy_work/topic/category/news.
9 Dan Gilmore, "Supply Chain News: Trip Report—NASSTRAC 2015," First Thoughts, *Supply Chain Digest*, April 16, 2015, http://www.scdigest.com/ASSETS/FIRSTTHOUGHTS/15-04-17.php?cid=9216.
10 Dan Gilmore, "Supply Chain News: Inventory Performance 2015—Some Interesting Comparisons," *Supply Chain Digest*, Aug. 20, 2015, http://www.scdigest.com/ASSETS/FIRSTTHOUGHTS/15-08-20.php?cid=9649.
11 Suzanne Bearne, "Updated: Tesco Axes Premium Clothing line," *Drapers*, March 26, 2012, http://www.drapersonline.com/news/womenswear/news/updated-tesco-axes-premium-clothing-line/5035129.article#.VhBoo3ldGUk; Joe Avella, "The One Reason Zara Is Dominating the Fashion Industry Right Now," video clip, *Business Insider*, July 14, 2015, http://www.businessinsider.com/zara-dominating-beating-competition-fashion-industry-2015-7; Ashley Lutz, "Zara Is Outsmarting H&M and Taking Over the World," *Business Insider*, June 13, 2013, http://www.businessinsider.com/zara-is-dominating-hm-2013-6.

APPENDIX: MANAGING INVENTORY

Single one-time order policies: For items such as fashion apparel and newspapers with uncertain demand, long lead times, and perishable inventory, there's often just a single window of ordering opportunity. We need to place orders for a line of women's tops on our vendors in China by November in order to get them by May next. That line turned out to be a hot seller this summer, but the long lead time did not allow us to obtain additional quantities in time. Could we have known to order more in that November order? The newsvendor (also called newsboy) model is a useful decision aid for determining the best order advance quantity in such situations.

Our friendly neighborhood newsvendor, Maria, complains that she has to throw away newspapers one day for want of customers, yet turn away customers the next day for want of sufficient stock. She has to order the papers the night before, and cannot reorder them on the day of issue. Let's help her find the optimum number of newspapers to order (in advance). There are four things we need to know:

- Recent demand data
- Cost of one paper to Maria
- Profit from one paper to Maria
- Salvage value, if any, for unsold papers

Maria shows us the demand figures from the past 20 days. She also tells us that the newspapers cost her $0.45 each, and she sells them for $0.65 each. Unsold papers are taken back by the paper distributor at a salvage value of $0.05/paper. If she runs out, customers, though annoyed, stay loyal to her conveniently located newsstand. For simplicity's sake, we assume that future demand is very unlikely to dip below the lowest recorded demand of 153 papers, or rise above the maximum recorded demand of 237 papers.

We can find the optimum number of papers to order in two ways—the long way, building a marginal profit analysis table, or a shorter way using the newsvendor model.

Marginal Profit Analysis

Cost of a paper to Maria = $0.45; selling price = $0.65
Profit = $0.65 selling price − $0.45 cost = $0.20/paper
Salvage value of each unsold paper = $0.05/paper
d = anticipated future demand; Q = number of newspapers that Maria can order for the future;
$P(d \geq Q)$ = The probability of future demand being equal to or $\geq Q$ (taken from table 8.3 below)

How many papers should Maria place an (advance) order for? She should buy 182 papers, for a total optimal profit of $682.40. We did not compute profits for the entire range of orders, since we can see that total profit maximizes at an order quantity of 182 papers, and declines for larger order quantities. The total profit for alternative order quantities can be computed by simply adding up the column totals in table 8.4 below.

A shorter way to compute the total would be as follows:

If Maria wants no waste and orders the minimum demand, i.e., 153 papers (Q) each day, the chances of demand being equal to or greater than 153 for each of the next 20 days would be 1.00 ($P(d \geq 153)$ = 100%, from column 1 of 'Historical Demand' table below), so all papers are sold.

Table 8.3 Historical Demand for the Past 20 Days

Demand over Past 20 days	Probability of this demand	If Maria would order this qty Q	Then the probability of future demand being equal to or > Q, i.e., P(d ≥ Q), would be
153	0.05 (1/20; Note 153 demand occurred just once in the 20 days of data)	153	$P(d = 153) + P$ (future demand being > 153) $= 0.05 + \sum[P(d = 162 \text{ papers}) + P(d = 171 \text{ papers}) + P(d = 178 \text{ papers}) + P(d = 181 \text{ papers} + \ldots\ldots\ldots\ldots\ldots.P(d = 237 \text{ papers})]$ $= 0.05 + \sum[P(d = 162) = 0.05 + P(d = 171) = 0.10 + P(d = 178) = 0.05 + P(d = 181) = 0.05 + \ldots\ldots\ldots. P(d = 237 \text{ papers}) = 0.05]$ $= 0.05 + 0.95$ $= 1.00$
162	0.05	162	$P(d = 162) + P$ (future demand being > 162) $= 0.05 + 0.90$ $= 0.95$
171	0.10 (2/20; 171 demand occurred twice in the 20 days of data)	171	$P(d = 171) + P$ (future demand being > 171) $= 0.10 + 0.80$ $= 0.90$
178	0.05	178	0.80
181	0.05	181	0.75
182	0.05	182	0.70
185	0.05	185	0.65
186	0.05	186	0.60
188	0.05	188	0.55
190	0.05	190	0.50
192	0.05	192	0.45
195	0.10 (2/20; 195 demand occurred twice in the 20 days of data)	195	0.40
196	0.05	196	0.30
197	0.05	197	0.25
198	0.05	198	0.20
218	0.05	218	0.15
225	0.05	225	0.10
237	<u>0.05</u> 1.00	237	0.05

Table 8.4 Marginal Profit Table

d	P(d ≥ Q)	153 $ Daily profit	162	171	178	181	182	185	186	188....
153	1.00	30.60[i]	27.00[iii]	23.40[vi]	20.60	19.40	19.00	17.80	17.40	16.60
162	0.95	30.60[ii]	32.40[iv]	28.80	26.00	24.80	24.40	23.20	22.80	22.00
171	0.90	30.60	32.40[v]	34.20	31.40	30.20	29.80	28.60	28.20	27.40
171	0.90	30.60	32.40	34.20	31.40	30.20	29.80	28.60	28.20	27.40
178	0.80	30.60	32.40	34.20	35.60	34.40	34.00	32.80	32.40	31.60
181	0.75	30.60	32.40	34.20	35.60	36.20	35.80	34.60	34.20	33.40
182	0.70	30.60	32.40	34.20	35.60	36.20	36.40	35.20	34.80	34.00
185	0.65	30.60	32.40	34.20	35.60	36.20	36.40	37.00	36.60	35.80
186	0.60	30.60	32.40	34.20	35.60	36.20	36.40	37.00	37.20	36.40
188	0.55	30.60	32.40	34.20	35.60	36.20	36.40	37.00	37.20	37.60
190	0.50	30.60	32.40	34.20	35.60	36.20	36.40	37.00	37.20	37.60
192	0.45	30.60	32.40	34.20	35.60	36.20	36.40	37.00	37.20	37.60
195	0.40	30.60	32.40	34.20	35.60	36.20	36.40	37.00	37.20	37.60
195	0.40	30.60	32.40	34.20	35.60	36.20	36.40	37.00	37.20	37.60
196	0.30	30.60	32.40	34.20	35.60	36.20	36.40	37.00	37.20	37.60
197	0.25	30.60	32.40	34.20	35.60	36.20	36.40	37.00	37.20	37.60
198	0.20	30.60	32.40	34.20	35.60	36.20	36.40	37.00	37.20	37.60
218	0.15	30.60	32.40	34.20	35.60	36.20	36.40	37.00	37.20	37.60
225	0.10	30.60	32.40	34.20	35.60	36.20	36.40	37.00	37.20	37.60
237	0.05	30.60	32.40	34.20	35.60	36.20	36.40	37.00	37.20	37.60
Total Profits (Column total)		$612.00	$642.60	$667.80	$679.00	$682.00	$682.40	$681.80	$681.00	$678.20

i. Ordered 153 papers, demand was 153 papers, and sold 153 papers.

    Profit   = 153 * $0.20/paper

            = $30.60

ii. Ordered 153 papers and sold 153 papers, even though demand was 162 papers.

    Profit   = 153 * $0.20/paper

            = $30.60

    We take profit in hand, and not the potential loss of turning customers away.

iii. Ordered 162 papers, demand was 153, thus sold only 153 papers, with 9 papers leftover

    Profit   = 153 * $0.20/paper − (162 − 153) papers * $0.45/paper + 9 papers * $0.05/paper salvage value

            = $27.00

iv. Ordered 162 papers, demand was 162 papers, sold 162 papers

    Profit   = 162 * $0.20/paper

            = $32.40

v. Ordered 162 papers and sold 162 papers, even though demand was 171 papers.

    Profit   = 162 * $0.20/paper

            = $32.40

vi. Ordered 171 papers, demand was 153, thus sold only 153 papers, with 18 papers leftover

    Profit   = 153 * $0.20/paper − (18) papers * $0.45/paper + 18 papers * $0.05/paper salvage value

            = $23.40

Total profit from sale of 153 papers * $0.20 profit/paper * 20 days = $612.00.

Alternatively, if Maria orders an additional 9 papers (i.e., 162 papers each day), 95 percent of the time all those additional 9 papers would be sold every day ($P(d \geq 162 = 0.95)$. However, 5 percent of the time, when demand is just 153 papers, those additional 9 papers would be returned as salvage at $0.05/paper. Thus, those marginal 9 papers that increase the original order quantity of 153 papers to 162 papers contribute:

Marginal profit = [0.95(0.20 profit/paper) − 0.05($0.45 cost/paper − $0.05 salvage value/paper)] * 9 papers * 20 days
= $30.60

Thus,

Profit for ordering 153 papers/day for 20 days   = $612
Profit from ordering an additional 9 papers (total 162 papers/day) for 20 days   = $30.60
Total profit from ordering 162 papers/day for 20 days   = $642.60

Maria should stop increasing the size of her orders when the marginal profit from the additional quantities turns negative—which happens when she increases the order size from 182 to 185 papers (Table 8.5). Note that even if Maria strays a bit from the ideal order quantity, the total profits do not change much. The optimal solution is relatively flat bottomed, accommodating minor errors in estimating costs.

B. Newsvendor Model

Maria will go on increasing the order size Q, as long as:

[Probability of selling additional unit * unit profit] $\geq$ [probability of not selling additional unit * unit loss], or

$[P(d \geq Q) * C_s] \geq [P(d < Q) * C_o]$, or

$[P(d \geq Q) * C_s] \geq [1 - P(d \geq Q)] * C_o$, or switching sides

$[1 - P(d \geq Q)] * C_o \leq [P(d \geq Q) * C_s]$, Opening up the LHS

$[C_o - (C_o * P(d \geq Q))] \leq [P(d \geq Q) * C_s]$, Adding $C_o * P(d \geq Q)$ to each side

$C_o * P(d \geq Q) + [C_o - (C_o * P(d \geq Q))] \leq [P(d \geq Q) * C_s] + C_o * P(d \geq Q)$

Simplifying, $C_o \leq [P(d \geq Q) * C_s] + C_o * P(d \geq Q)$ Dividing both sides by $(C_o + C_s)$

$C_o / (C_o + C_s) \leq [P(d \geq Q) * C_s]/(C_o + C_s) + [C_o * P(d \geq Q)]/(C_o + C_s)$

$\leq [P(d \geq Q) * C_s] + [C_o * P(d \geq Q)]/(C_o + C_s)$

$\leq [P(d \geq Q) (C_s + C_o]/(C_o + C_s)$,

Thus,

$C_o / (C_o + C_s) \leq P(d \geq Q)$

Expected revenue from ordering an additional paper ≥ Expected loss from ordering an additional paper, or
In other words, find that order quantity Q, where the probability of demand being equal to or greater than Q is $\geq C_o/(C_o + C_s)$.
$C_o/(C_o + C_s)$ is called the 'Critical Ratio.'

For Maria, profit = \$0.20/paper = cost of stock-out C_s
Cost of leftover excess stock = C_o = cost of a paper to Maria – salvage value = \$0.45 – \$0.05 = \$0.40/ paper
Order size = Q; demand = d

Substituting values of C_s = \$0.20; C_o = \$0.40/paper from Maria's business, the critical ratio becomes:

$$C_o/(C_o + C_s) = 0.40/0.60 = 0.67$$

From table 8.3, reproduced partially in table 8.5, find that order quantity Q (column 3) such that the probability of demand being equal to or greater than Q—that is, $(P(d \geq Q)$—is ≥ 0.67. To do that, first look at column 4 to identify that $P(d \geq Q)$ value that is equal to or immediately greater than the critical ratio 0.67. It is 0.70, corresponding to an order quantity Q of 182 papers (see column 3). We get the same result as from the marginal analysis table. Maria should order 182 papers every day in order to maximize her profit over the next 20 days.

Table 8.5 Partial Reproduction of Table 8.3—Historical Demand for Past 20 Days

Demand over past 20 days	Probability of this demand	If Maria would order this qty Q	Then the probability of future demand being equal to or > Q, i.e., P(d ≥ Q), would be
153	0.05 (1/20; Note 153 demand occurred just once in the 20 days of data) + ...	153	$P(d = 153) + P$ (future demand being > 153) $= 0.05 + \sum[P(d = 162) = 0.05 + P(d = 171) = 0.10 + P(d = 178) = 0.05 + P(d = 181) = 0.05$ $P(d = 237$ papers$) = 0.05]$ $= 0.05 + 0.95$ $= 1.00$
162	0.05	162	$P(d = 162) + P$ (future demand being > 162) $= 0.05 + 0.90$ $= 0.95$
171	0.10 (2/20; 171 demand occurred twice in the the 20 days of data)	171	$P(d = 171) + P$ (future demand being > 171) $= 0.10 + 0.80$ $= 0.90$
178	0.05	178	0.80
181	0.05	181	0.75
182	0.05	182	**0.70**
185	0.05	185	0.65
186.........			

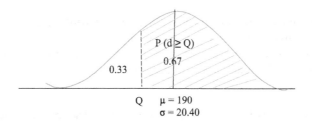

Figure 8.10 Distribution of Daily Newspaper Demand

If demand is distributed normally, the critical ratio represents the area under the demand curve, corresponding to the optimal z value and order size d. For example, the mean and standard distribution of Maria's historical 20 days demand data (table 8.5) is 190 and 20.40. If we assume that the data is normally distributed, then:

Critical ratio = 0.67
Corresponding z value = 0.44
$Q = \mu - 0.56* \sigma = 190 - 0.44 * 20.40 = 181.03$

So the optimal order size with the data normally distributed would be 181 or 182 orders. We observe that the optimal order quantity is lower than the average demand of 190 papers. Why is it so? Note that the profit margin/cost of stock-out C_s ($0.20/paper) is lower than the cost of leftover excess stock C_o ($0.40/paper). It's more expensive ($0.40/paper) to over-order and carry excess compared to the forgone profit ($0.20/paper) from running out. As such, we tend to order less than average demand. Conversely, products with high stock-out costs, C_s, (e.g., high profit margins or customers who'd leave us forever) relative to the cost of excess stocks, C_o, will tend to order more than the average demand. Low C_o's and very high C_s's seen in products such as designer dresses can drive ordering and stocking levels to average CSLs (cycle service level) of close to 1.00. The downside is that large orders and high stock levels translate into significant capital tied up in inventory. A high C_s leads to more capital being locked up by larger orders and higher inventory levels. Capital needs can be reduced by lowering the cost of stocking out (C_s) by offering similar profit margin substitutes to the customer, such that if a particular product becomes unavailable, the customer may buy the substitute. Designer dresses may not fit the bill, but men's shirts do.

Managers, though, may not always follow newsvendor model recommendations. Even if there is a high C_s, that is, high lost profits from not having enough stock, managers may prefer to under-order, since no record is usually maintained of customers who walk away, whereas excess inventory can be very visible in the store. Other times, managers order more than the newsvendor recommendation, even for items with a high C_o, that is, high cost of unsold stock. They seem to be psychologically unable to order less of an item when demand exists, even when inventory models tell them that it's economically beneficial, in fact, to turn some customers away.

Besides being used for determining a one-time single order placement, the newsvendor model's logic can be applied for other decisions such as establishing safety stocks, setting target inventory levels, determining a final production run, and making capacity decisions. The model can be applied where there's a single decision variable, random demand, and good estimates of stock-out and excess stock costs. Many extensions of the model exist, including the case when stock from one season can be carried over to the next.

In Summary

- Single-order quantity policies use marginal analyses that compare the expected profits from alternative order quantities for a given discrete distribution of demand.
- The newsvendor model fixes a single order quantity by continuing to add units to the order until the expected profit from ordering one more unit becomes zero.

Example:
Baruch College Bookstore sells T-shirts for college special events. The shirts are sold during the event at $20 each—unsold shirts are sold after the event for $4 apiece. The purchase cost to Baruch Bookstore is $8 for each T-shirt. Using the following empirical estimate of demand, how many T-shirts should the bookstore order (Q)?

Demand	Probability	$P(d \geq Q)$ *if* $Q = qty$ *in 'Demand' column.*
300	0.05	1.00
400	0.10	0.95
500	0.40	0.85
600	0.30	0.45
700	0.10	0.15
800	0.05	0.05

$C_o = \$8 - \$4 = \$4$; $C_s = 12$
$CR = 4/(12 + 4) = .25$; so order only so much such that the probability of demand > than order qty is 0.25. There's a 45 percent chance that d will be equal to or greater than 600, so order 600.

So order 500–600, based on this distribution.

Alternatively, compute the expected profit for each possible ordering level across the six levels of demand and choose that order level that maximizes the expected profit. For example, if we order 500, than the expected profit is:

Demand	Probability	Profit at 500 order level
300	0.05	$300 * 12 - 200 * 4 = \$2,800 * 0.05$
400	0.10	$400 * 12 - 100 * 4 = \$4,400 * 0.10$
500	0.40	$500 * 12 = \$6,000 * 0.40**$
600	0.30	$500 * 12 = \$6,000 * 0.30$
700	0.10	$500 * 12 = \$6,000 * 0.10$
800	0.05	$500 * 12 = \$6,000 * 0.05$
Expected Profit		$= \$5,680$ (sum of above)

** We have 500, so we sell 500 even though the demand is 600—do not include the potential lost profit from the 100 lost sales. Similarly, compute the expected profit at order levels of 300, 400, 600, 700 and 800. The expected profit maximizes at an order level of 600 ($6,000).

So order 600 T-shirts.

Alternatively, compute expected (= average) demand (545) and standard deviation of demand (112.25). Assume demand is normally distributed. $CR = 0.25$ = probability that demand would exceed order quantity.

Z corresponding to area of $0.75 = 0.67$
Order qty = expected demand + Z (std. dev) = $545 + 0.67 * 112 = 620$ T-shirts

EOQ with Volume Price Discounts

The traditional EOQ model can be extended to provide 'how much to order' recommendations when the supplier offers a price discount(s) at different order volumes. If we buy more, we spend less and place fewer orders but end up holding more inventory. So the basic question is: Is the price break large enough to compensate for the increased holding cost? In the traditional EOQ model, purchase price does not change with volume, so total cost is the sum of total ordering cost and total holding cost. However, in the volume price discounting model, since purchase price varies with volume,

Total cost = total ordering cost + total holding cost + total purchasing cost
Or,

TC = TOC + THC + TPC   (Equation 1)
   = $(D/Q) * S + (Q/2) * H$ + unit price * qty purchased
   = $(D/Q) * S + (Q/2) * H + P * D$

Where,
D = annual demand; Q = quantity of a single order; s = administrative cost of placing an order, H = cost of holding 1 unit for 1 year, P = unit price

The traditional EOQ total cost curve is a single curve with a minimum point. With the introduction of multiple price levels, there is a separate total cost curve for every price break level (discount levels), with different minimum points. We compute EOQs for all price levels, starting with the *lowest price* offered. We then compare total costs for possible purchase order quantities.

For example, a retail warehouse store is offering a discount on flavored water bottles:

Buy	Price
1–19 bottles	$1.60/bottle
20–39 bottles	$1.20/bottle
> 39 bottles	$0.99/bottle

Suppose our annual consumption (D) of flavored water is 300 bottles, ordering cost (S) = $1/order (going to store gas + time), and holding cost (H) = 60% of item cost (high, since you don't want to drink water that has been kept long).

Using the traditional formula, and beginning with the lowest price of $0.99/bottle:

At $0.99 purchase price

EOQ = $\sqrt{[(2 * D * S)/H]}$
    = $\sqrt{[(2 * 300 * 1)/(0.60 * \$0.99]}$
    = 31.78 = buy 32 bottles at a time

But buying 32 bottles is not possible @0.99 each, since the minimum order quantity at this rate is 40 bottles. So we compute the EOQ at the next price break point of $1.20/bottle.

At $1.20 purchase price:

EOQ = $\sqrt{[(2 * D * S)/H]}$
    = $\sqrt{[(2 * 300 * 1)/(0.60 * \$1.20]}$
    = 28.86 = buy 29 bottles at a time

$$TC = (D/Q) * S + (Q/2) * H + P * D \quad \text{(From equation 1 above)}$$
$$= (300/29) * 1 + (29/2) * 0.72 + \$1.20 * 300$$
$$= \$380.78$$

Now we can buy at \$0.99 if we buy a minimum of 40 bottles at a time. Let's compare the cost of doing that with the cost of ordering the EOQ of 29 bottles at a time at \$1.20/bottle.

Cost of buying 40 bottles at a time at \$0.99/bottle:

$$TC = (D/Q) * S + (Q/2) * H + P * D \quad \text{(from equation 1)}$$
$$= (300/40) * 1 + (40/2) * 0.594 + \$0.99 * 300$$
$$= \$316.38 \text{ (vs. \$380.78 for buying 29 bottles @\$1.20/bottle).}$$

We buy 40 bottles at \$0.99/bottle since that is the lowest total cost option. The total cost of buying at the remaining volume price of (1 to 19 bottles) at \$1.60/bottle is higher (EOQ = 25 bottles, which are actually priced at \$1.20/bottle).

Volume price discounts have to be approached carefully for perishable products like flowers or fish, where the holding costs are very high. A very large volume price discount is required in such cases. It may be better to negotiate price discounts on things other than order volume for perishable products, such as a discount for early payments or payment in cash.

When to Buy—JIT

A car plant makes about 240 cars per day. The cars are made in 2 shifts at 15 cars/hour per 8-hour shift. Each car requires a steering wheel. Since we know how much we generally need every shift, why can't we ask our supplier to deliver 120 steering wheels at the beginning of each shift? Better yet, why not ask for delivery of 60 steering wheels twice in a shift, or maybe even delivery of 15 steering wheels per hour. This is 'just-in-time' supply, popularly known as JIT. What it does is obvious—the plant's inventory and, thus, costs are dramatically reduced. Keeping a small safety stock to cover emergencies, the plant asks the supplier to begin supplying the steering wheels on an as-needed basis. If production is reduced for a time for any reason, the supplier is informed immediately or ahead of time and makes fewer steering wheels for that period. Of course, the swings in demand cannot be too large or frequent, as suppliers typically incur costs when adjusting production to demand. Similarly, the plant follows a JIT approach in its own production plans.

JIT says buy or make 'just in time' to meet demand. Popularized by Taiichi Ohno at Toyota, the just-in-time (JIT) philosophy has one basic goal—to unearth and remove waste in business operations. Waste, or '*muda*' in Japanese, according to Taiichi Ohno, comes in seven primary types: inventory, movement, waiting time, over-processing, over-production, and defects. Putting over-qualified people on a simple job is also considered a waste of human resources. A broader view is that waste is anything that adds a cost that the customer is not willing to pay for. Today, that cost is seen at a societal level, which we all pay directly or indirectly, as, for instance, the environmental damage caused by a coal-fired utility that supplies power to an auto plant, or the costs of collecting, transporting, and recycling/disposing discarded non-biodegradable bottles by municipalities. Focusing on inventory, Toyota's 'evils of inventory' checklist is well known:

- Inventory hides problems in the workplace by allowing workers to use inventory as a buffer against operational uncertainties, such as defectives, supplier problems, and workforce issues. A component was not made right—no problem, we have some good ones in stock. A machine broke down again—no problem, we have a back-up. The underlying problem of ineffective machine maintenance is, perhaps, not recognized widely since it is buffered by inventory from affecting immediate operations.

Figure 8.11 JIT Thinking

- Inventory removes the motivation to seek improvement. Few bother to find and address the root causes of machine breakdown or defective output because of the ready availability of inventory.
- Inventory causes delayed recognition of underlying problems.

Inventory is a buffer against just-in-case problems such as breakdowns and unanticipated disruptions in individual operations. Toyota says: remove inventory, uncover underlying problems, and eliminate root causes. Ultimately, there will be no need to carry inventory, since all major operational problems would have been uncovered and removed. With JIT, the usual inventory buffers are removed, meaning that operations can no longer be treated separately. A problem at one operation is now a problem for the whole system. But without inventory, costs will escalate—expediting, express freight shipments, split production lots and excessive setups, shortages, and stock-outs. So a better way may be to address more visible problems first and then reduce inventory *gradually*. A small amount of emergency inventory may be kept at strategic locations to be used in dire need, accounted for carefully, and analyzed for reason for use after the emergency is over. Lead time and ordering/set-up time reduction is a JIT prerequisite. The root causes for those problems that need addressing may lie in inefficient logistics, cumbersome plant layouts with excessive movement of material, ineffective machine maintenance, inefficient work processes, and misaligned worker compensation systems.

JIT asks that only what is immediately required be made. Consider the following:

Idle machines do not bother managers so much as idle employees. JIT takes a different approach. Nicole is not slacking off—that unused production capacity is there as a buffer for times when demand is greater than

Table 8.6 JIT—Prior and After

Before JIT	After JIT
• Nicole works an 8-hour shift.	• Nicole works an 8-hour shift
• Nicole makes 160 pieces during her shift. Today's demand is 120 pieces, so 40 pieces are kept in inventory.	• Today's demand is 120 pieces and Nicole makes 120 pieces
• Nicole's productivity = 160/8hr = 20 pieces/hr	• Nicole's productivity = 15 pieces/hr
• Nicole's a star!	• Nicole is a slacker! Unused capacity = 5 pieces/hr

100 pieces. What JIT has done is convert those 40 pieces of physical inventory into buffer capacity for peak demand periods. In the meantime, we should not fire Nicole or cut down her hours—instead, utilize that unused capacity to train her in quality and new techniques, teach her equipment maintenance, have her clean her workspace, encourage her to think of improvements in how she does her job and possible improvements in product design, engage her to mentor and train newer workers, and perhaps take her out to meet actual

customers once in a while. Note that demand is taken as a stable entity, a desirable goal for JIT systems. However, it is frequently not—which brings us to another principle of JIT—build in small and mixed lots.

A JIT system builds small lots of a variety of items, as and when demand dictates, instead of making large lots of one item and building stock. Imagine we work for an auto maker and were told to make the following models.

Table 8.7 Mixed Model Demand

Model	Weekly Demand
Aveo	250
Cruze	300
Malibu	400
Impala	190

We spend time and money to change machines, machine speeds, components, dies, and molds each time we switch to a different model. In a conventional system, for reasons of economies of scale, we would make one item for its full quantity before moving on to the next. Our production plan sequence for the week may look like this:

> Aveo, Aveo, Aveo, Aveo . . . complete 250 units of model Aveo, then,
> Cruze, Cruze, Cruze, Cruze . . . complete 300 units of model Cruze, then,
> Malibu, Malibu, Malibu, Malibu . . . complete 400 units of model Malibu, then,
> Impala, Impala, Impala, Impala . . . complete 190 units of model Impala

Whereas in a JIT system, we make just the quantity needed at the time required. Our production sequence would follow the demand pattern every day, which may look like this on a particular day of the week:

> Aveo, Aveo, Cruze, Impala, Malibu, Cruze, Malibu, Malibu, Aveo . . . Cruze

At the end of the week, we would have made the full weekly demand of all items, but only if those models and quantities were still required. We do not pick one model for bulk production at a time. Instead, we make in the daily or, in some cases, hourly sequence required by the market—what is called market-paced and mixed model production. The result is no inventory, and since we make on a daily demand pattern basis, no wasted production of any item, should there be an unanticipated change in the weekly demand mix of items. Well, what about those lost economies of scale, you may well ask? We compensate for that by drastic reductions in our inventory stocks, reductions in setup and lead times, and by identifying and resolving underlying waste-causing problems such as bad layouts and work procedures, poor quality materials, lack of standardization and sharing of components across models, and incompatible incentive schemes.

When to Buy—VMI

"Excuse me," you ask that person busy restocking a shelf at your local ShopRite/Kroger/Stop&Shop/Meijer, "could you please point me to the salsa aisle?" "Sorry," comes the response, "I am not a store employee." It is, in fact, a vendor's employee who is busy checking and replenishing his company's stock on the store's shelves. That product is VMI or vendor managed inventory. When to buy and stock is not the buyer's concern any more. The supplier owns and monitors inventory at site. Today, many plants have components and tools stock in secure locations inside the plant that is staffed by supplier personnel. Suppliers issue stock, monitor inventory, and place replenishment orders. The buyer pays only for material that is taken from the VMI stock. For small and low-value components, vending machines may be used, operated by codes or special passwords. Some VMI systems do not maintain local site inventory, but the decision to buy rests with the supplier. The buyer provides demand and inventory position data (usually via EDI or the Internet) to the supplier, allowing the supplier to reconcile buyer inventory position with buyer point-of-sale data. The supplier is responsible for placing an order (on itself) when it feels that inventory at the buyer site needs replenishment. Obviously, VMI provides a neat way to shift the cost and risk of holding inventory to the supplier. Pricing may be a bit higher, but the cost and risk avoidance compensates. There is of course, the risk of a stock-out, but there's usually an alternate supplier and contractual safeguards that would require the supplier to reimburse the buyer for the consequences of a stock-out. But what's in it for the vendor? Plenty, as it turns out. Boots and eyes inside your customers' stores can provide insights into customer demand patterns and store workings and offer opportunities to build relationships with store personnel, see how price discounts are passed on and work, monitor competitor actions on the ground, suggest better layout and presentation ideas to store managers, and, of course, ensure that your product is fully stocked and kept in a visible and accessible location at all times. Replenishment orders by vendors are, however, still better-driven by allowing them access to retail points of sale or real time plant usage data than by letting them estimate future demand from visits to the store/plant. Whether all customers would feel comfortable allowing such access to real time sales or usage data is another issue.

OM IN PRACTICE

VMI in the HD Drive Industry

The high tech hard disc drive industry faces market price declines of about 1 percent per week for some products. Keeping inventory is thus an expensive proposition. Retailers continue to push inventory ownership and responsibility to manufacturers, who, in turn, try to do the same to their own supply base. Seagate, the well-known disc maker, recently introduced a VMI system with its suppliers, using the services of a third party logistics provider (3PL). Seagate communicates real time demand to its 3PL provider, who communicates inventory and receipt data to Seagate plants and suppliers. The system uses a web-based collaboration platform. Lead times range from two hours to two days, and replenishments are made only when the user sees demand. Seagate now owns no component inventory and maintains no warehouses yet has been able to reduce flow time to the customer. Costs have gone down, and revenues have increased.

Adapted from: "Supply Chain Inventory Strategies Benchmark Report," *Aberdeen Group*, Dec. 2014.

9 Managing Quality

Managing Quality: A Road Map

Customer: *"Why should I choose you?"*
Business: *"Because we promise you that the quality of our products and services shall meet and surpass your expectations."*

9.1 What Is Quality?

"An iPhone, definitely!" called out most of my class. They were responding to my question asking them to choose between an HTC, Samsung, or iPhone. "Why?" Better quality, said Nikita. How so, I asked? Josh spoke up, "More apps." Others chimed in: features, looks, battery performance, price, feel, service, repair cost, carrier area coverage, or even that iconic "sent from my iPhone" line. What quickly became evident was that a) quality is defined in many ways and that b) specific quality dimensions appeal differently to different people. For manufactured products like phones, those individual differences are not too wide, can be measured in tangible terms (apps/features/battery life), and don't change that often. For service products, though, quality dimensions may frequently be much more intangible. How can one measure the experience of watching a movie or a concert? Let's take a closer look at both product and service quality.

9.1.1 Product Quality

Over the years, manufactured products and their users have been probed and prodded to get some common understanding of what quality stands for:

Performance: Is the product performing appropriate to the user's environment? Does the product fit and meet customer expectations regarding standards of use? Experiential reactions such as "It's difficult to use" or "Smells bad" or "Sounds flimsy" are less tangible yet important aspects of quality in product design and use.

Features: Any feature that matters to a user, including design and weight. Added features like wipers on car headlights, WIFI capability, or dual facing cameras or running 'Flash' on phones may differentiate a product. Features could include surprise and delight features (see discussion on Kano's model in chapter 3).

Reliability: Reliability means consistent performance over different operating conditions and increases with control over parts and components. It is particularly important for products that are generally repaired (not discarded) when they fail. Apple, as the sole maker of iPhones, exercises total control over development and integration of product and software. Google, in contrast, offers the open Android system to a number of phone manufacturers, including Motorola, HTC, Samsung, LG, and others. Different manufacturers mean hardware design differences and varying reliability.

Durability: Durability refers to the life of the product and can differ in different operating environments. Stop and go traffic generally wears out brake pads quicker as compared to driving on highways. Durability matters most for products that are used to their full life and then discarded (not repaired), such as light bulbs and batteries.

Serviceability: Ease of repair, particularly convenient location and easy access to consumable parts, and modular design for replaceable parts in a product design. For example, users cannot upgrade the memory or replace the batteries on their iPhones themselves. In Android phones, however, both batteries and memory can be changed by the user.

Aesthetics: Good looks and feel.

Brand: Brand benefits, ranging from assurance of quality to social status and re-sale value.

Conformance to: How well the manufacturer could make the product according to product design.
Specifications specifications—generally a concern of the manufacturer.

Can you update the list above? How about ethics, safety, security, confidentiality, and sustainability? Would you still buy that leather jacket if you knew that the workers who made it handled toxic leather tanning chemicals in the workplace? Would animal torture affect your perception of the quality of that burger you are putting into your mouth?

OM IN PRACTICE

Animal Welfare in Food Products

Sparboe Egg Farms were blacklisted by McDonald's for cruelty to hens. Hidden camera footage showed hens being stuffed into cages, beaks being burnt off, and other graphic incidents of animal mistreatment by workers. Sparboe Egg Farms has terminated the guilty employees and made changes to management. There are no laws that govern how an animal should be treated in such farms, but public reaction was probably a powerful factor in McDonald's decision. McDonald's states that its suppliers are charged with meeting "our stringent requirements for delivering high quality food prepared in a humane and responsible manner."

The incident has probably made other chicken purveyors like KFC and Popeyes re-examine their own supply lines. Target has since dropped Sparboe as a supplier of eggs to its stores. Ethical treatment of animals has long been an issue in fur apparel and cosmetic products. It is now emerging as an important element of quality for other products too. And Tyson is now directly conducting 'Farm Check' and 'Farm Animal Well Being' programs, auditing the treatment of animals at livestock and poultry farms with the help of veterinarians and animal welfare experts.

Another big buyer of eggs, Dunkin' Donuts aimed at 10 percent of eggs sourced for breakfast sandwiches in the U.S. will be cage-free by 2016's end—and is assessing how this can be done in its international operations too. In 2013 Dunkin' Donuts reached its goal to make 5 percent of its eggs cage-free by that year. Dunkin' Donuts has also committed by 2022 it will only source in the U.S. pork that does not use gestation crates, a metal pen that houses and confines a female pig.

Recently, Walmart made sweeping changes in its animal welfare rules. Concerned suppliers (and their suppliers, in turn) are required to investigate and comply with the 'Five Freedoms' of animal welfare by the Farm Animal Welfare Council:

1   *Freedom from Hunger and Thirst*—by providing ready access to fresh water and a diet to maintain full health and vigor.
2   *Freedom from Discomfort*—by providing appropriate environment including shelter and a comfortable resting area.
3   *Freedom from Pain, Injury or Disease*—by ensuring prevention or rapid diagnosis and treatment.
4   *Freedom to Express Normal Behavior*—by providing sufficient space, proper facilities and company of the animal's own kind.
5   *Freedom from Fear and Distress*—by ensuring conditions and treatment which avoid mental suffering.

In addition, antimicrobials should be limited to animals that are sick or at risk. The costs of the above policy, and how these costs shall be borne or distributed are not known yet. The benefit in terms of increased sales is also unclear, although avoiding negative press does have value for corporations.

Adapted from: Gina-Marie Cheeseman, "Walmart Adopts Groundbreaking Animal Welfare Policy," *Triple Pundit*, May 25, 2015, http://www.triplepundit.com/2015/05/walmart-adopts-groundbreaking-animal-welfare-policy/; "Dunkin' Donuts Eyes Shift to All Cage-Free Eggs Globally," *The Associated Press*, March 31, 2015. http://wwlp.com/2015/03/30/dunkin-donuts-eyes-shift-to-all-cage-free-eggs-globally/; Alise Blunk, "McDonald's Drops Egg Supplier after Animal Cruelty Footage," *NBCChicago.com*, Nov. 18, 2011, http://www.nbcchicago.com/news/business/McDonalds-Drops-Supplier-After-Animal-Cruelty-Footage-134128938.html; footage of mistreatment of animals at http://www.youtube.com/watch?feature=player_ embedded&v=r6E8H3C1CrU (warning: graphic), accessed Oct. 3, 2015.

Other factors like product carbon footprint and organic growing conditions have also become a part of the contemporary quality mosaic for products.

9.1.2 Service Quality

Beyoncé is fine as I rush to get ready in the morning, but Ariana Grande goes better with my evenings. Different singing styles spell better quality to me depending on the time of the day. Service quality is a complex phenomenon. We note that services are often consumed as experiences, and user reactions can vary widely in terms of taste and time. An opera sends this author reaching for Tylenol, while his spouse clasps her hands in joy. Yet other men around seem to enjoy that piercing coloratura soprano well enough (some fake it, I suspect). The challenge for a business is to find out which quality attributes appeal to the most customers, at a specific time or place, and to deliver on those attributes as consistently as possible. Identifying such attributes may be a problem, though. Users can tell if they like a song based on experienced feelings and sensations. Yet when pressed to state exactly what they like about the song, they cannot define it in words. Variance in delivery adds to the complexity of service quality. That chirpy checkout clerk we joshed with at the start of the 9 a.m. shift becomes unrecognizably impersonal and short-tempered by eight o'clock in the evening. Researchers grappling with such issues in service quality have surveyed thousands of businesses. From these studies, five generic dimensions of service quality have emerged:

Empathy: Provider's caring attitude, effort to understand customer's needs, ease of communication, and relational ties. For example, a plumber taking the time and thought to put on plastic wraps around his shoes before stepping into the house or a professor who allows a make-up test for a student who has been through a rough experience.

Assurance: Provider's knowledge and competence.

Responsiveness: Provider's timeliness in responding to user needs. For instance, responding to a student's email within a couple of hours or attending to a customer's phone call without delay.

Reliability: Consistency of provider performance and dependability. For example, making sure the cable guy turns up at the promised time or the #6 train comes on (or near) schedule every day.

Tangibles: Physical trappings surrounding the service that serve as cues about the quality of the service. For example, a UPS delivery person's service uniform represents the UPS company to the customer. Framed copies of license to practice and board certification in a doctor's office testify to the quality of the medical service provided. A single red rose on a spotless white tablecloth on a restaurant table signifies hygiene, organization, and taste.

We could add other service quality dimensions such as security, safety, and anonymity. Studies though, have shown that most users value reliability and responsiveness over service quality attributes such as tangibility or empathy. A well-dressed prof who cries with the student after a difficult exam is not of much use. You would definitely prefer a teacher who responds quickly to student concerns, displays consistency in teaching standards and grading practices, and is knowledgeable about the subject.

9.1.3 Quality's Heroes: Deming, Juran, and Crosby (and Notable Others)

Figure 9.1 W. Edwards Deming (CC license)

W. Edwards Deming (1900–1993), is widely considered to be the father of the quality movement in the U.S. and Japan. To him, the only meaningful definition of quality was what the consumer specifies, with as little variation around that as possible. But what if the customer does not know her needs, as Steve Jobs famously said while introducing Apple's novel products? Deming argued that while current needs are to be met, quality has a long-term component that is charged with anticipating the consumer's future needs. One way to do that, he said, would be to use his "Continuous Improvement Helix," based on the famous Deming PDCA Cycle (plan, do, study/check, act):

- Design the product.
- Manufacture the product and test it in the plant and the laboratory.
- Put it in the market.
- Test it in service. Find out what the user thinks of it, and why the nonuser has not bought it.

Figure 9.2 Joseph M. Juran (CC license)

Joseph M. Juran (1904–2008) was another quality guru and a contemporary of Deming. He defined quality as "fitness for use," meaning:

a) Product features that meet customer needs, and
b) Freedom from deficiencies.

Juran developed a quality trilogy to achieve these goals. Quality planning identifies the customer and his needs and designs a product accordingly for manufacture. Quality control ensures that the product is made according to design specifications. Quality improvement, the third part of the trilogy, involves evaluating customer reactions to the product, measuring gaps in performance, and providing feedback to control and plan for quality improvement. Juran also recognized the human factor in the quality trilogy and discussed the importance of manager education and training to overcome "cultural resistance," the human tendency to resist change.

Philip Crosby (1926–2001), a major contributor to the quality movement, took a more managerial view. Quality meant conformance to well-designed, well-defined, and well-communicated requirements. Crosby emphasized that quality has to be built in at the design stage. The guiding operating principle should be prevention of defects rather than detection and repair of defects during inspection. "Zero defects" is the goal, he said, not "close enough." This, Crosby said, could be achieved by educating the workforce about quality principles, the need to adhere to defined requirements, and close monitoring and documentation of failures.

Figure 9.3 Philip Crosby (CC license)

The three gurus of quality converged on the need to hear the customer and translate her voice into tangible quality dimensions. They also agreed on a customer feedback mechanism to ensure that product design and manufacturing could hear changes in customer needs. Their differences stem from differences in training and implementation. Deming, a statistician, stressed top-down driven application of quality principles, used statistical tools to monitor quality, and promoted the use of market research to determine customer needs. Juran, an engineer, focused more on product design and its ability to satisfy customer needs. Crosby, a manager, treated quality as a human-centered effort, with clear guidelines about quality standards. To illustrate, if hired as a consultant, Deming would typically have worked with top management to ensure company commitment and relied on a top-down organizational approach to drive quality through the organization. Businesses like McDonald's or service call centers with standardized processes and low skilled labor may be appropriate for Deming's top-down approach. But a company like Intel employing advanced engineering and scientific staff would benefit more from Juran's product design-based, engineering approach. Crosby may have been more successful in a human relations-intensive, high skill environment like a hospital. Perhaps he would begin with a townhall meeting to inform and enthuse employees and then bring them on board to accept and execute a "zero defect" make philosophy. Of course, the approaches can be mixed and matched to suit specific organizational conditions—the human relations element will be present to a degree in all situations.

There are other notable contributors to the quality movement. Armand Feigenbaum (1922–2014) examined the nature of quality costs and observed that the additional efforts in correcting quality failures amounts to having "a hidden plant" within a factory. Feigenbaum also pointed out that accountability is essential to quality management because when quality becomes "everybody's job," it may become "nobody's job." Walter Shewhart (1891–1967), Deming's teacher, introduced statistical process control charts as a tool to monitor quality in a production process. Shewhart spoke of the importance of reducing variation in a process. He also noted how continual process adjustment without first understanding the causes of variation could actually increase variation and degrade quality. Genichi Taguchi's (1924 - 2012) contributions include the "Taguchi loss function," which measures financial loss from variability in output, and other concepts in quality analysis. Kaoru Ishikawa (1915–1989) developed the Ishikawa diagram, which is used to investigate cause-and-effect relationships in tracing the root causes of quality problems. He also introduced the practice of workers forming quality circles to engage in off-work brainstorming.

KEY POINTS

- Quality for manufactured products is made up of dimensions such as performance, features, service, reliability, durability, aesthetics, and brand.
- Quality for services involves more subjective considerations of empathy, assurance, reliability, responsiveness, and tangibles.

- Service quality varies more than manufactured product quality since it is defined much more individually and is delivered by people.
- Deming characterized quality programs as a plan-do-check-act (PDCA) cycle. Juran espoused the quality trilogy of planning, control, and improvement. Crosby emphasized zero defects and getting it right the first time.
- While Deming preferred a top-down quality program introduction approach, Juran focused more on product and engineering. Crosby had a more strategic, people-oriented approach to quality initiatives.

9.2 Why Is Quality Important?

Quality is directly related to profits. Quality leaders can charge a premium on price for excellence in quality and create an upscale niche market or charge usual prices but provide higher quality to drive a market penetration strategy. Quality may also positively affect stock price, as found in several studies that looked at the effects of winning quality awards on share prices.

Quality has an after-life. A memory of poor quality accumulated over the years take years to change. A study of the Ford Mustang showed that quality improvements in the Mustang brand took more than two years to be recognized by car buyers.[1] It may even take longer, as seen in Hyundai's attempts to convince customers that it is a premium brand. Hyundai is haunted by a bad reputation dating back to quality problems in the 1980s and '90s, although it is up there with Lexus and Porsche in J.D. Power's initial quality rankings now.

Quality lowers cost and increases productivity. As explained by Deming, quality initiatives have a chain reaction through the enterprise. Costs go down through less rework, fewer mistakes, increased flow times, and better use of machines and material—leading to higher productivity, market growth, and higher employment.

Here's a typical job in the quality area:

Job Summary

The person hired for the position of **Quality Services Supervisor** will directly supervise and manage all functions involved in the testing of 3M products in an accurate, safe and economic fashion. Responsible for direct supervision, product quality, training, safety performance, cost control, employee communications, employee morale and productivity.

Primary Responsibilities include but are not limited to the following:

- Leads a quality team environment for employees by encouraging and implementing cross training programs, cooperation, flexibility and teamwork
- Schedules team to support testing of product on a 3 shift 5 days per week production environment (availability to resolve non-first shift issues)
- Implements quality programs within the plant that improves the customer experience, drives high quality product, improves productivity and reduces cost
- Coordinate necessary activities between plant functions to address quality, customer or compliance topics
- Supports plant production schedules to provide product in a timely manner, including investigating and resolving non-conforming material
- Assures quality tools and methodologies are consistently used, effectively and efficiently, across the plant

Basic Qualifications:

- Bachelor's degree or higher in an engineering and/or science discipline from an accredited university
- Minimum three (3) years of Quality and/or Manufacturing experience

Preferred Qualifications:

- Bachelor's degree or higher in a Science or Engineering discipline from an accredited University
- Minimum of five (5) years of Quality and Manufacturing experience in a medical device or another regulated environment
- Green Belt trained and/or previous statistical training
- Previous supervision experience
- Experience in a regulated environment, calibration systems, production testing and Certified Good Manufacturing Practices (cGMP)
- Skills include negotiation, statistical data analysis, Excel (intermediate), equipment and system troubleshooting, department budgeting and developing work instructions
- Experience leading cross-functional teams
- Excellent communications skills (oral, written and presentation)

Location: Irvine, CA

Source: Job listing on ASQ website, Sept. 29, 2015, http://careers.asq.org/jobs/7553338/quality-services-supervisor-irvine-ca, accessed Oct. 3, 2015.

9.3 How Is It Done?

Managing quality requires measurement, costing, analyzing, monitoring, and improvement. Let's look at these actions briefly, in turn.

9.3.1 Measuring Quality

How do we measure quality? When dimensions are known, metrics can be developed. For example, the 'tangibles' dimension of service quality could be measured through a combination of metrics such as:

- Are facilities attractive?
- Are staff dressed appropriately?
- Are written materials easy to understand?
- Does the technology look modern?

Product quality dimensions such as:

a) Reliability are measured in term of 'mean time between failures' (MTBF). A dishwasher fails, gets repaired, runs, fails again, gets repaired again, and so on—we compute the average time between failures.
b) Product durability is often measured as the 'mean time to failure' (MTTF). To find the MTTF for a battery, for example, several batteries are run until they fail, and the average time to failure is computed.

c)   In a mass production environment, service or manufacturing, quality is measured in terms of defectives parts per million (DPPM) or errors per million opportunities, or parts per million defective (PPM defective). What constitutes a defect or defective is up to the business to define.

d)   The technical measure of quality performance in a process is yield (see chapter 4, "Managing Processes"). Yield is simply the probability of making 'good' products/services.

Yield at a work step = # of good units/total # of units processed;

So, if a work step makes, say, 20,000 defective pieces of a total of 1 million pieces made in a specific time period:

Work step Yield = 980,000/1,000,000 = 0.98; that is on average, 98 pieces out of 100 made would be 'good,' while two pieces would be defective (at that work step).

Re-writing this in probability terms:

Probability of making a 'good' piece = 0.98

Probability of making a 'defective' piece = (1 – probability of making a 'good' piece) = 0.02

If there are other work steps involved in making the product, a total process yield could be computed, given the yields of individual work steps.

Yield can be very different for seemingly the same process. We take two situations:

1   The process will produce a defective piece if *any one work step* in the process makes an error.

Individual work steps cannot/do not return defects made by the preceding work step, but simply pass them along.

In a four-step process, assume the following yields (in parenthesis):

Step1→Step 2→Step 3→Step 4
(0.99) (0.99)   (0.99)   (0.99)

Step 1 makes one error on average for every 100 pieces made. All the 100 pieces, though, go on to Step 2, which works on the 99 good pieces received from Step 1. Step 2 has a yield of 0.99, so 99 percent of those 99 good pieces from Step 1 are processed correctly, meaning that 98.01 pieces (99 percent of 99 pieces) are made correctly—the one defective from Step 1 and the one defective from Step 2, too, pass on to Step 3. Step 3 similarly processes 99 percent of the 98 good pieces it gets from Step 2 correctly (97.02 pieces)—the two defectives it has received through Steps 1 and 2, and the one defective it makes itself, pass on to Step 4. Step 4, therefore, gets about 97 good pieces from Step 3 and in turn processes 99 percent of those 97 good pieces correctly, making 96 good pieces and one defective. Overall then, out of the 100 pieces entering the four-step process, 96 good pieces and four defectives emerge at the end. The yield of the process is the product of the yields of the individual work steps.

Process yield   = yield of Step 1 * yield of Step 2 * yield of Step 3 * yield of Step 4
= 0.99 * 0.99 * 0.99 * 0.99 = **0.96**

On average, this process will make 96 percent good pieces of the total number processed.

Process probability of making a 'good' piece = 0.96

Process probability of making a defective piece = (1 – probability of making a good piece) = 0.04

2   The process will produce a defective piece *only if every step* in the process makes an error:

Individual work steps *do* have the responsibility to catch and return defective pieces made by the preceding work step. This happens when quality checks are made at every step, such as the process of making sure that the right patient is picked for an operation. The nurse checks the patient's wrist tag (step 1), the stretcher attendant checks it again (step 2); the operating room nurse checks it yet again (step 3), and the final wrist-tag check is done by the operating surgeon (step 4). None of that absolutely guarantees that a heart patient will not get a fresh kidney, but the odds of making a mistake are considerably reduced. Note that an error can be made at any one step but is likely to be caught and rectified at the any of the following steps. The chances of the wrong patient being operated on would be very low, since every step would have to make an error in patient identification. In our four-step process from above,

Step1→Step 2→Step 3→Step 4
(0.99)   (0.99)   (0.99)   (0.99)

Process yield	= (1 − process probability of making a defective piece)
Process probability of making a defective piece	= (probability of an error at Step 1)
	*
	(probability of an error at Step 2)
	*
	(probability of an error at Step 3)
	*
	(probability of an error at Step 4)
Probability of making an error at a step	= (1 − probability of making a good piece)
	= (1 − yield of the step)

Therefore,

Process probability of making a defective piece	= (1 − 0.99) * (1 − 0.99) * (1 − 0.99) * (1 − 0.99)
	= (0.01) * (0.01) * (0.01) * (0.01)
	= 0.00000001, or 1 out of 100 million pieces will emerge defective at the end of the process and
Process yield	= (1 − probability of making a defective piece)
	= (1 − 0.00000001) = **0.99999999**

Multiple checks do improve quality (but do add to the work and increase costs).

QUICK CHECK

Cases have been reported of instruments or material left inside patients during operations. A hospital has instituted a standard operating procedure that has the surgeon, the operating nurse, and the assistant nurse each (and separately) count and account for the number of instruments and material used in an operation. The yield at the surgeon's and operating nurse's checkpoints is 0.99 each, while the assistant nurse's yield has been observed at 0.98.

  Which is correct?

a) The process will produce a defective piece if *any one work step* in the process makes an error.
b) The process will produce a defective piece *only if every step* in the process makes an error

What is the process yield?

Answer: b. Process probability of making an error = probability of surgeon making an error (1 − 0.99) * probability of operating nurse making an error (1 − 0.99) * probability of the assistant nurse making an error (1 − 0.98) = 0.000002

Therefore, process yield = (1 − process probability of making an error) = (1 − 0.000002) = 0.999998

It gets challenging to develop measures for more intangible dimensions such as sound and image, or dimensions that are felt but not expressed well by the user, such as a car ride that is not 'cushy enough.' Quality today has gone beyond technical failures like faulty parts and 'does not run well.' Poor quality could include things that are too hard to use, like an ill-placed radio knob, or a delayed delivery, or a car door that does not shut with that satisfying 'thunk' sound. In the Lexus plant in Ontario, one worker is dedicated to make sure the right sound—a reassuring thud—sounds when a passenger door slams shut. Have you ever thrilled to the *vroom-vroom* of a car engine exhaust as you floor that accelerator? Well, VW put in an artificial sound-making speaker that makes a mild-mannered engine sound like a V8 on steroids. That particular design innovation did not go over well with car enthusiasts, once discovered. At times, quality expectations are hard to fathom. Hummer owners knew about the miserable 10–13 mpg gas mileage prior to purchase but still downgraded the vehicle for 'excessive fuel consumption' after using it!

Whatever the metrics, measurements are compared to standards, and gaps are identified and investigated for improvement. The Malcolm Baldridge National Quality Award (MBNQA) is one such standard that evaluates quality on multiple dimensions.[2] Four U.S. companies—Price Waterhouse Cooper (PWC); Hill Country Memorial, Fredericksburg, Texas, (health care); St. David's HealthCare, Austin, Texas; and Elevations Credit Union, Boulder, Colo. (nonprofit)—were chosen as 2014 Baldrige Award recipients, from a field of 22 applicants. All applicants underwent rigorous evaluation by an independent board of examiners in seven areas defined by the Baldrige Criteria for Performance Excellence: leadership; strategic planning; customer focus; measurement, analysis and knowledge management; workforce focus; operations focus; and results. The Deming prize in Japan is a similarly coveted corporate quality rating and recognition award.

Quality standards are also embodied in the ISO (International Organization for Standardization) series of standards. Standards such as ISO 9000 and ISO 14000 prescribe and certify quality management and environmental quality management, respectively, among manufacturing and service organizations. Professional and accreditation bodies like the AACSB (Association to Advance Collegiate Schools of Business) and the AMA (American Medical Association) also prescribe and verify standards. Peer pressure is a more informal but powerful force for setting quality standards, especially in professional associations and teams. However, quality standards can become too exacting. Recently, workers at Foxconn, Apple's primary assembler, reportedly beat up plant quality inspection personnel for being faulted for microscopic scratches and tiny errors on the iPhones. The iPhone being made mandated an indentation standard of 0.02 mm—that's 25 times smaller than a grain of salt! Ultimately, iPhones and other electronics may demand precision manufacturing beyond human ability. Foxconn, Apple's primary manufacturing partner, has reportedly begun adding in-line x-ray imaging machines and has plans to add one million robots to its production lines. Neither human nor machine inspection, however, provide a 100 percent guarantee against defects.

Other raters do not set standards, as such, but provide detailed ratings, such as hotel reviews on TripAdvisor and consumer product reviews by Consumer Reports. Similar ratings are conducted by J.D. Power for autos, U.S. News "Best Colleges," and Castle Connolly in its annual ranking of top doctors. Data is collected and analyzed through user and peer feedback, technology-based stress testing, and destructive testing and inspections. Products are used, torn apart, or run to the ground in order to investigate the quality of parts and workmanship. Inspections are conducted by workers, testing/inspection machines, quality inspectors, NGOs (nongovernmental organization), and other third party agencies. Apple, for example, gets its own supplier quality and ethics internal ratings audited by the Fair Labor Association, an external independent body.

OM IN PRACTICE

Breast Implants: PIP's Jean-Claude Mas Gets Jail Sentence

Figure 9.4 Silicone Breast Implant

Source: FDA, April 1, 2009, http://www.fda.gov/ucm/groups/fdagov-public/documents/image/ucm259884.jpg.

Jean-Claude Mas, CEO of implant maker PIP, was sentenced to four years in prison for fraud by a French court in 2013. The company was found to have used industrial silicone gel—rather than medical-grade silicone—resulting in many implant ruptures around the world.

PIP (Poly Implant Prothese), French maker of breast implants, was regularly audited by external examiners for quality standards and performance. But instead of silicon, workers were pumping cheap industrial grade gel into implants. The toxic gel would be kept hidden away from quality examiner eyes in a separate warehouse and would also be loaded on trucks and driven around the city during auditor visits. Computer entries were changed, and workers celebrated with rounds of drinks after another "successful deception." The industrial grade gel costs $6.37/kg compared to the $52/kg cost of medical grade silicon that was supposed to be in the implants. The products ruptured after being implanted. After a massive recall of all PIP implants, the company declared bankruptcy.

Professionals suggest clarity in specifications and standards, a transparent process to know where rejects go, occasional presence at the production floor, formal supplier approval/certification, references, and required ISO certifications as ways to ensure that suppliers and manufacturers are meeting quality standards.

Adapted from: Heather Smith and Albertina Torsoli, "Europe Weighs Tougher Breast Implant Scrutiny," *Bloomberg Businessweek*, April 2–8, 2012, http://www.bloomberg.com/bw/articles/2012-03-29/europe-weighs-tougher-breast-implant-scrutiny/; "Q&A: PIP Breast Implants Health Scare," *BBC News*, Dec. 10, 2013, http://www.bbc.com/news/health-16391522.

9.3.2 The Cost of Quality

Instead of thinking about how much it costs to improve quality, let's ask a simple question: what are the costs of *not* having perfect quality? Any cost that would *not* have been incurred if there were no defects or failures or complaints, can be counted as a 'cost of quality.' We adopt Feigenbaum's classification to categorize all such costs under the respective costs of 'prevention,' 'appraisal,' and 'internal and external failure.' To illustrate:

Table 9.1 The Costs of Quality

Name	Description	Example
Appraisal costs	Any investment that helps to inspect and catch quality defects or failures, such as manual or machine inspection at the suppliers, inspectors at work, inspection of stocks, inspection of the final product.	A passenger walks through an airport security screening and is halted because she's carrying a filled water bottle. The cost to the airport is the wages of TSA inspectors as well as the cost of scanners.
Internal failure costs	Any cost that is incurred *after* a defective unit is caught during appraisal but *before* it reaches the customer, such as the costs of scrapping a unit, repair, re-inspection, and retesting, and discounting.	The passenger throws away the bottle, re-enters the security line and is cleared through security. The reappraisal (inspector wage/scanning cost) is classified as an *internal failure* cost (not an appraisal cost) because the cost was caused by a defective unit being reprocessed.
External failure costs	Any cost that is incurred when a defect/failure is discovered by the producer or consumer *after* the product reaches the market. Product recalls, warranty claims, discounts, returns and refurbishing costs, and legal class action suits are some such costs.	The passenger conceals a small bottle of water on his person during his second attempt at clearing security that is *not* detected at the security check. The bottle is noticed by a passenger in the plane, chaos ensues, and the plane returns to the airport. The passengers sue the airline and airport for security negligence and win.
Prevention costs	An investment that can *prevent* a defect or failure from happening *in the first place*, such as: training workers, redesigning products, and using better machines or suppliers.	The airport invests in warning signs, publicized penalties, and educative TV and web advertisements aimed at flyers. The goal is to ensure the passenger enters the security check line *without* any liquids *in the first place*.

Generally, external failure costs are the hardest to estimate since customers could react in many ways to a defect, from a simple acceptance of a replacement to a class action suit that bankrupts the company. Arthur Anderson, the accounting giant, disappeared from the business scene after external agencies found it culpable of irregularities at similarly bankrupted Enron Corporation. It has also been noticed that companies spent the least on prevention costs, although prevention is surely the best way to actually improve quality. One reason could be that prevention investments such as worker training take time to develop and deliver results, while hiring more inspectors or placating angry customers with freebies are readily visible and immediate problem-solving actions. Actions in prevention may also not have expected impacts if other costs are fixed. Consider the following scenarios:

Table 9.2 Quality Cost Interactions

Scenario	Prevention investments	Appraisal investments	Internal failure costs	External failure costs
IDEAL	Company trains workers and quality actually → improves.	Appraisal costs go down. Quality has → demonstrably improved, fewer inspectors are needed.	Go down since fewer defective products are → made, and thus fewer are found.	Go down since fewer defective products are made.
Fixed costs	Company trains workers and quality actually improves. →	Appraisal costs *remain unchanged*, since inspectors are unionized and cannot be → laid off or transferred to other jobs, or customer mandates 100% inspection (medicines, defense).	Go down since fewer defective products are made, and thus fewer are found. →	Go down since fewer defective products are made.
Wrong priorities	Company does not invest in prevention activities. →	Company adds inspectors. Appraisal costs go up. →	Internal failure costs *go up*, since more inspectors catch more defective products—note → that actual quality has not improved and the same # of defective products are being made. Sometimes adding more cops results in an increase in reported crime rate.	Go down since fewer defective products reach the market (most are caught internally by the added inspectors).

Deming and Juran thought that the rate of quality improvements from investing in prevention activities will eventually slow down as lower hanging fruit are plucked and opportunities become fewer and more expensive. Crosby, though, was of the view that price premiums and increases in market share would compensate for the costs of prevention investments, making quality improvements essentially 'free' for businesses.

KEY POINTS

- Quality performance is measured across multiple dimensions.
- Measures for intangible dimensions such as product sound and image are subjective and derived mainly from customer input.
- Evaluations and inspection are done internally as well as by external hired or independent raters, such as Malcolm Baldridge, ISO standard inspectors, and third party agencies.
- The cost of quality is best understood as the cost of not making a perfect product or service.
- Such costs can be classified into prevention, appraisal, and failure costs.
- Prevention costs aim to prevent defects from happening in the first place but take time to take effect.
- Appraisal costs are incurred during any kind of inspections at any stage.

- Failure costs accrue because of 'internal failures' where defects are caught and repaired/scrapped internally, and 'external failures' where the defect is detected by the customer.
- External failure costs are generally the highest and most difficult to estimate.
- Investing primarily in appraisal will not reduce the number of defectives being made.

9.3.3 Analyzing and Monitoring Quality

We can analyze quality using both nonstatistical and statistical tools. Here's a road map:

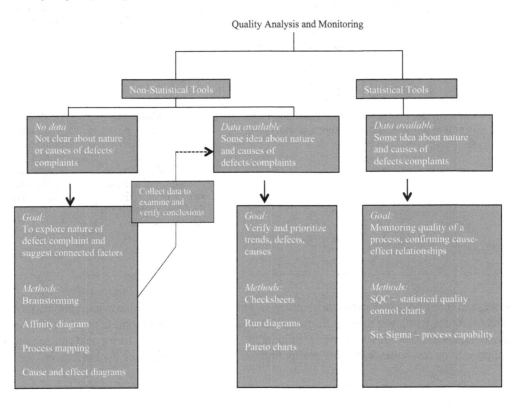

Figure 9.5 Quality Analysis Tools

Nonstatistical tools: Let's apply these tools to a quality complaint the NYC subway (MTA) often faces—train delays. MTA hosts a *brainstorming* session where employees and customers meet to discuss the issue and its causes. Basic rules such as no criticism apply, and perhaps a nominal group technique is followed where ideas are developed independently and then voted on, sometimes by anonymous ballot. These ideas can be consolidated into a smaller group of natural clusters such as 'equipment related,' 'passenger related' and so on—a technique called an '*affinity diagram.*' A *process map* is developed using flow diagrams and process charts (elaborated in chapter 4) to understand how trains are scheduled and run. The ideas developed by brainstorming are mapped onto the process map, identifying specific process steps where they occur/apply.

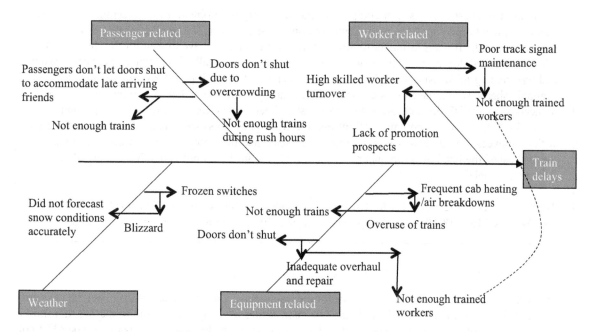

Figure 9.6 Cause and Effect Diagram

Finally, the gathered participants engage in an in-depth root cause analysis using a structured approach called the *cause and effect diagram*, also known as the 'fishbone chart,' based on its shape, or the 'Ishikawa diagram' after its developer, Professor Kaoru Ishikawa of the University of Tokyo.

As we can see, the head of the fishbone represents the central quality problem (train delays), while the four fins represent the cause categories possibly developed by an affinity diagram. The cause categories we use are up to us, typically examining issues of equipment, worker/user, material, and work methods, but should not be more than four to five to avoid confusion. We ask—why are trains delayed? We dig deep until most present agree on the root causes of the central quality concern. We do not need data to build a fishbone chart. The fishbone is particularly useful in surfacing basic causes and factors when the reasons for the quality issue are not well known or not well defined. The root causes suggested by this technique can then be verified by collecting data on relevant variables and looking for data-based relationships between such root causes and the quality problem.

OM IN PRACTICE

Applying Root Cause Analysis in the Hotel Industry

The general manager at the Four Seasons hotel at Dallas, TX, noticed that the front desk was slow in checking in arrivals. On asking, he found that rooms were not available, although the hotel was not at full capacity. Guests were checking out as scheduled. The GM tried to pin down the probable root cause(s) for the reduced availability of rooms. The GM kept probing, trying to see if there was an employee-, guest-, process-, or equipment-related underlying problem. In his meeting with housekeeping, a maid piped up: "Are we running low on king-size sheets?" The GM asked, "Why?" Well, replied the maid, "It takes us longer to turn over rooms because we have to wait for the sheets." After talking to several different functional groups in the hotel, he eventually found that a dryer had broken and was waiting for a spare part. The part was a special custom-built part. Fewer dryers meant fewer available sheets, which meant slower room cleaning and preparation by housekeeping, which, in turn, reduced room availability and caused the front desk to keep guests from checking in. The problem was solved in 24 hours. Open communications and the willingness to systematically look for root causes with employees directly involved in various processes made the difference. One wonders, though, if the GM asked the head of equipment maintenance, "Why did I, and not you, have to learn about this from your people?"

Adapted from: Peter Bregman, "The Real Secret of Thoroughly Excellent Companies," *Harvard Business Review Blog Network*, March 18, 2009, http://blogs.hbr.org/bregman/2009/03/the-real-secret-of-thoroughly.html.

Nonstatistical Tools (with Data)—Checksheets, Run Diagrams, Pareto Charts

Having identified a number of possible causes for the train delays, the MTA decides to collect data to verify these ideas. The first thing it does is to define what constitutes a 'delay.' According to the MTA, a train is considered to be delayed when it is late by six minutes or more at the last station on its route. The MTA collects data on the frequency of the root causes in the form of a *checksheet*, a sample of which is shown below:

Table 9.3 Checksheet

Cause	Week 1	Week 2	Week 3	Total
Train cab air conditioning failures	‖‖	‖‖	‖‖‖	12
Not enough skilled staff	‖‖‖ ‖‖	‖‖‖	‖‖	17
Door did not shut	‖	‖‖‖	‖‖‖	12
Total	15	13	13	41

What is the checksheet telling us? First, what's the most important cause for delay? The most common cause for delays appears to be lack of adequate skilled staff (17 counts). But the most important cause may be something else. If doors do not shut, the train does not move from the station, and all following trains have to stop. Air or heating failures may not bring the entire line down immediately. Second, is any one cause related to another? For example, would not having enough skilled workers affect the incidence of train cab air or heating failures? If so, taking care of the former would also solve the latter. What other inferences can we draw? The week does not seem to make a difference. A breakdown by day of the week, time of day, train line number, and age of train may help. Also, more data is required to make more definitive conclusions about patterns, if any.

Next, the MTA wishes to see if there's a trend in the data. A *run chart* can be used to see changes in observed data for a particular factor over a period of time. So the MTA collects more data and develops a run chart for the number of cab air/heating failures every week—the performance appears to be stable without any long term trend. The median can also be tracked (currently is week 5 data = 4 occurrences, approximately), and individual weekly data points compared to the median (above or below).

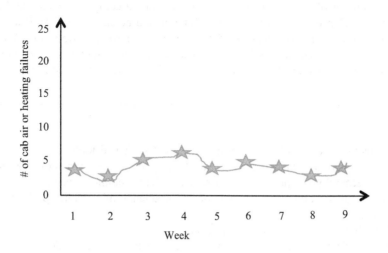

Figure 9.7 Run Chart

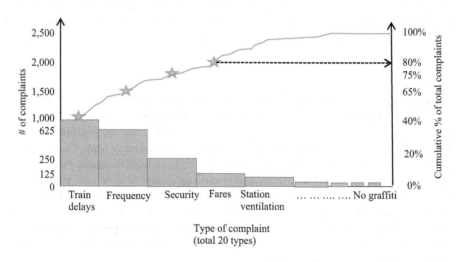

Figure 9.8 Pareto Chart

Besides train delays, the MTA also gets complaints about quality problems such as station cleanliness, security, fares, overcrowding, frequency, trains skipping stops, defective metro cards, broken down station stairs, slippery ceramic stairs, defective ticket machines, poorly ventilated stations, disruptions to traffic because of MTA work, smelly drivers/conductors, rude workers, tasteless ads in subway cars, wastefulness, no 'quiet' cars, slow moving tourists, and not enough decorative graffiti on drab station walls! The MTA uses Pareto's 80/20 rule to prioritize the type of complaint in descending order in the form of a Pareto chart (also discussed in earlier chapters). It finds that 80 percent of the total number of complaints received is about just 20 percent of the quality problems. That is, about 80 percent (2,000) of the total number of complaints received (say, 2,500), would concern just four (20 percent) of the 20 different types of complaints enumerated above. Accordingly, these four problems are treated first, resources permitting.

As we see above, just four types (20 percent of the 20 types) of complaints (train delays, frequency, security and fares) make up 80 percent of the total number of complaints received. The MTA weights each type of complaint equally in terms of consequence, so the most important complaint would be the one that has the highest number count. That would be train delays, which would be addressed first. But the MTA may treat security, for instance, as higher priority than train delays because of the more serious consequences associated—in which case the above chart will have to be revised, each type of complaint being weighted by both number count and some sort of a scale (e.g., 1 = low to 5 = high) reflecting severity of consequence.

KEY POINTS

- Quality analysis is done with both nonstatistical and statistical tools.
- The 'fishbone' chart is a nonstatistical tool for finding root causes, when the reasons for a quality problem are generally not precisely known or conflicting opinions exist.
- A checksheet collects and organizes data on the frequency of a quality problem—data patterns are examined.
- A run chart shows possible trends in the data.
- A Pareto chart identifies the few, most important, defects or causes of defects, based on Pareto's 80/20 rule.
- The 'importance' of a defect or complaint can be gauged not just by how often it occurs, but also by the relative severity of the consequences that follow from the defect or complaint.

Statistical Tools—SQC, Six Sigma

Statistical tools are used to a) monitor and signal when the quality performance of a process goes 'out of control' and b) identify relationships between the process variables and the quality performance variable.

SQC: Statistical quality control applies statistical sampling to monitor the performance of a product or service made by a process on a specific quality aspect—and sound a warning when that performance appears to go astray. Let's take the example of a hotel front desk. As the front desk manager, you find that the number of complaints about front desk delays in checking in guests has suddenly gone up—should you take action? SQC helps you to determine a) when to take action and b) when to leave the process alone, believing that performance will return to normalcy. What we need to understand is that every process, as proxied by its product or service, will have some amount of variation. It is impossible to produce absolutely identical outcomes in nature or business. The critical question is—"Is that variation 'normal' or 'abnormal'?" We answer that question by looking at the causes of variation.

Front desk delays can be caused by many factors, including:

1) Routinely under-staffed
2) Poorly trained staff
3) Frequent computer breakdowns
4) An employee who suddenly falls sick
5) A sudden rush of guests caused by a cancelled flight
6) A talkative guest who monopolizes the desk

Causes 1 to 3 can be anticipated by us, as managers, and should be our responsibility to fix and control. Reasons 4 to 6, on the other hand, are random events that cannot be predicted or anticipated well. We cannot control or address these issues easily. Deming calls the first types of causes *special* or *assignable*—causes that persist or happen fairly regularly. A special or assignable cause is one that is identifiable and predictable. As managers, we should be able to anticipate and control such causes. For instance, ill-trained staff can be sent for training or placed under an experienced mentor on the job. Similarly, frequent 'system is down' situations should be tackled by asking senior management for more reliable equipment and software. Random causes, in contrast, occur erratically, cannot be identified or predicted well, and are often beyond management control. A sudden sickness on the job cannot be anticipated or protected against—we could keep extra workers just in case, but that costs money! That random guest who decides to tell the story of her life to the front desk clerk cannot be anticipated or shooed away. Deming calls such random causes *'common causes.'* Common causes are natural factors that cause a natural range of variation. They are present in the environment but occur irregularly, without prior warning, and are generally unavoidable. Sometimes they can be hard to detect, such as natural internal wear and tear. There is no easy way to identify exactly how much life is left in a hard drive's components without taking it apart. And once they occur, common causes of variation can be difficult and expensive to control or protect against.

Deming said that, as managers, we should anticipate and take care of the special or assignable causes in the process. That's our job, and we cannot expect the worker to take responsibility. If we have done our job well as managers, the special causes should have been removed. Any remaining variation that we see in performance would be essentially normal and random, driven by common causes. These common causes cannot be anticipated or controlled well by managers. Under such conditions, the quality of a worker's output may zoom up one day and slip the next purely because of common causes over which she (and the manager) have no visibility or control. Why then penalize the worker for the 'normal' variation in output quality that occurs because of a common cause? According to Deming, we should not penalize (or reward) the worker for any positive/negative variation in performance.

In the context of our front desk checking-in time, both common and special causes will result in some variation around the mean checking-in time, with some earlier than usual check-ins, and some delayed check-ins. We have cause to worry if we find that the increase in customer complaints is being caused by special causes, meaning that we are not doing our job well enough. As managers, we should make sure that the special causes of variation have been tackled. This would reduce but not eliminate the variation around the mean checking-in time, since common causes would remain in the system. In the immediate run, we have no choice but to live with them and accept the fact some check-ins would be delayed, on a random basis. Over time, we may invest in technology or other areas to change the process, and remove the occurrence or impact of some common causes. For example, if the hotel invests in self-check kiosks, a sudden sick call out by a front desk employee will not make a difference to checking-in time.

In brief, our job as a manager is to reduce variation in performance outcomes. In doing so, we sort out the causes of variation into two buckets, common and special. We take care of the special causes, and learn to live with the remaining variation that is being driven by common causes. A system that is cleaned of special causes is called a 'clean' system (even though common causes remain) or a system that is in 'statistical control.' SQC is conducted on a system that has been bought into statistical control.

Quality control can be done by checking every unit that's made, but 100 percent inspection is costly, impractical, and not 100 percent reliable. SQC uses sampling. Sampling is more convenient and cost effective and nearly as reliable, when done properly. The basis for sampling is the *central limit theorem*, which essentially states that when enough samples of adequate size are taken from any process, the sample means would form a normal distribution. The average of the sample means distribution, thus formed, would be very close to the actual average of the process.

SQC watches over a system that is in statistical control, like an alarm system. It monitors movements in the system average on a regular basis by taking samples at intervals. It sounds a warning if it sees any unusual variations in sample readings, suggesting that a special cause has somehow crept back into the 'clean' system and rendered it 'out of statistical control.' SQC sets up charts made with data.

Table 9.4 Matching Type of Data with Type of SQC Chart

Type of data	Type of chart	What the chart does	Example
Variable	X-bar chart (averages chart)	Tracks sample averages	Average time for cops to respond to 911 calls over past month
Variable	R-chart (range chart)	Tracks sample ranges	Range of times cops took to respond to 911 calls over past month (difference between maximum response time and minimum response time)
Attribute	p-chart (proportion defective chart)	Tracks proportion of defectives*	Proportion of 911 calls responded to within, say, 10 minutes of receiving call at 911 call center—of all calls received over past month
Attribute	C-chart (count chart)	Tracks number of defects* in a piece	On average, how many defects (mistakes) did responders make on a 911 response call? For example, wrong address, wrong person, incorrect procedure, etc.

* A defect is an unsatisfactory outcome on a particular quality dimension—e.g., the Coca-Cola can did not contain 12 fluid oz. and/or the label on the Coca-Cola can was not printed legibly. A defective is a product or service that is considered unfit for reason of the presence of one or many types of quality defects. We could say a Coca-Cola can was a defective piece because it did not contain 12 fluid oz., or because it was not labeled properly, or perhaps because both types of defects were present. Typically, a defective product or service is discarded, or repaired, or replaced. Whether a particular defect is important enough to make an entire product or service defective is up to the business to decide (often based on customer reactions to that defect).

Data about the quality problem is collected in two forms: variable and attribute. Going back to our MTA example of train delays, the MTA could measure delays in two ways. One, count the actual length of the delay in terms of minutes for each train. Alternatively, it could just count the number of trains delayed, without noting the actual length of the delay. The former approach measures delay in terms of a continuous variable, time, which can be a fractional or decimal value; for example, a train is delayed by 2.35 minutes. The latter approach would just note that the train was delayed (or not)—an attribute measure that essentially classifies measurement into a discrete yes/no measurement category. Variable measures may tap dimensions like height, weight, diameter, speed, length, and direction of variation, while attribute measures apply a yes/no rule. A variable measure may measure the actual arrival times of Flight 601 at JFK over the past month and report the average variation around the actual scheduled arrival time. The corresponding attribute approach may just count the number of times Flight 601 did not come in on schedule in the past month. The attribute report would specify the proportion of flights that did not come in on schedule out of the total number of Flight 601 flights in that month. Similarly, an attribute measure of invoice accuracy may ask what proportion (or percentage) of invoices go out with errors exceeding ± 0.50 percent of the actual amount. Note that we define defective quality as 'an invoice that errs by more than ± 0.50 percent of the actual amount.' In contrast, a variable measure would show the magnitude and direction of the errors in those defective invoices—by *how much more* than ± 0.50 percent of the actual amount did the errors detected in those defective invoices vary? Obviously, variable measurement is preferable because it provides more information, but a simpler yes/no attribute measure is cheaper and quicker to do. The way we measure a quality aspect is important because SQC has separate charts for variable and attribute data.

KEY POINTS

- Variation around an 'ideal' specification is caused by common and special (assignable) causes.
- 'Normal' variation is driven by common causes that occur randomly and are difficult to predict or control.
- 'Abnormal' variation is due to special causes that can be anticipated and controlled by management.

- Managers are responsible for cleaning a process of 'special' causes, bringing it under 'statistical control.'
- SQC (statistical quality control) uses charts to monitor against special causes coming back into a system that has been brought under 'statistical control.'
- A quality characteristic can be measured in 'variable' (continuous) or 'attribute' (yes/no) format.

All the above SQC charts have a center line representing an average and upper and lower control limits that fix the limits of normal variation caused by the common causes that remain in a system in statistical control. Let us build and interpret a few types of charts to get a clearer understanding of how SQC works.

A 911 call center has been receiving customer complaints about delays in picking up phone calls. In consultation with the workers, the supervisor identifies and resolves special causes such as old equipment and new-hire training. The system is now considered to be in statistical control, and the remaining variation in call pick up time can be ascribed to common causes only. SQC charts are developed to monitor the average pick-up time and signal if and when the process goes out of control, that is, a special cause creeps back into the system. Since we're monitoring average pick-up time, X-bar and R-charts are used. Batches of 10 incoming calls are sampled at daily intervals to develop a series of sample mean pick-up times and sample pick-up time ranges. The data looks as follows:

X-bar and R-chart Example

Pick-up Times for Incoming 911 Calls

Sample the process to gather data
6 samples = # of samples (take one sample a day)
n = sample size = 10 calls per day (one sample/day)
$\bar{X}$ = Mean of the pick-up times across the 10 individual calls (not shown here) making up a sample
R = The difference between the maximum and minimum pick-up times (not shown here) in a sample of 10 calls

Sample#	$\bar{X}$	Sample R (range)
1.	10.2 seconds	1.0 seconds
2.	10.8	1.3
3.	11.4	1.8
4.	10.0	1.1
5.	10.9	1.6
6.	11.6	1.9
Total	64.90	8.7

Grand mean: 10.82 seconds   Average range: 1.45 seconds
    (64.9/6)   (8.7/6)

Use the data to make the chart
X-bar Chart
Upper control limit (UCL) = grand mean + 3 standard deviations
Lower control limit (LCL) = grand mean − 3 standard deviations

Equivalent formula using factor chart

UCL = grand mean + (A$_2$ * avg. range) = 10.82 + (.31 * 1.45) = 11.27   (Equation 9.1)

LCL = grand mean − (A$_2$ * avg. range) = 10.82 - (.31 * 1.45) = 10.37   (Equation 9.2)

R-chart

UCL = D$_4$ * avg. range = 1.78 * 1.45 = 2.58   (Equation 9.3)

LCL = D$_3$ * avg. range = 0.322 * 1.45 = 0.32   (Equation 9.4)

A$_2$, D$_3$, and D$_4$ are read from the 'factor chart for X and R-charts'—*see appendix*. Use the sample size (10 observations per day) to read off the relevant values of the factors. The UCL and LCL in both charts represent ±3 standard deviations from the center line grand mean/average range figures.

Using the above data:

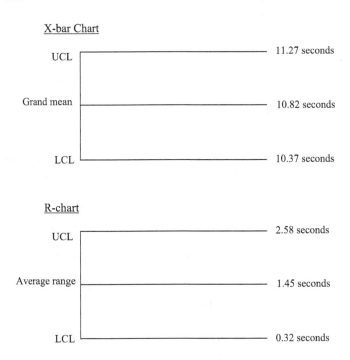

X-bar Chart

UCL ——————————————— 11.27 seconds

Grand mean ——————————————— 10.82 seconds

LCL ——————————————— 10.37 seconds

R-chart

UCL ——————————————— 2.58 seconds

Average range ——————————————— 1.45 seconds

LCL ——————————————— 0.32 seconds

Figure 9.9 SQC Charts

The charts show that the average time to pick up a call is 10.82 seconds. This time can vary between 10.37 seconds and 11.27 seconds. The variation is on account of the common causes present in the system. Similarly, the average range or the difference between the fastest individual call pick-up time and the slowest is, on average, 1.45 seconds. This difference can vary between 0.32 seconds to 2.58 seconds. This is the quality performance standard of the 911 call process when it is in statistical control. We cannot reduce the variation or improve the process mean without attacking the common causes of variation, a task that would likely require a complete and expensive revamp of the process. So we have to live with our process as it is, at least in the short term. We wish to make sure, though, that the process mean has not shifted and that the process variation has not increased. To do so, we use charting, watching the process, collecting *fresh* samples at regular intervals and plotting the sample means and sample ranges of the call pick-up times on the respective X-bar and R-charts. We sample more frequently initially and gradually space our samples if the process continues to behave. If anytime the sample mean and/or range goes out of the UCL or LCL boundaries, it signals that the process mean and/or process variability has shifted and that the process is no longer in statistical control.

We use both the charts together since the X-bar tells about the average, while the R-chart tells about the spread. An average can be misleading without information about the spread. In the Sahara, night temperatures could drop to 30°F while day temperatures could zoom to 120°F. Taking the average, it would be a pretty balmy Hawaii afternoon at 75°F. That is absurd, of course—the range (120°F–30°F) is too wide to treat the average temperature as a real figure.

We draw fresh samples and proceed to plot sample means and ranges on the X-bar and R-charts. The results are shown below. As we can see, the mean of our day 5 sample is out of the LCL bound, suggesting that the mean time for a call pick-up has shifted from 10.82 seconds. The process has gone out of control. The range, though, remains in control.

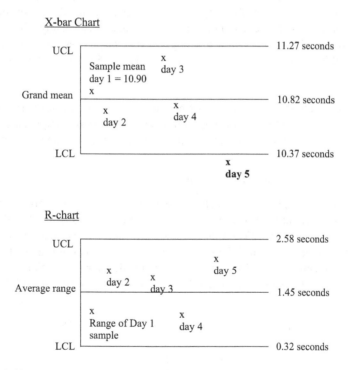

Figure 9.10 Using SQC Charts

A few commonly asked questions in such situations:

- Who plots the sample points on the chart?

  Answer: Typically a worker in the process, after being trained in SQC basics. The task of taking samples and plotting sample data on the SQC chart may be rotated among process workers. Managers should resist using the chart results for penalizing or rewarding individual workers—after all, if the process is in statistical control, any individual worker's performance will vary randomly. Besides, workers may not report out-of-control points if they fear penal action.

- What should we do?

    Answer: We should stop the process or isolate that part of the process.

- Why?

    Answer: Because a special cause has come back into our 'clean' process.

- Are you sure? Why not continue to collect samples and wait to see if another sample mean falls out of bounds?

    Answer: With ± 3 standard deviations ULC and LCLs, we are pretty sure that a sample data point that falls outside these limits indicates that the process has gone out of statistical control. Because the UCL and LCL are ± 3 standard deviations from the grand mean, covering 99.73 percent (0.9973) of the total area in a normal distribution (1.0000), the remaining area outside the UCL and LCL is only 0.27 percent (1 – 0.9973 = 0.0027) taken together. This means that there is only a 0.135 percent (0.27%/2) probability that a sample data point will fall outside the limits by chance when the process is still centered on the grand mean and is actually still in statistical control. In other words, the chances of making a wrong call, that the process has gone out of statistical control, while it still is actually in statistical control, is only 0.135 percent. This is called a 'type 1 error.'

- Is it good news or bad news?

    Answer: Statistically speaking, any out-of-bounds data point is bad news. However, from a practical point of view, the fact that the average call pickup time for the sample taken on day 5 is less than 10.37 seconds is good news! Of course, it would have been bad news all around if the data point happened to fall outside the UCL.

- What should we do after we stop or isolate the process?

    Answer: Have a game plan ready and have clear instructions for workers. Who should be contacted first? To whom should the worker report the out-of-control situation? Will there be a meeting? Where and who will attend? We want to find out the special cause that is responsible for the process going out of statistical control. However, since the special cause is actually reducing the pick-up time, we do not eliminate it. Instead, we nurture and develop the special cause and try to propagate it in our process. Perhaps we find that the special cause is a new hire with lots of experience who

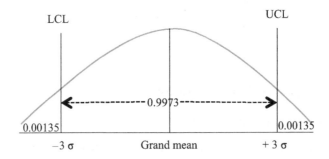

Figure 9.11 Chances of Making a Type 1 Error

has just joined the call center. Let's try to learn from her and have her mentor other workers. Of course, if the day 5 sample mean had fallen outside the UCL, we would have tried to identify and eliminate the guilty special cause.

- Does a sample data point have to fall outside the UCL or LCL for a process to be deemed to be out of statistical control?

   Answer: No—there are other indications, too. The variation in an 'in control' process is supposed to be driven by common (random) causes only. Therefore, we would expect that the data points from the samples should not form a pattern (because the variation is being driven by random causes). Here are a few examples of processes that display patterns in sample data points, suggestive that the process may be going out of statistical control.

Out-of-control process – trend (5 to 7 points)

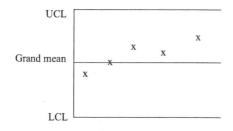

Out-of-control process – data points are concentrated above or below center line

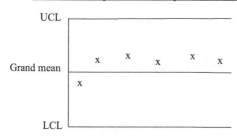

Out-of-control process – several data points near the UCL or LCL

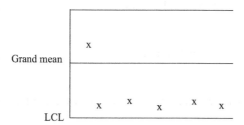

Figure 9.12 Indications of an Out-of-Control Process

For that matter, any discernible data pattern in a chart is a tip-off that the process may be going out of statistical control. The process should be examined for the return of a special cause(s).

Let's tackle a p-chart next. We follow the same procedure as we did for the other charts.

P-chart Example Attribute Data

"Were the front desk staff courteous?"
Respond either "Yes" or "No"
$n = 50$ guests per week
6 samples of 50 each

Sample #	Number defective	Fraction (or proportion) defective
1.	5	.10
2.	3	.06
3.	6	.12
4.	10	.20
5.	8	.16
6.	6	.12
	38	.76

Average proportion defective $\bar{p}$ = total # defective/total # of guests sampled
= 38/300
= .13

Alternatively:

Average proportion defective = total fraction defective/# of samples
= .76/6
= .13

Standard deviation = $\sqrt{[\text{avg. prop. defective} * (1 - \text{avg. prop. defective})/\text{sample size}]}$
= $\sqrt{[0.13 * 0.87)/50]}$
= 0.05

UCL = average proportion defective + Z * standard deviation   (Equation 9.5)
= .13 + (3 * 0.05) = 0.28

LCL = average proportion defective − Z * standard deviation   (Equation 9.6)
= .13 − (3 * 0.05) = (−)0.02 = 0

Note that the chart is not symmetrical because we truncate the LCL at 0 (we cannot have less than 0 proportion defective!).

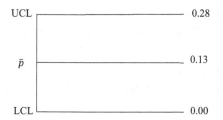

Figure 9.13 P-chart

After constructing the chart, we continue to sample the process and plot the sample proportion defectives on the chart. The chart is interpreted and used in the same manner as an X-bar or R-chart.

Let's do a c-chart next. C-charts are used to track the number of defects in a product/service. For example, a dining table may have surface marks, wood imperfections and veneer spots. The maker knows that the customer will tolerate imperfections, but not too many—hence, he wishes to count and monitor the average number of defects on a piece. After bringing the manufacturing process under statistical control (eliminating special causes), he develops a c-chart for this purpose. The underlying distribution is the Poisson, based on the notion that the defects occur randomly on each piece.

Building a C-chart

Monitoring the average # of defects on a piece
$n = 1$ piece
6 samples of 1 each

Sample #	Number of defects
1.	5
2.	3
3.	6
4.	2
5.	8
6.	6
	30

Average # of defects/piece $\bar{c}$ = total # defects/total # of pieces sampled
= 30/6
= 5
Standard deviation = $\sqrt{\bar{c}}$
= 2.24

UCL $= \bar{c} + 3$ standard deviations   (Equation 9.7)
       $= 5 + 3(2.24) = 11.72$ (using the normal approximation to the
                              Poisson distribution)

LCL $= \bar{c} - 3$ standard deviations   (Equation 9.8)
       $= 5 - 3(2.24) = (-)1.72 = 0$ (cannot have negative # of defects)

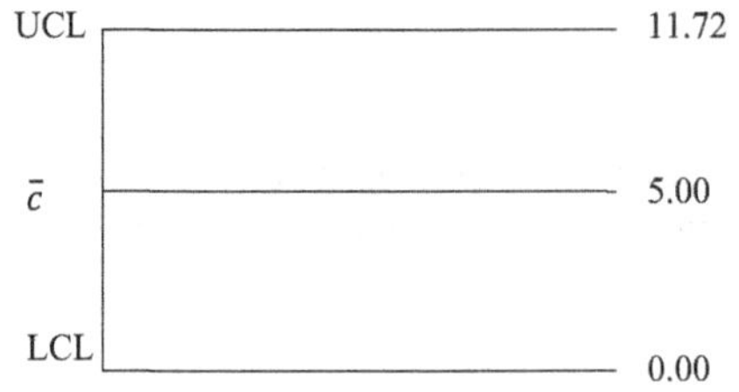

UCL ─────────────────── 11.72

$\bar{c}$ ─────────────────── 5.00

LCL ─────────────────── 0.00

Figure 9.14 C-chart

As with the other charts, we continue to sample the process and plot the results. The chart is interpreted and used in the same manner as an X-bar or R-chart.

SQC charts have many applications, such as lab test accuracy in a hospital, check processing accuracy in a bank, claim processing time and accuracy in an insurance company, response time for ambulances, and so on. Trading algorithms in Wall Street use SQC limits, as do autopilot software programs in airplanes.

Some cautions: Avoid starts or ends of working days for data collection—give the process some time to settle down. Single haywire units can slip through since sampling is employed. Also, one chart can track just one quality dimension in one product/service. A single auto gear can have up to 142 quality dimensions, calling for 142 SQC charts—we'll need a special chart room! Some quality aspects cannot be measured objectively, and some processes have very low defective rates. Workers will get tired of charting if defects are not detected once in a while. In such cases, it is better to conduct a quality audit from time to time, instead of continuous SQC charting. Another problem is that production runs of individual products may be too short for SQC in today's high variety-low sales markets. But perhaps the greatest lacuna in SQC charts is the absence of customer input. The UCL and LCL represent the natural range of what the process makes, but that spread may not be what the customer is willing to accept. A capable process is one that makes a product to the customer's ideal, with UCL and LCL variation that the customer will tolerate. We expand on process capability in the next section.

KEY POINTS

- SQC uses X-bar and R-charts to track the mean and range of a specific quality characteristic that has been measured in a variable format.
- Both p and c-charts use attribute data to monitor process proportion defective and mean number of defects/piece, respectively.

- SQC is not appropriate for operations that are low volume or have an extremely low proportion of defects.
- X-bar, R, *p*, or c-charts do not reflect the voice of the customer—they just tell us about whether the variation in a process has increased to a point where the process is statistically out of control.

Process capability and Six Sigma:

Going back to our 911 call center process, the current 'in statistical' control picture looks like this:

Figure 9.15 X-bar Chart

So how good *is* our process?

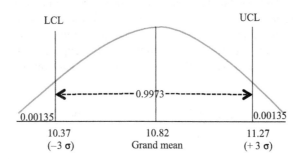

Figure 9.16 UCL and LCL Mapping on a Normal Curve

Moving the vertical axis by 90° allows us to map a normal curve over the process mean and process spread.

We can see that almost all (99.73 percent) of the 911 calls are picked up between 10.37 seconds and 11.27 second. That seems pretty good—but is it? Well, a survey says that callers are comfortable with a 10.82 second wait in general, but will not accept any wait beyond 10.97 seconds. They, of course, have no problem with a

0 second pickup time. In other words, the callers expect calls to be picked up in about 10.82 seconds but have tolerance limits (also called specification limits) that range between 0 seconds to 10.97 seconds. Mapping this on our current process:

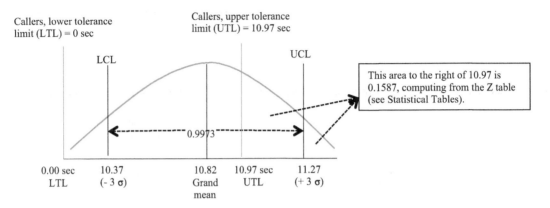

Figure 9.17 UTL and LTL Mapping on a Process

Practically none of the incoming calls are picked up in 0 seconds. That's OK, but about 15.87 percent of calls are picked up after 10.97 seconds and are defective pick-ups, from the customer's perspective. The 15.87 percent is calculated as follows. The process standard deviation = 0.15 seconds (from earlier), and thus 10.97 seconds would be the mean + 1 σ (area to the left of that = 0.8413, from Z table), and the area beyond that is 0.1587 (1 − 0.8413). The redeeming feature is that the process happens to be centered on 10.82 seconds, which is what the caller expects in general. A formula can compute the process capability index (C_{pk}), a measure of how well the process delivers on the customer's tolerances. The C_{pk} considers a) how far away the process mean is from what customer normally expects and b) what proportion of units are being made/delivered/performed within the customer's upper and lower tolerance limits (also called specification limits).

$$C_{pk} = \text{the minimum of} \left[\frac{\text{Grand Mean} - \text{LTL}}{3\sigma} \quad \text{or} \quad \frac{\text{UTL} - \text{Grand Mean}}{3\sigma} \right] \qquad \text{(Equation 9.9)}$$

In our case,

$$C_{pk} = \text{the minimum of} \left[\frac{10.82 - 0}{3(0.15)} \quad \text{or} \quad \frac{10.97 - 10.82}{3(0.15)} \right]$$

$$= \text{the minimum of } [24.04 \quad \text{or} \quad 0.333]$$
$$= 0.333$$

not a good capability index!

The higher the C_{pk}, the better the fit of the process output to the customer's needs. In our process, almost 16 percent of pickup times are not acceptable to the callers. We need to either persuade the callers to be more lenient in their standards (unlikely) or increase the C_{pk} of our process such that all calls are picked up within 10.97 seconds, the callers' UTL. How to do so? Looking at the C_{pk} formula above, one way would be to reduce the standard deviation of our process, making it tighter, and ensuring that everything (99.73 percent) is made with minimum variation from the process mean. Since the standard deviation would be reduced, the upper and lower control limits would naturally be lower numbers (mean ± 3 standard deviations), and the process spread would be minimized.

Consider, if our process standard deviation can be reduced to 0.05 seconds from 0.15 seconds:

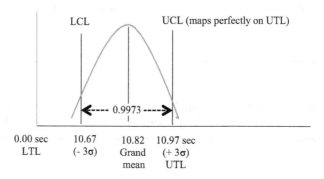

Figure 9.18 Perfect FIT between UTL and UCL

The C_{pk} for this improved process is 1.00.

If we could also lower the average process mean time to, say, 9.82 seconds from 10.82 seconds, and maintain our tightened standard deviation of 0.05, our C_{pk} would be further increased to 7.67 (see Figure 9.19).

$$C_{pk} = \left(\frac{UTL - \text{Grand Mean}}{3\sigma} \right) = \left(\frac{10.97 - 9.82}{3 \times 0.05} \right) = 7.67$$

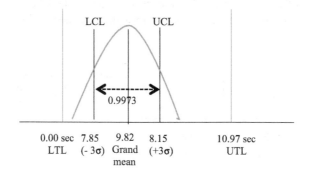

Figure 9.19 Process UCL and LCL Fall within Customer UTL and LTL

Companies like Motorola and Intel have achieved such low standard deviations that not just 99.73 percent ($\pm$ 3σ), but 99.9999998 percent ($\pm$ 6σ) of the process output falls within the customer's tolerance limits. The Six Sigma quality program is built on this premise. In a process making, say, one billion pieces a month, Six Sigma quality means that 99.9999998 percent of the output would be within customer tolerance limits (LTL to UTL), leaving just two pieces outside the tolerance limits. For Six Sigma, shifts in the mean to the extent of $\pm$1.5 standard deviations are acceptable, in which case about 3,400 parts per billion would fall outside the customer tolerance limits. The challenge is that customer expectations do not stay static. Demanding customers are less and less tolerant of products that do not deliver exactly what they want. Consequently, the supplying process has to be tightened and centered continuously in order to be able to deliver almost every piece very close to the customer's wish. We can figure out current sigma levels and by how much the standard deviation of a process needs to be lowered in order to achieve a Six Sigma process.

Computing Process Sigma

If we drop off our clothes by 7 a.m., Same Day Drycleaners promises to have them ready by 5 p.m. the same day. We can tolerate delays up to two hours—picking up our clothes latest by 7 p.m. on our drive back home. But this promised 10-hour turnaround is now actually averaging 11 hours, with a standard deviation of 2 hours.

a) *Is Same Day delivering Six Sigma quality to its customers?*

Seems unlikely, but let's do the numbers:
Customer's tolerance = 2 hrs around promised 10-hr turnaround
UTL = 12 hrs (10 hrs + 2 hrs); LTL = 8 hours (10 hrs − 2 hrs)
Process mean = 11 hrs, process standard deviation σ = 2 hrs,
Thus, current sigma levels are,
ZUTL = (UTL − mean)/σ = (12 − 11)/2 = **0.50**
and,
ZLTL = (mean − LTL)/σ = (11 − 8)/2 = **1.5** = use (−)1.5 since it's to the left of the mean.
The process is nowhere near Six Sigma! In fact, taking the UTL Z value, delivery is delayed beyond our (customer's) UTL of 12 hours almost 31 percent of the time. The LTL Z value does not have any practical significance here, since we have no problem with our clothes being made ready earlier than our UTL time.

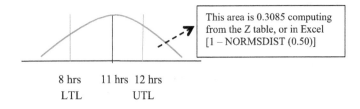

This area is 0.3085 computing from the Z table, or in Excel [1 − NORMSDIST (0.50)]

8 hrs   11 hrs   12 hrs
LTL   UTL

Figure 9.20 Process Capability

b)   *To what extent should the standard deviation be reduced to make this a Six Sigma process?*

We have to lower the mean from 11 hours to the promised 10 hours. But prior to that, we could reduce the standard deviation.

In a Six Sigma process, 99.9999998 percent of the output lies within the LTL and UTL ($\pm 6\sigma$). That is, the distance from the mean to the UTL and the LTL should be at least 6 standard deviations, respectively. Right now,

Distance of UTL from mean = 12 − 11 hrs = 1 hr, and

Distance of LTL from mean = 11 − 8 = 3 hrs

So,1 hr should represent at least a Six Sigma distance away from the mean, i.e.,

$6\sigma = 1$;

Therefore, our desired $\sigma = 1/6 = 0.1667$ hrs.

In order to achieve a Six Sigma process, Same Day Drycleaners will have to reduce the standard deviation of its delivery time from the existing 2 hrs to 0.1667 hrs.

To verify, we plug in the desired σ:

ZUTL = (UTL − mean)/σ = (12 − 11)/0.1667 = **5.999**, and

ZLTL = (mean − LTL)/σ = (11 − 8)/0.1667 = **17.996, so both sigma levels are ≥ 6**

The C_{pk} approach to quality measurement echoes Taguchi's take on process capability. Customers, according to Taguchi, want perfection every time. To the extent that there is variation from perfection, customer satisfaction declines. This view contrasts sharply with the traditional LTL-UTL school. The latter frames customer satisfaction as a yes/no phenomenon, with zero satisfaction if quality falls even a tad outside the LTL-UTL, and 100 percent satisfaction if it falls anywhere within those limits.

Figure 9.21 Traditional View of Acceptable Variation in Quality

Figure 9.22 Taguchi's View of Acceptable Variation in Quality

Perhaps more realistically, Taguchi's says that customers get increasingly upset as the quality of the product or service moves away from what they consider to be ideal. Taguchi calculated the cost (nonlinear) of moving away from this 'ideal' as the 'Taguchi Loss Function.'[3] A zero loss would correspond to a process where every piece is made and delivered to perfection, with zero variation.

Six Sigma is a popular catchword—phrases like "have a Six Sigma weekend" or a "Six Sigma date" are pretty common around a Six Sigma workplace. But Six Sigma is easier said than done. Recall that these processes are supposed to be in statistical control, that is, only common causes of variation operate, since all identifiable special causes have already been removed. As we know, common causes are notoriously difficult to anticipate or control—a mood swing in a worker or a customer who cannot make up his mind—cannot be typically predicted or controlled. We would have to retool our process to match the process mean to the customer's 'ideal' expectation. We would also have to reduce common causes, such that the variations around that mean fit within customer LTL and/or UTL. Six Sigma programs follow a roadmap called DMAIC: *Define* the problem in the process, *measure* process performance, *analyze* to ascertain root causes, *improve* by eliminating the root causes, and *control* with failproofing and SQC—which brings us to the challenge of improving quality.

KEY POINTS

- A measure of process capability is C_{pk}. It measures the extent to which:

  a) product mean deviates from the customer's 'ideal' and

  b) the LCL − UCL of the product's range of variation fits within customer tolerances.

- C_{pk} can be improved (increased) by:

  a) centering the process mean closer to the customer 'ideal' and

  b) by reducing the variance of the process (LCL − UCL spread) relative to the customer's tolerance limits (LTL − UTL).

- Six Sigma means the standard deviation of the process has been improved to such a small number that even output that falls as far away as ± 6 standard deviations from the process mean is acceptable to customers, that is, 99.9999998 percent of process production falls within a range that is acceptable to the customer.
- Taguchi opines that customer satisfaction declines the minute we move away from the customer's 'ideal,' disputing the traditional view that the customer stays happy as long as we remain within his LTL-UTL range.

9.3.4 Improving Quality

Who is responsible for improving quality? Deming tasked managers with removing as much variance as possible in the workplace by identifying and eliminating special causes of variation. Workers live their work processes day in and day out. What the manager has to do is draw upon the deep process understanding that the worker possesses. Workers contribute when motivated and treated as thinking human beings.

We have seen public places like foodcourts with overflowing bins. The janitor has to empty out the bins very often. Why doesn't it occur to him to suggest a larger trash bin? Probably because, at some point, he may have asked why and was told "because we have always done it this way here." This author remembers working in his college cafeteria, throwing out perfectly good food that didn't get sold—like complete trays of pork chops. As a perpetually hungry (and poor) student, I asked one of my supervisors, "Why"? Back came the curt response: "Because we said so." I shut up. Another supervisor later explained why—we could not give it to anyone for legal/safety reasons. Also, management thought allowing employees to eat or take away excess food might encourage us to make more intentionally. This supervisor was approachable and talked freely with everyone about their ambitions and backgrounds. She knew that I was working towards a degree in operations management, and asked if I had any ideas. *Workers have good ideas.* I did a simple forecasting exercise with seasonality for the most expensive items we made. The supervisor tried it out, and it worked! We threw away less—waste was reduced! I was applauded and got a raise. Lesson: Good managers motivate and provide opportunities and tools to workers to encourage them to contribute to process quality improvement. Deming propagated a TQM implementation program with 14 steps. The ones that stood out were a) the need to remove fear from the minds of workers and b) removing competition as a basis for work rewards and replacing it with cooperation. Ishikawa developed the practice of quality circles where workers could gather in self-governed teams to brainstorm improvements and receive a portion of the resultant savings. Managers saw that good ideas came from quality circles that received quick feedback and recognition.

Three Levers for Improving Quality

A simple equation identifies the three main levers for improving quality.

Quality improvement = CS + ES + CI, where
CS = customer satisfaction, ES = employee satisfaction and CI = continuous improvement.

Each area is measured, benchmarked, and then tasked for improvement. Let's begin with CS.

CUSTOMER SATISFACTION

If we consider customer satisfaction primarily as a product of quality, then:

CS = perceived quality = actual quality *minus* expected quality = AQ − EQ

In services we can work out CS quickly since consumption is immediate and actual quality is immediately experienced, e.g., a doctor's visit, taking a flight, watching a movie, or eating a hotdog. Consumers can experience actual quality in dimensions such as reliability, responsiveness, assurance, empathy, and tangibles as they consume the service. They can then compare actual quality, as experienced, to their a priori expectations in these dimensions. The larger the (positive) gap between AQ and EQ, the higher is the level of perceived quality that emerges from this comparison,

CS = perceived service quality = AQ − EQ

In fact, the above equation has been developed into a service quality evaluation instrument called 'SERVQUAL'[4]:

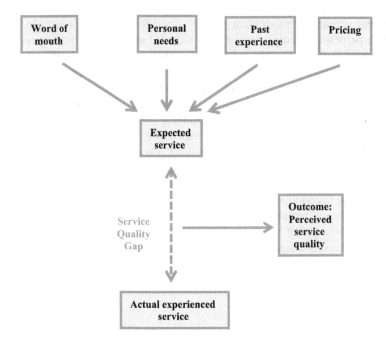

Figure 9.23 An Abbreviated Servqual Model

Perceived service quality = experienced service *minus* expected service. To increase perceived service quality, we can increase actual experienced service (AQ), and/or manage expected service (EQ). Deliberately lowering customer expectations through actions such as price reductions and offering a bare bones product is possible but can be dangerous to reputation and sales.

But CS is not that simple to measure in consumer durables and manufactured products. The average life expectancy of a car is now about 10 years. It'll take most of those years to evaluate and pass judgment on the actual quality of a car. Since actual quality is not known, CS for durables, at the point of purchase, is primarily a function of expected quality at the time. Which fact gives rise to some interesting scenarios:

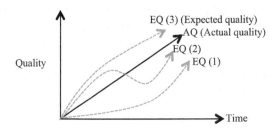

Figure 9.24 The Evolution of Expected Quality Compared to Actual Quality

Even though most businesses steadily increase the actual quality of their products over time, expected quality can take many trajectories. We assume that customer perceptions of expected quality would eventually meet reality (actual quality) at some point in time. Until that happens, however, expectations about quality need to be managed.

Situation EQ(1): When actual quality is higher than expected quality. Even though the actual quality of U.S. car makers has improved markedly over the past decade, perceptions of quality have not caught up fully. Car buyers generally still think and expect less of U.S. cars compared to Honda or Toyota cars.

Situation EQ(2): Expected quality is higher than actual quality at the beginning, but later drops below actual quality. Hyundai cars came in with a bang, riding on the success of Honda and Toyota in the 1980s. The public expectation was that anything 'Asian' (and sounding like 'Honda') must be better. But the first Hyundai cars were not well made, and quality perceptions of Hyundai cars soon plummeted. Today, Hyundai makes some of the finest cars in the world but is still laboring to completely lift its expected quality out of the shadow of the past.

Situation EQ(3): Expected quality is higher than actual quality and persists. A case in point is Toyota, where years of building good cars has built an enviable reputation for quality. Recent cracks in Toyota's armor (brake issues and recalls) have emerged, suggesting that actual quality may not be as high as thought of, but try to tell that to the car-buying public!

For durables, AQ takes a long time to be experienced by the customer, so we manage the evolution of EQ. Of the three situations, it makes most sense to pursue and maintain *EQ(3)* if possible. In other situations, too, EQ can be managed strategically through advertisements, warranties, and such to minimize the lag time between EQ and AQ. AQ, of course, has to be improved consistently in all cases. CS can be measured using a variety of methods, including claims, returns, surveys, focus groups, post service calls, and interviews.

We can try to improve CS using conceptual tools like Kano's model (see chapter 3—process design). Kano speaks of product features in terms of dis-satisfiers (must haves), satisfiers (more is better), and delighters (surprise quality). Anything less than 100 percent of 'dis-satisfier' features can damage CS, so we use *poka-yokes* and other failproofing methods to ensure that these are always present in our product. We also establish service-recovery programs for the inevitable failures, offering warranties, no-question-asked refunds, and other forms of compensation to affected customers. The challenge that remains is—how do we increase 'satisfiers' and create 'delighters' without breaking the bank? An innovative employee can often answer this question. But innovative workers cannot be dis-satisfied workers, which brings us to the second part of the quality equation: employee satisfaction (ES).

Employee satisfaction: While some studies report that happy workers do not guarantee a productive workplace, common sense suggests that dis-satisfied and, therefore, unhappy workers *will* guarantee poor performance. This effect becomes very visible when a dis-satisfied employee takes it out on the customer. ES can be measured with in-house surveys and with metrics such as employee turnover, absenteeism, employee morale, and number of employee suggestions. Employee satisfaction can be improved through equitable reward systems, appropriate training, and employee empowerment. An important element of employee satisfaction, especially in services, is dignity of work. A janitor in a hospital will feel better about his job and respond better when told that he is contributing to the medical task of maintaining the patient's health. The author has a friend who used to travel to Japan often (business or first class)—apparently, the airline he frequented paused the in-flight movie when he went to the restroom. The flight attendant also asked him what time he would like to have dinner! My friend ruminated—why do these people take such initiative? Don't they know that they are *not* important? Dignity of work and management appreciation makes an employee see how his/her own work connects to the customer's well-being and satisfaction—and that makes for a satisfied employee.

Continuous improvement: The third part of the equation, CI, essentially means never standing still. To paraphrase Lexus, CI is the "relentless pursuit of perfection." As a Honda CEO once said: The moment we say we have achieved quality perfection is the moment we begin to die. CI can be measured in different metrics depending on how the business and its customers define quality. It can be implemented in different ways, including:

- Supply chain management initiatives using better materials and suppliers
- Benchmarking against internal and external best-in-class processes and companies
- Process improvement through removing waste and cycle time reduction
- Activity-based costing that estimates product contribution margins more accurately than standard costing by allocating overhead costs per the exact amount of overhead consumed by a product
- Statistical and nonstatistical tools, as described earlier
- Reducing inventory, thus exposing faults and defects earlier in the process (elaborated on in chapter 8, section 8.3.3)
- Product redesign with fewer parts, improving product reliability, reducing manufacturing complexity, and reducing opportunities for failures
- Increased parts sharing among different products, although this may boomerang when a defective part shared across multiple products disables a wide range of products at the same time.

We begin to build a quality strategy by identifying the quality attributes that the customer wants. We then identify and classify order-winning attributes, benchmark ourselves, and target those attributes that we wish to compete on. Finally, we invest resources, as needed, in structural areas like technology and equipment as well as in infrastructural areas like the workforce, supply chain management, and quality management systems.

KEY POINTS

- Taking the initiative to improve quality is principally a management (not worker) responsibility.
- Quality improvement = (customer satisfaction + employee satisfaction + continuous improvement)

   Customer Satisfaction = (Actual Quality minus Expected Quality)

- Actual quality of services is experienced as soon as they are consumed.
- Since consumer durables are consumed over many years, quality improvements take time to register with consumers.
- Relative to services, consumer purchases of consumer durables are more dependent on expected quality, since actual quality is not completely known at the time.
- Employee empowerment and equitable compensation systems can increase employee satisfaction.
- Continuous improvement is pursued through many approaches, including process analysis, the use of quality tools, benchmarking, and supply chain management
- SERVQUAL describes a measurement process for evaluating consumers' opinions about service quality.

9.4 Was It Done Right?

Despite all the ways we can 'git 'er done,' quality improvement outcomes do not always meet expectations. Why not? Sometimes, the quality attributes that the customer actually prizes are not that obvious. Courtesy is a highly regarded quality attribute in all service businesses (barring *Seinfield*'s 'soup nazi' types). A call center handling technical calls spent a lot of money training its representatives on customer courtesy. Surprisingly, it then found that employees who stressed courtesy were being rated lower by callers compared to employees who were more factual and direct. There was no difference in technical abilities among the employees. Customer problems were similar, too, as also the time required to resolve them. The call center's investigation observed a few calls:

Polite employee	Direct employee
"Hello, It's a great day at XYZ co! How are you? How can I help you?"	"Hello? What's the problem?"
"You said that you get an error message while installing our software. We are so sorry for your trouble. I'll do my best to help you out right away. Let me look into it."	"You said that you get an error message while installing our software. Let me look into it."
Two minutes pass "I apologize for the delay—am still working on it."	*Does the same diagnosis* . "Well, I am now looking at the . . . . at our site. Oh, that doesn't show anything. Well, let me try this . . . .
Another three minutes pass "Still working in it"—"thanks for your patience"	"That worked , but I can't get your address inserted . . . let me try to . . . Can you try to do that on your computer too? Did it work? No—well, then—I'm
Two minutes later	going in deep. OK, now . . . we got you installed, but there's still a glitch in page recognition speed."
"Good news! I found out the reason. Here's what you need to do. . . ."	"I am now going to change the specs to conform to your particulars. Hang on. . . . got it! Here's what you need to do. . . ."
"Thanks for calling, and remember that we're always here 24/7 to serve you. Take care and have a great day!"	"Well, then, everything should be OK now. Bye."
Total time: 7 minutes	*Total time: 7 minutes*

The technical analysis, corrective actions, and the outcomes were identical for both employees. Why, then, did callers seem to prefer the more direct spoken customer representative?[5]

What else could go wrong? Implementation. Employees and customers barraged by slogans and messages about quality tune out. Ever ignored those safety preflight seatbelts and oxygen masks announcements on a plane? You're not alone. Airlines have tried everything to make passengers take notice of these routine preflight announcements—by making it nonroutine. Air New Zealand experimented with videos of naked flight attendants and exercise guru Richard Simmons leading a disco number. Cebu Airlines live-choreographed preflight announcements to Lady Gaga and Katy Perry recordings. On the ground, companies struggle to make quality initiatives meaningful for workers and believable for customers. It takes time, money, and visible commitment. Visible investments in worker training, consistent follow-up, management passion, and clear links of rewards to quality milestones and targets help.

Worker-manager disconnects can make matters worse. The author recalls visiting a plant with a colleague some years ago. We listened to glowing management descriptions of plant quality initiatives and were shown many performance charts. On our way out, we saw something that intrigued us—pools of bluish liquid around some machinery. We stopped and asked the operators what it was—"coolant," came the reply. Why is coolant spilled all around the machines, we asked? After some conversation, we put the pieces together. The workers were being compensated on a piece-work basis, so they wanted to operate flat out in order to make as much as possible. Not wanting to stop for any reason, they put coolant in running machinery—hence the spillage. The machines weren't getting fluids or maintenance and were being run to the ground. Product quality suffered, but the unspoken emphasis was on getting the 'stuff out of the door.' In that atmosphere, there was a clear disconnect between plant management quality exhortations and worker perceptions of the reality of quality priorities.

Six Sigma has also posed some unexpected problems. Centering and continuous tightening of the process to make everything as close to the customer's ideal as possible has, no doubt, improved quality. Yet it may have also created a working 'hell' for employees, placing them under constant and intense pressure to work harder and harder with less. Continuous improvement demands a relentless focus on efficiency, aiming to squeeze every little bit of variance out of the system. It can come with serious side-effects. Toyota's vaunted production system came under fire by an insider[6] who uncovered a culture of intimidation and subservience and a high rate of injuries due to inadequate training, fast line speeds, and crowded factories. Another troubling feature about Six Sigma is that process efficiency could discourage creativity and innovation. While Six Sigma emphasizes routine, waste reduction, and variance reduction, innovation thrives on experimentation and variance, and creates inevitable waste. Some companies strategically keep their regular process operations and Six Sigma initiatives completely separate from their innovation centers.

KEY POINTS

- What the customer considers important may not be readily apparent—observations help uncover deeper wants and causes.
- Worker and customer belief in quality initiatives requires visible and consistent commitment of resources by management.
- Six Sigma programs can stress variance reduction at the cost of employee creativity and innovation.

9.5 Current Trends in Quality Management

Formal quality initiatives are now emerging in health care, food, and supply chain management. Health care and food experience wide variances in standards, while quality failures in the supply chain are now quickly connected to company reputation. Technology has enabled quality advances in these areas.

- Quality in health care: Performance metrics in health care are resisted. The reasons are a lack of standardization of practices and apprehensions about being sued if found wanting against those metrics. Patients are ill informed about the quality of service and acceptable standard of care they will receive. The American Recovery and Reinvestment Act is changing things. Under the act, doctors and hospitals will have to move from paper charts to electronic records. A cardiologist, for example, would be able to access a patient's medical record from his or her primary care doctor. Easier and more complete access to medical records is expected to deliver standardized, evidence-based, best-practice care. The act reimburses part of the expense to convert to electronic format, provided the doctors show that they are actually using it. Doctors and hospitals that haven't made the move to electronic health records will receive lower payments from Medicare and Medicaid. Prepare to see more doctors with iPads.

- Food quality: Two dimensions in food quality have been getting much attention lately—food safety and animal welfare. The problem in ensuring food safety is traceability. An outbreak of salmonella in April 2008 led the FDA to point the finger toward raw tomatoes. After a three-month investigation, the FDA found that jalapeño peppers, not tomatoes, were the actual cause. In the meantime, more than 1,000 people fell sick, and many small tomato producers were wiped out. In July–August 2012, two died and many were sickened by eating cantaloupes infected with salmonella. The infection was ultimately traced to a farm in Indiana, but the fruit had been shipped to 21 states and points further. No one knew exactly where all the infected cantaloupes eventually went. The 2011 Food Safety Modernization Act created the first mandatory national safety standards for produce, but resource constraints hamper required federal inspections at farms and other food-handling facilities. Recent technological advances are helping. IBM's InfoSphere system attaches a unique QR bar code to foods that can track a product all the way from farms through slaughterhouses, shipping containers, and trucks to the grocery store. New tests from the Dutch RIKILT food institute can tell whether an egg or a ham is organic or not. The tests can also trace the geographical origins and authenticity of products such as cheese, butter, olive oil, *halal* meat, and wild salmon. We, as consumers, can also use certifying services while shopping. For example, products labeled by "Where Food Comes From" carry a unique QR Code that can be scanned and read by any smartphone, providing information about the people and processes behind the product.[7] In Ghana and Nigeria, rife with counterfeit medicines, mPedigree has launched a mobile verification service. Medicines come with scratch-off labels containing codes that users text to a system that checks and verifies the authenticity of the drug.

- Compliance act: Compliance is affecting raw material supply chains. The Conflict Minerals Act of 2010 charges users to identify and confirm that rare minerals are not being sourced from war zones in Congo. Conflict minerals are cassiterite (for tin), wolframite (for tungsten), coltan (for tantalum), and gold ore extracted from the Eastern Congo and processed and sold through a chain of intermediaries to electronics companies. These minerals are used in consumer electronics and other devices. Prior to the act, warring warlords could mine and sell freely—in 2009, tantalum mined in the Kivus and Katanga sold at $132/kg. Now, with legal constraints and monitoring mechanisms, conflict zone sellers find it difficult to find Western buyers, instead reportedly selling to Asian supply chains at an approximately 30 percent to 60 percent discount. The difficulty in monitoring point of origin is that these minerals are obtained and processed in hundreds of smelting companies—how can Intel or Apple possibly know the origin of each rare metal that comes out of a smelter? It can at best rely on the statements and record keeping of its smelters, who in turn must rely on the statements of their own suppliers for such metals. The Conflict Minerals Act and many companies are grappling with such practical problems—but it is here to stay.

OM IN PRACTICE

Sometime in mid-2011, Taiwanese food inspectors found chemicals called plasticizers in foods, beverages, and medicines being exported to countries including the U.S., China, and South Korea.

Plasticizers are industrial chemicals used to soften plastic containers. Taiwan's reputation for food safety was in jeopardy. President Ma Ying-jeou said the fact that "it ended up in our food products is unimaginable."

The plasticizers contamination was ultimately traced to two downstream suppliers, who used them as an alternative to more-expensive palm oil.

> Taiwan since introduced a mandatory food-tracking system, together with increased oversight of food manufacturers and plasticizer makers, more inspections, and tougher penalties.
>
> In the U.S., the FDA reportedly has been screening suspect products from Taiwan for DEHP—a toxic plasticizer—since 2011.
>
> Adapted from: Paul Mozur and Jenny Hsu, "Taiwan to improve food-tracking system following scare," *Wall Street Journal*, June 9, 2011, http://www.wsj.com/articles/SB10001424052702304259304576373104011409920.

- Ethics and morality: Ethics and morality have been part of the consumer's perception of quality—recall the recent furor over Apple's contract manufacturer, Foxconn's, treatment of workers. Of late, YouTube and social media driven exposures of animal mistreatment has extended such quality concerns to animals too. Demands for 'animal friendly' food chains are growing,[8] the logic being that while eating an animal may be natural, torturing it is not. Such sensitivities have compelled companies to take a hard look at supplier practices. McDonald's, in association with the Humane Society of the U.S., recently began pushing its pork suppliers to stop confining pigs in standing-room-only pens. Recently, In-N-Out severed ties with a California meat supplier after an abuse video surfaced showing mistreatment of animals. Food businesses like Chipotle and Campbell Soup are also active in this area. The moral and ethical dimensions of quality have become too visible and too important to reputation for businesses to ignore any longer.
- Big data: In all these and related problems in service and product quality, big data's role is becoming important and evident. Beyond Six Sigma and other variation-reducing initiatives, big data analysis has discovered relationships and patterns that are providing quality-related insights previously not possible. Particularly complex production processes like chemicals, pharmaceuticals, and mining can have hundreds of variables that affect yield. The 'internet of things' is providing real-time data to companies, which, when integrated and analyzed, helps identify patterns and relationships among process steps and inputs. This knowledge can be used to track and optimize processes and products. In bio-pharma, for example, a company collected detailed data about its production process, including materials, methods, and machinery. It stored the data centrally and applied data-mining techniques to find relationships and the effect of such relationships on process yield. The results led to process changes in selected parameters that increased yield by more than 50 percent—and millions of dollars in savings.[9]

KEY POINTS

- The American Recovery and Reinvestment Act is pushing medicine to move from manual to electronic operations, helping to track quality and standardize treatments.
- Tracing food recalls and infectious outbreaks to food origins is getting a boost from newly available technologies.
- Consumers now consider including animal welfare in addition to worker welfare as a part of product quality.
- Legal regulations like the Conflict Minerals Act are imposing accountability on supply chains.
- Big Data analysis offers opportunities to improve yields by discovering hidden inter-dependencies among process and product parameters.

9.6 Conclusion

Customer: *"Why should I choose you?"*
Business: *"Because we promise you that the quality of our products and services shall meet and surpass your expectations."*

What have we learned about how to define, measure, and improve quality? Quality is evaluated along many dimensions, some subjective, like taste and aesthetics. Consumer quality perception is a function of the difference between actual quality and expected quality. Consumers can evaluate service mostly immediately, but product durables take a longer time to experience and evaluate. We now are familiar with the tools used to analyze and monitor quality. We recognize that quality programs call for improvements in customer satisfaction, employee satisfaction, and continuous improvement. We understand that we can access a variety of statistical and nonstatistical tools to evaluate and control quality. We also understand that a process gains in capability as it moves its mean and tightens its variance to get as close to the customer ideal as possible.

As a manager, you would need all this knowledge, but implementation may be your biggest challenge. Build a compelling vision, provide consistent support with resources, and get out of the way. Evaluate results, and provide feedback with complete candor. As Jack Welch, the well-known ex-CEO of GE says: "Good business leaders create a vision, articulate the vision, passionately own the vision, and relentlessly drive it to completion."[10] Ignite your people's passion, and watch your quality programs zoom!

What Have We Learned?

What Is Quality?

- Quality is made up of many dimensions.
- The major dimensions of manufacturing quality include performance, features, reliability, durability, serviceability, aesthetics, brand, and conformance to manufacturing specifications. Ethics and morality are also emerging as elements of quality.
- The major dimensions of service quality include empathy, assurance, responsiveness, reliability, and tangibles.
- Deming, Juran, and Crosby were the three gurus of the quality movement. Deming saw variation as the principal evil and advocated a plan-do-check-act process for improving quality. Juran emphasized customer-based product design, using the customer to benchmark product quality in terms of a quality trilogy of planning, quality control, and quality improvement. Crosby focused on zero-defects as a principal quality goal, with an emphasis on getting the product right "the first time around."

Why Is It Important?

- Quality affects profits, enabling higher pricing or increased market share through lower production costs.
- Quality has a memory. Memories of poor quality linger on in the minds of consumers even when quality improves.

How Is It Done?

Measurement

- Each dimension of quality can be measured using specific metrics. Metrics for service quality and intangible 'experience' dimensions are more subjective.

- Quality ratings are conducted through quality awarding institutions such as the Malcolm Balridge National Quality Award, various ISO standards, and independent raters such as J.D. Power and third-party audit agencies.
- Yield is the probability of making a good unit at a particular work step or for an entire process.

Costs

- Not making perfect quality has a cost, classified as prevention costs, appraisal costs, and the cost of internal and external failure.
    - Prevention costs are investments made to prevent defects from happening in the first place.
    - Appraisal costs are investments made in inspection equipment, people, and the cost of external hiring of rating agencies.
    - Internal failure costs represent the expense of repairing or scrapping defectives caught in internal inspections.
    - External failure costs represent the expense of meeting warranty claims, loss of reputation, lawsuits, etc., when defectives are detected by the external customer/user.

Tools

- Quality analysis tools include nonstatistical (with and without data) and statistical tools.
- Nonstatistical tools include brainstorming, process mapping, and cause-and-effect diagrams. These are exploratory tools, applied without formal data collection.
- Data based nonstatistical tools include checksheets, run diagrams and Pareto (80/20 rule) charts.
- Statistical tools include SQC charts and process-capability evaluations:
    - X-bar charts and R-charts are used to track the mean and range of a process on a quality characteristic that is being measured using variable (continuous) data,
    - P and c-charts track the proportion of defectives and number of defects/piece, respectively, based on a quality characteristic that is being measured using attribute (yes/no) data.
- Variation from 'ideal' or 'average' quality standard is caused by a combination of common and special (assignable) causes:
    - Common causes are natural causes that occur randomly and cannot be predicted or controlled in the short run.
    - Special or assignable causes can be identified, predicted, and controlled by management.
    - It is management's responsibility to clean a process of special causes. Common causes cannot usually be eliminated or reduced in the short run. Attempting to do so would need significant changes to be made in the process.
    - A process that has been cleaned of special causes is called a process that is 'in statistical control.'
    - There is still (reduced) variation in a process in statistical control—caused by the residual common causes (which cannot be removed easily).
    - SPC (statistical process control) is undertaken on a process that is 'in statistical control.'
- All SQC (statistical quality control) charts have a center line representing the process mean and upper and lower control limits (UCL and LCL) that are normally drawn $\pm 3\sigma$ limits from the mean.
    - SQC is appropriate for high volume processes that have measureable defective levels.

- SQC charts monitor an 'in control' process and warn when it appears to be going out of control (due to a special cause coming back into the system).
- The chance of mistakenly calling a process 'out of statistical control' when it is actually in statistical control is only 0.135 percent.
- Any kind of emerging data pattern in a control chart is suggestive of a process that is not in statistical control.

- 'Process capability' is measured on the extent to which the process mean is centered on the customer's 'ideal' desire and the extent to which production is within customer tolerances (UTL and LTL).
- Process capability improves as the process mean moves closer to the customer's 'ideal' and as the standard deviation of the process is reduced.
- Six Sigma calls for extending the process UCL and LCL to $\pm 6\sigma$, implying that 99.9999998 percent of process production falls within a range that is acceptable to the customer.

Improving Quality

- Quality improvement = (customer satisfaction + employee satisfaction + continuous improvement).
- Each dimension has to be measured, benchmarked and targeted for improvement. Customer satisfaction = perceived quality = (actual quality minus expected quality).
- SERVQUAL is a measurement model that explains and assesses the perceived quality of services.
- The actual quality of a service can be evaluated as soon as the service is consumed. Perceived quality is a function of actual quality minus expected quality.
- On the other hand, actual quality of consumer durables is not evident immediately since these are consumed/ used over a long period of time. Thus initial purchases are made on the basis of expected quality.
- Empowered employees supported by equitable reward systems are likely to increase employee satisfaction.
- Continuous improvement is pursued using a combination of quality tools, process analysis, benchmarking, and supply chain management.

Was It Done Right?

- Quality outcomes fall short of expectations if what the customer prizes is not immediately apparent and thus not identified properly.
- Announcements and programs become routine after some time and are ignored by employees and customers. Visible and sustained commitment of resources together with clear reward systems are required.
- Six Sigma can impact creativity and innovation adversely because of its stress on variance reduction and efficiency.

Current Trends

- Quality initiatives are growing in fields like health care and food supply, pushed by regulation and public concern.
- Advances in tracking technology are enabling tracing of quality recalls and failures along the supply chain.

Key Formulas/Equations

X-bar chart: UCL = grand mean + (A$_2$ * avg. range); LCL = grand mean − (A$_2$ * avg. range)

R-chart: UCL = D$_4$ * avg. range; LCL = D$_3$ * avg. range

p-chart:

Average proportion defective $\bar{P}$ = total # defective/total # of units sampled

Standard deviation = $\sqrt{}$ [(avg. prop. defective * (1 − avg. prop. defective))/sample size]

UCL = average proportion defective + Z * standard deviation

LCL = average proportion defective − Z * standard deviation

c-chart

Average # of defects/piece $\bar{c}$ = total # defects/total # of pieces sampled

Standard deviation = $\sqrt{\bar{c}}$

UCL = $\bar{c}$ + 3 standard deviations

LCL = $\bar{c}$ − 3 standard deviations

$$C_{pk} = \text{the minimum of} \left[\frac{\text{Grand Mean} - \text{LTL}}{3\sigma} \quad \text{or} \quad \frac{\text{UTL} - \text{Grand Mean}}{3\sigma} \right]$$

Computing sigma levels:

Z_{UTL} = (UTL − mean)/σ

Z_{LTL} = (mean − LTL)/σ

Customer satisfaction = perceived quality, and

Perceived quality = actual quality *minus* expected quality = AQ − EQ

Discussion Questions

1 Briefly explain the differences between service quality and manufacturing quality.

2 Provide examples of dimensions that are a) common to and b) unique to both service and manufacturing quality.

3 List three reasons why quality matters to a business.

4 Can you think of a real product or service where quality improvement is not necessary?

5 Describe and contrast the quality themes and approaches of Deming, Juran, and Crosby.

6 Write a short memo to your boss explaining your preference for Deming or Juran or Crosby's approaches in organizing a Taylor Swift concert.

7 Try estimating prevention, appraisal, and failure costs at your place of work—where is the most money being spent now? Why?

8 Provide one good reason why knowledge about quality management would be important to a) a finance major, b) an accounting major, c) a marketing major, d) an HR major e) a computer science major.

9 Provide one application each of a cause-and-effect diagram, a run chart, a checklist, and a Pareto chart.

10 What is the purpose of SQC?

11 Can we apply SQC to a medical clinic? Which process in such a clinic might be appropriate for SQC?

12 Airlines build delays into their flight schedules to guard against weather and other disruptions, effectively adding safety buffer stock between flights. How might this buffer inventory affect flight timeliness quality improvement initiatives?

13 Taichi Ohno, Toyota's process guru, would "spend an hour or even two hours at one spot. [He] would keep looking at things for as long as it took to figure out what the problem was."[11] Do you see any difference between Ohno's approach to quality and statistical sampling methods?

End of Chapter Problems

1 Color pictures generally fade with time relative to black and white pictures. Which quality-related product characteristic would you emphasize if you were selling black and white film only?

   a) Reliability
   b) Durability
   c) Excellence
   d) Assurability
   e) Compatibility

2 Investing money in appraisal activities alone (without investing in prevention costs) would likely:

   a) Not significantly impact internal and external failure costs.
   b) Increase internal failure costs but cause external failure costs to decline.
   c) Cause both internal and external failure costs to decline.
   d) Increase external failure costs but not affect internal failure costs.

3 You are the student representative in a team put together by the registrar to help identify the (yet unknown) causes and resolve the problem of inordinate delays in some registration cases. What would be the best quality tool, in your opinion, to begin with?

   a) Checklist/check sheet
   b) Pareto chart
   c) Process map
   d) Cause-and-effect (fishbone chart) diagram

4 Student complaints about mistakes in the registration process are growing. I wish to find out if there is a pattern in the complaints, identify the complaints that affect students the most, determine the root causes for those complaints, and take corrective action, in that order. What is the best *sequence* of application of the quality tools described below to fulfill my objective?

   a) Check sheet—Pareto chart—cause-and-effect diagram
   b) Cause-and-effect diagram—Pareto chart—check sheet
   c) Pareto chart—cause-and-effect diagram—check sheet

5 Evaluating the quality of which item below would *particularly* call for the use of the SERVQUAL model?

   a) The quality of an automobile
   b) The quality of a movie
   c) The quality of a sandwich
   d) The quality of a student's performance in a final exam

6   A *poka-yoke* is a tool or method or an aspect of product design used to failproof an operation, i.e, make sure that failures do not happen, or if they do, automatically get resolved to a significant extent. Which situation best represents the above description of an effective *poka-yoke*:

   a)   A nurse verbally counting the number of operating instruments used by a surgeon before and after an operation
   b)   What happens to a stair escalator at your college during a power failure
   c)   A free cheeseburger for every order of burnt fries at the Baruch Cafeteria
   d)   A smile from that hot cashier after he/she makes a mistake on your payment amount due

7   Deming felt that worker incentive/penalty plans are essentially a 'lottery' because:

   a)   The manager has no control over common or special causes.
   b)   The worker will manipulate the system to gain an unfair advantage.
   c)   The manager usually removes both common and special cause variation from the process and thus deserves the credit—rewarding a worker would be redundant and can lead to favoritism.
   d)   In a system in 'statistical control,' variation in worker output quality is a random phenomenon driven by common causes over which the worker has no control.

8   Which of the following is NOT a 'variable' (and thus an 'attribute') measure of quality?

   a)   Proportion of late flights
   b)   Weight of a Big Mac
   c)   Diameter of a ball
   d)   Temperature of a Heineken or a Bud Light

9   Generally speaking, using a 'variable' measure of quality is preferable to using an 'attribute' measure because:

   a)   Variable measures provide more information.
   b)   Variable measures are easier to track.
   c)   Variable measures are more easily developed.
   d)   The above statement is not true—that is, the fact is that variable measures are actually not preferred over attribute measures.

10   Which of the following would most likely be a 'common' cause of variation in a McDonald's?

   a)   A worker who calls out regularly for various reasons
   b)   A regularly malfunctioning fryer
   c)   A customer who changed her order three times in a row
   d)   Poor quality raw materials

11   Which of the following would most likely be an 'assignable or special' cause of variation in a McDonald's?

   a)   A sudden rush of customers
   b)   A regularly malfunctioning fryer
   c)   A customer who changed her order three times in a row
   d)   High humidity due to unexpected rains causing the french fries to lose their 'crispiness'

12 In Kano's model, *poka-yokes* (foolproofing) would be particularly useful for ensuring that:

    a) Delighters are always present in the product/service
    b) Dis-satisfiers are always present in the product/service
    c) Satisfiers are always present in the product/service
    d) $e = mc^2$

College Bakers Inc. employs process control in its muffin baking process. Each hour, a sample of four muffins is taken to collect data about the weight of muffins in the process. The results for Thursday's work are presented below: Use the data to answer the following questions.

Sample time	Weight observations				X-bar	R
	1	2	3	4		
8 a.m.	12.60	13.00	12.40	12.70		
9 a.m.	12.30	12.60	12.80	12.50		
10 a.m.	13.10	12.60	12.30	12.80		
11 a.m.	12.40	12.50	13.00	12.80		
12 noon	12.90	12.70	12.40	12.50		
1 p.m.	12.70	12.60	12.90	12.30		
2 p.m.	13.00	12.30	12.70	12.60		
3 p.m.	12.50	13.00	12.70	12.90		
			Grand mean	12.659	Mean R	0.60

13 What is the sampling mean for the 10 a.m. sample?

    a) 12.400
    b) 12.600
    c) 12.659
    d) 12.675
    e) 12.700

14 What is the sample range for the 8 a.m. sample?

    a) 0.5
    b) 0.6
    c) 0.7
    d) 0.8
    e) 0.9

15 Using the standard table for control chart factors, the UCL for the X-bar chart is ____.

    a) 13.259
    b) 13.096
    c) 13.005
    d) 12.659
    e) 12.222

16 Using the standard table for control chart factors, the UCL for the range chart is ____.

    a) 0
    b) 1.268
    c) 1.369
    d) 1.544
    e) 1.666

17 Using the standard table for control chart factors, the LCL for the range chart is ____.

    a) 0
    b) 1.268
    c) 1.369
    d) 1.554
    e) 0.6

18 Using 3-sigma control limits compared to 2-sigma control limits ____ the probability of Type I error (Type 1 error: When you say there is an assignable cause though none exists, and the process is actually still in statistical control).

    a) Increases
    b) Decreases
    c) Makes no difference to the Type I error probability
    d) Either a) or b) can result.

19 After getting the process into statistical control, a range chart was developed (3-sigma limits) with LCL = 0 and UCL = 2.50. Similarly, an average chart was developed (3-sigma limits) with LCL = 15 and UCL = 24. Five monitoring samples subsequently taken read as follows: sample ranges: 1.75, 2.42, 1.82, 2.04, 2.80, and sample means: 19.5, 22.3, 17.4, 20.1, 26, respectively. What can you tell management from this analysis?

    a) The process variability is out of control but the process average is in control.
    b) The process average is out of control but the process variability is in control.
    c) Both the process average and the process variability are out of control.
    d) We cannot tell from the data provided.

A furniture manufacturer has collected data on dining tables, noting a total count of 190 painting defects across those 25 tables. He wishes to develop a c-chart.

Use the above information to answer the following questions.

20 The recommended center line for the appropriate control chart is ____.

    a) 1.9
    b) 3.8
    c) 7.9
    d) 25
    e) 7.6

21 The lower control limit for the control chart is ____.

    a) −0.67
    b) 0.00

c) 0.67

d) 4.84

e) 7.60

22 What *minimum* number of defects on a dining table would signify an out-of-control situation (how many defects would it take to *first* set off the alarm)?

a) 5

b) 8

c) 19

d) 25

e) 28

23 Of late, customer complaints about delayed deliveries in your courier service have increased. You decide to monitor the *proportion* of late deliveries to investigate and control the severity of the problem. Which chart would you prepare and use to do so?

a) c-chart.

b) Pareto chart.

c) p-chart.

d) R-chart.

e) X-bar chart.

24 You correct the problem described in the question above, but you also decide to monitor the range of delivery times to maintain consistency of service. You have recently found that several data points have been recorded at or near the lower control limit (= 0) in the R-chart. Which of the following do you most agree with? The data points:

a) Suggest that no special cause of variation is present.

b) Can be ignored because they signify better than average quality.

c) Suggest that the process lower control limit is inappropriate.

d) Should be investigated because a special beneficial cause of variation might be present.

25 Narrow control limits like ± 1-sigma are not very common. Where would you most likely encounter such limits?

a) Retail shop, e.g., Macy's

b) Auto manufacturing plant—e.g., Ford

c) Drug manufacturing—e.g., Pfizer

d) Food preparation and cooking process in a cafeteria

26 If some proportion of the items produced in a manufacturing process always fall *outside* the upper and lower tolerance limits, the process capability measure C_{pk} must be

a) > 1.

b) < 1.

c) = 1.

d) Infinite

e) Depends on the variance of the process

27 A beer maker's cans should contain beer at 40 psi (at 60°F). The filling process has an upper tolerance limit of 45 psi and a lower tolerance limit of 33 psi (for storage and customer can-opening safety reasons). SPC finds that the beer can filling process actually results in an average can pressure of 41 psi with a standard deviation of 2 psi. Find out the process capability of the beer maker's can-filling process.

Answer:

$$C_{pk} = \text{the minimum of} \left[\frac{\text{Grand Mean} - \text{LTL}}{3\sigma} \quad \text{or} \quad \frac{\text{UTL} - \text{Grand Mean}}{3\sigma} \right]$$

$$= \frac{(45 - 41)}{3*2} = \frac{4}{6} = 0.667$$

Using the process mean found through SPC sampling, the probability of making a defective can (>45 psi or < 33 psi), given a process average of 41 psi and a standard deviation of 2 psi, is: Probability of going > 45 psi + probability of being < 33 psi

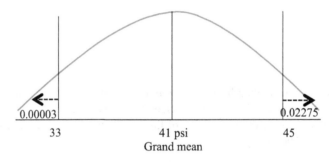

33   41 psi   45
         Grand mean

Figure 9.25 Probability of Going > 45 PSI + Probability of Being < 33 PSI

$Z = (x - \bar{x})/\sigma$
So for probability of going > 45psi, z = (45 − 41)/2 = 2,
corresponding to an area of (1 − 0.97725) = 0.02275 (1 − NORM.DIST(45,41,2,TRUE)
And, probability of going < 33 psi, z = (33 − 41)/2 = (−)4,
corresponding to an area of 0.00003 (NORM.DIST(33,41,2,TRUE)
So the probability of making a defective can = 0.02275 + 0.00003 = 0.02278 = 2.28%, approximately.

Answers:

1—b	2—b	3—d	4—a	5—b	6—b	7—d
8—a	9—a	10—c	11—b	12—b	13—e	
14—b (13 minus 12.40)		15—b	16—c	17—0	18—b	19—c
20—e	21—b	22—c	23—c	24—d	25—c	26—b

Suggested Class Projects

1   Visit and describe the dimensions of quality as you experience it in a:

   a)   Auto repair workshop
   b)   McDonald's
   c)   Class lecture

2   In your visits, could you find a process suited to the use of SQC? Please explain, with some data, if possible.

Suggested Case

Process Control at Polaroid (A), HBS case 9-693-047

Notes

1   R. Narasimhan, S. Ghosh, and D. Mendez, "A Dynamic Model of Product Quality and Pricing Decisions on Sales Response," *Decision Sciences*, 24(5), 1993, 893–908.
2   See clips of winning companies at http://www.nist.gov/baldrige/index.cfm.
3   G. Taguchi, S. Chowdhury, and Y. Wu, *Taguchi's Quality Engineering Handbook, Part III : Quality Loss Function,* (New Jersey: John Wiley & Sons: 2005), 171–198.
4   A. Parasuraman, V.A. Zeithaml, and L.L. Berry, "A Conceptual Model of Service Quality and Its Implication," *Journal of Marketing*, 49(Fall), 1985, 41–50.
5   You're right! The direct representative kept her caller posted continuously about what she was doing. The other representative was definitely more courteous. However, he kept the caller hanging during those long minutes of silence during which he worked to resolve the issue. People like to know what's going on. The call center found that continuous feedback, rather than a focus on courtesy, was among the order-winning quality attributes for their business.
6   Darius Mehri, *Notes from Toyota-Land: An American Engineer in Japan,* (Ithaca, NY: Cornell University Press, 2005).
7   Learn about Where Food Comes From at http://www.wherefoodcomesfrom.net/index.aspx and http://wherefoodcomesfrom.com/what-we-do/source-verification/, accessed Oct. 3, 2015.
8   Watch a video about animal cruelty at Tyson Farms at http://www.youtube.com/verify_age?next_url=/watch%3Fv%3DbNY4Fjsdft4%26feature%3Dplayer_embedded. (*Warning –graphic content.*)
9   Eric Auschitzky, Markus Hammer, and Agesan Rajagopaul, "How Big Data Can Improve Manufacturing," *McKinsey*, July 2014, http://www.mckinsey.com/insights/operations/how_big_data_can_improve_manufacturing.
10   Jack Welch quote from http://www.searchquotes.com/quotation/Good_business_leaders_create_a_vision,_articulate_the_vision,_passionately_own_the_vision,_and_relen/11834/, accessed Oct 3 2015.
11   John Shook, Michikazu Tanaka of Daihatsu on 'What I Learned from Taiichi Ohno,' " *Lean Enterprise Institute*, April 8· 2009, http://www.lean.org/shook/displayobject.cfm?o=910.

APPENDIX: FACTOR CHART FOR $\bar{X}$ AND R-CHARTS

Constants for Average Range Charts Based on the Average Range

n	A_2	D_3	D_4
2	1.88	0	3.268
3	1.023	0	2.574
4	0.739	0	2.282
5	0.577	0	2.114
6	0.483	0	2.004
7	0.419	0.076	1.924
8	0.373	0.136	1.864
9	0.337	0.184	1.816
10	0.308	0.223	1.777

10 Supply Chain Design

Chapter Take-Aways

- Importance
- How to design
- Templates
- The design process
- Design tools
- Cautions

Supply Chain Design: A Road Map

- Suggested class projects
- Suggested cases

Customer: *"Why should I choose you?"*
Business: *"Because we promise you that the product you purchase is made, transported, and distributed to meet your needs in the most efficient, reliable, timely, ethical, and sustainable manner possible."*

That is some promise! So, how do we deliver? The way we design our supply chain has a lot to do with converting promise into reality.

10.1 What Is Supply Chain Design?

Take a look below at J.B. Hunt's (a leader in distribution and logistics) conceptualization of the domestic portion of a typical supply chain design. Overseas suppliers are not shown but could be represented by the ships docked at the ports. Suppliers would have their own associated storage, distribution, and logistics facilities.

Designing a chain design is about choosing the number and location of supply, R&D, manufacturing, assembly, warehouse, and distribution centers involved in the transformation and movement of a product from raw material/component stage to assembly, storage, distribution, and returns. We design different configurations and

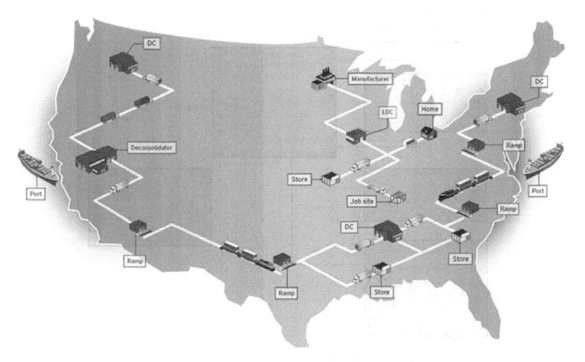

Figure 10.1 A Supply Chain Design

DC: national/regional distribution center; LDC: local distribution center; Ramp: loading/unloading/transfer point; Deconsolidator: location where large consignments are broken down and repackaged into smaller consignments.

Source: Reproduced, with permission, from J.B. Hunt Transport Services Inc.

choose that specific network that optimizes performance, in terms of cost or time or risk or other factors. The factors that we consider in developing a design include facility location, transportation loads and costs, currency fluctuations, location tax differences, speed to market, flexibility to adjust/adapt to disasters and interruptions, warehouse size, manufacturing production plans, and costs. All firms may not have the choice to design their own supply chains, perhaps having inherited one or perhaps being dominated by a larger or more powerful firm that is part of its supply chain (think Intel and small specialty PC makers). But most firms can and do make design changes to their supply chains. Which brings us to the question: What exactly is a supply chain?

Have you ever thought about who makes your Apple iPhone? It's not Apple, by the way. About where it's made? And how it comes to you? And why it costs what it does? The iPhone is an end product representing the collective contribution of many firms to its design, components supply, logistics, assembly, marketing, distribution, and returns. These tasks are performed in some sequence, giving rise to the term 'supply chain,' a chain or network of firms that work together to eventually supply an end product to the consumer. Apple's supply chain for the iPhone consists of more than 14 major component suppliers around the world. Although some of the suppliers are incorporated in the U.S. and do the design work here, the actual manufacturing is undertaken in plants and contract manufacturers in China, Taiwan, Korea, and other Asian countries.

Besides manufacturing and assembly locations, iPhone's physical supply chain also consists of logistics, transportation, storage, and distribution facilities owned by various companies. iPhone's supply chain has many

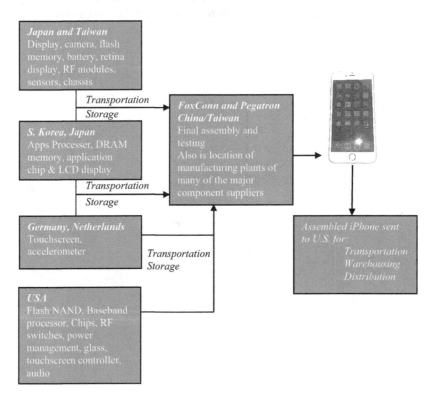

Figure 10.2 Apple's Supply Chain for the iPhone 5

Source: "Many iPhone 5 Components Change, But Most Suppliers Remain the Same, Teardown Reveals," press release, *IHS Technology*, Sept. 25, 2012, https://technology.ihs.com/411502/many-iphone-5-components-change-but-most-suppliers-remain-the-same-teardown-reveals.

types of flows: the flow of human labor to factories, the flow of raw materials that are turned into parts, the flow of those parts to make finished phones, the flow of orders from retailers like AT&T and direct buyers, and the flow of cash payments from the customer to the last supplier in the chain. There's also a flow of design knowledge from Apple and other firms to the manufacturers, and information exchange flows about demand forecasts, production schedules, and shipping dates through the chain of companies in the supply chain. When the focal firm is capable, active and fair in its dealings, there also exists a flow of camaraderie and relationships among the firms that make up the supply chain. While supply chain design focuses primarily on the arrangement of physical facilities and logistics, globalization and shortened product life cycles have introduced explicit and early considerations of information, risk, and cash flows as important design elements. Well, now we know where the innards of the iPhone are made and assembled. But who makes the most money in the supply chain? Looking at a supply chain from the perspective of profit centers—a value chain perspective—who captures the most value, and where? Below is an estimation of how an iPhone's costs and profits are distributed:

The Sum of iPhone Parts

iSuppli costed the first basic iPhone in 2007 at $217.73. Apple has kept a tight leash on costs despite significant advances in phone features and performance. Below is an estimate of the cost of the iPhone 6.

Total est. cost $227

Selling price retail in U.S. (estimated without plan)	= $649, minus
COGS	= $227
Selling, general & administrative expenses (SG&A)	= $42*
R&D	= $19*
Apple's estimated operating profit/margin	= **$361 per phone**

Apple's $178 billion cash hoard (Jan 2015) accounted for nearly 10 percent of the corporate cash held by U.S. nonfinancial companies.

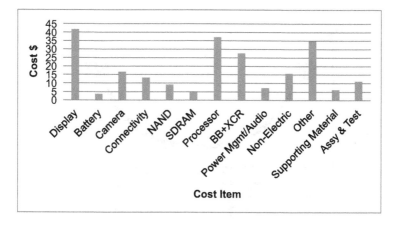

Figure 10.3 iPhone 6 Cost Breakdown

Flash, display, and wireless component suppliers (such as LG Display, Sharp, Samsung, Qualcom) likely make the most margins among Apple's suppliers for iPhone parts.

Adapted from: Ben Berkowitz, "Apple Posts Blowout Quarter, Will Ship Watch in April," *CNBC*, Jan. 27, 2015, http://www.cnbc.com/2015/01/27/apple-earnings-306-per-share-vs-expected-eps-of-260.html; Jim Edwards, "Apple's Manufacturing Costs Reveal The Profits It Will Make On iPhone 6," *Business Insider*, Sept. 24, 2014, http://www.businessinsider.sg/analysis-iphone-6-plus-costs-prices-and-profits-2014-9/#.VhCpQXldGUk; Joshua Sherman, "Spendy but Indispensable: Breaking Down the Full $650 Cost" of the iPhone 5, *Digital Trends*, July 26, 2013, http://www.digitaltrends.com/mobile/iphone-cost-what-apple-is-paying/.

Even though essentially most of its manufacturing activity is located in China, the bulk of an iPhone's value accrues to the designers and marketers outside China. Profit accumulates where design, branding, and marketing knowledge reside.

The 'smile curve' shows the value chain for Apple products—the proportion of profit captured by value-adding activities in the supply chain. Apple, being the product designer as well as the marketing and customer service provider, captures much of the profit from the product. Apple component suppliers like Sony, Samsung, LG, Sharp, Broadcom, and Qualcomm, which supply crucial sub-systems like processors, wireless components, displays, and cameras, collect the next round of profits. At the lowest point of the curve is the assembler, Foxconn/Pegatron for Apple, who gets only a small fraction of the profit.

It's difficult to map a supply chain in its entirety, considering the many supply, manufacturing, assembly, and distribution points involved from raw material to finished product. Dr. Johnson at the Warwick Business School meticulously traced the supply chain for the tennis balls used at Wimbledon and found that they traverse 50,570 miles in the making. While the tournament is played in Wimbledon, UK, the balls are made and shipped in cans from Bataan, Philippines. Costs are kept low since most of the production and raw material are clustered around Bataan, Philippines. A significant part of those 50,570 miles is consumed in transporting premium wool for the balls from New Zealand for processing into felt in the UK (the felt is then sent to Bataan).

Deciphering a supply chain is a difficult task for more complex products or services like an auto, airplane, or a multi-artist concert, all of which have hundreds or even thousands of components and tasks involved.

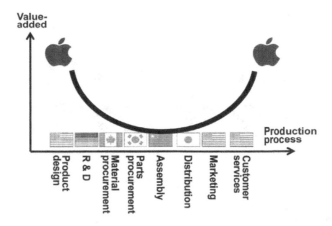

Figure 10.4 Apple's Smile Curve: Who Makes the Money?

Source: With permission from Satoshi Inomata, "Trade in Value Added East Asia Perspective" *ADBI*, December 2013.

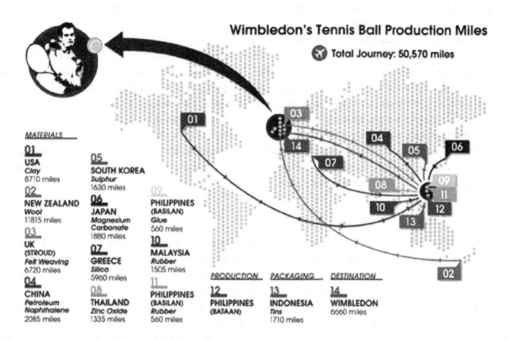

Wimbledon's Tennis Ball Production Miles

Total Journey: 50,570 miles

MATERIALS

01
USA
Clay
8710 miles

02
NEW ZEALAND
Wool
11815 miles

03
UK
(STROUD)
Felt Weaving
6720 miles

04
CHINA
Petroleum
Naphthalene
2085 miles

05
SOUTH KOREA
Sulphur
1630 miles

06
JAPAN
Magnesium
Carbonate
1880 miles

07
GREECE
Silica
5960 miles

08
THAILAND
Zinc Oxide
1335 miles

09
PHILIPPINES
(BASILAN)
Glue
560 miles

10
MALAYSIA
Rubber
1505 miles

11
PHILIPPINES
(BASILAN)
Rubber
560 miles

PRODUCTION

12
PHILIPPINES
(BATAAN)

PACKAGING

13
INDONESIA
Tins
1710 miles

DESTINATION

14
WIMBLEDON
6660 miles

Figure 10.5 How a Tennis Ball Gets to Wimbledon

Source: With permission from Dr. Mark Johnson, Warwick Business School, April 27, 2015, http://www.wbs.ac.uk/news/the-50000-mile-journey-of-wimbledons-tennis-balls/.

10.2 Why Is Supply Chain Design Important?

Companies are looking at supply chain design as a strategic instrument to gain competitive advantage, spread risks, and create options for alternative sourcing.

> Competitive advantage = company's own area of competence + supply chain design + supply chain management

10.2.1 The Effects of Supply Chain Design on Performance—Agility, Efficiency, and Adaptability Advantage

Microsoft's core competence is software design and marketing. When the Xbox first came out, Microsoft outsourced manufacturing to Flextronics, the well-known global contract manufacturer, who, in turn, sourced manufacturing in Mexico and Hungary. Speed to market was important in order to get the new product out for release by the Christmas deadline, and the supply chain was designed to meet that need for speed. Xbox's design features and performance created a splash in the market, and sales shot up. A key competitor, Sony, watched the situation and reacted with deep discounts on its Play Station 2. Competition in the game box arena suddenly switched from innovation to cost. In response, Flextronics moved the manufacturing of the Xbox away from Eastern Europe and Mexico to China, a lower cost location. In effect, Microsoft was competing with its supply chain, first designing a quick response network of manufacturers and suppliers to meet market exigencies and later shifting to a low-cost supply chain designed to meet its competitor's moves. An adaptable supply chain design enabled Microsoft, a newcomer, to attack and gain ground from Sony, an entrenched competitor in the game box market.

Besides cost, supply chain agility, or speed of response to changes in product design or demand (or lack thereof), also affects competitive advantage. Speed of response is especially critical in volatile product markets such as apparel and electronics. Clothing retailers like Zara and H&M and manufacturers like Samsung have flourished because of their ability to spot changes in market preferences early *and* because they have designed their supply chains to respond in quick time. In such fickle product markets, today's hot items become yesterday's leftovers. Apple reacted quickly to shortages in supply after product launch—its supply chain design had the capability to ramp up to meet the surge in volume. Note that it was not simply a task of adding hands to the assembly operations at China but also of finding new and reliable suppliers of raw materials and newly designed parts. Agility, though, sometimes becomes victim to quality, as Toyota found a few years ago when quality problems escalated with global expansion.

10.2.2 Jobs in Supply Chain Design

Supply chain design jobs are interesting, career enhancing, and well paying. Any company of a reasonable size has a global supply or customer network, with associated distribution networks. Job titles include positions such as supply chain analyst, supply chain optimizer, distribution specialist, port security, port management and operations (including container logistics), and intermodal logistics.

For a finance major, supply chain design might mean designing a lean capital chain, organizing and costing financing of goods, inventory and transportation along the supply chain. An accounting major may find herself speeding up the invoicing and settlements process, increasing the velocity of working capital, and factorizing and securitizing accounts receivables for cash flow. A marketing major may find himself responsible for designing a supply chain for a marketing promotion program, that involves sourcing and integrating print suppliers, IT sourcing, assembly of promotional material, and distribution to retailers nation-wide. Product pricing decisions also draw on supply chain capabilities and costs, current and anticipated. Companies recruit actively for supply chain design positions. Here's a typical job posting:

MCKINSEY & COMPANY

Operations–Supply Chain Associate—North America

Overview

McKinsey & Company is a management consulting firm that helps leading corporations and organizations make distinctive, lasting and substantial improvements in their performance. With consultants deployed from more than 90 offices in more than 50 countries, McKinsey advises companies on strategic, operational, organizational, and technological issues.

Detailed Description

Progressive experience and proven results in optimizing transportation and warehousing including:

- Hands-on experience in line haul and small parcel transportation management including network modeling; mode optimization, truck utilization, and/or zone improvement; 3PL/carrier sourcing (RFP, negotiations) and management, experience with transportation management systems (TMS)

- Prior experience in warehouse network design; warehousing productivity and process improvements, e.g., shift balancing, lean; strategic sourcing; experience with warehouse management system (WMS), e.g., SAP, Oracle, RedPrairie, Manhattan Associates, Sterling commerce WMS; experience with supply chain security solutions for high value items
- Prior experience in designing solutions for multiple customers/industries (e.g. part of operations, pre-sales support, solutions design, industrial engineers teams, not sales), or equivalent hands-on experience prior to joining 3PL/carrier
- Defining new organizational structures, roles and processes across global supply chain/network organizations. This may involve: upgrading line and staff skills, changing the structure of reporting relationships, developing improved processes and procedures, and instituting rigorous target-setting and performance-monitoring systems
- Working with the client to realize immediate savings by building and executing network strategies
- Rationalizing operational assets and networks to achieve the higher levels of effectiveness and efficiencies.

Desired Skills

All operations practice consultants possess common characteristics consistent with our firm-wide hiring mission. We are seeking individuals who are:

- Passionate and committed to operations and technical excellence
- Strategic and creative thinkers
- Comfortable and adept with quantitative analysis
- Proven leaders with the ability to inspire others, build strong relationships, and create a true followership
- Able to grasp and communicate complex ideas clearly
- Collaborative team players, capable of working well with others but also autonomously with little direction
- Results-driven achievers
- Comfortable with extensive travel (greater than 80%)
- Bachelor's or master's degree (strongly preferred)
- 5+ years of experience
- Minimum level of responsibility: manager or manager-level specialist/contributor
- Understanding and exposure to supply chain concepts
- Experience assessing and driving transformational improvements across operational settings
- Insights/experience in managing key transformation factors (e.g., performance management systems, mindsets/behaviors)
- Particular interest in network design, sales and operations planning (S&OP), inventory, or physical flow management
- Clear demonstration of having led operations improvements/transformations

Source: Job listing on McKinsey & Company, accessed Oct. 3, 2015, https://mckinsey.secure.force.com/EP/job_details?jid=a0xA0000002JdM51AKBottom_of_Form.

In summary, supply chains have to be designed, and how that is done will affect everything from product pricing to customer service and profit margins.

KEY POINTS

- Supply chain design selects and integrates suppliers of raw material, components, assembly, logistics, distribution, and warehousing capabilities into a coherent configuration that delivers value to the consumer.
- Supply chain management coordinates and motivates the entities in a supply chain to work together for common goals.
- A value chain describes the activities that capture the most value in a supply chain, where such value resides, and to whom it accrues.
- Supply chain design is dynamic, anticipating and changing shape with changes in the demand and supply markets.

10.3 How to Design a Supply Chain

There are several frameworks in supply chain design that we can use: Hau Lee of Stanford University identified the three key objectives of supply chain design as agility, adaptability, and alignment; Charles Fine of MIT[1] believes that the structure of a product and its rate of change of technology determine the structure of its supply chain. Marshall Fisher (1997) of Wharton prescribed efficient supply chains for commodity products and responsive chains for innovative products, while Salvador et al. (2004) matched different levels of product customization to different configurations of supply chain design. Others have combined supply chain designs into lean-agile structures that serve both cost and responsiveness goals at different stages of the supply chain.[2] We integrate the various prescriptions into a guideline for the supply chain designer, using a product of every-day use, the telephone, as an example.

10.3.1 A Template for Supply Chain Design

There are three distinct elements in supply chain design: supply network, assembly, and distribution. Designing each begins with understanding the nature of the market and designing a product that fits market demands.

Look at the market first. The landline phone market shows a trend of steady declining demand. Demand being a *steady* trend, forecasting accuracy increases, and thus markdowns and stock-outs are infrequent. Profit margins are low. It is a *functional* market. Contrast that with the market for smartphones, with exploding variety and high demand uncertainty at the individual product level. Profit margins are high, but the costs and probability of designs becoming obsolete or of being unable to meet demand for bestsellers are relatively high. It is an *innovative* market. The market for other cell phones is somewhere in the middle in terms of forecasting accuracy, supply-demand mismatch, and consequent costs. It is a *hybrid* market.

Let's look at the products for these different types of markets. Product design follows specific market condition. A *functional* product like a traditional landline phone would be based on a fairly established dominant design that has evolved over the years. Variety would be limited and offered through component swapping and component sharing on a basic design platform. Then there are *hybrid* products such as cell phones that offer more variety than functional products, but less so than an innovative product like a smartphone. Cell phone (not smartphone) designs have matured into clamshells (flip-open) or cards (one piece) shapes, differentiated by interchangeable faceplates and similar accessories that are inserted on a basic design platform. Such phones still account for a large part of phone sales in developing markets. Hybrid products might see high demand uncertainty for certain components like differently colored/designed faceplates but stable demand for standard components such as batteries. Both functional and hybrid phone designs are 'old,' and manufacturing lines for such products have existed for a long time. It would be difficult and expensive to change manufacturing lines in order to make radical design changes on a frequent basis. Customers compare products primarily on the basis of price and are reluctant to pay premiums for incremental design upgrades. In sharp contrast, smartphones are *innovative* products, in the growth stage of the product life cycle, with ongoing battles for market share and design dominance raging among leaders like Apple and Android-based phones such as Samsung's Galaxy line. Demand is uncertain at the product level, and so is design. Design complexity and specification tolerances are tight, with new features constantly being added to already feature-packed platforms. Design obsolescence is high, with newer versions being launched often and low potential for swapping or sharing parts among different phones. Manufacturing lines are in constant flux to keep pace with design changes. Time to market launch is critical since competitors may preempt with their own new designs. At the same time that products are being designed, the design of the supporting supply chain also begins. Supply, assembly, and distribution nodes are selected, developed, and configured into networked supply chain designs that target cost/efficiency or time/responsiveness objectives.

Let's now look at the *supply network* for these different product types. The supply network is designed based on how the product is put together and the ease of disassembly, that is, product architecture. The first issue is the extent to which parts of the product can be outsourced to suppliers. Products that are modular in design, that is, can be broken down into sub-units, are best suited to outsourcing. Each module or sub-system of a modular product can be manufactured independently in different locations and then assembled at a central point. Charles Fine's framework describes product modularity as the main driver of outsourcing, with independent sub-systems being distributed to different suppliers for manufacture. Most electronic products are modular by design, as are products such as automobiles and garments. Complex products with tightly integrated parts such as jet engines are not easily decomposable into independent sub-units and are not suitable for dispersed outsourcing. At times, critical modules that are highly profitable, quality sensitive, or use proprietary technology or are 'best sellers' are kept for in-house manufacturing, while the more routine or lower volume modules are outsourced. When several products share common modules, suppliers obtain volume and repetitive manufacturing economies of scale.

The second issue in designing a supply network is the choice between efficiency (lean) and agility. Supplier proximity to the market is desirable where agility is required, typical of new, uncertain volume, rapid-design-change products with fickle consumer preferences. Proximity can be a function of time, distance, or culture. iPhone components are sourced across the world, but supply lead times are kept short through air shipments and timely information exchanges that are understood and acted on by a global, multi-cultural supply network. Lean supply networks, on the other hand, are organized to deliver at least cost, and locations are usually global. Needs change with time. Furniture is an example of a product that used to demand an agile, close proximity supply network. But the furniture industry now operates with a lean network based mostly in far-off but low-cost China. Even though furniture is a heavy, large volume product, container shipping has reduced unit shipping costs and shipping times from China to make supplier proximity a secondary factor. A product could use a mix of lean (low cost) and agility (responsive to changes in demand and specifications) to create a 'le-agile' supply chain design. A hybrid product like the cell phone described in

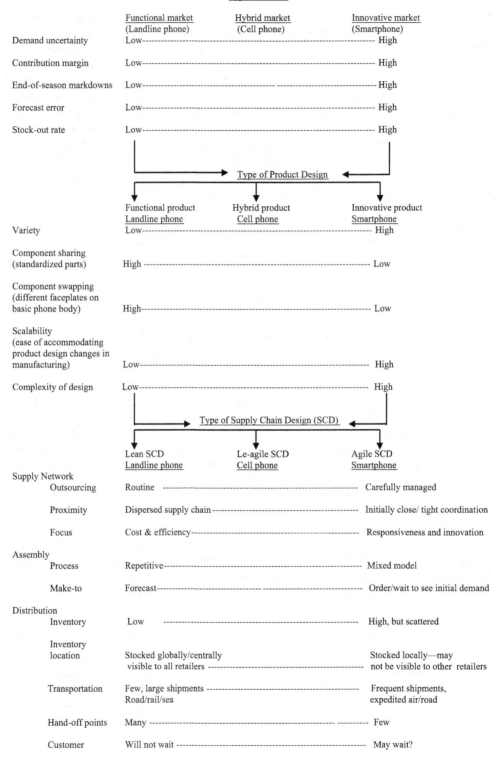

Figure 10.6 A Template for Supply Chain Design

Figure 10.6 may have both lean and agile supply networks for significant components. The use of specific interchangeable faceplates is driven by transient customer preferences. The small, variable numbers for specific faceplate types demand an agile supply network that is close to the assembly area. High volume standardized items such as batteries, semi-conductors, or power cords that go into multiple variants of a cell phone can be sourced from global low-cost locations. Demand for such standardized items is not affected by changes in consumer preferences. Such le-agile supply networks are not as efficient as cost minimization driven pure lean versions, but afford some flexibility and responsiveness to market changes. Lean supply networks typically focus on single sourcing, with the supply base optimized to a few carefully chosen and developed suppliers who are closely engaged with high volumes, repeat business, and process and logistics efficiency. Agile networks typically follow a 'keep a bird in the hand' policy, maintaining alternative sources of supply but keeping local supply sources as standbys with small higher priced purchases. Companies could also develop both lean and agile supply networks for the same product to meet market conditions. A shirt can be probably made most cost-effectively today by buying the textile from China, sending it for stitching to lower labor cost Bangladesh, and returning it to Hong Kong for consolidated shipment to the customer. But if the same shirt becomes a best seller requiring rapid replenishment at retailers, both sourcing and manufacturing can be performed in China for quicker, but higher cost, supply.

The *assembly network* is the second element of supply chain design. Assembly network design calls for choices about the type and location of product assembly points. Depending on the product, the final assembly of a finished product could be carried out at a factory, by a sub-contractor, a warehouse or distributor, a logistics carrier, a retailer, or even the customer (think IKEA). From our template above, assembly of a functional product like a landline phone, with fewer variants, can be centralized in an assembly plant. A hybrid cell phone, volume permitting, can be assembled partially at a central location before being sent to distributors or retailers for accessorizing with snap-on different color plates, chargers, and screen protectors. Functional and hybrid products can be made to stock, given the comparative stability in demand, higher forecast accuracy, and customer tendency to look elsewhere if the product is not readily available. Smartphones, an innovative and high variety product, would be most suited to a mixed model centralized assembly process, where flexible machinery and versatile labor allow rapid switching between a range of variants. Such flexibility would suit 'hot' hi-tech or customized products like consumer electronics, apparel, and custom vehicles. Mass assemblers like FoxConn, with access to cheap and large labor pools, can afford to rapidly build separate production lines for different varieties.

OM IN PRACTICE

Flexible Assembly Networks

Factories in Asia "can scale up and down faster" and "Asian supply chains have surpassed what's in the U.S."

—Unnamed Apple Executive

2007: An annoyed Steve Jobs looks at scratches made on his iPhone glass screen by the keychain in his pocket. He demands scratch proof glass—it does not exist. Apple works with Corning USA to develop large panes of scratch-proof glass. But a problem remains: how to cut up those large panes into millions of iPhone screens? In mid-2007, after a month of experimentation, Apple's engineers finally perfected a method for cutting strengthened glass so it could be used in the iPhone's screen. Now came the problem of finding a cutting plant and workers who could do the job quickly enough on a mass scale. Glass cutting and grinding is precision work. Then a bid for the work arrives from a Chinese factory. When an Apple team visited, the Chinese plant's owners had samples ready with engineers on hand and a brand new facility with worker dorms—all this in anticipation of a contract. They got it. The glass screens would be cut and grinded down to Apple's perfection and supplied to Foxconn's assembly plant.

Then Apple redesigns the iPhone's screen. The glass cutters respond in quick time. The first truck-loads of redesigned screens glass arrive at Foxconn City late at night. "A foreman immediately roused 8,000 workers inside the company's dormitories," according to an Apple executive. Each employee was given a biscuit and a cup of tea, guided to a workstation, and within half an hour started a 12-hour shift fitting glass screens into beveled frames. Within 96 hours, the plant was producing over 10,000 iPhones a day. "The speed and flexibility is breathtaking," the executive said. "There's no American plant that can match that." Foxconn has assembled over 400 million iPhones since 2007. Work conditions are not bad, but work pressure is reportedly extremely high.

Figure 10.7 Foxconn Shenzhen

Source: Photo by: Steve Jurvetson, "Electronics Factory in Shenzhen," 2005, Jurvetson (flickr), Menlo Park, USA, via *Wikimedia Commons*, https://commons.wikimedia.org/wiki/File:Electronics_factory_in_Shenzhen.jpg.

Adapted from: Charles Duhigg and Keith Bradsher, "How the U.S. Lost Out on iPhone Work," *The New York Times*, Jan. 21, 2012, http://www.lipa.cz/doc/29/09.pdf.

The distribution network is the final element in supply chain design. Where in the network are products to be stored, and how are they to be distributed? Product storage and movement happen both within the firm's own manufacturing/assembly/warehouse locations and from such locations to the firm's dealers, retailers, and end-customers. Material in a traditional supplier(s)-manufacturer-distributor-dealer-retailer network goes through multiple hand-off points (nodes). Inventory builds up at such locations where material is handled and stored. For a typical consumer product, distributors are a few national or regional companies, dealers are regional or local and more in number, and retailers number in the hundreds or thousands. Product options and variants are many. The customer is accustomed to ready availability. Manufacturers/assemblers mostly ship direct to a few chosen distributors. The logistics costs and management of direct supply of different products to many dealers or retailers, involving thousands of destinations, would be dauntingly high and complex. Distributors generally ship to regional or local dealers instead of directly to retailers for the same reason. Dealers carry inventory for local retailers and direct ship to them. Consumers like to have choices, and retailers wish to keep everything in stock for fear of missing a sale. But retailers cannot carry much for reasons of capital, space, and risk of obsolescence. So dealers function as inventory back-ups for retailers, and distributors, in turn, provide inventory back-ups for the dealers. The system is convoluted and inefficient but does succeed in spreading inventory, carrying costs and risk across many locations in the distribution network, and enables retailers to replenish stocks in small lots of changing product designs.

The conventional manufacturer-distributor-dealer-retailer distribution is being challenged. Big box retailers like Best Buy and Walmart cut out the distributor and dealer (and associated costs) and get direct shipments from the manufacturer in big lots but then organize the redistribution of smaller volumes of product to their many retail outlets themselves. Companies like UPS now offer to break down shipments at the port of entry into customer-specific packages and ship directly to large retail outlets/distribution centers like Home Depot. In China, a country without big box retailers or malls, Nike has opened more than 5,000 small boutique shops with local partners—margins are higher since there is no big box store competition. Companies may prefer direct shipments to dealers or retailers for reasons of control, especially with proprietary technologies. Apple has a short and direct distribution network since it wishes to maintain tight control over a manageable number of distribution nodes. Traditional manufacturer-distributor-dealer-retailer networks work well when markets are not too volatile, product variety is limited, and an agile supply network exists to respond rapidly to market-driven changes in the product mix. Too much market volatility or too much product variety would clog the traditional network with unsold inventories.

E-tailers like Amazon get manufacturers to ship to Amazon's warehouses, but some products may also be shipped directly from the manufacturer/assembler to the customer (drop shipments), such as a keyboard or a printer for a computer purchase. When lower price or scarcity induces a customer to wait, inventory can be kept in a centralized place(s) and shipped direct from the manufacturer to the customer. Such items, for the most part, are light-weight, compact, and easy to transport. Products like digital cameras, for example, are express-mailed from a single or a handful of centrally located distribution facility(ies) direct to the customer. Direct shipping has caught on with consumer products such as home appliances, including 3D TVs, washing machines, and refrigerators. Buy a washing machine online from Best Buy and they'll ship it free to your home, install it, and cart away your old machine. Although shipping direct to thousands of customers can be expensive for a manufacturer compared to shipping to a few distributors, third-party providers like UPS, FedEx, and USPS have highly efficient logistics systems that deliver reliably up to the last mile. The cost of direct shipments is usually borne by the customer, although free shipping is fast becoming a deal maker nowadays. In fact, direct shipments work out better for large and expensive products, since logistics would account for a lower proportion of total product cost. Paying $100 for transportation and delivery of a $1,500 TV is psychologically more acceptable to the customer than paying the same $100 for a $300 couch. Dealers would exist to primarily install and perform maintenance service on such sales. Of course, the risk of carrying stock is then borne by the manufacturer. But shorter direct shipments mean fewer hand-off points and thus lower overall inventory levels and lower overall mark-ups in the network. This prompts lower costs that allow e-retailers to offer lower prices. Lower prices persuade customers to suppress their instinctive wish for instant gratification and wait for delivery. Direct shipments are on the rise for almost every type of consumer product.

10.3.2 Adaptability in Design

One dimension of supply chain design remains to be examined—the aspect of adaptability or having options to exercise in case of need. The figure below shows an adaptable supply chain design.

Each link connecting specific suppliers to specific assemblers, distributors, and retailers represents a unique supply chain, which requires active managing. For example, supplies from plant a_{11} can go through assembler a_{21} (or alternatively a_{22}) and distributor a_{31} (or alternatively a_{32}) to eventually reach retailer a_{41}. More branching means increased choice and potentially, increased adaptability. Simulation results suggest that the adaptability gains from, say, 20–30 percent linkages is close to the gains from 100 percent linkages—so it's not necessary to link all nodes to each other to obtain a significant degree of supply chain adaptability. Adaptability can be designed to different extents at different networks depending on perceived risk, e.g., if the assembly network is relatively vulnerable to delays and shut-downs, back-up assemblers should be consigned to each retailer. Note, though, that the planned adaptability may not be achieved if the assembly nodes themselves are strongly inter-correlated in their vulnerability to causes of delays or disruption. If all the assemblers are affected by, say, foreign exchange risk, as happened in the Asian currency crisis in the 1990s or the near breakdown of global commerce in 2007–8, they would all collapse together. There would be no unaffected 'back-up' sources left. Adaptability calls for a trade-off between efficiency and risk reduction. Resorting to multiple sources reduces economies-of-scale efficiencies, compromises optimization goals, and increases management complexity. Adaptability can be examined at the supply chain design stage by modeling alternative chain structures and simulating their performance under different operational scenarios. Executing an adaptable supply chain design requires processes that provide rapid risk prediction and identification information, as well as enhanced visibility, at critical locations along the supply chain. These attributes go together with analytical capabilities and an organizational structure that can use such information to make quick-response decisions.

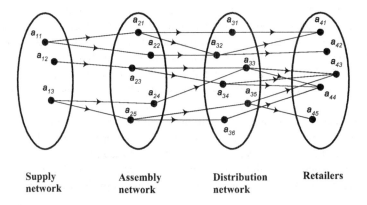

Figure 10.8 An Adaptable Supply Chain Design

OM IN PRACTICE

Adaptability in Supply Chain Design

When flood waters rose in Thailand in late 2011, Walmart stores in Japan ran out of mouthwash. Mouthwash is manufactured in Thailand for Asia. About 1/3rd of global hard disk production also went underwater. Auto components makers supplying Toyota, Honda and GM were submerged, and divers were sent to retrieve expensive production molds. When the tsunami and earthquake hit Japan in 2011, shortages of obscure but vital chemicals hit many industries including phone and auto makers.

During 2011, the turmoil in Egypt forced P&G to temporarily shut its plants there and spice maker McCormick to look for an alternate source of spices supply. In February 2012, Iran threatened to close the Hormuz Straits to shipping. The Los Angeles port strike in spring 2015 caused McDonald's in Japan to run out of french fries.

Companies are taking a hard look at the traditional supply model of clustering supply sources in a particular region. The benefits in terms of quality, costs, and ease of management could be offset by the considerable risk of losing all supply sources at the same time. The challenge is to establish an adaptable supply network that balances efficiency with the additional costs of dispersion/some duplication. Companies are responding. The research firm UBM TechInsights said it took apart several new iPads since they went on sale and found components with the same functions made by at least three manufacturers (at different locations) in different tablets. Outsourcing shops with supply chains that comprise call centers and software design and service shops are designing adaptable chains. Bangalore (India)-based Wipro has developed call centers in the Philippines, and other companies are following

Figure 10.9 NASA Satellite View of Tsunami in Northeastern Japan on March 13, 2011

Source: NASA Goddard Space Flight Center. "Satellite Feed of Northeast Japan after Tōhoku Earthquake and Tsunami," March 13, 2011, https://www.flickr.com/photos/gsfc/5523171908/.

suit both to spread risks and reduce costs. Dell has teams working with the impacted suppliers in Thailand to resume hard drive supplies and is also actively seeking and qualifying new sources and routes of supply. Companies are using tools such as geographical risk analysis and global risk maps (AON Inc.) to design adaptable supply chain designs. Companies, though, find it difficult to justify adding supply chain redundancies in anticipation of a supply chain disruption, unless the pain of a disruption has been recently and significantly felt. They are happy, though, to dole out advice to their suppliers about de-clustering manufacturing facilities and creating alternative sources of supply.

Adapted from: "The New iPad—Generation 3 Teardown and Apple A5X IC Analysis," *TechInsights*, April 16, 2013, http://techinsights.com/teardowns/new-apple-ipad-gen3-teardown-analysis/; "Supply chain disruption risk map," *AON.com*, Quarter 3, 2015, htttp://www.riskmap.aon.co.uk/political_riskmap.aspx#; Bill Powell, "The Global Supply Chain—So Very Fragile," *Fortune*, Dec. 12, 2011.

10.3.3 The Process of Supply Chain Design

From a 'how to' or process perspective, supply chain design begins with an analysis of the market and the product characteristics suited to that market. Questions include:

- Who are our customers?
- What are their expectations?
- How well are we meeting their expectations?
- How do we stack up compared to our major competitors?
- What products/services/tasks should be kept in-house and what should be outsourced?
- How do we see our responses to these questions changing over the next two to three years?

Your school distributes a service, education, with a specific supply chain design. Here's one perspective. The supply network is formed by schools supplying PhD profs to your school. The assembly network consists of various academic conferences that bring together and provide a critical mass of PhDs (finished products) to hiring schools. The distributing network comprises the individual hiring schools that 'buy' the service and distribute it to you, the consumer. Based on a review of market and competitor trends, product profiles, and level of customer service, your school would have specific cost and revenue goals for its supply chain design. It would then typically gather operational and cost data on student demand, supplier capacity, and costs (different schools producing PhDs), assembly capacity and costs (PhD job seekers at different conferences plus recruitment and interviewing costs), and distribution capacities and costs (how many PhDs it can hire, from where, and costs of alternative location and premises). Although, strictly speaking, suppliers do not 'charge' distributors for their products in education, the products themselves, fresh PhDs, come with varying price tags. A Harvard PhD would be much more expensive to hire than a state school supplied product. Your school would develop a baseline model of its existing supply chain and validate that with existing data. It would then model alternative configurations, sometimes numbering in the hundreds, of alternative supply, assembly and distribution possibilities—PhDs from different schools, different conferences and recruitment procedures, number and location of (teaching) distribution locations, and so on. The objective would be to develop alternative supply chain designs, compare, and find out which supply-assembly-distribution design offers the best possibility of meeting school cost and quality targets in meeting the education needs of students.

For a business, the process consists of listing all feasible sourcing, manufacturing/assembly and distribution facility capacities, locations, and linkage choices. These data are used to simulate supply chain designs that are compared with baseline models, tested for robustness, and evaluated to find a currently optimal design. The primary elements of a solution are location, number, capacity, inventory storage, and logistic linkages of manufacturing, assembly, and distribution facilities. At this level, averages are employed. The performance parameters are usually total operating cost and speed, and sensitivity analysis examines the sensitivity of these outcomes to changes in the primary elements. The solution must include external factors such as tax and currency factors and also the anticipated cost of transitioning from the existing network to the optimal one. The human aspect, though difficult to model, needs consideration as well. For example, a logistics design that has the potential to bring truck drivers back to their homes on a regular basis would have significant effects on driver morale and productivity.

Once an optimal design emerges, detailed planning and modeling of the design begins with specific operational data and costs on all supply chain elements: facilities, logistics, staffing, transition costs. The model is run with detailed operational data to verify its feasibility for day-to-day operation. Cross-functional teams together with area expert consultants are involved in the supply chain design process. It is absolutely essential to consult and involve line managers who would actually execute the design and manage the supply chain in design decisions. During implementation, transition steps and roll-out phases have to be clearly defined. Which events will come first, and which can come later? How should the implementation be phased to minimize disruption to suppliers, employees, and customers? Who is accountable for executing different steps of the redesign? What incentives or dis-incentives have been developed to prevent people from falling back into old habits? Are the benefits of the supply chain design/redesign visible to all supply chain members, and are they seen as being shared equitably? The design process needs to have clear planning and implementation phases, with accountability, roll out timing, and resources clearly defined for each phase.

OM IN PRACTICE

How Furniture Companies Redesigned Their Supply Chains

Prior to the 1990s, the furniture industry in the U.S. made most of their product in the Carolinas and northeastern Mississippi. Beginning with the late 1990s, challenged by low-cost global competition and facilitated by the reduction in shipping costs enabled by the introduction of containers, supply chain designs moved most manufacturing to China and, later, Vietnam. The high labor content of furniture manufacture was well suited to the much lower labor costs in these regions. Eventually, many large furniture companies outsourced all their manufacturing to China, keeping design, brand management, and marketing as core in-house functions.

Four primary supply chain designs have emerged in the U.S. furniture industry. Large retailers such as Macy's and Walmart follow the direct sales mode, cutting out distributors, reportedly buying direct from large overseas assemblers. In the manufacturer outsourcing mode, other—smaller—companies route their requirements to overseas manufacturers through agents while retaining limited domestic capacity for fast-moving items. Other smaller companies follow the distributor/agent outsourcing mode and buy all their requirements through distributors/agents who import from overseas manufacturers. Finally, the direct investment mode has seen companies like Ashley and La-Z-Boy build their own manufacturing capacity in China. The distribution network is the longest for small companies, with small volume orders traversing the manufacturer to distributor/agent-dealer route. Costs are relatively higher, but delivery times are quicker, since agents consolidate orders from several buyers and import and hold inventory locally. Large volume container loads can be ordered only by the larger companies to avail of lower logistics costs and volume discounts on purchase prices.

Globalized supply chains have meant radical changes in logistics, risks, management tasks, and delivery dates. Logistics, for instance, becomes tri-modal—rail, sea, and road. A shipment would arrive from China at the Los Angeles port, move by rail to Tennessee, and be sent by truck to different companies in the region. Of late, lower domestic energy prices, impatient customers, U.S. port and truck strikes, escalating international labor rates, and simultaneously declining domestic labor rates have encouraged manufacturers to come back home. Tax and employee training incentives by state authorities also play a role. The supply chain for furniture appears to be readying for another major redesign.

Source: Various news reports; for a look at furniture currently being made in China, see http://fafa88.en.made-in-china.com.

10.3.4 Ownership

Who owns what in a supply chain? And why? Professor Charles Fine of MIT offers an interesting framework for location of ownership in a supply chain based on the relative clockspeed of the chain's different members. 'Clockspeed' refers to the speed of change in technology in an industry. The industry with the highest clockspeed would drive a supply chain's evolution and occupy the most valuable and influential position in the chain. So in the TESLA electric car, for example, the car battery probably represents the fastest-moving technology. To follow Professor Fine, Tesla should exercise some form of ownership or control over the electric car battery industry. Not to do so may be to lose substantial revenues down the road, as IBM did when they did not buy out Intel, the fastest-changing technology in the PC. In fact, Tesla Motors is building a massive car battery plant in Nevada, perhaps for this reason. Applying a value chain perspective, a firm should study the clockspeeds of the various components in its supply chain, identify the ones with the fastest clockspeeds, and invest in such locations, either through vertical integration or through some other form of ownership and control, such as financing or exchange of personnel. If firms do not have resources for this task, consultants can perform an analysis at the time of supply chain design, and periodically thereafter. For example, Disney uses a variety of technologies to constantly upgrade the quality of its theme park attractions. These technologies change at different rates. Disney designs most mechanical technologies, such as the pirates in the perennial favorite Pirates of the Caribbean ride and keeps such designs stable for periods of time. Animation and software technology, on the other hand, mutate rapidly. Proprietary animations are kept in-house, while other designs are outsourced to firms such as Silicon Graphics. Perhaps Disney would benefit from a value chain analysis based on clockspeed differences in its different technologies. Disney, of course, is invested heavily in animation, but the slower mechanical technologies could be divested to other firms while the high clockspeed software and animation are retained in-house for greater control and competitive advantage.

Besides profits, product architecture also underlies supply chain ownership decisions. Highly complex, tightly engineered products are not easily broken down into separate outsourceable parts and are therefore typically not suited to outsourcing. Ownership of manufacturing resides with the firm or with one or two contract manufacturers that are controlled by the firm. Modular products with easily disassembled parts, like bicycles or home audio-visual systems, can be distributed for manufacture and are thus more amenable to widespread outsourcing. Ownership or control of a node in a supply chain is also influenced by such factors as the need to acquire or protect intellectual property and critical technology and quality or delivery concerns with suppliers. Quality drives Lindt chocolate's ownership of practically its entire supply chain, beginning from beans from Africa, Central America, and South America to its new 350,000 square foot plant in Stratham, New Hampshire, where the beans are processed into cocoa liquor and then processed into the Lindt Truffles and chocolate bars.

Firms wish to control any factor that can potentially lower sales revenue or profits, including loss of reputation, loss of margin, creation of competitors, quality and safety liabilities, risks, and varied costs. Walmart, for example, is taking ownership of the logistical network between its distribution centers (DC) and its suppliers.[3] The desire to control and participate in profit points can be realized through direct ownership or, to reduce risk exposure, through limited equity participation, joint ventures, marketing assistance, and the building of deep and enduring relationships with supply chain members through trust, transparency, fair treatment, and personal initiatives. A company should, of course, weigh the benefit of control against the costs of controlling larger parts of the supply chain—opportunity costs, nonperforming and obsolete assets if technology/tastes change, and the costs of increased management complexity.

10.3.5 Tools for Supply Chain Design

Supply chain designers use a variety of quantitative modeling techniques starting from simple spreadsheets, to statistical analysis, linear and mixed integer programming, simulation, and expert programs and heuristics. What one chooses to apply typically represents a trade-off between speed, complexity, and accuracy. We test supply chain designs, making alternative load and node decisions about where to locate facilities, what modes of transportation to use, and long-term sourcing choices. We can simulate the relative sensitivity of chain and node performance to changes in critical parameters and finding out "tipping points"—when and which changes in key parameters such as costs and delivery times will necessitate changes in the supply chain design. Simulation, for example, could incorporate global warming rates and develop a tipping point for global temperature rise that could impact shipping times and costs dramatically, causing openings and closings in the supply, assembly, and distribution network.

OM IN PRACTICE

Arctic Shipping Lanes and a New Silk Road

Melting ice in the Arctic sea is making it easier for shippers. Shipping from Shanghai to Rotterdam via the Northern Sea route is shorter by 40 percent, or some 2,500 nautical miles, compared with the alternative via the Suez Canal. Journeys between Asia, Europe, and America could be cut by as much as half.

The extreme left and right lines represent recently open shipping lanes, while the line in the middle shows a more direct route once the ice is gone (estimated 2040–2050). Rapid ice melting may advance the timetable. The cost savings are significant. More than 70 ships (mostly oil tankers) sailed through the Northern Sea Route in 2013, saving about 5,000 nautical miles. As more do, global supply chains will be redesigned. Faster service means less dependence on forecasts, reduced inventory, and more responsiveness to market demands.

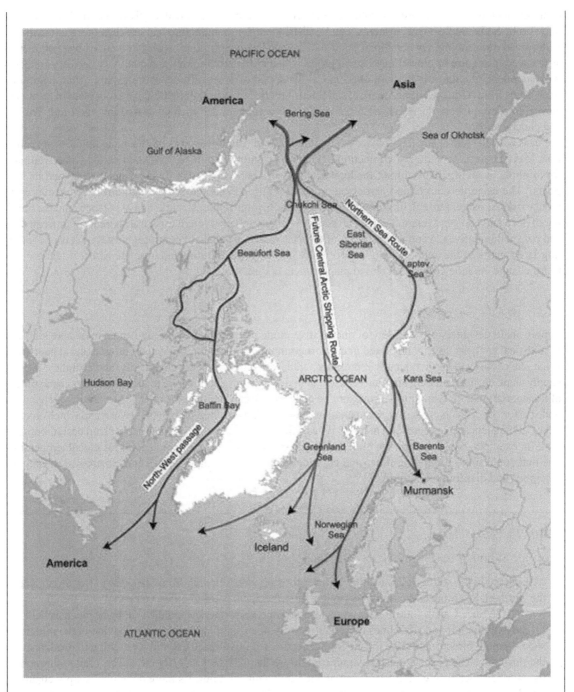

Figure 10.10 Ice Melt and New Shipping Routes

Source:"213 DSCTC 10 E—Security at the Top of the World: Is There a NATO Role in the High North?" *NATO Parliamentary Assembly*, from the 2010 annual session, http://www.nato-pa.int/default.asp?SHORTCUT=2082.

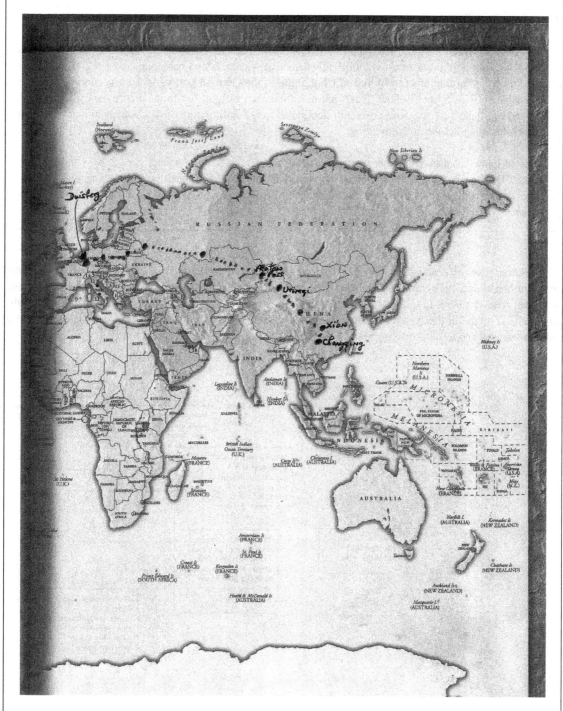

Figure 10.11 The New Silk Road

Source: Author. Based on information from Pearl Forss and Anthony Morse, "In Pictures: China's New Silk Road," *Channel News Asia*, Oct. 3, 2015, http://www.channelnewsasia.com/news/asiapacific/in-pictures-china-s-new/2167304.html and Fu Ying, chairperson of Foreign Affairs Committee, National People's Congress, "China's New Silk Road Promises Prosperity Across Eurasia," *The World Post*, July 31, 2015, http://www.huffingtonpost.com/fu-ying/china-silk-road-eurasia_b_7899236.html.

It's not all ocean freight, though. China's new Silk Road opened in 2014. Instead of sending iPads and Nikes through pirate-infested, politically sensitive waters, China has organized a 6,200-mile-long rail link from the manufacturing hub of Chongqing to the German port of Duisburg, running through Kazakhstan, Russia, and Poland. Costs are more than sea freight, but times are cut down to 15 days instead of 30 days by sea. Rail costs will decline as freight volume increases and manufacturers open more sites inland closer to Chongqing.

Adapted from: Adam Pasick, "Your Next iPhone Might Be Delivered from China via a 2,000-year-old Trade Route," Quartz.com, May 2, 2014; various news reports; "Global Rules Urged for Arctic Shipping," *Waterloo Region Record*, Feb. 28, 2012, http://www.therecord.com/news-story/2599089-global-rules-urged-for-arctic-shipping/, NATO records.

Advanced network simulation can show, for example, what would happen across the network if a supplier or assembler or logistics carrier suddenly failed; or if a customs approval took twice as long as anticipated; or if fuel costs doubled. Like flight simulators that allow pilots to practice using various scenarios modeled in a realistic model of the system, simulation allows managers to model processes and test the robustness of these processes in alternative scenarios.

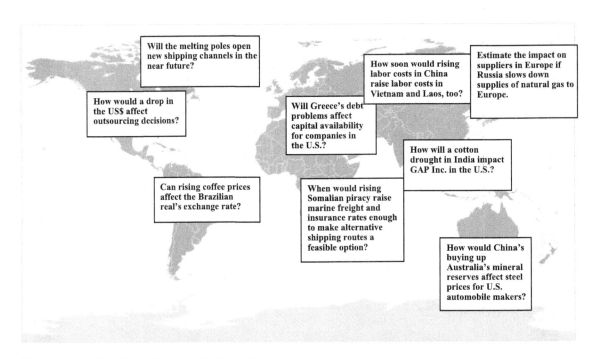

Figure 10.12 A Simulation Situation with Scenarios

Source: Map from Wikipedia, accessed Oct. 3, 2015, http://vignette3.wikia.nocookie.net/juego-de-mapas/images/8/87/Mapa.png/revision/latest?cb=20130202202449&path-prefix=es.

Optimization tools help develop and contrast different configurations of supply, assembly, and distribution locations to optimize performance across the entire supply chain. Users of network design tools tend to be companies with large, tiered distribution networks and globally distributed manufacturing and supply networks. Network design tools are also much used among companies that seek to identify redundant facilities after acquiring competitors—e.g., DOW, Nike, Levi, Whirlpool, and the like. Coca-Cola, Japan, modeled close to 100 bottling lines and distribution centers to come up with a design configuration of bottling and warehousing locations to best meet demand and changes in demand. Design tools create surprises—for instance, it may be less expensive to airfreight a small load than to send it by road as a non-FTL/FCL (full truck or full container) load. A simulation of a U.S. furniture company's supply chain design suggested that even with 100 percent outsourcing, it would be advantageous to keep a local (higher cost) domestic source of supply in view of overseas lead time uncertainty.[4] The most time-consuming and difficult task in simulation and optimization is gathering detailed, accurate data about forecasted demand, product and facility information, manufacturing, assembly distribution flow rates, capacities, and costs and understanding interrelationships among entities to enable basic model building.

OM IN PRACTICE

Super Models!

In 2008, an MIT network design researcher developed a complex super model of the entire distribution networks of two HP printers, evaluating the impact of changes in labor costs in Asia, fuel price increases, exchange rate appreciations of Asian currencies, and shorter required supply times. The results: Thailand edged out China for some production locations if labor costs increase; significant increases in fuel costs converted Mexico and Brazil into viable production centers; and Germany emerged as a production location when duties increased, labor costs rose in Asia or lead time was curtailed. Another exercise looked at the impact on the supply chain design of an apparel business if there would be changes in labor rates in China, fuel price hikes, doubling or removal of all tariffs/duties, and an increase in the price of cotton. Thailand and Bangladesh disappeared as manufacturing locations, while China and Romania grew in manufacturing importance.

Reality has since caught up with the simulations. Reports show that a surging Chinese economy has raised labor costs by 30 percent over a year in some sectors, with labor protests rising. Shipping costs have increased owing to a container shortage and longer port clearance times, the renminbi is steadily rising in value, and Chinese manufacturers are experiencing rapid employee attrition. Despite their considerable investment in developing reliable supply chains in China, some U.S. companies are moving to lower cost climates like Mexico, Vietnam, and Thailand, as predicted by the simulation models. Meanwhile, U.S. labor wages and U.S. domestic energy prices are in decline, with increasing labor concessions and the recent shale gas finds.

Adapted from: Keith Bradsherjan, "Even as Wages Rise, China Exports Grow," *The New York Times*, Jan. 9, 2014, http://www.nytimes.com/2014/01/10/business/international/chinese-exports-withstand-rising-labor-costs.html; SCDigest Editorial Staff, "Supply Chain News: Rise in China Wages Now Means Labor Costs about 20% Lower in Mexico, New Study Finds," *Supply Chain Digest*, April 8, 2013, http://scdigest.com/ontarget/13-04-08-1.php?cid=6913.

Analytical models also need to be tempered with field experience. A supply chain design done for the supply of malaria medicines in Africa, for example, recommended keeping stocks at local distribution locations to enable quick response to changes in demand. But, in practice, managers noted that direct distribution from a centralized location worked better. The reason was that local distribution points grew lax, secure in the knowledge of readily accessible local stock, leading to stock-outs and mismanagement. Centralization proved to be the best configuration for both inventory management and proper packaging of the meds. Of course, local objections to the loss of 'power' and decision making had to be considered and overcome.

KEY POINTS

How to Design a Supply Chain

- Market and product characteristics determine the shape of supply chain design.
- Adaptability is a valuable attribute of supply chains, affording an option to switch to alternative supply chains in times of need.
- A supply chain design consists of three basic networks: supply, assembly, and distribution.
- A high rate of technology change at a supply chain position represents value and attracts ownership interest.
- A modular product with easily separable components is more suited for outsourcing.
- Network design uses simulation and optimization tools to model and find best-performing configurations of supply, assembly, and distribution networks.

10.4 Was It Done Right?

Supply chain designing is fraught with risks—mostly brought on by continuous changes in the market and in the elements of the supply chain. Let's take a look at some of the pitfalls of supply chain design.

10.4.1 What Could Go Wrong in Supply Chain Design?

Let's take a look at some classic supply chain design disasters. They include Webvan, a now defunct direct grocery service whose $25 million automated warehouses were a poor fit with the high variety-low volume nature of their market; Nike's 2001 demand-planning system disaster with technology provider i2 that double-ordered old style shoes and led to a drop in Nike's share price; and Aris Isotoner's catastrophic supply chain re-design in 1994, when parent company Sara Lee revised its supply network and assembly network designs to move to lower cost but, as it later found, lower quality destinations. Revenues plummeted 50 percent, and the division was soon sold. Why supply chain designs go wrong can be a matter of dysfunctional technology or algorithms, but a common reason is the human factor:

- Functional biases: The IT and purchasing people generally regard supply chain design as a matter of connectivity and relationships. The logistics and distribution people, on the other hand, have a long history of analyzing data and building optimization models. The approaches are necessary and complementary. But training and backgrounds make it difficult for two perspectives to mix well. The quants would want to model at a detailed level, but qualify their recommendations with lots of ifs and buts about operational conditions. The non-quants would question the practical value of such assumption-laden model outcomes and prefer "I've been doing this stuff for 15 years" rationales.

- Risk: Design changes also touch multiple functions and are therefore messy—not too many people wish to get involved in complex changes that will disrupt everyday work and may not turn out well.
- Ignorance: Designers may not be aware of the minutiae of what happens in the field. Ignorance leads to inaction when designers cannot see how their supply chain design is performing in everyday conditions. People also become chained to habit and do not look at or re-examine design premises regularly. Even if they have the inclination, coping with day-to-day problems could leave managers with no time to look at strategic design issues. The need to review and change usually assumes urgency with a new CEO or new technology or when a supply chain crisis erupts.
- Self-preservation: Managers and decision makers do not want to design themselves or their friends out of a job. Relocating sourcing to another supplier may not affect buyer personnel employment directly, but shutting down an assembly or distribution center may mean direct lay-offs. The best design may remain on paper if the human costs are not explicated and handled.
- Implementation: When supply chains are redesigned, the new design can be rolled out in stages or in a 'big bang' manner, where all parts of the organization have to change at the same time. Typically, big bang approaches have been found to result in poor implementation and performance.

10.4.2 Operational Metrics

What constitutes evidence of a 'correctly done' supply chain design? Starbucks focuses on five high-level categories of metrics to evaluate supply chain performance: safety in operations, service measured by on-time delivery and order fill rates, total end-to-end supply chain costs, energy and natural resource footprint, and enterprise savings. Enterprise savings are cost reductions from non-logistics areas such as purchasing, marketing, or research and development innovation. More generally, supply chain designs are being evaluated on total end-to-end cost, on-time delivery, service quality, innovation, sustainability, and safety. Cost comparisons are meaningful if performed on the same basis on a period-to-period comparison basis. Even so, factors beyond the supply chain designer's control could confuse performance evaluations. Shipment size can affect shipping costs. Distribution costs can change based on order size, destination changes and mode of freight changes. Supply network logistics costs can change because of changes in supplier location. Another performance measure is cash velocity, measuring the time elapsed between receiving a customer order and receiving payment after satisfactory delivery. Cash velocity is a fairly comprehensive measure since it is based on the effectiveness of the supply, assembly, and distribution networks.

10.4.3 Strategic Metrics

Ultimately, a supply chain design proves itself on two basic counts—is the design matched to product and market needs, and is the design capable of keeping pace with changes in operational and market conditions? The initial supply chain design may itself be inadequate, failing to match existing product-market features. An efficient supply chain design will perform poorly for a product that comes in large variety—women's apparel fashions, for instance. Rapid changes in consumer tastes would be best met with a supply chain that can respond quickly to surprises in design and volume. An agile supply chain, on the other hand, would ill suit a product that serves a mature, stable demand, cost-conscious market—canned soup, for example. And a supply chain design that is not adaptable to market or network risk and changes would collapse under the pressure of unexpected events.

Figure 10.13 Supply Chain Design Goals

Efficiency, agility, and adaptability in supply chain design typically cannot be prioritized simultaneously. Practically speaking, one among these three characteristics becomes the dominant choice, depending on the nature of the market. From a strategic standpoint, adaptability may be of most value in current times. Events move quickly, and a rigid supply chain handicaps competitiveness. Food chains have learnt to activate alternate supply and distribution sources quickly in response to an unexpected weather or food safety-related crisis. On March 20, 2010, Iceland's Eyjafjallajökull volcano began to erupt, soon spewing ash columns thousands of feet into the atmosphere, disrupting traffic and commerce around the world. Tulips rotted in Amsterdam, and $3 million of flowers and produce were dumped at Kenya's airports. But some flower and fish buyers had established alternate supply sources with orchid growers and salmon fisheries in New Zealand, even as the Iceland volcano eruption shut down mainstream Dutch and Norwegian supply lines. Similarly, fashion houses have learned to respond to frequent changes in customer tastes and preferences. The problem with adaptability is that it is the most expensive aspect to design into a supply chain, since alternative supply, assembly, and distribution sources have to be identified, vetted, monitored and, if need be, integrated in a hurry into the supply chain.

How can a company design a resilient supply chain? Cisco first undertakes risk analytics to estimate the probability of occurrence of risk events and the consequences of the event. It then examines the capability of major nodes in the supply, assembly, and distribution networks to withstand the event, using TTR (time to recover) as a measure of node resiliency. TTR is a factor of inventory on hand, alternate prequalified location availability, capacity options, and time needed to replace or repair critical infrastructure. Cisco strategically designs its supply chain to feature redundancies and replications of supply and assembly sources while consolidating production of low-volume products at a single site for economies-of-scale reasons. Optical service routers, with customization and quick delivery market requirements, need a more adaptive and resilient supply chain, with switchable suppliers and a short TTR. Simple routers sell on price and would need a more efficient supply chain with fewer redundancies and higher TTR levels. Cisco also develops a forward-looking anticipation of its future supply chain footprint, including the location and capabilities of key supply, assembly, and distribution network nodes relative to anticipated risks and future demand. With all the planning and preparations, risk may still strike in unexpected ways. Recovery is an important facet of supply chain design, popularly addressed through 'hot state,' 'warm state,' or 'cold state' goals.[5] Hot state recovery requires duplication and a state of readiness for all key elements of the supply, assembly, and distribution networks. It is also an expensive strategy in view of the extensive duplication of sources. Warm state recovery requires advance identification and certification of alternate manufacturing and logistic locations, with a transition plan. Cold state recovery largely depends on reacting to events as they unfold. The best supply chain designs map out the supply chain to identify the critical materials, tasks, storage points, and transports for which there are few sources. Once identified, hot or warm state recovery plans are developed, including multiple sourcing, reserving advance capacity, and designing products and packaging that minimize dependence on scarce resources or high-risk regions. Simulation and optimization models can be used to evaluate the potential performance of the recovery plans. For example, energy price fluctuations can be met by switching production capacity between various locations. These plans are triggered by event occurrence or through early warning systems that monitor leading signals such as delayed shipments, supplier silence, and stock write-offs.

KEY POINTS

Was It Done Right?

- Human weaknesses such as inertia, functional biases, and self-interest may compromise supply chain design.
- Total end-to-end supply chain cost, on-time delivery, customer service level, and quality are conventional measures of supply chain design performance.
- Cash velocity, safety, energy usage, and innovation are other measures of interest.
- The defining measure of supply chain design performance is the ability of the chain to keep pace with market changes.
- Risk analysis and recovery planning are key tasks in developing a resilient supply chain design.

10.5 Current Trends in SCD

Let's look at current trends in supply chain design in two dimensions: trends that affect supply chain design and trends that are appearing in supply chain design. First, the trends that are shaping supply chain design:

10.5.1 Trends Influencing SCD

- *Rate of change*: Supply chains do not stand still, and there is no one-fits-all supply chain design. Some years ago, a complete skirt used to be made in China. Now, the cloth for a skirt may be purchased in China, sent to Bangladesh for sewing, and then sent to Hong Kong or Singapore to make use of high-speed, reliable port clearance and shipping advantages. Chasing changing labor costs and growing labor skill levels around the world means switching supply, assembly, and distribution jobs to different locations at different times. Rapid rates of change are also seen in commodities today, with volatility hampering long-term contracts and the formulation of long-term business plans. Similarly, rapid changes in tax rates, tariffs, and duties are endangering established supply chain designs. Logistics costs have also experienced significant volatility in the past few years, driven by economic bust-boom cycles and fuel price volatility.
- *Risk* has increased multifold, springing from the globalization of supply chains and increased exposure to such factors as exchange rate variations, piracy of ideas and property, political uncertainties, weather, and coordination complexities. Cyber-attacks are now feared on key supply chain nodes. In the first reported case of a digital attack on a business resulting in destruction of physical equipment, hackers struck a steel mill in Germany in Christmas 2014. The hackers hijacked the plant's control systems and actually damaged the mill's furnaces. Calls are being made to develop software firewalls separating business and production networks, but that, of course, defeats the very purpose of efficient and integrated operations.
- *Climate change* is posing an exponentially increasing risk to vulnerable mining, agricultural, and energy chains. Water shortages, flooding, fires, and drought can impact both production and transportation as well as create social unrest. The earth had its warmest December in 2014 since the late 1800s.

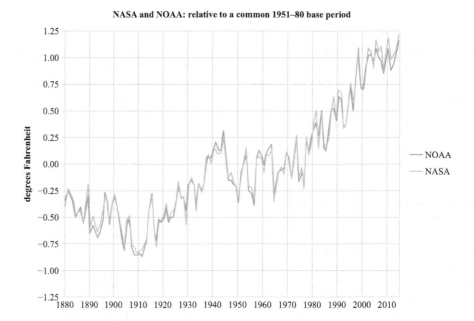

Figure 10.14 Global Land Temperature Anomalies

Source: "Climate at a Glance," National Oceanic and Atmospheric Administration, U.S. Department of Commerce, accessed Oct. 3, 2015, http://www.ncdc.noaa.gov/cag/time-series/global/globe/land/12/8/1880-2015?trend=true&trend_base=10&firsttrendyear=&lasttrendyear=.

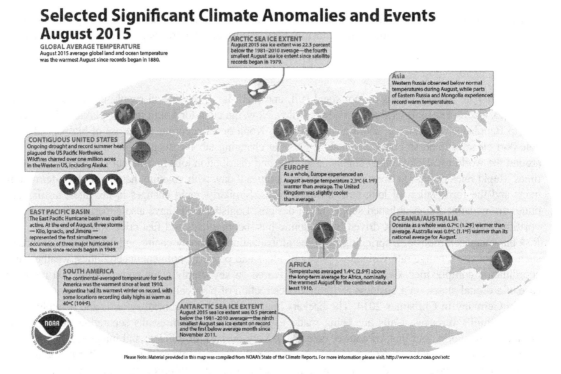

Figure 10.15 Significant Climate Anomalies and Events

Source: "Selected Significant Climate Anomalies and Events," *National Oceanic and Atmospheric Administration*, U.S. Department of Commerce, accessed Oct. 3, 2015, http://www.ncdc.noaa.gov/sotc/service/global/extremes/201508.gif.

- Compliance responsibilities have exploded. The U.S. pharmaceutical industry, for example, had to comply with the new Drug Quality and Security Act, which took effect Jan. 1, that will require drug manufacturing companies to keep records of the transaction history of drugs moving through their systems. By 2020, it will extend to drug distributors, hospitals, doctors, nursing homes, pharmacies, and other businesses involved in the journey from manufacturer to patient. All this costs money, but community, customer, and government concerns about ethics, safety, and sustainability have mandated different expectations and regulations worldwide. Easily available global communication technologies have made it possible for individuals to reveal and revile powerful noncompliant multinationals.

- Product variety has proliferated, largely to satisfy demanding consumers and stave off growing low-cost competition. McKinsey reports that cell phone makers introduced 900 more varieties of phones in 2009 compared to what they introduced in 2000. Variety means increased complexities in sourcing, forecasting, pricing, manufacturing, inventory and distribution, raised risks, and more rapid changes in supply chain design.

- 'Made here' pressures are growing as a counterpoint to globalization. To an extent, it makes business sense for products that have short life cycles, are not labor intensive, have high obsolescence costs, and are sold to time-sensitive markets to be made in the country of consumption. Electronics and high fashion apparel fit the bill. But businesses carefully weigh the benefits of shorter production and delivery lead times, lower transportation costs, energy savings, and currency exchange risk considerations against the very real and significant labor cost savings available in other locations worldwide. That's why electronic products like smartphones, laptops, and digital cameras sold in the U.S. are made in China. On the other hand, IKEA crunched the numbers and opted for U.S. manufacturing for its North America market over lower cost manufacturing locations, citing "reducing sourcing costs, reducing overall lead times, reducing currency exposure, transportation concerns and [developing a] secure supply for IKEA's growing demand" as some of the reasons behind the $281 million, four-manufacturing facility phased plan.[6]

- 'Build close' to the customer is a recent mantra driven by same-day/hour delivery expectations. To this end, we see the development of mini-distribution centers, perhaps with existing businesses, growing applications of new production technologies like 3D printing, and rapid deliveries by drone/cabs/ Uber and the like. Amazon is reportedly developing mobile 3D production trucks and experimenting with various methods of rapid delivery.

10.5.2 Responding to Trends: Flexibility in Design

Supply chain design is responding to such trends. Flexibility has become a mantra in supply chain design, replacing the old focus on costs and costs alone. But the ability to respond quickly to changes in demand, supply, logistics, and political/government regulations does not come cheap. Capacity redundancies in the form of alternate suppliers, plants, and distributors have to be created and maintained and capacity made more versatile. Even Toyota, of just-in-time inventory fame, has taken to keeping small reserves of inventory at strategic locations in its supply chain. More flexible distribution networks are also being developed with dynamic logistics routing between different modes, such as rail and road and between-sea routes, in step with changing conditions. Completion of the deepening of the Panama Canal will enable 14,000 TEU ships to take advantage of this sea route 'short cut' connecting the Atlantic and Pacific oceans. One TEU represents the cargo capacity of a standard shipping container, 20 feet (6.1 m.) long and 8 feet (2.44 m.) wide. Nestlé developed a new distribution system using a river barge that carried 300 different goods, stopping at 18 markets of 800,000 potential customers along the Amazon river in Brazil. Another interesting phenomena is the development of assembly, packaging, and repair and return capabilities by the distribution network, enhancing network capacity and building agility in the chain. Toshiba laptops are being repaired and serviced at distribution centers being run by UPS. Flexibility in supply chain design also requires flexible leadership—a flexible mind-set on the part of the designers and the management team. Managers must be willing to tolerate the organizational and personal disruption that typically accompanies change.

Companies are splintering long dedicated supply chains into shorter and more flexible chains. Going against the conventional wisdom of single sourcing and economies of scale, a U.S. consumer company splintered its single supply chain into four parts, based on a volatility-volume analysis: high volume, stable demand products were retained for China, volatile demand items were allocated to the domestic U.S. supply chain, and low volume-low demand items were consigned to Mexican and U.S. supply chains. High volatility items benefitted from being made in the U.S. since their markets paid a premium for quick delivery, agility in meeting specification changes, and more complex manufacturing. Similarly, Dell cast aside its finely tuned, efficiency-geared direct order supply chain design to carve separate supply chains based on customer segment needs for service, speed, and pricing. Splintering supply chains into smaller units aids visibility, and the smaller number of products and entities in a particular supply chain makes it easier to manage and redesign. For example, companies that make both basic and fashion clothing will want to deliver their basic products through an efficient supply chain and deliver their fashion products through a highly responsive supply chain. Each segment will have different forecasting and stocking policies. Similarly, two-speed supply chains are being talked about now—a slower, stable one for established but stagnant Western markets and another for fast-growing Asian markets with much faster response, adaptability, and agility attributes. Quality may be defined differently in these different markets/supply chains.

Real options theory, a way of estimating the comparative value of alternative courses of action/decisions, is being employed to estimate the value of flexibility in supply chain design.

OM IN PRACTICE

Real Options in Supply Chain Design

Evaluating a choice between locating a plant in Germany or Switzerland, the company's home, Flexcell Ltd. chose the latter since labor and regulations differences meant that the Switzerland plant could be built months quicker. In options language, that meant Flexcell had an option to delay building at Switzerland for several months vis-à-vis Germany and collect valuable information about the market in that time. Given a target completion date for building the plant, Germany would have required an immediate start to building, a disadvantage strong enough to offset a cost saving of about 15 percent over the Switzerland plant. Being closer to home also afforded easier management and control, and quicker response time to disruptions. Unlike the traditional discounted cash flow approach to evaluating competing projects that considers cash flows only, real options theory allowed Flexcell to place a dollar figure on the value of these flexibility options. Their plant in Switzerland is reportedly doing very well.

Adapted from: S.D. Treville and L. Trigeorgis, 2010, "It May Be Cheaper to Manufacture at Home," *Harvard Business Review*, October 2010, 84–87.

Visibility, or the ability to track the movement of goods, production plans of suppliers, and stocks held at different locations in real time, is essential to flexibility—and safety. The cause of the nationwide salmonella outbreak some time ago was initially attributed to contaminated tomatoes. As it turned out, peppers from Mexico were the culprits. It took U.S. authorities more than a month and 1,300 people stricken across the country to identify the root cause of the outbreak. To capture and monitor product movement and storage points, the food supply chain is experimenting with radio frequency identification, laser etchings on products, and micro-percussion markers that make tiny indents on produce. Unfortunately, visibility may conflict with flexibility. Visibility calls for fixed communication software and hardware investments in specific supplier, assembly, and distribution locations, while flexibility discourages heavy specific chain investments since alternative chains have to be developed.

10.5.3 Sustainability and Other Considerations

Supply chain designs are heeding calls to include sustainability as an important design criteria. The goal is to create a design that minimizes habitat destruction and consumption of natural resources and maintains a low energy and low air/noise pollution footprint. Distribution networks focus on reducing energy use as well as air and noise pollution through innovative packaging, more efficient route planning, and the use of energy efficient modes of transport. Companies such as Walmart and P&G have introduced programs to select, acquaint, train, and evaluate suppliers on sustainability metrics. Efforts are underway to persuade key suppliers to drive sustainability standards down to the smaller, lower tier suppliers in the supply chain. Motorola manufactures a carbon-free handset for Sprint's green manufacturing program, meeting or surpassing criteria on the use of sustainable materials, sustainable packaging, recyclable content, and energy efficiency. Timberland redesigned its shoe boxes to save 15 percent on material costs, and they sell 25 million pairs of shoes annually. Contributing to sustainability goals but driven by customer service motives, reverse supply chain designs are being re-examined and revamped to ensure easy collection of product returns and recalls and proper disposal and recycling of materials. Traditionally designed on lowest cost basis for the key tasks of collection, sorting, movement, storage, repair/refurbish, and inspection, reverse supply chains were suited to slower moving, technologically stable products like office machines. But agile supply chain designs are being developed for products that are vulnerable to rapid obsolescence in terms of technology or selling trends (e.g., cellphones).

Innovative thinking in logistics and intermodal transport are changing supply chain designs.

OM IN PRACTICE

Drones and Tube Logistics—Pipe Dreams?

Jeff Bezos introduced a working concept of Amazon Prime service recently—a drone picks up your package (up to 5 lbs.) and delivers it by air to your doorstep. In Mumbai, a pizza place is already flying pizza-carrying drones over crowded Mumbai streets. Book rental company Zookal will deliver books to its customers on drones flying across the vast expanses of Australia. USPS repurposes its mail vans as drone mother ships that park in a neighborhood and deliver by drone—fancy or future fact? Legal hurdles are being resolved, and the technology is evolving to balance cost, distance, and safety issues.

Moving goods takes an enormous amount of energy and contributes to pollution. It also takes time. Dr. Cotana at the University of Perugia, Italy, proposed to solve all that with the introduction of an 'old' technology—moving materials through pipelines. Pipenet, as his system is called, envisages moving a pair of jeans or shoes or an iPhone in capsules that speed below cities at 1,000 mph using induction motors with magnetic technology. The cost is estimated to be one-tenth of the cost of building a high speed rail transport system and has added benefits such as reducing congestion and pollution. The concept is controversial, with concerns ranging from terrorist threats to underground rodents as well as anticipated high installation and repair costs. In the long term, can we expect steak grown in Argentina to be delivered in New York City through a trans-oceanic pipeline?

Adapted from: Paul Clinton, "USPS Considering Drone Delivery Vehicle," *Business Fleet*, May 13, 2015, http://www.businessfleet.com/news/story/2015/05/usps-considering-drone-delivery-vehicle.aspx; Kelsey D. Atherton, "Amazon Wants to Begin Drone Deliveries as Soon as They're Legalized," *Popular Science*, June 17, 2015, http://www.popsci.com/amazon-wants-drone-delivery-soon-legally-possible; "The Amazing Pizza Delivery Drone" *The Telegraph*, May 22, 2014, http://www.telegraph.co.uk/technology/technology-video/10848992/The-amazing-pizza-delivery-drone.html; Dean Nelson, "Indian Restaurant Uses Aerial Drone to Deliver Pizza to Skyscraper," *The Telegraph*, May 22, 2014, http://www.telegraph.co.uk/news/worldnews/asia/india/10848680/Indian-restaurant-uses-aerial-drone-to-deliver-pizza-to-skyscraper.html; Staff, "Pipedream," *Supply Chain Quarterly*, Quarter 1, 2011, http://www.supplychainquarterly.com/print/scq201101forward_pipedream/.

A shipment today can be moved through a combination of road, ship, and air, depending on cost, convenience, and speed needs. Container ships, trains, and trucks have made movement more compact, fast, and safe. A shipment can be air-freighted from Hong Kong to Paris at a cost of approximately $10,000 or sent by sea at a cost of $3,000. An alternative solution may involve an intermodal distribution route that air-freights the shipment to Taiwan and then ships it from Taiwan to Paris at a total cost of $5,000, with a transit time that markedly improves on the original all by sea route delivery time. One problem with transportation is the growing congestion and aging in U.S. infrastructure—both ports and roads. There has not been a significant new port built in the U.S. for years. In contrast, China is building about eight new ports at the moment. The same goes for road construction. The charts below show the increasing congestion in road traffic (with little action to expand the national highway system significantly). Again, in contrast, the expressway network of China (about 70,000 miles) surpassed the overall length of the American Interstate Highway System in 2011, with about 4,600 miles being built in 2014 alone.

Tax-efficient supply chain designs are becoming popular and constitute a hot area for consultants. Companies are moving production and concentrating warehousing and distribution in specific countries like Singapore and Thailand to take advantage of tax efficiencies, lower tariff rates, and tariff-free access to the country's regional free trade agrement partners. Suzuki pays about 12 percent tariff on parts imported into India for its vehicles made there. In contrast, Hyundai pays just 1 percent to 5 percent, benefitting from South Korea's free trade agreement with India. Companies can stand to make millions just by switching tasks and inventory to tax beneficial locations. Of course, such moves must be made after considering the effects of the switch on logistics costs, delivery times, and the costs of reduced physical proximity to the end user.

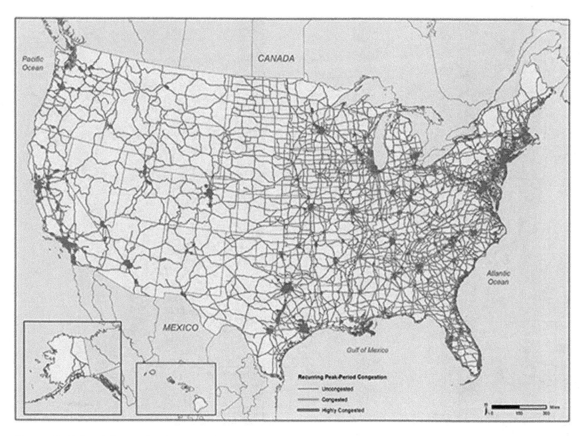

Figure 10.16 Road Congestion 2011 on U.S. National Highway System

Source: U.S. Department of Transportation, Federal Highway Administration, Office of Freight Management and Operations, *Freight Analysis Framework*, version 3.4, 2013, accessed Oct. 3, 2015, http://www.rita.dot.gov/bts/publications/passenger_travel/chapter3/figure3-2.

10.6 Conclusion

Customer: *"Why should I choose you?"*
Business: *"Because we promise you that the product you purchase is made, transported, and distributed to meet your needs in the most efficient, reliable, timely, ethical, and sustainable manner possible."*

To recapitulate, designing a supply chain requires identifying and choosing from a selection of supply, assembly, and distribution networks, involving choices on the number and location of supply, manufacturing, assembly, warehouse, and distribution centers. The choice of design considers facility location, transportation loads and costs, currency fluctuations, location tax differences, speed to market, flexibility to adjust/adapt to disasters and interruptions, warehouse size, manufacturing production plans, and costs.

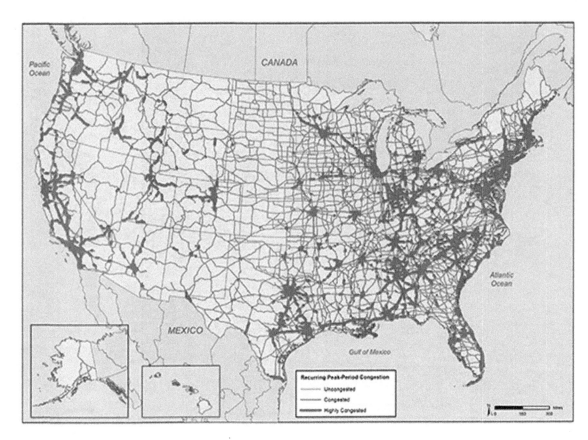

Figure 10.17 Anticipated Road Congestion 2040 on U.S. National Highway System.

Source: U.S. Department of Transportation, Federal Highway Administration, Office of Freight Management and Operations, *Freight Analysis Framework*, version 3.4, 2013, accessed Oct. 3, 2015, http://www.rita.dot.gov/bts/publications/passenger_travel/chapter3/figure3-2.

Supply chains are organic entities that live, breathe, and change. Changes in the operating environment can strip away a supply chain design's rationale in weeks. All it takes is a stroke of a pen somewhere in the world to introduce a tariff or a law that suddenly wrecks the cost and availability structure of a product. Good anticipation, good signaling systems, and built-in agility and adaptability in supply chain design help cope. The supply chain design principles of efficiency, agility, and adaptability discussed in this chapter highlight the importance of such capabilities. Today, 80 percent of the cost of a product is determined by its design *and* its supply chain design. Both product design and supply chain design run, or should run, concurrently, for maximum effect. And because supply chains never stand still for long, supply chain designing never stops.

What Have We Learned?

What Is Supply Chain Design?

- Supply chain design involves finding the 'best' configuration of supply, assembly, and distribution facilities to make, store, finance, and move a product from raw material to finished product in the hands of the consumer.
- A value chain identifies the most profitable position in a supply chain design—who makes/will make the most money and where.

Why Is It Important?

- How facilities and flows are selected and organized in a particular supply chain design would affect a company's competitive advantage—cost, quality, speed and reliability of delivery, and the ability to cope with changes in demand and supply—while satisfying desired customer service levels.
- All business study majors are connected to supply chain design. Product pricing, product availability, product and logistics financing, tax efficiency analysis, and personnel management and training are tasks that interface with majors such as marketing, finance, tax accounting, and HR.

How Is It Done?

- Supply chain design involves the design of supply, assembly, and distribution networks.
- Supply chain design should be concurrent with product design.
  - Lean supply chain designs that focus on efficiency best support functional standardized products that serve functional, low demand volatility markets.
  - Agile supply chain designs that focus on responsiveness best support short product life cycle, high variety products that serve innovative, high volatility markets.
  - Some products can be broken down into standardized and customized components or making processes, requiring a mix of lean and agile supply chain designs.
  - Some products may require separate efficient and agile supply chain designs, the latter to meet emergencies and sudden surges in demand.
- Adaptability in supply chain design, the capability to find, develop, and access alternative supply chains when normal networks are disrupted or become infeasible, is of value to both lean and agile types of supply chains.
- Shorter distribution networks, seen in e-tailing business models, mean lower overall cost, but local inventory is not available to satisfy immediate consumer wants.
- Supply chain design recommends potentially advantageous positions of ownership along a supply chain. These positions of profit or power are generally identifiable by rapid rates of technology change or the need to protect/acquire technologies of value or ensure quality and availability of supplies.
- Simulation and optimization models are the preferred tools of supply chain design, enabling performance comparisons and sensitivity analysis among different possible configurations of supply, assembly, and distribution networks.

Was It Done Right?

- Supply chain designs are rendered ineffective or weakened by changing operational conditions such as the emergence of lower cost suppliers outside the chain, changes in tax, tariffs, and currency exchange rates, fuel cost increases, and natural disruptions.
- Human self-interest, work biases, and inertia are also reasons for supply chain design failures.
- Supply chain design performance metrics are difficult to separate from supply chain management metrics—cost, time, quality, and cash-to-cash cycle time.
- Supply chain design performance is also measured in terms of network resiliency—the ability to absorb and recover from disruptions. Time to recover (TTR) is estimated by inventory, capacity, and routing options in the network.

Current Trends in Supply Chain Design

- Globalization has increased the length, number of nodes, and time to supply aspects of supply chain designs.
- Volatility in commodity prices, fuel costs, labor rates, currency exchange rates, and market demand conditions raise risks, increase costs, and hamper long term planning.
- International compliance burden has grown, with new financial and regulatory laws being enacted in different regions of the world.
- In response to these forces, supply chain designs have become more flexible, with capacity redundancies and the transfer of some assembly and repair tasks to the distribution network.
- Long, extended supply chain designs have also evolved into shorter, local chains with increased visibility on real time information and increased proximity to high value, high volatility markets.
- Technology advances such as RFID enable greater visibility into supply chain member activities. Connectivity and knowledge generation and sharing across and among chains are valued even when monolithic supply chains are splintered into shorter ones.
- Warehousing and distribution are increasingly being located on the basis of country and region tax and tariff efficiencies.

Discussion Questions

1 Give an example of a product that is best suited for a:

   a) Lean supply chain design
   b) Agile supply chain design
   c) A Le-Agile supply chain design

2 Suggest two practical measures, each, of the following in a supply chain design:

   a) Efficiency
   b) Agility
   c) Adaptabilty

3 Suggest two ways to increase agility and adaptability in a supply chain design. Discuss the advantages and disadvantages of increasing agility and adaptability in supply chain design.

4 Read the following news piece.

UPDATE: Mars: Ivory Coast Cocoa Ban to Have No 'Short Term' Effect

NEW YORK (Dow Jones)—Candy maker Mars Inc. said Tuesday that a call by Ivory Coast's presidential claimant for a month-long ban on cocoa exports won't affect production in the near term.

Over the weekend, Alassane Ouattara, who is widely held to have won the Nov. 28 election, called for the ban to financially corner his challenger, incumbent Laurent Gbagbo.

Ivory Coast supplies about a third of the world's cocoa, and the export ban sent prices on the Intercontinental Exchange to one-year highs on Monday.

In an emailed statement, Mars, the maker of Snickers and M&Ms, said: "We expect that a complete understanding of the export ban and its implications will require some time, but we are certain that in the short term this will not impact our ability to manufacture the chocolate products that our consumers desire."

Agriculture company Cargill Inc. announced Monday that it was temporarily suspending purchases in Ivory Coast. Archer Daniels Midland Co. (ADM) and Barry Callebaut AG (BARN.EB) said they are evaluating the situation. Switzerland-based Barry Callebaut, however, said it has sufficient cocoa stocks to cover its processing needs.

Hershey Co. (HSY) declined to comment on the situation.

On Monday, the U.S. State Department said it endorsed the ban.

"It is part of our strategy to deny Laurent Gbagbo the resources so that he could continue to buy support from the military and political actors," Assistant Secretary Philip J. Crowley said in a briefing. "We hope that this will convince him to step aside."

ICE cocoa for March delivery was recently 1.7 percent higher on the day at $3,367 a ton.

Adapted from: Leslie Josephs, "Mars: Ivory Coast Ban to Have No Short Term Effect," *Dow Jones Newswires.*

What would you do as the supply chain designer for Mars?

Suggestions could range from finding cocoa substitutes to marketing promotions for non-cocoa products to finding alternative sources of supply and locking up available stocks by paying more.

Suggested Class Projects

1 Pirates are an active danger, especially near Somalia. Identify Somalia on a world map—trace the origin and destination points of cargo ships that move through that area—and redraw the supply chain to suggest alternative viable routes. Estimate the additional costs and times of these alternative routes.

2 Draw the supply network, assembly network and distribution network for

    a)   An auto manufacturer in the U.S.

    b)   An auto manufacturer in Europe

    c)   A pair of Levi's jeans

    Who captures the most value in the supply chain design?

3 The Panama Canal is being deepened to accommodate 14,000-plus TEU ships. Examine the impact this would have on U.S.-bound cargo, with reference to specific ports on the two coasts and what the ports need to do as well as the impact on costs and lead times for importers in the U.S.

Points for Discussion

Currently, most cargo from Asia goes to Los Angeles/Long Beach, where it is moved by rail and truck to the Midwest and East Coast. But the new canal will change that route. Ships coming from Asia will be able to bypass the West Coast and sail directly into Gulf of Mexico and East Coast ports. Direct sea deliveries to the East Coast would cut out the expense and hassles of road and rail transportation from West Coast ports to the East Coast. And it's not just shipping from Asia but also shipping to Asia—coal exports to Asia are increasing rapidly, but West Coast ports are ill-equipped to handle the traffic. The deepened Panama canal would further move Asia-going shipping away from the West Coast ports to the East Coast.

Recognizing the threat, Long Beach is investing $3 billion over the next 10 years to increase and streamline port capacity and processing times. And the East Coast ports are not prepared to handle the larger ships. The "post-Panamax" ships require depths of up to 50 feet of water to enter the ports when fully loaded. The only East Coast port that has that capacity now is the one in Norfolk, VA. Other ports have plans to expand. The port of New York/New Jersey has a $2.3 billion project under way to deepen its harbor to 50 feet but also needs another $1.3 billion to raise the Bayonne Bridge, under which ships must pass. The port of Mobile is undergoing a $600 million improvement project, building a new container terminal and a turning basin for large ships. The port of Savannah is midway through an eight-year, $500 million expansion that will double its container capacity and is embarking on another project to deepen the Savannah River along the 35 miles between the ocean and the port. Similarly, the ports of Charleston, New Orleans, and Miami are either planning or undertaking significant port improvement projects to accommodate deeper draught and increased traffic from Asia.

Suggested Cases[7]

Supply Chain Optimization at Hugo Boss A, HBS, Product# 609029-PDF-ENG

Description

We evaluate the impact of a supply chain pilot implemented at Hugo Boss. This pilot entailed altering the way in which Hugo Boss orders from its suppliers. We explore the challenge of assessing the impact of supply chain change, the link between operational performance and firm performance, and the relationship between sales, inventory, and product availability.

Learning Objective

To understand the effects of supply chain redesign on firm performance.

Evolution of the X Box Supply Chain, HBS, Product# GS49-PDF-ENG

Description

In November 2005, Microsoft prepared for a global launch of its next-generation game console, the Xbox 360. Microsoft's original Xbox had been introduced a year after Sony's Playstation but would beat Sony's next-generation system to market by a substantial amount. It would also play an important part in Microsoft's future strategy, where the home entertainment system was seen as a major growth opportunity. Describes the evolution of the video game console business and the evolution of the Xbox, both from a design and manufacturing perspective. Microsoft's decisions for the original Xbox supply chain are described, together with the changes in the supply chain that were made for the Xbox 360. Asks questions about the motivation for changes to the supply chain, the risks and benefits of global rather than regional launch, and the use of contract manufacturers.

Learning Objective

To illustrate how supply chains must evolve to support changing corporate strategy. Uses the changes in the Xbox supply chain to facilitate discussion of how changes in the competitive environment, and in corporate strategy, lead to changes in the supply chain.

Notes

1 C. H. Fine, "Clockspeed-Based Strategies for Supply Chain Design," *Production and Operations Management*, 9(3), 2000, 213–221; M. L. Fisher, "What Is the Right Supply Chain for Your Product?" *Harvard Business Review*, March–April 1997, 105–116; F. Salvador, M. Rungtusanatham, and C. Forza, "Supply-chain Configurations for Mass Customization," *Production Planning & Control: The Management of Operations*, 15(4), 2004, 381–397.

2 M. Christopher and D. R. Towill, "Supply Chain Migration from Lean and Functional to Agile and Customized," *Supply Chain Management: An International Journal*, 5(4), 2000, 206–213.

3 C. Burritt, C. Wolf, and M. Boyle, "Why Wal-Mart Wants to Take the Driver's Seat," *Bloomberg Businessweek*, May 31–June 30, 2010, 17–18.

4 B. Eksioglu, S. Eksioglu, J. Zhang, and M. Jin, "A Simulation Model to Analyze the Impact of Outsourcing on Furniture Supply Chain Performance," *Forest Products Journal*, 60(3), May 2010, 258–265.

5 L. Solomon and J. McLain, "Designing Your High Tech Supply Chain with Risk in Mind." *Logistics Spectrum*, 43(1), 2009, 8–11.

6 Karen M. Koenig, "Inside Swedwood: IKEA's First U.S. Plant: IKEA Manufacturing Subsidiary Swedwood Opens the Doors to its 930,000-square-foot Facility in Danville, VA, Part of a Four-phase, $281 Million Plan," May 2008, http://www.thefreelibrary.com/Inside+Swedwood%3A+IKEA's+first+U.S.+plant%3A+IKEA+manufacturing..-a0179694070.

7 hbr.org/Case-Studies

11 Managing Supply Chains

Chapter Take-Aways

- The importance of supply chain management
- Types of uncertainties in a supply chain
- How to manage uncertainties in a supply chain
- Ways to assess supply chain health
- Emerging trends in supply chain management

Managing Supply Chains: A Road Map

Customer: *"Why should I choose you?"*

Business: *"Because we promise that you will find our product on the right shelf, at the right time, and at the right cost, without concerns about child labor, toxic chemicals, animal cruelty, or unsafe worker conditions being a part of what you buy from us."*

Delivering on this promise depends on intelligent management of the supply chain we designed in the previous chapter.

11.1 What Is Supply Chain Management?

That OJ carton calling to you in the juice aisle does not tell you how it got there. Behind the accomplishment of placing that juice carton in the right shelf, at the right time, and at the right cost lies a story of orchestrated purchasing, supply, production, storage, and logistics effort. In other words, supply chain management!

Supply chain management (SCM) = managing the (SUPPLY network + ASSEMBLY network + DISTRIBUTION network) + the HUMAN network

11.1.1 Challenges

A supply chain is a network of organizations embodying a chain of capabilities that serve to build and deliver products and services to markets. Supply chain management is the coordination, alignment, and orchestration of the supply, assembly, and distribution networks of a supply chain to synch with customer needs. It also involves the management of one other network—the human network embedded in the other three networks. The goal in managing supply chains is to build and move product, information, knowledge, and cash in a smooth, no-waste flow from the source to the customer on demand. In short, supply chain management aims to match supply with demand in a way designed to maximize revenue and profit at minimum environmental and social cost. So what's the problem? Not one, but many, as you may imagine. For one thing, one would be lucky if supply and demand actually and precisely match just one day in a year. For the most part, they trend in opposite directions, and companies find themselves either engorged or starved for supplies. Customers demand quicker and more accurate fulfillment while demand grows ever more volatile, driven by changing economic conditions and growing product variety. On the supply side, increasingly globalized supply, assembly, and distribution networks make supply markets more volatile and exposed to an increasing variety of political, economic, technological, climatic, and safety risks. Managing a supply chain is a complex task. It requires managing the flow of goods, cash, and technology in the chain as well as the management of intellectual property, risk, human emotions, political factors, and safety and sustainability concerns. Companies that have done it well (like Apple and McDonald's, Gartner's 2014 Supply Chain of the Year) stand out. But problems do arise with complex global supply chains. Take Boeing's management of its supply chain for the highly advanced Dreamliner 987 passenger airplanes, for example. Read on to find out how events unfolded.

Global Partners Bring the 787 Together

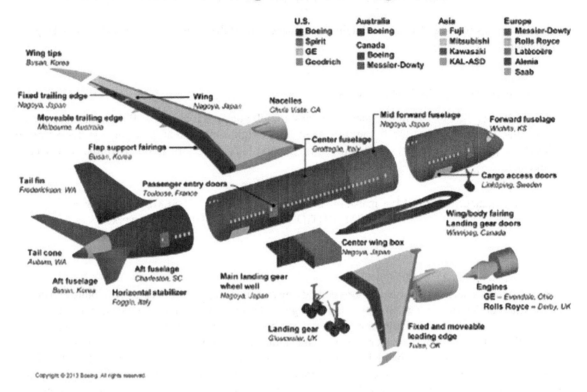

Figure 11.1 Global Partners Bring the 787 Together

Source: With permission from www.BoeingImages.com

Boeing Press Release, Oct 12, 2007 (abbreviated)

AUCKLAND, New Zealand—Clearly, as our company's top executives expressed this week, the 787 schedule change is disappointing for all of us at Boeing. . . .

Still, this six-month delivery delay from our original target of May 2008 stings a bit. . . . The first 787 is now due to fly by the end of the fourth quarter of 2008.

The issues that led to this week's announcement are essentially the same ongoing challenges we talked about last month, including out-of-sequence production work on the structure of the first airplane and shortages of parts. What we discovered is that the work has gone more slowly than we had anticipated. And it became clear that we'd used up the margin to accommodate any unexpected issues.

Boeing Press Release, April 9, 2008 (summary)

Boeing Revises 787 First Flight and Delivery Plans; Adds Schedule Margin to Reduce Risk of Further Delays

- First flight moved into fourth-quarter 2008; deliveries to begin third-quarter 2009.
- Production plan now targets approximately 25,787 deliveries in 2009.
- Slower than expected completion of work that traveled from supplier facilities into Boeing's final assembly line, unanticipated rework, and the addition of margin into the testing schedule.
- "We have taken significant action to improve supply chain and production system performance. . . ."

Boeing Press Release, Dec. 11, 2008 (summary)

Boeing Schedules 787 Dreamliner First Flight for Second Quarter 2009; First Delivery for First Quarter 2010

- Updated schedule moves the commercial jet's first flight into the second quarter of 2009 and first delivery into the first quarter of 2010. Approximately a further six month delay.
- New schedule reflects the impact of disruption caused by the recent Machinists' strike along with the requirement to replace certain fasteners in early production airplanes.
- "We're laser focused on what needs to be done to prepare for first flight," said Pat Shanahan, 787 program vice president.

Boeing Press Release, April 27, 2010 (summary)

Boeing Sets 787 First Delivery Date for Mid-First Quarter 2011

- Now expects delivery of the first 787 in the middle of the first quarter 2011.
- Cumulative impact of a series of issues, including supplier workmanship issues related to the horizontal stabilizer and instrumentation delays and delayed availability of engines from Rolls Royce could push first delivery of the 787 . . . to mid-first quarter 2011

Boeing Press Release, Jan. 18, 2011(summary)

Boeing Sets 787 First Delivery for Third Quarter

- Expects delivery of the first 787 Dreamliner in the third quarter of this year.
- Continued delay reflects the impact of an in-flight incident during testing last November and includes the time required to produce, install, and test updated software and new electrical power distribution panels in the flight test and production airplanes.

(All Nippon Airways took delivery of the first 787 jet on Sept. 25, 2011.)

As of 2015, Boeing was making about 10 Dreamliners per month and had not yet managed to bring costs down to below selling price. Why did Boeing deliver more than a full three years after its original May 2008 first jet delivery date? Well, for one thing, keeping track of the extensive supply network and monitoring quality and delivery schedules proved more difficult than Boeing had anticipated. It has about 1,200 "tier-one" suppliers that supply parts directly from 5,400 factories in 40 countries. These factories, in turn, are fed by thousands more "tier-two" suppliers, which themselves receive parts from many others. Did the sheer number of suppliers and outsourced components overwhelm Boeing's supplier monitoring, coordination, and development capabilities? Failure to synchronize delivery of seemingly minor items like fasteners led to ripple delay effects in production. Repeated quality and delivery failures point to inadequacies in Boeing's supplier quality control system. Boeing vetted all the contractors but left it to its partners to vet the subcontractors. Boeing admits that, in hindsight, too much of the Dreamliner program was contracted out to other firms. In fact, Boeing has now purchased manufacturing operations from suppliers like Vought Aircraft and Global Aeronautica LLC. On the other hand, Boeing alone cannot afford to vertically integrate all the key suppliers: The capital investments would be huge. Farming out product manufacturing is a model that Walmart does exceptionally well; can it really be applied to something as complex as plane manufacturing? Can Boeing learn something from Walmart's legendary logistical and supplier coordination capabilities? In hindsight, other questions arise, too, about the adequacy of their risk analysis process and second sourcing planning for critical parts. To be fair, Airbus, Boeing's chief competitor, also suffered from similar delays in its Airbus 380, the largest commercial plane at this time. In a sense, Boeing's transparency about the delays afflicting its building process is re-assuring to its customers. Its willingness to address criticism and not cut corners to speed up deliveries, testifies to the meticulous attention that Boeing pays to quality of manufacture and flight in its products. Planes generally have a long product life cycle, and Boeing will, most likely, recoup its financial losses. Boeing has since become much more aggressive in stress-testing supplier manufacturing capabilities, adding 200 engineers and supply chain specialists who regularly verify that suppliers have the required skills, processes, and capabilities. Still, quality issues such as battery fires and engine icing problems persist.[1]

11.1.2 Supply Chain Management vs. Supplier Management

How is managing supply chains different from traditional purchasing? Unlike managing a few immediate suppliers with a competitive-bidding, lowest-price process, actively managing a supply chain requires:

- A focus on end-to-end process—requiring a holistic integrative perspective of the supply chain.
- More intense and committed supplier relationships, especially if larger suppliers are expected to monitor and manage smaller suppliers.
- Greater information sharing between buyer-suppliers and among suppliers. A delay in one component could lead to other suppliers having to delay their own deliveries of matching components.
- Greater focus on performance monitoring and measurement of key suppliers and the purchasing organization—costs, cash flows, quality defects, supplier process capability metrics, inventory.
- Greater focus on the total cost of ownership in buying items (item cost + cost of transport + duties/tariffs + cost of defects + cost of delayed delivery + cost of overseeing and monitoring + opportunity cost).
- Aligned incentives along the supply chain to achieve focus on end-customer service and satisfaction.

11.2 Why Is Supply Chain Management Important?

Companies are looking at supply chains as a strategic means to gain competitive advantage, spread risks, and create options for alternative sourcing.

Competitive advantage = own area of competence + supply chain design + supply chain management

Supply chains, when managed well, can deliver decisive competitive advantage by way of cost, innovation, speed, reliability, and flexibility to meet changing customer needs.

11.2.1 Importance for Businesses

A supply chain can be directly responsible for up to 60 percent to 80 percent of a company's total cost structure. How it is managed has direct performance effects. A study of supply chain disruptions over time found that such disruptions impact stock returns on average by nearly (-)10 percent.[2] Recovery is slow, and perceived risk goes up. It is no surprise that supply chain management ranks high on CEOs and COO's list of priority attention areas.

Supply chain managers are charged with reducing operating costs and inventory levels, improving service and product quality, speeding up delivery times, reducing risk, and achieving a greener supply chain footprint. Some of these goals are in conflict with others—increasing customer service while reducing inventory is usually a contradiction in terms. It is noteworthy that senior executives expect so much from their supply chains—a supply chain manager's job has become a front-line responsibility, much like marketing. It is in the limelight, highly visible, and important.

Brand and marketing can only carry a company so far—when market turbulence hits and/or customers become more demanding, supply chain excellence provides a sustainable competitive edge. Success stories like Zappos were enabled by effective supply chain management, ensuring that differentiation advantages built on fast delivery and easy product returns were maintained consistently. Done well, supply chain management can facilitate access into new markets and increase revenue from existing markets. It can also increase asset productivity by maximizing utilization of assets and converting fixed assets into variable ones (outsourcing). Supply chain management can identify and exploit tax and currency efficiencies in manufacturing, assembly, and distribution worldwide—buying, building, and storing materials in tax friendly locations. Hong Kong offers an extremely low corporate tax of 16.5 percent (by comparison, the U.S. corporate tax rate is 39 percent plus state and local tax), taxing new investments at the even lower rate of 4 percent. There is no sales tax, no capital gains tax, and income tax caps at 20 percent. Other countries like Singapore and Ireland have attracted overseas investments and business by offering low corporate tax rates and a business-friendly environment.

11.2.2 Importance for You

There is probably no better time than now to begin a career in supply chain management. Companies are desperate for revenue growth and focused on cost cutting at the same time. Supply chains, managed with thought and care, can deliver both—and their managers would be visible to top management. Companies like McKinsey that deal with strategy makers in the C-suite now routinely talk about SCM, indicating its visibility and importance to top management. In terms of career growth, senior supply chain positions are typically located near the apex of the organizational pyramid, reporting directly to the CEO or the COO.

Jobs in supply chain management are available in a wide variety of industries.

Boeing is the world's largest aerospace company and leading manufacturer of commercial airplanes and defense, space and security systems. We are engineers and technicians. Skilled scientists and thinkers. Bold innovators and dreamers. Join us, and you can build something better for yourself, for our customers and for the world.

Boeing's 737 Supply Chain Management team has an exciting opportunity to be on the leading edge of supply chain and manufacturing solutions.

The Supply Chain Management Analyst will be responsible for, but may not be limited to, the following:

- Proactive, team player with good communication, analytical skills and ability to manage multiple supply chain work packages supporting aggressive 737 Program Manufacturing rates, representing the 737 Materials Management organization.
- Responsible for managing ordering and provisioning plans to drive synchronization of the supply chain between international or domestic organizations, customers and suppliers.
- Utilizes Supply Chain Management (SCM) systems, methodologies, processes and tools.
- Creates orders to satisfy demand requirements through analysis of manufacturing build rates to determine optimum and accurate inventory requirements balancing costs associated with transportation, inventory levels and inventory turn rates to drive the most efficient and on-time flow of parts from an internal/external supply chain.
- Develops and controls inventory plans based on integration of company, customer and supplier capabilities to optimize inventory levels, maintain high turn rates and reduce unit cost while ensuring accurate requirements and supply chain adherence to committed delivery schedules.
- Applies knowledge of processes associated with regulating/distribution of goods through the entire manufacturing cycle to the delivery of finished products.
- Introduces new SCM tools and techniques by working with complex processes and establishing and maintaining cross-functional relationships to increase supply chain performance.
- Candidate must be highly motivated, a problem solver, and have an ability to identify and lead process improvements utilizing project management principles and methodologies

Boeing is the world's largest aerospace company and leading manufacturer of commercial airplanes and defense, space and security systems. We are engineers and technicians. Skilled scientists and thinkers. Bold innovators and dreamers. Join us, and you can build something better for yourself, for our customers and for the world.

Division

BCA Airplane Programs

Qualifications

Typical education and experience:

Bachelor's degree and typically 3 or more years' related work experience, a master's degree and typically 1 or more years' related work experience or an equivalent combination of education and experience.

This position must meet Export Control compliance requirements, therefore a "U.S. Person" as defined by 22 C.F.R. § 120.15 is required.

- A degree in supply chain or similar field of study is desired, but not required.
- Experience working in Supply Chain or Materials Management is required.
- Working knowledge of supply chain management software is required.
- Familiarity with supply chain & Lean concepts and methodologies is highly desired.

Location

Renton Washington United States

Source: Job listed on Boeing website, accessed Oct. 5, 2015, https://jobs.boeing.com/job/renton/supply-chain-management-analyst-2-3/185/854482.

APICS (The Association for Operations Management) has developed a competency model that identifies the skills required to be a supply chain professional. Knowledge of operations management subjects such as supply chain management, location, process improvement, and project management (all included in this text) rank high as required professional skills. Check it out for an idea of what it takes to attain competence in the field.[3]

Most college majors would interface with some aspect of the supply chain, either directly (e.g., marketing) or in a support role (e.g., finance and accounting). A basic knowledge of how supply chains are designed and managed would be very useful in all functions.

KEY POINTS

- Supply chain management is the coordination, alignment, and day to day management of the supply, assembly, distribution, and human networks that constitute a supply chain.
- Challenges include increasingly demanding and fickle customers, product proliferation, economic uncertainty, volatile labor and commodity costs, and the risks of global supply markets.
- Managing a supply chain requires an end-to-end focus, greater information sharing, use of incentives to align members, and a focus on total supply chain performance.
- Effective supply chain management can convert fixed costs into variable costs, ease entry into new markets, create new markets, and reduce working capital needs.

11.3 How to Manage a Supply Chain

What exactly do we manage in a supply chain, in everyday terms? We manage the business processes that run within a supply chain, part embedded inside company walls, part extending to the supply base or customer, as the case may be. Specifically, we manage, that is, design, monitor, measure, benchmark, communicate, and improve the steps in these processes. Within a company, a supply chain engages a company's procurement, production, logistics, design and engineering, finance, accounting, HR, and marketing/sales functions with each other and with the company's key suppliers, distributors, and customers (see figure 11.2). Procurement and, at times, production, typically directly interface with suppliers, while marketing/sales and finance/accounting directly engage with distributors and customers. Logistics is involved in all inbound and outbound flows. Product and cash flow through the chain, while information exchanges facilitates such flows.

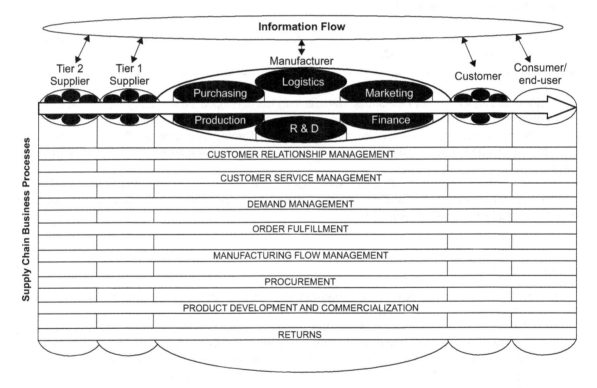

Figure 11.2 What We Manage in a Supply Chain

Source: D.L. Lambert, M.C. Cooper, and J.D. Pagh, "Supply Chain Management: Implementation Issues and Research Opportunities", The International Journal of Logistics Management, Vol 9(2), 1998, pg. 2.

To illustrate, the procurement process *inside* a company may involve the following steps:

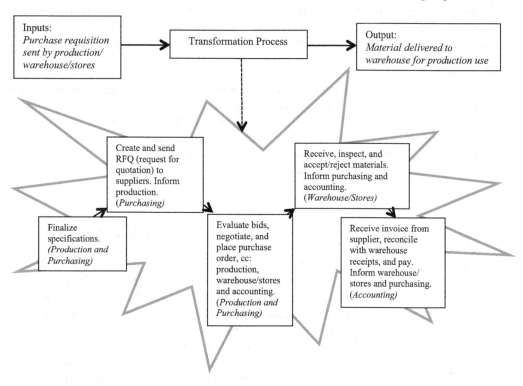

Figure 11.3 Procurement Process

But managing a supply chain requires us to identify and manage key steps in the procurement process that happen *beyond* company boundaries, too. Some of those inbound process steps from the supplier to our receiving warehouse may include:

Process steps taken by supplier	Action taken by us
Order acknowledgment by supplier	Compare acknowledgment with purchase order specs
Raw material receipt at supplier	Monitor quality and delivery in time
Supplier production scheduling	Monitor and match with order delivery schedule
Supplier production runs	Monitor, check for quality, check for completion date
Supplier final product quality control	Request intimation and details; intimate production
Advanced shipment notice (ASN)	Match ASN with purchase order, inform receiving, inspection, production, accounting
Supplier sends invoice	Match with purchase order and hold for receipt of supplies
Logistics to port of shipment	Monitor
In-transit status	Monitor
Customs clearance	Monitor
Logistics to company warehouse	Monitor

The monitoring at both supplier location and in-transit is done through a combination of visibility software, manual checks, and third party reports. We would similarly manage steps both within and outside the company for other processes. Managing the order fulfillment process, for instance, would include managing the internal steps to receive, fill, and ship orders to customers, as well as the outbound steps that happen after the shipment leaves our dock (intransit-status, transhipments, proof of delivery to customer, customer invoice status, bank interactions, returns).

We obviously make hundreds of decisions every day in managing a supply chain. What are the key decisions, though? The first two decisions in managing a supply chain are strategic. One is 'value partitioning' or 'make-buy'—determining *what* part of the value of the product should be made in-house. The second decision is *when* to start the supply chain motor, either after getting a firm indication of demand or in anticipation of demand (pull vs. push). The remaining decisions in managing a supply chain center on synchronizing supply with demand, using a variety of approaches and techniques.

11.3.1 Make-Buy

Make-buy calls for a preliminary evaluation of in-house areas of core competence. These are tasks that are performed best internally for reasons of cost, quality, or time or proprietary knowledge. Anything that an outsider can do better in terms of cost or quality or delivery should be actively considered for outsourcing. Outsourcing is different from purchasing/buying in that outsourcing tasks can potentially be done in-house but are sent out for specific reasons. A car maker normally would not have the equipment or know-how to make steel and therefore buys steel from steel suppliers. But it can certainly choose to make an engine in-house, if it makes business sense to do so, over outsourcing an engine from another manufacturer. Conceptually, it makes sense to make when the cost of internal production (through vertical or horizontal integration) is less than the combined cost of buying the product and managing suppliers (market costs). Trade-offs between make and outsourcing demand careful examination of cost/revenue issues, the nature of the supply market, technology issues, and internal factors:

Table 11.1 Reasons to Outsource (or Not)

Factor	Reasons to Make	Reasons to Outsource	Reasons to both make and outsource
Cost/Revenue			
Cost (high volume Items)	Lower total cost.	Lower total cost Supplier enjoys economies of scale.	Keep some portion in-house to gain knowledge of actual making costs.
High fixed costs	To fully utilize fixed assets and spread fixed costs over a higher volume.	None, unless price difference is really significant. Note a 'vicious cycle' of outsourcing may begin when unit fixed costs of remaining in-house items keep going up as more and more items are outsourced.	Gradually sell-off/retire assets and convert fixed costs into variable costs. Buy by the 'drink', not make and store.

Factor	Reasons to Make	Reasons to Outsource	Reasons to both make and outsource
High margin Item	Retain for profit. Retain for leverage. When customer asks for cost cut, we have high margin in-house items that we can negotiate.	Supplier makes it cheaper, so profit to buyer increases.	Outsource some portion only if supplier is significantly lower priced.
Supply Market			
Few suppliers	Increase competition.	Supplier economies of scale. Gain information about competitor buys.	Make some portion internally to create competition.
Suppliers operating at low capacity		Supplier may need volume to break-even and offer unusually low price.	
New market (typically foreign)	Local suppliers of quality do not exist.	Not familiar with intricacies of market. If you set up own captive plant, locals will beat you every time. Political pressures from host country/distributors.	Go with make, using joint ventures, but exercise caution—partners can churn out fake or similar products on their own using other plants.
Technology/Complexity			
Complex product (difficult to describe or make; integrative architecture)	Retain (and improve) know-how in-house.	Supplier ahead on learning curve: much better quality and lower cost supplier.	If capability gap can be filled, retain some portion in-house. Learn from supplier. Make some in-house to retain making knowledge and skills for a) emergencies and b) to check supplier quality, costs and evaluate requests for price increases
Proprietory/core technology (e.g., Rolex watch movements)	Retain in-house. Supplier may learn and become a competitor.	None.	Political or to open a market. Draw cast-iron contracts and monitor excessively. Demand separate, shielded, assembly lines
High rate of technology change	None.	Keep options open to change to supplier with most current technology. Don't lock up resources in rapid obsolescence technologies	Retain a small portion in-house (experimental lines) to be able to have enough knowledge to carry on an intelligent conversation with a hi-tech supplier or consultant. Or use as a visible deterrent against supplier threats.
Internal			
Volume uncertainty			Utilize internal capacity and keep supplier to meet surges in demand.

(*Continued*)

Table 11.1 (Continued)

Factor	Reasons to Make	Reasons to Outsource	Reasons to both make and outsource
Unionized plant	No choice.	If unions can be won over and outsourcing is in-house otherwise preferable.	Outsource some portion to benchmark make performance against market Also use as as leverage in union negotiations
Managerial Focus		Managers can focus on things of core value that they do well in-house	
Employment		Move surplus employees to work for supplier. Help them keep their jobs.	
CEO ego	Likes big empire to govern.	None.	None.
Transition plan	Core items for in-house: Flag green. Will not outsource. If in-house not best-in-class, develop in-house capability.	Items for outsourcing: Flag red. Also identify items for potential outsourcing. Flag yellow and ask employees to show why items should be retained in-house.	Items for hybrid sourcing: Flag blue (deliberate decision to split between in-house and supplier)

Make/outsourcing decisions are also aided by numerical analysis, using tools such as break-even analysis.

Using Break-Even Analysis for Outsourcing Decisions

Total cost to outsource = unit landed cost (price + freight + insurance . . .) * reqd. qty.
$\qquad = C * D$

Total cost to make $\quad$ = total fixed cost + variable cost/unit * reqd. qty.
$\qquad = FC + VC * D$

Break-even point is where:
Total cost to outsource = total cost to make
$C * B$ (break-even qty.) $= FC + VC * B$

Therefore:

$$B = \frac{FC}{(C - VC)}$$

e.g. D $\quad$ = 30,000 units; FC = \$300,000 (facility + equipment + administative costs)
$\qquad$ VC = \$80/unit; C = \$90/unit

1 $\quad$ *To make or buy?*

TC to outsource $\quad$ = \$90 * 30,000 = \$2,700,000
TC to make $\qquad$ = \$300,000 + (\$85 * 30,000) = \$2,850,000

Outcome: Outsource because it saves $150,000 over making in-house.
Decision: Consider other costs of outsourcing including increased managerial oversight costs.

Also consider the impact of spreading the in-house fixed cost of $300,000 over the remaining
products still being made in-house. Unit fixed costs of these items will increase.
Consider any additional advantage of outsourcing: quality, delivery. . . .

2   *Break-even point?*

B (break-even qty.) $= \dfrac{FC}{(C - VC)}$

$= \dfrac{\$300,000}{(90 - 85)} = 60,000$ pieces, that is, at 60,000 units, the cost of making would
be equal to the cost of outsourcing; making would be cheaper
at more than 60,000 pieces.

The company then has to decide whether to get the job done within the country (in-shoring) or outside
country borders (off-shoring). Note that off-shoring may not always equate to outsourcing, since the offshore
unit may be owned by the company.

QUICK CHECK

A company has just received a quote from China for an important new part that it can also make in-
house. The landed cost from China is $70, while the variable cost of making it in-house is $65. It would
take special tooling worth $100,000 to make the part in-house. The expected production volume for
the part is 10,000 pieces/year. The China supplier will provide the tooling free of charge, if picked for
the order.

a)   Make a make/buy recommendation for the part.
b)   Would your recommendation hold if the volume increases to 15,000 pieces? Or drops to 5,000 pieces?
c)   At what volume would your recommendation of a) above change?

Answer:

a) | *Make/buy recommendation* | *Make* | *Buy* |
|---|---|---|
| Fixed cost (FC) | $100,000 | $0 |
| Unit variable cost (VC) | $65 | $70 (C) |
| Annual demand (units) | 10,000 | 10,000 |

Total cost to outsource = unit landed cost (price + freight + insurance . . .) * reqd. qty.

$$= \$70 * 10,000$$
$$= \$700,000$$

Total cost to make = total fixed cost + variable cost/unit * reqd. qty.

$$= \$100,000 + \$65 * 10,000$$
$$= \$750,000$$

Recommendation: *Buy,* BUT,

First, consider strategic nature of item and whether it's necessary to keep the design in-house. Give in-house a chance to bring the cost down—the unit VC difference is only $5. Also consider additional lead time, possible rise in inventory holdings, and cost of coordination, control, and quality monitoring for China manufacturing. Consider how easy and quick it would be to change production volumes if manufacturing is done by the supplier in China. Consider impact of foreign exchange rate changes and political and ethical risks in China.

b) *Volume changes*

Demand increases to 15,000 units

Total cost to outsource = unit landed cost (price + freight + insurance ...) * reqd. qty.

$$= \$70 * 15,000$$
$$= \$1,050,000$$

Total cost to make = Total fixed cost + variable cost/unit * reqd. qty.

$$= \$100,000 + \$65 * 15,000$$
$$= \$1,975,000$$

Recommendation remains: *Buy*

Also consider that supplier may offer a volume discount and that in-house variable cost may also decline with increased volume due to learning curve effects and other efficiencies. Do not assume that supplier will be able to ramp-up to 15,000 pieces (a 50 percent increase over 10,000 pieces) immediately or without cost to company.

Demand declines to 5,000 units

Total cost to outsource = $70 * 5,000 = 350,000$

Total cost to make = $100,000 + 65 * 5,000 = 425,000$

Recommendation remains: Buy, but consider that unit variable cost for in-house as well as for the supplier are likely to increase with the smaller volume.

c) B (break-even qty.) $= \dfrac{FC}{(C - VC)} = \dfrac{\$100,000}{(\$70 - \$65)} = 20,000$ units.

Recommendation would change from buy to make at any volume above 20,000 units.

Outsourcing implies no ownership stakes. Nonetheless, an off-shoring option demands rational evaluation:

Table 11.2 Reasons to Offshore

Market reasons	Product reasons	Labor cost/skills reasons	Logistics reasons	Other reasons
Importance of time to market—off-shoring is out, if there is a need for speed in responding to changing customer preferences.	Digital—software, X-rays, document processing, expert opinion.	High labor content item. Low labor wages.	Infrastructure exists.	To open up or meet demands of foreign markets.
	Low complexity or low integration part that does not need intricate joining with other parts (e.g., car battery) or repeated iterations of samples (e.g., not custom designs).	Developed supply network available.	Containerization. Container ships. Container ports. Dedicated roads and rails.	Spread risk.
	Low weight/volume preferred, although shipping advances have made higher weights and volumes easier/less expensive to transport.	Skills not available readily locally (special machining, tool/ die making skills are dying in the U.S. with the decline in manufacturing).		Avoid domestic regulations Competition does it.
	Longer life cycle—few volume and design changes.	Suppliers of parts do not exist locally.		Customer has no domestic political stakeholders to answer to.

Companies like Nike and Apple offshore practically all manufacturing and focus on their core competence—product design. At the other extreme, companies like Acrelor Mittal, the global steelmaker, are vertically integrating into iron ore mines, infrastructure development, and distribution. In between are companies that do some manufacturing or asssembly work in-house, based on a variety of reasons, and outsource/offshore the rest. Off-shoring has escalated in the past decade for reasons of cost, quality, and manufacturing flexibility. High wage differentials existed even 30 to 40 years ago between the U.S. and Asia, but the high cost of goods movement and a poor global communication system made global flows of materials and information a time-consuming and impractical process. The real breakthrough in shipping came during the 1990s, when cargo was filled into containers and carried on huge container ships that were then transhipped seamlessly on rail and road to retail shelves across the U.S. Logistics costs per piece plummeted, container ports like those in Los Angeles and New Jersey sprang up to handle container traffic, and, suddenly, new manufacturing regions became feasible around the globe. The combination of high-labor-content goods, low wages, low transport costs, and speedy handling reduced U.S. retail prices for a host of products. Asian workers gained experience and skills as their workload increased, and quality levels rose to match global standards. The advent of the Internet completed the trifecta of globalization—low labor wages, reliable and low cost transportaton, and easy web connectivity. The web connected the world digitally and enabled information and capital to move rapidly around the world to facilitate and finance product flows.

Services that do not require physical proximity to the consumer are especially attractive for offshoring. Lost your food stamps or got a problem with Medicare? In Minnesota, some time ago, you would have been transferred to a person in India to sort it out. Even back in 2004, callers to the California state welfare hotline could either press 1 for English and speak with a worker in India or press 2 for Spanish and speak with a worker in Mexico. This author recently called a company to cancel his store card—a process requiring transfers across multiple continents. After speaking to the service associate in India, he was transferred first to a center in the Philippines, and then finally to Miami, FL, where extensive efforts were made to get him to change his mind. Apparently, different centers have different skill and job specialties, and the 'hard sell' is perhaps best done by domestic experts.

Businesses are off-shoring services primarily for cost reasons. However, the risks of off-shoring need careful evaluation and attention. 'Atrophy' risk refers to a loss of in-house technological and managerial expertise and competence in important technologies and integrative performance. This can happen if offshore operations are not self-owned. Even when suppliers have been located in or near internal company operations, formerly hands-on company engineers have been observed to turn into 'supervisors' of supplier technical personnel and gradually lose experiential expertise. Shadow engineering (overseeing technical tasks) and technology listening posts (monitoring technology developments) are no substitute for a deep undersanding of technology and the 'how it works and interacts with other system components' learning that hands-on experience begets. Other types of risk exist. 'Location' risk refers to country-specific economic and political risks. 'Behavioral' risk refers to the complexity and challenges of managing employees and suppliers in a culturally and socially different milieu. 'Legal' risks refer to the difficulty of understanding and adhering to local laws, courts, and regulations, particularly in regard to intellectual property integrity, employee firings, and environmental issues. Such risks are real and a prime reason for companies preferring local suppliers or joint ventures with local partners in off-shoring projects, at least initially. Off-shoring, understandbly, evokes strong reactions at home. Telstra, an Australian telecom company, moved IT jobs to India. "It's shocking, you know, you have your family, your home loan, the career path you've chosen to develop—to have it taken from you is a bit of a shock," an employee of 16 years with Telstra says. "Once it starts, where does it stop? If the companies are just making purely economic decisions based on shareholder dividends and money, then the country will have no work at all because of course we can't compete with India when someone over there is being paid a pittance," he said.[4] This reaction is typical of wherever jobs are being lost to overseas workers, and there is no good answer. For similar reasons, states like Indiana and Ohio were forced to cancel large off-shoring projects even though a clear business case existing for off-shoring the work. Near-shoring, where the work is done in nearby countries, is becoming more competitive because of rising labor and supply chain monitoring cost in China. Average wages in Mexico, for example, were 19.6 percent lower than China in 2013, whereas in 2003 they were 188 percent higher than China.[5] Add to that lower supply chain monitoring, logistics costs, and speed of response. China, though, has developed deep domestic complementary supply chain networks for many products, an advantage that Mexico cannot match at this time. China itself is now off-shoring production to places like Africa, where an average worker's wage can be just 25 percent of Chinese worker rates—attractive enough to consider moving production, even after accounting for lower productivity and infrastructural demands. Meanwhile, in the USA, energy costs are plumetting, unions are more willing to accept concessions, and states are offering larger incentives to businesses to build at home. U.S. wages in new manufacturing plants have also gone down considerably. Re-shoring, or moving facilities from one country to another, however, may not be as easy as it seems.

OM IN PRACTICE

Leaving Town? Not so Fast!

The CEO of a U.S.-headquartered medical supplies business decides to re-shore manufacturing from China to India. The workers see the machinery being packed for shipment and lock him up in his office. No lights, constant banging on walls, no bathroom, and no breaks—for days—until all dues are paid. Dues also include taxes and any other debt owed to suppliers or bodies. Law also states that the business liquidates and de-registers per regulations. Permissions may have to be obtained from the party in power and could take months or years. Designs, tools, and molds, essential for starting manufacturing elsewhere, may not be considered company property, even if they had been imported at the time of setting up the plant. They are not allowed to be taken out unless clearly and a priori-specified in a documented agreement. The same designs, tools, and molds can then be used by a business in the host country to make identical products for both domestic and foreign markets. Realistically, there may be no IP protection and no practical recourse. Such exit costs are often not evident or estimated in advance of re-shoring decisions. They are real, and should be.

Adapted from: R. Coates, "What Happens When You Decide to Leave China?" *Supply & Demand Chain Executive*, December 2014, 8–11. http://www.nxtbook.com/nxtbooks/acbusinessmedia/sdce_201412/#/8.

Inshoring, where work is outsourced to other lower-cost, but domestic, locations, is also gaining traction. Caterpillar, Ford and NCR have all announced plans to bring back some overseas manufacturing home, but likely would engage or open facilities in low-cost U.S. locations. However, economics largely dictates business decisions on where to get work done, and as long as business can readily and inexpensively connect large, eager low-wage labor markets with growing skill sets to the needs of developed (and emerging but rapidly growing) markets, off-shoring will remain a reality.

KEY POINTS

- Make-buy is the determination of what portion of the value of a product should be outsourced, what portion made in-house, and what portion made both in-house and purchased from outside sources.
- 100 percent outsourcing is preferred for cost, quality, or superior supplier technology reasons.
- 100 percent making in-house is preferred if strong unions exist, or the technology bestows core competitive advantage, or high fixed costs cannot be reduced easily.
- Splitting volume of a product between concurrent in-house making and outsourcing is preferred if the maker desires to retain some technical skills for testing and inspection purposes or retain some leverage over the supplier, component technology changes at a rapid pace, or the company has surplus workers it can ask the suppliers to use.
- Off-shoring can be performed with both supplier and self-owned assets. In either case, cost is the prime driver. Digital products, low weight/volume products, and longer-life cycle products are natural fits.

11.3.2 Push vs. Pull

Once the make-buy determination is made, it is time to make a decision on when to turn on the ignition and start the supply chain engine. Two basic approaches prevail—push, where the supply chain acts without waiting for customer orders, and pull, where it starts only after demand becomes visible. When to do which depends on a volume–volatility trade-off.

Volatility of Demand

	High	**Low**
High	**PUSH & PULL** High volatility Low forecast accuracy High volume Economies of scale **CARS I**  *Figure 11.5* Source: (CC license).	**PUSH** Low volatility High forecast accuracy High volume Economies of scale **PRINTER PAPER II**  *Figure 11.6* Source: Author.
Low	**PULL** High volatility Low forecast accuracy Low volume No scale economies Make to order **III** **CUSTOMIZED CABINETS**  *Figure 11.7* The Children's Museum of Indianapolis [CC BY-SA 3.0] (http://creativecommons.org/licenses/by-sa/3.0)], via *Wikimedia Commons*, http://commons.wikimedia.org/wiki/File%3A The_Childrens_Museum_of_Indianapolis-Child_size_%.	**PUSH & STOCK** Low volatility High forecast accuracy Low volumes, but can make long runs to forecast Economies of scale possible, but inventory locks up capital **IV** **TEXTBOOKS**  *Figure 11.8* (CC license).

*(Left margin: **Volume required**, with **High** at top and **Low** at bottom)*

Figures 11.4–11.8 A Push-Pull Guidance Framework

Cars are sold in high volumes, yet demand is volatile at the individual car model level since so many varieties and models are offered for sale. Yet a deeper look reveals that variety declines at the component level. This author was quoted $132 for a sensor for a Lexus model. Digging around, he found that a Toyota Corolla uses the exact same sensor priced at about $75. Parts sharing or, more correctly, parts commonality, translates into high volume demand for a part that is shared across several product families. The high volume allows a push manufacturing approach for the sensor. Forecasts of aggregate demand for that part for Lexus and Corolla models combined would be more accurate than if the makes did not share the same sensor and separate forecasts had to be made for different sensors. Thus, the sensor could be made on a push basis at high volume based on more accurate forecasts, while different cars could be made on a pull basis, with colors and option configurations completed after receiving customer preferences if the customer could be incentivized to wait.

A pure pull system (Quadrant III see figure 11.4) waits for the customer's order and suits a high volatility demand market that does not offer enough volume to get economies of scale. A customized product such as custom-fitted ordered cabinets fit the bill.

A pure push system is suited to conditions in quadrants II and IV. Stable demand facilitates more accurate demand forecasts in both quadrants. In Quadrant II, high volumes enable natural economies of scale. Since demand is predictable, Quadrant IV's low volumes could also be made in high volume runs and kept safely as inventory for future sales,. Economies of scale would have to be weighed against the additional inventory-holding costs.

A push-pull approach could also be used on different networks in the supply chain. Customized furniture can be made on a pull basis in the supply and assembly network stages but shipped on a push basis in the distribution network to take advantage of scale economies in logistics.

These guidelines are not set in stone but would hold for a large variety of volume-volatility conditions. Realistically, management earns its pay by managing quadrants I and III. A supply chain for a high volume-low volatility product can be set on auto-pilot in normal conditions, and a low volume-low volatility combination is usually not very challenging, either. A pull policy for running the supply chain has one major vulnerability, however—it can run short of supplies if significant supply disruptions or sudden price hikes or demand surges occur.

11.3.3. Synchronizing Supply with Demand

Starting the ignition does not guarantee a smooth drive—a supply chain requires regular maintenance, emergency repairs, and an alert hand on the wheel. The goal is to match supply with demand. It is very difficult to do so, on a consistent basis. Quality scares with baby milk formula in China led to Chinese students in Australia buying milk formula in bulk to send back home—resulting in panic buying and shortages in several cities in Australia.[6] In the U.S., demand for premium American whiskeys has shot up, but such products require several years of barrel aging. Jim Beam's plans to meet demand for their flagship Makers Mark whiskey by watering down content was abandoned in the face of consumer outcries.[7] Companies are installing capacity for the future and raising prices in the present to manage demand. Drinkers may switch to other products while supply matures in oak barrels for five to 10 years. It is entirely possible that we could see a glut of fine American whiskey a few years from now, once again the result of a mismatch between supply and demand.

The primary reason for a mismatch between supply and demand is uncertainty in both markets. Professor Hau Lee of Stanford University suggests a comprehensive approach to the challenge.[8]

Demand Uncertainty

	Higher	Lower
Higher Supply Uncertainty **Lower**	Wind energy Music Smart apps **I**	Fruit and produce Hydro-electric power **II**
	Plastic surgery Fashion Movies **III**	Staples: milk, bread, eggs, men's underwear **IV**

Figure 11.9 Uncertainty Analysis

Adapted from: Hau Lee, "Aligning Supply Chain Strategies with Product Uncertainties," *California Management Review*, 44(3) (2002): 105–119.

Where is the right place to be in the above framework? Quadrant IV is the safest position for a business, with low demand and low supply uncertainty. It is, however, likely the lowest margin position, with businesses competing primarily on cost and efficiency. Margins would be highest in quadrant I, a demanding position with high demand and high supply uncertainty. Life would be stressful—but rewarding—for those few businesses that can decipher and manage the high levels of risk well.

Managing Risk

Risk = f (probability of occurrence, probability of early detection, estimated time to impact operations, consequences, estimated recovery time).

To the extent these elements of risk can be quantified, a total risk index can be developed for every important node in the supply network. In order to do so, we need to first understand the drivers of demand and supply uncertainty.

MANAGING DEMAND UNCERTAINTY

When P&G examined the order patterns for their Pampers diapers, they found that sales at retailers fluctuated, but not excessively—after all, babies are born and use diapers at a steady rate. But, surprisingly, retailer orders on P&G distributors showed more variance, while orders from distributors to P&G varied even more. In turn, the fluctuations in order quantities for orders placed by P&G on their diaper manufacturer saw even greater swings. The net result were inventory pile-ups, increasing in size from retailer to manufacturer, as supply chains members tried to buffer against the fluctuations in the order quantities received by them. P&G called these excessive swings in order quantities "the bullwhip effect." A whip crack begins as a mere flick of the wrist, the oscillation traveling down the length of the whip, magnified, until it reaches the tip, which oscillates at a rate that cracks the sound barrier—hence the sharp explosive sound of the whiplash. Variability in a supply chain may begin as a small fluctuation in demand at the end consumer level and then travel along the chain, swelling in size, until it cascades upon the upstream manufacturer.

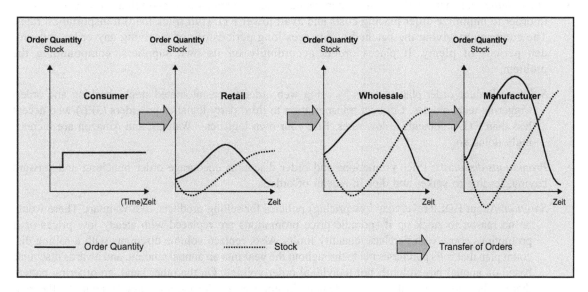

Figure 11.10 How a Bullwhip Effect Ripples through a Supply Chain

Source: Grap, "Visualization of Bullwhip Effect," [CC], via *Wikimedia Commons*, March 2010, http://commons.wikimedia.org/wiki/File%3ABulwhip_efect.jpg.

The bullwhip effect has been felt in many industries, including electronics (HP printers) and construction machinery (Caterpillar). It is commonly measured as the ratio of the variance of the order rate to the variance of the demand rate.

Bullwhip effect = Variance of order quantities/variance of demand

Why does a blip in demand at the customer level escalate into major demand uncertainties for the upstream supply chain members? The bullwhip effect, on closer study, is seen to arise from one or a combination of the following factors:

- *Forecasting inaccuracy*: When end demand is not visible to upstream companies, forecasts then are based on what the company sees at its immediate customer level. When a sudden downturn in end demand happens, firms upstream are not immediately aware of it and continue producing and placing orders on their own suppliers. A glut eventually forms, and now the upstream companies react sharply and cut down production and their own orders to upstream suppliers. When demand at the end-customer eventually picks up, supply falls short.

    Solution: Place retail POS (point of sale) data on a web site that key supply chain members can access. Share information about end demand with all key members of the supply chain so that everyone can plan and respond to actual market conditions.

- *Order batching*: Instead of placing orders as needed, companies wait and release orders in a batch in order to minimize order placing costs and avail lower FTL (full truck load) transportation rates. The company receiving the batched orders sees long periods of not receiving any order and sudden periods of plenty. It places orders accordingly on its own suppliers, compounding the problem.

  Solution: Reduce order placing costs by using web ordering or automated stock checking and order-triggering technologies. Contract transportation to third party logistics providers (3PL) who accept less than FTL shipments at low rates. Run your own logistics—Walmart and Amazon are increasingly doing so.

- *Promotions/discounts*: Price promotions and order discounts encourage order bunching and forward buying, leading to spikes and dips in receipt of orders.

  Solution: Adopt EDLP (everyday low pricing) policies for selling products, like Walmart. There would be no reason to stock up if sporadic price promotions are replaced with steady low prices or if promotions come with purchase quantity limits. Also, replace volume discounts with a rolling discount plan that rolls purchases made throughout the year into an annual amount, and awards discounts based on annual buy volume, not individual order volume. On the other hand, an ordering pattern that is inherently seasonal, like high demand in stores on weekends, for example, could be theoretically smoothed out with the use of price promotions or similar order-shifting demand management initiatives.

- *Sales people incentives*: There are times when sales commissions and monthly/quarterly targets push sales people to sell products ahead of actual demand (forward sales)—some of those 'sales' are returned by the customer in the next quarter. Conflicting incentives also create problems. Logistics, being rewarded on freight cost reduction, may delay shipments until enough builds up to qualify for a full truck load rate. Meanwhile, the customer waits.

  Solution: Such manipulation of incentive plans can be avoided by offering a plan that rewards sales people based on final sell-through rather than forward sales. For example, P&G may decide to pay its sales people part of their commission when they sell P&G product to the retailer and part when the product gets sold by the retailer to the end consumer. A sell-through commission system depends on accurate tracking of final retail sales and reconciliation of sold stocks with retailer orders, working best when products do not stay on the retailer's shelf for long.

- *Shortages*: Experienced or anticipated shortages can make buyers order more than they need in anticipation that what they actually get would be less than the quantity they order. It becomes a second-guessing game, with the manufacturer trying to gauge whether the larger than normal order they received from their immediate customer is an inflated order or reflects an actual increase in market demand.

  Solution: Analyze orders received for abnormal variations. In a shortage situation, it makes sense to allocate per past sales, that is, if dealer A normally orders 500 and dealer B orders 1,000, allocate product in a 1:2 ratio, even though dealer A's current order may be an inflated 1,000 pieces. Also, try to shorten replenishment time through quicker production and rush deliveries. Dealers then would not be tempted to over-order and over-stock, fearing that supplies may not be replenished fast enough if sales for a product suddenly took off.

OM IN PRACTICE

The Mazda Bullwhip

The best-selling two-seat convertible sports car in history, Mazda's Miata roadster became a hot-seller and ran short in dealers' lots. Strong demand reportedly put customers on pre-order lists and may have led to instances of dealer price markups.

Figure 11.11 Mazda Miata

Source: IFCAR, "Mazda Miata," (Public domain), via *Wikimedia Commons*, May 28, 2011, http://commons.wikimedia.org/wiki/File%3A2nd_Mazda_Miata_--_05-28-2011.jpg.

Considering the circumstances and hypothetically speaking, a typical bullwhip effect would have unfolded as follows: Dealers respond by placing larger orders on Mazda. Mazda could not ramp up production quick enough and was only able to fill about 50 percent of the order quantities. Dealers take note and respond by placing bigger orders on Mazda, knowing that they would likely receive only about 50 percent of the quantity ordered. So if a dealership thought actual demand would be 300 cars next week, it would place an order for 600 cars, anticipating an actual supply of 300 cars. Mazda thinks it is seeing demand surge at an increasing rate, and would ramp up production to meet a demand of 600-plus cars per week, per dealer. That takes some time, but eventually Mazda is able to supply 600 cars/week. The dealer does not need the 600 delivered cars right now, so he stops ordering for a while. For Mazda, it is like seeing orders go down from 600/week/dealer to zero. Mazda (over)reacts by slashing production capacity. But once dealers run through their excess inventory and ordering returns to normal levels, Mazda finds itself short of capacity, leading to a shortage situation once again. Dealers numbered in the hundreds, and it is impossible for Mazda to understand the nuances of individual dealer order quantity variations in such a dispersed distribution network. The effects of the whipsaws in dealer ordering patterns is felt by Mazda's suppliers, who also see wide fluctuations in orders received from Mazda.

Sources: "News from Mazda," *Mazda Global*, April 2, 2011, http://www2.mazda.com/en/publicity/release/2011/201102/110204a.html; "Mazda MX-5," Wikipedia, Sept. 29, 2015, https://en.wikipedia.org/wiki/Mazda_MX-5.

- *Cognitive reasons:* The human mind, even a trained professional's, cannot remember certain things well. A study found that experienced supply chain managers remembered the orders they had pending for supply up to a maximum of three pending orders. So if five orders were still outstanding, the buying manager would place a fresh order for current/anticipated demand without taking the soon-to-be received supplies from two of those pending orders into account. Functional biases, mistrust, or lack of access to information may also prevent insights into other points of view. Marketing may not see or appreciate supplier problems. Lack of perspective or lack of communication impairs the ability to see and think holistically.

   Solution: Use technology to keep tabs and raise flags on ordering and supply status. Rotate personnel among different functions at the beginning of their careers. Job rotation/training or communication alone are not sufficient—they need to be done together

Bullwhips can also happen in reverse, where minor delays in supply are amplified downstream. For example, a supplier's manufacturing process might not be able to fill an order completely on time because a quality issue lowered yield (# of good units/total # of units made) by 2 percent for that production run. That 2 percent variation, although minor, leads to a shortfall of good units. Delay cascades. The next batch of that product is scheduled for manufacturing a week later, so manufacturing the required missing good units is delayed for a week. Further waits may be experienced at the shipping dock to bundle the consignment into a larger consignment for transportation convenience, which may lead to a later cargo flight and delayed customs clearance. Since manufacturing and shipment in single units is bad economics, the necessary batching and missed scheduled runs cumulatively escalate delays along the supply chain. Eventually, the minor delay of perhaps just one week in production may build up into a delay of weeks for the end consumer—a bullwhip in reverse traveling from the manufacturer to the end consumer.

Supply contracts can be used to disperse risk stemming from demand uncertainty. Take a buy-back contract. Supposing HP contracts with Best Buy to accept any unsold products at some percentage of the cost paid by Best Buy. Naturally, that would transfer some of the demand uncertainty risk to HP, and Best Buy would now order more from HP. How much more would depend on the historical probability of low/high retail sales at Best Buy, the margins at Best Buy and HP, and the benefit to HP from higher sales due to increased availability of products on the Best Buy shelves.

Using Supply Contracts to Distribute Risks

BB buys printers from HP at $100/unit. BB sells them retail at $140/unit. Printers that BB cannot sell at full price are donated (nominal tax savings). Technology changes fast in the printer business, and discounts do not attract significant additional customers.

The retail probabilistic demand forecast is as follows:

Demand	5,000	8,000	10,000	12,000	15,000
Probability	0.08	0.25	0.28	0.30	0.09

Without Buy-back

a) *How many printers should BB buy from HP?*
   Unit profit = selling price (SP) − cost = $140 − $100 = $40
   Unit loss = cost − salvage value = $100 − $0 = $100

Suppose BB buys 8,000 printers from HP, and

i. Demand turns out to be 5,000 (so 3,000 printers are over-ordered);
   Total profit = (qty sold at full price * unit profit) − (excess qty ordered * unit loss)
   $$= (5,000 * \$40) - (3,000 * \$100)$$
   $$= (-)\$100,000$$

ii. Or demand turns out to be 8,000 (so 0 printers are over-ordered);
   Total profit = (qty sold at full price * unit profit) − (excess qty ordered * unit loss)
   $$= (8,000 * \$40) - (0 * \$100)$$
   $$= \$320,000$$

iii. Or demand turns out to be 10,000 (so 0 printers are over-ordered, but, remember, BB sells only the 8,000 it bought);
   Total profit = (qty sold at full price * unit profit) − (excess qty ordered * unit loss)
   $$= (8,000 * \$40) - (0 * \$100)$$
   $$= \$320,000$$

Profit for demands of 12,000 and 15,000 would also be limited to $320,000, respectively, since BB would have bought only 8,000 printers to sell. We consider profit made on actual sales and not any potential loss due to lost sales.

The expected profit for an order quantity of 8,000 printers and the probabilistic demand pattern shown above would thus be:

Expected profit for an order quantity of 8,000 = $\sum$(prob. of demand = 5,000 * total profit)
$$+ \text{(prob. of demand = 8,000 * total profit)}$$
$$+ \dots \text{(prob. of demand = 15,000 * total profit)}$$
$$= \sum(0.08 * (-)100,000) + (0.25 * 320,000) + (0.28 * 320,000)$$
$$+ (0.30 * 320,000) + (0.09 * 320,000)$$
$$= \$286,400$$

Expected profit for BB for an order quantity of 8,000 printers = $286,400.

Similarly, we can compute the expected profit for order quantities of 5,000, 10,000, 12,000, and 15,000 (see online Excel worksheet 'SCM BuyBack Contract Excel Analysis'). The order quantity that results in the maximum expected profit for BB ($286,400.00) is 8,000 printers.

b) *What would be the profit for HP if BB buys 8,000 printers?*

   Assume HP's variable cost/unit = $70 (ignore fixed costs, since they'd be incurred even if BB does not buy any units):
   HP's selling price to BB = $100/unit
   HP's profit = units ordered by BB * unit profit = 8,000 * $30 = $240,000

With Buy-Back

a)   *How many printers should BB buy from HP if HP agrees to buy back unsold printers from BB at $65/unit. Recall BB's cost of purchase from HP is $100 and it sells the printers retail for $140.00.*

So now unit profit for BB remains at $40, but unit loss = $100 – $65 = $35/unit
Suppose BB buys 8,000 printers from HP, and

i.   Demand turns out to be 5,000 (so 3,000 printers are over-ordered);
       Total profit = (qty sold at full price * unit profit) – (excess qty ordered * unit loss)
                  = (5,000 * $40) – (3,000 * $35)
                  = $95,000

ii.   Or demand turns out to be 8,000 (so 0 printers are over-ordered);
       Total profit = (qty sold at full price * unit profit) – (excess qty ordered * unit loss)
                  = (8,000 * $40) – (0 * $35)
                  = $320,000

The profit would stay at $320,000 for the higher demand levels of 10,000, 12,000, and 15,000, as explained earlier.

The expected profit for BB for an order quantity of 8,000 printers and the probabilistic demand pattern shown above would thus be:

$\sum$(prob. of demand = 5,000 * total profit) + (prob. of demand = 8,000 * total profit) + . . . (prob. of demand = 15,000 * total profit)
= $\sum$(0.08 * 95,000) + (0.25 * 320,000) + (0.28 * 320,000) + (0.30 * 320,000) + (0.09 * 320,000)

Expected profit for BB an order quantity of 8,000 printers = $302,000
Similarly, we can compute the expected profit for order quantities of 5,000, 10,000, 12,000, and 15,000 (see online Excel worksheet 'SCM BuyBack Contract Excel Analysis').

BB should order 10,000 printers from HP since that order quantity results in the maximum expected profit for BB = $332,500

b)   *What would be the profit for HP if BB buys 10,000 printers?*
       HP's variable cost/unit   = $70 (ignore fixed costs, since they'd be incurred even if BB does not buy any units).

       HP's selling price to BB = $100/unit; HP's buy-back cost = $65/unit

       HP's profit   = (units ordered by BB * unit profit) – (expected # of units returned by BB * buy-back cost)

Given that BB orders 10,000 units from HP and the returned quantity = order quantity − demand:

Expected # of units returned = $\sum$(prob. of demand = 5,000 * (return qty:10,000 − 5,000)) + (prob. of demand = 8,000 * 2,000) + (prob. of demand = 10,000 * 0) + (prob. of demand = 12,000 * 0) + (prob. of demand = 15,000 * 0)

$\qquad = \sum$(0.08 * 5,000) + (0.25 * 2,000) + (0.28 * 0) + (0.30 * 0) + (0.09 * 0)

$\qquad$ = 900 units

Thus, HP's profit $\qquad$ = (units ordered by BB * unit profit) − (expected # of units returned by BB * buy-back cost)

$\qquad$ = (10,000 * 30) − (900 * \$65)

$\qquad$ = 241,500.00

We see that adding a buy-back clause to the contract between HP and BB resulted in gains for both HP and BB:

	HP	BB	*Total supply chain profit*
Profit w/o buy-back	\$240,000	\$286,400	\$526,400
Profit with buy-back	\$241,500	\$332,500	\$574,000

There are additional costs such as returns inspections, logistics, and disposal that can also be factored in here. The underlying retail demand forecast would inevitably vary from reality and thus affect the profit figures.

We can experiment with different buy-back rates to find out that rate which maximizes the total profit.

c) *Another way:*

We can also use the newsvendor model's critical ratio (CR) for BB and the 'supply chain' to find out the optimal profit-maximizing order quantity (at which the probability of demand being less than the order quantity is equal to or greater than the CR). We assume a buy-back of \$65 here.

CR for BB = Cu/Co + Cu, where Cu = cost of running out and Co = cost of over-ordering.
Cu for BB = profit margin = retail price − cost of purchase from HP = (\$140 − \$100) = \$40/unit
Co for BB = loss = cost of purchase from HP − salvage value (buy-back) = (\$100 − \$65) = \$35/unit

Therefore, CR for BB = \$40/(\$35 + \$40) = 0.53
We need to find that order quantity where the (cumulative) probability of demand being less than the order quantity is 0.53 (or greater). Looking at the demand forecast provided (reproduced below):

Demand	5,000	8,000	10,000	12,000	15,000
Probability	0.08	0.25	0.28	0.30	0.09
Cumulative probability.	*0.08*	*0.33*	*0.61*	*0.91*	*1.00*

10,000 is that order quantity where the cumulative probabilty of demand being less than the order quantity is at least 0.53.

d) *Total supply chain profit with newsvendor*

Another way to look at it is to imagine if BB weren't there—if the entire supply chain was HP alone (manufacture and retailing), how much would HP make (and sell) to maximize its profits, given the probabilistic retail demand forecast reproduced below?
    The retail probabilistic demand forecast is as follows:

Demand	5,000	8,000	10,000	12,000	15,000
Probability	8%	25%	28%	30%	9%

So, now HP's unit VC = $70 and its retail SP = $140. There is no salvage value for unsold printers. What is the optimal profit quantity to make and sell?
    CR for supply chain = Cu/Co + Cu, where Cu = cost of running out; Co = cost of over-ordering
    Cu for supply chain = profit margin = retail price − variable cost of making = ($140 − $70) = $70/unit
    Co for supply chain = loss = variable cost of making − salvage value = ($70 − $0) = $70/unit
    CR for supply chain = $70/($70 + $70) = 0.50
    Again 10,000 is that order quantity where the cumulative probabilty of demand being less than the order quantity is at least 0.50.

In addition to such buy-back contracts, revenue-sharing contracts and contracts that offer incentives if sales cross a certain limit offer similar risk-sharing arrangements. Such contracts call for more intensive information sharing on actual retail revenue achieved, necessary technology, and independent revenue figure verification mechanisms.

Pooling and postponement are other strategies for coping with demand uncertainty. Pooling exploits the benefits of centralization. Imagine a distribution network with individual distribution centers (DCs) serving individual markets. A sudden demand surge in market A may result in a stockout at DC A. Simultaneously, a sudden dip in demand in market B may result in left-over stock at DC B. The demand uncertainties faced by the distribution network can be reduced by pooling (centralizing) several DCs into one mega-DC.

Demand across the markets remains unaltered, but is now met by one large DC. The benefits of pooling are:

1   *Lower levels of safety stock.* Each individual DC used to carry a safety stock of inventory in anticipation of demand surges in its individual market. With the mega DC, a sudden increase in demand in market A can be offset by a sudden decline in demand in another market. The overall uncertainty of total demand thus goes down due to the off-setting effects of one market's behavior on another. The mega warehouse would be able to increase or maintain the same customer service level as before while keeping less inventory. To enable the pooling effect, demand in the markets should be negatively correlated. Also, as the number of markets being fed from the mega DC increase, the chances of one market off-setting another market increases.

2   *Reduced transportation costs from plant to DC.* Earlier, loads had to move out to many DCs, whereas pooling creates a single route. Economies of scale in transportation apply, too. The logistics costs of

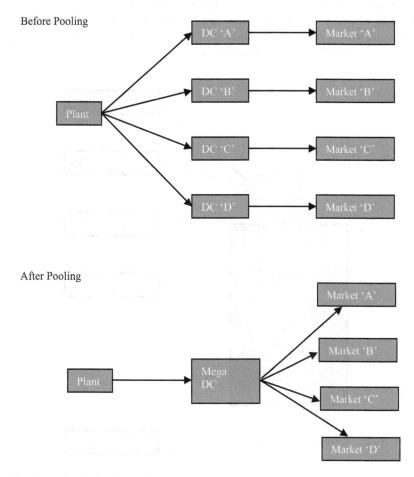

Figure 11.12 Pooling in a Distribution Network

moving loads from DC to market(s) may be higher in the pooled situation, but the increase in distance traveled may be compensated by centralized transportation rate negotiations with a single carrier.

With a mega DC, though, a fire or labor strike can disrupt shipments to all markets. Also, the intimacy of relationship and deep market knowledge that came from having individual DCs dedicated to individual markets may be lost. Companies work around this by forming dedicated teams for different regions in a mega DC network. Virtual pooling can also be undertaken through electronic communications among individual DCs, and by centralized stocking of common parts that fit into many different products (that have negatively correlated demand).

Postponement involves deferring the decision to customize products for specific markets and thus allows the option of delaying commitment until demand becomes a bit more visible. Decisions such as customer-specific labeling, packaging, assembly, or accessory attachment are postponed until the last possible moment, waiting to get a clearer picture of demand. HP printers were manufactured with different built-in power units, each appropriate to a country's specific electrical power type (AC/DC; 110 or 220V), and different plug-socket systems. A printer manufactured for one market could not be used in another. HP experienced problems matching supply to demand in individual markets. HP alleviated the problem by redesigning the printer so that the power unit would be a separate add-on. It manufactured generic printers

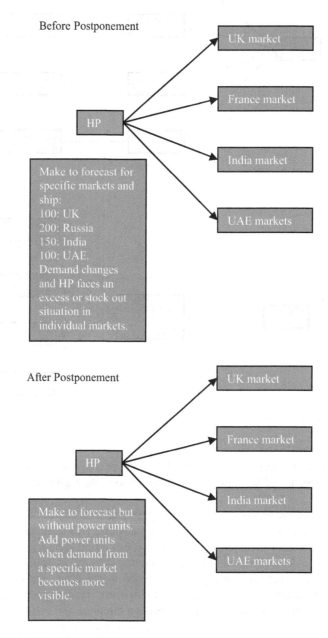

Figure 11.13 Postponement to Meet Demand Uncertainty

and then fitted them with country specific power units, as and when needed. In effect, it postponed the addition of power units to the printers until market specific demand firmed up. Adding the power units could be done at country DCs since it was not a particularly complex operation. The result? Fewer stock-outs, less excess inventory, and increased customer service levels. Costs: printer redesign and DC personnel training in power unit assembly and fitment.

The advantages of postponement should be weighed against the cost of product redesign and the costs of any additional step in the manufacturing or assembly process. Country tariffs often favor import of goods in SKD or CKD kits (semi-knocked down or completely knocked down into constituent parts), which is another point in favor of delayed differentiation at local assembly sites through postponement.

KEY POINTS

- The bullwhip effect amplifies small uncertainties in retail demand into large demand swings for supply chain members.
- Bullwhip effects can be mitigated through information sharing, stable retail pricing, replacing order-quantity-size-based discounts with annual spend discounts, equitable rationing in shortages, and basing salesforce commissions on end-consumer off-take, not sales made to the retailer.
- Pooling reduces demand uncertainty through increasing the probability of a demand surge in one market being offset by a dip in demand in another.
- Postponement reduces demand uncertainty by delaying final assembly/accessorizing and thereby being able to wait until demand becomes more visible.

Managing Supply Uncertainty

According to the *Supply Chain Quarterly*,[9] the top five causes of supply chain delays or disruptions are adverse weather, IT outage, transport network disruption, earthquake or tsunami, service provider failure, and loss of talent/skills. As supply chains grow more global and complex, quality failures, foreign exchange fluctuations, intellectual property theft, compliance issues, commodity price and availability volatility, component obsolescence, and political events also increase supplier uncertainty levels. Physical threats such as piracy on the high seas, warehouse thefts, and truck hijackings are escalating.

Piracy—A Very Real Threat

Piracy attacks have cost numerous lives and disrupted global supply chains. Shippers are reluctant to engage in firefights since cargo can be inflammable and lives are at risk. Marine insurance insures the cargo but only if it is proven to be 'irretrievably' lost—not just held for ransom. And it is the buyer's risk. Once the cargo goes over the ship rails in the source port, ownership passes from the supplier on to the buyer. The cost of insuring a container passing through the region increased more than ten-fold between 2007 and 2014, with shipping companies adding a piracy risk surcharge ranging from $130 to

Figure 11.14 'Captain Jack Sparrow'

Source: Gage Skidmore, "Captain Jack Sparrow at Phoenix Comicon," [CC], via *Wikimedia Commons*, May 26, 2011, http://commons.wikimedia.org/wiki/File%3ACaptain_Jack_Sparrow_(5764018454).jpg.

Figure 11.15 Real Pirates

Source: Jan van Rijn, "A Somali Pirate with Weapons aboard a Vessel," [public domain], via *Wikimedia Commons*, 2008, http://commons.wikimedia.org/wiki/File%3ASompirgnbt.jpg.

$300/TEU (one TEU = cargo capacity of a standard intermodal container). Additional marine kidnap and ransom (K&R) insurance incurs.

Costs run far beyond the ransom amounts that are generally paid. While actual ransom paid remains low relative to prevention costs, the costs of the loss of human lives and the impact to companies of delayed or disrupted shipments is incalculable. Actions by international navies, security on ships, and a better political climate in Somalia have since reduced the number of attacks off the Horn of Africa. Somali pirates, however, are believed to still be holding 50 hostages, and the threat still remains.

Adapted from: Different newscasts; Mike Schuler, "Somali Pirates' First Hijacking Attempt of 2014 Ends with Arrests," *gCaptain*, Jan. 20, 2014; One Earth Future Foundation, "The Economic Cost of Somali Piracy" (working paper), *Oceans Beyond Piracy*, 2011, http://oceansbeyondpiracy.org/publications/economic-cost-somali-piracy-2011; Janice Kowell, "Ocean Marine Cargo Insurance and Modern Day Piracy on the High Seas," *Marsh Global Marine*, May 20, 2010.

Specific actions to deal with supply uncertainties range from vertical integration to collaborative forecasting and hedging and insurance. Companies also keep reserves of stock or capacity in supply, assembly, and distribution networks. A low probability-high consequence disruption like the 2011 Thailand floods requires reserve capacity in the form of alternate suppliers and routes.

Sony was hard hit by the Thailand floods due to a lack of alternative supply sources. On the other hand, Seagate, the disk manufacturer, though affected by the flooding, was able to better weather the disruption with its diversified supply chain. Recent supply chain disruptions in Asia-based supply chains include violent worker protests at Chinese-owned factories in Vietnam due to China setting up an oil rig in disputed waters. Supplies to global retailers such as Nike and Walmart have been affected. Political unrest in Thailand and safety concerns in Bangladesh have also impacted U.S. companies.

Figure 11.16 Submerged Industrial Estate—Floods in Thailand

Source: Cpl. Robert J. Maurer, "Floodwaters Inundated Rojana Industrial Park in Ayutthaya Province, Thailand, in the 2011 Floods," [public domain], U.S. Marine Corps, via *Wikimedia Commons*, Oct. 16, 2011, http://commons.wikimedia.org/wiki/File%3AFlooding_ of_Rojana_Industrial_Park%2C_Ayutthaya%2C_Thailand%2C_October_2011.jpg.

Inventory is an expensive premium to pay for risk, especially low probability risks. Even so, if holding and opportunity costs are low, prices are not trending downwards, and product obsolescence is not an issue, inventory reserves can counter delay and disruption supply risks. Coal and steel may fit the bill—flowers and semiconductors don't. Companies use a combination of inventory, capacity, and logistics to combat uncertainty. Cisco keeps some high-value-item assembly capacity in the U.S. to respond quickly to demand or can fly in high value items on short notice. It also keeps local inventories of low value-high demand items made in lower cost foreign locations. Toyota and Honda use 60/20/20 or 80/10/10 or similar splits of supply orders to their suppliers and also strategically invest in suppliers of critical parts.

Intellectual property (IP) theft is harder to guard against—fine print contracts often cannot be easily enforced in other countries. Some buyers insist on dedicated production lines that are concealed from other workers and managers; others exercise control over suppliers by locking up sources of inputs or customizing manufacturing or testing equipment with proprietary software and machine modifications. Dell used to keep final assembly in-house. Apart from the risk of IP theft and/or forward integration by suppliers, counterfeit parts/products are a major supply chain risk for high priced or highly valued items such as medicines, aircraft parts, currency, and brand names. OEMs (original equipment manufacturers, e.g., Caterpillar, Ford) do not want to be identified as being the recipients or users of fake parts, even if it happens inadvertently. To counter counterfeiting, anti-counterfeiting experts recommend that a company should set up a mechanism for early notification when fakes are first detected in the supply market. It should also have the genuine product specifications and information and testing capabilities available in the field to quickly determine if components are counterfeits. An EOL (end-of-life) notice from genuine manufacturers of parts, indicating that a part would no longer be made, is often a flag for the emergence of counterfeiting in the parts after-market. EOLs from suppliers can be handled with 'through-life' contracts with availability guarantees.

Compliance risk is the risk of suppliers infringing sustainability, safety, and ethics regulations set by governments or world bodies like the United Nations. Skirts made by 7-year-olds and carpets woven in toxic conditions by 5-year-old fingers are no longer acceptable to customers or society. Such conduct used to be hidden from public view in earlier times, but NGO (nongovernmental organizations) monitoring on the ground and easy point-click-shoot-disseminate technologies have made exposure and mass dissemination possible. Governments in the U.S., Europe, China and other countries have introduced sustainability, ethics, and safety regulations. The U.S. has enacted a Conflict Minerals Act that asks companies to certify due diligence and source control over material from Congo or near-abouts (conflict or war zones) that has entered their product. It has created tremendous difficulties for many manufacturers since visibility and control/influence upstream down to a specific mining location level can be very limited. Government anti-terrorism mandates represent another form of compliance risk. In 2013, the U.S. Customs and Border Protection's Customs-Trade Partnership Against Terrorism (C-TPAT) program conducted 2,129 validations involving thousands of physical site visits in 75 countries throughout the world.

The challenge for supply chain managers is the lack of knowledge and lack of direct control over the worker management methods and materials used by their immediate first tier suppliers. Second or third tier supplier behavior is much more opaque. Supplier capillaries have crept outwards from established supplier locations, moving to remote locations, challenging the monitoring capacities of their customers. Compliance documentation requires significant resources in order to obtain a deeper understanding of the actual material composition of parts and products and their manufacturing and disposal processes. Global supply chains are developing web-based supplier compliance programs where every supplier, manufacturer, and distributor has to complete and regularly update a role-specific compliance questionnaire.

Another supply risk, price volatility, can be managed through hedging strategies. Hedging is appropriate for inputs where a small shift in supply or in demand results in a large price change because of a lack of substitutes. Companies like GM have been using hedging, options, and derivatives for the past 60 years to stabilize prices for commodities. A company can lock in fuel prices at current rates for the next six months but can also purchase a protective hedge against prices falling in that period. But hedging is not *always* necessary or beneficial. Suppose the marketing division of a business decides to hedge its foreign-exchange exposure from the sale of $600 million in goods to Australia. But, unbeknownst to marketing, the purchasing division of the same business is simultaneously sourcing about $450 million of goods from Australia. The net foreign exchange risk to the company as a whole is actually $150 million, and it wastes resources on unnecessary hedging of the entire sales amount of $600 million. Besides direct costs such as bid-ask spreads and broker fees, hedging contracts often mandate a company keep additional capital reserves to meet potential future obligations. The opportunity cost can be significant, and is tied to the price volatility of the hedged product. If oil prices fluctuate between 20 and 30 percent in a year, hedging a volume of $100 million would require an additional capital reserve of up to $30 million. The opportunity cost of $30 million at 8 percent works out to $2.4 million a year. Hedging can be combined with other nonfinancial risk management initiatives such as transferring uncertainty through insurance covers.

Manufacturing and customer substitution are also remedies for supply uncertainty. In one-way or manufacturing substitution, if a part runs out, the customer is provided a superior part at no extra cost. For example, Dell can supply a laptop with a 200 GB HD if it runs out of the 150 GB HD machine a customer has ordered. Most customers will not complain about the substitution, and the shortage of 150 GB HDs is not allowed to impact sales. Of course, if both HDs come from the same supplier, the manufacturer is probably out of luck. Two-way or customer substitution transfers the power to substitute to the customer. Dell would present a range of substitute products if the one on order is not available, and the customer would make a choice. Costs and quality perceptions are important considerations in such substitution strategies.

Buying the umbrella before it rains is sound policy, but what happens if it doesn't rain for a long time (and it's an expensive umbrella)? The boss is not likely to fire you for not preparing for an earthquake in New York city or a political uprising in Thailand. However, she may do so if you failed to anticipate price increases for the commodities you buy. Most executives choose to focus on controllable risks. Asked in confidence, many would agree that they tend to focus on risks that can impact their jobs or careers—risks that they can be held accountable for. In the final analysis, protection against all risks is not feasible, but a process that identifies risks early, has a plan to deal with it, and can mobilize resources quickly is the core of a risk management strategy for supply chains.

Despite all the information technology and legal contracts and optimization models in the world, a supply chain cannot be managed well unless its members really accept and act on the need to exchange information and improve the supply chain. IT provides a conduit for information exchange but cannot guarantee that companies will actually exchange useful information. The supplier may be happy that you let him access your retail point-of-sale sales information in real time. But does he share information with you equally openly and promptly, particularly when it's bad news? When there's a fire at his plant overseas; or when one of his key suppliers goes bankrupt; or when he knows than a consignment has restricted materials? Avoiding such 'surprises' or uncertainties requires collaboration. Ask your supply chain partners:

"What would you be doing differently if we were part of the same company?
And why aren't we able to do it now? "

TRUST

Suppliers have deep knowledge in their own specialties and intelligence on competitor actions. Building trust is essential. Of course, building intimacy indiscriminately with all suppliers is not necessary or beneficial. Samsung or Apple, for example, may not be very inclined to develop long-term relationships with suppliers of chips or other technology-sensitive components in their short life-cycle gadgets. Suppliers often change as designs and specifications evolve rapidly, and collaborative initiatives do not last from one model to the next. In more stable environments, trust must originate with the buyer. The buyer typically has more power, and suppliers need to be convinced about long-term intentions and commitment before investing in dedicated resources or sharing proprietary information. J. Ignacio Lopez, ex-buying chief at GM Motors, was notorious for obtaining proprietary designs from auto suppliers and then posting the designs in public view for open biddings. Affected suppliers vowed never to let GM see their most important breakthroughs, preferring instead to share innovations with the likes of more considerate Toyota and Honda, the latter automakers being known for assisting suppliers with engineering expertise and finance to lower product design, material, and production process costs and sharing these cost gains with their suppliers. A framework for collaboration with clear guidelines on what can be shared (sales) and what cannot (prices, core technology advances) helps clarify and bring transparency to relationships. Collaboration should also be explored outside traditional design and cost reduction issues to include logistic sharing possibilities and joint procurement of generic inputs such as steel and commodities. Collaboration deepens into intimacy and anticipatory intelligence with time—it helps getting a heads up on surprises like the sole supplier of a small-volume but critical part coming up to say: "I'm closing up shop and retiring to Florida next month."

KEY POINTS

- Supply chain risks include input price volatility, intellectual property (IP), compliance, and political risks.
- Hedging is a strategy to manage price volatility.
- Dedicated production lines, contractual safeguards, and good ground information scanning capabilities reduce IP risks.
- Compliance risks are managed by rigorous documentation and independent audits and certifications all along the supply chain.
- Collaboration and long-term contracts help build abiding relationships in stable supply markets.

11.4 Was It Done Right?

In 1995, Apple ran out of Power Mac PCs. Not many remember that Apple, not IBM or Compaq, often led the PC market in sales during the 1990s. But poor supply chain management was a major reason for dethroning them from that position. Apple introduced the new Power Mac just before the December holidays in 1995. Burned by their earlier experience with Power Book laptops, when excess inventory had piled up, Apple decided to play it safe this time around. Capacity and inventory were set to conservative forecasts. But Power Mac sales took off, and soon Apple found itself with $1 billion worth of unfilled orders. Suppliers could not ramp up fast enough, and Apple found that it did not have enough flexibility or adaptability in its supply chain. Apple faced a supply chain disaster. Its share price plummeted 50 percent. Beset by furious customers, stressed suppliers, and share-holder lawsuits, Steve Jobs, Apple's CEO, was thrust out. It eventually took an iPod to return both the CEO and Apple's stock to a position of respect.

11.4.1 What Could Go Wrong in Managing a Supply Chain?

Where's the pain in the chain? While the above example can be considered as a fundamental demand-supply mismatch failure, bad management policies can damage supply chain performance.

Silo thinking can conflict with supply chain performance. A business set its sales targets on a quarterly basis. Customers quickly took note and delayed ordering till the last days of the quarter, when desperate supplier salespeople would be more likely to offer deep discounts or most-favored delivery terms. The resultant order-bunching created demand volatility problems for the supply chain. Similarly, sales promises of expedited delivery led to increased distribution costs because of less than FTL loads and worker overtime. A company found that its lead customers did not really value a reduction of a day or two off a 10-day delivery schedule.

What really made a difference to the customer was when delivery could be completed in a 24-hour window. The business stayed with its normal delivery schedules but created an 'express' lane for special 24-hour delivery consignments to customers that desired such, at an extra charge. Such insights and policy making can only happen when sales, marketing, and supply chain managers forecast and plan jointly to bring perspective and demand and supply market intelligence to the table.

Paying off suppliers too early or too late can affect cash flows. If a supplier's cost of funds is high, early payment can obtain significant discounts from the supplier. Receiving and inspection processes at the buyer should be informed about the importance of paying suppliers in time and also be incentivized to conduct timely inspections to enable timely payment. A history of bad accounts payable can mean suppliers padding their prices and/or cutting corners on delivery, quality, returns, or order quantities. Large companies are now using their clout with bankers to facilitate account payable collateral backed loans to their smaller suppliers.

Supply chain 'savings' may not be reflected appropriately with financial P&L statements. A framework for quantifying and accommodating direct and indirect supply chain gains in financial statements has to be worked out between supply chain and finance managers.[10]

> Supply chain 'savings' = cost savings + cost avoidance + deferred cost savings
> Cost savings = realized gains from reduced prices, quality, and delivery terms for that year.
> Deferred cost savings = cash savings from asset and equipment purchases that are depreciated. Savings from spending that is depreciated or amortized should be treated the same as spending that starts on the balance sheet and migrates to P&L over time.
> Cost avoidance = cost increases avoided by retaining favorable prices and terms, for that year.
> All the above recognized on P&L as: Realized P&L + deferred P&L + avoided P&L

The baseline for assessing gains (or loss) could be last year's figures or current industry averages, or some combination.

High purchasing overheads and a lack of organizational compliance with company ordering policy can also hurt supply chain performance. Centralized contract negotiation and decentralized contract operation often provide the best outcome. For high value items, inventory can be stored centrally and made visible to users.

Shrinkage or pilferage ail all supply chains and grow as the supply chain becomes longer and more complex. Consumer electronics, food, medicines, and apparel are the most pilfered products. More serious is the case with fakes, especially fake medicines. In 2012, authorities identified a supply chain that allowed fake Avastin, a cancer drug, to reach U.S. clinics. The global route began with a possible China-based manufacturer, with transshipments and handling through Turkey and Egypt and Swiss and Danish wholesalers, before it reached a UK wholesaler, according to pharmaceutical-industry and law-enforcement officials. The UK wholesaler then shipped the Avastin to U.S. doctors through a Tennessee distributor. Robust inventory visibility and data collection systems, combined with a careful analysis and fortification of the weak points in the supply chain, can help reduce shrinkage. Reducing the number of hand-off points in the logistics and distribution chain also helps.

An ever-present danger in supply chains, unexpected supplier bankruptcy, has grown in recent years owing to the funding crisis, commodity price volatility, and the cost-driven chase to unfamiliar suppliers in far-away lands. Realistically, not many suppliers communicate internal financial troubles in advance. Some warning signs:

- Your supplier is restating earnings and future outlooks.
- Your supplier's larger customers or their industries are not doing well.
- Your supplier's accounts payable is trending upwards. If your supplier is delaying payments or order placement on its suppliers, it may run out of raw material or cut corners on quality.

- Your supplier is making significant and unusual price concessions to you/other customers.
- Your supplier is offering heavy discounts for earlier payment of its accounts receivables.
- Your supplier is making large cuts in R&D, IT, equipment or resources, with no balancing investments elsewhere.
- Your supplier is conducting unusually high employee layoffs.
- Your supplier is invested in large fixed-assets projects that are delayed or have long payback periods.
- Your supplier's capacity utilization level suddenly increases or declines. A sudden increase may be driven by a desperate supplier offering deeply discounted prices to new customers. A sudden decline may signal the loss of a significant customer.
- Your supplier's premises show poor housekeeping, poor landscaping maintenance, haphazardly stowed inventory, too clean (unused) equipment and aisles, declining utility bills, lower labor payments (check for delays), and the like.
- Extreme product commitment ratio: the percentage of the supplier's total product category sales to a given customer divided by the percentage of customers' product category that is purchased from the supplier. A ratio of 1.0 indicates a balanced partnership. Extreme ratios like 100/1 or 1/100 suggest high-risk scenarios.

Finally, switching off a global supply chain when demand falls short of forecasts is a difficult task. An overheated supply chain is like a missile—once the products are launched across oceans, they will arrive a few weeks later, regardless of whether the market for them still exists or not. Huge and expensive inventory buildups occur. Good planning anticipates forecast errors and develops alternate channels of disposal.

11.4.2 Supply chain performance metrics

Companies build different dashboards to report supply chain performance at different levels. The popular SCOR model (supply chain operations reference) developed by the Supply Chain Council details performance metrics at strategic (level 1), tactical (level 2), operational (level 3), and shop floor (level 4) levels. SCOR dimensionalizes supply chain performance into two perspectives—customer facing and internal facing. Each performance area is then measured with its own level 1 metrics that, in turn, drill down to more detailed metrics. A sampling of metrics, restricted to level 2 for simplicity, is shown in Table 11.3.

"SCOR omits financials, so a 'shareholder facing' dimension can be added with metrics such as ROA and EVA (economic value added). While fill rate and on-time delivery metrics benchmark against customer requirements, it is important to understand that customer expectations may exceed contractual requirements. Competition may sense this and exploit the shortfall. The level of effort in achieving a particular metric target goal should also be understood. For example, a credit note issued to a customer for an error, say an inaccurate shipped order, usually requires a "reason code" to be used. Using such error codes, let us estimate overall order accuracy by examining the accuracy rates of the reasons underlying order accuracy."

Reason: Order entry accuracy = 99 percent
Reason: Pick & ship accuracy = 99 percent
Reason: On-time delivery = 99 percent
Reason: Shipped without damage = 99 percent
Reason: Invoicing accuracy = 99 percent

Therefore, overall order accuracy is = $0.99 \times 0.99 \times 0.99 \times 0.99 \times 0.99 = 95.01\%$, despite near perfect accuracy rates.

Table 11.3 SCOR Metrics of Supply Chain Performance (Sampling)

Performance dimension	Level 1 metric	Description	Level 2 breakdown
Customer facing			
Supply chain reliability	Perfect order fulfillment lead time	% of orders delivered on-time, complete, accurate, of right quality, correctly invoiced	i) Order completeness: % of orders delivered in full ii) Order fill rate: % of orders delivered in time or % of line items on order shipped on time iii) Quality accuracy: % of orders delivered in perfect condition iv) Documentation accuracy: % of orders delivered with full match of supplier invoice and packing list with price, description, quantity with buyer order
Responsiveness	Order fulfillment cycle time	Time period from receipt of order to receipt of material by customer	Source cycle time Make cycle time Deliver cycle time Delivery retail cycle time
Internal facing			
Supply chain cost	Total supply chain management cost Cost of goods sold	Total cost of supply chain outcomes per $1,000 of revenue	(per $1,000 of revenue) Cost to plan Cost to source Cost to make Cost to deliver Cost to return from customer Cost to return to supplier

Adapted from: "SCOR Framework," *Apics Supply Chain Council*, accessed Oct. 5, 2015, http://www.apics.org/sites/apics-supply-chain-council/frameworks/scor.

Getting the supply chain to perform at 100 percent accuracy requires resources, but when accomplished, it can streamline operations and flows with significant realized gains in terms of improved customer service, fewer returns and chargebacks, lower inventory levels, and fewer arguments with customer receipt and accounting. That level of accuracy requires extremely close coordination among sales, order taking, warehouse operations, shipping, and outstanding IT-enabled process visibility across the supply chain. And everyone has to be measured on the same metric—if sales is rewarded on orders obtained, documentation flaws in order execution is not their concern, unless, of course, their compensation or performance evaluation or budget is tied to the cost of customer claims and chargebacks on discrepancies between order, documented shipment, and actual receipts. The potential for manipulation of metrics should also be noted: For example, shipments might be deliberately delayed in order to get a perfect 'order completeness' and 'order fill rate' score.

Other metrics that look across the supply chain, both downstream and upstream, could include customer market growth and profitability, total profit margin of supply chain, and profit margins of supply chain partners, inventory levels at different hand-off nodes, length of time FGI (finished goods inventory) waits between shipping dock at plant and shipment to the customer, information sharing across supply chain, and the adoption of new technologies by supply chain partners. Year-to-year cash-to-cash cycle time also affords a measure of how quickly goods are moved through the supply chain and converted into cash.

> C-to-C time = number of days of accounts receivable + plus the days of inventory held − the number of days of accounts payable.

Metrics assume that data is accurate, available, and accessible at all key supply chain nodes. They also assume that someone is standing at a central vantage point where they can see the entire supply chain. More likely, data, when available, will be in the form of averages or estimates for only a part of the chain. These estimates or averages could be more easily obtained and processed separately for the supply, assembly, and distribution nodes and then collaboratively coalesced and analyzed for the entire supply chain. The purpose of a metric is to provide advance warning of events with potential for supply chain damage or early detection of such events that have already happened. These warnings and intimations have to be provided to decision makers in the front lines quickly so that they can evaluate alternatives quickly, collaboratively, and effectively for decisive and timely action. And finally, a word of caution: A majority of managers, just as the rest of us, when asked, tend to think that their performance is better than average!

11.5 Current Trends in Supply Chain Management

Reading and listening to supply chain experts, scholars, front-line managers, and various supply chain groups such as ISM, Gartner, and the Supply Council reveal a surprising convergence of thoughts on supply chain trends.

The compelling need for *speed and flexibility* in anticipating and responding to fast-moving technologies and fast-moving events is a challenge to supply chain managers. Integrative practices such as collaborative forecasting, collaboration in running promotions, consulting supply chains for product pricing, collaborative new product introductions and customized offerings, cutting replacement and repair times, and smaller, more frequent replenishments are gaining momentum. The customer end itself is being investigated, analyzed, and segmented in much greater intensity for understanding demand and matching it with appropriately designed supply chains.

Visibility into supply, assembly, and distribution operations has become necessary for achieving supply chain speed and flexibility. Yet the increasing number of hand-offs in complex supply chains has reduced transparency of end-to-end supply chain data. The customer wants to know where the shipment of blue stone-washed jeans in size large, ordered three weeks ago, is, and when she can expect your truck to pull into her receiving dock. How rapidly can you connect with key nodes in the supply chain? How quickly can you exchange contacts, data specifications, volumes, and integration points internally and in the supply chain? Information and product visibility is enabled by advances in communication and information technologies. Quicker loading and unloading means keeping to scheduled arrival and departure times. A loading delay at Chittagong port at Bangladesh could mean that the ship misses high tide and is delayed 12 hours at departure. That initial delay of 12 hours would snowball into delays in arrival port time and delays in unloading and customs clearance schedules. Track and trace technologies like radio frequency identification (RFID) sensors now keep tabs on cargo in transit as well as individual pieces on a retailer's shelf. Sensors help keep tabs on perishable cargo in containers; and let the customer monitor and request a change in the temperature en route.

OM IN PRACTICE

Transparency in Shipping Containers

Consider the common steel shipping container and the amount of time spent on inspecting and verifying its contents at shipping docks, ports, trains, customs, and transshipment. Now think of a transparent shipping container, which can be inspected without having to open it or submit it to X-rays. Westbound Shipping Services have developed the first transparent shipping container in the world—made of shatterproof high density, scratch-resistant Perspex cast acrylic—and equipped with a small solar powered power pack. The power pack sends a small continuous electrical current through the Perspex, which keeps the container opaque. A shipper or inspector simply shuts off the current using a unique container-specific code, and the container becomes completely transparent. Security, time, and cost all benefit.

Adapted from: G. Tyler, "How Transparent Shipping Containers Could Impact Port Operations," *Lojistic*, April 3, 2015, https://www.lojistic.com/blog/how-transparent-shipping-containers-could-impact-port-operations.

Product visibility also assists in supply and production scheduling. A known delay in receipt of a seating harness would let a car maker stagger the delivery of associated parts that are received from other suppliers. Sensor technology has evolved to next-generation 2D bars codes such as the Microsoft tag that are scanned directly by mobile devices and instantly connect the user to compliance information, inventory and location information, and live feeds of warehouses and assembly centers. It is similar to the smart codes that you would read with your smartphone.

The recent deluge of *data* from regular sources, social media, and the supply chain and the consequent storage, access, and analysis requirements demand exponential increases in computing power. Companies like Li & Fung, Hong Kong-based supply chain managers for major brands and retailers worldwide, manage over 80 offices, over 13,000 employees, and thousands of suppliers in more than 40 economies across North America, Europe, and Asia. To ensure visibility on network operations, petabytes of information flow through their network. But instead of buying and maintaining vast hardware and software installations, such companies are turning to cloud technology for their data storage and analysis needs. A cloud is a server farm that is maintained by a third party like Google or IBM. A cloud cuts down the need for local storage. Many of the more than 1 million apps for the iPhone are small programs that connect to programs and data stored on a cloud. A business can securely store data in a cloud and use cloud-provided analytical tools to analyze and share data. Multiple and simultaneous access is possible, meaning members of a supply chain can post, look at, update, and analyze the same data together. This results in enhanced visibility along the supply chain, on a budget. Security concerns have limited the use of cloud technology in banks and other sensitive businesses, but security improvements are on-going.

Speed and response times also depend on quick transshipments and cross-docking in warehouses. New design warehouse *robots* are emerging for high volume picking operations. Zappos, Diapers.com, Staples, and Gap warehouses have adopted advanced robotic technologies to pick and ship products from mega-warehouses. Speed and accuracy of service is the selling edge.

OM IN PRACTICE

Robots in the Warehouse

With manufacturing increasingly being done elsewhere, companies are concentrating on distribution efficiencies. Warehousing automation has grown from simple forklifts and pallet loaders to sophisticated automatic storage and retrieval robotic systems (AS/RS) and Kiva robots. AS/RS can travel to item location and pick by item type and quantity. Kiva robots are short squat orange lifters that glide under storage racks, lifting and moving them where they need to go. They're guided by a very simple grid of stickers attached to the floor. Wi-Fi communications between bots and clusters of servers keep robots from colliding on the grid—no easy task, considering that a single warehousing company could use up to 500 of the little lifters. With KIVA, the racks are brought to the human workers instead of the other way around. Instead of having many workers work on the same order, the KIVA system allows for a single touch approach.

Figure 11.17 Stingray Shuttle Warehouse Automation

Source: Stefan Kiefer, "Stingray Shuttle AS/RS Technology for TGW," [CC], via *Wikimedia Commons*, 2013, http://commons.wikimedia.org/wiki/File%3ATGW-Stingray-Shuttle.jpg.

How Kiva's robots run a warehouse:

- To complete an order, Kiva's squat orange robots fetch tall movable shelves, or pods, that have the items needed, bringing them to the human "picker."
- A laser pointer tells the human which item needs to be picked from each shelf. The worker, who stays in one place, scans a bar code to confirm it is the right item. It's placed in the order box, which sits on another one of the mobile pods.
- New pods arrive steadily with additional items as needed. Items are grouped together to fulfill the orders.
- Pods filled with completed orders are taken by the robots to the shipping door, where a human tapes them closed in preparation for final transport.

With fewer hands used on each order, productivity increases, errors decrease, and the work process is streamlined. Zappos (a Kiva customer) claims order-to-ship times of as little as 12 minutes. And GAP, Quiet Logistics, and Amazon (which owns Kiva now) are all users of the little bot. A large part of Amazon's recent same-day 'local express' delivery initiatives and Sunday deliveries is being enabled by robotic warehousing efficiencies. About 10,000 little Kivas will be scurrying around Amazon's distribution centers.

"They have sensors, and they're supposed to stop if they see you," says one user, "but it's better to stay out of their way. They're very quiet, and you don't hear them coming." Retailer Crate & Barrel prefers Kiva robots because they can work in the dark, saving money on lighting and air-conditioning.

Adapted from: http://www.kivasystems.com; Thad Rueter, "Amazon Will Deploy Thousands More Robots in Its Warehouses This Year," *Internet Retailer*, May 23, 2014; Lauren Sherman, "The Robot Ballet Powering Fulfilment for Fast-Growing Fashion Start-ups," *Business of Fashion (BoF)*, July 10, 2013; "Robots in the Warehouse," *Robotland*, Feb. 21, 2012.

The *low-cost* regimes that supply chain managers have become accustomed to are coming to an end. Some economists say that low-cost favorite, China, is fast approaching the 'Lewis' turning point (named after Nobel Prize winner economist, Arthur Lewis), when surplus labor supply dries up and wages, prices, and inflation consequently increase. Companies like Honda and Foxconn faced labor strikes for better wages and improved working and living conditions in their China plants recently. Some companies are pushing into China's countryside, seeking new cheap sources of labor. Others are employing a China + 1 strategy, opening just one plant in another country. Chinese businesses themselves are investing in Africa, drawn by cheap labor and market growth prospects. However, China is still hard to beat, with its well-developed domestic supplier networks and reliable infrastructure that provide parts and personnel at factory doorsteps.

On the raw materials front, commodity price increases have seen wide fluctuations. For the future, supply chain managers can expect increasing volatility in commodity price trends and have to think of coping strategies. Companies are responding by reducing sizes (cereal), using substitutes (polyester instead of cotton), moving operations closer to consumer points to save on freight costs, and using technology to increase labor productivity. Co-opetition or leveraging volume with other businesses is also emerging as a cost-cutting strategy. Pepsi and Anheuser-Busch jointly purchase goods and services ranging from electronics to travel in the U.S. Shared warehouses and distribution routes are other co-opetitive possibilities.

Outsourcing in sensitive industries like insurance and legal work is increasing. Vendors are moving up the food chain, offering skills and security at much lower cost. Services are better served by off-shoring, since wage differentials can be significantly high. Despite reactions like Connecticut's 2011 bill to prevent "unlicensed" offshore workers for drafting, reviewing, or analyzing of legal documents for patrons in that state, the market for LPO (legal process outsourcing) is estimated at $2 billion at this time. Businesses in more sensitive or high skill-high touch areas such as health care and insurance services are actively considering outsourcing options. Life insurance companies spend a great deal on 'legacy books,' where existing life insurance policies are maintained and managed till the policy ceases or a claim is made. The maintenance time can stretch till 50 years or more, representing a considerable and recurring cost to the insurance company. Insurance companies are outsourcing 'legacy books,' freeing up capital and availing of the lower costs of specialized high volume outsourcing providers.

Compliance requirements are escalating. Till recently, only large corporations had the 'big picture' on globalization and could keep unsavory working conditions and news hidden from the everyday consumer. Today, ordinary consumers can see dead fish in polluted streams, tumors growing on toxic waste victims' faces, and little overworked fingers weaving carpets—instantly via Twitter, YouTube, Facebook and smartphones—and are demanding changes. Consumer pressure and government regulations now require companies to establish global practices for their supply chain that comply with a comprehensive set of compliance regulations from worldwide regulatory agencies.

OM IN PRACTICE

Seeking the "Ethical Smartphone"

John Wood, at the Trades Union Congress in the UK, has a problem—he cannot find an 'ethical' smartphone. He probed Apple, HTC, Samsung, Nokia supply-chain realities. He speaks of Taiwan's Young Fast Optoelectronics, who make those real-life picture touchscreens for brands like HTC, Samsung, and LG. Problem is, Mr. Wood says, Young Fast Opto is also faced with allegations of forced overtime, unsafe working, child labor, and union busting. He cites reports of worker suicides in companies like Foxconn, the debilitating effects of toxic chemicals used by iPhone screen supplier WinTek, and the horrors of rape and worker abuse in warlord-ravaged Congo, the source of the tantalum used in electronics manufacturing. All phones, he thinks, are ethically "shades of gray," including his own considered choice, the Samsung Galaxy Note—a choice that disappointed, when he found out later that Samsung, too, has been criticized for its labor practices and use of toxic chemicals.

Supply chain leaders are taking action. Tim Cook of Apple says "Apple takes worker conditions very seriously, and we have for a very long time." Apple prohibits underage labor, monitors workplace safety, and forbids forced overtime in its supplier plants. It has the Fair Labor Association begin inspections of FoxConn and other assembly suppliers in "probably the most detailed factory audit in the history of mass manufacturing." Apple, he stresses, will invest the same effort in supply chain ethics as it does in the design of its beautiful products. No doubt, interested observers, with dual lens iPhones at the ready, will be watching.

Adapted from: John Innit, "Ethical Smartphones: An Upgrade Dilemma," *Occasional Scrapbook of a Labor Geek* (blog), June 3, 2011, http://www.johninnit.co.uk/2011/06/03/ethical-smartphones-an-upgrade-dilemma; Andrew Leonard, "There Is No Ethical Smartphone," *Salon*, Feb. 23, 2012, http://www.salon.com/2012/02/23/there_is_no_ethical_smartphone/; Macworld Staff, "This is Tim: Apple CEO Talks at Investment Conference," *Macworld*, Feb. 14, 2012, http://www.macworld.com/article/1165379/this_is_tim_apple_ceo_talks_at_investment_conference.html.

Rapidly developing economies (RDE) like China, Brazil, and India are increasingly attractive markets for MNCs (multi-national companies), but average income levels are still too low to afford developed-country product prices. Companies like GE and P&G have responded to RDE needs by developing low-cost, but effective, product designs. GE Healthcare's Mac 400 portable and robust electrocardiogram machine was successfully developed for rural India. GE Healthcare improved upon the Mac 400 and introduced the new model, the Mac 800, into the U.S., where it found new markets, such as use at accident sites. This is known as reverse innovation, and it is an emerging trend. Creating entry-level products for developing nations and then repackaging them for sale in developed markets reduces product development costs and increases global revenues. But creating such cost-frugal products takes a special kind of supply chain design and management. Different and more difficult conditions in both demand and supply markets pose special challenges to the supply chain manager. RDEs do not have developed or reliable logistics and utility infrastructure in all parts of the country, though China is making great strides toward improving their logistics and infrastructure. Distribution networks in RDE do not have huge automated warehouses, or loading systems, or refrigerated 18-wheelers to move goods quickly, safely, and cheaply. Rather, a motorcycle or bicycle may be the mode of transport for final delivery. Retail points number in the millions in RDEs, with mom-and-pop stores forming the last mile. Forecasting is more difficult since data collection systems are nonexistent or unreliable, or just too expensive to develop from scratch. Electronic payments and goods tracking in RDEs is often not possible, leading to cash-on-delivery or manual ledger keeping of accounts payables/receivables. Local supplier quality is spotty and difficult to monitor. However, the rapid growth of RDE markets have made global companies seek suitable points of entry to these markets. And although much of growth in global supply chains is unidirectional, that is, originating from low-cost countries to a developed buying country, the RDE product needs a local supply chain for a locally developed product. When introduced in developed markets, the RDE product still requires the same low-cost supply chain to source and make it.

Sustainability has become a compliance, energy savings, reputational, and competitive concern in supply chain management. Sustainability reports and updates are now regularly published by companies like Coca-Cola and Walmart, and a quick glance at almost any business website will notice a prominent mention of sustainability. P&G's supplier scorecard, modeled after major customer Walmart's sustainability index, uses nine key metrics including energy use, water use, waste disposal, and greenhouse gas emissions, and sustainability innovation ideas on an annual basis. Use of the scorecard has resulted in improvements such as eliminating plastic windows on a brand's cartons, manufacturing scrap waste reduction, replacing petroleum-based materials with certified Roundtable on Sustainable Palm Oil (RSPO) material, and more efficient logistics. European suppliers led the ratings.

Mandating sustainability to the supply, assembly, or distribution network rarely works on a consistent basis. Why couldn't Apple find and stop the use of child labor at one of its suppliers in China? Why did Walmart's extended supply chain balk at being forced to adopt the retail giant's sustainability standards? The two issues are the lack of visibility into supply chain capillaries and the lack of incentive or capability in the supply chain to understand, accept, and adhere. Mattel's lead paint on toys catastrophe was traced to an unapproved supplier to Mattel's established manufacturer in China. Mattel's manufacturer did not test for lead because it reportedly accepted a forged certification without feeling the need to conduct due diligence. That lack of follow-up attests to indifference at best and complicity at worst. The reasons could be many, ranging from misplaced trust from personal relationships (important in Asia) to simple inertia. MNCs (multi-national companies) often leave the supply network to cope with sustainability mandates on its own. Suppliers understand the mandates but are also quite aware that the MNC would have little hesitation in switching to a lower cost supplier if the opportunity presented itself. Competition is fierce among suppliers in low-cost regions, and such buyer behavior is expected and quite consistent with the rationales of low-cost jurisdiction off-shoring. Why, then, would the supply network invest scarce resources on sustainability when cost is the prime criteria for continued business? Additionally, lax environmental laws and lax enforcement of laws create opportunities for manipulation. There are companies that take a comprehensive approach. Even when the buying company establishes offices abroad, their top local executive is generally an expatriate living in a city and assisted by a small group of locals. The expats lack first-hand knowledge of the world beyond the city, and visits to the field are too short to uncover situational realities. The solution lies with the supply chain manager. MNCs must a) provide auditing personnel and technical and financial help to suppliers; b) maintain a clear preference for compliant suppliers, even at higher cost, through additional volume and longer term contracts; c) share the additional compliance costs incurred by local suppliers; d) take help from local NGOs and governments to keep tabs on second- and third-tier suppliers; e) keep a managerial eye and foot on the ground—mix and mingle, and f) do the things the supplier cannot—root-cause analysis and long-term solutions. Companies can also lead by example. IKEA is switching from timber to lighter weight cardboard pallets in its warehouse-like retail centers, reducing transportation costs and squeezing in more pallets in the same warehouse space. IKEA's suppliers will be able to watch the transition and feel confident about doing the same at a later time.

OM IN PRACTICE

How Esquel Met the Sustainability Challenge

Esquel, a leading shirt contractor for companies and brands like Nordstrom, Lands' End, Hilfiger, Nike, and Abercrombie & Fitch, wanted to reduce the water and pesticide content in its shirts by switching to organically grown cotton. Most of Esquel's cotton was grown in the Xinjiang province of China, an impoverished region, where pesticides were used to kill insects and vermin in the cotton fields. Growing organic cotton would mean a reduction in cotton yields and additional processing with toxic chemicals. Esquel could not pass on the additional costs to its customers and would not allow the chemical processing, either. Instead of half-solutions and temporary fixes, Esquel decided to do it the right way, which was also the hard way. It helped the cotton farmers of Xinjian change to drip irrigation that used less water; they developed and introduced pest- and disease-resistant strains of cotton seeds and persuaded farmers to handpick the cotton for a cleaner harvest. Esquel also teamed up with the Standard Chartered Bank to provide micro-financing to the cotton growers and guaranteed purchase of whatever cotton was grown at a guaranteed price or the prevailing spot price, whichever turned out to be higher at the time of harvesting. The cotton farms that Esquel worked with flourished—yields of organic cotton doubled, grower incomes almost doubled, and the company secured a reliable supply source for a commodity that has since seen price increases of over a 100 percent. Esquel followed up its sustainability initiatives at the raw material level with improvements to its own manufacturing processes, reducing water and chemical usage in the spinning and fabric-making processes. Esquel also runs mobile workshops that educate local populations on the importance of sustainability and simple ways to promote it, like tree planting.

Adapted from: http://www.esquel.com; Hau Lee, "Don't Tweak Your Supply Chain—Rethink It End to End," *Harvard Business Review*, October 2010.

For a Wall Street perspective on sustainability, check out the Dow Jones Sustainability Indices, the first global indices to track the financial performance of the leading sustainability-driven companies worldwide.

KEY POINTS

- Sensor and robotic technology advances are bringing increased visibility, information, and product flow speeds, as well as flexibility, to supply chains.
- Cloud computing is reducing IT costs and enhancing supply chain visibility, flow speed, and reliability along the chain.
- Cost increases are percolating through the supply chain to the consumer.
- Companies are using substitute materials, productivity increasing technology, reduced packaging size, and increased outsourcing to cope with cost increases.
- New, frugal supply chains in RDEs are challenging supply chain managers.
- Assistance and rigorous auditing by buyers is necessary for supply chain members to accept and adhere to sustainability and compliance goals.

11.6 Conclusion

Customer: *"Why should I choose you?"*

Business: *"Because we promise that you will find our product on the right shelf, at the right time, and at the right cost, without concerns about child labor, toxic chemicals, animal cruelty, or unsafe worker conditions being a part of what you buy from us."*

The supply chain of the future would be a perfectly balanced, instantly responsive network, where the sale of a shirt in NYC triggers the planting of cotton in a field in China. With the help of sensors, information technology, risk-sharing contracts, and working capital access, the trade-off between perfectly responsive and lowest cost may be resolved sooner than we think. Till then, the matching of supply to demand remains a difficult objective. Toward this end, supply chain managers can employ a range of strategies to try to manage demand and supply uncertainties more effectively. Supply chain managers are becoming coordinators of global networks of dispersed manufacturers, assemblers, and distributors, picking and activating specific networks depending on the time and cost priority of the customer. Orchestration skills are becoming key in coordinating supply chain members and showing member companies how they would benefit if they play to the conductor's (supply chain manager's) score. Managers who can learn to orchestrate great networks of globally dispersed, independent, supply, assembly, and distribution organizations are valued and rewarded. With this chapter, you are on your way!

What Have We Learned?

What Is Supply Chain Management?

- Managing a supply chain design involves coordinating and orchestrating the build and movement of product, information, knowledge, and cash in a smooth, no-waste flow from the source to the customer on demand, and at a profit.
- Supply chain management = managing the (SUPPLY network + ASSEMBLY network + DISTRIBUTION network) + the HUMAN network
- Demand and supply uncertainties create challenges in matching supply to demand.

- Competition today is between supply chains, not just in-house competencies.
- Supply chain performance has a direct effect on financial performance.

How Is It Done?

- Supply chain managers are paid to make the right decisions in three basic decision areas: Value-partitioning (Make-Buy), push vs. pull, and the synchronization of supply with demand.
- Value-partitioning is a strategic decision on dividing product values among in-house, outsourced, and combined in-house-outsourced manufacture and supply.
  - Outsourcing is asking an external agency to do a job that can be done in-house.
  - Factors such as manufacturing in new, foreign locations, complex integrative product architecture, proprietary technology/design, and strong unions or customer pressure can keep a product in-house, even if outsourcing offers a better cost argument.
- Push vs. pull is a decision that requires a trade-off between making to economies of scale (push) and making to order after demand becomes known (pull).
  - Low demand volatility products are best made to stock—that is, products are pushed through the supply chain by demand forecasts and economies-of-scale-based production runs.
  - High demand volatility—low volume products are best made after demand becomes visible (pull).
  - High volatility-high volume products can be made in a divided push-pull approach, with the product components split between high volume standardized or common-to-many-products components and components that are special to that product.
- The standardized components can be made to forecast, availing economies of scale (push), while manufacturing of the remaining components and final product assembly can be done to order (pull).
- Synchronizing supply with demand
  - A high demand uncertainty-high supply uncertainty position is a premium segment if a company can manage those uncertainties well.
  - Uncertainty begets risks. *Risk = f(probability of occurrence, probability of early detection, consequences, estimated time to impact operations, estimated time to recovery)*
  - The bullwhip effect amplifies retail-level variations in demand as demand travels upstream in the supply chain.
  - Bullwhip remedies include better forecasting, stable pricing, connecting sales force commission to sales to the end-customer, supply allocations during shortages based on past usage, and exposing different functions to each other's perspectives.
  - Buy-back and revenue contracts between the retailer and manufacturer can also help share the risks of demand uncertainty.
  - Pooling centralizes supply and reduces overall experienced demand uncertainty by offsetting demand movements in negatively correlated markets.
  - Postponement reduces the effects of demand uncertainty by delaying the final assembly point and allowing time for demand to become more visible.
  - Supply uncertainties include foreign exchange fluctuations, intellectual property theft, compliance issues, commodity price and availability volatility, a long supply chain with multiple global hand-off points, component obsolescence, political risks, and natural events.
  - Local reserve capacity and air freight are employed to counter supply uncertainties in high value-high uncertainty items. Low value-high volume items are stored in local inventory stock.

- Hedging is a preferred strategy to combat input cost volatility but requires a careful consideration of the costs of hedging.
- Uncertainties can be reduced through collaboration, but long-term supplier relationships and contracts in high-speed, high-tech industries may be detrimental to staying current.

Was It Done Right?

- Silo thinking can lead to conflicting behavior by different functions or among members of a supply chain. Collaboration is the key to effective supply chain management.
- Supply chain financial performance, including cost savings, cost avoidance, and deferred cost savings, requires visibility in financial statements.
- Too many product variants can strain the supply chain.
- Suppliers' financial health can be monitored indirectly by watching how their key customers are faring, supplier accounts payable and receivable behavior, and factors such as sudden fluctuations in capacity utilization and unusually heavy price discounts.
- Supply chain performance is evaluated using a combination of customer-facing, internal-facing, and shareholder-facing metrics.
- Metrics that can be applied across the supply chain include cash-to-cash cycle time, working capital deployment, customer growth and profitability, cycle time accumulation, and adoption of new technologies.

Current Trends in Supply Chain Management

- Speed and flexibility in supply chains demand visibility—facilitated by sensor and cloud technologies and advances in robotic warehousing and tracking technologies.
- Rising labor and input costs have encouraged co-opetition, the sharing of resources among companies for economies of scale and scope.
- Outsourcing is growing at a fast pace in sensitive industries like insurance and health.
- Compliance regulations are increasing, leading supply chain managers to scrutinize and monitor their supply chains more closely.
- Developing and managing supply chains in rapidly developing economies (RDEs) is becoming necessary and represents a challenge for managers with developed economy backgrounds.
- Pushing sustainability behavior through global supply chains requires significant investments in auditing, long-term commitments to suppliers, and visible preference for sustainability over cost in supplier selection and contract awards.

Discussion Questions

1   Connect the dots: How could instability in the Middle East affect demand or supply uncertainty?

   Answers: Disruption in oil supplies, higher oil prices; higher shipping rates, ships run at slower speeds increasing delivery times; disruption in shipping channels (Suez Canal), and the SUMED oil pipeline running alongside the canal leading to increased shipping distance and rates, exposure to piracy, and increases in insurance premiums; disruption in commodity supplies like Egyptian cotton and Israeli fruits and high-tech components; greater geo-political risk drives money to safe havens like the U.S. and Japan, dollar and yen exchange rates rise in the world, global demand for goods made in the U.S. and Japan declines, and so on. . . . . Also unrest rooted in food inflation and youth unemployment—Middle East governments may hoard up grain and other food commodities, leading to price increase in foodstuffs and increase in social support or entrepreneurship programs for youth. Also, to pay for these additional stocks and projects, may temporarily increase oil output leading to temporary decline in oil prices. Also, unrest may spread to other countries in region.

One way to estimate geo-political risk is to look at the spread between U.S. Treasuries and emerging market bonds. The 2008 global crisis led to an October 2008 high of 891 basis points between the JP Morgan EMBI Global index (tracks emerging market bonds) and comparable U.S. Treasuries.

2   Read the following:

The publishing industry realizes there are problems with its business model, but there are few alternatives. When a new book is released, bookstores need copies to sell to customers. The industry has significantly more retail outlets now than it did a few years ago. Each of the hundreds of Barnes & Noble stores gets copies of new releases. Unsold books are boxed up and shipped back to the publishers. The publishers shred some books and sell others to discounters. This involves significant expenses for shipping, transportation, and labor. These inefficiencies affect the profitability of publishers, but tradition is difficult to change. The practice dates back to the Depression era, and now 34 percent of adult hardcover books are returned to publishers. It is difficult for publishers to determine in advance which titles will be blockbusters, and they don't want to run short of inventory at the bookstore. One suggested solution is to run the book business similar to other retail enterprises, where the store buys inventory and then marks it down instead of returning it. Bookstores are reluctant to change because, currently, the publishers shoulder the risks if a title doesn't sell. Publishers also worry that customers might wait until the book goes on sale instead of paying full price.

Questions:

i)   What are the elements that constitute demand and supply uncertainty in the book (not textbook) business?
ii) Place the book-selling industry (bookstores) in a suitable quadrant in the demand-supply uncertainty matrix.
iii) Detail your strategies for managing demand and supply uncertainties in the book selling business

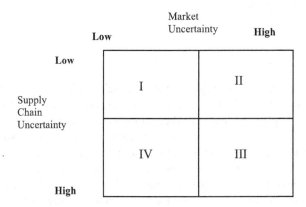

Figure 11.18 Demand-Supply Uncertainty Matrix

Answers: Examine why stores wish to keep large inventories—fear of slow replenishment in case a title becomes an instant bestseller. Bestsellers have a limited sales window. Why publishers push inventory to stores—they print to get economies of scale and do not have adequate storage capacity. Remedies: better forecasting (how?), reduce manufacturing and transportation lead time, pooling DCs, redesign books and book manufacturing process for postponement options, incentives for customer to wait, keep limited 'demo' model in stores and so on.

End of Chapter Problems

Use figure 11.18 to answer questions 1 and 2.

1   Which one of the following choices is most appropriate for this framework?:

   a)   I Milk, II Petroleum, III Hotel rooms, IV GM's hydrogen powered cars
   b)   II Milk, I Petroleum, IV Hotel rooms, III GM's hydrogen powered cars
   c)   I Milk, IV Petroleum, II Hotel rooms, III GM's hydrogen powered cars
   d)   I Milk, II1 Petroleum, IV Hotel rooms, II GM's hydrogen powered cars

   Answer: c

2   Why would any business possibly *prefer* to remain in quadrant III rather than move to quadrant 1?

   a)   Because quadrant I represents an environment that needs agile, responsive supply chains that require considerable time and cost to develop, as well as one that needs hard-to-get superior forecasting skills.
   b)   Because quadrant III represents an environment where it's relatively easy to do business in.
   c)   Because quadrant III may offer price and profit premiums for competent firms.
   d)   Because both quadrants represent similar profit and growth opportunities, so there is no reason to opt for movements between quadrants (change is always disruptive).

   Answer: c

3   Typically, the best way to *anticipate* (not react to or just cope with) market uncertainty is to:

   a)   Develop improved forecasting abilities.
   b)   Develop an agile supply chain (quick supplier responses to changes in product specifications).
   c)   Reduce supplier lead time (quick supplier response to changes in market demand volume).
   d)   Reduce supplier lead time uncertainty.

   Answer: a

4   Typically, the best way to reduce supply chain uncertainty (in today's cost-competitive world) is to:

   a)   Make most things yourself.
   b)   Develop strategies to reduce supplier lead times.
   c)   Offer promotional discounts to market customers to buy in the off-season.
   d)   None of the above.

   Answer: b

5   The *principal* advantage in risk pooling is:

   a)   Overall reduction in uncertainty from offsetting across markets resulting in lower inventory holdings.
   b)   Reduced logistics costs between plant and mega-warehouse.

   c) Everyone in the supply chain shares risks equally.

   d) None of the above.

Answer: a

6   One possible disadvantage of risk pooling is:

   a) Increased logistics costs between plant and warehouse.

   b) Higher stock levels at the mega-warehouse.

   c) Reduced understanding of individual market nuances and dynamics.

   d) Increased mega-warehouse warehouse operating cost as compared to cost of operating individual warehouses.

Answer: c

7   Which of the following diagrams is most representative of the bullwhip effect?

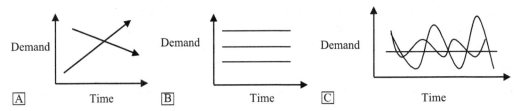

   a) Figure A

   b) Figure C

   c) Figure B

   d) None of them

Answer: b

8   Millhiser Castings makes cast iron skillets and a few other products. The fixed cost at its plant in Tennessee is $3 million while the variable cost per skillet is $4. Faced with increasing demands for cost reduction by major retailers who carry its skillets, Millhiser Castings explored the cost of offshoring manufacturing to China. Making the skillets in China would cost an annual fixed amount of $1 million and a variable cost of $6 per skillet delivered in the U.S. Would it make economic sense to offshore the manufacturing of the skillets? Annual demand for the skillets is about 500,000 pieces. Assume quality and delivery times are acceptable for the off-shoring option.

a)   Where should we make the skillets?

   Answer:

      TC to outsource = FC + VC = $1,000,000 + $6 * 500,000 = $4,000,000

      TC to make   = FC + VC = $3,000,000 + $4 * 500,000 = $5,000,000

Outcome: Outsource because it saves $1 million over making in-house.

Decision: Consider other costs of outsourcing, including increased managerial oversight costs. Also consider the impact of spreading the in-house fixed cost of $1 million over the remaining products still being made in-house. Unit fixed costs of these items will increase. Consider returns and warranty logistics.

b) What is the break-even quantity for deciding between the two locations?

Answer:

Break-even point is where:
Total cost to outsource = total cost to make
$FC_{out} + VC_{out}$ * qty for outsourcing = $FC_{make} + VC_{make}$ * qty for making
Say B is the break-even quantity;
$FC_{out} + VC_{out}$ * $B = FC_{make} + VC_{make}$ * B
$B = (FC_{make} - FC_{out}) / (VC_{out} - VC_{make}) = (\$3,000,000 - \$1,000,000) / (\$6 - \$4) = 1,000,000$ units

In other words, it would take an annual production quantity of over 1,000,000 skillets to make it economic to make in Tennessee. At the break-even quantity, we are indifferent to where we make it (realistically, we'd make in Tennessee for reasons of delivery and control). Since the annual demand of 500,000 skillets is less than the break-even quantity of 1,000,000 units, China would be the more economic manufacturing location.

9 ABC Inc buys phone speakers from Bass-Bose at $70/unit. ABC sells them retail at $120/unit. Retail demand is normally distributed with a mean of 2,000 and a standard deviation of 500.

Without Buy-back

Assume ABC does not offer any discounted sales for strategic reasons. It sells off excess units to a third party for $30 each for export markets.

a) How many speakers should ABC buy from BB (Bass-Bose) in order to maximize its profit?

Answer: Cost of running out, Cu = lost profit

Unit profit = SP − cost = $120 − $70 = $50
Thus Cu = $50
Cost of excess units, Co = loss from unsold units
Co = unit loss
Unit loss = cost − salvage value = $70 − $30 = $40
Thus Co = $40
And the
Critical ratio (CR) = $Cu/(Co+Cu)$ = 50/(40 + 50) = 0.5556

We need to find that order quantity where the (cumulative) probability of demand being less than the order quantity is 0.556 (or greater).

Procedurally, we need to find the Z value first for a F(Z) of 0.5556 or greater. F(Z) is the probability of demand being equal to or less than the order quantity represented by that Z value. We look under the F(Z) 'area under curve' columns in a standard normal distribution table.

Looking at the standard normal distribution table, the Z values for F(Z)s of 0.5517 and 0.5557 are 0.13 and 0.14, respectively. We always round up when using a critical ratio.

So Z for a CR/F(Z) of 0.5556 = 0.14; in Excel, use NORM.S.INV(0.5556)
Mean demand (given) = 2,000, standard deviation (given) = 500; Z value = 0.14
So the order qty = mean demand + Z * standard deviation = 2,000 + 0.14 * 500 = 2,070 units

b) What would be ABC's profit for an order quantity of 2,070 units?

Answer: The procedure for normally distributed demand is as follows:

    i) Find the Z value corresponding to the order quantity.
    ii) Use this Z value to look up the 'expected lost sales,' L(Z), from the Standard Normal Loss Function Table. Or in Excel, use NORMDIST(Z,0,1,FALSE) − Z * NORMSDIST(−Z)
    iii) The expected lost sales = standard deviation * L(Z)
    iv) Expected sales (demand) = mean − expected lost sales
    v) Expected leftover units = order qty − expected sales
    vi) Expected profit = (expected sales * unit profit) − (expected leftover * unit loss)

Thus:

    i) We know (from above) that the Z value corresponding to an order quantity of 2,070 = 0.14
    ii) L(z) for a Z value of 0.14 = 0.3328; in Excel NORMDIST(z,0,1,FALSE) − Z*NORMSDIST(−Z), where Z = 0.14
    iii) Expected lost sales = standard deviation * L(Z) = 500 * 0.3328 = 166.4 = 165 units
    iv) Expected sales (demand) = mean demand − expected lost sales = 2,000 − 165 = 1,835 units
    v) Expected leftover units = order qty − expected sales = 2,070 − 1,835 = 235 units
    vi) Expected profit = (expected sales * unit profit) − (expected leftover * unit loss)
             = (1,835 *$50) − (235*$40) = $82,350.00

c) What would be Bass-Bose's profit if ABC orders 2,070 units?

Answer: Assume BB's unit variable cost of production at $40/unit (ignore fixed costs). It sells to ABC at $70/unit.

Unit profit = SP − cost = $70 − $40 = $30/unit
BB's total profit = $30 * 2,070 units = $62,100.00

d) What is the total supply chain profit?

Answer: Supply chain profit = ABC profit + BB profit = $82,350.00 + $62,100.00 = $144,450.00

With Buy-Back

a) How many speakers should ABC buy from BB if BB agrees to buy back unsold speakers from ABC at $50/unit? Recall ABC's cost of purchase from BB is $70, and it sells the speakers retail for $120. ABC does not sell unsold units to a third party ($30/unit) now since BB pays them more to return unsold units ($50/unit).

Answer: So now unit profit for BB remains at $50, but unit loss reduces to $20/unit

Cost of running out, Cu = lost profit = unit profit = SP − cost = $120 − $70 = $50
Thus $Cu = 50
Cost of excess units, Co = loss from unsold unit = unit loss = cost − buy-back value
    = $70 − $50 = $20
Thus $Co = 20

And the,

Critical ratio (CR) = Cu/(Co + Cu) = 50/(20 + 50) = 0.7143

So Z for a CR/F(Z) of 0.7143 = 0.57; in Excel use NORM.S.INV(0.7143)

Mean demand (given) = 2,000, standard deviation (given) = 500; Z value = 0.57

So the order qty = mean demand + Z * standard deviation = 2,000 + 0.57 * 500 = 2,285 units

b) What would be ABC's profit for an order qty of 2,285 units?

> *Answer:* Following prescribed procedure for normally distributed demand:
>
> i) We know (from above) that the Z value corresponding to an order qty of 2,285 units = 0.57
>
> ii) L(Z) for a Z value of 0.57 = 0.1771; in Excel, NORMDIST(Z,0,1,FALSE) – Z * NORMSDIST(–Z), where Z = 0.57
>
> iii) Expected lost sales = standard deviation * L(Z)= 500 * 0.1771 = 88.55 = 89 units
>
> iv) Expected sales (demand) = mean demand – expected lost sales = 2,000 – 89 = 1,911 units
>
> v) Expected leftover units = order qty – expected sales = 2,285 – 1,911 = 374 units
>
> vi) Expected profit = (expected sales * unit profit) – (expected leftover * unit loss) = (1,911 * $50) – (374 * $20) = $88,070.00

c) What would be Bass-Bose's profit if ABC orders 2,285 units?

Answer: Assume BB's unit variable cost of production at $40/unit (ignore fixed costs). It sells to ABC at $70/unit. It takes back unsold units from ABC at $50/unit. BB sells these unsold units to a third party for $30/unit.

Unit profit = SP – VC of production = $70 – $40 = $30/unit

Cost of returns = $50/unit – $30/unit (salvage value) = $20/unit

BB's total profit = (unit profit * qty sold) – (returns qty * cost of return/unit)

From b) above we know that the expected return = 374 units (leftover units at ABC).

Thus:

BB's total profit = $30 * 2,285 units - $20 * 374 units = $61,070.00

d) What is the total supply chain profit at the given buy-back rate of $50/unit?

Answer: Supply chain profit = ABC profit + BB profit = $88,070 + $61,070 = $149,140 (with buy-back)

Supply chain profit = ABC profit + BB profit = $82,350 + $62,100 = $144,450 (no buy-back)

The supply chain profit increases with the buy-back, but BB's profit declines.

e) Is there an optimal buy-back rate that will lead the retailer (ABC) to order the supply chain profit-maximizing order quantity?

What would be an optimal buy-back rate to maximize profit for the total supply chain?

The critical ratio (CR) determines the order quantity. When demand is normally distributed, that rate occurs when the CR for the retailer equals the CR for the supply chain.

CR for retailer (BB) = Cu/(Co + Cu)

Cost of running out, Cu = lost profit = unit profit = selling price (Sp) − purchase cost (Pc)

Thus Cu = Sp − Pc

Let b = the supply chain optimal buy-back rate

Cost of excess units, Co = loss from unsold unit = purchase cost − buy-back rate

Thus Co = Pc − b, and

CR for retailer = Cu/(Co + Cu) = (Sp − Pc)/[(Pc − b) + (Sp − Pc)] = (Sp − Pc)/[(−b) + Sp)] = (Sp − Pc)/
(Sp − b) . . . (1)

CR for supply chain = Cu/(Co + Cu)

From a supply chain perspective, we assume full collaboration between the retailer and manufacturer. We assume that there is effectively no intermediary profit and that the total supply chain profit will be shared (hopefully eqitably) by the parties in the supply chain. There is no buy-back involved, since we assume no intermediary retailer. We intend to find out that buy-back rate that would maximize this total supply chain profit pool, given a specific purchase cost (Pc).

So, now BB (manufacturer) theoretically sells at the retail price = Sp

BB's unit variable cost = Vc

Let's assume that unsold units salvage value = Sv.

CR for supply chain = Cu/Co + Cu,

Where,

Cu for supply chain = profit margin = retail price − variable cost of production = Sp − Vc

Co for supply chain = loss = variable cost of making − salvage value = Vc − Sv

Thus:

CR for supply chain = Cu/Co + Cu = (Sp − Vc)/[(Vc − Sv) + (Sp − Vc)] = (Sp − Vc)/(−Sv + Sp)
= (Sp − Vc)/(Sp − Sv) . . . (2)

Setting the retailer CR(1) equal to supply chain CR(2), we get:

(Sp − Pc)/(Sp − b) = (Sp − Vc)/(Sp − Sv)

Cross-multiplying:

(Sp − Pc) * (Sp − Sv)] = (Sp − Vc)*(Sp − b)

Reversing:

(Sp − Vc) * (Sp − b) = (Sp − Pc) * (Sp − Sv), or

(Sp − b) = [(Sp − Pc) * (Sp − Sv)]/(Sp − Vc), or

−b = {[(Sp − Pc) * (Sp − Sv)]/(Sp − Vc)} − Sp, or

b = Sp − {[(Sp − Pc) * (Sp − Sv)]/(Sp − Vc)} . . . (3)

'(3)' is the formula for 'b,' the optimal buy-back rate for the supply chain.

Applying (3) in this case, if BB (manufacturer) sets a purchase cost of $70/unit,

Sp = retail price = $120/unit; Pc = purchase cost = $70/unit; Sv = salvage value = $30; Vc = variable cost of production = $40/unit (all given values taken from the beginning sections of this problem)

b = Sp − {[(Sp − Pc)*(Sp − Sv)]/(Sp − Vc)}
= 120 − {[(120 − 70)*(120 − 30)]/(120 − 40)}
= $63.75

b = $63.75/unit, the buy-back price for a given purchase cost, variable cost of production, and salvage value, that will result in BB ordering the supply chain optimal-profit ordering quantity.

f)   So what is the optimal supply chain order quantity for BB to order from ABC at a buy-back rate of $63.75?

   Answer: Purchase cost to BB = $70; retail price = $120; buy-back rate = $63.75
   Cost of running out, Cu = lost profit = unit profit = SP − cost = $120 − $70 = $50
   Thus Cu = $50
   Cost of excess units, Co = loss from unsold unit = unit loss = cost − buy-back value = $70 − $63.75
      = $6.25
   Thus Co = $6.25
   And the
   Critical ratio (CR) = Cu/(Co + Cu) = 50/(6.25 + 50) = 0.8889
   So Z for a CR/F(Z) of 0.8889 = 1.23; in Excel, use NORM.S.INV(0.8889)
   Mean demand (given) = 2,000, standard deviation (given) = 500; Z value = 1.23
   So the order qty = mean demand + Z * standard deviation = 2,000 + 1.23 * 500 = 2,615 units

g)   What would be ABC's profit for an order quantity of 2,615 units?
   Unit profit = $50, and unit loss = $6.25.

   Following prescribed procedure for normally distributed demand:

   i)   We know (from the previous questions) that the Z value corresponding to an order quantity of
         2,615 units = 1.23
   ii)   L(Z) for a Z value of 1.23 = 0.0527; in Excel, NORMDIST(Z,0,1,FALSE) − Z *NORMSDIST(−Z),
         where Z = 1.23
   iii) Expected lost sales = standard deviation * L(Z)= 500 * 0.0527 = 26.35 = 27 units
   iv)   Expected sales (demand) = mean demand − expected lost sales = 2,000 − 27 = 1,973 units
   v)   Expected leftover units = order qty − expected sales = 2,615 − 1,973 = 642 units
   vi)   Expected profit = (expected sales * unit profit) − (expected leftover * unit loss)
                    = (1,973 * $50) − (642 * $6.25) = $94,637.50

h)   What would be Bass-Bose's profit if ABC orders 2,615 units?

   Answer: Unit profit = SP − VC of production = $70 − $40 = $30/unit

   Cost of return = $63.75/unit − $30 (salvage value) = $33.75/unit
   BB's total profit = (unit profit * qty sold) − (returns qty * cost of return/unit)
   From g) we know that the expected return = 642 units (leftover units at ABC)
   Thus:
   BB's total profit = $30 * 2,615 units − $33.75 * 642 units = $56,782.50

i)   What would be the total supply chain profit at the buy-back rate of $63.75/unit?

   Answer: Supply chain profit = ABC profit + BB profit

No buy-back	*$50/unit buy-back*	*$63.75/unit buy-back*
$144,450	$149,140	$151,420
$82,350 + $62,100	$88,070 + $61,070	$94,637.50 + $56,782.50
ABC profit + BB profit	ABC profit + BB profit	ABC profit + BB profit

The problem here is obviously that ABC and BB should devise a way to share the total supply chain profit more equitably.

Try f),g),h), and i) with a buy-back rate of $65/unit—you will find that the total supply chain profit declines to $151,410. The buy-back rate of $63.75 optimizes the total supply chain profit, with the given values of the other parameters.

Q#9) Verifying optimal buy-back quantity.

j)   So what is the optimal supply chain order quantity for BB to order from ABC at a buy-back rate of $65?

Answer: Purchase cost to BB = $70; retail price = $120; buy-back rate = $65

Cost of running out, Cu = lost profit = unit profit = SP − cost = $120 − $70 = $50
Thus: *Cu* = $50
Cost of excess units, Co = loss from unsold unit = unit loss = cost − buy-back value = $70 − $65 = $5
Thus: *Co* = $5
And the,
Critical ratio (CR) = Cu/(Co + Cu) = 50/(5 + 50) = 0.9090
So Z for a CR/F(Z) of 0.9090 = 1.34; in Excel, use NORM.S.INV(0.9090)
Mean demand (given) = 2,000, standard deviation (given) = 500; Z value = 1.34
So the order qty = mean demand + Z * standard deviation = 2,000 + 1.34 * 500 = 2,670 units

k)   What would be ABC's profit for an order quantity of 2,670 units?

Answer: Unit profit = $50, and unit loss = $5

Following prescribed procedure for normally distributed demand:

vii) We know (from above) that the Z value corresponding to an order quantity of 2,670 units = 1.34
viii) L(Z) for a Z value of 1.34 = 0.0418; in Excel, NORMDIST(z,0,1,FALSE) − Z *NORMSDIST (−Z), where Z = 1.34
ix) Expected lost sales = standard deviation * L(Z)= 500 * 0.0418 = 20.90= 21 units
x)   Expected sales (demand) = mean demand − expected lost sales = 2,000 − 21 = 1,979 units
xi) Expected leftover units = order qty − expected sales = 2,670 − 1,979 = 691 units
xii) Expected profit = (expected sales * unit profit) − (Expected leftover * Unit loss)
                     = (1,979 * $50) − (691 * $5) = $95,495

l)   What would be Bass-Bose's profit if ABC orders 2,670 units?

Answer: Unit profit = SP − VC of production = $70 − $40 = $30/unit

Cost of return = $65/unit − $30 (salvage value) = $35/unit
BB's total profit = (unit profit * qty sold) − (returns qty * cost of return/unit)
From k), we know that the expected return = 691 units (leftover units at ABC)
Thus:
BB's total profit = $30 * 2,670 units − $35 * 691 units = $55,915.00

Total supply chain profit = $151,410 (< than the $151,420.00 with a $63.75 buy-back rate)

Suggested Class Projects

1 Depict the supply chain for a bank offering mortgage products. Who are the major companies in that supply chain? What are their objectives? How can you, as the supply chain manager of the bank, reconcile these objectives and align them?

2 Take a product that you use in class—trace its supply chain as far back as possible. How is member power distributed in the chain?

3 Environmental groups in China have singled out Apple as a failure for ignoring environmental and labor standards in its supply chain.

How would you, as Apple's supply chain manager, a) respond to this criticism, b) control the actions of your dispersed supply chain?

Suggested Cases[11]

Zappos.com: Developing a Supply Chain to Deliver WOW!

By Michael Marks, Hau Lee, David W. Hoyt; publication date: Feb. 13, 2009. Prod. #: GS65-PDF-ENG.

Description

Zappos was founded in 1999, during the Internet boom, to sell shoes online. The company's founding premise was to provide the ultimate in selection to its customers—all brands, styles, sizes, and colors. Zappos organized all aspects of its business (including recruiting, culture, call center, inventory, website, and supply chain) to provide the best possible service—it wanted to "wow" everyone who interacted with the company, from customers to employees to corporate partners. Zappos grew rapidly, and by 2008 was profitable with net sales (after returns) of about $650 million. The company faced a number of issues as it looked forward. While it had penetrated only about 3 percent of the U.S. market for shoes, Zappos had expanded its product lines to items such as camping gear and video games. It needed to determine whether those elements of its strategy had contributed to its success in shoes and whether it would be able to duplicate that success in other product lines. It also needed to determine how it could scale its business—much of the effort it had made to "wow" its customers was labor intensive and expensive—could this be scaled to a company with revenues of tens of billions? Finally, the economic landscape changed dramatically in late 2008, with the financial market collapse and recession. The service-intensive Zappos.com business was based on sales at little to no discount, unlike many websites that relied on selling at the lowest possible price. Would the company need to make changes to respond to the changed economic environment, and if so, what were those changes? The case provides an opportunity to evaluate the core competences of an Internet retailer that has experienced rapid initial success. The case enables students to consider supply chain issues, which are critical to the company's success, in the broader context of the business: the bases of Zappos' success, its core competencies, culture, and competitive environment.

Learning Objective

The case highlights an Internet retailer that has grown rapidly but faces significant issues, including scope of product offerings, supply chain costs, customer service costs, and scalability. The teaching objective of the case is to examine these issues and the considerations that the company must make in choosing a way forward.

Crocs: Revolutionizing an Industry's Supply Chain Model for Competitive Advantage

By Michael Marks, Chuck Holloway, Hau Lee, David W. Hoyt, and Amanda Silverman; publication date: June 18, 2007. Prod. #: GS57-PDF-ENG

Description

Discusses the astounding growth of Crocs, Inc., a manufacturer of plastic shoes, from 2003 through early 2007. Much of the company's growth was made possible by a highly flexible supply chain that enabled Crocs to build additional product within the selling season. The normal model used within the fashion industry was to take orders well in advance of each selling season and produce to those orders, with relatively little additional production. If demand was far in excess of this production, there would be stock outs, and the company would lose the ability to capture revenue for that season. The product might or might not be in fashion the following year, when production would again be based on preseason orders. Crocs' ability to build additional shoes within the season enabled it to take advantage of strong customer demand, resulting in the company filling in-season orders totaling many times that of the initial prebooked orders.

Learning Objective

To illustrate use of supply chain management as a central factor in a company's strategy and examine the uses of in-sourcing and outsourcing and the factors involved in constructing a flexible supply chain to address a global market.

Notes

1   "Boeing: Faster, Faster, Faster; The Planemaker Struggles to Fulfil a Rush of Orders," *Economist*, Jan. 28, 2012; Mike M. Ahlers, Aaron Cooper, and Thom Patterson, "Another Battery Incident Troubles Boeing's 787 Dreamliner," *CNN*, Jan. 14, 2014, updated 5:52 p.m.
2   K. B. Hendricks and V.R. Singhal, "An Empirical Analysis of the Effect of Supply Chain Disruptions on Long-Run Stock Price Performance and Equity Risk of the Firm," *Production and Operations Management*, Spring 2005.
3   Supply chain professional skills: "APICS Competency Models," accessed Oct. 5, 2015, http://www.apics.org/careers-education-professional-development/careers/competency-models.
4   Stephanie March, "Telstra Workers Protest Against Offshore Jobs," *ABC News*, Feb. 17, 2012, 15:47:48.
5   "Mexico Hourly Wages Now Lower Than China's—Study," Update 1, *Reuters*, April 4, 2013, 4:59 p.m.
6   Sue Dunlevy, "Danone Nutricia's Karicare and Aptamil Baby Formula Shortage," *News Corp Australia*, April 24, 2014.
7   Daniel Ferry, "The Great American Whiskey Shortage—Should Investors Belly Up?" *The Motley Fool*, May 10, 2014. http://www.fool.com/investing/general/2014/05/10/the-great-american-whiskey-shortageshould-investor.aspxm.
8   Hau Lee, "Aligning Supply Chain Strategies with Product Uncertainties," *California Management Review*, 44(3), (2002): 105-119.
9   "Supply Chain Resilience 2011 Study," Zurich Financial Services Group and Business Continuity Institute, reported in CSCMP's *Supply Chain Quarterly*, Nov. 23, 2011.
10 Editorial staff, "Partial Disconnect between Cash Savings and P&L is Part of the Problem: A Calculation Framework," *Supply Chain Digest*, Jan 12, 2011.
11 hbr.org/Case-Studies

Part IV

Finding the Right Location

12 Location Decisions

Chapter Take-Aways

- How to describe the location of a place in different ways
- Service and manufacturing location decisions
- Methods to help in location decision making
- Behavioral aspect of location decision making
- Indicators of a 'good' choice of location
- Latest trends in location

Location: A Road Map

Customer: *"Why should I choose you?"*
Business: *"Because we promise you an easy-to-get-to, safe, clean, and cheerful location."*

12.1 What Is Location?

From an operations management perspective, location is the position of a place (or a person or object) on the earth's surface. We can describe location in a number of ways.

12.1.1 Ways to Describe a Location

The location of Baruch College in New York City is at:

Mailing/Google address: One Bernard Baruch Way, New York, NY 10010
Absolute location: Position on Earth's surface using the coordinate system of longitude (that runs from North to South Pole) and latitude (that runs parallel to the equator).

41 degrees latitude and 74 degrees longitude, or

Relative location: Position on Earth's surface relative to other features.

1 mile from NY Penn station, heading SE, or
6 blocks SE from the Empire State Building

The physical and demographic attributes of a location:

The main campus at Baruch College is a 17-floor, 800,000-square-foot structure, with over a hundred high-tech classrooms, TV studios, a performing arts complex, and an underground Olympic-size swimming pool with a complete rec and sports center. The college also includes a 1,450-seat, 330,000-square-foot library, with a full-fledged financial trading floor and conference facilities. The Baruch population is about 17,000 students who speak 110 languages and come from 170 countries. The college ZIP code, 10010, shows a surrounding population of 32,784, median age 34.5 years, median income $94,600, and an individual consumer spend of about $70,000. ZIP code 10010 has a majority of 'Cosmopolitans' and 'American Dreams.' 'Cosmopolitans' are older, ethnically diverse high-income couples without live-in children. They are likely to shop at Macy's, vacation abroad, read *Audubon Magazine*, watch *Masterpiece*, and drive a Lincoln Town Car Flex Fuel. 'American Dreams' represent young to middle age professional couples with a college education and kids, ethnically diverse, and speaking multiple languages. They shop at Kaiser Pharmacy, visit the zoo, read the *Tribune*, watch E! Entertainment TV, and drive a Volkswagen Tiguan.[1]

12.1.2 How to Identify a Location

Your parents looked up a location by thumbing through a printed map or asking for directions at the gas pump. You would probably use technology tools such as a GPS, or satellite maps, or Google street views, or augmented reality GPS apps on cell phones (iPhone, Android). Or, of course, ask a passer-by or a gas station (genetically, men never get 'lost' and are not pre-disposed to this approach).

12.2 Why Is Location Important?

When asked which chain, Home Depot or Lowe's, they like better, a majority said Lowe's. But more people went to Home Depot than Lowe's simply because Home Depot had more convenient locations.[2] Better location may actually drive customers to places that they otherwise may not patronize. Location is an important decision for businesses.

12.2.1 Importance for Businesses

You were just hired for the operations manager job at Delicious Donuts! Your manager hands you your first assignment—to help him decide the location of the next Delicious Donuts outlet. Your friend was just hired for the operations manager job at CMW Auto, a car maker. Her manager ask her to help decide the location of the next CMW manufacturing plant in the USA. What is the difference in terms of picking a location for a service vs. a manufacturing business? Let us see:

1   *Customers*: CMW can locate in Alabama and sell its cars all over the world. But Delicious Donuts cannot. Its customers live nearby, or are local traffic. So location for Delicious Donuts is a matter of daily revenue generation, of being physically close to its customers. CMW does not depend on walk-in customers to stop by and pick up a car. Its choice of location will be more influenced by the costs of the location, including land, taxes, infrastructure development, logistics, training, and labor costs. Thus, closeness to the customer is required in many service businesses' locations, including perishable goods providers (such as flower or fish stores), but generally much less so in manufacturing locations. Reasonable proximity to the customer may be required for manufacturing businesses that sell products with high distribution costs, such as cement or gravel. Back-offices of companies also do not interact directly with customers and usually pick locations on the basis of cost and employee convenience.

2   *Frequency*: Delicious Donuts opens a few hundred outlets a year, while CMW opens a new plant once in five to 10 years or more.

3   *Size of investment*: Delicious Donuts invests a million dollars opening a new outlet, while CMW spends a few billion dollars.[3]

4   *Commitment*: Delicious Donuts could close or relocate an outlet fairly quickly, easily, and inexpensively if that location does not work out. But CMW cannot close its manufacturing facilities easily because of city, state, and federal laws, heavy investments in machinery and other fixed assets, impact on community, and the difficulty of finding a buyer for an asset so large and permanent.

5   *Incentives*: Countries and states compete for investment dollars and jobs. For a town or community, a new CMW plant would be expected to generate long-term and significant economic growth for the region, while a Delicious Donuts outlet opening, like many other fast food chains, is a pretty routine event. The Volkswagen (VW) manufacturing plant in Chattanooga, TN, which opened in May 2011, has made a significant economic impact on the community. Over 3,200 people have been hired and 9,500 estimated

indirect supplier jobs created, with tens of millions of dollars of related benefits to the community.[4] Delicious Donuts, though, does not expect or get suitors with bags of money pleading to get the company to open their next outlet in their neighborhood. In fact, cities like Los Angeles are now pushing to limit the number of fast food outlets in certain city areas, for reasons of community health.

OM IN PRACTICE

Tesla Motors in Nevada

Tesla Motors Inc. chose Nevada as the site for the largest battery manufacturing plant in the world for its electric cars. The plant may cost as much as $10 billion, with Nevada chipping in with a tax and abatement relief package of about $1.3 billion. At about an estimated $200,000 a job, the package does not seem to compare well with similar deals by other states. South Carolina invested $120 million in Boeing for adding 2,000 jobs at their plant near Charleston, which works out to about $60,000 a job. Volkswagen adds 2,000 jobs at its plant at Chattanooga, TN, rewarded by a $178 million break in taxes and similar benefits. The estimated cost per job? Around $90,000/job. However, Nevada hopes to see considerable multiplier effects in its economy as the plant begins to function. As of March 2015, Tesla Motor Inc. said that construction of its billion-dollar battery plant in Nevada remains on schedule, although unions on site report significant delays and possible scaling down of the scope of the project.

Adapted from: "Tesla Says Nevada Battery Plant on Track Despite Report of Delay," *Reuters*, March 6, 2015; Matthew L. Waldsept, "Nevada Woos Tesla Plant in Tax Deal, but Economic Benefits Prompt Debate," *New York Times*, Sept. 13, 2014.

There are, as you can see, differences in what services and manufacturing consider important in location decisions. Essentially, manufacturing looks at costs while services look for revenues. The latter typically requires being closer to customers.

12.2.2 *Importance of Location Knowledge for You*

Location decisions can affect you directly. Business globalization means that you could be asked to set up an office in a new region or country—knowledge of basic location-decision approaches and factors would be a valuable skill. Typical jobs in location include titles such as GIS analyst, operational manager, and site acquisition specialist. Consulting companies also require location experts to advice clients about supply chain design, outsourcing, and relocation.

Location Specialist Job Requirements

Job Title: Retail Site Location Analyst
Company: Leading Specialty Retailer

Job Description (abbreviated)

Retail Site Location Analyst works closely with the respective real estate managers and directors to ensure sites submitted support the overall real estate strategic plan.

Responsibilities

Sales forecasting for new store development with associated knock-off analysis

Market screening and optimization analysis for new stores and relocations

Data maintenance for sales forecasting model

GIS graphic support

Analyze local market dynamics, develop appropriate geographic trade areas, and calculate sales potential

Develop appropriate geographic trade areas

Perform field work as required for new sites and competitive reviews

Stay abreast of important developments impacting market research

Prepare related materials to support site work required for committee approvals

Present, explain, and defend such work, as called upon

Additional responsibilities include maintenance of system for new stores, closings, conversions, and data updates.

Qualifications

BS degree in geography, business, urban planning

2 to 3 years' experience with sales forecasting for new store development

Adapted from: http://www.doostang.com/signups/signup_syndicate/193560?utm_source=Juju&utm_campaign=Juju&utm_medium=sponsored

---

KEY POINTS

- Location is important for service firms to reach customers and ensure sufficient revenue flows.
- Location is important for manufacturers to ensure cost efficiencies.
- Services and manufacturing location decisions also differ in terms of frequency, size of investment, and exit costs.
- Globalization and outsourcing make it likely that locations will change or be expanded—your knowledge of location decision making will be useful to the business and your career.

12.3 How to Make Location Decisions

We consider factors such as traffic, cost, visibility, access, incentives, and location demographics while making a location decision. And we rely on experience. What should we learn to be able to make a good choice of location? Where do we start? Let us begin by treating a location decision as a systematic process comprising four well-defined stages.[5]

12.3.1 The Location Decision Process

Abigail (Abby), a site selection specialist, is entrusted with picking an appropriate location for a company's new office. She knows the four-stage drill: form a location project team and formulate location criteria and objectives, screen potential candidate sites, evaluate short-listed sites, and, finally, conduct due diligence on the selected site.

Stage 1: *Team forming and criteria selection*

Abby gathers a location project team that includes key stakeholders. Her team begins by defining the essential criteria and location objectives such as revenue targets, cost goals, minimum space/size needs, and employee relocation start dates. Base case and current/future scenarios for criteria are considered, and assumptions are noted.

Stage 2: *Screening*

Abby and her team define a geographic search by region, employing essential criteria filters to create a list of initial candidates. Applying more restrictive criteria further narrows the field of potential location candidates to 8 to 10 areas. The team then uses survey/market intelligence, project team familiarity, and methods such as weighted factor scoring model (described later) to develop a short list of three to four candidates.

Stage 3: *Evaluation*

At this point, Abby's project team assesses shortlisted areas through field-based due diligence evaluation including interviews with comparable employers and other pertinent entities. Among the evaluated factors are revenue potential along with traffic, income segments, competition, and infrastructure (e.g., utilities). A comparison of the shortlisted locations made is based on:

- Company's internal needs
- Area's most prominent assets/liabilities
- Business operating costs (multi-year)
- Labor market—demand/supply, quality/stability
- Cost
- Unionization
- Transportation costs
- Services
- Utilities (cost, capacity, reliability)
- Electric power
- Telecommunications
- Natural gas
- Water/sewer
- Taxation
- Practices
- Rates
- Incentives
- The package savings
- Disaster risk
- Quality-of-life/cost-of-living

Abby sets some milestone dates, consults with human resources and real estate, and commences negotiations in one or two areas. She chooses a best location area and a leading alternate location and identifies specific sites and buildings in these locations.

Stage Four: *Site selection*

Abby, together with HR and environmental/building inspection specialists, conduct due diligence on the chosen property. She conducts a variety of mainly local tasks that lead up to acquisition of the property.

- Acquisition/lease plan
- Budget forecast

- Field visits/property reviews
- Shortlist properties
- Developer/owner request for proposals (RFPs)
- Incentives negotiation
- Additions
- Local counsel retained
- Due diligence reviews
- Final negotiations
- Final occupancy plan
- Site building acquisition
- Decision announcement

Abby recommends a final choice of site and building. In this process, Abby and her team make use of a variety of evaluation and selection methods that we will examine later in the chapter.

OM IN PRACTICE

How Fleetguard Made a Location Decision

Fleetguard was looking for a southeast location in the U.S. to set up an auto parts making facility. They had 12 possible candidate locations in mind and hired WDG Consulting to finalize a location.

WDG ran a comparative analysis of data including population, educational level, number of semi-skilled and unskilled manufacturing workers, unemployment rate, utility costs, real estate costs, tax rates, air quality, transportation, incentives, manufacturing wage rates, unionized operations, union election results, roster of major industrial employers, and anticipated new manufacturing plants (a signal of future labor market competition). Data came from WDG Consulting's proprietary database, published/online sources, and each location's economic development agency. Three locations emerged.

Next, WDG went to the three locations for a boots-on-the-ground due diligence evaluation. This included confidential interviews with existing manufacturers in those locations about operational conditions and possible insights on future business conditions. Interviews were similarly held with government officials, education/training officials, state job services, utility representatives, truckers, real estate owners, and economic planning bodies.

These interviews were followed by detailed examinations of geotechnical maps and satellite imagery for specific sites and buildings and physical inspections of locations. Lead economic development bodies for each location were asked to offer incentive packages. After comparing each location on various criteria, Waynesboro, GA (20 miles south of Augusta) was chosen for the new auto parts plant. The choice of location has been validated by actual performance in terms of lower wage rates and logistics costs, lower workforce turnover, and about $11 million in savings from the incentive package obtained.

Adapted from: "Fleetguard Nelson (Cummins Filtration)," Project case study, *WDG Consulting*, http://www.wdgconsulting.com/WDGC_Project_case_studies_FleetgardNelson.htm

---

12.3.2 Location Decision Methods

A manufacturing location decision is quite different from a service location decision. Here we discuss established location decision methods, keeping in mind the type of business involved.

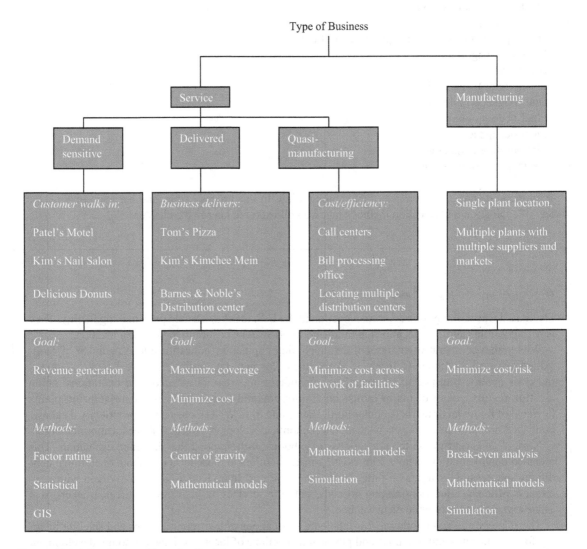

Figure 12.1 A Road Map of Location Decision Methods

Adapted from: R. Metters, K. King-Metters, M. Pullman and S. Walton, *Successful Service Operations*, (Thomson-South Western, USA: 2006), pg. 329.

Let us go through the map, starting with service businesses.

Demand-Sensitive Business

Consider Kim's Nail Salon, a demand-sensitive service relying on walk-in customers to bring in the cash. Kim has three salons and wishes to open a fourth one. She has three site options in mind—we have to help her find the 'best' one. We will use three methods: factor rating, statistical, and GIS (geographical information systems)—there is no particular sequence or order in using these methods.

- *Factor rating*: This method (also called the scoring method) is generally used to narrow the choice of sites. No one location can possible satisfy all that Kim is looking for, so we use the factor rating method to identify the best composite choice among the possible location sites.

Step 1: Identify the factors (location criteria):

Kim considers five factors—foot traffic,[6] crime rate, site size, visibility from intersection, and lease cost—as the most important 'factors' in making a location decision.

Step 2: Decide the relative importance of the factors:

Based on her experience, Kim weights the five factors, splitting 1.00 into different weights (see table below). This is a subjective judgment.

Step 3: Evaluate the three sites:

We visit the three alternative sites with Kim and grade the sites on how well they satisfy her five factors (see table). Use a scale of 1 (poor) to 10 (excellent). In a team setting, individual grades may be averaged to arrive at a single 'grade' for that factor, for a specific location (see later remarks, too, in this connection).

Step 4: Compute weighted factor scores for the three sites:

We multiply the site grades with the factor weights and add the results column-wise to obtain a composite factor score for each of the three sites. The site with the highest composite score is the 'best' one (see table).

The 'best' site is B, with the highest score of 6.65. Note, though, that C is pretty close, with a composite factor score of 6.35. It would be unwise to reject C outright since a small change in the grades or in the factor weights (both of which were fixed by us) could reverse the result. It would be reasonable to say that the factor score method led us to reject location A, and narrow our choice down to locations B or C. We can ask for more information about the two remaining sites to make a final decision.

Understand that objective data on a relatively 'hard' factor such as crime rate can be readily obtained from the local police precinct. Consider, though, the essential subjectivity of a factor such as 'ambience.' 'Soft' factor evaluations should be performed by a seasoned team with experience and deep knowledge about the business. For Kim's Nails, Kim's long experience in that business would make her opinion about location ambience much more valuable than that of, say, an external consultant. In fact, for 'soft' factors, it is advisable to accord different weights to different evaluator opinions based on an individual's experience and understanding of the

Table 12.1 Factor Rating Method

Factors (Step 1)	Step 2 Weights (total up to 1.00)	Step 3 Evaluate Location A Scale of 1 to 10	Step 4 Composite score for Location A (multiplying steps 2 and 3)	Step 4 Composite score for Location B*	Step 4 Composite score for Location C*
Foot traffic	0.30	4	4 * 0.30	7 (* 0.30)	7 (* 0.30)
Crime rate	0.25	2	2 * 0.25	8 (* 0.25)	7 (* 0.25)
Site size	0.15	1	1 * 0.15	9 (* 0.15)	6 (* 0.15)
Visibility	0.20	6	6 * 0.20	5 (* 0.20)	7 (* 0.20)
Lease cost	0.10	3	3 * 0.10	2 (* 0.10)	2 (* 0.10)
Composite score			3.35	**6.65**	6.35

We evaluate locations B and C, similarly as in Step 3, and compute their weighted composite scores, in Step 4. Step 3 has not been shown separately for locations B or C, but the scores can be seen in their Step 4 columns; e.g., Location B has been evaluated as a '7' on a 1–10 scale for foot traffic, and so on. Note that the weights and scores shown above are completely imaginary.

dynamics of that particular business. Experience also helps in spotting the finer details. Noticing that the subway (underground city train) exit is on the left side of the street is important—people would tend to walk on the left side of the street.

QUICK CHECK

Khan's Kabobs wants to open a new location. Khan has narrowed it down to either one of two spots—one near a college (A) and the other at downtown (B). Having collected information about the two sites, they wish to use the factor rating method to identify the 'best' location. The rating scale goes from 1 (poor) to 5 (excellent).

Factor	Weights	Location A Ratings	Location B Ratings
Lunch traffic	0.40 x	3	5
Competition	0.20 x	5	3
Rental	0.15 x	3	5
Visibility	0.25 x	4	3
Composite score		3.65	**4.10**

Recommendation: *Pick location B.*

Cautions: Look at other factors such as option to expand, ability to exit, ease of transportation, availability of workers, and likelihood of increase in competition.

• *Statistical methods*: When a business has past data from existing outlets on important factors, we can use regression to refine our location choices. Kim knows from experience and observation that the five factors identified by her are important to sales. Let's suppose that Kim had several years' data on all the above five factors, as well as sales data, for each of her existing three nail salons. She wants to pick the location that would offer the highest sales potential. We could use the available historical data to model the relationship between the 5 factors and sales, using regression analysis (using Excel or any stats package).[7] The regression model may look like the following (all figures assumed):

Sales (\$) = 2.0 + 5 foot traffic − 4 crime rate + 2 site size + 3 visibility − 1.5 lease cost

---

The practical importance of the above model lies in its regression coefficients. The term '5 foot traffic' simply means that a unit increase in foot traffic, say one more pedestrian/hour, would see an increase in mean sales by \$5, on average.[8] Similarly, a unit reduction in crime rate (say one fewer robbery/day) would see an increase in mean sales of \$4, on average. We can now collect current data on the above five factors for each location A, B, and C, and plug the data into the regression model above to find out the highest potential mean sales location.

For example,

Table 12.2 Applying the Regression Model

Factors	Data for Location A	Data for Location B	Data for Location C
Foot traffic	40/hr	65/hr	60/hr
Crime rate	20/day	5/day	8/day
Site size	500 sq. ft.	1,000 sq. ft.	900 sq. ft.
Visibility	6 (1–10 scale)	5 (1–10 scale)	7 (1–10 scale)
Lease cost	$20/sq. ft.	$15/sq. ft.	$15/sq. ft.

So using the regression model we developed earlier:

Sales ($) = 2.0 + 5 foot traffic − 4 crime rate + 2 site size + 3 visibility − 1.5 lease cost

$ Potential mean sales (location A) = 2.0 + 5 (foot traffic for A) − 4 (crime rate for A) + 2 (site size for A) + 3(visibility for A) − 1.5 (lease cost for A)

= 2.0 + 5(40) − 4(20) + 2(500) +3(6) − 1.5(20) = $1,110

Similarly:

$ Potential mean sales (location B) = 2.0 + 5(65) − 4(5) + 2(1,000) + 3(5) − 1.5(15) = $2,299.50 (highest), and

$ Potential mean sales (location C) = 2.0 + 5(60) − 4(8) + 2(900) + 3(7) − 1.5(15) = $2,068.50

Location B seems to be the best choice of location based on predicted sales. We can rule out location A but perhaps keep location C as a standby. It is also possible to break down a factor into two or more factors to glean more information about its influence. For example, we may have reason to believe that the morning and evening rush hour crowds consist of higher income people than the afternoon pedestrian. We could divide foot traffic into time-separated traffic counts, say traffic count 'between 8 a.m. and 10 a.m.,' 'between 11 a.m. and 4 p.m.,' and 'between 4 p.m. and 8 p.m.' factors. We would then have three regression coefficients for each of the three traffic count predictive factors and would know how traffic at different times of the day contributes differently to sales.

QUICK CHECK

Khan's Kabobs now wishes to find out if customer income is a relevant factor to consider in its location evaluation. Khan collects historical data on weekly sales as well as for a variety of independent variables including customer average income for his current locations around town. A regression model is developed (assume model satisfies statistical criteria):

Sales = 0.16 + 0.36 lunch traffic + (−) 0.15 competition + (−) 0.10 rental + 0.23 visibility + 0.18 customer average income

a) Why are the regression coefficients for competition and rental negative?

b) Use the model to pick a new location. The data for the new locations being considered is as follows:

	Location A	Location B
Lunch traffic	400 customers	600 customers
# of competitors	10 casual food shops	25 casual food shops
Rental	$1,300/mo	$4,000/mo
Visibility	4	3
Customer average income	$30,000 annual	$50,000 annual

c)   Additional info is now available from current locations' historical data on customer income in terms of the proportion of customers earning an income below $30,000, between $30,000 and $50,000, and above $50,000. The regression model is modified to describe income as three different independent variables:

$Weekly Sales = 0.11 + 0.30 Lunch Traffic + (−) 0.10 Competition + (−) 0.09 Rental + 0.18 Visibility + (−) 0.11 Proportion of customers with income below $30,000 + 0.22 Proportion of customers with income between $30,000 and $50,000 + (−) 0.16 Proportion of customers with income above $50,000.

Explain the above model.

Answer:

a)   The regression coefficients are negative because increased competition and higher rentals reduce sales (based on historical data) in this particular case. In other cases, it could very well be that more competition (variety of options) attracts more customers (as in food courts).

b)   Location A sales = 0.16 + 0.36 (400) + (−) 0.15 (10) + (−) 0.10 (1,300) + 0.23 (4) + 0.18 (30,000)
= $5,413.58,

which is the forecasted average weekly sales for location A given the above values of the independent variables observed for location A.

Location B sales = 0.16 + 0.36 (600) + (−) 0.15 (25) + (−) 0.10 (4,000) + 0.23 (3) + 0.18 (50,000)
= $8,813.10,

which is the forecasted average weekly sales for location B given the above values of the independent variables observed for location B.
Location B's average weekly sales estimate is higher, based on the regression model.

c)   With the other coefficients retaining their original signs, the regression coefficients of 'proportion of customers with income below $30,000' and 'proportion of customers with income above $50,000' are negative, while that of 'proportion of customers with income between $30,000 and $50,000' is positive. A simple interpretation is that kabobs may be a middle class food.

A note of caution: Regression cannot anticipate future events and requires clean data. Regression's main advantage over the factor rating method is that we use actual data instead of judgment to measure and validate the importance of chosen location factors to location sales/profits.[9]

•   *Geographical information systems* (GIS)[10] are useful spatial location aids, marketed by companies such as Tactician (tactician.com), Unisys, and ESRI, who obtain census data and integrate it with geographic maps to offer geo-demographic information. Let's take a look at how to use GIS. Kim desires to brand her new salon as an upscale 'hip' place for the young, affluent crowd. GIS can help her find out if there are 'young, affluent' crowds in the vicinity of the locations she has in mind.

1   Register (free) on www.tactician.com and sign in (use Internet Explorer, not Mozilla).
2   Select 'quick reports'
3   Specify Kim's salon location, e.g., 55 Lexington Ave., New York, NY 10010 (or any ZIP of your choosing to get your own report).

4   Pick up to three trade areas to look at—e.g., within .25 miles, .50 miles, and 1 mile of Kim's salon.
5   Choose the nature of information required—in this case, 'sample income' and geography ('block groups'—ZIPs are too wide). Note that we can obtain information on traffic count, crime rate, lifestyle, consumer expenditure, and many other factors if we choose to pay for the service.
6   Create a title for the report—'Finding a location for Kim's Salon.'
7   Pick an additional map display feature—say, 'cosmetic store.' The result will show all cosmetic stores in the area.
8   Hit 'generate report.' Look at the HTML view of the report.

It is good news and bad news for Kim. There are plenty of financially sound people over 16 years old, but a closer look reveals that it's actually the 55plus years group that constitute the financially high income group

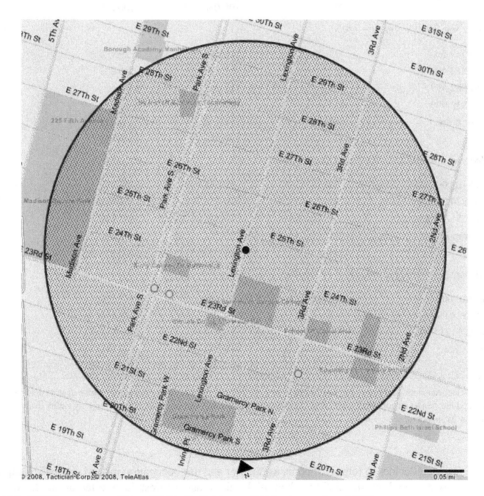

Figure 12.2   GIS Map of Area within .25 Mile Radial Area of 55 Lexington Ave., NYC

Table 12.3 Demographics of Population Living within .25 Miles of 55 Lexington Ave., NYC.

Description	Radial Trade Area, 0.25 mile		United States	Area
	Number	Percent	Percent	Index
Earnings by Sex: Male Age 16+ (2000)				
$1 to $2,499 or loss	216	7.8%	19.0%	41.20
$10,000 to $12,499	185	6.7%	17.8%	37.73
$20,000 to $22,499	263	9.5%	19.3%	49.50
$35,000 to $39,999	422	15.3%	24.0%	63.69
$100,000 or more	1,670	60.6%	19.9%	304.97
Total	2,755	100.0%	100.0%	
Earnings by Sex: Female Age 16+ (2000)				
$1 to $2,499 or loss	429	16.6%	29.7%	55.99
$10,000 to $12,499	302	11.7%	26.2%	44.61
$20,000 to $22,499	314	12.2%	22.1%	54.87
$35,000 to $39,999	554	21.5%	17.7%	121.49
$100,000 or more	984	38.1%	4.4%	872.31
Total	2,583	100.0%	100.0%	
Age by Income: Householder Age Less Than 25 (2000)				
Less than $10,000	233	59.2%	64.2%	92.19
$20,000 to $24,999	82	20.7%	31.6%	65.59
$100,000 to $124,999	58	14.8%	3.1%	474.38
$200,000 or more	21	5.3%	1.0%	511.77
Total	394	100.0%	100.0%	
Age by Income: Householder Age 55—64 (2000)				
Less than $10,000	192	37.8%	37.2%	101.39
$20,000 to $24,999	47	9.2%	23.1%	39.87
$100,000 to $124,999	106	20.8%	25.9%	80.30
$200,000 or more	164	32.2%	13.8%	234.20
Total	508	100.0%	100.0%	

(32.2 percent). Kim decides to remove income as a factor and use occupation instead (choose 'sample labor' in step 5)—how do you think she did? She then thinks about using 'lifestyle' as a factor but decides against it, since she finds it's a pay-for option.

GIS can identify customer segment by location, provide data on competing or complementary businesses, and estimate cannibalization figures for same stores, combining geographical data with demographic and business data. YUM! Brands, Inc. the world's largest restaurant chain, uses GIS to find locations for Pizza Hut and

Taco Bell outlets. FedEx uses GIS to locate drop box sites. GIS works in international locations, too, but be cautioned that maps can become outdated fairly rapidly because of road and building construction booms. A human foot-on-the ground check of local sites by a reliable local person helps keep information current.

KEY POINTS

- Factor rating scores locations applying weighted criteria to location scores on those criteria. Subjectivity in criteria importance ranking and site scoring can be a drawback. Used to screen out 'bad' sites.
- Regression develops models that employ historical data to forecast location performance on outcome criteria such as sales or profits. Historical data presumes perpetuation of current conditions. Used to screen sites.
- GIS is a geo-spatial tool that provides information on demographics and competitive/complementary factors in selected locations. Requires current information.

Delivered Services

Delivered services are businesses where the primary business comes from deliveries to the customer at his/her location. The center of gravity method is a popular technique to help locate a single point from which to serve multiple markets.

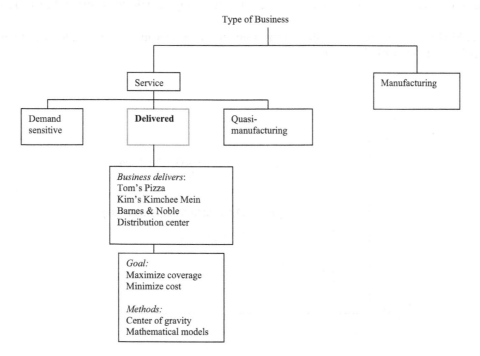

Figure 12.3 A Road Map of Location Decision Methods

Adapted from: R. Metters, K. King-Metters, M. Pullman and S. Walton, *Successful Service Operations*, (Thomson-South Western, USA: 2006), pg. 329.

- *Center of gravity* With her profits from the nail salons, Kim diversified into a Korean-Chinese fusion fast food place. Kim's Kimchee Mein delivers to three different neighborhoods in NYC. With market changes over the years, Kim wishes to relocate her place to better serve her customers and minimize delivery cost. We use the center of gravity (COG) method to find out the 'best' location for Kim's take-out restaurant. The center of gravity method balances distance, market size, and logistics costs to find the approximately best location that minimizes the total incremental cost of serving several markets from a distribution point.:

Kim's delivery customer segments are:	Volume	Unit delivery cost/mile
SoHo (South of Houston Street):	200 customers/day	$1.50
TriBeCa (Triangle Below Canal Street):	350 customers/day	$2.00
Washington Square (NYC)	400 customers/day	$2.50

Step 1: Obtain a current geographical map of NYC from an atlas/web. Mark the location of the neighborhoods on a transparency of the map.

Step 2: Take the transparency of the map and place it over a piece of grid paper. Scale the X and Y axis of the grid using any scale of your choice. Mark the locations of the neighborhoods off the map onto the grid paper. At this point, it should look something like the grid below (ignore the COG point). We could also use a map scale factor K (e.g., 1 interval on the grid = 0.25 mi), but that would require multiplying the K factor with the volume and unit delivery cost/mile of market, while computing the total cost of the COG solution—see step 5.

Step 3: Find out the coordinates of the center of gravity (COG) location. This location will represent the central point location of Kim's restaurant.

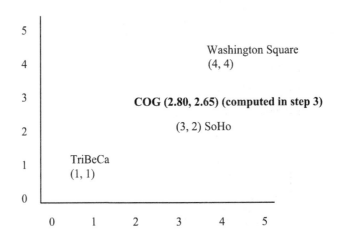

Figure 12.4 Grid Paper Map of Markets

Calculating the COG coordinates:

X coordinate of the COG = (Unit delivery cost to Soho * SoHo's market size * *X* coord. of SoHo +

Unit delivery cost to Tribeca * TriBeCa's market size * *X* coordinate of TriBeCa +

Unit delivery cost to Wash. Sq.* market size of Wash Sq * *X* coord. of Wash. Sq.)

(Unit delivery cost to Soho * SoHo's market size +

Unit delivery cost to Tribeca * TriBeCa's market size +

Unit delivery cost to Wash. Sq. * market size of Wash. Sq.)

Thus,

X coord. of COG = $(1.50 * 200 * 3 + 2.00 * 350 * 1 + 2.50 * 400 * 4)/(1.50 * 200 + 2.00 * 350 + 2.50 * 400)$

= 5,600/2,000 = **2.80**

The *Y* coordinate of the COG point is also found similarly, using the *Y* coordinates of the three markets in the numerator. Thus,

Y coord. of COG = $(1.50 * 200 * 2 + 2.00 * 350 * 1 + 2.50 * 400 * 4)/(1.50 * 200 + 2.00 * 350 + 2.5 * 400)$

= 5,300/2,000 = **2.65**

The relevant formulas are:

$$X\text{cog} = \frac{\sum_{j=1}^{n} c_j w_j x_j}{\sum_{j=1}^{n} c_j w_j} \qquad \text{(Equation 12.1)}$$

and,

$$Y\text{cog} = \frac{\sum_{j=1}^{n} c_j w_j y_j}{\sum_{j=1}^{n} c_j w_j} \qquad \text{(Equation 12.2)}$$

Where:

*X*cog = *x* coordinate of the center of gravity location

*Y*cog = *y* coordinate of the center of gravity location

x_j = *x* coordinate of market *j*

y_j = *y* coordinate of market *j*

c_j = delivery cost per mile from the center of gravity location to market *j*

w_j = volume or demand of market *j*

Step 4: Convert the COG coordinates on the grid into real geographic street and neighborhood information by superimposing the grid on the map. If you do this using a real map of NYC, the COG will be roughly northwest of SoHo (maybe Varick Street and Vandam Street?). Kim's Kimchee Mein would minimize the total incremental cost of serving the three target markets if it relocates in the vicinity of this location.

Step 5: Calculate the total cost of the COG solution. Thus, locating Kim's Kimchee Mein restaurant at or close to the COG point would imply a total incremental cost ($930.50/day) of serving the three markets. That would be the minimum cost point.

Total Cost of COG Solution

$$TIC = \sum_{j}^{n} c_j w_j Kd_j = \sum_{j}^{n} c_j w_j K \sqrt{(Xcog - Xj)^2 + (Ycog - Yj)^2} \qquad \text{(Equation 12.3)}$$

Where:

TIC = total incremental cost

c_j = delivery cost per unit per mile from the center of gravity location to market j

w_j = volume or demand of market j

K = 0.25 (map scaling factor to convert grid coordinates into miles: For this case, we take 1 grid interval = 0.25 miles on map)

d_j = travel distance from center of gravity location to market j.

$$= \sqrt{(Xcog - Xj)^2 + (Ycog - Yj)^2} \qquad \text{(Equation 12.4)}$$

Market j volume wj	K	Delivery cost/unit/mile c_j	Xcog	X_j	Ycog	Y_j	d_j	TIC
SoHo 200 customers/day	0.25	$1.50	2.80	3	2.65	2	0.68	$51.00
TriBeCa 350 customers/day	0.25	$2.00	2.80	1	2.65	1	2.44	$427.00
Wash. Sq. 400 customers/day	0.25	$2.50	2.80	4	2.65	4	1.81	*$452.50*
							Total cost	$930.50

e.g. TIC for SoHo $= c_j w_j K d_j$

$$= c_j w_j K \sqrt{(Xcog - Xj)^2 + (Ycog - Yj)^2}$$

$$= 1.50 \times 200 \times .25 \times \sqrt{(2.80 - 3)^2 + (2.65 - 2)^2} \qquad \text{(Equation 12.5)}$$

$$= \$51.00$$

We can perform sensitivity analysis on the COG point by varying delivery cost and market volume. The COG technique finds use in many areas, including locating cell phone towers, warehouses and ambulance centers. A drawback is that a COG point could be geographically anywhere—on top of a building, in the ocean, or on a highway. Additionally, this methods uses the Euclidean distance (remember calculating the hypotenuse on a triangle?), which may not reflect the reality of urban street distances. Further, the COG approach does not consider the fixed costs at different locations, which is likely to be different. The COG point provides the general vicinity of the 'best' location but not the mathematically optimal spot. So we can take a walk around the COG point and try to find an available location nearby. It is possible to compute an exact COG solution though a more involved optimal COG procedure. The method described here works well, though, that is, provides close to optimal solutions if the number of markets is large and no one market is disproportionately larger than any other market being considered. An extension of the COG method is also available for determining the locations of multiple distribution centers for multiple markets, which, however, lies outside the scope of this text.

COG or other locations need not be fixed. In fact, movable assets are often redeployed to match patterns in demand. For example, ambulances may be located in the city during work hours but repositioned to the suburbs at night in order to match supply with demand. Conceivably, one could have two COGS for different locations at different times of the day. New York City experiences a dramatic shift of population from a booming Manhattan downtown during the day to the suburb boroughs in the evening. Manhattan has the highest U.S. county day/night population ratio, at 1.92.

Quasi-manufacturing and Manufacturing Locations

Quasi-manufacturing covers service operations whose locations are picked on the basis of cost, similar to manufacturing location decisions. Examples include call centers, IT development and maintenance, and medical diagnostics such as X-ray readings. The approaches to location decisions for quasi-manufacturing and manufacturing location decisions are similar.

- *Mathematical and simulation approaches*

Simulation and mathematical approaches provide guidance when we need to locate multiple outlets, call center networks, or distribution centers with many supply points or multiple markets. Established models include the gravity model used for locating retail outlets based on estimation of consumer demand and expected profit for each competing location; the cross-median approach which minimizes weighted travel distances; the location set-covering approach that finds the minimum number of locations required to service different demand points within a specified radial distance; and the maximal covering location approach that seeks to maximize population coverage. Detailed coverage of these methods is outside the scope of this text.

Simulation is a modeling tool that allows multiple runs of a system of locations with different factor values. Revenue- or cost-impacting events at a location such as political changes, tariff changes, currency changes, or sudden changes in logistical costs can be hard to forecast. But if we can estimate a range of values with associated probabilities (distribution type) for important location-related factors, simulation enables us to develop thousands of 'what if' scenarios and make a location decision based on the robustness of overall results. The transportation method is a popular technique that uses linear programming to optimize shipment locations in a network of supply sources and multiple points of receipt. It shows the cost

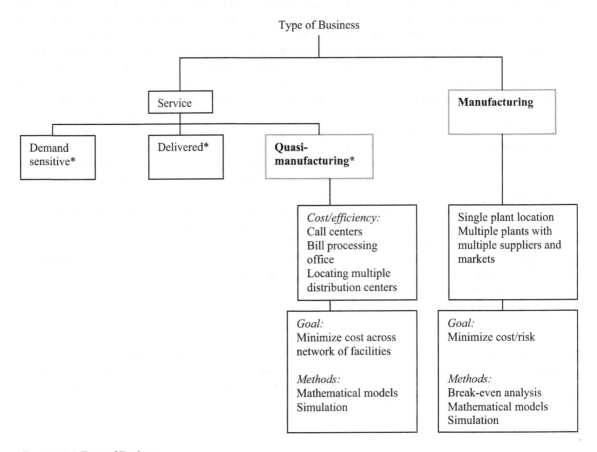

Figure 12.5 Type of Business

implications of adding new supply or receipt locations to an existing network but lies outside the scope of this text.

- *Break-even analysis (BEA)*

BEA is useful for any cost- or profit-based location analysis. Typically used in a location decision where cost is a key factor, BEA evaluates the total cost associated with alternative location sites. Revenues are assumed to be similar across locations and, thus, the revenue line does not appear in the BEA graph. A conventional BEP with sales revenue and cost curves is discussed in chapter 6, Capacity Planning ("Evaluating capacity planning alternatives for Lady RA-RA").

Figure 12.6 shows the total cost lines associated with different levels of production volume for locations A, B, and C. As you may recall, the total cost lines comprise a fixed cost component (the 'y' intercept value) and a variable cost/piece component (slope of the line). The break-even point in the figure is that production point where the total cost of production would be identical for any two (or three) locations, that is, 8,000 pieces for locations A and B, and about 20,000 pieces for locations A and C.

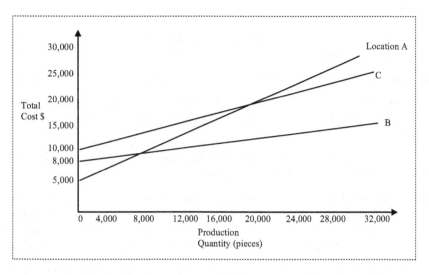

Figure 12.6 Break-Even Analysis Based on Location Costs

At 8,000 pieces, the break-even point for location A and B, the total production cost would be:
Total cost at BEP of A&B = fixed cost + variable cost
$\qquad$ = \$5,000 + variable cost/piece * # of pieces made
$\qquad$ = \$5,000 + slope of line A * 8,000 pieces
$\qquad$ = \$5,000 + 0.50 * 8,000
$\qquad$ = \$9,000
Slope of line A = rise/run
Run X axis = say from 0 to 8,000 pieces
$\qquad$ = 8,000
Corresponding rise
on Y axis = from 5,000 to 9,000 approx.
$\qquad$ = 4,000 approx.
Slope = 4,000/8,000 = 0.50 approx.

Let's further interpret the break-even analysis:

i) What is the total fixed cost associated with location C?[11] (for answers) With location B?
ii) Which location would you choose for a production quantity of 16,000?
iii) How would you know the variable cost per unit associated with a particular location?
iv) If your favorite uncle agreed to pay for the fixed cost, which location would you choose, irrespective of production quantity?

A few cautions:

i) Variable cost/unit may not remain constant at all production levels. Learning and experience lowers material used, material costs, and labor costs as production increases (learning curve effects).

> *Lesson:* Ask for lower prices per piece from suppliers, e.g., as buying volumes go up.

ii) Total fixed costs may also not remain fixed at all production levels. Capacity limits may force an increase in total fixed costs, e.g., leasing an additional warehouse when we run out of space in our current warehouse.

> *Lesson:* Do what-if scenario planning for fixed investment utilization levels in the future to identify possible new fixed investment needs.

iii) BEA typically assumes instantaneous payment of costs (and instant revenue from sales). But customers may ask for extended payment terms, while suppliers may insist on advance payment (especially with small start-up businesses). Thus, cash outflow may be much higher than cash inflows at a particular production/sales quantity level, even though the BEA may show a theoretical profit at that level. Bankruptcy results.

> *Lesson:* Get more working capital, cash required for payroll, suppliers, and day-to-day expenses, than you think you'd need.

BEA can also be used to select locations based on net present value comparisons. Anticipated cash flows from revenues and payments are converted into present value, and a net present value (revenue less cost) figure is developed for each location. Locations below a certain net present value benchmark are rejected from further consideration. It's also just another step to add transportation costs from each location to a market(s) to the total cost of each location, in case that is relevant to the analysis.

12.3.3 Guidelines: Choice of a Method

Let's do a quick recap of what works best, and when?

- Methods like factor rating can be used for both service and manufacturing locations. Factors for service location evaluations would be primarily revenue based, such as local traffic, its income, and the intensity of nearby competition. Factors for manufacturing location decisions would be essentially cost and risk based.
- Regression and GIS are best suited for services that are demand sensitive, and depend on customer walk-ins. Applications could include hotels, salons, and restaurants. Regression demands clean and considerable historical data, which may be a matter of concern for smaller or newer businesses.
- Center of gravity (COG) is appropriate for locating a single center that services several markets. Examples may include location decisions for an ambulance center, a fire station, a pizza place, or a distribution warehouse.
- Break-even analysis (BEA) is a method that has traditionally found use in manufacturing location decisions. Yet, like factor rating, BEA can be used for service location decisions, too. The difference, of course, is that for services, location determines revenue, the life-blood of services, while manufacturing location choices typically affect costs much more than revenues.
- Mathematical models and simulation are best suited for network location decisions such as designing a system of distribution warehouses for Barnes & Noble with multiple supply sources and shipments

to multiple retail stores. These methods grow rapidly in sophistication and complexity in practical usage and are usually handled by specialized consultants. Professional association sites such as www. ISM.ws (/tools/directories/supplier directories/consulting services) and APICS.org (/resources/consultants directory) provide extensive listings.

Remember, no matter what type of location method used a tool can aid but not substitute for experience and judgment. A deep understanding of the business and how it works is essential to making that final location decision.

KEY POINTS

- Demand-sensitive services use factor rating, regression and GIS methods.
- Delivered services use center of gravity and mathematical methods.
- The center of gravity method identifies a location that minimizes market-size-weighted travel cost of serving multiple markets. COG does not consider fixed costs and provides approximate, not optimal, outcomes.
- Quasi-manufacturing services and manufacturing use a variety of optimization and simulation methods. Mathematical approaches provide optimal locations based on provided inputs. The outcome is as good as the quality of input information and how reasonable underlying model assumptions are.
- Simulation runs iterations based on selected specific distributions. It does not identify an optimal location but suggests on-average 'best' locations based on the magnitude and probability of selection criteria/input values.
- Methods such as break-even analysis find use in all types of services as well as in manufacturing location decisions.

12.3.4 Behavioral Considerations

The psychology of location extends to region and country brand image—teens drag their parents to a Beverly Hills auto dealership just to get a coveted 90210 license plate frame. The possible negative effects of a 'made in Mexico' image persuaded Mercedes Benz to locate their plant in the U.S. and not in lower cost (and comparable quality) Mexico. Similarly, buyers of super-luxury goods may not like a 'made in China' cachet since China houses a large counterfeiting industry.[12] Many businesses may also get their routine or back office work performed in lower cost countries of excellent quality but do not necessarily tell the customer about these arrangements. Patients may react badly if they knew that their prestigious city hospital is sending their digitized X-rays to be read in a developing country, or that the mortgages they applied for, containing personal information, are being processed in a foreign country like India or Malaysia.

Cultural intangibles matter, too. MCI's debacle with their technical staff location move from diverse Washington, DC, to beautiful Colorado Springs, Colo., is a well-documented lesson in cultural snafus.[13] Technical R&D personnel from Asian, South American, and other backgrounds found Colorado to be a beautiful place for a vacation, but not for regular living—the primary reason being the relative lack of cultural diversity.

Location issues may also involve matters of spiritual or cultural interest.[14] In Abu-Dhabi, for instance, don't build or lease a location that has a bathroom facing towards Mecca. A bathroom is considered an 'unclean' place and should not face a holy site. It's likely that you'll visit or deal with China and other Eastern cultures some time during your career. When making location choices in those parts of the world, many organizations consider feng shui as an important location factor. Feng shui strives to balance the forces of yin or yang.[15] An inhabited house, for example, is classified as yang, while a gravesite is classified as yin. The house of the living (yang) should be separated from the house of the dead (yin). Lesson—do not locate a business close to a cemetery, funeral home, or a hospital! Excessive yang is not good, either. Premises such as prison complexes, police stations, power generation plants, and petroleum refineries fall into this category. A similar concept is found in the role of *vastu* in location choice and construction design in South East Asia. One need not suscribe to these beliefs, but many local customers and employees will. It is advisable to take such beliefs into consideration while locating physical facilities in these regions.

Special considerations figure in overseas location decisions. Many manufacturing businesses, such as POSCO, Caterpillar, and John Deere, are locating plants in hot growth markets like India and China. China's hinterland lacks adequate infrastructure. Yet China, being a top-down command political system, has speedier project implementation times and relatively better infrastructure than India, a democracy with many conflicting voices. Besides political uncertainties, infrastructural weaknesses including erratic power availability and bad road conditions also compel closer attention to overseas location decisions. It would be unwise to extrapolate U.S. transit times to developing country locations. Poor roads, weak bridges, interminable local tariff stops, lack of refrigerated trucks, and corrupt local officials can combine to make a two-day transit time U.S. estimate turn into a nightmarish month of transit delay. A poorly chosen location could lead to slow and erratic inputs supply, high safety stock inventory levels, burgeoning costs, unreliable delivery times, and low levels of customer service.

12.3.5 Sources of Data and Information

Data intelligence is available from various sources. Observation is one, such as traffic count at an intersection location under consideration. Location-specific crime data is available on the web or from the local police precinct.[16] GIS companies such as Mapscape.com and PitneyBowes Map info provide detailed information on demographics, competition, crime, transportation sites, and many factors relevant to location decisions. Community development and road and train construction plans are usually available from town municipalities and transport authorities. For instance, anyone considering locating a business in South Brunswick, NJ, should be aware of the proposal to build a new rail stop in the area. The New Jersey Transit Authority could provide reliable intelligence on expected completion dates, progress made, frequency of stops, and other key aspects of the development plan.

Real estate agencies and lawyers usually have current information about planned area developments. Real estate agencies are also a good source for information on rent and lease availabilities and costs. Lately, companies like American Express have started selling location-related data intelligence to businesses, data mining their extensive databases on customer credit card spending patterns to identify high-spending customer areas. It's also always a good idea to possibly engage in conversations with the HR departments of companies who are already located in the region for information on employee quality, turnover, rates, and such.

International location intelligence is available from trade/commercial officers in country embassies and consulates. Consultants can, of course, provide information and analysis together in a foreign location advice package. In international location decisions, it is always a good idea to visit potential location choices more than once to keep up with the rapid pace of infrastructural, construction, and social change in those areas of the world.[17]

Figure 12.7 Dubai—A Picture in Contrasts

Source: Mark, "Sheikh Zayed Road in 1990," [CC], via *Wikipedia*, http://en.wikipedia.org/wiki/File:Sheikh_Zayed_Road_in_1990.jpg#/media/File:Sheikh_Zayed_Road_in_1990.jpg.

Figure 12.8 Dubai—A Picture in Contrasts

Source: Fabio Achilli, "Sheik Zayed Road, Dubai Sheik Zayed Road, Dubai, United Arab Emirates," [CC], via *Flickr*, Aug. 18, 2012.

KEY POINTS

- Country and region image biases can be reason for highlighting or downplaying the supply source.
- Culture and traditions influence location choice and design, especially in foreign locations (feng shui in China, *vastu* in India).
- Infrastructural factors and political conditions should never be overlooked in foreign location choices, to avoid logistics, lead times, and political 'surprises.'

> • Sources of information for location decisions are available from online specialist companies, GIS sites, local business bureaus, real estate agencies, location consultants, and consulates. Local visits to HR departments of existing companies in the region can provide tacit information on current and future conditions.

12.4 Was It the Right Choice of Location?

Location pitfalls can be avoided by due diligence. Still, things do go wrong in a changing world.

12.4.1 What Could Go Wrong?

Some business can pack up and relocate relatively easily. Others cannot. An example of a bad location decision was when Tata Motors, of the world's cheapest car fame—the Nano—recently abandoned a manufacturing plant location at Singur in the state of West Bengal, India, after sinking more than $350 million in the project. Some 40,000 protestors descended on the Nano plant, effectively shutting it down.[18] Politicians instigated the local populace to protest the 'exploitation' of land-owning villagers, and development at that location ground to a halt.

The key action to avoid such outcomes is to be able to identify important KSFs (key success factors) in the location decision and develop forecasts for changes in these factors. Simulation can help in examining the impact of changes in these factors on important location outcomes such as sales or costs. From a practical perspective, location 'surprises' happen for a variety of reasons, including placing undue emphasis on incentives, failing to geographically balance the supply chain, a rising exchange rate, and a follow-the-crowd mentality. Engaging in the currency arbitrage game can also bring disadvantages in time. Craig Barrett, former chairman at Intel, observed that "out of the 14 reasons Intel came to Ireland two decades ago, only one remains: a low corporate tax rate of 12.5 percent."[19]

12.4.2 Indicators of Location Performance

Beyond the obvious indicators such as lower-than-expected traffic or higher-than-forecasted costs, poor location decisions can manifest in other ways. Employees coming in late regularly, supply trucks getting parking tickets, frequent visits by health inspectors, rain water accumulation near the front, and frequent power outages in the summer that could affect perishable goods are signs of a flawed location decision. Other metrics include labor rate stability and a good flow of qualified applicants.

KEY POINTS

- Reasons for picking a specific location may fade away in time.
- Identify important KSFs (key success factors) in the location decision and develop forecasts for changes in these factors.
- A rigorous scenario analysis of foreign exchange rates, labor costs, infrastructural promises, and political conditions is required in foreign location choices.
- Look at unconventional indicators, too, such as employees being late consistently—if your worker finds it difficult to reach your location, imagine the trouble your customer faces in coming to your business.

12.5 Current Trends in Location

Globalization has wrought changes in how we approach location choices. Demand-sensitive businesses such as hospitals need to attract walk-ins. But lowered travel costs and times as well as improvements in service quality have made it possible to locate such businesses in low-cost locations and still attract walk-ins. The rise of 'medical tourism' is a case in point, where patients go abroad to high quality but lower cost hospitals in Thailand, India, and Singapore for procedures such as bypass surgery and organ transplants.[20] Manufacturing is more difficult to move, but there are emerging reports of China gradually losing its manufacturing preeminence because of lower cost alternative locations becoming available in countries such as Vietnam. Mobile locations are coming up that offer low cost and no travel restrictions. Blueseed is creating a living and work space physical community on a cruise ship in international waters 12 nautical miles from the coast of San Francisco. The location allows startup entrepreneurs from anywhere in the world to launch or grow their companies near Silicon Valley, without the need for a U.S. work visa. As companies mature, Blueseed will offer legal services, including immigration, tax and incorporation, to help a transition over to the U.S. mainland. So far, over 1,500 entrepreneurs from 500 startups in 70-plus countries have expressed interest in living on Blueseed.[21]

Figure 12.9 International Entrepreneurs in International Waters

Source: "International Entrepreneurs in International Waters," *Blueseed*, http://blueseed.com/.

12.5.1 Co-location

Another expanding phenomenon is that of retail co-location. Cost considerations are persuading retailers to team up on locations. In 2008, FAO Schwarz placed a location inside Macy's flagship Chicago store, with plans to expand into more Macy's stores countrywide. Besides exploiting customer traffic synergies and affording Macy's rental for excess store space, a single location for diverse shopping needs cuts down on customer driving costs. In May 2009, Toys"R"Us Inc. acquired FAO Schwarz, and FAO Schwarz withdrew from Macy's. Toys"R"Us has a separate area in its stores for FAO brand toys. The FAO brand is considered distinct enough that cannibalization of sales is not considered a major issue. Co-location is not such a new phenomenon in manufacturing, though, which has long co-located suppliers in assembly plants for reasons of time, quality, inventory, communication, and ease of management.

12.5.2 Clustering

There *is* a Starbucks on every corner. Why? Clustering is a popular location strategy seen with 'urge' purchase businesses such as Au Bon Pain, Starbucks, and Dunkin' Donuts. Coming across a Starbucks around the corner, one feels an urge for a latte—we ignore that urge. Walking on, we see another Starbucks at the next corner and succumb. Clustering can also lock up attractive sites from access by competition. Clustering with competition such as McDonald's and Burger King is also good for business, because customers gravitate to locations that provide a wider choice. Cross-store sales cannibalization is considered a necessary cost, but one that is compensated by higher overall sales (of course, not if the stores are individually owned). Another longer term cost may be loss of brand value from over-exposure.

Clustering is also seen in manufacturing and research and design centers, with interconnected companies, workforce skills, universities, and cities teaming up to create work-centers that offer synergies and innovation bandwidth far beyond that available from standalone establishments, or even virtually connected ones. Silicon Valley is, of course, a world famous example of clustering, but locations such as the Spartanburg corridor in South Carolina have formed successful manufacturing clusters. Clustering also results from location by mimicry of leading competitor location decisions. Anecdotal accounts abound of Wendy's following McDonald's locations, and Lowe's setting down stores near existing Home Depot stores.

12.5.3 Pop-ups

Have you noticed how Halloween stores seem to pop-up right about the time you need a Halloween costume? Pop-ups are temporary retail location sites that have a short but exciting life—typically built to take advantage of a seasonal fashion, mark a special event, advertise a movie launch, or to convey a subversive, urban alter-ego for an established company. Younger businesses may use a pop-up to attain market visibility. They also save on rent. Designers like the buzz generated by pop-ups.

12.5.4 Locating Online Businesses

A web site can replace physical locations, housing thousands of products for viewing and purchase by customers around the world. Shipping availability, costs and times, and return logistics become concerns, though, when distances grow large. Larger organizations like Amazon maintain physical distribution centers, while others route deliveries direct from the manufacturer/supplier to the customer.

Figure 12.10 Kate Spade's NYC Bryant Park 3-Week Pop-Up Igloo

Source: *The Snob Magazine* and http://www.wallpaper.com/gallery.

OM IN PRACTICE

Cobblers Go Online

From a location standpoint, a cobbler was traditionally a demand-sensitive business where the customer walked into the store. Now, online shoe repair businesses are transforming the location choice into a delivered service or even quasi-manufacturing cost-based location decision. Easy logistics using FedEx or UPS with tracking has made it possible to centralize operations and reap economies of scale.

Resole America, American Heelers Inc., and NuShoe Inc. are a few shoe repair shops in the U.S. that perform shoe 'renewals' and extras such as polishing, cleaning and waterproofing. Charges and lead times are fairly competitive, 8 to 10 business days. The ladies 'ultra' package at NuShoe, for instance, costs just $60 for replacing the leather heel cover, heel tips or flats, new Italian leather half-soles, and a sole guard option. All the work is done in shops in the U.S. The next logical step would be to send the shoes in batches to a low-cost country for repairs, with a final prep and quality check in the U.S.

Adapted from: http://www.nushoe.com/ladies-shoe-repair.html#D; http://www.resole.com.

Traditional grocery stores are now using e-wall displays in public locations that consumers can 'touch' to order while waiting for a train or walking. Orders are delivered within a day.

OM IN PRACTICE

Real Groceries from a Virtual e-Wall

Figure 12.11 Peapod Virtual Grocery Stores

Source: Peapod, used with permission, http://www.peapod.com/site/companyPages/our-company-overview.jsp.

Forgot to pick up those eggs? No problem—just find and zap them with your phone on the seven-foot-high virtual grocery wall created by Peapod at a Chicago Transit Authority (CTA) "L" station, as an experiment. Your previously downloaded Peapod app will price those eggs (and any of the other 70 item images on the virtual wall) and offer a checkout option. Items will be delivered at your door within a day. Busy consumers love the idea. "I think it's really cool, being able to walk by, scan something and shop." "It's kind of interesting. I feel like I'm actually in a store right now." Peapod carries more than 12,000 items in its regular store, so the e-Wall is pretty limited in its offerings right now—but just like those electronic billboards that rotate ads, one may see different products being rotated depending on the time of the day and expected demand.

Figure 12.12 Kate Spade Saturday Stores

Source: Photo courtesy of Kate Spade for *Untapped Cities*, http://untappedcities.com/2013/06/29/kate-spade-saturday-pop-up-nyc/.

High fashion purveyor Kate Spade took on a more casual look with its touchscreen 'Kate Spade Saturday Stores' in NYC. These were pop-up stores with a limited lifespan. Customers browse on the touchscreen on the shopfront and pay through Paypal. The 'shop' does not have any employees and remains open 24/7. Items can be delivered in an hour.

Adapted from: Robert Channick, "Peapod Unveils Virtual Grocery Store Aisle at CTA State/Lake Tunnel," *Chicago Tribune*, May 4, 2012; Catherine Ku, "Touch Screen 'Window Shopping' at Kate Spade Saturday Pop-Up in NYC," *Untapped Cities.com*, June 29, 2013, http://untappedcities.com/2013/06/29/kate-spade-saturday-pop-up-nyc.

It may be soon be possible to send coupons in real time to such E-wall customers. And how would a store know where a prospective customer is at that moment? Answer—a smartphone. Small cheap Wi-Fi transmitters called beacons are being tested for use in retail aisles. A beacon can send a signal to a smartphone and sense its location to within a few inches, allowing companies to present coupons or direct customers to certain displays right on the spot. Macy's, American Eagle and others are testing the technology even now.[22] Ever wonder how much of a discount is required to draw customers in? A recent study puts it at approximately 1 percent off for every 100 meters away from the store.[23]

What else that used to be tied down to a physical location is going online? Well, people for one. Consider the company Automattic Inc., a web services business (http://automattic.com/). It has 123 employees working in 26 countries, all from home. There is an office in San Francisco for sporadic use, but project management, brainstorming, and water-cooler chatter take place on internal blogs/Skype or chat. There are some intangible downsides of working from home, including feelings of social isolation and loss of nonverbal communications. To keep things real, such businesses often have periodic get-togethers where employees get to meet and greet each other in the flesh. On the plus side, companies can spot and use talent on a global bandwidth and cut down significantly on real estate and commuting costs. Similarly, doctors can now both diagnose and prescribe online, with the patient perhaps hundreds of miles away. According to Cisco, a provider of virtual health presence technology, virtual medicine is a familiar practice that allows access to highly specialized medical expertise. In some places, such as Northern California, families sometimes wait as long as nine months to see a pediatric specialist. "This system allows areas such as ours that are underserved in that regard to bring in as needed pediatric specialists from Stanford," said Amanda Spencer, a patient who made use of the technology. "We can ask questions. He can reply, just like he was standing in the room."[24]

12.5.5 Ethical Considerations

Locations with a reputation for child labor or environmental laxity may carry attached stigma, even if the locating firm does not engage in such practices. For example, Apple admitted that some of its manufacturers located in China were found to employ child labor both in 2008 and 2009, used toxic chemicals that poisoned workers, and engaged in harsh punitive practices that led to worker suicides. While Apple itself has strict rules against the employment of child labors, its suppliers have been caught falsifying records and in violation of ethical and safety regulations and norms. Apple has since taken steps for third-party monitoring of key suppliers and a series of actions to encourage compliance with environmental, safety, and ethics regulations. Public health concerns also figure. Los Angeles, CA, is in the midst of an on-going health-driven debate on not allowing further openings of fast food places in certain low-income locations in the city.

12.5.6 When Locations Close Down

"Poor real estate decisions that were made . . .," explained Starbuck CEO Howard Schultz in a memo to employees that preceded the closure of over 950 stores in the U.S. and abroad.[25] How does management determine the locations to exit and the locations to keep? Revenue performance and growth prospects are key, of course. So are fixed costs. Several boutiques that used to define the trendy SoHo district in New York City were forced to move out or shut down after the 2008–2009 recession because their current revenue stream could not meet fixed leasing costs—and landlords were yet to recognize that rents have to fall to meet economic conditions. Result: a lot of empty store fronts. Of course, store closures also present opportunities—the demise of brick-and-mortar Circuit City led to a lot of empty locations in prize spots, which were quickly taken up by stores such as P.C. Richards, a Northeast-based electronics chain. On the other hand, FAO

Schwarz did shut down for some time a few years ago but did not vacate its prime and well-known longstanding location at Fifth Avenue and 58th Street in New York City. Some locations do matter.

Manufacturing locations lose their luster mostly for reasons of cost. The Caterpillar plant in London, Ontario (Canada) was shut down because it could no longer count on a weak currency to create a cost advantage. In 1998, Canada's dollar was worth as little as 63 cents (U.S.). It had strengthened to about 90 cents (U.S.) by March 2014. On the other hand, intellectual property concerns, quality concerns, and changes in cost structures, including rising labor rates abroad, reduced U.S. energy costs, and high overseas transportation costs are also bringing back manufacturing business to the U.S. FoxConn of China plans to open a $30 million high tech manufacturing plant in Pennsylvania, while GE has brought some appliance manufacturing from China back to the U.S.[26]

12.6 Conclusion

Recall our promise to our customer?

Customer: *"Why should I choose you?"*
Business: *"Because we promise you an exceptionally easy-to-get-to, safe, clean, and cheerful location."*

We saw in this chapter that operations management provides a variety of tools for delivering on that promise. Combine these tools intelligently with human judgment and experience in the location decisions that you may make in your life and career. And let us know when you come across other approaches.

What Have We Learned?

What Is Location?

- Location can be described in absolute (latitude-longitude), and relative (1 mile north of St. Paul's Cathedral) terms.
- We can measure the distance between locations in terms of Manhattan (taxicab distance) distance and Euclidean (straight line) distance, among other ways.

Why Is It Important?

- Location drives revenues for walk-in, as well as delivered, service businesses.
- Location drives cost for a manufacturing or quasi-manufacturing facility.
- With increased globalization and outsourcing, location decision-making knowledge equips you with the capability to understand and make intelligent location decisions in your job and life.

How Is It Done?

- Location decision making is a systematic process with sequenced steps, beginning with basic criteria definition, screening, and shortlisting of potential candidates, evaluation on additional factors, and, finally, site visits for the final selection.
- Demand-sensitive businesses such as hair and nail salons depend on attracting walk-in customers.
- Factor rating, regression, and GIS are some location-aid tools for demand-sensitive businesses.

- Delivered businesses such as pizza and warehouses deliver their products or services to their customers.
- Center of gravity is a useful technique that helps identify the lowest total cost location for a delivered business.
- Manufacturing and quasi-manufacturing businesses can apply break-even analysis, mathematical modeling and simulation tools in location decision making.
- Behavioral considerations such as country-of-origin bias, culture, and traditions are especially important to international location decisions.
- Demographic and other profiles of alternative locations can be developed using information from consulting companies, local business bureaus, personal visits to firms in the vicinity, embassies, and online sources.

Was It the Right Choice of Location?

- Bad location outcomes manifest in lost sales, increased costs, or sunk investments.
- Early warning signals could range from employee absenteeism to a scarcity of qualified applicants and supplier complaints about delivery access.
- Incentives should not sway location decisions away from a full consideration of revenue, infrastructure, and foreign exchange and cost stability.
- Factors that affect costs and revenues significantly should be identified and scenario-analyzed to estimate the impact of future changes in such factors on revenue and costs.

Current Trends in Location Decisions

- Clustering is a distinct location strategy that aims to a) afford multiple opportunities for consumption and b) lock out competition from attractive location sites and markets. The downsides are additional investment in multiple locations, increased supervisory responsibilities, and cannibalization of revenue from own stores.
- Co-location is a phenomenon where businesses locate within other businesses' premises for mutual revenue traffic and leasing cost sharing benefits. Product substitutability and brand image damage are concerns in this practice.
- Pop-ups are a means to showcase new brands or businesses without making large permanent investments and to avail of seasonal markets. Established firms often do pop-ups to create a buzz and refresh store personality.
- Online businesses' virtual location may not relieve them of the costs of managing distribution centers and forward and return logistics.

Key Terms

Demand-sensitive services: A business where the customer comes into the premises to transact business.

Delivered services: A business where the product or service is delivered to the customer at his/her location.

Simulation: A technique that makes repeated runs of a model with different values of variables.

Factor rating method: A technique that develops composite weighted score for alternative location option.

Center of gravity method: A technique that identifies the best approximate location for a single location from which to supply different surrounding markets.

Break-even analysis: A technique that identifies the production point where production costs are equal at two competing locations. In nonlocation applications, BEA identifies that production point where sales revenue and production costs are equal to each other.

Co-location: Businesses locating in the premises of another business.

Clustering: When a business saturates an area with its own locations, or when competing businesses locate near each other in order to attract maximum customer traffic.

Discussion Questions

1 Why do you think this location was chosen for your college?

2 Did location matter when you chose the college? How important was location relative to other criteria in your choice of college?

3 Is your college in a good or poor location, in your opinion? What are some of the location attributes that may have changed over the years at this location?

4 Name two possible drawbacks (besides the ones mentioned in the text) of:

a) break-even analysis
b) factor rating method
c) regression
d) center of gravity method

5 Manufacturers locate on the basis of cost, while services locate to be near their customers. Can you think of a counter-example in each case?

6 Give two reasons why reading this chapter might be useful for a marketing major; a finance major; an accounting major; and a HR major.

End of Chapter Problems

1 In Vietnam, six laborers, each making the equivalent of $3 per day, can produce 40 units per day. In China, 10 labors, each making the equivalent of $4 per day, can produce 75 units. In Cincinnati, two workers, each making $60 per day, can make 100 units. Based on labor costs only, which location would be most economical to produce the item?

Answer:

Vietnam: Unit variable cost = 6 workers * $3 per day/# of units made per day = $18/40 units = $0.45

China: Unit variable cost = 10 * $4/75 = $0.53

Cincinnati: 2 * $60/100 = $1.20

Pick Vietnam, the lowest unit variable cost location.

2 Refer to problem 1.: Shipping cost from Vietnam to New York, the final destination, is $1.50 per unit. Shipping cost from China to New York is $1.25 per unit, while the shipping cost from Cincinnati to New York is $0.30 per unit. Considering both labor and transportation costs, which is the most favorable production location?

Answer:

Vietnam: Total cost = unit VC + unit transportation cost = $0.45 + $1.50 = $1.95
China: Total cost = $0.53 + $1.25 = $1.78
Cincinnati: Total cost = $1.20 + $0.30 = $1.50
Pick Cincinnati.

3   Kareena and Jim are a couple looking at rental options. They have three rental alternatives that they have rated on a 1 to 5 scale (5 = best). Which rental option is the most preferred, using the factor rating method?

Location factor	Factor weight	A	B	C
Rent	0.25	3	1	2
Quality of life	0.20	2	5	5
Schools	0.05	3	5	3
Proximity to work	0.10	5	3	4
Proximity to recreation	0.15	4	4	5
Neighborhood security	0.15	2	4	4
Utilities	0.10	4	2	3

Answer:

Factor score for rental option A = 0.25 * 3 + 0.20 * 2 + 0.05 * 3 + 0.10 * 5 + 0.15 * 4 + 0.15 * 2 + 0.10 * 4 = 3.1
Factor score for rental option B = 3.2
Factor score for rental option C = 3.7

Rental C has the highest factor score and is the most preferred option. Of course, any change in ratings or weights may cause the factor scores to change and suggest a different location.

4   Made Here Manufacturers, a maker of iPhone high-end accessories, is considering expansion to a larger location. Two competing locations have been shortlisted: a) Albany, NY, with annual costs of $400,000 per year and a unit variable cost of $10,000/unit; b) Allentown, PA, with annual fixed costs of $500,000 and variable costs of $9,000 per standard unit. The accessories sell for an average price of $50/each, irrespective of where they are made. Assume transportation and other costs to be identical for the two locations.

a)   What is the break-even production quantity at which the two locations become equivalent?
b)   For what volume of production would Albany/Allentown be a better location?

Answer:

Since revenue does not depend on location, disregard the price and revenue elements.
Let x be the volume produced

Albany: Total cost = FC + VC = $400\,000 + $10\,000 * x$ units
Allentown: Total cost = $500,000 + $9,000 * x$ units

a)   At break-even, TC at Albany = TC at Allentown

$400,000 + $10,000 * x = $500,000 + $9,000 * x$
$1,000x = 100,000$
$x = 100$ units = break-even production quantity

b)   At 101 units,

TC at Albany = $400,000 + $10,000 * 101 = $1,410,000
TC at Allentown = $500,000 + $9,000 * 101 = $1,409,000
So Allentown is cheaper at any volume above 100 units.
At 99 units,
TC at Albany = $1,390,000
TC at Allentown = $1,391,000
So Albany is cheaper for a volume of 99 or fewer units.
Note that the total cost difference around break-even point will be nominal—that cost difference will grow as we move further away from the break-even point.

5   A location decision for a typical retail store (e.g. Duane Reed or Ace Hardware) would tend to have a(n)

a)   cost focus
b)   revenue focus
c)   labor focus
d)   environmental focus
e)   education focus

6   A location decision for an automaker would tend to have a(n)

a)   cost focus
b)   revenue focus
c)   labor focus
d)   environmental focus
e)   education focus

7   If a facility is well managed, it will succeed regardless of location.

a)   True
b)   False

8   The basic center of gravity method does **not** take into consideration

a)   the location of markets
b)   the volume of goods shipped to the markets
c)   the value of the goods shipped
d)   the combination of volume and distance

Dr. Nilofer Ahmed has narrowed down the choice of location of her new emergency out-patient clinic to the following three locations (45 Lexington Avenue; 56th Street & Broadway; 17 Lexington Avenue)

Location factor	Importance of criteria	Scored on each location factor			Weighted factor scores		
		45 Lexington Avenue	56th Street & Broadway	17 Lexington Avenue	45 Lexington Avenue	56th Street & Broadway	17 Lexington Avenue
Land availability	15	3	7	8			
Parking availability	40	8	7	9			
Traffic patterns	15	9	8	8			
Lab facility availability	30	5	7	7			
		(1 = poor; 10 = excellent)					

Use this information to answer questions 9. and 10.

9 Analyzing the above information using the factor rating system, which location would she prefer?

a) 45 Lexington
b) 56th & Broadway
c) 17 Lexington
d) None
e) Either 56th & Broadway, or 45 Lexington

10 What significant caution would you like to emphasize to Dr. Ahmed about the above method?

a) Future competition will render the location unsuitable.
b) The criteria weights are essentially subjective.
c) Traffic patterns data are usually subjective.
d) The 1 to 10 scale used to rate each location is incorrect.

After some time, Dr. Ahmed realizes that there are many immobile patients who need medical services at their homes and decides to open a mobile urgicare medical center, using several specially outfitted vans. She anticipates that these patients will be drawn mostly from four surrounding neighborhoods and therefore would like to locate her new mobile center at an overall 'best' central point from which all four neighborhoods can be served.

Neighborhood	Neighborhood Coordinates		Anticipated in-patient
	x	y	volume
A	2	18	1,500
B	15	17	1,200
C	2	2	2,250
D	14	2	*3,300*
			8,250

Use this information to answer questions 11. and 12.

11 Using the center of gravity method, what is the x-coordinate for the 'best' location for the new clinic?

a) 7.09
b) 9.82
c) 8.69
d) 6.47
e) none of the above

12 Using the center of gravity method, what is the y-coordinate for the 'best' location?

a) 8.69
b) 6.47
c) 7.09
d) 9.82
e) none of the above

COG x-coordinate: $\sum d_{ix} V_i / \sum V_i$
COG y-coordinate: $\sum d_{iy} V_i / \sum V_i$

Where:

i = 1 to n neighborhoods
d_{ix} = x-coordinate of the ith neighborhood
d_{iy} = y-coordinate of the ith neighborhood
n = number of neighborhoods
V_i = anticipated in-patient volume from neighborhood i

Use Figure 12.13 to answer questions 13. to 15.

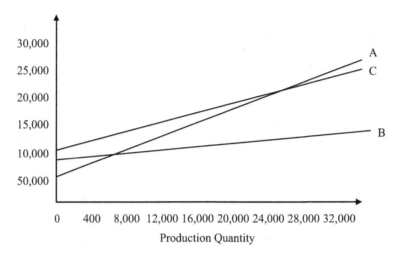

Figure 12.13 Question 13 Break-Even Chart

13 Based on the chart, for what production quantity is location C appropriate?

a) Below 8,000
b) Between 8,000 and 12,000, approximately
c) Above 20,000
d) None of the above

14 Based on the chart, for what production quantity would the decision maker be indifferent to choosing between location A and location B?

a) About 8,000
b) About 12,000
c) About 28,000
d) None of the above

15 Supposing the Small Business Bureau agrees to foot all the fixed-cost expenses (that is, fixed costs are 'free' for you), which location would you prefer for production on a volume that may range from 4,000 to 32,000 units?

a) Location A
b) Location B
c) Location C
d) Cannot determine from the information provided

16 Which of the following examples best describes a delivered service firm?

a) Back-office processing centers of banks
b) The Baruch College bookstore
c) Hotel reservation systems—web-based
d) UPS
e) All of the above

17 Competitive clustering, the notion of locating close to competitors, *primarily* benefits demand-sensitive businesses because:

a) One can monitor competitor prices easily.
b) Customers like to go to places where they can make comparisons among many alternatives and have choices.
c) If our competition is there, it must be a good site!
d) Logistics costs go down since suppliers can make bulk deliveries to several businesses at a time.

18 Starbucks has adopted a strategy of saturation location, grouping outlets tightly in urban areas. What's a true problem with this location strategy?

a) Stores cannibalize (steal away) customers from one another, affecting individual store sales (assuming individual store manager performance evaluation is based on individual store revenue).
b) Customers tune out because they get fed up with seeing so many outlets.
c) Locating so many outlets together is not beneficial from a real estate cost perspective.
d) Expenses for advertising and supervision by senior management increase.
e) Starbucks shuts out competitors from prime space, who can then sue Starbucks.

Answers: 5–b; 6–a; 7–b; 8–c; 9–c; 10–b; 11–c; 12–c; 13–d; 14–a; 15–b (lowest unit VC); 16–d; 17–b; 18–a

Suggested Class Project

Student teams are assigned to recommend a location for various businesses, such as:

a) A new McDonald's (walk-in fast food)
b) A new Olive Garden (walk-in sit-down)
c) A new post office (serving several customer zones)
d) A new branch office for a bank
e) A new ATM location
f) A new back office bill processing center for a hospital (quasi-manufacturing business—cost driven)

Students are encouraged to collect actual data (distances, traffic count, time of the day and direction of traffic flows, number of nearby competitors, town/municipality/neighborhood development restrictions and future development plans, neighborhood crime rate, and income and age levels) while analyzing location alternatives and making a recommendation. Use of at least one location technique is mandatory.

Suggested Cases

Site Selection at La Quinta Hotels

Richard Metters, rmetters@mays.tamu.edu

Description

Location analysis for demand-sensitive service industries. The old adage of the three most important aspects of real estate being "location, location, location" is never more true than in the transient hotel business. The physical site is an essential attribute of a new hotel—no amount of marble in the foyer can bring customers to a poor location and a good location could profit under mediocre management.

Unfortunately, there is considerable disagreement over which sites are better than others. While everyone could agree that a Death Valley Hotel probably would be a poor choice, it is difficult to determine exactly what makes for a good choice. To be considered beyond the most preliminary investigation, each potential site must have a number of positive aspects. Historically, selecting a site for new La Quinta inns has been decidedly more art than science. Although objective data could be gathered, sifting through the data and finding a good site still requires "gut feel"—and everyone's gut feel is a little different. With more difficult economic times and increased industry capacity squeezing La Quinta's profits in early 1987, location decisions required more scrutiny. La Quinta decided to try a new approach to selecting sites: utilizing regression analysis of the current performance of their installed inn base to determine sites for new inns.

Whelan Pharmaceuticals: Tax Factors and Global Site Selection

G. Peter Wilson; Jane Palley Katz

Source: Harvard Business School
Publication Date: Nov 13, 1991
Product #: 192066-PDF-ENG
Discipline: Business & Government Relations
Length: 12 p, English PDF
Revision Date: Aug 5, 2005

Description

Whelan Pharmaceuticals, a U.S. company with $3 billion in sales, must decide where to manufacture its newest product. In considering possible sites, both foreign and U.S., the firm must identify and make trade-offs between tax, marketing, and manufacturing factors.

Are We Ready for an Automotive Plant?

Yi-Chia Wu; Joo Y. Jung

Format: PDF
Also Available In: English Hardcopy Black & White
Source: Ivey Publishing
Publication Date: Jan 26, 2010

Product #: 909D14-PDF-ENG
Discipline: General Management
Length: 15 p, English PDF

Description

The case addresses a wide range of issues regarding site selection factors within the automotive industry. Depending on the format of how the case is presented and used, the case presents one or more teaching objectives: To examine essential factors for site location of different industries including the automotive industry; to evaluate the potential sites based on a quantitative method such as the relative aggregate score; to understand other qualitative factors that can affect the decision. The case can be used in undergraduate, graduate, and executive levels. This case would be more suitable for courses and workshops concerning operations management, supply chain management, production management, project management, decision science, and management science. Depending on the audience, a different level of case can be provided; for example, the case can be given as is for an undergraduate level, or, for graduate and executive levels, some (or even all) exhibits can be omitted, requiring the students to research and come up with their own factors. Further, another industry instead of automotive can be explored for site selection, which would result in different factors.

The city of McAllen, Texas, and its partners have worked on attracting an automotive assembly plant to the region for over 15 years. Under the North American Free Trade Agreement (NAFTA) provision, this region enjoys the advantages offered by both sides of the Mexican-U.S. border. Even during the economic downturn of 2007 to 2008, McAllen experienced a lower unemployment rate compared to other cities in the United States. One of the primary reasons was its close proximity and economic ties to Mexico. Lower labor cost, a right-to-work state and proximity to Mexico were some of this region's strengths, while a high illiteracy rate, limited numbers of automotive suppliers and small workforce were among its weaknesses. Based on publicly available data and aggregate score evaluation methods, McAllen is compared to other potential sites. The case addresses a wide range of issue regarding site selection factors within the automotive industry. Teaching objectives include: 1) to examine essential factors for site location of different industries, including the automotive industry; 2) to evaluate the potential sites based on a quantitative method, such as the relative aggregate score; 3) to understand other qualitative factors that can affect the decision. The case is suitable for courses and workshops concerning operations management, supply chain management, production management, project management, decision science, and management science. Exhibits can be omitted for graduate and executive levels, requiring the students to research and come up with their own factors.

Notes

1 "Who are my customers?" *Prizm*, http://www.claritas.com/MyBestSegments/Default.jsp.
2 "Home Depot vs. Lowe's: Location Advantages," *Wall Street Journal*, Sept. 12, 2007, B5C.
3 See an overview of BMW's auto plant in South Carolina, including how much it has invested there: https://www.bmwusfactory.com/manufacturing/production-overview/?r=1395771167807#stats
4 See Volkswagen's facts about its Chattanooga, TN, factory: http://www.volkswagengroupamerica.com/facts.html.
5 This process was adapted with permission from WDG Consulting: http://wdgconsulting.com/Site_Location_decision_process.htm.
6 Data source for foot traffic and crime rate can be found at www.tactician.com, among others.
7 *(For instructors)* Here the instructor may provide a quick and dirty refresher on independent variables, dependent variables, and how to interpret a complete regression model, including R square, statistical significance, intercept, and standardized/unstandardized coefficients—see the forecasting chapter (chapter 5).
8 Unstandardized coefficients.

9 Regression can be used even when relationships are not linear by way of transforming factors into linear forms (*log* transformations), or by modeling curvilinear relationships.

10 GIS: Instructor—Go to mapscape.com, register and work through a GIS example. For a more rigorous treatment of the tool, and for cases, consult ESRI's site for GIS for higher education: http://www.esri.com/industries university/ index.html. Customer demographic packages are available from other sources (e.g. PRIZM at http://www.claritas. com/MyBestSegments/Default.jsp). Also see http://www.tetrad.com/demographics/usa/ claritas/prizmne.html? gclid =CN25lInn0p8CFVw55QodmBMscw for a comprehensive description of GIS and related tools.

11 *Answers:* i) C $10,000, B $8,000; ii) B (lowest total cost); iii) Variable cost/unit = the slope (rise/run) of the total cost line; iv) Since the fixed cost becomes 0 for all locations, pick location 'B', the one with the flattest slope, and therefore the lowest variable cost/unit.

12 Mark Turnage, "A Mind-Blowing Number Of Counterfeit Goods Come From China," *Business Insider*, Jun. 25, 2013, http://www.businessinsider.com/most-counterfeit-goods-are-from-china-2013-6; S.C., "Luxury goods in China Chinese malconsumption ," Free Exchange (blog), *Economist*, June 22, 2012, http://www.economist.com/ blogs/freeexchange/2012/06/luxury-goods-china.

13 Alex Markels, "Long Distance; Innovative MCI Unit Finds Culture Shock in Colorado Springs," *Wall Street Journal*, June 25, 1996.

14 *Instructor:* I have found it informative and entertaining to ask my international students about cultural and spiritual issues in location decisions—makes the 'quiet' students in the class surprisingly vocal!

15 The material on feng shui has been adapted from www.absolutelyfengshui.com.

16 To see NYPD crime statistics, visit http://www.nyc.gov/html/nypd/html/crime_prevention/crime_statistics.shtml.

17 View video of the pace of construction in Dubai: Bruce Fenton, "That's FAST: 6 Months of Construction—Dubai BEFORE and AFTER, UAE, Middle East," *YouTube*, June 12, 2007, www.youtube.com/watch?v=ndbdKswDm_s.

18 "Tata Suspends Work at Nano Plant at Singur," *Tata.com,* Sept. 2, 2008, http://www.tata.com/article/inside/ 7VqcQt58pCw=/TLYVr3YPkMU=; A K Bhattacharya, "Singur to Sanand," *Business Standard*, Aug. 6, 2011, http:// www.business-standard.com/article/beyond-business/singur-to-sanand-111080600026_1.html.

19 Kerry Capell, "Goodbye Ireland," *Businessweek*, Feb. 22, 2010, 52.

20 "Globalization and Healthcare: Operating Profit," *The Economist*, Aug. 16, 2008, 74–76, http://www.economist.com/ node/11919622

21 Read more about the company's plans: "International Entrepreneurs in International Waters," http://blueseed.com.

22 Harry McCracken, "Nowhere to Hide" *Time*, March 31, 2014.

23 "Mobile Marketing: Location Matters—But How Much?" *Knowledge@Wharton Today*, March 9, 2012.

24 Alexis Raymond, "Cisco Technology Allows for Virtual Visits with Medical Specialists", Cisco Blogs, Oct 22, 2013, http://blogs.cisco.com/csr/cisco-technology-allows-for-virtual-visits-with-medical-specialists.

25 Andrea James, "Starbucks Releases First Store Closure List," *Seattle Times*, July 11, 2008, http://www.seattlepi.com/ business/article/Starbucks-releases-first-store-closure-list-1279122.php; Melissa Allison, "Howard Schultz says No More Layoffs Planned at Starbucks," *Seattle Times*, March 3, 2009, http://www.seattletimes.com/business/ howard-schultz-says-no-more-layoffs-planned-at-starbucks/.

26 Charles Fishman, "The Insourcing Boom," *The Atlantic*, Nov. 28, 2012; Brian Wingfield & Romy Varghese, "Apple Supplier Foxconn to Invest Millions in Pennsylvania," *Bloomberg Businessweek,* Bloomberg.com, Nov 22, 2013.

Part V

Working with Projects

13 Managing Projects

Managing Projects: A Road Map

- Suggested class projects
- Suggested cases

Customer: *"Why should I choose you?"*
Business: *"Because we will build and deliver your project at cost, on time, and to your specification."*

13.1 What Is Project Management?

There is often some confusion about what is (and what is not) a project. Let's try to clear some of that first, and then talk about project management.

13.1.1 What Is a Business Project?

Formally speaking, a project is a unique and structured work effort to accomplish a specific goal. How would you recognize a project when you see one? Look for a task that is fairly unique and nonrepetitive, has a clear start and finish, has specific goals, and has linked work steps with a specified timeline. Look for a task that involve teams with interdependent activities that have to be coordinated and directed to a common project goal. Look for teams that draw on different functions for a specific task, and disband after that task is over. Look for conflict involving differences between and among clients, project teams, and other stakeholders.

Let's try to identify a few projects. For example, developing Windows 8 was a project—while looking for a cure for cancer is probably not (since we do not know when we shall reach that goal). From your perspective, getting a business degree is a project—maintaining your Facebook page is not. A regular commute to school or work is not a project—a family vacation is. An operation or task that is repetitive, continuous (does not end), and standardized is likely not a project. Running an assembly line for cars is not a project—it would be a process consisting of hundreds of steps that are done over and over again. Similarly, preparing invoices for customers is a process. Also, unlike a process, where everyday goals are usually achieved, project goals change, and outcomes are usually more uncertain. There are three key performance dimensions of a project: cost, scope, and time. Usually, improvements in one dimension require compromises on the other two.

13.1.2 What Is Project Management?

Formally defined, project management is the art of orchestrating time and resources to meet and manage stakeholder goals, project risks, and project changes. Managing multiple projects is called program management.

Although we generally think that managing projects is mostly about managing people, project managers manage three things—performance, people, and change.

How do they do it? In consultation with the client, the project manager sets and monitors cost, quality, and time standards of performance and output. Performance goals include softer aspects such as team morale and client employee morale. To succeed in today's project environment, technical skills aren't enough. People management is important. Project teams are built co-opting people with expertise to fit the tasks on hand. Roles and expectations are clearly defined. Communicating within and outside the team is important. Short everyday reviews and regular meetings to evaluate progress and identify impediments help. Inevitable conflicts spring up within teams and with client personnel. The project manager must resolve such problems with tact, consistency, and integrity while maintaining enthusiasm and focus among the troops. Managers with high levels of emotional intelligence have been found to be more successful. Changes are also inevitable. Changes

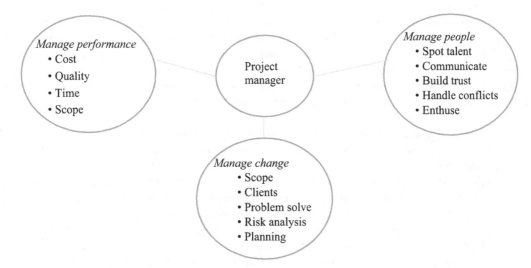

Figure 13.1 Managing Projects

are created by technical or engineering surprises uncovered along the way, client changes in cost, scope, or time, and changes in project personnel. Risk analysis and scenario planning can anticipate or help prepare for some changes.

OM IN PRACTICE

Project Management Best Practices at NASA

Never mind those pics of Mars sent by Curiosity. The Cassini-Huygens Saturn spacecraft landed a probe on Titan, Saturn's largest moon years ago, and it is still sending spectacular pictures back to earth.

Figure 13.2 Titan Moon Orbiting Saturn

Source: Image taken by Cassini spacecraft, NASA, May 23 2013, http://www.nasa.gov/mission_pages/cassini/multimedia/pia14922.html.

"How do you get a five-ton spacecraft safely to Saturn and land a probe on its largest moon when your project involves three space agencies, 17 countries, 18 separate scientific payloads, and 250 scientists working across 10 time zones?" The physics is indeed rocket science, but the management centers on projects. As Dr. Edward J. Hoffman, chief knowledge officer at NASA, says, "We are dealing with grand challenges, and the only way we can deal with them is with a project approach."

PMI (Project Management Institute) found specific project management best practices at NASA that can be applied to any business project. Prominent among those were:

- Running a rigorous project selection and prioritization process, especially critical in today's resource-constrained environment. For example, the shuttle program was shut down in favor of the Mars project.
- Obtaining strong and widely spread project sponsors, with important stakeholders and supporters at NASA, the external scientific community, and industry. Sponsors lend support at critical junctures, helping to obtain financial, technical, and people resources.
- Endowing project management teams with decentralized resource-allocation and exchange authority. Each of the 18 task leaders in NASA's Saturn project could exchange resources.
- Developing talent. NASA's in-house project leadership development program identifies the 4 A's—ability, attitude, alliances, and assignments. A technical star with a noncollaborative attitude would not become a team member. Alliances for knowledge sharing and consulting are essential and encouraged. As project managers evolve, they are challenged with assignments of increasing difficulty.

Now, scientists want to send a follow-up mission to explore the liquid methane lakes of Titan. The TALISE project (Titan Lake In-situ Sampling Propelled Explorer) would land a boat, propelled by wheels, paddles, or screws, to move around Ligeia Mare, the largest lake on the moon.

Adapted from: "2012 Pulse of the Profession," *Project Management Institute*, 2012, https://www.pmi.org/~/media/PDF/Research/2012_Pulse_of_the_profession.ashx; NASA news.

13.2 Why Is Project Management Important?

13.2.1 Importance for Businesses

Some years ago, the Motorola Razr appeared in the market. The cell phone was an instant and enduring hit. Motorola sold more than 130 million units over a period of four years. At that time, cell phone manufacturers could design a new cell phone in about six to 12 months and could hope to sell it over the next few years. During that extended selling period, they had the time to design, test, and refine another two to three models (each model design taking about six months to a year). Today, phone makers launch new models every few months. If they don't, they are likely to lose market share to a competitor's fresh product, as Motorola's Razr and RIM's BlackBerry did. The problem is that while the time required to design a new cell phone still hovers around six months to a year, the product life cycle for a new design has collapsed to a few months. The only way phone makers can introduce a new phone every few months is to have two or three overlapping new

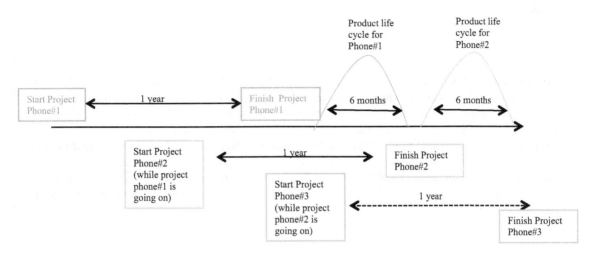

Figure 13.3 Managing Multiple Projects[1]

phone design projects. And not one project can afford to come in late, since a new design is needed every few months.

Managing multiple projects to successful and timely completion has never been so important to business survival than now. It is not easy, to do so, though. PMI reports that organizations are losing an average of US$109 million for every US$1 billion spent on projects, and that a staggering 44 percent of strategic initiatives reportedly fail.[2] For every failure, however, there are companies like Coca-Cola, Apple, and Nike, who, while making practically nothing themselves, have developed a set of outstanding project management skills. These successful project managers orchestrate complex manufacturing and distribution supply chains to work together in projects that develop and launch new products around the world.

13.2.2 Importance for You

Every business undertakes projects of some kind. Construction, aerospace, consumer electronics, and consulting companies work all the time on building, development, or new product projects. Food, retailing, and textiles are less project-oriented, but new distribution center and retail outlet openings and IT system revamps keep happening all the time.

With life-time employment becoming rarer, you probably will be working a lot with teams from around the world on short, focused projects. Learn some project skills now.

Project Manager—Medical Center Houston, TX

Job Title: Project Manager
Job ID: 135951
Location: Medical Center Houston, TX
Full/Part Time: Full-Time
Regular/Temporary: Regular

Shift: 8 a.m. to 5 p.m. FT
Salary Grade: 14

About Texas Children's

Texas Children's Pediatrics is the nation's largest primary pediatric care network with more than 200 physicians in 48 locations throughout the greater Houston area. Providing the finest pediatricians dedicated to meeting the health care needs of infants to teenagers, our expert physicians offer full-service pediatric care. As part of its goal to build a community of healthy children, Texas Children's Pediatrics Community Cares Program provides trusted, high-quality pediatric medical services for children who otherwise would seek care from emergency centers or possibly go without care or treatment due to low family incomes and/or lack of health insurance. For more information on Texas Children's Pediatrics, visit texaschildrenspediatrics.org. Get the latest news from Texas Children's Pediatrics by visiting the online newsroom.

Position Summary

We are searching for our next Project Manager—someone who is not afraid to jump right in to work in a fast-paced hospital environment. In this position you'll lead integrated, complex, multiple system project(s) and manage the on-going maintenance of a group of related applications. We need someone who has knowledge of current business practices and computing systems, interfaces, and health plan standard software.

Sound like the job for you?

Job Duties & Responsibilities

- Manages multiple mandatory, essential, high, moderate and/or low business priority projects
- Responsible for adherence to the IDS Project Governance guidelines and Enterprise Project Methodology, including the approvals processes and project and reporting structures. Establishes project specific governance and conducts steering and work team meeting
- Determines staff resource needs for analysts, programmers, vendors, user personnel, consultants, and equipment by assessing the size, duration, scope, and complexity of the project
- Formulates, administers and maintains the detailed Project Plan, using Project Management tool, which will include all required activities, tasks, risks, issues and resources requirements, leading to a successful and timely implementation. Provides regular project status reports as required
- Facilitates, communicates, listens and works with project team members and other Project Managers to continuously update the detailed project plan in addition to the risk and issues plan
- Analyzes project standards, methodologies, and impacts
- Determines, analyzes, and formulates current practices, user needs, and workflow processes, issues and potential solutions on projects
- Coordinates activities and information dissemination with committees, management, and other necessary participants
- Serves as Business Operations representative as a participating member of designated committees—Perioperative Services

Requirements

- Bachelor's degree in business administration, healthcare administration, nursing or other related field, BSN is preferred
- Five (5) years of experience in Healthcare, is preferred—Perioperative Experience
- Nursing experience is preferred
- An equivalent combination of education and related work experience may be substituted for those specified
- Familiarity with various operating systems, used by data processing techniques and practices, and a working knowledge of a variety of hardware and software environments and of the healthcare industry is also required.
- Ability to demonstrate expertise in project management and planning and process mapping
- Ability to demonstrate group presentation, leadership, team building, written and verbal communication, analytical, and organizational skills
- Ability to analyze the functionality of systems and their fit with specifications, and to demonstrate the ability to work independently with minimal supervision

Source: Job for Texas Children's Pediatrics listed at https://eapps.texaschildrenshospital.org/psp/hcmprdca/ EMPLOYEE/HRMS/c/HRS_HRAM.HRS_CE.GBL?Page=HRS_CE_JOB_DTL&Action=A&JobOpeningId= 135951&SiteId=1&PostingSeq=1 (accessed Oct. 6, 2015).

To specialize in project management as a career, take a few more project management courses and acquire a CAMP (Certified Associate in Project Management), followed by a PMP (Project Management Professional) certification after you gain some experience. Both certifications are awarded by the Project Management Institute (PMI). PMI reports that jobs in project management have grown by about 30 percent over the past five years. You can also put your project management skills to use on personal projects like planning for studying and vacations to more complex tasks such as organizing a party or a wedding.

KEY POINTS

- A project is a temporary job with specific goals, linked work steps, limited resources, and a clear start and finish. Projects are fairly unique and nonrepetitive.
- Project managers manage three things—performance, people, and change.
- Project performance has three dimensions: cost, scope, and time. Seeking improvement in one dimension requires acceptance of deteriorated performance on the others.
- With constantly shortening product life cycles but static product development times, multiple projects have to be launched and successfully completed in overlapping times. Failure to come in on time may jeopardize market share and financial success.

13.3 How Is It Done?

Broadly speaking, a project manager creates an organizational structure, develops plans, identifies tasks, budgets required resources, determines timelines, and deals with the team and client(s). Chronologically, project management activities move through distinct phases.

13.3.1 Moving Through the Phases

A project passes through four different phases, from initiation to closure. Each phase has to be managed according to its unique tasks and requirements.

- Initiation
- Planning
- Implementation
- Closure

We begin the *initiation* phase after a project receives the go-ahead. We create a project charter with a formal high-level description of the objectives, deliverables, and governance of the project. We also specify the scope of the project, indicating what will and will not be included as part of the project. This is perhaps the most important part of the initiation phase. Poorly defined scope results in many changes and extensions of work down the line later ('scope creep'). Scope creep leads to delays and arguments, affecting cost, morale, and customer relationships. However, even with a well-defined project scope, it is inevitable that shifting needs and circumstances will call for adjustments and new tasks. An explicit change-management article will lay out a formal and agreed upon process for tackling changes in project scope or other issues. We develop a resource projection for the project over its duration that includes purchases, lease costs, training, and maintenance. We also identify high-level risks and highlight key assumptions. A list of key personnel is prepared. The charter document represents the formal agreement for the project. It is signed by all parties, marking the end of the initiation phase.[3]

The next phase, *planning*, is when project details are thrashed out and documented. Although it is tempting to cut short on planning and begin execution, lack of preparedness creates problems and failures down the road. We prepare individual plans for important project dimensions like risk, quality, vendor management, communication and coordination, and task planning. We also identify interdependencies among plans for future use, as changes in one plan can ripple through other plans. We prepare a project organization plan, defining team composition and staffing, roles and responsibilities, and performance measures. The tools available for planning range from work breakdown structures to Gantt charts to PERT/CPM network diagrams, which we'll explore later in the chapter.

Implementation, the following phase, is about plan execution. Plans face challenges and changes. It is here that the project manager's real mettle is tested. A good plan provides discipline and milestones, and a good change management protocol helps deal with the inevitable changes from plan that happen during execution. Best practices, codified from earlier projects, are used. Tools such as PERT and CPM track and monitor project progress and cost/time deviations from plan. Every milestone achieved typically calls for a small celebration among employees and involves clients and suppliers.

During the final phase, *project closure*, we hand over the final deliverables to the client and intimate formal project closure to all stakeholders. Working out bugs, continuing client requests, and other issues can prolong closure. A clear project scope helps closure. Supplier contracts are closed, and project staff releases and transfers are made. Communicating release dates and transfer plans to project workers is important. Otherwise, project employees may spend their time during execution and closure looking for the best next place to work. Lessons learned are discussed and recorded for future use. A celebration is usually held to mark successful project closure and honor workers and key client personnel. Important project documents are archived in a safe and accessible place. Sometimes, project maintenance or continued operation is also required after closure, but that usually forms a separate contract.

13.3.2 Organizing for Projects

How is a project staffed and organized? Generally, people resources are estimated in terms of FTEs or 'full-time equivalents.' We first estimate the number of days it would take one person to complete an activity ('person day estimate of effort'). We next determine the required completion date and compute the FTEs staffing requirement. For example:

Required completion time for a project activity = 2 months

Person day estimate of effort for that project activity = 200 person days, that is, it would take one person 200 working days to complete the activity, working alone.

So, how many full time equivalents (people) would be required to finish the activity in the required two months?

$$\text{\# of FTEs required} = \frac{\text{person day estimate of effort}}{\text{required completion time} \times 22 \text{ working days/mo}} \qquad \text{(Equation 13.1)}$$

$$= \frac{200 \text{ person days}}{2 \text{ months} \times 22 \text{ days}} = 4.55 \text{ FTEs}$$

Thus, 4.55 full time equivalents would be required to complete the activity in two months.

Typically, people are pulled in from different areas of a company to staff a project. They are organized as a project team. Some join earlier or later according to when their expertise is required. Such project teams, built with many different talents, usually follow either a matrix organization or a functional organization structure.

QUICK CHECK

a)   Experience Reports suggest that it'd take 20 'person day estimate of effort' days to finish the team term paper. What does that mean?

b)   The team term paper has to be turned in five days from now. The team consists of three students. They can work in parallel. Will they be able to turn in the paper in time?

Answer:

a)   It would take one person 20 days to complete the paper, working by herself.

b)   # of FTEs required = person day estimate of effort

required completion time * 22 working days/mo

= 20/5
= 4 FTEs.

A three-student team will not be able to complete the paper in five days (they would take 20/3 = 6.67 days).

In a matrix organization, the project leader is the boss, and every team member reports to and is evaluated by him/her. In a functional format, team members may still report to the project leader but would also report to their functional bosses for evaluation, raises, and career growth purposes. This often creates dual loyalties and conflicts between the project leader and the functional boss. Members in functional structures are also often working on other projects. Matrix organizational structures work better since reporting and accountability lines are clear and simple. Members are not shared with other teams or their functional home areas. On the other hand, dedicating a functional expert to every project in the business would call for many experts and places a strain on company personnel resources. Team members in a matrix structure may also feel orphaned after the project ends, having lost touch with their erstwhile pre-project functional 'home.'

After forming a team, making the team work well is the next challenge. Good project managers can spot strengths and weaknesses in teams. They plug gaps by managing, obtaining, and allocating talent as needed. They manage emerging issues to forestall them from becoming problems. Experienced project managers can see and show how project goals connect to overall firm business goals. They monitor changes in project scope, specifications, risks, and costs and understand their implications for firm business goals.

KEY POINTS

- A project passes through four different phases from initiation to closure.

    - Initiation creates a project charter that outlines the project scope, resource projection, deliverables, and governance.
    - Planning involves preparing individual plans for risk, quality, task sequencing, project staffing, communication, and coordination.
    - Execution means monitoring using tools and motivational techniques.
    - Closure happens with the handover of deliverables to the client, vendor contact termination, project staff releases, and document archiving.

- We estimate the number of days it would take one person to complete an activity. We divide that number by the required activity completion time in working days to compute the FTE requirement for the activity.
- Project teams are organized in a functional or matrix structure.

    - A functional structure retains team member accountability and reward at the member's functional home—good for morale and career development
    - A matrix structure allows the project manager full control over the team member's evaluation and rewards—resources are dedicated to a project team.

- Project managers have to SWOT (strengths, weaknesses, opportunities, and threats) analyze a team and plug gaps with required talent.

13.3.3 How to Select a Project

What should we go with? Developing new product A or new product B? Opening an outlet at location A or at location B? Companies have to select from competing projects at all times. Comparing projects usually involves comparing cash flow projections.

The simplest method is the *payback period*, which examines how soon the investment in the project will be returned, similar to a break-even analysis. Projects with shorter payback periods are obviously more attractive. The *net present value* (NPV) approach introduces the time value of money by applying a cost of capital rate to cash inflows and outflows. The NPV is calculated as the present value of the project's cash inflows minus the present value of the project's cash outflows. The project with the higher NPV is ranked higher. A return on investment (ROI) figure can also be calculated using the NPV as the numerator and the present value of the cash outflows as the denominator. The third technique, the *internal rate of return (*IRR), calculates the rate of return that equates the estimated cash inflows to the investment made in the project. IRR is used more to accept or reject projects. Projects with IRRs that meet the company's expectations of a minimum rate of return are chosen. However, IRR (and ROI) can bias selections to favor a project with a high rate of return even though the absolute value of the return may be comparatively smaller. For example, a $100,000 investment returning $500,000 will have a higher IRR (and ROI) than a $1 million investment returning $2 million. IRR generally compares projects of similar durations. NPV and IRR could point to different directions when comparing projects due to differences in the timing of cash flows for each project and differences in project size. These methods are best used when cash flow projections are fairly predictable.

Picking a Project—Payback, NPV, and IRR

A concert promoter has to pick among three alternative projects: a six-month concert series by Lady Daga or a similar concert series staging Sailor Swift or Austin Bieber. The cash flow projections are as follows:

Alternatives	Cash flow projections ($ thousands)								
	Upfront cost	Cash inflow from concerts							
		month 0	mo1	mo2	mo3	mo4	mo5	mo6	Total cash inflow
Lady Daga	$500		$150	$100	$200	$140	$80	$220	$890
Sailor Swift	$500		$100	$120	$150	$100	$220	$200	$890
Austin Bieber	$500		$200	$120	$180	$30	$150	$210	$890

Using Payback Period

Lady Daga	Cost = $500
	First 4 months of revenue = $150 + $100 + $200 + $140 = $590
	Payback in 4 months
Sailor Swift	Cost = $500
	Payback in 5 months ($690)
Austin Bieber	Cost = $500
	Payback in 3 months ($500)

Pick the Bieber project since it has the shortest payback period.

Using NPV

Assume cost of capital at 2 percent per month (private sources of funding with relatively high interest rates). The NPV is calculated as the present value of the project's cash inflows minus the present value of the project's cash outflows.

$$NPV = CF_0 + CF_1/(1 + r) + CF_2/(1 + r)^2 + CF_3/(1 + r)^3 + \ldots + CF_t/(1 + r)^t \qquad \text{(Equation 13.2)}$$

Where CF_t = cash flow at time t, and r = cost of capital

Thus, Lady Daga's NPV = $(-)\$500 + \$150/(1 + .02)^1 + \$100/(1 + .02)^2 + \$200/(1 + .02)^3 +$
$\$140/(1 + .02)^4 + \$80/(1 + .02)^5 + \$220/(1 + .02)^6$
$= (-)\$500 + \$828.79$
$= \$328.79$

Sailor Swift's NPV $= \$ (-)\$500 + \$823.97$
$= \$323.97$

Austin Bieber NPV $= \$ (-)\$500 + \$831.09$
$= \mathbf{\$331.09}$

Bieber ROI = NPV/PV of cash outflows = ($\$331.09/\$500$) * 100 = **66.21%**

In this theoretical example, we would choose to go with Austin Bieber, since he has the highest NPV. In practical terms, the differences in NPV are so little that we would probably use additional project selection criteria. Such criteria could be the relative reliability of cash flow estimates, which artist is easier to work with, or artist dependability.

Using IRR

Internal rate of return (IRR) is the interest rate at which the net present value of all the cash flows (both positive and negative) from a project equal zero. IRR is found by using trial-and-error to identify the appropriate rate at which NPV becomes zero. Financial calculators and spreadsheet programs have an inbuilt IRR function.

$$0 \text{ (NPV)} = CF_0 + CF_1/(1 + IRR) + CF_2/(1 + IRR)^2 + CF_3/(1 + IRR)^3$$
$$+ \ldots + CF_t/(1 + IRR)^t \qquad \text{(Equation 13.3)}$$

Computing Lady Daga's IRR,

$$0 = (-)500 + \$150/(1 + IRR) + \$100/(1 + IRR)^2 + \$200/(1 + IRR)^3 + \$140/(1 + IRR)^4 +$$
$$\$80/(1 + IRR)^5 + \$220/(1 + IRR)^6$$

Lady Daga's IRR = 19% (rounding off errors included)

(In Excel, enter *all* the cash flows in one column and go to formulas/financial/irr. Enter the cell numbers in the 'values' section of the box that opens up. You could similarly select NPV for an NPV computation but enter just the cash flows after period 0 into the column. Take the resultant NPV figure from Excel and manually subtract the cash outflow in period 0 from that figure to get the actual NPV.)

Similarly,

Sailor Swift's IRR   = 17%

Austin Bieber's IRR   = 20%

If we assume that the promoter's required minimum threshold IRR for accepting any project is (arbitrarily) say, 15 percent, then all the three projects pass the threshold IRR test. The project with the highest IRR would be chosen.

When cash flows are so uncertain that we cannot estimate probabilities, we look at envisaged best, moderate, and worst case scenarios. For example, assume that the NPVs from our six-month concert series projects above represent the 'best' future. We then estimate cash flows for each project in two other possible situations—moderate and worst—and compute the resultant NPVs.

Project selection under uncertainty (all figures in $ thousands)

Project	Best NPV	Moderate NPV*	Worst NPV*
Lady Daga	$329	$300	$250
Sailor Swift	$324	$290	$270
Austin Bieber	$331	$300	$240

*moderate and worst NPVs are arbitrary numbers

Taking the *maximin* approach, we simply look at the 'Worst NPV' column, and pick the best of the worst—the guaranteed minimum. That would be the Sailor Swift project at $270,000. Alternatively, we could use the *maximax* approach that looks at the 'Best NPV' column and picks the best of the best—the most optimistic view. We would thus choose the Austin Bieber project at an NPV of $331,000. We could, of course, compute an average NPV for each project and choose the one with the highest average NPV (*Laplace method*). However, that assumes that we know that the best, moderate, and worst scenarios are equally likely to happen (equal probabilities). In a truly uncertain world, we cannot estimate probabilities of future events at all.

We could also use the *minimax regret* approach that attempts to minimize regrets or opportunity loss. We look at each NPV column above and compute a regret number for each project. For example, the maximum NPV is $331,000. Choosing Lady Daga or Sailor Swift would lead to a loss of $2,000 ($331,000 minus $329,000), and $7,000, respectively. Thus:

Minimax regret: Project selection under uncertainty (all figures in $ thousands)

Project	Regret under best NPV	Regret under moderate NPV	Regret under worst NPV
Lady Daga	$2 ($331 − $329)	$0	**$20** ($270 − $250)
Sailor Swift	$7 ($331 − $324)	*$10* ($300 − $290)	$0
Austin Bieber	$0 ($331 − $331)	$0	**$30**

Reading horizontally, we can see that the maximum regret for Lady Daga's project is $20,000, while Sailor Swift and Austin Bieber's maximum regrets are $10,000 and $30,000, respectively. The minimax regret approach would ask us to pick the project with the *smallest* maximum regret, that is, the best of the worst. We choose the Sailor Swift project.

Finally, when probabilities can be attached to cash flows, companies can develop multiple cash flow scenarios using a single cost of capital rate and then compute an expected cash flow projection, also called the EMV or 'expected monetary value.' We equate NPV with EMV in this case.

Project selection with probabilities

Project	Best NPV (20%)*	Moderate NPV (50%)*	Worst NPV (30%)*	Expected NPV
Lady Daga	$329	$300	$250	**$290.80** $\{(0.20 \times 329) + (0.50 \times 300) + (0.30 \times 250)\}$
Sailor Swift	$324	$290	$270	**$290.80**
Austin Bieber	$331	$300	$240	$288.20

Estimated probability of a best/moderate/worst condition situation emerging in the future (arbitrary figures).

We pick the project with the highest expected NPV (EMV), in this case a tie between Lady Daga and Sailor Swift. We could resolve the tie using other criteria, such as payback period or more qualitative considerations. Sensitivity analysis can be used to see the impact on NPV by varying the cost of capital and probabilities (see Table 13.1 for a summary).

Table 13.1 A Summary of Project Selection Methods

Short to medium-term projects with predictable cash flows

Method	What it does	Issues
Simple Payback period	Computes the time required to break-even	Ignores time value of money. Does not consider cash flows beyond the payback period.
Net present value (NPV)	Incorporates the time value of money. Computes the net present value of projects. Present value of inflows *minus* the present value of cash outflows.	Changing interest rates can change original NPV figure. Long term projects are not appropriate because the predictability of cashflows decline. Does not directly compute or compare ROI.
Internal rate of return (IRR)	The rate of return at which the present values of cash outflows and inflows are equal to each other. Shows the return on the initial investment	Assumes rate of return will remain stable over life of project. Can get two IRRs if there are negative cash inflows. Used to accept or reject projects rather than rank projects Ignores absolute size of return.

Projects with unpredictable cash flows where probabilities cannot be estimated

Method	What it does	Issues
Maximin	Compute competing project values in worst case scenarios. Pick project that has the highest worst scenario value.	Pure pessimistic approach. Ignores upside potential of project performance
Maximax	Compute competing project values in best case scenarios. Pick project that has the highest best scenario value.	Pure optimistic approach. Ignores downside pitfalls of project performance
Minimax regret	Computes the maximum opportunity loss of a project over best, moderate and worst scenarios. Picks the project with the smallest maximum regret figure.	Minimizing regret is psychologically comfortable, but may not maximize returns

Projects with unpredictable cash flows where probabilities can be estimated

Method	What it does	Issues
Expected monetary value (EMV)	Estimates the expected project value. Weights values in different scenarios with probabilities associated with those scenarios. Cash flow projections can be similarly weighted.	Probabilities can change. Provides an 'expected value' that would be representative if such decisions were made repeatedly over a long period of time. For example, tossing a coin for a 'heads you win $100' game would have an expected value of $50 (.50*$100 + .50*$0). If we were to play the game x times, add up the wins and no-wins, and and divide that figure by x, the resulting average would be $50, the EMV.

Understand, though, that it is possible for a project to come in at specification, at cost, and on time—the hallmarks of a successful project—and yet have a negative NPV. One reason could be unanticipated changes in revenues. Companies may, too, use additional, noneconomic, reasons to pick one project over another. Risk tolerances, potential to enter new markets or appease powerful constituents, potential to generate employment, and other such reasons may prevail. Once we select a project, we have to know how to plan for one.

KEY POINTS

- Project evaluation typically involves assessing and comparing cash flows.
- Evaluation methods used for projects with predictable cash flows include the payback period, the NPV, the ROI, and the IRR, the latter three considering the time value of money.
- Evaluation methods used for projects with cash flows that are too uncertain to estimate probabilities include the maximin, maximax, and the minimax regret. Each estimates cash flows in best case, worst case, and moderate case scenarios.

- Evaluation methods used for projects with uncertain cash flows with estimated probabilities include the EMV, which weights cash flows with their estimated probabilities.
- Nonfinancial evaluation criteria may include risk tolerances, potential market development options, or political reasons.

13.3.4 How to Plan a Project

Think about leading one of the many building, water salination, or energy projects in a fast-growing location such as Dubai or Qatar. Temperatures in the summer can exceed 124° F. Consider, too, that many in your team, as well as your sub-contractors and suppliers, may be fasting during the holy month of Ramadan. Fasting means no food and no water from sunrise to sunset. The local law does not allow work shifts beyond six hours (although some employers reportedly ignore these rules). Productivity can drop by 50 to 60 percent. As project managers, we would have to plan carefully to work around such events and conditions. We could schedule critical tasks before or after Ramadan, plan to hire more workers during that period, and keep plenty of cold

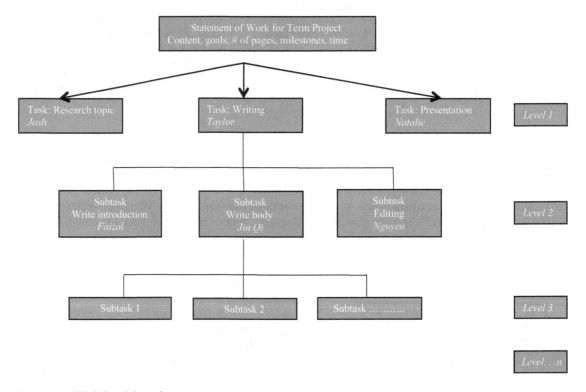

Figure 13.4 **Work Breakdown Structure**

water and air-conditioned cooling sites. The client has to be kept posted on likely schedule changes. We can use three popular techniques to plan for and monitor a project. These are the WBS, the Gantt chart, and the PERT/CPM network diagram.

The first step in planning for a project is to prepare a work breakdown structure (WBS). A WBS breaks down a project into a statement of work, tasks, and sub-tasks. Take a project that we all do at school—writing and presenting a business project as a group term paper assignment.

As we can see above, the WBS shows the tasks and component sub-tasks, with accountability. Taylor is the team leader for the writing task and has allocated writing-related sub-tasks to her team, consisting of Faizal, Jin Qi, and Nguyen. In theory, these sub-tasks can be further decomposed into lower-level smaller tasks as long as they constitute standalone activities of practical size and significance performed by an individual(s). What a WBS does not usually show is timeline, sequence, and interrelatedness of activities. Some of that is provided by the Gantt chart, which uses the WBS as a base document:

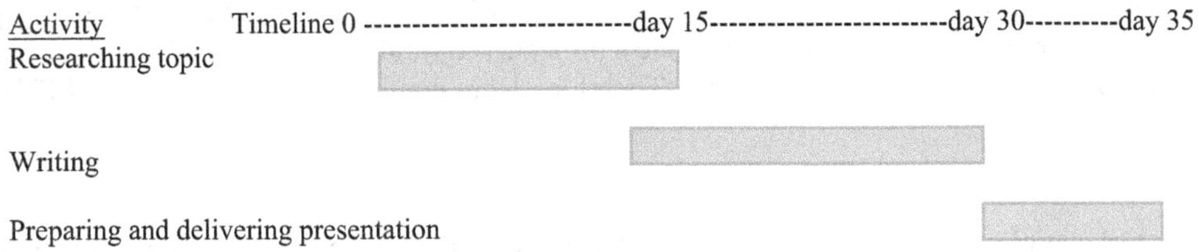

Activity	Timeline 0 ------------------------------day 15------------------------day 30----------day 35
Researching topic	
Writing	
Preparing and delivering presentation	

Figure 13.5 Gantt Chart

The Gantt chart tells us a few things:

a) *Project completion time*: The entire term paper project is expected to take 35 days.
b) *Activity completion times*: Research, writing, and presentation are estimated at 15, (about) 18, and five days, respectively.
c) *Sequence of activities*: Research precedes writing, and writing precedes presentation
d) *Activity interdependencies*: Writing is not 100 percent dependent on research. We do not have to wait for research to be completed in order to begin writing. Preparing and delivering the presentation is 100 percent dependent on writing. We generally do not begin this task without having written out the paper.
e) We could also color an activity or task bar in different colors to show the percent of each activity or task completed, if using the chart for monitoring progress.

Gantt charts are visually simple and popular with smaller projects where the chart(s) is short enough to be read easily. What they do not show are complex task interdependencies, task costs, or the tasks that have the highest risk of delay or failure.

KEY POINTS

- A work breakdown structure (WBS) identifies major activities and the tasks and sub-tasks involved, describing people responsible for such activities and tasks.
- A Gantt chart describes the sequence of activities, the extent of their interdependence, how long they may take, and the estimated project completion time.

From the WBS and Gantt, we proceed to PERT/CPM network diagramming. PERT was developed by the US Navy for planning and managing the Polaris missile project. PERT reads as the 'program evaluation and review technique.' DuPont developed the CPM method to plan plant maintenance projects. CPM stands for 'critical path method.' CPM, as developed, provided firm timelines for tasks since DuPont had years of experience with plant maintenance tasks. On the other hand, the Polaris missile project was the first one of its kind. The Navy used estimates of uncertain task times in PERT and activity sequence to develop a network of activities required to be done to complete a project. Today, almost all network diagramming techniques work with estimated and not exact times. Therefore, let us confine our attention to the PERT method.

PERT

First, let's pick a project. Imagine we are cadets at the police academy. We have been taught that in order to catch a criminal, we have to first put ourselves in their shoes. There are few things more heinous to a cop than a donut crime. As a learning exercise, we sketch out a detailed donut store heist project plan. We note the following: Robberies are generally done at night; cops patrol on the hour; and there is absolutely no violence. The project requires a team of three villains—a security system expert, a donut taster, and Mr. Muscles. Here are the project activities based on a prior WBS and Gantt chart description (not shown here).

Table 13.2 Project Activities—The Great Donut Robbery

Activity	Expected time	Description	Who does the job
A	15 min	Disarm door alarm and camera	Security expert
B	20 min	Prise open door lock	Security expert
C	10 min	Taste donuts on shelves	Donut taster
D	5 min	Take selected donuts out from shelves and place in getaway bag	Mr. Muscles
E	12 min	Disable storeroom camera	Security expert
F	5 min	Empty donuts from storeroom shelves into getaway bag	Mr. Muscles
G	*5 min*	Gather, wipe prints, and RUN!	All
	72 min		

1   Should we go ahead with the project?

The initial reaction is, of course, no! It'll take 72 minutes to pull it off, while the cop patrols come around every 60 minutes. We cannot distract or bribe security. But wait—note that some jobs can be done simultaneously, so the actual total time may be lower than 72 minutes.

2   What is the expected time for completing the project?

We develop a PERT chart (fig 13.6) (shown below) to work out the expected project completion time after accounting for activities that can be performed in parallel.

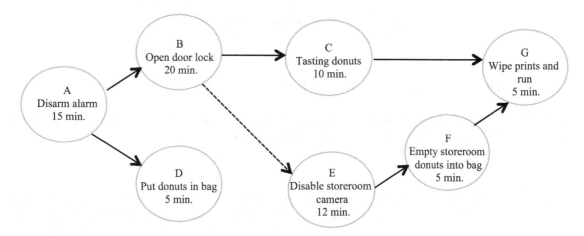

Figure 13.6 PERT Chart—The Great Donut Robbery

There's something missing. Note the arrows identifying activity interdependencies. But are there resource dependencies as well? Yes—our security expert will have to finish activity B before he can move on to activity E, as shown by the dotted arrow. Looking at the PERT chart, we can find out the expected project completion times in two ways:

a)   Find out the longest duration (not # of activities) path(s) in the below network diagram.
b)   Find out the critical (most important) activities and the associated critical path(s).

Taking the first approach, we list out the paths in the above project:

Path   A→B→C→G   = 15 + 20 + 10 + 5   = 50 minutes
Path   A→D→E→F→G = 15 + 5 + 12 + 5 + 5   = 42 minutes
Path   **A→B→E→F→G** = 15 + 20 + 12 + 5 + 5 = **57 minutes**

All the paths need to be completed, so the longest path determines the expected time it'll take to finish the project. That path is **A→B→E→F→G**, and thus the expected project completion time is 57 minutes. This path is called the *critical path*. Can there be more than one longest path in a project? Sure, if they are all of

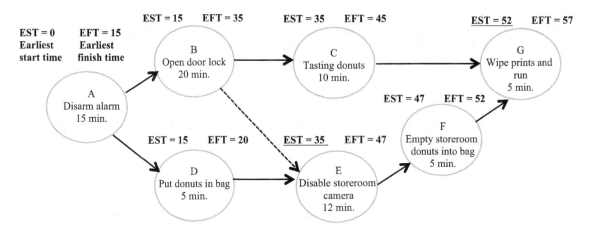

Figure 13.7 PERT Chart 'Forward Sweep'—The Great Donut Robbery

equal duration. We are under 60 minutes, the cop patrol time, so perhaps we can go ahead with the project. If so, what are the activities that we should pay special attention to?

3   What are the most important tasks in the project?

We define 'importance' as being most impactful on project timeliness. There are some activities where some amount of delay will not affect the project completion time. Delays in others will impact project time immediately and directly. These activities where no delay can be tolerated are called *critical activities*. Finding them is a two-step process, requiring a 'forward' sweep and a 'backward' sweep.

First, let's do a 'forward' sweep.

*   A starts at time zero and takes 15 minutes to complete. The earliest we can begin A is time 0 (EST), and the earliest we can finish A is 15 minutes (EFT).
*   B can then begin at minute 15 and takes 20 minutes to do, meaning an EST of 15 minutes and an EFT of 35 minutes.
*   C can start as soon as B is over. Its EST = 35 minutes and EFT = 45 minutes.
*   D is dependent on A but does not have to wait for B. Thus D's EST = 15 minutes and EFT = 20 minutes (takes 5 minutes to do).
*   E *cannot* start until the completion of *two* predecessor activities (B and D). D finishes at minute 20 (EFT), but we have to wait for B to finish, too (EFT = 35 min). So E's EFT = 35 minutes and EFT = 47 minutes.
*   F can begin as soon as E is done, so it has an EST of 47 minutes and an EFT of 52 minutes.
*   G can start *only* after both C and F are finished. Although C finishes at minute 45 (EFT), F ends at minute 52. Thus, activity G's EST = 52 minutes and EFT = 57 minutes.

Project completion time = the time the end activity is completed = 57 minutes.

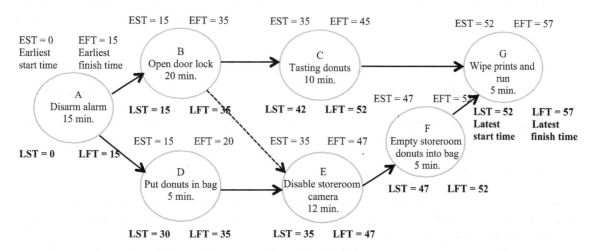

Figure 13.8 PERT chart 'Backward Sweep'—The Great Donut Robbery

We still need to do one more step in order to find the critical activities. That step is called a 'backward' sweep.

- Moving backwards, the end activity G has to be completed by minute 57 (in order to meet the expected project completion time of 57 minutes). The latest finish time (LFT) for G is thus 57 minutes. G takes 5 minutes, which means that it has to be started latest by minute 52 in order to be completed by the LFT of 57 minutes. The latest start time (LST) is therefore 52 minutes.
- F requires to be done by minute 52 to meet G's LST of 52 minutes. It takes 5 minutes to do, so F's latest start time (LST) is 47 minutes, while its LFT = 52 minutes. C's LST = 42 minutes, seeing it takes 10 minutes to get done.
- E's LFT = 47 minutes, since its successor F has to start at the latest by minute 47. E takes 12 minutes to do, so its LST = 35 minutes.
- D can finish as late as minute 35, since E has a LST of 35 minutes. It takes 5 minutes to complete D, so its LST = minute 30.
- C needs to be completed at the latest by 52 minutes in order to satisfy G's LST of 52 minutes. Its LST = minute 42.
- B feeds two activities, C and E. While C can be started at the latest by minute 42, E has an LST of 35 minutes. Thus, B has to be completed by minute 35 (its LFT). It takes 20 minutes to finish B, so it has to begin at the latest by minute 15, its LST.
- Finally, A, which drives both B and D, requires completion at the latest by minute 15, since B has to begin by minute 15.

We can see that there is a time cushion in some activities, and no cushion in others. We call this cushion 'slack.' Activities with slack can be delayed up to the slack period without affecting expected project completion time. However, we cannot afford delays in activities with no slack, since any slippage will adversely affect project completion time proportionately. An activity with zero slack is called a *critical* activity.

$$\text{Slack} = \text{LFT} - \text{EFT, or}$$

$$= \text{LST} - \text{EST} \qquad\qquad\qquad \text{(Equation 13.4)}$$

As table 13.3 shows, our *critical* activities are A, B, E, F, and G. The path that connects these critical activities,

$$A \rightarrow B \rightarrow E \rightarrow F \rightarrow G,$$

is called the *critical* path. The critical path is the longest path in the project network, in terms of time. The duration of this path equals 57 minutes, the expected project completion time. A project may have multiple critical paths, all of the same duration.

We pay very close attention to critical activities since any delay (or early completion) in these will be detrimental (beneficial) to project completion time. We can afford to be more lax for activities that have substantial slack. Delays (or early completions) up to the slack period, will not affect project completion time. Activities that have very little slack are called *near-critical* activities. These are monitored regularly, since delays may consume the small amount of slack quickly. Our current project does not have any near-critical activities.

Table 13.3 Critical Activities —The Great Donut Robbery

Activity	Slack	Critical Activity?	Remarks
A	0 min (LFT—EFT = 15—15 = 0) Or, (LST—EST = 0—0 = 0)	Yes	A delay of 1 min e.g., will delay the project completion time by 1 min, i.e., to 58 min instead of 57 min. Likewise, a saving of 1 min. will shorten project completion time to 56 min. Try re-computing the project completion time with times of 16 min or 14 min for A.
B	0 min	Yes	Same as A above
C	7 min (52—45 = 7); Or, (42—35 = 7)	No	Even if C is delayed by 7 min, the project completion time (57 min) will stand. Try re-computing the project completion time with times of 11 or 9 min for C.
D	15 min	No	Delay of up to 15 min will not delay project completion time.
E	0 min	Yes	Delay's detrimental to project completion time
F	0 min	Yes	Same as E above
G	0 min	Yes	Same as F above

4   What is the probability of being able to finish the project in 55 minutes?

The current expected project completion time of 57 minutes seems to be cutting it too close for safety—remember, the cops come around every 60 minutes. We shall be more comfortable with a larger margin of safety, say, five minutes. So what is the probability that we shall be able to pull it off in 55 minutes? Recall that 57 minutes is the *expected* completion time for our donut heist project. This time is based on the sum of the individual activity times of the critical activities. The individual activity times, in turn, are the means of multiple estimates for individual activity completion times.

We collect three time estimates for every activity from our (experienced) team members, one each for the most optimistic (a), most likely (m), and most pessimistic (b) scenarios. We base these estimates on what is possible with current available resources. In other circumstances, we may also consult subcontractors and others with deep experience in that activity. Using the three estimates, we develop the mean and variance of each activity time. Individual activity times are distributed as a beta distribution, where:

$$\text{Mean} = \frac{a + 4m + b}{6} \qquad \text{(Equation 13.5)}$$

$$\text{and Variance} = \frac{(b-a)^2}{(6)^2} \qquad \text{(Equation 13.6)}$$

Project variance does not include noncritical activities, since they have time cushions that can accommodate (some) variance.

Now, what we wish to know is the probability of being able to complete the project within 55 minutes. We wish a buffer of at least 5 min, to escape being caught by the cops on their every 60 minutes patrols. Project completion times are distributed in our familiar bell shaped normal curve shape.

Table 13.4 Activity Expected Times—The Great Donut Robbery

Activity	Most optimistic time 'a'	Most likely time 'm'	Most pessimistic time 'b'	Mean	Variance
A	13 min	15 min	17 min	15 min*	0.45 min*
B	14 min	21 min	22 min	20 min	1.78 min
C	8 min	10 min	12 min	10 min	0.45 min
D	5 min	5 min	5 min	5 min	0.00 min
E	8 min	11 min	20 min	12 min	4.00 min
F	4 min	5 min	6 min	5 min	0.11 min
G	3 min	4 min	11 min	5 min	1.78 min

* Mean for A = $\frac{a + 4m + b}{6} = \frac{13 + 4*15 + 17}{6} = 15\,\text{min}$

* Variance for A = $\frac{(b-a)^2}{(6)^2} = \frac{(17-13)^2}{(6)^2} = 0.45\,\text{min}$

Project variance = $\sum \sigma_p^2$ = sum of variance of critical activities = (0.45 + 1.78 + 4.00 + 0.11 + 1.78) = 8.12

Project standard deviation = $\sqrt{\text{Project variance}} = \sqrt{\sum \sigma_p^2} = \sqrt{8.12} = 2.85$

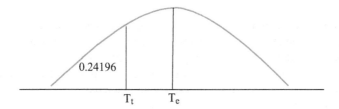

Figure 13.9 Distribution of Project Completion Times

T_t = desired target time = 55 min
T_e = expected project completion time = 57 min
$\sqrt{\sum \sigma_p^2}$ = project standard deviation = 2.85 min (from table 13.4)
Now how many standard deviations removed is T_t from T_e? Or other words, convert T_t into a Z variable.

$$Z = \frac{T_t - T_e}{\sqrt{\sum \sigma_p^2}}$$ (Equation 13.7)

$$Z = \frac{55 - 57}{2.85} = (-)0.70$$

The area to the left of a Z value of $(-)\,0.70 = 0.24196$ (from normal curve table, or using Excel).

The probability of being able to complete our donuts heist project within 55 minutes is just 24.20 percent. This is low—a sure route to Rikers prison, if anyone were to attempt it! So now we ask . . .

5   How can we increase the probability of being able to finish the project in 55 minutes?

We do it by reducing project activity expected times, adding more resources (people/tools) to our project. We call it *crashing* a project. Which activities should we target for crashing? Critical ones, obviously, since a reduction of activity time in a noncritical activity would simply add to the safety cushion (slack) that already exists in the latter. On the other hand, shaving off a minute from a critical activity would reduce total expected project completion time by a minute. Assume that our experts have come up with estimates of possible time reductions and associated costs for crashing our project (table 13.5). We need to reduce the project completion time from 57 minutes to 55 minutes, that is, get a two-minute reduction. Which activity should we crash? The critical activity that has the lowest crash cost/minute.

In this case, we can crash G by a maximum of one minute at a cost of $40. We need to reduce the project time by one more minute. We also crash B, the next cheapest crash cost activity, by one minute. It costs us $60. We have our two minute reduction at a total *additional* cost of $100. We can add a 10 to 15 percent cushion to this $100 additional cost estimate to cater to unanticipated events. Be aware that crashing a critical activity may, at times, change the critical path in a project. Some existing critical activities may become non-critical, while some noncritical activities may become critical. In our case, this does not happen, since the target time reduction is only two minutes, compared to the much greater slack available in the noncritical activities. What if two critical activities have the same cost/minute crash cost? One might choose to crash the one with the larger variance (risk).

Table 13.5 Project Crashing—The Great Donut Robbery

Activity	Normal expected time (NT)	Normal cost (NC)*	Crash time (CT)⁺	Crash cost (CC)⁺	Maximum possible crash period	Crash cost per minute*
A	15 min	$100	14 min	$120	1 min	$120/min
B	20 min	$150	18 min	$270	2 min	$60/min
C	10 min	$120	2 min	$160	2 min	$20/min
D	5 min	$100	1 min	$128	4 min	$28/min
E	12 min	$280	11min	$350	1 min	$70/min
F	5 min	$ 80	5 min	$ 80	0 min	–
G	5 min	$100	4 min	$140	1 min	$40/min

*Crash cost per minute $= \frac{CC-NC}{NT-CT}$

⁺Costs and crash times are all assumed.

After crashing, our project's critical path remains unchanged at

$$A \rightarrow B \rightarrow E \rightarrow F \rightarrow G,$$

but now the total duration of these paths equals 55 minutes instead of the original 57 minutes. The new, reduced, expected project completion time is now 55 minutes, and the probability of completing the project within this time is now 50 percent. This probability is a huge improvement over the earlier 55 minutes completion probability figure of 24.20 percent, but is it enough? What completion time would give us a good chance of pulling off the project without getting caught by the every-60-minutes cop patrols? We call a 'good chance' as, say, a 90 percent probability. So, we need to find that desired target time, x, that translates into a probability of 90 percent. Working with the post (after) crashing project time figures:

T_t = desired target time = x min
T_e = expected project completion time = 55 min
$\sqrt{\Sigma\sigma^2_p}$ = project standard deviation = 2.85 min (unchanged from table 13.4)
Desired probability of completing the project within x minutes = 90% = 0.9000
Z associated with a probability of 0.9000 = 1.30 (from normal curve table, or using Excel)
Thus:

$$Z = \frac{T_t - T_e}{\sqrt{\Sigma\sigma^2_p}}$$

Or,

$$1.30 = \frac{x - 55}{2.85}$$

$x = (1.30 \times 2.85) + 55 = 58.72$ minutes

With a (crashed) expected project completion time of 55 minutes, there is a 90 percent chance that we'll be able to carry out the project successfully within 58.72 minutes. That's still too uncomfortably close to that cop patrol every 60 minutes. We'll have to put more resources to crash the expected project completion time (T_e) to lower than 55 minutes—say, to 52 minutes. In that case, our computed target time (T_t) for a 90 percent probability of success would be:

$$Z = \frac{T_t - T_e}{\sqrt{\Sigma \sigma_p^2}}$$

Or,

$$1.30 = \frac{x - 52}{2.85}$$

$$(T_t) = x = (1.30 \times 2.85) + 52 = 55.70 \text{ min}$$

So crashing the project to an expected completion time of 52 minutes would give us a 90 percent probability of pulling off our donuts project within 55.70 minutes. This target time of 55.70 minutes provides, to our reckoning, an acceptable margin of safety over the 60-minute-window constraint imposed by the cop patrols. The question now is, of course, does our payoff from the donut heist compensate for the increased cost of the crashed project? That depends on how much we like donuts!

With multiple critical paths, we'll have to crash each path by the same amount of time in order to crash the project expected completion time. Our project, though, has just one critical path.

KEY POINTS

- PERT (or CPM) develops project diagrams that show activities, activity times, and activity precedence.
- The critical path(s) in a PERT project diagram is the path(s) of the longest duration path(s). The duration of the critical path is the expected duration of the entire project.
- Every activity that falls on a critical path(s) is called a critical activity. A critical activity has zero slack (LFT − EFT or LST − EST = 0). A noncritical activity has positive slack.
- Since critical activities have zero time cushions, they are watched and monitored carefully. A minute's delay (or reduction) in a critical activity means a corresponding minute's delay (or reduction) in the overall duration of a project.
- Activity time estimates are built on three estimates: optimistic, most likely, and pessimistic. These can be used to estimate the probability of finishing a project within a target time.
- We crash a project by reducing critical activity times. We reduce the expected duration of critical activities by adding more resources (dollars) to such activities.
- Critical paths can change when we crash critical activities.

13.4 Was It Done Right?

A perfect project completion would mean an 'on time, within budget, and to specifications' delivery to satisfied users by a satisfied project team. Perfection, though, is hard to achieve. The PMI's 'project of the year' is a good place to look for project success stories.

OM IN PRACTICE

"Shave US$100 million from a project's budget and your stakeholders will likely be thrilled. Shave another US$100 million from the budget, and the entire project management profession will likely take notice," wrote Cyndee Miller of PMI in a blog post about the organization's annual Project of the Year Award in 2011. Larry Catalano, city projects manager for the Prairie Waters project of Aurora, CO, and his project team did just that. The project was delivered two months ahead of schedule for US$653 million, $200 million less than the budgeted $853 million. How? "Excellent project management" and "a little bit of luck," said Catalano as he accepted the award.

The project scope included constructing a 34-mile, 60-inch pipeline, four pump stations, a natural purification area, and a state-of-the-art water-treatment facility. The project manager had to organize, coordinate, and satisfy multiple stakeholders and resources, included one program management firm, construction managers, city project managers, design engineering firms, general contractors, various attorneys, regulatory agencies, property easements, permits, and city council members representing 330,000 people "that weren't too happy about their water bills being increased," according to Catalano. Working closely, the project team and contractors tried to discover cost savings without collateral damage. Such cost savings were split evenly with the city and the contractors.

In a world where public projects are usually associated with waste and inefficiencies, the Prairie Waters project stands out as a testimony to the value and importance of excellence in project management.

Adapted from: Cyndee Miller, " 'Miracle' Project Wins PMI Project of the Year Award," blog post, *PMI,* Oct. 23, 2011, http://www.projectmanagement.com/blog/Voices-on-Project-Management/8742/ (watch videos of award ceremonies at http://www.pmi.org/About-Us/Our-Professional-Awards/Project-of-the-Year-Award.aspx).

Yet reports of projects failing to meet their original goals and business intent abound. In September 2012, UK officials abandoned what is considered to be the world's largest public IT project of all time. The project, begun in 2002, was a massive undertaking by the UK's National Health System (NHS) to provide electronic health records for all UK citizens. It was axed as targets on dates, functionality, usage, and levels of benefit had been delayed or reduced, and it did not fit NHS's current needs. The cost overruns were more than double the original budget of £6.2 billion.[4] The project was seen as a top-down decision to impose centralization on a decentralized system of administering medicine to widely different patient segments. Political and technical problems debilitated the project, which at the end served as an example of "what not to do." Closer to home, the recently introduced New York City 911 digital system is being blamed for causing delayed ambulance response times, allegedly leading to fatalities. Montclair State University in New Jersey recently sued Oracle over a PeopleSoft project, a planned replacement for its legacy system. Who, or what, is to blame for project failures?

The reasons could be placed in three categories: scope, process, and people.

Scope is defined by specifications and the statement of work drawn up at the planning stage. Sometimes, the scope entirely misses a not-so-obvious yet fundamental factor for project success. For example, a project designed to improve learning by providing iPads to school children may not work well in poor regions. Kids cannot focus if they are hungry. Free school lunches (and perhaps dinners) need to be provided, but this association may not have naturally occurred to project planners. Other times, unforeseen issues come to the fore as the project is executed. This author's kitchen cabinet replacement project turned into a complete kitchen counter-top, floor and appliances replacement job, since the old appliances did not 'match' the new cabinets. Late realizations and epiphanies lead to 'scope creep' or, in the case of product design, 'feature creep.' It is impossible to foresee all changes and eventualities, so some amount of scope creep is inevitable. This underlines the importance of having a formal process for handling change issues with project stakeholders.

Process failures happen when reality and expectations clash during execution. Sometimes the business case is founded on shaky grounds. *The Economist* reports that projections of passenger traffic used to justify various rail projects were up to 400 percent higher than what eventually was experienced.[5] Overly optimistic assumptions about activity times and costs are made to win a project. The average budget overrun for producing the Olympic Games since 1976 has been around 200 percent. Closer to home, the Boston Big Dig came in 324 percent over cost, while the Verazzano Bridge in NYC exceeded initial estimates by 384 percent. The highest reported cost overrun happened with the Canadian Firearm Registry project. It was originally estimated to cost $2 million and was completed with a massive 36,917 percent higher cost overrun.[6] In general, people underestimate the level of effort required for a task, especially when they do not have enough experience in that job. Remember your experience completing your first term paper project in college? We also tend to forget that we cannot work at 100 percent all the time. We need to accommodate unexpected events such as team member sickness, sick kids, travel delays, babysitter no-shows, supplier/subcontractor issues, special training, equipment problems, information delays, and other accidents and emergencies. A 16-hour job that technically requires, say, two FTEs' worth of effort may actually take four FTEs to accomplish. Process failures also happen when risks are not anticipated or managed properly. Contingency buffers of time and cost are necessary to absorb what cannot be foreseen. The size of and justification for such buffers will be determined by past experience. While the technically recommended way to estimate activity completion time is by taking three estimates, optimistic, most likely, and pessimistic, practice may deviate. Managers look at times taken for similar activities in other projects. Given that we may not initially know if an expert or novice will be available to do a particular activity, the three estimate approach takes a conservative approach to time estimation. Another misconception is that uncertainty in activity times will be offset over a period of time—that a randomly high completion time for an activity will be offset by a randomly low completion time in another activity, and so the average times will prevail. This is not likely to happen.

Activities A and B run *at the same time*, and *both have to be completed* in order to deliver the product.

Activity A has a 50 percent probability of completion in five days and a 50 percent probability of completion in nine days.

Activity B has a 50 percent probability of completion in four days and a 50 percent probability of completion in eight days.

What is the expected product delivery time? Activities are independent.

Event	Probability	Combined probability	Days required to deliver product
1. A takes 5 days	0.50	0.25	5 days (A takes longer)
B takes 4 days	0.50		
(Best case)			
2. A takes 9 days	0.50	0.25	9 days
B takes 4 days	0.50		
3. A takes 5 days	0.50	0.25	8 days (B takes longer)
B takes 8 days	0.50		
4. A takes 9 days	0.50	0.25	9 days
B takes 8 days	0.50		
(Worst case)			

Expected delivery time = 0.25 * 5 days + 0.25 * 9 days + 0.25 * 8 days + 0.25 * 9 days = 7.75 days

The best case is 1., when both activities are done early. Cases 2. and 3. represent instances of highs and lows of both activities, respectively—but note that the delivery periods are similar—and similar to 4., the worst case situation. There's just a 25 percent chance that the best case (1.) would happen.

A has an average time of seven days (0.50 * 5 days + 0.50 * 9 days) and B similarly has an average time of six days. Recall that they run at the same time, so the average delivery time computes to seven days (A's time). But the expected delivery time with uncertainty is not seven days but rather 7.75 days. So a high in one activity does not offset a low in another, and the average *does not* prevail.

Multi-tasking is another culprit in project delays.[7] Switching people back and forth among different tasks or projects creates friction. Besides the time lost in mentally switching from one job to another, the cumulative effect on individual job times is significant. For example, there are three tasks in different projects that need an expert. In single tasking, the expert does the tasks in order of arrival.[8]

$$\frac{\text{Single tasking}}{\text{Expert takes}} \quad \frac{\text{Project A}}{\text{5 days}} \quad \text{moves on to} \quad \frac{\text{Project B}}{\text{5 days}} \quad \text{moves on to} \quad \frac{\text{Project C}}{\text{5 days}}$$

Total time taken to
do task in Project A   *5 days*

In multi-tasking, our expert jumps between jobs:

$$\frac{\text{Multi-tasking}}{\text{Expert does}} \quad \frac{\text{Project A}}{\substack{\text{50\% of A} \\ \text{in 2.5 days}}} \quad \text{switches to} \quad \frac{\text{Project B}}{\substack{\text{50\% of B} \\ \text{in 2.5 days}}} \quad \text{switches to} \quad \frac{\text{Project C}}{\substack{\text{50\% of C} \\ \text{in 2.5 days}}} \quad \text{returns to} \quad \frac{\text{Project A}}{\substack{\text{completes} \\ \text{A in 2.5 days}}}$$

Total time taken to
do task in Project A   *10 days* (2.5 days + 5 days waiting while expert works on Projects B and C
+ 2.5 days to complete remaining work at Project A)

People failures are perhaps the most difficult to pinpoint in advance and to treat. A senior sponsor suddenly loses interest in the project. Project Management Institute research shows that having "actively engaged executive sponsors is the top driver of project success. Yet this research also shows that fewer than two-thirds of projects and programs have assigned executive sponsors."[9] Many among those projects have suffered from sponsor overextension (sponsor for multiple projects), lack of communication between the sponsor and project manager, and inadequate resources allotted for sponsor development in the organization. People failures happen at the project level, too. A weak team member derails and demoralizes the entire team. A 'superstar' creates motivation and coordination problems for the whole team. A friend of this author who has led and managed large projects for 20 years has a firm principle. No one is indispensable. A team member was not regular in attending team meetings or visiting clients. The employee was a client favorite but was fired nevertheless. The client was informed about the reasons and reassured that the project would not be allowed to be affected. Most clients understand since they have faced similar situations themselves. Then there are 'heroes,' who can also deliberately delay activities or go on 'suicide' missions to get a chance to shine in an emergency. Such 'suicide missions' should not be rewarded, as a routine feature. People also tend to conceal bad news. An intimidating project manager may not even hear about bad news from subordinates until it's too late in the day. Another common manager practice, especially in bigger organizations with large resources, is to throw people at a delayed task. There are natural limits to team size and activity reduction potential beyond which added personnel create conflict, confusion, and other dysfunctionalities. A two-person team requires just one communication channel—add another two people, and the number of communication channels jumps to six! So, too, rise the chances of miscommunications, misunderstandings, confusion, conflict, and delay.

Too many cooks can indeed spoil the broth! People-level incompatibilities with clients also affect project performance. A techie may not have the nicest personality—keep him away from direct client contact. Sometimes, we do not know who in the client's organization will eventually declare the project a success or failure. Find the real stakeholders early and keep them apprised of project progress. Other times, every stakeholder assumes that the project will give them everything they wanted. Conflicting requirements and necessary compromises have to be clarified early on.

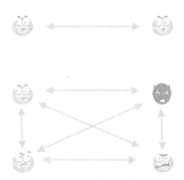

Figure 13.10 Team Size and Communication Issues

The best executed project will fail if it's not accepted and used by the organization. A structured plan on how to persuade employees to understand and accept changes in routines and practices is called change management. The PMI stresses that change management should address both the "hearts and minds of employees." "Minds" listen to reason and incentives, including rewards, disincentives, metrics, organizational structure and responsibilities, and training. The "hearts" aspect deals with questions such as "why do we have to change," crafting a "story of change" that tells about what it will mean to individual jobs and contributions, discovering and developing homegrown 'change champions,' and keeping morale up in times of change. Change management is not linear but iterative in nature, requiring continuous communication, feedback, and engagement right from the early stages of a project.

Projects will fail sometimes. Like star athletes, a standout characteristic of good project managers is the ability to recycle and rebound quickly after a failure. They analyze the reasons, remove the memory of failure, and apply lessons learned to the next job. What went well? What did not? If we had to do it all over again, what would we do differently? What lessons have we learned that we can codify, document, and use in other projects? If we can query and learn, the next project is more likely to be done 'right.'

KEY POINTS

- Projects fail because of deficient scope, process, or people.
- Scope creep leads to incremental addition of features and work effort.
- Process failures arise when task times are underestimated or utilization of resources is overestimated.
- Multi-tasking creates friction and extends individual task completion durations.
- People problems include prima donnas and weak team members, personality incompatibilities, and unrealistic (but not yet clarified as such) stakeholder expectations.

13.5 Current Trends in Project Management

What's happening in the world of project management? In a recent study, PMI found a positive trend among companies for emphasizing change management and risk management issues in project planning. More companies created a formal PMO (program management office) to evaluate, select, oversee, and coordinate a portfolio of projects. The use of EVM (earned value management—see appendix at end of chapter) and other formal project management approaches also showed an increase. What declined, ironically, were company investments in formal programs to develop project management competencies in managers. Where would these companies get qualified people to staff and run their PMOs? My friends in industry complain about how large organizations aggravate problems by throwing more personnel at project delays without first training them in project management principles. In smaller organizations, project personnel may acquire deep expertise that is limited to a few specific types of projects or are spread thin over multiple projects and thus don't really learn much.

In other trends, globalization has created huge opportunities for project managers to directly manage far-flung projects. Project managers are charged with program management, overseeing and orchestrating a portfolio of projects scattered around the world. Responsibilities extend to project portfolio selection and evaluation, vendor bid scrutiny and personnel skill set evaluation for awarding projects, resource allocation, external mentoring, and fiduciary responsibilities, all in a climate of constant change. Perhaps because of the current economic/political uncertainties in all world markets, another trend is towards smaller, shorter time horizon projects, aimed at tomorrow rather than multiple years ahead. Projects are now easier to conduct with advances in visual and audio communication technology. When Hurricane Sandy hit New York City and New Jersey in October 2012, this author noticed many cars parked with people inside around functioning libraries. They were using the library's wireless network to remotely connect to their office computers and work with their project teams around the world. Eventually, work slowed down, as office computers were gradually taken offline in order to conserve scarce generator gas for office emergency operations.

13.5.1 Project Evaluation Using Real Options

Rising uncertainties in the business environment have complicated project outcome evaluation. Real options theory offers a new way to add on to the traditional NPV and similar project evaluation methods. Real options represent the opportunity in a project to take some decision in the future. There is, however, no obligation to do so when that time in the future arrives. There may be a small price to pay for reserving the option to make a decision later, without having to make it now. Managers may have an intuitive feel about such options but may not make an explicit, comprehensive examination of projects using options criteria. Some of these options are:[10]

- *Growth*: A project has the potential to generate more projects or follow-on revenue and growth opportunities.
- *Stage*: Project investment is made in stages such that large 'sunk costs' are not incurred early on.
- *Scale*: Scope, budgets, timelines, and resources can be ramped up or down relatively easily. IT and web projects are commonly scalable since incremental costs are low.
- *Switch*: A project can be put to alternative use, if required or, in the case of a production project, can use different-than-planned-for inputs without losing value, e.g., a power plant that can switch between natural gas and coal.
- *Defer*: Project start can be deferred without losing the opportunity and reasons to invest—a wait-and-see investment approach to changing conditions, where the opportunity also will wait for us to accept or reject at a later time. An example, is deferring the decision to build a distribution center for a year to better study traffic and demand changes. An option to lease the land would probably be purchased.
- *Abandon*: The flexibility to abandon an on-going project and re-deploy or sell the remaining project resources and expected future cash flows elsewhere is particularly useful for capital-intensive projects like airlines, power plants, and railroads.

Computing option values is not in the scope of this introductory text. Option valuation is based on the well known Black-Scholes option-pricing model (ring a bell, finance majors?).[11] However, common sense can tell us if the presence or absence of an option hurts or benefits a particular project. Specific projects may weight these options differently. Also, projects with high uncertainties and borderline NPVs may pay more attention to real options in order to strengthen the case for selection. High NPV projects are an easy approval decision and may not even need the support of potential real option values. Sometimes though, an absence of options is bad news:

OM IN PRACTICE

A Project Without an Abandonment Option

A deserted construction site in NJ marks the unfinished mouth of the abandoned ARC commuter rail-road tunnel beneath the Hudson river, to make another connection from New Jersey to Manhattan, New York. The project was designed to alleviate the frequent rush hour and bad weather/tunnel maintenance caused waiting of stalled trains at the existing rail tunnels connecting NJ with NY. After an initial expenditure of about half-billion dollars, NJ State and NJ Transit, a partially state funded agency, abandoned the $9.8 billion project in 2010 because of anticipated cost overruns. The overruns may have added another four billion taxpayer dollars to the project. The problem was that the project planners did not seem to have considered an abandonment option while evaluating project viability. The outcomes from resources spent could not be deployed elsewhere and there was no significant salvage value. In fact, NJ Transit is still paying out millions of dollars in closing costs.

The federal authorities claimed $271 million as reimbursement of money it had spent on project work—settled for $95 million by NJ. Land owners in Hoboken and Weehawken, NJ, were awarded $8.15 million to compensate them for eminent domain property take-overs by the state. The agency also agreed to pay $5.6 million to a design company, BJJV, who reportedly had completed more than half of the final design plans, drawings and reports. The only redeeming feature was a possibility that the design documents could still be used if the project was ever resuscitated. But that's about the only salvage value from the abandoned project. No one had apparently taken a hard look at potential abandonment options while evaluating the NJ-NYC Hudson rail tunnel project.

Adapted from: Mike Frassinelli and Jennifer Brown, "NJ Transit Still Paying Price for Canceled Hudson River Rail Tunnel," *The Star-Ledger*, Oct. 16, 2012.

13.5.2 Critical Chain Project Management

If asked to estimate time for an activity, an experienced hand would probably pad that estimate with a safety buffer to allow for surprises. The late Dr. Eliyahu M. Goldratt asked why, then, are so many projects delayed? His observations suggested that such safety buffers are eaten away by human faults. We know that we have a safety buffer and so delay beginning the task or do the work slower. Sometimes we multi-task several activities or projects, and that, too, consumes safety buffers. Other times we do the task early but deliberately delay announcing the early finish for fear of pressurizing or overloading the person doing the next task. Goldratt's book *Critical Chain*[12] proposed a new way to manage projects that extended the traditional PERT/CPM focus on critical path to include the critical chain.

The critical chain project management (CCPM) considers both the critical activities and resource constraints. CCPM works backward from a completion date, with each task beginning as late as possible (LST). Two times are estimated for a task. One uses an aggressive time with a 50 percent chance of completion probability and the other a time that has a 90 to 95 percent chance of completion probability. Resources are assigned to each task, keeping the aggressive 50 percent completion time estimates. The longest sequence of resource-leveled tasks that lead from beginning to end of the project is then identified as the critical chain. The difference between the 90 to 95 percent completion probability time estimates and the 50 percent completion probability time estimates is collected and positioned as a pooled buffer. Using the aggressive 50 percent probability task times to time and monitor individual task performance means elimination of all slack. No slack forces focus on the task at hand. The objective is to remove the temptation to delay work or to do extra work when there seems to be time. Employing 50 percent completion probability task times means that some tasks will not be completed in time. The task leader can then request the project manager to release some of the pooled safety time. For the project manager, monitoring becomes a simple matter of keeping track of who asks for more time from the collective buffer. If the rate of buffer consumption is low, the project is on target. If high, measures need to be taken at the task level to see what the problem is and resolve it.

CCMP is being adopted by more businesses, reportedly with promising results.

KEY POINTS

- Smaller and quicker deliverables projects are becoming more popular.
- Portfolio selection and management skills are becoming valuable in overseeing and orchestrating a global portfolio of projects.
- Real options theory from finance is finding use in valuing project growth, deferment, stage, scale, switching, and abandonment options. This goes beyond conventional NPV valuations.
- Critical chain project management (CCPM) removes time cushions in individual activity time estimates but provides a pooled time buffer that everyone can draw on. The advantage is that the project manager can identify and question large 'withdrawers' and also react quickly when the pooled buffer sees a lot of withdrawal requests.

13.6 Conclusion

Customer: *"Why should I choose you?"*
Business: *"Because we will build and deliver your project at cost, on time, and to your specification."*

Our readings have told us a little about how to keep that promise to the customer. We define a project as a time-bound, temporary job, unique and consisting of interrelated activities with specific goals, scope, and budget. A project passes through four phases: initiation, planning, implementation, and closure. During these phases, project managers manage three things—performance, people, and change. Performance is evaluated in three key dimensions: cost, scope, and time. Softer goals may include team and client people motivation, integrity, trust, and other parameters. People in projects are organized in functional or matrix structures, team members reporting in varying degrees to functional heads or to the project manager, as the case may be. We evaluate a project using different methods depending on the level of uncertainty of cash flows and the duration of the cash flows. We describe a project with a work breakdown structure (WBS), which in turn, evolves into a Gantt chart and a detailed PERT or CPM network diagram. PERT can provide estimates for project completion time, critical activities, critical paths, probability of completion within a certain time, and resources required to shorten project duration. Once a project starts, we can monitor its progress using the EMV suite of methods that track variances of cost and schedule. Projects run into problems when resources multi-task or delay tasks, taking comfort in inbuilt time safety cushions. The critical chain project management (CCPM) approach attempts to resolve these problems by holding individual task times to a stringent schedule while simultaneously keeping an available common pool of buffer time that people can draw on, but on special request. People issues in projects are particularly sensitive and complex to manage. Team composition and how superstars are managed affects both team morale and performance.

Remember times when you worked all-nighters cheerfully and willingly with others, with little sleep and lots of pizza? There was a camaraderie and shared enthusiasm that made us connect intensely with the job, our team, and our goals. Rewards were not the chief concern at the time—living the experience was. You can call yourself a good project manager when you can make that happen for your team and your clients.

What Have We Learned?

What Is Project Management?

- A project is a work job of interrelated work activities that is unique, temporary, has clear goals, a clear start and end, and a defined cost and time budget.
- Project goals are defined in terms of scope, cost, and time.
- Project management involves the planning, scheduling, and coordination of project scope, project activities, project resources, project risk, and project clients toward the achievement of project performance goals.

Why Is It Important?

- There is little room for project failure, considering the short product life cycles of today.
- Project work—short, focused, temporary work jobs—are replacing the stable corporate jobs of yesterday.

How Is It Done?

- Each project moves through four phases: initiation, planning, implementation, and closure.

  - Initiation creates a project charter describing scope, goals, deliverables, and governance.
  - Planning involves plans for tasks, risks, quality, communication, and vendor management.
  - Implementation involves monitoring and managing change and cost/time variances.
  - Closure requires final deliverables, termination of vendor contracts, release plans for project personnel, lessons-learned sessions and document archiving.

- Projects teams are organized in functional or matrix fashion, the latter placing members directly under the project manager's control for task execution and evaluation and reward purposes.
- Work effort is reckoned in terms of FTEs (full time equivalents).
- Payback period, NPV, and IRR are typical techniques used for evaluating projects. Uncertain cash flows require maximin, maximax, minimax regret, and expected monetary value calculations.
- Work breakdown structure (WBS) breaks down tasks into subtasks, with accountability.
- Gantt charts provide visual information on activity and project completion time and activity inter-dependencies.
- PERT/CPM network diagrams show activity times and relationships, the expected completion time, and the probability of completing a project within a certain time.

- A critical activity in a PERT chart is one that has no slack (spare time). Any delay (early completion) would directly and proportionately delay (shorten) project completion time.
- The path(s) that links critical activities together is called a critical path(s). It is the path(s) with the longest duration in a project.
- Crashing a project reduces completion time by crashing critical activities with additional resources, lowest-crash-cost critical activities being reduced first.
- Projects fail because of scope, process, and people issues.
- Real options evaluates the value of possible options to defer, stage, grow, scale, switch, or abandon projects
- CCPM (critical chain project management) proposes building and monitoring a centralized safety time buffer to replace the time buffers often built into individual activity time estimates.

Key Formulas

$$\textbf{\# of FTEs } required = \frac{Person\ day\ estimate\ of\ effort}{Required\ completion\ time \times \#\ of\ working\ days/mo}$$

$$\textbf{NPV} = CF_0 + CF_1/(1 + r) + CF_2/(1 + r)^2 + CF_3/(1 + r)^3 + \ldots + CF_t/(1 + r)^t$$

Where, CF_t = cash flow at time t, and r = cost of capital
ROI = NPV/PV of cash outflows
IRR computation (solve for IRR)

$$0\ (NPV) = CF_0 + CF_1/(1 + IRR) + CF_2/(1 + IRR)^2 + CF_3/(1 + IRR)^3 + \ldots + CF_t/(1 + IRR)^t$$

PERT
Slack = latest finish time (LFT) − earliest finish time (EFT), or
    = latest start time (LST) − earliest start time (EST)
Activity expected time = mean time = $\dfrac{a + 4m + b}{6}$

Variance of activity time = $\dfrac{(b-a)^2}{(6)^2}$

Where a = most optimistic time m = most likely time   b = most pessimistic time,
Probability of completing a project in time task in T_t

$$Z = \frac{T_t - T_e}{\sqrt{\Sigma\sigma_p^2}} = \frac{55 - 57}{2.85} = (-)0.70$$

T_t = desired target time
T_e = expected project completion time
$\sqrt{\Sigma\sigma_p^2}$ = project standard deviation
Crash cost per minute = $\frac{CC-NC}{NT-CT}$, where CC = crash cost; NC = normal cost; NT = normal time;
NC = normal cost

Discussion Questions

1 From all that you see around you in college and elsewhere, identify work that looks like a project. Similarly, identify work that looks like a process. State your reasons for such classifications.
2 Briefly explain the comparative utility of WBS, Gantt charts and PERT diagrams.
3 By definition, all critical activities should be monitored equally closely. But given that we have just enough resources to monitor one of two critical activities, how should we pick the one to focus on?

(Instructor—could be the activity with the higher time variance (higher uncertainty), or the activity with the higher potential for political damage, or the activity that the client is monitoring more closely, or. . .?)

4 Why might you like to be the team leader of a critical activity? Why would you rather not?
5 Project A has a lower NPV than project B, with a similar risk profile. Name at least two business reasons why I should choose project A over project B.
6 What are some of the factors that make a project manager's job more challenging than that of a traditional manager?
7 Why might you like to be assigned to work in a project that follows a functional organization? Why would you rather work in a project with a pure matrix organization?

End of Chapter Problems

1 How many FTEs of work effort would a project estimated to take 500 person days require in order to be completed in four months? Assume 20 working days in a month.

Answer:

Required completion time for a project activity = 4 months
Person day estimate of effort for that project activity = 500 person days, that is, it would take one person 500 working days to complete the activity, working alone.

$$\text{\# of FTEs required} = \frac{Person\ day\ estimate\ of\ effort}{Required\ completion\ time \times 20\ working\ days/mo} = \frac{500\ person\ days}{4\ months \times 20\ days}$$

$$= 6.25\ \text{FTEs}$$

Thus, 6.25 full time equivalents would be required to complete the activity in 4 months.

2 We have to choose between two competing projects. Project A's initial cost is $500,000, and annual cash inflows of $55,000 are anticipated for 10 years. Project B's initial cost is estimated at $800,000, with anticipated annual cash inflows of $120,000 for eight years.

Our cost of capital is 10 percent annually, and we would like a payback period of three years.

a) Using payback period criteria, which project should we pick (if any)?

Answer:

Project A: cost = $500,000
Revenues at $55,000/yr
Time required to recover cost =500,000/55,000 =9.09 yrs

Project B: Cost = $800,000
Revenues at $120,000/yr
Time required to recover cost = 800,000/120,000 = 6.67 yrs
Neither project provides a payback within three years.

b) Using NPV, which project(s) should we pick (if any)?

Answer:

Annual Cost of capital = 10%

$NPV = CF_0 + CF_1/(1 + r) + CF_2/(1 + r)^2 + CF_3/(1 + r)^3 + \ldots + CF_t/(1 + r)^t$ (From Equation 13.2)

Where CF_t = cash flow at time t, and r = cost of capital

Project A NPV = (−) 500,000 + 55,000/(1 + 0.10) + 55,000 (1 + 0.10)^2 + . . . 55,000 (1 + 0.10)^{10}
= **(−) $147,317.10 (use Excel formulas in toolbar)**

Project B NPV = (−) 800,000 + 120,000/(1 + 0.10) + 120,000 (1 + 1.10)^2 + . . . 120,000 (1 + 0.10)^8
= (−) $145,280.78

Neither project offers a positive NPV.

c) Using IRR, which project(s) should we pick?

$0 (NPV) = CF_0 + CF_1/(1 + IRR) + CF_2/(1 + IRR)^2 + CF_3/(1 + IRR)^3 + \ldots + CF_t/(1 + IRR)^t$ (From Equation 13.3)

Answer:

Project A, using the same values as in b) and solving for IRR (use Excel formulas)
IRR = 0.01772 = 1.77% approximately
Project B, using the same values as in b) and solving for IRR (use Excel formulas).
IRR = 0.04239 = 4.24% approximately
Project B has a higher IRR.

3   Which of the following *best* fits the description of a project?

a) Running the assembly line of an auto plant
b) Contributing to Wikipedia at times
c) Surfing the web searching for old OM test questions
d) Developing a cure for cancer
e) Developing a vaccine for cervical cancer

Answer: e; more specific goal than d; a, b, c have no end or finish goalpost.

4   Work breakdown structures (WBS) break down project goals into sub-goals and attach accountability to the performance of these sub-goals and activities.

a) True
b) False

Answer: a

5   A Gantt chart typically DOES NOT add which of the following to the WBS?

a) Sequence among sub-goals and activities
b) Start and finish time for each activity

c)   The extent of interdependence among activities

d)   The probability of not being able to complete an activity on time.

Answer: d

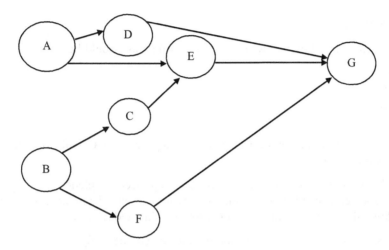

Figure 13.11 PERT Chart for Questions 6. to 9.

Activity	Expected time (weeks)
A	4.0
B	5.5
C	3.5
D	2.0
E	6.5
F	9.0
G	4.5

Use the diagram in figure 13.11 to answer questions 6. to 9.

6   The critical path of this network consists of activities

a)   A-E-F

b)   B-F-G

c)   B-C-E-G

d)   A-E-G

Answer: c. (longest period path)

7   The total expected time of the critical path is ____ weeks.

    a) 40
    b) 38
    c) 20
    d) 25

    Answer: c. 20 weeks

8   If activity C were delayed by two weeks, the project duration would be

    a) reduced
    b) increased
    c) unchanged
    d) cannot say

    Answer: b (because C is on the critical path, and any delay in C will affect the project duration proportionately)

9   Your client demands that you reduce the expected total project completion time by 10 days. You have some spare resources available (labor, money) to throw at a few jobs in order to achieve such a reduction. What kind of activities would you target for task time reduction?

    a) Invest resources for task time reduction on critical activities only.
    b) Invest resources for task time reduction on noncritical activities only.
    c) Invest resources for task time reduction on both critical and noncritical activities.
    d) Reducing activity times, whether critical or noncritical, does not reduce the expected total project completion time.

    Answer: a (because reducing times for critical activities reduces project duration proportionately. Reducing times for noncritical activities does not—because they have slack time).

10   We are preparing to host a concert at school. The PERT chart for our concert prep plan shows six distinct paths (individual activities not shown):

Path#	Expected completion time (days)	Variance (days)
1	20	3.5
2	18	2.8
3	25	3.4
4	12	2.2
5	17	3.1
6	10	1.9

    a) Which path is the critical path?
    b) What is the probability of completing the project within the expected completion time?
    c) What is the probability of completing the project within 30 days? Within 23 days?

Answers:

a) The longest path − Path 3 (25 days)
b) 98.38%

Probability of completing a project in time task in T_t

$$Z = \frac{T_t - T_e}{\sqrt{\sum \sigma_p^2}} = \frac{30 - 25}{\sqrt{3.4}} = 2.71 \quad \text{(which is the project variance for path 3)}$$

T_t = The desired target time
T_e = The expected project completion time
$\sqrt{\sum \sigma_p^2}$ = Project standard deviation (square root of the variance)

From the normal distribution table a Z value of 2.71 covers an area of 0.9838 (area to the left of the Z value).

Similarly, for a target time of 23 days,

$$Z = \frac{23 - 25}{\sqrt{3.4}} = (-) \, 1.09$$

The area to the left of Z for a positive Z value of 1.09 = 0.8621
The area beyond this Z = 1 − 0.8621 = 0.1379 (since 1 is the area covered by the entire curve)
Since the normal distribution curve is symmetrical, the area to the left of (−) 1.09 would also be 0.1379.
So the probability of completing the project within 23 days is 13.79% only.

11 Given the following activities and precedence information,

Activity	Immediate predecessors	Expected completion time
A	−	4
B	−	3
C	A	2
D	A	5
E	B	6
F	C, D	4
G	D, E	5
H	F, G	4

a) Develop a PERT chart of the project.
b) Compute ES, EF, LS, LT times for all activities.
c) Identify critical activities and the critical path(s).
d) State the expected completion time for the project.

12 Consider the following EVM chart (this question is for the appendix section)

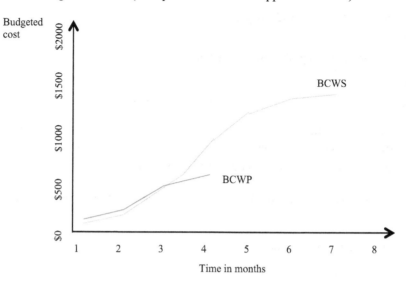

Figure 13.12 EVM Chart

Assume the following:

- At month 4, BCWP = $500; BCWS = $1,000; ACWP = $450
- BAC = $1,500
- OD = Month 7

   a) Approximately till what period of time was the project doing well?
   b) What is the approximate EV at week 4? Is it good news or bad news?
   c) What is our cost variance? Are we over budget or under budget?
   d) What is the SV at week 4?
   e) How late are we running (time variance) at week 4?
   f) What's the CPI? Is it good news or bad news? Why?
   g) What's the EAC?
   h) What's the SPI?
   i) What's the ETTC?

   Prepare a brief report on the health of the project as on month 4, based on the above EVM metrics.

13 You have to choose between competing projects A and B. The required rate of return is 11.00 percent for project A and 10.50 percent for project B. Which project should you accept and why?

Year	Project A	Project B
0	−$48,000	−$126,900
1	$18,400	$69,700
2	$31,300	$80,900
3	$11,700	$0

Suggested Class Projects

1   Prepare a WBS and Gantt chart for a group project that you are doing in any of your classes.
2   Prepare a Gantt chart for the academic curriculum leading to your college degree. What is the expected completion time?

Suggested Cases

Project Management Simulation: Scope, Resources, Schedule

By Robert D. Austin

Publication Date:	Product number:
Sep 01, 2009	3356-HTM-ENG
Discipline:	Length:
Operations Management	90min

Description

In this single-player simulation, the students' primary objective is to bring a competitive product to market on time and on budget, ahead of the competition. Explores trade-offs among the three major project management levers: scope, resources, and schedule. Illustrates importance of and trade-offs associated with level, timing and type of communication Shows the value of coaching and training and examines importance of team member morale on productivity. Aids in illustrating the concept of earned value management. Highlights importance of appropriately timing changes in project resource allocation. Forces students to navigate projects through uncertainty and unanticipated events. Illustrates the concept that correcting problems early in the course of the project provides significant benefit.

Boeing 767: From Concept to Production (A)

By David A. Garvin, Lee C. Field, Janet Simpson
HBS 688040, 19p, B case 688041, TN 689027
Seattle, WA, airplane manufacturing Fortune 500
$9 billion revenues 1970–1981

Description

Describes the evolution of the Boeing 767 from the conception of the project to the start of manufacturing. Shows how the company manages an enormously complex and risky project and introduces students to a variety of estimating and management tools. Subjects: Aircraft; learning curves; manufacturing; operations management; project management.

Other Cases

1   See brief tutorial on Microsoft projects software: http://www.youtube.com/watch?v=sPwURRG9_ Gs&feature=related, accessed April 24, 2015
2   See Dilbert's "why projects fail" at: htttp://www.youtube.com/watch?feature=endscreen&v=52yjQEE dnso&NR=1, accessed April 24, 2015

Notes

1 Adapted from the late Dr. Eliyahu Goldratt's various writings on project management, including the *Critical Chain*. Eliyahu Goldratt, *The Critical Chain*, (Great Barrington, MA: North River Press, 1997).
2 Project Management Institute, "The High Cost of Low Performance 2014," *PMI's Pulse of the Profession,* February 2014, http://www.pmi.org/~/media/PDF/Business-Solutions/PMI_Pulse_2014.ashx.
3 See http://www.workforce.com/articles/sample-project-charter for a specimen project charter document (accessed April 24, 2015).
4 Kirsty Walker, "Will NHS Axe £7bn Electronic Records? Ministers Ready to Pull the Plug on Computer Fiasco," *Daily Mail,* Aug. 3, 2011, http://www.dailymail.co.uk/news/article-2021768/Will-NHS-axe-7bn-electronic-records-Ministers-ready-pull-plug-fiasco.html.
5 "Overdue and Over Budget, Over and Over Again," *The Economist,* June 11, 2005.
6 "15 of the World's Biggest Cost Overrun Projects," / *CIMA*, Jan. 23, 2013, http://www.fm-magazine.com/infographic/prime-number/15-world%E2%80%99s-biggest-cost-overrun-projects#.
7 Goldratt, *Critical Chain.*
8 *CIMA*, "World's Biggest."
9 Project Management Institute and the Boston Consulting Group, "Executive Sponsor Engagement," *Pulse of the Profession@In-Depth Report*, Executive Summary, October 2014, http://www.pmi.org/~/media/PDF/Knowledge%20Center/PMI-Pulse-Executive-Sponsor-Engagement.ashx.
10 R. Fichman, M. Keil, and A.Tiwana, "Beyond Evaluation: Real Options Thinking in IT Project Management," *California Management Review*, 47(2) (2005): 74–96.
11 I found Timothy Luehrman's well-presented "Investment opportunities as real options," *Harvard Business Review,* July–Aug 1998, useful for more advanced classes
12 Goldratt, *Critical Chain.*

APPENDIX: MANAGING PROJECTS

EVM—Earned Value Management

Evaluating the Health of an Ongoing Project

(Optional and to be used at the instructor's discretion.)

We track and estimate the progress of a project using four items: a cost and time budget, actual cost data, actual time data, and forecasts. These are integrated for objective measurement of project health using a method called earned value management (EVM). We can use EVM to answer a variety of questions about project progress and health from both a cost and a time perspective. EVM is particularly appropriate in projects with high labor content and activity variance, where things change often and prompt regular checks.

Question 1: Our actual costs as of today are lower than budget—that's good, right?

Not always. We need to see what percentage of the work scheduled to be completed at that point of time has actually been done. If we have completed 100 percent of the jobs budgeted till that point in time, and done so at a cost lower than budget, let's pat ourselves on the back. But spending less than the budgeted amount could also simply mean that we have not completed 100 percent of the work that was budgeted/scheduled to be done till that point in time. For example, in a project,

- Our budget plan states that x amount of work is scheduled to be completed by week 4.
- The budgeted value of that x amount of work scheduled for completion in week 4 is, say, $100. This is formally called the BCWS (budgeted cost of work scheduled) at that point in time.

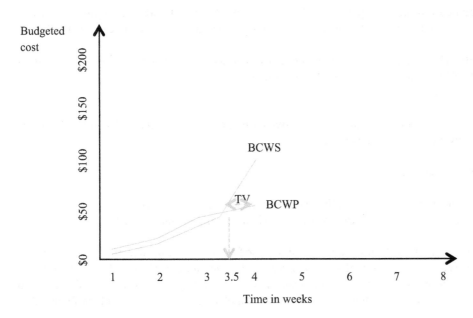

Figure 13.13 EV Computations in a Project

- But after the project begins, we find that only 50 percent of that *x* amount of work scheduled by week 4 has actually been completed by week 4. This is formally called the BCWP (budgeted cost of work performed) at that point in time.

  BCWP = 0.50 * $100 = $50

The earned value (EV) of the project at week 4 is the BCWP figure of $50, or 50 percent of the BCWS. Earned value is the budgeted value of the percent of work actually completed out of the amount of work originally scheduled to be completed by a particular point in time. The EV of a project before work starts is, of course, zero.

We are currently at week 4. As figure 13.13 shows, up to a little beyond week 3, the BCWP line was above the BCWS line. Up to that time, the work *actually* performed in budget dollar terms (BCWP) was ahead of the work *scheduled* to be performed in budget dollar terms (BCWS). After that, the work actually performed, BCWP, fell behind the work scheduled to be performed (BCWS). At the current time (week 4):

  BCWS at week 4 = $100
  BCWP at week 4 = $50
  Thus, *EV* at week 4 = 50% of work scheduled = $50

This is bad news. We have accomplished just 50 percent of the work value scheduled to be completed by week 4.

Question 2: How do our actual costs compare with budget?

Suppose that the actual cost of the work performed (ACWP) by week 4 is $80 (arbitrary figure). We would have actually spent $80 for doing work that is valued at $50 using budgeted rates/value (BCWP). So, our

Cost variance = (BCWP, i.e., budgeted value of work performed within a specific reporting period) *minus*
(ACWP, i.e., actual cost of work performed)
= $50 − $80 = (−) $30

A negative cash variance means *over budget*. A positive cash variance means *under budget*. Effectively, our project is running over cost by $30 at week 4.

Question 3: How late are we?

SV (schedule variance) at week 4 = BCWP − BCWS = $50 − $100 = (−)$50
A negative schedule variance means *late*. A positive schedule variance means *early*.

According to Figure 13.13, week 4 shows a BCWP of $50. So $50 of work, valued at budget, was *actually performed* by week 4. When was that $50 of work *originally scheduled* for completion? The BCWS line in the chart shows that $50 of work should have been done by week 3 1/2, approximately. We took week 4 to actually perform that $50 of work scheduled for week 3 1/2 completion, so we are behind by about half a week.

Time variance = [Time within which a specific budgeted $ amount of work (BCWS) was scheduled to be performed]
minus
[Time when that value of work (BCWP) was actually performed]
Time variance for
a BCWS of $50 = (BCWS of $50: scheduled by week 3 ½) − (BCWP of $50: performed by week 4)
= (−) ½ week

In practice, BCWPs and variances are computed for individual activities or packages of activities. Added up, they present a complete picture of the cost and time performance of the project at every reporting period.

Question 4: Our actual costs as of today are higher than budget—what would be the likely final cost of the entire project?

If actual costs have been seen to be higher till now, using the budgeted cost rates for future work would provide erroneously low project completion cost figures. Re-estimating the cost for each remaining task in a project would be very time consuming. So what we do to is develop an estimated-cost at-completion (EAC) figure. First we compute a cost performance index (CPI) for the project based on data available at this time:

$$CPI = \frac{BCWP}{ACWP} = \frac{\$50}{\$80} = 0.63$$

A CPI of 0.63 means that for every $ actually spent, only 63 cents of value is being created, costed at budget. A CPI below 1.00 means that the actual cost of work completed is higher than planned. A CPI of greater than

1.00 indicates the cost efficiency of the project is better than planned (budgeted). Very high CPIs, though, may indicate that the budget costs were originally over-estimated.

Next we apply the CPI to find the estimated cost at completion (EAC):

$$EAC = ACWP + \frac{(BAC - BCWP)}{CPI}$$

BAC is budget-at-completion, the original budgeted cost of the entire project. Let's suppose that was $200. To recap, our cost figures are:

ACWP = $80; BCWP = $50; CPI = 0.63; BAC = $200. So,

$$EAC = \$80 + \frac{(\$200 - \$50)}{0.63} = \$318.10$$

The actual estimated cost of the *entire* project, based on current (not budgeted) cost efficiency, would be $318.10. This compares to our original budgeted project cost of $200. Experience has shown that the CPI for a project stabilizes within 20 percent of project start time, and does not typically improve after that. In fact, it may well deteriorate. We are not doing well, and may do worse.

Question 5: We are running behind scheduled time. When would the project likely be completed?

We compute the estimated time to completion (ETTC), the estimated *overall* duration of the project. We first compute the scheduled performance index (SPI), a measure of how efficiently the project is running, schedule-wise:

$$SPI = \frac{BCWP}{BCWS} = \frac{\$50}{\$100} = 0.50$$

Like the CPI, an SPI value below 1.00 is bad news. It means that the schedule (time) efficiency of project performance is running below planned performance (SPI > 1.00 is good news).

We next use the SPI to compute the ETTC, the total estimated time to complete the project.

$$ETTC = \frac{OD}{SPI}$$

OD = Original budgeted duration of the project = assume as 8 weeks
SPI = Scheduled Performance Index = 0.50

$$ETTC = \frac{8 \text{ weeks}}{0.50} = 16 \text{ weeks}$$

The estimated overall duration of the project is now estimated at 16 weeks, given the time efficiency rating of 0.50, instead of the budgeted 8 weeks.

We developed all our forecast estimates using straight-line projections of the cost and time efficiency indices. They do not include any information about emerging situations or future events. Efficiency rates are unlikely to increase, but may well decline. In that case we would have to use curve-based projections of cost and time efficiency rates. The table below summarizes our analysis.

As of week 4, our project is doing poorly. Reasons could range from changes in external conditions, problems revealed during work, or unanticipated sub-contractor failures. Threatening project employees may result in cover-ups and future misreporting. We should involve them and stakeholders in resolving the causes for slippage. We should also recognize the reality that goals and 'success' criteria change as a project evolves through multiple changes. It is also often the case that negative cost variances are the result of seeking positive schedule variances. We trade cost for time savings.

We may declare a project a success. But the client decides not to award us any more projects. And our project team members vow never to work with us again. Why? Performance has two aspects—goal related and people related. Our goals concerning cost, time, and quality may well have been achieved, but perhaps

Table 13.6 EVM Metrics—Evaluating Project Performance

EVM Metric	Explanation/Formula	Value
BAC Budget at Completion	The sum of all planned project costs at project start.	$200 (assumed)
OD Original Budgeted Duration	Budgeted duration of entire project, or part of a project, or an individual project activity	8 weeks (assumed)
BCWS Budgeted Cost of Work Scheduled.	The total planned cost for work scheduled to be completed by a specific point in time	$100 by week 4 (from Figure 13.11)
BCWP Budgeted Cost of Work Performed	The total budgeted cost of work actually completed by a point in time	$50 by week 4 (from Figure 13.11)
ACWP Actual Cost of Work Performed	The total actual cost of work actually completed by a point in time	$80 by week 4 (assumed)
Cost Variance	(BCWP − ACWP) at a point in time	(−)$30 at week 4
Schedule Variance	(BCWP − BCWS) at a point in time	(−)$50 at week 4
CPI Cost Performance Index	Cost efficiency metric at a point in time $$\frac{BCWP}{ACWP}$$	0.63 at week 4
SPI Schedule Performance Index	Time schedule efficiency metric at a point in time $$\frac{BCWP}{BCWS}$$	0.50 at week 4
EAC Estimated Cost at Completion	Total estimated cost of project at completion, recalculated at a point in time $$ACWP + \frac{(BAC - BCWP)}{CPI}$$	$318.10
ETTC Estimated Time to Completion	Total estimated duration of project, recalculated at a point in time $$\frac{OD}{SPI}$$	16 weeks

we faltered handling people issues. Did we manage challenges and changes through acrimony and legalities, or through communication and relationship building? Did we celebrate small successes along the way with our people and our clients? Did we appreciate the social dimensions of team and client management? In short, did we, as project managers, pay attention to the softer yet so important issues of client morale, project team morale, team spirit, trust, responsiveness, communications, conflict resolution, integrity, and sociability? These factors are often, subjectively and subtly, considered as part of project performance. They can and should be measured/estimated, weighted relative to goal related performance criteria, and included in a broader definition of project success.

KEY POINTS

- EVM (earned value management) tracks project health by tracking cost and time variances in activities, relative to budget, and provides revised projections of cost and time schedules.
- EVM computes the *earned value* of a project. Earned value = BCWP (budgeted cost of work actually performed).
- EVM computes *cost variance* = BCWP – ACWP (actual cost of work performed). A negative cost variance indicates a cost over-run.
- EVM computes *schedule variance* = BCWP – BCWS (budgeted cost of work scheduled). A negative schedule variance indicates a time over-run.
- EVM computes time variance = (time within which a specific budgeted $ amount of work (BCWS) job was scheduled to be done) minus (time within which that work (BCWP) was actually done). A negative time variance shows the extent of the delay.

Key Formulas

EVM

Cost variance = (BCWP, i.e., budgeted value of work performed within a specific reporting period) *minus*
(ACWP, i.e., actual cost of work performed)

Schedule variance = BCWP – BCWS (budgeted cost of work performed till that specific reporting period of time)

Time variance = [Time within which a specific budgeted $ amount of work (BCWS) was scheduled to be performed] *minus*
[Time when that value of work (BCWP) was actually performed]

Cost performance index $CPI = \dfrac{BCWP}{ACWP}$

Estimated time at completion $EAC = \text{ACWP} + \dfrac{(BAC - BCWP)}{\text{CPI}}$, where BAC = budget-at-completion (original budget cost)

Scheduled performance index $SPI = \dfrac{\text{BCWP}}{\text{BCWS}}$

Estimated time to complete the project $ETTC = \dfrac{\text{OD}}{\text{SPI}}$, where OD is the original budgeted duration of the project

Statistical Tables

Infinite Source Values for L_q and P_o Given λ/μ and M

λ/μ	M	Lq	Po	λ/μ	M	Lq	Po	λ/μ	M	Lq	Po
3.8	5	1.519	.017	4.6	5	9.289	.004	5.3	8	0.422	.005
	6	0.412	.021		6	1.487	.008		9	0.155	.005
	7	0.129	.022		7	0.453	.009		10	0.057	.005
	8	0.041	.022		8	0.156	.010		11	0.021	.005
	9	0.013	.022		9	0.054	.010		12	0.007	.005
3.9	4	36.859	.002		10	0.018	.010	5.4	6	6.661	.002
	5	1.830	.015	4.7	5	13.382	.003		7	1.444	.004
	6	0.485	.019		6	1.752	.007		8	0.483	.004
	7	0.153	.020		7	0.525	.008		9	0.178	.004
	8	0.050	.020		8	0.181	.008		10	0.066	.004
	9	0.016	.020		9	0.064	.009		11	0.024	.005
4.0	5	2.216	.013		10	0.022	.009		12	0.009	.005
	6	0.570	.017	4.8	5	21.641	.002	5.5	6	8.590	.002
	7	0.180	.018		6	2.071	.006		7	1.674	.003
	8	0.059	.018		7	0.607	.008		8	0.553	.004
	9	0.019	.018		8	0.209	.008		9	0.204	.004
4.1	5	2.703	.011		9	0.074	.008		10	0.077	.004
	6	0.668	.015		10	0.026	.008		11	0.028	.004
	7	0.212	.016	4.9	5	46.566	.001		12	0.010	.004
	8	0.070	.016		6	2.459	.005	5.6	6	11.519	.001
	9	0.023	.017		7	0.702	.007		7	1.944	.003
4.2	5	3.327	.009		8	0.242	.007		8	0.631	.003
	6	0.784	.013		9	0.087	.007		9	0.233	.004
	7	0.248	.014		10	0.031	.007		10	0.088	.004
	8	0.083	.015		11	0.011	.077		11	0.033	.004
	9	0.027	.015	5.0	6	2.938	.005		12	0.012	.004
	10	0.009	.015		7	0.810	.006	5.7	6	16.446	.001

(*Continued*)

Infinite Source Values for L_q and P_o Given λ/μ and M (Continued)

λ/μ	M	Lq	Po	λ/μ	M	Lq	Po	λ/μ	M	Lq	Po
4.3	5	4.149	.008		8	0.279	.006		7	2.264	.002
	6	0.919	.012		9	0.101	.007		8	0.721	.003
	7	0.289	.130		10	0.036	.007		9	0.266	.003
	8	0.097	.013		11	0.013	.007		10	0.102	.003
	9	0.033	.014	5.1	6	3.536	.004		11	0.038	.003
	10	0.011	.014		7	0.936	.005		12	0.014	.003
4.4	5	5.268	.006		8	0.321	.006	5.8	6	26.373	.001
	6	1.078	.010		9	0.117	.006		7	2.648	.002
	7	0.337	.012		10	0.042	.006		8	0.823	.003
	8	0.114	.012		11	0.015	.006		9	0.303	.003
	9	0.039	.012	5.2	6	4.301	.003		10	0.116	.003
	10	0.013	.012		7	1.081	.005		11	0.044	.003
4.5	5	6.862	.005		8	0.368	.005		12	0.017	.003
	6	1.265	.009		9	0.135	.005	5.9	6	56.300	.000
	7	0.391	.010		10	0.049	.005		7	3.113	.002
	8	0.133	.011		11	0.017	.006		8	0.939	.002
	9	0.046	.011	5.3	6	5.303	.003		9	0.345	.003
	10	0.015	.011		7	1.249	.004		10	0.133	.003

Tables of the Normal Distribution

Z	0.00	0.01	0.02	0.03	0.04	0.05	0.06	0.07	0.08	0.09
0.0	0.5000	0.5040	0.5080	0.5120	0.5160	0.5199	0.5239	0.5279	0.5319	0.5359
0.1	0.5398	0.5438	0.5478	0.5517	0.5557	0.5596	0.5636	0.5675	0.5714	0.5753
0.2	0.5793	0.5832	0.5871	0.5910	0.5948	0.5987	0.6026	0.6064	0.6103	0.6141
0.3	0.6179	0.6217	0.6255	0.6293	0.6331	0.6368	0.6406	0.6443	0.6480	0.6517
0.4	0.6554	0.6591	0.6628	0.6664	0.6700	0.6736	0.6772	0.6808	0.6844	0.6879
0.5	0.6915	0.6950	0.6985	0.7019	0.7054	0.7088	0.7123	0.7157	0.7190	0.7224
0.6	0.7257	0.7291	0.7324	0.7357	0.7389	0.7422	0.7454	0.7486	0.7517	0.7549
0.7	0.7580	0.7611	0.7642	0.7673	0.7704	0.7734	0.7764	0.7794	0.7823	0.7852
0.8	0.7881	0.7910	0.7939	0.7967	0.7995	0.8023	0.8051	0.8078	0.8106	0.8133
0.9	0.8159	0.8186	0.8212	0.8238	0.8264	0.8289	0.8315	0.8340	0.8365	0.8389
1.0	0.8413	0.8438	0.8461	0.8485	0.8508	0.8531	0.8554	0.8577	0.8599	0.8621
1.1	0.8643	0.8665	0.8686	0.8708	0.8729	0.8749	0.8770	0.8790	0.8810	0.8830
1.2	0.8849	0.8869	0.8888	0.8907	0.8925	0.8944	0.8962	0.8980	0.8997	0.9015
1.3	0.9032	0.9049	0.9066	0.9082	0.9099	0.9115	0.9131	0.9147	0.9162	0.9177
1.4	0.9192	0.9207	0.9222	0.9236	0.9251	0.9265	0.9279	0.9292	0.9306	0.9319
1.5	0.9332	0.9345	0.9357	0.9370	0.9382	0.9394	0.9406	0.9418	0.9429	0.9441
1.6	0.9452	0.9463	0.9474	0.9484	0.9495	0.9505	0.9515	0.9525	0.9535	0.9545
1.7	0.9554	0.9564	0.9573	0.9582	0.9591	0.9599	0.9608	0.9616	0.9625	0.9633
1.8	0.9641	0.9649	0.9656	0.9664	0.9671	0.9678	0.9686	0.9693	0.9699	0.9706
1.9	0.9713	0.9719	0.9726	0.9732	0.9738	0.9744	0.9750	0.9756	0.9761	0.9767
2.0	0.9772	0.9778	0.9783	0.9788	0.9793	0.9798	0.9803	0.9808	0.9812	0.9817
2.1	0.9821	0.9826	0.9830	0.9834	0.9838	0.9842	0.9846	0.9850	0.9854	0.9857
2.2	0.9861	0.9864	0.9868	0.9871	0.9875	0.9878	0.9881	0.9884	0.9887	0.9890
2.3	0.9893	0.9896	0.9898	0.9901	0.9904	0.9906	0.9909	0.9911	0.9913	0.9916
2.4	0.9918	0.9920	0.9922	0.9925	0.9927	0.9929	0.9931	0.9932	0.9934	0.9936
2.5	0.9938	0.9940	0.9941	0.9943	0.9945	0.9946	0.9948	0.9949	0.9951	0.9952
2.6	0.9953	0.9955	0.9956	0.9957	0.9959	0.9960	0.9961	0.9962	0.9963	0.9964
2.7	0.9965	0.9966	0.9967	0.9968	0.9969	0.9970	0.9971	0.9972	0.9973	0.9974
2.8	0.9974	0.9975	0.9976	0.9977	0.9977	0.9978	0.9979	0.9979	0.9980	0.9981
2.9	0.9981	0.9982	0.9982	0.9983	0.9984	0.9984	0.9985	0.9985	0.9986	0.9986
3.0	0.9987	0.9987	0.9987	0.9988	0.9988	0.9989	0.9989	0.9989	0.9990	0.9990

(Continued)

Tables of the Normal Distribution (Continued): Far Right Tail Probabilities

Z	P{Z to oo}	Z	P{Z to oo}	Z	P{Z to oo}	Z	P{Z to oo}
2.0	0.02275	3.0	0.001350	4.0	0.00003167	5.0	2.867 E-7
2.1	0.01786	3.1	0.0009676	4.1	0.00002066	5.5	1.899 E-8
2.2	0.01390	3.2	0.0006871	4.2	0.00001335	6.0	9.866 E-10
2.3	0.01072	3.3	0.0004834	4.3	0.00000854	6.5	4.016 E-11
2.4	0.00820	3.4	0.0003369	4.4	0.000005413	7.0	1.280 E-12
2.5	0.00621	3.5	0.0002326	4.5	0.000003398	7.5	3.191 E-14
2.6	0.004661	3.6	0.0001591	4.6	0.000002112	8.0	6.221 E-16
2.7	0.003467	3.7	0.0001078	4.7	0.000001300	8.5	9.480 E-18
2.8	0.002555	3.8	0.00007235	4.8	7.933 E-7	9.0	1.129 E-19
2.9	0.001866	3.9	0.00004810	4.9	4.792 E-7	9.5	1.049 E-21

Cumulative Poisson Distribution Table

Table shows cumulative probability functions of Poisson Distribution with various α. Example: to find the probability $P(X \leq 3)$ where X has a Poisson Distribution with $\alpha = 2$, look in row 4 and column 4 to find $P(X \leq 3) = 0.8571$ where X is Poisson(2).

					α					
x	0.5	1	1.5	2	2.5	3	3.5	4	4.5	5
0	0.6065	0.3679	0.2231	0.1353	0.0821	0.0498	0.0302	0.0183	0.0111	0.0067
1	0.9098	0.7358	0.5578	0.4060	0.2873	0.1991	0.1359	0.0916	0.0611	0.0404
2	0.9856	0.9197	0.8088	0.6767	0.5438	0.4232	0.3208	0.2381	0.1736	0.1247
3	0.9982	0.9810	0.9344	0.8571	0.7576	0.6472	0.5366	0.4335	0.3423	0.2650
4	0.9998	0.9963	0.9814	0.9473	0.8912	0.8153	0.7254	0.6288	0.5321	0.4405
5	1.0000	0.9994	0.9955	0.9834	0.9580	0.9161	0.8576	0.7851	0.7029	0.6160
6	1.0000	0.9999	0.9991	0.9955	0.9858	0.9665	0.9347	0.8893	0.8311	0.7622
7	1.0000	1.0000	0.9998	0.9989	0.9958	0.9881	0.9733	0.9489	0.9134	0.8666
8	1.0000	1.0000	1.0000	0.9998	0.9989	0.9962	0.9901	0.9786	0.9597	0.9319
9	1.0000	1.0000	1.0000	1.0000	0.9997	0.9989	0.9967	0.9919	0.9829	0.9682
10	1.0000	1.0000	1.0000	1.0000	0.9999	0.9997	0.9990	0.9972	0.9933	0.9863
11	1.0000	1.0000	1.0000	1.0000	1.0000	0.9999	0.9997	0.9991	0.9976	0.9945
12	1.0000	1.0000	1.0000	1.0000	1.0000	1.0000	0.9999	0.9997	0.9992	0.9980
13	1.0000	1.0000	1.0000	1.0000	1.0000	1.0000	1.0000	0.9999	0.9997	0.9993
14	1.0000	1.0000	1.0000	1.0000	1.0000	1.0000	1.0000	1.0000	0.9999	0.9998
15	1.0000	1.0000	1.0000	1.0000	1.0000	1.0000	1.0000	1.0000	1.0000	0.9999
16	1.0000	1.0000	1.0000	1.0000	1.0000	1.0000	1.0000	1.0000	1.0000	1.0000

					α					
x	5.5	6	6.5	7	7.5	8	8.5	9	9.5	10
0	0.0041	0.0025	0.0015	0.0009	0.0006	0.0003	0.0002	0.0001	0.0001	0.0000
1	0.0266	0.0174	0.0113	0.0073	0.0047	0.0030	0.0019	0.0012	0.0008	0.0005
23	0.0884	0.0620	0.0430	0.0296	0.0203	0.0138	0.0093	0.0062	0.0042	0.0028
3	0.2017	0.1512	0.1118	0.0818	0.0591	0.0424	0.0301	0.0212	0.0149	0.0103
4	0.3575	0.2851	0.2237	0.1730	0.1321	0.0996	0.0744	0.0550	0.0403	0.0293
5	0.5289	0.4457	0.3690	0.3007	0.2414	0.1912	0.1496	0.1157	0.0885	0.0671
6	0.6860	0.6063	0.5265	0.4497	0.3782	0.3134	0.2562	0.2068	0.1649	0.1301
7	0.8095	0.7440	0.6728	0.5987	0.5246	0.4530	0.3856	0.3239	0.2687	0.2202
8	0.8944	0.8472	0.7916	0.7291	0.6620	0.5925	0.5231	0.4557	0.3918	0.3328
9	0.9462	0.9161	0.8774	0.8305	0.7764	0.7166	0.6530	0.5874	0.5218	0.4579
10	0.9747	0.9574	0.9332	0.9015	0.8622	0.8159	0.7634	0.7060	0.6453	0.5830
11	0.9890	0.9799	0.9661	0.9467	0.9208	0.8881	0.8487	0.8030	0.7520	0.6968
12	0.9955	0.9912	0.9840	0.9730	0.9573	0.9362	0.9091	0.8758	0.8364	0.7916
13	0.9983	0.9964	0.9929	0.9872	0.9784	0.9658	0.9486	0.9261	0.8981	0.8645
14	0.9994	0.9986	0.9970	0.9943	0.9897	0.9827	0.9726	0.9585	0.9400	0.9165

(Continued)

Cumulative Poisson Distribution Table (Continued)

x										
15	0.9998	0.9995	0.9988	0.9976	0.9954	0.9918	0.9862	0.9780	0.9665	0.9513
16	0.9999	0.9998	0.9996	0.9990	0.9980	0.9963	0.9934	0.9889	0.9823	0.9730
17	1.0000	0.9999	0.9998	0.9996	0.9992	0.9984	0.9970	0.9947	0.9911	0.9857
18	1.0000	1.0000	0.9999	0.9999	0.9997	0.9993	0.9987	0.9976	0.9957	0.9928
19	1.0000	1.0000	1.0000	1.0000	0.9999	0.9997	0.9995	0.9989	0.9980	0.9965
20	1.0000	1.0000	1.0000	1.0000	1.0000	0.9999	0.9998	0.9996	0.9991	0.9984
21	1.0000	1.0000	1.0000	1.0000	1.0000	1.0000	0.9999	0.9998	0.9996	0.9993
22	1.0000	1.0000	1.0000	1.0000	1.0000	1.0000	1.0000	0.9999	0.9999	0.9997
23	1.0000	1.0000	1.0000	1.0000	1.0000	1.0000	1.0000	1.0000	0.9999	0.9999
24	1.0000	1.0000	1.0000	1.0000	1.0000	1.0000	1.0000	1.0000	1.0000	1.0000

α

x	10.5	11	11.5	12	12.5	13	13.5	14	14.5	15
0	0.0000	0.0000	0.0000	0.0000	0.0000	0.0000	0.0000	0.0000	0.0000	0.0000
1	0.0003	0.0002	0.0001	0.0001	0.0001	0.0000	0.0000	0.0000	0.0000	0.0000
2	0.0018	0.0012	0.0008	0.0005	0.0003	0.0002	0.0001	0.0001	0.0001	0.0000
3	0.0071	0.0049	0.0034	0.0023	0.0016	0.0011	0.0007	0.0005	0.0003	0.0002
4	0.0211	0.0151	0.0107	0.0076	0.0053	0.0037	0.0026	0.0018	0.0012	0.0009
5	0.0504	0.0375	0.0277	0.0203	0.0148	0.0107	0.0077	0.0055	0.0039	0.0028
6	0.1016	0.0786	0.0603	0.0458	0.0346	0.0259	0.0193	0.0142	0.0105	0.0076
7	0.1785	0.1432	0.1137	0.0895	0.0698	0.0540	0.0415	0.0316	0.0239	0.0180
8	0.2794	0.2320	0.1906	0.1550	0.1249	0.0998	0.0790	0.0621	0.0484	0.0374
9	0.3971	0.3405	0.2888	0.2424	0.2014	0.1658	0.1353	0.1094	0.0878	0.0699
10	0.5207	0.4599	0.4017	0.3472	0.2971	0.2517	0.2112	0.1757	0.1449	0.1185
11	0.6387	0.5793	0.5198	0.4616	0.4058	0.3532	0.3045	0.2600	0.2201	0.1848
12	0.7420	0.6887	0.6329	0.5760	0.5190	0.4631	0.4093	0.3585	0.3111	0.2676
13	0.8253	0.7813	0.7330	0.6815	0.6278	0.5730	0.5182	0.4644	0.4125	0.3632
14	0.8879	0.8540	0.8153	0.7720	0.7250	0.6751	0.6233	0.5704	0.5176	0.4657
15	0.9317	0.9074	0.8783	0.8444	0.8060	0.7636	0.7178	0.6694	0.6192	0.5681
16	0.9604	0.9441	0.9236	0.8987	0.8693	0.8355	0.7975	0.7559	0.7112	0.6641
17	0.9781	0.9678	0.9542	0.9370	0.9158	0.8905	0.8609	0.8272	0.7897	0.7489
18	0.9885	0.9823	0.9738	0.9626	0.9481	0.9302	0.9084	0.8826	0.8530	0.8195
19	0.9942	0.9907	0.9857	0.9787	0.9694	0.9573	0.9421	0.9235	0.9012	0.8752
20	0.9972	0.9953	0.9925	0.9884	0.9827	0.9750	0.9649	0.9521	0.9362	0.9170
21	0.9987	0.9977	0.9962	0.9939	0.9906	0.9859	0.9796	0.9712	0.9604	0.9469
22	0.9994	0.9990	0.9982	0.9970	0.9951	0.9924	0.9885	0.9833	0.9763	0.9673
23	0.9998	0.9995	0.9992	0.9985	0.9975	0.9960	0.9938	0.9907	0.9863	0.9805
24	0.9999	0.9998	0.9996	0.9993	0.9988	0.9980	0.9968	0.9950	0.9924	0.9888
25	1.0000	0.9999	0.9998	0.9997	0.9994	0.9990	0.9984	0.9974	0.9959	0.9938
26	1.0000	1.0000	0.9999	0.9999	0.9997	0.9995	0.9992	0.9987	0.9979	0.9967
27	1.0000	1.0000	1.0000	0.9999	0.9999	0.9998	0.9996	0.9994	0.9989	0.9983
28	1.0000	1.0000	1.0000	1.0000	1.0000	0.9999	0.9998	0.9997	0.9995	0.9991
29	1.0000	1.0000	1.0000	1.0000	1.0000	1.0000	0.9999	0.9999	0.9998	0.9996
30	1.0000	1.0000	1.0000	1.0000	1.0000	1.0000	1.0000	0.9999	0.9999	0.9998
31	1.0000	1.0000	1.0000	1.0000	1.0000	1.0000	1.0000	1.0000	1.0000	0.9999
32	1.0000	1.0000	1.0000	1.0000	1.0000	1.0000	1.0000	1.0000	1.0000	1.0000

Normal Distribution and Loss Function Table

F(Z) is the probability that a variable from a standard normal distribution will be less than or equal to Z, or alternately, the service level for a quantity ordered with a z-value of Z.

L(Z) is the standard loss function, i.e. the expected number of lost sales as a fraction of the standard deviation. Hence, the lost sales = L(Z) × σ_{DEMAND}

z	F(Z)	L(Z)	z	F(Z)	L(Z)	z	F(Z)	L(Z)	z	F(Z)	L(Z)
−3.00	0.0013	3.000	−1.48	0.0694	1.511	0.04	0.5160	0.379	1.56	0.9406	0.026
−2.96	0.0015	2.960	−1.44	0.0749	1.474	0.08	0.5319	0.360	1.60	0.9452	0.023
−2.92	0.0018	2.921	−1.40	0.0808	1.437	0.12	0.5478	0.342	1.64	0.9495	0.021
−2.88	0.0020	2.881	−1.36	0.0869	1.400	0.16	0.5636	0.324	1.68	0.9535	0.019
−2.84	0.0023	2.841	−1.32	0.0934	1.364	0.20	0.5793	0.307	1.72	0.9573	0.017
−2.80	0.0026	2.801	−1.28	0.1003	1.327	0.24	0.5948	0.290	1.76	0.9608	0.016
−2.76	0.0029	2.761	−1.24	0.1075	1.292	0.28	0.6103	0.274	1.80	0.9641	0.014
−2.72	0.0033	2.721	−1.20	0.1151	1.256	0.32	0.6255	0.259	1.84	0.9671	0.013
−2.68	0.0037	2.681	−1.16	0.1230	1.221	0.36	0.6406	0.245	1.88	0.9699	0.012
−2.64	0.0041	2.641	−1.12	0.1314	1.186	0.40	0.6554	0.230	1.92	0.9726	0.010
−2.60	0.0047	2.601	−1.08	0.1401	1.151	0.44	0.6700	0.217	1.96	0.9750	0.009
−2.56	0.0052	2.562	−1.04	0.1492	1.117	0.48	0.6844	0.204	2.00	0.9772	0.008
−2.52	0.0059	2.522	−1.00	0.1587	1.083	0.52	0.6985	0.192	2.04	0.9793	0.008
−2.48	0.0066	2.482	−0.96	0.1685	1.050	0.56	0.7123	0.180	2.08	0.9812	0.007
−2.44	0.0073	2.442	−0.92	0.1788	1.017	0.60	0.7257	0.169	2.12	0.9830	0.006
−2.40	0.0082	2.403	−0.88	0.1894	0.984	0.64	0.7389	0.158	2.16	0.9846	0.005
−2.36	0.0091	2.363	−0.84	0.2005	0.952	0.68	0.7517	0.148	2.20	0.9861	0.005
−2.32	0.0102	2.323	−0.80	0.2119	0.920	0.72	0.7642	0.138	2.24	0.9875	0.004
−2.28	0.0113	2.284	−0.76	0.2236	0.889	0.76	0.7764	0.129	2.28	0.9887	0.004
−2.24	0.0125	2.244	−0.72	0.2358	0.858	0.80	0.7881	0.120	2.32	0.9898	0.003
−2.20	0.0139	2.205	−0.68	0.2483	0.828	0.84	0.7995	0.112	2.36	0.9909	0.003
−2.16	0.0154	2.165	−0.64	0.2611	0.798	0.88	0.8106	0.104	2.40	0.9918	0.003
−2.12	0.0170	2.126	−0.60	0.2743	0.769	0.92	0.8212	0.097	2.44	0.9927	0.002
−2.08	0.0188	2.087	−0.56	0.2877	0.740	0.96	0.8315	0.090	2.48	0.9934	0.002
−2.04	0.0207	2.048	−0.52	0.3015	0.712	1.00	0.8413	0.083	2.52	0.9941	0.002
−2.00	0.0228	2.008	−0.48	0.3156	0.684	1.04	0.8508	0.077	2.56	0.9948	0.002
−1.96	0.0250	1.969	−0.44	0.3300	0.657	1.08	0.8599	0.071	2.60	0.9953	0.001
−1.92	0.0274	1.930	−0.40	0.3446	0.630	1.12	0.8686	0.066	2.64	0.9959	0.001
−1.88	0.0301	1.892	−0.36	0.3594	0.605	1.16	0.8770	0.061	2.68	0.9963	0.001
−1.84	0.0329	1.853	−0.32	0.3745	0.579	1.20	0.8849	0.056	2.72	0.9967	0.001
−1.80	0.0359	1.814	−0.28	0.3897	0.554	1.24	0.8925	0.052	2.76	0.9971	0.001
−1.76	0.0392	1.776	−0.24	0.4052	0.530	1.28	0.8997	0.047	2.80	0.9974	0.001
−1.72	0.0427	1.737	−0.20	0.4207	0.507	1.32	0.9066	0.044	2.84	0.9977	0.001
−1.68	0.0465	1.699	−0.16	0.4364	0.484	1.36	0.9131	0.040	2.88	0.9980	0.001
−1.64	0.0505	1.661	−0.12	0.4522	0.462	1.40	0.9192	0.037	2.92	0.9982	0.001
−1.60	0.0548	1.623	−0.08	0.4681	0.440	1.44	0.9251	0.034	2.96	0.9985	0.000
−1.56	0.0594	1.586	−0.04	0.4840	0.419	1.48	0.9306	0.031	3.00	0.9987	0.000
−1.52	0.0643	1.548	0.00	0.5000	0.399	1.52	0.9357	0.028			

(Continued)

Normal Distribution and Loss Function Table (Continued)

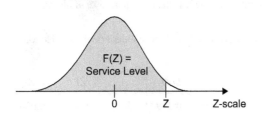

Z & L(z) for special service levels		
Service Level F(z)	z	L(z)
75%	0.67	0.150
90%	1.28	0.047
95%	1.64	0.021
99%	2.33	0.003

Poisson Loss Function Table

	Mean									
S	0.05	0.10	0.15	0.20	0.25	0.30	0.35	0.40	0.45	0.50
0	0.05000	0.10000	0.15000	0.20000	0.25000	0.30000	0.35000	0.40000	0.45000	0.50000
1	0.00123	0.00484	0.01071	0.01873	0.02880	0.04082	0.05469	0.07032	0.08763	0.10653
2	0.00002	0.00016	0.00052	0.00121	0.00230	0.00388	0.00602	0.00877	0.01219	0.01633
3	0.00000	0.00000	0.00002	0.00006	0.00014	0.00028	0.00051	0.00084	0.00131	0.00194
4	0.00000	0.00000	0.00000	0.00000	0.00001	0.00002	0.00003	0.00007	0.00011	0.00019
5	0.00000	0.00000	0.00000	0.00000	0.00000	0.00000	0.00000	0.00000	0.00001	0.00002
6	0.00000	0.00000	0.00000	0.00000	0.00000	0.00000	0.00000	0.00000	0.00000	0.00000

	Mean									
S	0.55	0.60	0.65	0.70	0.75	0.80	0.85	0.90	0.95	1.00
0	0.55000	0.60000	0.65000	0.70000	0.75000	0.80000	0.85000	0.90000	0.95000	1.00000
1	0.12695	0.14881	0.17205	0.19659	0.22237	0.24933	0.27741	0.30657	0.33674	0.36788
2	0.02122	0.02691	0.03342	0.04078	0.04901	0.05812	0.06813	0.07905	0.09089	0.10364
3	0.00276	0.00379	0.00508	0.00664	0.00850	0.01070	0.01325	0.01620	0.01955	0.02334
4	0.00029	0.00044	0.00063	0.00089	0.00121	0.00162	0.00212	0.00274	0.00347	0.00435
5	0.00003	0.00004	0.00007	0.00010	0.00015	0.00021	0.00029	0.00039	0.00052	0.00069
6	0.00000	0.00000	0.00001	0.00001	0.00002	0.00002	0.00003	0.00005	0.00007	0.00009
7	0.00000	0.00000	0.00001	0.00001	0.00002	0.00002	0.00003	0.00005	0.00007	0.00009
8	0.00000	0.00000	0.00001	0.00001	0.00001	0.00002	0.00003	0.00004	0.00006	0.00008

	Mean									
S	1.25	1.50	1.75	2.00	2.25	2.50	2.75	3.00	3.25	3.50
0	1.25000	1.50000	1.75000	2.00000	2.25000	2.50000	2.75000	3.00000	3.25000	3.50000
1	0.53650	0.72313	0.92377	1.13534	1.35540	1.58208	1.81393	2.04979	2.28877	2.53020
2	0.18114	0.28096	0.40165	0.54134	0.69795	0.86938	1.05366	1.24894	1.45356	1.66609
3	0.04961	0.08980	0.14562	0.21802	0.30729	0.41320	0.53511	0.67213	0.82313	0.98693
4	0.01134	0.02416	0.04481	0.07514	0.11672	0.17077	0.23815	0.31936	0.41454	0.52357
5	0.00221	0.00558	0.01191	0.02249	0.03870	0.06195	0.09353	0.13462	0.18619	0.24901
6	0.00038	0.00113	0.00278	0.00592	0.01134	0.01993	0.03270	0.05070	0.07501	0.10662
7	0.00006	0.00020	0.00058	0.00139	0.00297	0.00574	0.01026	0.01719	0.02728	0.04134
8	0.00001	0.00003	0.00011	0.00029	0.00070	0.00149	0.00292	0.00529	0.00902	0.01460
9	0.00000	0.00000	0.00002	0.00006	0.00015	0.00035	0.00076	0.00149	0.00273	0.00472
10	0.00000	0.00000	0.00000	0.00001	0.00003	0.00008	0.00018	0.00038	0.00076	0.00141
11	0.00000	0.00000	0.00000	0.00000	0.00001	0.00002	0.00004	0.00009	0.00020	0.00039
12	0.00000	0.00000	0.00000	0.00000	0.00000	0.00000	0.00001	0.00002	0.00005	0.00010
13	0.00000	0.00000	0.00000	0.00000	0.00000	0.00000	0.00000	0.00000	0.00001	0.00002
14	0.00000	0.00000	0.00000	0.00000	0.00000	0.00000	0.00000	0.00000	0.00000	0.00001
15	0.00000	0.00000	0.00000	0.00000	0.00000	0.00000	0.00000	0.00000	0.00000	0.00000

(*Continued*)

Poisson Loss Function Table (Continued)

						Mean						
S	3.75	4.00	4.25	4.50	4.75	5.00	5.25	5.50	5.75	6.00	6.25	6.50
0	3.75000	4.00000	4.25000	4.50000	4.75000	5.00000	5.25000	5.50000	5.75000	6.00000	6.25000	6.50000
1	2.77352	3.01832	3.26426	3.51111	3.75865	4.00674	4.25525	4.50409	4.75318	5.00248	5.25193	5.50150
2	1.88523	2.10989	2.33915	2.57221	2.80840	3.04717	3.28804	3.53065	3.77467	4.01983	4.26593	4.51278
3	1.16230	1.34800	1.54286	1.74579	1.95575	2.17182	2.39316	2.61903	2.84877	3.08180	3.31763	3.55582
4	0.64606	0.78147	0.92907	1.08808	1.25763	1.43684	1.62483	1.82073	2.02371	2.23300	2.44788	2.66766
5	0.32361	0.41030	0.50919	0.62019	0.74303	0.87734	1.02260	1.17824	1.34362	1.51806	1.70086	1.89134
6	0.14649	0.19543	0.25413	0.32312	0.40277	0.49330	0.59479	0.70716	0.83024	0.96374	1.10727	1.26038
7	0.06021	0.08476	0.11582	0.15417	0.20052	0.25548	0.31958	0.39320	0.47663	0.57004	0.67348	0.78690
8	0.02259	0.03363	0.04839	0.06758	0.09192	0.12211	0.15882	0.20268	0.25426	0.31402	0.38238	0.45966
9	0.00778	0.01226	0.01861	0.02732	0.03893	0.05402	0.07318	0.09704	0.12620	0.16126	0.20276	0.25123
10	0.00247	0.00413	0.00662	0.01023	0.01529	0.02219	0.03136	0.04326	0.05842	0.07733	0.10056	0.12862
11	0.00073	0.00129	0.00219	0.00356	0.00559	0.00849	0.01253	0.01801	0.02528	0.03471	0.04673	0.06178
12	0.00020	0.00038	0.00067	0.00116	0.00191	0.00304	0.00469	0.00702	0.01026	0.01462	0.02040	0.02790
13	0.00005	0.00010	0.00019	0.00035	0.00061	0.00102	0.00165	0.00257	0.00391	0.00579	0.00838	0.01187
14	0.00001	0.00003	0.00005	0.00010	0.00018	0.00032	0.00054	0.00089	0.00141	0.00217	0.00325	0.00477
15	0.00000	0.00001	0.00001	0.00003	0.00005	0.00010	0.00017	0.00029	0.00048	0.00077	0.00119	0.00181
16	0.00000	0.00000	0.00000	0.00001	0.00001	0.00003	0.00005	0.00009	0.00015	0.00026	0.00042	0.00066
17	0.00000	0.00000	0.00000	0.00000	0.00000	0.00001	0.00001	0.00003	0.00005	0.00008	0.00014	0.00022
18	0.00000	0.00000	0.00000	0.00000	0.00000	0.00000	0.00000	0.00001	0.00001	0.00002	0.00004	0.00007
19	0.00000	0.00000	0.00000	0.00000	0.00000	0.00000	0.00000	0.00000	0.00000	0.00001	0.00001	0.00002

						Mean						
S	6.75	7.00	7.25	7.50	7.75	8.00	8.25	8.50	8.75	9.00	9.25	9.50
0	6.75000	7.00000	7.25000	7.50000	7.75000	8.00000	8.25000	8.50000	8.75000	9.00000	9.25000	9.50000
1	5.75117	6.00091	6.25071	6.50055	6.75043	7.00034	7.25026	7.50020	7.75016	8.00012	8.25010	8.50007
2	4.76025	5.00821	5.25657	5.50525	5.75420	6.00335	6.25268	6.50214	6.75170	7.00136	7.25108	7.50086
3	3.79599	4.03784	4.28109	4.52551	4.77090	5.01711	5.26399	5.51142	5.75931	6.00759	6.25618	6.50502
4	2.89176	3.11961	3.35072	3.58466	3.82103	4.05949	4.29974	4.54153	4.78462	5.02882	5.27395	5.51988
5	2.08880	2.29260	2.50210	2.71672	2.93589	3.15912	3.38593	3.61589	3.84863	4.08378	4.32105	4.56015
6	1.42257	1.59331	1.77203	1.95815	2.15112	2.35036	2.55532	2.76549	2.98036	3.19947	3.42238	3.64868
7	0.91016	1.04302	1.18519	1.33631	1.49597	1.66373	1.83912	2.02167	2.21087	2.40625	2.60732	2.81362
8	0.54606	0.64173	0.74671	0.86095	0.98434	1.11669	1.25777	1.40726	1.56485	1.73015	1.90277	2.08229
9	0.30712	0.37082	0.44267	0.52292	0.61174	0.70924	0.81546	0.93037	1.05387	1.18580	1.32597	1.47411
10	0.16204	0.20132	0.24694	0.29932	0.35885	0.42586	0.50062	0.58334	0.67418	0.77321	0.88047	0.99594
11	0.08031	0.10280	0.12973	0.16156	0.19876	0.24175	0.29094	0.34671	0.40936	0.47920	0.55644	0.64127
12	0.03746	0.04945	0.06427	0.08232	0.10403	0.12983	0.16013	0.19537	0.23593	0.28221	0.33454	0.39326
13	0.01648	0.02245	0.03007	0.03965	0.05152	0.06603	0.08354	0.10445	0.12913	0.15798	0.19137	0.22968
14	0.00685	0.00964	0.01332	0.01809	0.02418	0.03185	0.04137	0.05304	0.06718	0.08413	0.10422	0.12782

Poisson Loss Function Table (Continued)

S	6.75	7.00	7.25	7.50	7.75	8.00	8.25	8.50	8.75	9.00	9.25	9.50
						Mean						
15	0.00270	0.00392	0.00559	0.00783	0.01077	0.01459	0.01947	0.02561	0.03326	0.04266	0.05409	0.06783
16	0.00101	0.00152	0.00223	0.00322	0.00456	0.00636	0.00872	0.01178	0.01569	0.02063	0.02678	0.03436
17	0.00036	0.00056	0.00085	0.00126	0.00184	0.00264	0.00372	0.00517	0.00706	0.00952	0.01266	0.01663
18	0.00012	0.00020	0.00031	0.00047	0.00071	0.00105	0.00152	0.00217	0.00304	0.00420	0.00573	0.00770
19	0.00004	0.00007	0.00011	0.00017	0.00026	0.00040	0.00059	0.00087	0.00125	0.00177	0.00248	0.00342
20	0.00001	0.00002	0.00004	0.00006	0.00009	0.00014	0.00022	0.00033	0.00049	0.00072	0.00103	0.00145
21	0.00000	0.00001	0.00001	0.00002	0.00003	0.00005	0.00008	0.00012	0.00019	0.00028	0.00041	0.00059
22	0.00000	0.00000	0.00000	0.00001	0.00001	0.00002	0.00003	0.00004	0.00007	0.00010	0.00016	0.00023
23	0.00000	0.00000	0.00000	0.00000	0.00000	0.00001	0.00001	0.00001	0.00002	0.00004	0.00006	0.00009
24	0.00000	0.00000	0.00000	0.00000	0.00000	0.00000	0.00000	0.00000	0.00001	0.00001	0.00002	0.00003

Index

Note: figures and tables are denoted with italicized page numbers.